International Institutions

International Organization **Readers**

Issues and Agents in International Political Economy, edited by Benjamin J. Cohen and Charles Lipson

Theory and Structure in International Political Economy, edited by Charles Lipson and Benjamin J. Cohen

International Institutions, edited by Lisa L. Martin and Beth A. Simmons

INTERNATIONAL INSTITUTIONS
An *International Organization* Reader

edited by
Lisa L. Martin and Beth A. Simmons

The MIT Press
Cambridge, Massachusetts and London, England

Library of Congress Cataloging-in-Publication Data

International institutions : an international organization reader / edited by Lisa L. Martin and Beth A. Simmons.
    p. cm.—(International organization readers)
  Includes bibliographical references.
  ISBN 0-262-63223-3 (pbk. : alk. paper)
  1. International agencies. 2. International organization. I. Martin, Lisa L., 1961– II. Simmons, Beth A., 1958– III. Series.
JZ4850 .I583 2001
341.2—dc21

00-067893

Contents

Contributors

Volume Editors

Lisa L. Martin is Professor of Government at Harvard University.

Beth A. Simmons is Associate Professor of Political Science at the University of California, Berkeley.

Contributors

Karen J. Alter is Assistant Professor of Government at Northwestern University, Chicago, Illinois.

Michael N. Barnett is Assistant Professor of Political Science at the University of Wisconsin, Madison.

Peter N. Barsoom is a Ph.D. candidate in the Department of Politics at Princeton University, Princeton, New Jersey.

Abram Chayes (1922–2000) was Professor of Law at Harvard University, Cambridge, Massachusetts.

Antonia Handler Chayes is Adjunct Lecturer in Public Policy at the Kennedy School of Harvard University, Cambridge, Massachusetts, and Senior Advisor and Director at Conflict Management Group (CMG), a nonprofit conflict resolution consulting firm.

George W. Downs is Professor of Politics at New York University.

Martha Finnemore is Associate Professor of Political Science at George Washington University, Washington, D.C.

Giulio M. Gallarotti is Associate Professor of Government at Wesleyan University, Middletown, Connecticut.

Harold K. Jacobson is Professor of Political Science and Senior Research Scientist at the Center for Political Studies at the University of Michigan, Ann Arbor.

Jeffrey H. Kaplan is a Research Staff Attorney for the Illinois Appellate Court, 2nd District, in Elgin, Illinois.

Friedrich Kratochwil is Professor of International Politics at the Geschwister-Scholl-Institut of the University of Munich.

Ronald Mitchell is Associate Professor of Political Science at the University of Oregon, Eugene.

David M. Rocke is Professor of Management in the Graduate School of Management at the University of California, Davis.

John Gerard Ruggie is James T. Shotwell Professor of Political Science at Columbia University, New York, New York.

Cheryl Shanks is Assistant Professor of Political Science at Williams College, Williamstown, Massachusetts.

James McCall Smith is Assistant Professor of Political Science and International Affairs at The George Washington University, Washington, D.C.

Oran R. Young is Professor of Environmental Studies and Director of the Institute on International Environmental Governance at Dartmouth College, Hanover, N.H.

Abstracts

Political Leadership and Regime Formation: On the Development of Institutions in International Society (1991)
by Oran R. Young

Leadership plays a critical but poorly understood role in determining the success or failure of the processes of institutional bargaining that dominate efforts to form international regimes, or more generally, institutional arrangements in international society. An examination of the nature of institutional bargaining serves as a springboard both for pinpointing the role of leadership in regime formation and for differentiating three forms of leadership that regularly come into play in efforts to establish international institutions: structural leadership, entrepreneurial leadership, and intellectual leadership. Because much of the real work of regime formation occurs in the interplay of different types of leadership, the study of interactions among individual leaders is a high priority for those seeking to illuminate the processes involved in the creation of international institutions. Not only does such a study help to explain the conditions under which regimes form or fail to form, but it also provides an opportunity to bring the individual back into an important area of international affairs.

Interests, Power, and Multilateralism (1992)
by Lisa L. Martin

Multilateralism characterizes, to varying degrees, patterns of interaction among states and the formal organizations they construct. The utility of multilateral norms or organizations varies with the type of cooperation problem states confront. Thus, the functional logic of international cooperation leads to hypotheses about the conditions under which the institution of multilateralism may be a feasible and efficient solution, as in coordination problems, and those under which it will not, as in collaboration problems. Within these constraints, powerful states choose institutions that will serve their interests, with multilateral arrangements becoming more attractive as the future is valued more highly. Multilateral institutions should be stable in circumstances of changing distributions of power, relative to more hierarchical institutions. The vulnerability of patterns of international cooperation to various exogenous changes depends on the type of strategic interaction underlying state behavior.

International Organizations as Teachers of Norms: The United Nations Educational, Scientific, and Cultural Organization and Science Policy (1993)
by Martha Finnemore

Most explanations for the creation of new state institutions locate the cause of change in the conditions or characteristics of the states themselves. Some aspect of a state's economic, social, political, or military situation is said to create a functional need for the new bureaucracy which then is taken up by one or more domestic groups who succeed in changing the stated apparatus. However, changes in state structure may be prompted not only by changing conditions of individual states but also by socialization and conformance with international norms. In the case of one organizational innovation recently adopted by states across the international system, namely, science policy bureaucracies, indicators of state conditions and functional need for these entities are not correlated with the pattern for their adoption. Instead, adoption was prompted by the activities of an international organization which "taught" states the value of science policy organizations and established the coordination of science as an appropriate, and even a necessary, role for states. This finding lends support to constructivist or reflective theories that treat states as social entities and shaped by international social action, as opposed to more conventional treatments of states as autonomous international agents.

Regime Design Matters: Intentional Oil Pollution and Treaty Compliance (1994)
by Ronald B. Mitchell

Whether a treaty elicits compliance from governments or nonstate actors depends upon identifiable characteristics of the regime's compliance systems. Within the international regime controlling intentional oil pollution, a provision requiring tanker owners to install specified equipment produced dramatically higher levels of compliance than a provision requiring tanker operators to limit their discharges. Since both provisions entailed strong economic incentives for violation and regulated the same countries over the same time period, the variance in compliance clearly can be attributed to different features of the two subregimes. The equipment requirements' success stemmed from establishing an integrated compliance system that increased transparency, provided for potent and credible sanctions, reduced implementation costs to governments by building on existing infrastructures, and prevented violations rather than merely deterring them.

Inertia and Change in the Constellation of International Governmental Organizations, 1981–1992 (1996)
by Cheryl Shanks, Harold K. Jacobson, and Jeffrey H. Kaplan

Hardly anyone expects public institutions to die. Yet a census reveals that fully one-third of the international governmental organizations (IGOs) in existence in 1981 had in fact become defunct by 1992. Most Eastern bloc and many regional developing country organizations vanished or became inactive. During this period a slightly larger number of new organizations was born. Not governments but other IGOs spawned most of the new offspring. Wealthy democratic countries increased their IGO memberships while poor unstable countries increasingly dropped out. This bifurcation was accompanied by greater reliance by all on a set of core universal-membership institutions dominated by Western values. Functionalism, organizational ecology, and realism each partly help us to understand these trends but leave important dynamics unexplained.

Who Are the "Masters of the Treaty"? European Governments and the European Court of Justice (1998)
by Karen J. Alter

To what extent can the European Court of Justice, an international court, make decisions that go against the interests of European Union member states? Neofunctionalist accounts imply that because the Court is a legal body it has vast political autonomy from the member states, whereas neorealist accounts imply that because member states can sanction the ECJ, the

Court has no significant political autonomy. Neither theory can explain why the Court, which was once politically weak and did not stray far from the interests of European governments, now boldly rules against their interests. In explaining how the Court escaped member state control, this article develops a general hypothesis of the autonomy of the ECJ, focusing on how differing time horizons of political and judicial actors, support of the Court within the national judiciaries, and decision-making rules at the supranational level limit the member states' ability to control the Court.

The Politics of Dispute Settlement Design: Explaining Legalism in Regional Trade Pacts (2000)
by James McCall Smith

Dispute settlement mechanisms in international trade vary dramatically from one agreement to another. Some mechanisms are highly legalistic, with standing tribunals that resemble national courts in their powers and procedures. Others are diplomatic, requiring only that the disputing countries make a good-faith effort to resolve their differences through consultations. In this article I seek to account for the tremendous variation in institutional design across a set of more than sixty post-1957 regional trade pacts. In contrast to accounts that emphasize the transaction costs of collective action or the functional requirements of deep integration, I find that the level of legalism in each agreement is strongly related to the level of economic asymmetry, in interaction with the proposed depth of liberalization, among member countries.

On Compliance (1993)
by Abram Chayes and Antonia Handler Chayes

A new dialogue is beginning between students of international law and international relations scholars concerning compliance with international agreements. This article advances some basic propositions to frame that dialogue. First, it proposes that the level of compliance with international agreements in general is inherently unverifiable by empirical procedures. That nations generally comply with their international agreements, on the one hand, or that they violate them whenever it is in their interest to do so, on the other, are not statements of fact or even hypotheses to be tested. Instead, they are competing heuristic assumptions. Some reasons why the background assumption of a propensity to comply is plausible and useful are given. Second, compliance problems very often do not reflect a deliberate decision to violate an international undertaking on the basis of a calculation of advantage. The article proposes a variety of other reasons why states may deviate from treaty obligations and why in many circumstances those reasons are properly accepted by others as justifying apparent departures from treaty norms. Third, the treaty regime as a whole need not and should not be held to a standard of strict compliance but to a level of overall compliance that is "acceptable" in the light of the interests and concerns the treaty is designed to safeguard. How the acceptable level is determined and adjusted is considered.

Is the Good News About Compliance Good News About Cooperation? (1996)
by George W. Downs, David M. Rocke, and Peter N. Barsoom

Recent research on compliance in international regulatory regimes has argued (1) that compliance is generally quite good; (2) that this high level of compliance has been achieved with little attention to enforcement; (3) that those compliance problems that do exist are best addressed as management rather than as enforcement problems; and (4) that the management rather than the enforcement approach holds the key to the evolution of future regulatory cooperation in the international system. While the descriptive findings above are largely correct, the policy inferences are dangerously contaminated by endogeneity and selection problems. A high rate of compliance is often the result of states formulating treaties that require them to do little more than they would do in the absence of a treaty. In those cases where noncompliance does occur and where the effects of selection are attenuated, both self-interest and enforcement play significant roles.

The Legalization of International Monetary Affairs (2000)
by Beth A. Simmons

For the first time in history, international monetary relations were institutionalized after World War II as a set of legal obligations. The Articles of Agreement that formed the International Monetary Fund contain international legal obligations of the rules of good conduct for IMF members. Members were required to maintain a par value for their currency (until 1977), to use a single unified exchange-rate system, and to keep their current account free from restrictions. In this article I explore why governments committed themselves to these rules and the conditions under which they complied with their commitments. The evidence suggests that governments tended to make and keep commitments if other countries in their region did so as well. Governments also complied with their international legal commitments if the regime placed a high value on the rule of law domestically. One inference is that reputational concerns have a lot to do with international legal commitments and compliance. Countries that have invested in a strong reputation for protecting property rights are more reluctant to see it jeopardized by international law violations. Violation is more likely, however, in the face of widespread noncompliance, suggesting that compliance behavior should be understood in its regional context.

International Organization: A State of the Art on an Art of the State (1986)
by Friedrich Kratochwil and John Gerard Ruggie

International organization as a field of study is where the action is. The analytical shifts leading up to the current preoccupation with international regimes have been both progressive and cumulative. And the field is pursuing its object of study in innovative ways that are bringing it closer to the theoretical core of more general international relations work. As we point, out, however, the study of regimes as practiced today suffers from the fact that its epistemological approaches contradict its basic ontological posture. Accordingly, more interpretive strains, commensurate with the intersubjective basis of international regimes, should be included in the prevailing epistemological approaches. In addition, as a result of its enthusiasm for the concept of regimes, the field has tended to neglect the study of formal international organizations. Interpretive epistemologies can also help to link up the study of regimes with the study of formal international organizations by drawing attention to the roles these organizations play in creating transparency in the behavior and expectations of actors, serving as focal points for the international legitimation struggle, and providing a venue for the conduct of global epistemic politics.

The Limits of International Organization: Systematic Failure in the Management of International Relations (1991)
by Giulio M. Gallarotti

Contributors to the literature on international organization (IO) have traditionally been overly optimistic about the ability of mutlilateral management to stabilize international relations and have tended to ignore the destabilizing effects of IO. While recent revisionist scholarship has acknowledged both the potential for organizational failure and the conditionality of management, it has tended to focus on how IO fails within specific issue-areas and institutions. This article offers a typology of the inherent (systematic) failures of IO across issue-areas and institutions and thereby seeks to bridge the gaps in our understanding of why many different institutions and managerial schemes have adverse effects. It argues that IO is prone to failure (1) when it attempts to manage complex, tightly coupled systems; (2) when it serves as a substitute either for more substantive and long-term solutions to international problems or for responsible domestic or foreign policy; (3) when it intensifies international disputes; and (4) when it generates moral hazard. In offering a general theoretical approach to understanding the destabilizing effects of IO, the analysis is intended to serve both as a focal point for understanding critical approaches to the study of IO and as an alternative rationale for eliminating the excess of multilateral management.

The Politics, Power, and Pathologies of International Organizations (1999)
by Michael N. Barnett and Martha Finnemore

International Relations scholars have vigorous theories to explain why international organizations (IOs) are created, but they have paid little attention to IO behavior and whether IOs actually do what their creators intend. This blind spot flows logically from the economic theories of organization that have dominated the study of international institutions and regimes. To recover the agency and autonomy of IOs, we offer a constructivist approach. Building on Max Weber's well-known analysis of bureaucracy, we argue that IOs are much more powerful than even neoliberals have argued but that the same characteristics of bureaucracy that make IOs powerful can also make them prone to dysfunctional behavior. IOs are powerful because, like all bureaucracies, they make rules, and, in so doing, they create social knowledge. IOs deploy this knowledge in ways that define shared international tasks, create new categories of actors, form new interests for actors, and transfer new models of political organization around the world. However, the same normative valuation on impersonal rules that defines bureaucracies and makes them powerful in modern life can also make them unresponsive to their environments, obsessed with their own rules at the expense of primary missions, and ultimately produce inefficient and self-defeating behavior. Sociological and constructivist approaches thus allow us to expand the research agenda beyond IO creation and to ask important questions about the consequences of global bureaucratization and the effects of IOs in world politics.

Theories and Empirical Studies of International Institutions (1998)
by Lisa L. Martin and Beth A. Simmons

Studies of international institutions, organizations, and regimes have consistently appeared in the pages of *International Organization*. We review the theoretical and empirical work on international institutions and identify promising directions for the institutionalist research program. Early studies of international institutions were rich with empirical insights and often influenced by theoretical developments in other fields of political science, but lacking an overarching analytical framework they failed to produce a coherent body of scholarship. Current efforts to reinvigorate the study of international institutions draw on a new body of theory about domestic institutions. We argue that the assumptions of this new approach to institutions are more appropriate to international studies than those of earlier attempts to transfer theories across levels of analysis. We suggest that the most productive questions for future research will focus on specifying alternative mechanisms by which institutions can influence outcomes and identify particular sets of questions within this agenda that are especially promising.

Preface

Lisa L. Martin and Beth A. Simmons

Theories and empirical studies of international institutions, regimes, and organizations are at the heart of the study of international relations. Scholars debate the origins of institutions, their roles and functions, their impact on state behavior and other outcomes, and their design and dynamics. International Organization *has been at the center of the burgeoning and highly productive new study of international institutions. A selection of the articles published there since the mid-1980s provides a firm foundation for understanding developments in the study of institutions and international relations theory more generally.*

In this reader we collect fourteen articles published since 1986 that exemplify the major approaches to the modern study of international institutions. Since so many articles on this topic have been published, we obviously had to make hard choices, and many high-quality articles could not be included here. Instead, we chose articles that cover as wide a range of theoretical perspectives and empirical applications as possible. For example, International Organization *has published numerous studies from an institutionalist perspective on the European Union (EU)[1]; however, we include just one example of this literature, an analysis of the European Court of Justice (ECJ).*

A brief definitional comment may be in order. Although we use the term international institutions *in the title of this reader, the articles included explicitly discuss international regimes and organizations as well as institutions. Are these distinctions significant? In some cases, no—many authors use the words interchangeably. Generally speaking, however, it is desirable to draw a distinction between institutions or regimes, on the one hand, and organizations, on the other. International institutions and regimes refer to sets of rules that regulate state behavior. These rules may be formal and explicit or informal and implicit. The term* international regimes *has been used to refer to rules and norms within a particular issue-area; thus general-purpose organizations such as the UN would not be considered regimes. Instead, organizations like the UN encompass a number of issue-specific regimes, such as those for peacekeeping, development, and environ-*

---

1. For example, see Pollack 1997; Moravcsik 1999; Meunier 2000; and Alter 2000.

mental issues. International organizations (IOs) are the formal embodiment of institutions and regimes. They are housed in buildings, employ civil servants and bureaucrats, and have budgets. They have varying degrees of agency, sometimes being able to take influential actions without explicit authorization from their member states. As the articles in this reader show, since the early 1980s the field has seen a shift from the study of regimes, including those that are highly informal, to the study of particular IOs.[2]

We organize the articles in this reader into four sections. The first section includes three articles developing alternative theoretical perspectives on international institutions. Oran Young, building directly on early work on regimes, argues that political leadership is a necessary and neglected ingredient in the successful establishment of regimes. Lisa Martin draws on an analysis of static collective-action problems to argue that the form of international institutions will respond in predictable ways to the dilemmas that states face. Martha Finnemore rounds out this theoretical survey with a self-identified constructivist model that sees IOs as promoters of international norms reaching deeply into the structure of national governments.

The second section turns from theoretical analysis to empirical studies. We have chosen articles that cover a broad spectrum of international politics. The articles here study environmental, economic, and regional integration problems as well as a general survey of the population dynamics of IOs. Ronald Mitchell finds that the design of regimes has a direct influence on their effectiveness in environmental affairs. Cheryl Shanks, Harold Jacobson, and Jeffrey Kaplan provide a statistical analysis of the population of IOs. They find a surprisingly high degree of turnover in this population, with individual IOs dying and being created continuously. Karen Alter provides one of many intriguing analyses of the ECJ, showing that its ability and willingness to act in opposition to the interests of EU member states has increased substantially over time. She attributes this change to relations with national courts and changes in supranational decision-making procedures. Finally, James McCall Smith turns to economic organizations, regional trade agreements in particular. He examines the legalization of dispute-resolution procedures in these pacts, finding that their form responds to asymmetries of economic power among their members and to the depth of cooperation required.

The third section focuses on an especially vibrant and important debate among institutional theorists: compliance with international rules. This debate is in one sense central to the study of institutions, since with low levels of compliance institutions might have little effect. It also illustrates the interaction between legal scholars and political scientists that increasingly characterizes studies of institutions. Abram Chayes and Antonia Handler Chayes approach the analysis of compliance from the perspective of legal scholars. They present a powerful

---

2. In contrast, Kratochwil and Ruggie, in this volume, identify a shift away from the study of formal to informal regimes. The pattern over the last two decades might therefore be described as the swing of a pendulum.

argument against attempts to quantify precisely levels of compliance or to develop hypotheses about how self-interest drives patterns of compliance. Instead, they begin from the assumption that compliance is generally good and argue that attention should turn to interpretation of the "acceptable" level of compliance in different international treaties. From this perspective, enforcement measures are not terribly important, and too much attention to enforcement provisions can even backfire. George Downs, David Rocke, and Peter Barsoom take on this claim, arguing that the inferences Chayes and Chayes draw are contaminated by severe selection problems and endogeneity. Although rates of compliance are high, we cannot infer from this fact that enforcement is unnecessary. In fact, enforcement is most important precisely when compliance would change patterns of state behavior most significantly. Beth Simmons contributes an empirical study of compliance issues, concentrating on international monetary affairs. She finds that the standard analysis of institutions in terms of the need to signal credible commitments and reputational considerations provides a good explanation for the evolution of legalistic rules in the international monetary system.

The final section concentrates on critiques of standard theories of international institutions. Friedrich Kratochwil and John Gerard Ruggie, presaging the explosion of work on institutions from a sociological or constructivist perspective in the 1990s, argue for a return to the study of formal IOs. This return would allow analysts to take more seriously the intersubjective nature of international institutions and identify new roles for them. Giulio Gallarotti challenges the "optimistic" view of most modern work on international institutions. He instead identifies patterns of systematic failure in international organization and reasons that IOs will often be ineffective or even backfire. Michael Barnett and Martha Finnemore criticize theories of IOs for neglecting their essentially bureaucratic nature. Drawing on Weberian analysis of bureaucracies, they argue that IOs have much deeper influences on states than assumed in the standard rationalist approach. Finally, Lisa Martin and Beth Simmons, in a survey of articles on international institutions and IOs published in the first fifty years of International Organization, *find both promise and problems in this body of work. They point to new directions for research, including drawing more explicitly on models of domestic institutions and developing new typologies of institutional effects.*

References

Alter, Karen J. 2000. The European Union's Legal System and Domestic Policy: Spillover or Backlash? *International Organization* 54 (3):489–518

Meunier, Sophie. 2000. What Single Voice? European Institutions and EU-U.S. Trade Negotiations. *International Organization* 54 (1):103–35.

Moravcsik, Andrew. 1999. A New Statecraft? Supranational Entrepreneurs and International Cooperation. *International Organization* 53 (2):267–306.

Pollack, Mark A. 1997. Delegation, Agency, and Agenda Setting in the European Community. *International Organization* 51 (1):99–134.

I.
Theories

Theoretical developments in international relations in recent years have often taken the form of arguments about the role of institutions. Theorists have focused on a number of issues related to institutions: their sources and dynamics, their impact on state behavior, and their form. Much of the modern theoretical work on international institutions can trace its roots to initial arguments put forth by Robert Keohane and in a collected set of essays on international regimes.[1]

One of the important steps in this new theoretical work was to identify institutions as solutions to collective-action problems faced by states. Theorists thus strove to distinguish their arguments from those of "idealists" who saw institutions as having enforcement powers and as overcoming the tensions of power politics and state interests. Instead, newer theories—initially under the label "neoliberal institutionalism"—accepted that states remained the major actors in international politics, that they were self-interested, and that they faced conflicts of interest. However, by focusing on aspects of the international environment, such as pervasive uncertainty, that made it difficult for states to achieve joint benefits even when they existed, theorists identified a role for institutions. They could reduce transaction costs, increase the value of a good reputation, increase the shadow of the future, set standards, provide information about the behavior of other states, and in other ways change aspects of the international environment, thus allowing cooperation for mutual gains.

These ideas excited researchers and gave rise to substantial theoretical and empirical developments. However, they also led to criticism from a number of directions. On the one hand, realists such as John Mearsheimer argued that institutions lack the capacity to change important aspects of the international environment and therefore could have little effect on patterns of state behavior.[2] On the other hand, critics, including constructivists, argued that the effects of institutions go much deeper than theorists had initially argued. Rather than just improving

---

1. See Keohane 1984; and Krasner 1983.
2. Mearsheimer 1994/1995.

the environment so that states could realize common interests, perhaps institutions could change state definitions of their own interests and identities in more fundamental ways. These theorists departed from the relatively strict definition of strategic rationality assumed by neoliberal institutionalists.

We include three articles published in International Organization *that exemplify these theoretical developments. Oran Young (Chapter 1) contributes to the emerging literature on international regimes by bringing the issue of political leadership into focus, thus shifting the emphasis away from states as actors to the interaction of individual leaders. While much of the initial regimes literature concentrated on changes in existing regimes, Young draws our attention to the creation of new regimes. He also insists that we need to take bargaining processes seriously. He argues that we cannot understand the conditions under which attempts to create regimes succeed or fail without considering leadership. Beyond contributing to our understanding of regime formation, Young develops a more general typology of political leadership. Leaders can exercise influence in a number of ways: by bringing material resources to bear, by framing issues, and by producing new systems of thought. Only the appropriate interaction of these types of leadership during the process of institutional bargaining will lead to the successful formation of institutions.*

Lisa Martin (Chapter 2) draws directly on analysis of collective-action problems to develop propositions about the form and role of institutions in different settings. She argues that the form of an institution—in particular, whether it conforms to principles of multilateralism[3]—depends on the specific type of problem that members of the institution are trying to solve. If they confront problems of monitoring and incentives to renege, the institution will need to be able to discriminate and single out violators in order to prevent widespread reneging. If the central problem is the need to coordinate on particular standards of behavior, in contrast, multilateral principles of nondiscrimination and generalized operating principles will be more effective. Often, analysis of symmetric collective-action dilemmas is inappropriate for the analysis of institutions because power asymmetries within these institutions are so intense. In this case a powerful state may find itself in a situation where it has incentives to provide collective goods unilaterally but prefers to induce other states to contribute to their provision as well. In this circumstance institutions can perform the function of allowing the powerful to link issues and to provide a veneer of multilateralism to cover the exercise of power.

Martha Finnemore (Chapter 3) theorizes that the effects of international institutions go well beyond manipulating external factors such as discount rates and information. Foreshadowing developments in more recent work, she analyzes IOs as agents rather than as institutions with sets of rules. She identifies a role of organizations that has proven vital historically but has not received much sustained analysis: the ability of organizations to develop and promote international norms.

---

3. Ruggie 1992.

In her self-identified constructivist approach, she moves away from the view of states as autonomous actors to consider them as entities shaped by interaction with others in the international arena. So, for example, the creation of new policymaking institutions on the domestic level is not just a functional response to demands to address new problems but also a social response to the activities of international norm promoters, including those in IOs. She concentrates on the issue of science policy and the role of UNESCO in teaching states to think of science as an appropriate area for state policy, therefore requiring the establishment of state science bureaucracies. This challenge to a purely rationalist account of the effects of institutions moves away from the consideration of interests to highlight processes of socialization and pressures to conform to international norms.

References

Keohane, Robert O. 1984. *After Hegemony: Cooperation and Discord in the World Political Economy.* Princeton, N.J.: Princeton University Press.

Krasner, Stephen D., ed. 1983. *International Regimes.* Ithaca, N.Y.: Cornell University Press.

Mearsheimer, John J. 1994/1995. The False Promise of International Institutions. *International Security* 19 (3):5–49.

Ruggie, John Gerard. 1992. Multilateralism: The Anatomy of an Institution. *International Organization* 46 (3):561–98.

Political Leadership and Regime Formation: On the Development of Institutions in International Society
Oran R. Young

Leadership, I argue in this article, is a critical determinant of success or failure in the processes of institutional bargaining that dominate efforts to form international regimes or, more generally, institutional arrangements in international society. Yet leadership is also a complex phenomenon, ill-defined, poorly understood, and subject to recurrent controversy among students of international affairs. The discussion to follow therefore seeks to elucidate the nature of leadership in the context of institutional bargaining and, in so doing, to deepen our understanding of the politics of regime formation at the international level.

The article begins with a brief discussion of the nature of institutional bargaining, an account that serves as a springboard both for pinpointing the role of leadership and for differentiating three forms of leadership that regularly come into play in efforts to establish international institutions: structural leadership, entrepreneurial leadership, and intellectual leadership. There follows an assessment of the contribution of each form of leadership to regime formation and an exploration of the interactions among them in bargaining of the sort associated with the formation of international institutions. In the process, I endeavor to bring the individual back in to the study of an important area of international affairs, without in any way diminishing the role of collective entities, such as states, international organizations, nongovernmental organizations, and multinational corporations.

This article originated in a presentation prepared for the 1989 annual meeting of the Academic Council on the United Nations System. It evolved during 1990 into a paper delivered at the annual meeting of the International Studies Association and a presentation developed for a joint Harvard/MIT seminar on international institutions. For constructive comments and advice, I am indebted to several anonymous reviewers as well as to Stephen Krasner, Gail Osherenko, and the members of the research team that has worked over the last two years on a project funded by the Ford Foundation and entitled "International Cooperation in the Arctic: The Politics of Regime Formation."

International Organization 45, 3, Summer 1991, pp. 281–308

Institutional bargaining

The phrase "institutional bargaining" refers to efforts on the part of autonomous actors to reach agreement among themselves on the terms of constitutional contracts or interlocking sets of rights and rules that are expected to
govern their subsequent interactions.[1] Occasionally, these contracts take the
form of broad, framework agreements encompassing the basic order or
ordering principles of an entire social system. In the case of international
society, the constitutional contracts articulated at Westphalia in 1648, Vienna
in 1815, and San Francisco in 1945 all belong to this class of comprehensive or
framework agreements. In all these cases, as it happens, the contract identifies
the sovereign state as the fundamental unit of international society and sets
forth a set of basic rights and rules intended to guide interactions among
states.[2] But there is nothing sacred about the state system; history is replete
with large-scale systems based on other ordering principles.

More often, however, institutional bargaining centers on efforts to reach
agreement on the provisions of more specialized institutional arrangements or
regimes covering particular issue-areas in contrast to the basic ordering
principles of international society. To illustrate, international regimes currently
in place deal with nuclear proliferation, international trade, telecommunications, air transport, ozone depletion, trade in endangered species, whaling,
Antarctica, and pollution control in the Mediterranean Basin. Efforts are
presently under way to establish similar regimes to deal with global climate
change and threats to biodiversity. As these examples suggest, international
regimes vary widely in terms of membership, functional scope, geographical
domain, complexity, administrative structure, and stage of development. The
regime for international trade, as formalized in the General Agreement on
Tariffs and Trade (GATT), for instance, includes a large number of members
and covers most of the world, though it is functionally restricted to matters
pertaining to trade and establishes only a modest administrative apparatus of
its own. The regime articulated in the Mediterranean Action Plan, by contrast,
is limited to eighteen members, is restricted geographically to the area
encompassed by the Mediterranean Basin, and covers matters pertaining solely
to environmental quality.[3]

Regardless of the character of the issues at stake in specific instances,
institutional bargaining in international society is marked by a number of

1. On the concept of a constitutional contract, see James M. Buchanan, *The Limits of Liberty*
(Chicago: University of Chicago Press, 1975), especially chap. 5.

2. For analyses of these framework agreements, which stress the role of social order in the
international system, see Hedley Bull, *The Anarchical Society: A Study of Order in World Politics*
(New York: Columbia University Press, 1977); and Ian Clark, *The Hierarchy of States: Reform and
Resistance in the International Order* (Cambridge: Cambridge University Press, 1989).

3. Peter M. Haas, *Saving the Mediterranean: The Politics of International Environmental
Cooperation* (New York: Columbia University Press, 1990).

distinctive features.[4] Those engaging in this type of bargaining normally operate under a unanimity rule in contrast to some form of majoritarian rule. In other words, once the problem is defined and the identity of the participants is settled (a process that may give rise to hard bargaining of a preliminary sort), actors endeavoring to formulate the terms of constitutional contracts make a concerted effort to devise packages of provisions that all the participants can accept.[5] What saves the resultant bargaining processes from yielding nothing but broad formulas containing little content or eventuating in outright failure is that regime formation in international society typically involves a large element of integrative (or productive) bargaining in contrast to distributive (or positional) bargaining[6] and proceeds under a (more or less thick) veil of uncertainty.[7] The participants in institutional bargaining do not begin with a clear picture of the locus and shape of a welfare frontier or contract curve, and they ordinarily seek to reach agreement on institutional arrangements encompassing enough issues or expected to remain in place long enough so that it is difficult for those negotiating on behalf of an individual participant to make confident predictions about the impact of particular options on that participant's own welfare.

Actors endeavoring to reach agreement on the terms of constitutional contracts seldom make a sustained effort to perfect the information at their disposal concerning the locus and shape of the contract curve before embarking on serious bargaining. They normally focus instead on a few key problems and seek to work out approaches to these problems that each of the participants can accept as fair in the sense that "patterns of outcomes generated under such arrangements will be broadly acceptable, regardless of where the participant might be located in such outcomes."[8] More often than not, this eventuates in the development and refinement over time of a negotiating text that serves as an organizing device for the sequence of discrete negotiating sessions that make up the overall process in specific instances of institutional bargaining.[9]

---

4. For an extended discussion of institutional bargaining, see Oran R. Young, "The Politics of International Regime Formation: Managing Natural Resources and the Environment," *International Organization* 43 (Summer 1989), pp. 349–75.

5. On processes of prenegotiation at the international level, see Janice Gross Stein, ed., *Getting to the Table: The Processes of International Prenegotiation* (Baltimore, Md.: Johns Hopkins University Press, 1989).

6. Richard Walton and Robert B. McKersie, *A Behavioral Theory of Negotiations* (New York: McGraw-Hill, 1965), chaps. 2–5.

7. Unlike the Rawlsian veil of ignorance, which stipulates that individual participants do not know their roles in society, the veil of uncertainty arises from factors that make it difficult for individuals to predict how specific institutional arrangements will affect their interests over time. See Geoffrey Brennan and James M. Buchanan, *The Reason of Rules: Constitutional Political Economy* (Cambridge: Cambridge University Press, 1985), pp. 28–31.

8. Ibid., p. 30.

9. Howard Raiffa, *The Art and Science of Negotiation* (Cambridge, Mass.: Harvard University Press, 1982), especially pp. 211–17.

The record clearly shows that institutional bargaining can and sometimes does yield positive results in the form of institutional arrangements that become effective as determinants of collective outcomes in international society. Consider, just to name some prominent examples, the postwar trade and monetary regimes and the more limited arrangements governing telecommunications, air transport, and human activities in Antarctica. The prognosis seems favorable as well for more recently developed regimes dealing with transboundary environmental problems, such as the long-range transport of airborne pollutants in Europe and the depletion of stratospheric ozone. Moreover, there appears to be no reason to reach pessimistic conclusions about the prospects for institutional bargaining dealing with emerging issues centered on global environmental change.

It is equally clear, however, that success is hard to come by in efforts to work out the terms of constitutional contracts, even when the participants readily acknowledge the existence of a sizable zone of agreement or contract zone. Institutional bargaining, in international society as in other social settings, is fraught with collective action problems that can and often do delay or block efforts to reach agreement on institutional arrangements that go beyond mere expressions of noble sentiments.

The operation of the unanimity rule, by itself, engenders incentives for ambitious or greedy actors to hold out in the hope that others will offer significant concessions to avoid stalemate and the resultant outcome of no agreement. But other considerations loom equally large as obstacles to success in institutional bargaining. The initiation of institutional bargaining proper, for example, is often delayed by problems of negotiation arithmetic or, in other words, diverging preferences regarding the composition of the group of participants and the contents of the agenda.[10] There is a world of difference, to take a current case in point, between negotiations intended to produce a series of regimes dealing with the long-range transport of airborne pollutants, ozone depletion, and climate change and efforts to develop a single, comprehensive regime of the sort envisioned by those who speak of a law of the atmosphere. Similar observations are in order regarding the nature of the product sought by participants in institutional bargaining. Consider, in this context, the gap between those who advocate starting with broad statements of principle to be fleshed out by adding substantive protocols over the course of time and those who prefer a more substantive approach in which an effort is made to reach agreement on solutions to problems treated as integrated packages from the outset.[11]

---

10. See James K. Sebenius, "Negotiation Arithmetic: Adding and Subtracting Issues and Parties," *International Organization* 37 (Spring 1983), pp. 281–316. See also Stein, *Getting to the Table.*

11. For a sophisticated treatment of this subject, drawing on experience with the law of the sea and the ozone depletion negotiations, see James K. Sebenius, "Negotiating a Regime to Control Global Warming," working paper, Kennedy School of Government, Cambridge, Mass., September 1990.

What is more, the parties to institutional bargaining at the international level are all collective or corporate entities, such as sovereign states or international organizations. This fact raises the prospect of what has recently been called the logic of two-level games or, to put it more descriptively, bargaining among divergent groups within a participating entity concerning positions to be taken by that entity in institutional bargaining proper.[12] Under the circumstances, it is hardly surprising that parties regularly differ in their ability to focus on specific instances of institutional bargaining and that it is difficult to structure events in such a way that the key participants are able simultaneously to summon the political will needed to reach closure on the terms of constitutional contracts. At a time when some participants are anxious to conclude the bargaining process, others may be paralyzed by internal disagreements over the terms of the proposed contract. Similarly, domestic elections or civil strife may divert the attention of some participants from institutional bargaining just as the political context within others makes it easy for them to exercise the political will required to bring the bargaining process to a close.

Taken together, these obstacles to success in institutional bargaining set the stage for the emergence of leadership. Leadership, as I will use the term in this article, refers to the actions of individuals who endeavor to solve or circumvent the collective action problems that plague the efforts of parties seeking to reap joint gains in processes of institutional bargaining. By themselves, the actions of leaders are not sufficient to guarantee that institutional bargaining will yield positive results; it is easy enough to point to instances of failure despite masterful performances on the part of one or more leaders. Consider the long-standing effort to reach agreement on a comprehensive nuclear test ban regime and the attempt to devise a regime for deep seabed mining in the context of the law of the sea negotiations as cases in point. Yet leadership does raise the probability of success, often dramatically, in efforts to devise provisions for constitutional contracts that all the participants are willing to accept. It follows that those desiring to understand the politics of regime formation in international society will do well to invest some of their time and energy in a study of the activities of those who assume leadership roles.[13]

The nature of leadership

Students of international politics are not likely to react with surprise to the proposition that leadership looms large in the context of institutional bargain-

12. Robert D. Putnam, "Diplomacy and Domestic Politics: The Logic of Two-Level Games," *International Organization* 42 (Summer 1988), pp. 427–60.

13. The discussion to follow places primary emphasis on factors that determine whether or not institutional bargaining succeeds in the sense that it results in a mutually acceptable constitutional contract. Two other concerns, however, are relevant to this treatment of the role of leadership. Leaders often influence the timing of the move toward closure on the terms of a constitutional contract. Similarly, leadership is a significant factor in accounting for the substantive content of the provisions incorporated into international regimes.

ing. Leadership, after all, is thought by many to constitute one of the key elements of all politics. Even so, recent efforts to elucidate the role of leadership in international society have engendered more confusion than illumination. At the outset, therefore, it is important to clear away some conceptual underbrush that has come to obscure our view of the role of leadership in institutional bargaining at the international level.

Part of the problem arises from the fact that it is easy to fall prey to post hoc reasoning in thinking about leadership. Students of international affairs often direct their attention toward cases in which institutional bargaining has succeeded and reason that leadership refers to actions on the part of one or another of the participants who apparently played a role in producing successful results. But this tack is fatally flawed as an approach to formulating and testing ideas about the role of leadership as a determinant of the success or failure of institutional bargaining. By conflating leadership with success in the formation of regimes, such reasoning effectively precludes the development of propositions dealing with the relationship between the activities of leaders on the one hand and the outcomes of institutional bargaining on the other. What is needed instead is a conception of leadership focusing on well-defined forms of behavior that can be identified without reference to the outcomes flowing from institutional bargaining. Only then will the role of leadership in determining the success or failure of institutional bargaining emerge as a viable topic for research on the part of those seeking to understand the formation of international regimes.

Another source of the problem lies in the preoccupation of many students of regime formation with the idea of hegemony or, to use Charles Kindleberger's term, dominance.[14] A hegemon, in the material sense, is a state that possesses a "preponderance of material resources."[15] Unlike individuals who become leaders in international affairs, hegemons are relatively scarce in individual issue-areas, much less in international society as a whole.[16] What is more, the principal inferences that analysts have drawn from the theory of hegemonic stability do not stand up well to empirical testing.[17] It is not difficult, for example, to identify cases that run contrary to the central hypothesis that the

14. Charles P. Kindleberger, *The International Economic Order* (Cambridge, Mass.: MIT Press, 1988), chap. 14.

15. The quotation is from Robert O. Keohane, *After Hegemony: Cooperation and Discord in the World Political Economy* (Princeton, N.J.: Princeton University Press, 1984), p. 32. Note that this discussion focuses exclusively on hegemony in the structural sense, in contrast to hegemony in the cognitive or Gramscian sense.

16. For an important discussion of the extent to which power is fungible and therefore applicable across issue-areas or is issue-specific, see David A. Baldwin, *Paradoxes of Power* (New York: Basil Blackwell, 1989), especially chap. 2.

17. For an early but excellent discussion, see Duncan Snidal, "The Limits of Hegemonic Stability Theory," *International Organization* 39 (Autumn 1985), pp. 579–614. For a more recent discussion, see Isabelle Grunberg, "Exploring the 'Myth' of Hegemonic Stability," *International Organization* 44 (Autumn 1990), pp. 431–77.

presence of a hegemon constitutes a necessary condition for the formation of effective institutional arrangements in international society.

Equally important is the fact that the recent emphasis on hegemony and, more generally, structural determinants of collective outcomes in international society has had the effect of diverting attention from the roles that individuals play as leaders who are able to exercise significant influence over processes of institutional bargaining. To avoid the resultant pitfalls of reification, it is important to bear in mind the relationship between individuals and collective entities, such as states and international organizations. Those who become leaders in institutional bargaining frequently act in the name of or as agents of states or international organizations. But in the final analysis, leaders are individuals, and it is the behavior of these individuals which we must explore to evaluate the role of leadership in the formation of international institutions.

These shortcomings in recent studies of regime formation have not gone unnoticed. Although there is a sense in which his work on the Great Depression stimulated the thinking of the hegemonists, Kindleberger stands out in this context for his persistent effort to distinguish between hegemony (or dominance) and leadership.[18] Yet even Kindleberger fails to lay bare the essential elements of leadership in institutional bargaining at the international level. He does not take a clear stand on the question of whether leaders are individuals or collective entities. He suggests that leaders are motivated "by ethical training and by the circumstances of position," a tack that encourages the formulation of propositions that are, at best, difficult to test.[19] He focuses on the roles leaders assume within existing institutional arrangements (for example, the role of stabilizer in the international monetary system), a move that shifts attention toward the roles leaders play once institutions are in place while diverting attention from the process of regime formation.[20] And his analysis often devolves into an effort to differentiate leadership from exploitation, an issue of intrinsic interest but not one that goes to the heart of the role of leadership in institutional bargaining. Refreshing as these ideas are as an antidote to the heavy-handed arguments of the hegemonists, therefore, Kindleberger's exploration of leadership leaves the essence of the leader's role or roles in institutional bargaining unspecified.

To overcome the resultant confusion concerning the contributions leaders make to regime formation, I argue, we must approach leadership in behavioral terms, focusing on the actions of individuals, differentiating analytically among several forms of leadership, and then analyzing the interactions among them. I call these forms of leadership structural leadership, entrepreneurial leadership, and intellectual leadership.[21] The structural leader is an individual who

18. See Charles P. Kindleberger, *The World in Depression, 1929–1939* (Berkeley: University of California Press, 1973); and Kindleberger, *The International Economic Order,* chaps. 11 and 14.

19. Kindleberger, *The International Economic Order,* p. 157.

20. Kindleberger, *The World in Depression,* especially chap. 14.

21. A fourth type of leadership, recognized by students of domestic politics, is often described as charismatic leadership. The charismatic leader exercises influence through force of personality and

acts in the name of a party (ordinarily a state) engaged in institutional bargaining and who leads by devising effective ways to bring that party's structural power (that is, power based on the possession of material resources) to bear in the form of bargaining leverage over the issues at stake in specific interactions. The entrepreneurial leader, by contrast, is an individual who may or may not act in the name of a major stakeholder in institutional bargaining but who leads by making use of negotiating skill to influence the manner in which issues are presented in the context of institutional bargaining and to fashion mutually acceptable deals bringing willing parties together on the terms of constitutional contracts yielding benefits for all. And the intellectual leader is an individual who may or may not be affiliated with a recognized actor in international politics but who relies on the power of ideas to shape the way in which participants in institutional bargaining understand the issues at stake and to orient their thinking about options available to come to terms with these issues.

These distinctions are analytic in nature. Although the roles typically fall to different individuals, leaders in actual instances of institutional bargaining may endeavor to devise strategies that draw on two or more of these forms of leadership at the same time. Nonetheless, an analysis of the differences among structural, entrepreneurial, and intellectual leadership will not only help us to grasp clearly the roles leaders play in institutional bargaining at the international level, but it will also open up fruitful avenues for research on the part of students of international affairs. In a later section of this article, I begin to explore these opportunities by considering interactions among the three forms of leadership in the context of institutional bargaining.

Structural leadership

Structural leaders are experts in translating the possession of material resources into bargaining leverage cast in terms appropriate to the issues at stake in specific instances of institutional bargaining. Because they act as agents of parties (ordinarily states) that are principals in the bargaining process, it is natural for such leaders to espouse institutional arrangements that seem well suited to the interests of the states they represent. But a preference for some particular set of institutional arrangements is not the essential feature of structural leadership. The opportunity to engage in integrative bargaining under a veil of uncertainty generally ensures that none of the stakeholders will be able to make confident predictions at the outset regarding the incidence of

---

seeks to impose a vision, often messianic in character, on those who become his or her followers. Whatever the relevance of this phenomenon in other social settings, I can see no evidence that it plays a significant role in institutional bargaining at the international level. For an account of charismatic leaders as spellbinders, see Ann Ruth Willner, *The Spellbinders: Charismatic Political Leadership* (New Haven, Conn.: Yale University Press, 1984).

the benefits likely to flow from alternative institutional arrangements. At the same time, the presence of collective action problems typically ensures that it will be hard to achieve consensus under the conditions associated with institutional bargaining. The essential feature of structural leadership, then, lies in the ability to translate structural power into bargaining leverage as a means of reaching agreement on the terms of constitutional contracts in social settings of the sort exemplified by international society.

In a general way, it makes sense to view the link between structural power and bargaining leverage as stemming from the existence of asymmetries among the participants or stakeholders in processes of institutional bargaining. While there are many ways to think about such asymmetries, two broad categories stand out because they engender distinctive leadership strategies. We may describe these categories in terms of what Kindleberger labels, in a colorful though unflattering phrase, "arm-twisting and bribery."[22] More specifically, a party enjoying relative invulnerability in the sense that it has less to lose than others from an outcome of no agreement can bring pressure to bear by threatening to stall the bargaining process unless others accept its preferred institutional provisions and by making use of committal tactics to enhance the credibility of its threats.[23] A party with more to gain than others from the successful conclusion of institutional bargaining, on the other hand, can exercise bargaining leverage by offering side-payments or promising to reward others for throwing their support behind the institutional arrangements it prefers.[24]

These observations give rise to several immediate points of clarification regarding the role of structural leadership in institutional bargaining. Bargaining leverage is necessarily relational; the important thing is what an actor stands to lose or gain relative to what others stand to lose or gain from institutional bargaining. An agent acting on behalf of a party badly in need of some suitable arrangement may nevertheless be able to play a leadership role if other participants stand to lose even more from an outcome of no agreement. Similarly, an agent acting in the name of a party that is in line to benefit substantially from the adoption of a particular arrangement may find it difficult to use side-payments effectively when some other party stands to gain even more from the choice of an alternative arrangement. Any effort to explain or predict the roles structural leaders play in institutional bargaining must therefore rest on an assessment of the relative, in contrast to the absolute, circumstances of the participants.

It follows, as well, that a number of individuals may function simultaneously

---

22. Kindleberger, *The International Economic Order,* p. 186.

23. For a seminal account of this type of bargaining power, see Thomas C. Schelling, *The Strategy of Conflict* (Cambridge, Mass.: Harvard University Press, 1960).

24. While this type of bargaining power may seem counterintuitive at first, it resembles Zeuthen's well-known conception of risk willingness. See Frederik Zeuthen, "Economic Warfare," in Oran R. Young, ed., *Bargaining: Formal Theories of Negotiation* (Urbana: University of Illinois Press, 1975), pp. 145–63.

as structural leaders in the effort to devise generally acceptable institutional arrangements in a given issue-area. Those who speak of hegemony presumably have in mind situations in which asymmetries in structural power are so extreme that those acting on behalf of a single actor can exercise overwhelming bargaining leverage, leaving others with virtually no leverage at all. Needless to say, an actor that qualifies as a hegemon in this sense will be well placed to impose the terms of international regimes on others. But these comments also make it clear why hegemony is an extreme type. Hegemony is the terminus of a spectrum, a point at which the relevant asymmetries reach their ultimate values. Far more common, in actuality, are situations in which two or more parties possess substantial, though not necessarily equal, structural power and the prospects for success in institutional bargaining turn on the ability of those acting on behalf of these parties to make use of bargaining leverage to foster agreement on the provisions of mutually acceptable constitutional contracts.

It is a relatively simple matter for those negotiating on behalf of a hegemon or dominant power to exercise structural leadership; they need only lay out the provisions of proposed constitutional contracts that others are in no position to oppose. The role of Henry Morgenthau, who represented the United States at the 1944 Bretton Woods negotiations on the postwar international monetary regime, is easy to understand in these terms. In other cases, however, the conversion of structural power into bargaining leverage framed in terms relevant to particular instances of institutional bargaining is a complex and uncertain process requiring both acumen and a capacity for sophisticated political action on the part of individuals desiring to act as leaders. As the following discussion makes clear, even those negotiating on behalf of an actor possessing great structural power, such as the United States during much of the postwar era, are not likely to achieve impressive results if they simply assume that their efforts to exercise bargaining leverage in specific situations will succeed.

Structural leadership is in part a matter of timing and the ability to deploy threats or promises in ways that are both carefully crafted and credible. During the mid-1980s, when the dangers associated with stratospheric ozone depletion were still subject to considerable scientific controversy, for example, American negotiators tried without success to induce Britain, France, Germany, and others to accept plans for a comprehensive reduction in the use of chlorofluorocarbons (CFCs). The result was the 1985 Vienna convention, a framework agreement containing little substantive content. By 1987, however, new scientific evidence had strengthened the case for restricting all major uses of CFCs, and Dupont (the largest producer of CFCs) had accepted the force of this argument. At this stage, Richard Benedick, negotiating on behalf of the United States, was able to make good use of threats to restrict access to the American market as a means of gaining acceptance of the principle of across-the-board cuts in the production and consumption of CFCs, a formula that ultimately became the centerpiece of the bargain articulated in the

Montreal protocol.[25] And by 1990, negotiators representing China and India, actors that seem relatively weak in conventional structural terms, were able to exercise considerable bargaining leverage in the process of hammering out the terms of the London amendments, including a compensation fund for developing countries prepared to phase out CFCs, by capitalizing on the fact that reductions on the part of major developed countries would come to naught without the cooperation of key developing countries.

The conversion of structural power into bargaining leverage is also in part a matter of forming effective coalitions and taking appropriate measures to prevent the emergence of blocking or counter coalitions.[26] Institutional bargaining during the Third United Nations Conference on the Law of the Sea revolved, in large measure, around efforts to devise a complex package deal acceptable to coalitions representing developing countries, maritime powers, landlocked countries, and so forth.[27] It is not surprising, therefore, that when American negotiators representing the newly installed Reagan administration sought in 1981 to reopen the carefully crafted law of the sea package to change provisions pertaining to deep seabed mining that Elliot Richardson had accepted on behalf of the Carter administration, their efforts were rejected by representatives of most of the other participants in the negotiations. By contrast, negotiators representing a coalition of advanced industrialized states, led by Britain and Germany, played a key role during the spring of 1990 in bringing pressure to bear on the Bush administration in the United States to accede to the creation of a fund designed to assist developing countries prepared to phase out the use of CFCs. It will come as no surprise, under the circumstances, that individuals who have the ability to put together and nurture coalitions of this sort regularly emerge as influential structural leaders in institutional bargaining.

The need for insight and creativity in efforts to convert structural power into bargaining leverage is reinforced by the common occurrence of political differences within the structural leader's own state that complicate efforts to bring pressure to bear on other participants in institutional bargaining. There can be no doubt that the United States has possessed great structural power in connection with many instances of institutional bargaining at the international level during the postwar era. Yet it is common knowledge in the international community that the promises made by American negotiators in the interests of winning over other parties to a treaty are not always credible, since the U.S.

25. See Peter M. Haas, "Ozone Alone, No CFCs: Epistemic Communities and the Protection of Stratospheric Ozone," *International Organization,* forthcoming. But note that the American success at this juncture was facilitated by the growing impact in Germany of the scientific case against CFCs and the consequent erosion of the earlier common stance of Britain, France, and Germany.

26. For an account that stresses the importance of preventing the emergence of blocking coalitions, see Sebenius, "Negotiating a Regime to Control Global Warming."

27. See James K. Sebenius, *Negotiating the Law of the Sea: Lessons in the Art and Science of Reaching Agreement* (Cambridge, Mass.: Harvard University Press, 1984); and Robert L. Friedheim, *Negotiating the New Ocean Regime,* forthcoming.

Senate may find the terms of the treaty unacceptable and therefore refuse to ratify it. In some cases, American negotiators have actually turned this constraint to good account, using it as a source of bargaining leverage rather than treating it as a liability. The evidence suggests, for instance, that those conducting arms control negotiations on behalf of the United States (such as Gerard Smith in the strategic arms limitation talks [SALT] of the late 1960s and early 1970s and Max Kampelman in the intermediate nuclear forces [INF] negotiations during the 1980s) have sometimes raised the specter of Senate opposition as an effective bargaining lever. But in other cases, internal complications of this sort have restricted the efforts of American negotiators to exercise bargaining leverage. As the influence of protectionism has grown stronger in American domestic politics, for instance, the ability of negotiators on behalf of the United States to operate effectively as structural leaders in international trade negotiations (such as the Uruguay Round) has declined.

The achievements of Henry Morgenthau, William Clayton, and other leaders who negotiated the postwar monetary and trade regimes on behalf of the United States at a time when American structural power was at its zenith were relatively straightforward, though the institutions they created certainly produced lasting effects. But the same cannot be said of more recent instances of effective structural leadership on the part of Americans, such as Curtis Bohlen's performance as the chief American negotiator of the 1973 polar bear regime, Paul Warnke's role as one of the American architects of the 1979 SALT II treaty, Tucker Scully's efforts as the principal American negotiator in the institutional bargaining eventuating in the 1980 Convention on the Conservation of Antarctic Marine Living Resources, Richard Benedick's performance as the American negotiator in the bargaining that produced the 1987 Montreal protocol on ozone depletion, and the efforts of Clayton Yeutter and Carla Hills to reach a mutually acceptable conclusion to the Uruguay Round of trade negotiations. Nor should we overlook the structural leadership of Elliot Richardson in the context of the law of the sea negotiations, despite the fact that his efforts failed to produce a deep seabed mining regime acceptable to the Reagan administration and therefore played a role in the eventual refusal of the United States to sign the 1982 Convention on the Law of the Sea.

On this account, there is no need to resort to vague notions such as "ethical training" or the "circumstances of position" to explain the behavior of structural leaders. No doubt, the role of structural leader will appeal to those brought up to value public service above other forms of achievement as well as to those deeply concerned about either a specific issue-area or the importance of international cooperation more generally as a means of avoiding destructive conflicts under the conditions of complex interdependence prevailing in the world today. At the same time, structural leaders are normally public servants who are compensated well to negotiate on behalf of states, whether or not the negotiations produce mutually acceptable institutional arrangements in a timely manner.

This suggests that self-interest, a concept based on the idea that individuals act to promote their own values, may well suffice to explain or predict the behavior of structural leaders. Yet several clarifying observations are in order in this context. Structural leaders are frequently drawn to their role for reasons having little to do with the pursuit of material rewards (some are wealthy in their own right). Rather, their incentives to strive toward agreement on the terms of constitutional contracts are apt to center on more intangible rewards, such as the satisfaction of seeing progress toward goals they espouse, the receipt of accolades from their peers, or the achievement of a place for themselves in history. In an important sense, this is good news for those concerned about recruiting the best and the brightest to act as structural leaders, since competent governments are often able to provide substantial rewards in intangible currencies, even when they are beset by persistent deficits or shortfalls that curtail their ability to pay in material terms.

Entrepreneurial leadership

Turn now to the entrepreneurial leader, an individual who relies on negotiating skill to frame issues in ways that foster integrative bargaining and to put together deals that would otherwise elude participants endeavoring to form international regimes through institutional bargaining. The source of the entrepreneurial leader's role lies in the existence of a bargainer's surplus coupled with more or less severe collective action problems plaguing efforts on the part of the principals to strike the bargain needed to capture the surplus.[28] A bargainer's surplus exists whenever an identifiable set of parties can reap joint gains by coordinating their behavior in a mutually agreeable fashion. In cases in which the relationship among the parties is fully specified, the bargainer's surplus will coincide with the area of the contract zone or zone of agreement. But even in the less well defined situations characteristic of institutional bargaining in international society, it takes no great acuity to see that the bargainer's surplus will often be substantial.

Most conventional theories of bargaining assume that rational parties will find ways to reach agreement on their own under such conditions, thereby reaping the bargainer's surplus without any need for entrepreneurial leaders to assist in the process.[29] In institutional bargaining of the sort under consideration here, however, problems arising from the need for innovative thinking to determine the scope of the contract zone, the propensity of the principals to

---

28. For a general account of entrepreneurial leadership under such conditions, see Norman Frohlich, Joe A. Oppenheimer, and Oran R. Young, *Political Leadership and Collective Goods* (Princeton, N.J.: Princeton University Press, 1971).

29. For a survey of these theories, see Young, *Bargaining.*

engage in positional bargaining, and the operation of the unanimity rule ensure that the existence of a bargainer's surplus is seldom sufficient (though it is undoubtedly necessary) to guarantee that efforts to reap mutual benefits will succeed. This provides an opening for entrepreneurial leaders to assume various roles in helping those engaged in institutional bargaining to reap the bargainer's surplus.

One immediate implication of this line of thinking is that leadership in institutional bargaining is by no means confined to situations involving the supply of public goods, as some of those who write on hegemony or dominance imply.[30] Institutional bargaining may indeed concern cost-sharing arrangements relating to the supply of international public goods, such as a stable system of exchange rates or a generally acknowledged system of rules pertaining to the use of marine resources. Still, such cases are no more than a subset of the overall domain of institutional bargaining. In international society, as in every other social setting, bargaining occurs when gains from trade are available and the terms of trade are subject to agreement on the part of the parties themselves.

Just what do individuals who act as entrepreneurial leaders do to help participants reap the bargainer's surplus in institutional bargaining processes? For the most part, they function as (1) agenda setters shaping the form in which issues are presented for consideration at the international level, (2) popularizers drawing attention to the importance of the issues at stake, (3) inventors devising innovative policy options to overcome bargaining impediments, and (4) brokers making deals and lining up support for salient options. Consider, in this connection, the efforts of entrepreneurial leaders such as Hamilton Amerasinghe, Tommy Koh, Jens Evensen, and Alan Beesley during the law of the sea negotiations, Stjepan Keckes in the process of developing the pollution control regime for the Mediterranean Basin, Mustafa Tolba in the negotiations leading to the Vienna convention and the Montreal protocol on ozone depletion, and Christopher Beebe in the effort to hammer out a minerals regime for Antarctica.

Keckes played an active role in devising a means to bring scientific ideas to the attention of policymakers within individual countries. Tolba provided a key link in translating the rapidly evolving scientific picture regarding ozone depletion into terms that were relevant to processes of institutional bargaining at the international level. For their part, Amerasinghe, Koh, Beebe, and the others became expert brokers of the interests of numerous states in their roles as custodians and refiners of the key negotiating texts relating to the law of the sea and Antarctic minerals. As the cases of stratospheric ozone depletion and global climate change suggest, entrepreneurs cannot achieve these results single-handedly. It helps, for instance, to be backed by an atmosphere of

30. Kindleberger, *The International Economic Order,* chaps. 9 and 14.

urgency or crisis, as in the case of ozone depletion following the discovery of the "ozone hole" over Antarctica in 1985, or by an emerging consensus in the scientific community, as in the case of global climate change.[31] Even so, it is hard to avoid the conclusion that entrepreneurs play key roles as facilitators of bargaining processes that can all too easily bog down or get diverted into blind alleys in the absence of skillful measures to keep them on track.[32]

Because their roles resemble each other in some respects, it is worth spelling out at this juncture the distinction between entrepreneurial leaders and mediators. Although they share with mediators an interest in working to overcome bargaining impediments, entrepreneurial leaders are not third parties. Unlike mediators, they are typically agents of actors that possess stakes in the issues at hand and participate in the relevant negotiations in their own right. Under the circumstances, entrepreneurs may be affected by the constraints of agency, but they are under no obligation to act in a manner that will seem impartial to all the principals. Equally important, entrepreneurial leaders do not limit themselves to efforts to assist or facilitate negotiations among the principals. They work to frame the issues at stake and intervene energetically in the substance of the negotiations, endeavoring to invent attractive options and to persuade the parties to back the options they espouse. It follows that entrepreneurial leaders are not bound by a number of restrictions that constrain the efforts of mediators or other third parties.

There are cases in which the work of the entrepreneurial leader is facilitated by being an agent of a powerful state participating in the bargaining process. When it is necessary to supplement entrepreneurship with "strong elements of both arm-twisting and bribery," to use Kindleberger's phrase, the backing of a powerful state is undoubtedly critical. Yet it is important to recognize that such backing is not a necessary condition for exercising entrepreneurial leadership in international society. For a classic example, we can turn to the role of Talleyrand, who represented the losing side in the negotiations following the Napoleonic Wars, in devising the terms of the Treaty of Vienna in 1815.[33] What is more, there are cases in which the backing of a powerful state would actually hinder rather than help the efforts of the entrepreneurial leader. It seems evident, for example, that entrepreneurs who gain stature from their association with intergovernmental organizations, such as Mustafa Tolba (who was executive director of the United Nations Environment Programme during the negotiations on ozone depletion) and Janos Stanovik (who was executive

31. See Sharon L. Roan, *Ozone Crisis: The 15 Year Evolution of a Sudden Global Emergency* (New York: Wiley, 1989); and Dean Edwin Abrahamson, ed., *The Challenge of Global Warming* (Washington, D.C.: Island Press, 1989).

32. See also Winfried Lang, "Negotiations on the Environment," in Victor Kremenyuk, ed., *International Negotiation: Analysis, Approaches, Issues* (San Francisco: Jossey-Bass, 1991), pp. 343–56.

33. Charles Webster, *The Congress of Vienna* (New York: Barnes & Noble, 1966).

director of the Economic Commission for Europe during the negotiations on long-range transboundary air pollution), would suffer from becoming too closely associated with one or another of the great powers.

As the preceding observations suggest, entrepreneurial leaders are individuals rather than states that are important by virtue of their dominant position in some social setting. To be sure, those individuals who become entrepreneurial leaders are typically agents in the sense that they act in the name of states, intergovernmental organizations, or nongovernmental organizations. This means that their efforts will be circumscribed by the interests of the organizations they represent and that they will be subject to removal if they neglect these interests in their efforts to ensure that parties reap the bargainer's surplus in international negotiations. Nonetheless, the fact that entrepreneurial leaders are individuals has enormous significance for the study of institutional bargaining in international society. It means, above all, that we can analyze the behavior of entrepreneurial leaders and even model their utility functions without worrying about reification on the one hand or the miasma of intraparty bargaining on the other.[34] It also means that we can apply our knowledge of individual behavior to the study of entrepreneurial leadership in institutional bargaining. To offer a single illustration, it seems reasonable to expect that the role of entrepreneur in situations that are poorly specified (so that the size of the bargainer's surplus is unknown and the invention of new policy options is critical) will prove more appealing to individuals who are risk takers than to those who are risk averse.

Frequently, the organizations that entrepreneurial leaders represent are governments. This was true, for example, in the cases of Amerasinghe, Koh, and Beebe referred to above. But this hardly obviates the need to inquire about the motivations of such leaders. Unlike Kindleberger, I assume that entrepreneurial leaders are self-interested: they are motivated or driven to exercise leadership to further their own values or goals rather than to fulfill some sense of ethical responsibility to the community. Of course, self-interest is a broad concept; it includes a devotion to intangible values, such as the achievement of a peaceful world, as well as to tangible concerns, such as the maximization of monetary rewards. Still, there is a sense in which the fact that entrepreneurial leaders are self-interested is a source of comfort rather than a problem. Individuals who act out of self-interest are far more reliable and predictable than those who respond episodically to some other motivating force, a fact that bodes well for the prospects of constructing a robust theory of entrepreneurial leadership in international society.

The existence of a bargainer's surplus ensures that the parties to institutional bargaining will be in a position to compensate those who function as

---

34. For a sophisticated account of the complications associated with intraparty bargaining, see Putnam, "Diplomacy and Domestic Politics."

entrepreneurial leaders. Although the actual terms may be subject to separate negotiations, the principals can offer rewards for these services and still come out ahead of the game, so long as the sum of the payments to entrepreneurs does not exceed the aggregate bargainer's surplus. This relationship is relatively straightforward when the leaders are agents of the actual parties to negotiations. It becomes a little more complex in the case of entrepreneurs who work for intergovernmental or nongovernmental organizations that are unlikely to emerge as parties to institutional arrangements in their own right, a fact that heightens the importance of the observation that entrepreneurial leaders are often willing (and sometimes even eager) to take their compensation in intangible currencies such as prestige, political influence in domestic arenas, or progress toward the achievement of some larger personal goal (for example, the uniting of Europe or the preservation of species). This undoubtedly helps account for the behavior of leaders such as Fridtjof Nansen in connection with the plight of international refugees, Jean Monnet in the context of efforts to achieve European integration, and the Duke of Edinburgh with regard to the protection of wildlife. It reminds us also that the achievement of success in striking a bargain may in itself constitute a form of payment for entrepreneurial leaders (who stand to benefit in terms of their reputations as skillful negotiators), quite apart from the more tangible income streams we usually consider in analyzing the behavior of individuals. This fact can only serve to enhance the scope for entrepreneurship in a wide range of international negotiations.

Those who talk of hegemony necessarily restrict leadership to the actions of a single dominant state. Even Kindleberger, who has sought repeatedly to differentiate his views from those of the hegemonists, characteristically speaks of a single leader (for example, Great Britain or the United States), though he appears to admit the possibility of a small coalition of key states handling the leadership function and to view the leader as the principal member of a cast including a number of supporting actors.[35] When we turn to entrepreneurial activities, by contrast, there is no barrier to the emergence of multiple leaders; simultaneous efforts on the part of a number of individuals endeavoring to frame the issues, invent options, or broker the interests of the principals constitute a common occurrence in international negotiations. On balance, the presence of multiple leaders is likely to prove more constructive when it involves popularizing issues and brokering interests than when it centers on the invention of new options. The introduction of a multiplicity of options in an uncoordinated fashion can easily divide the parties into competing factions supporting incompatible action plans, thereby hindering rather than helping efforts to reap the bargainer's surplus. Moving an issue to the top of the policy agenda for all relevant parties, by contrast, often requires the efforts of

---

35. Kindleberger, *The World in Depression*.

numerous entrepreneurs. And several brokers may be more efficient in working out the terms of a viable deal than a single individual who attempts to take into account all the interests in a complex negotiation.

Intellectual leadership

An intellectual leader is an individual who produces intellectual capital or generative systems of thought that shape the perspectives of those who participate in institutional bargaining and, in so doing, plays an important role in determining the success or failure of efforts to reach agreement on the terms of constitutional contracts in international society. Those who become intellectual leaders are necessarily individuals, though they may maintain some association with states or other corporate entities. It is possible as well to identify cases in which a single individual emerges not only as an intellectual leader but also as a structural or entrepreneurial leader. John Maynard Keynes appears to have played a dual role, articulating during the 1930s the intellectual bases for a mode of economic thought that has become known as embedded liberalism and then serving as a representative of Great Britain in the negotiations leading to the postwar monetary regime. And it may well be that analogous comments are in order with regard to Henri Dunant's activities in connection with the establishment of the International Committee of the Red Cross, Jean Monnet's efforts to set in motion the uniting of Europe, and Arvid Pardo's role in elaborating the concept of the common heritage of humankind and bringing it to bear on the development of the law of the sea.

For the most part, however, there is a clear distinction between intellectual leadership on the one hand and entrepreneurial or structural leadership on the other. This is in part a consequence of the fact that intellectual leadership ordinarily operates on a different time scale than the other types of leadership involved in institutional bargaining. Intellectual leadership is a deliberative or reflective process; it is difficult to articulate coherent systems of thought in the midst of the fast-paced negotiations associated with institutional bargaining. It is also in part due to the fact that new ideas generally have to triumph over the entrenched mindsets or worldviews held by policymakers, so that the process of injecting new intellectual capital into policy streams is generally a time-consuming one. None of this is meant to diminish the power of ideas and therefore the influence of intellectual leaders. On the contrary, as Keynes and others have often reminded us, the impact of generative systems of thought can continue to grow even after their creators have passed from the scene.[36]

36. There is, of course, a lively debate concerning the extent to which interested parties control the development and dissemination of ideas. In this article, I take the view that the causal relationships are reciprocal. While interested parties strive to control ideas, ideas can and often do operate as an independent force in human affairs.

To lend substance to the idea of intellectual leadership in connection with the establishment of international institutions, it will help to consider some prominent examples. While attempts to devise cooperative international arrangements to halt the spread of cholera, the plague, and other communicable diseases made little headway in the absence of agreement regarding causal mechanisms and effective responses, negotiations moved rapidly toward a successful conclusion with the triumph toward the end of the nineteenth century of the ideas of the contagionists, such as Robert Koch, over those of the miasmatists.[37] The constitutional contracts spelling out the provisions of the postwar international trade and monetary regimes could not have been formulated in the absence of the ideas associated with embedded liberalism, which provided a coherent argument in support of free trade and spurred the establishment of a system of adjustable exchange rates as an alternative to the preexisting gold standard.[38]

Similar observations are in order regarding the role of ideas pertaining to population dynamics and, more specifically, the role of the concept of maximum sustainable yield (MSY) from renewable resources (for example, fish and marine mammal stocks) in shaping efforts to come to terms with the dilemma of common property resources or the tragedy of the commons at the international level during most of the twentieth century.[39] This example is also instructive as an illustration of the persistent influence of ideas and of the intellectual requirements for bringing about change in institutional arrangements. So long as the concept of MSY reigned supreme in the minds of those concerned with the management of renewable resources, international regimes designed to conserve these resources focused on rules governing the harvesting of fish or animals rather than on broader issues relating to habitat protection or the interactions between targeted species and other components of the relevant ecosystems. This is why the "whole ecosystems" approach built into recent institutional arrangements, such as those set forth in the Convention on the Conservation of Antarctic Marine Living Resources, is widely regarded as a development of great significance.[40] In effect, it stands as a symbol of a switch from one set of guiding precepts to another whose implications when it comes to formulating the provisions of institutional arrangements diverge sharply from those of the earlier orthodoxy.

---

37. Richard N. Cooper, "International Cooperation in Public Health as a Prologue to Macroeconomic Cooperation," in Richard N. Cooper et al., eds., *Can Nations Agree?* (Washington, D.C.: Brookings Institution, 1989), pp. 178–254.

38. See also John G. Ruggie, "International Regimes, Transactions, and Change: Embedded Liberalism in the Postwar Economic Order," in Stephen D. Krasner, ed., *International Regimes* (Ithaca, N.Y.: Cornell University Press, 1983), pp. 195–231.

39. J. A. Gulland, *The Management of Marine Fisheries* (Seattle: University of Washington Press, 1974).

40. M. J. Peterson, *Managing the Frozen South* (Berkeley: University of California Press, 1988), chap. 5.

With these observations in mind, we can easily grasp the significance of several conceptual developments which are currently coming into focus and which seem likely to alter the intellectual capital available to those engaged in regime formation in international society during the foreseeable future. Consider, in this connection, the ideas of sustainable development, environmental security, and global change. Sustainable development, as articulated in the report of the Brundtland Commission and a barrage of subsequent publications, is a concept that forces negotiators to devote increased attention both to the links between economic issues and environmental issues and to the long-term consequences of current actions in formulating the terms of constitutional contracts.[41] The idea of environmental security, which suggests the need to redefine the concept of security to include a broader array of concerns, raises profound questions about the functionalist strategy of decoupling issues and dealing with them separately in the formation of international regimes.[42] For its part, the movement that has arisen around the theme of global change may well result in a dramatic restructuring of international agendas, with issues involving interactions between humankind and the environment moving toward center stage while the salience of conventional security concerns (for example, problems of arms control and nuclear proliferation) declines.[43] Whatever structural leaders and entrepreneurial leaders may do, it is apparent that the power of ideas is such that these new visions and the concerns they engender are likely to loom larger and larger in institutional bargaining processes at the international level.

The distinction between structural leadership and intellectual leadership is straightforward. While the structural leader seeks to translate power resources into bargaining leverage, the intellectual leader relies on the power of ideas to shape the intellectual capital available to those engaged in institutional bargaining. But we are now in a position to add some clarifying observations regarding the distinction between entrepreneurial leadership and intellectual leadership. Both the entrepreneurial leader and the intellectual leader rely on their wits to make their efforts felt. Whereas the entrepreneurial leader is an agenda setter and popularizer who uses negotiating skill to devise attractive formulas and to broker interests, however, the intellectual leader is a thinker who seeks to articulate the systems of thought that provide the substratum underlying the proximate activities involved in institutional bargaining. Accordingly, entrepreneurial leaders often become consumers of ideas generated by

41. See World Commission on Environment and Development, *Our Common Future* (New York: Oxford University Press, 1987).

42. See Richard H. Ullman, "Redefining Security," *International Security* 8 (Summer 1983), pp. 130–53; and Jessica Tuchman Mathews, "Redefining Security," *Foreign Affairs* 68 (Spring 1989), pp. 162–77.

43. See Cheryl Simon Silver and Ruth S. DeFries, *One Earth, One Future: Our Changing Global Environment* (Washington, D.C.: National Academy Press, 1990); and Ruth S. DeFries and Thomas F. Malone, eds., *Global Change and Our Common Future: Papers from a Forum* (Washington, D.C.: National Academy Press, 1989).

intellectual leaders. Occasionally, the two roles come together in the efforts of a single individual. But even in these uncommon instances, the leader's work as an intellectual innovator is apt to precede his or her work as an entrepreneurial leader.

All this makes it clear that numerous individuals can and often do seek to provide intellectual leadership regarding a given issue-area. What is more, there will usually be a more tenuous relationship between intellectual leaders and the principals in institutional bargaining processes than that obtaining between structural leaders or even entrepreneurial leaders and the principals. While those who provide intellectual leadership may be associated with interest groups possessing some stake in specific instances of institutional bargaining, they are just as likely to make their professional home in institutions of higher learning where they have the time for reflection needed to develop internally consistent and well-grounded intellectual constructs. As this observation suggests, intellectual leaders may confine their efforts to the generation of ideas in contrast to the application of these ideas to specific instances of institutional bargaining. Conversely, they generally have little ability to control the uses that others make of their ideas, a fact that can become a source of irritation or even acute frustration on the part of those who dislike the way in which their ideas are applied to actual cases.[44]

Still, intellectual leaders typically derive a sizable portion of their income stream from the sense of efficacy and the prestige that come from the development of ideas that subsequently play a role in shaping the course of institutional bargaining. This, in turn, suggests a final distinction of some relevance to our effort to illuminate the role of intellectual leaders. While the intangible benefits accruing to an intellectual leader are apt to be particularly satisfying when he or she single-handedly generates the intellectual capital needed to form a particular regime, the likelihood of achieving success in this realm rises dramatically when the ideas of an array of thinkers coalesce into an identifiable school of thought that carries the imprimatur of many prominent individuals and acquires interpreters able and willing to translate the essential ideas into forms accessible to an educated lay audience.[45] As the ongoing efforts to forge international responses to global changes such as ozone depletion and the greenhouse effect clearly attest, for example, the influence of scientists in processes of institutional bargaining depends heavily on the ability of the scientific community to reach consensus regarding the central issues at stake in various issue-areas.[46] Given the ethos of intellectual thrust and parry pervading much of intellectual life, at least in Western cultures, it will come as no surprise

44. On factors affecting the role of ideas in regime formation, see Judith Goldstein, "Ideas, Institutions, and Trade Policy," *International Organization* 42 (Winter 1988), pp. 179–217.

45. For a study of the political influence of Keynesian economics, see Peter A. Hall, ed., *The Political Power of Economic Ideas: Keynesianism Across Nations* (Princeton, N.J.: Princeton University Press, 1989).

46. S. Andersen and W. Ostreng, eds., *International Resource Management* (London: Belhaven Press, 1989).

that intellectual leadership is a chancy phenomenon and that it is difficult to purchase the talents of intellectual leaders in the same way in which the principals in institutional bargaining can pay those with recognized negotiating skills to apply their talents to a particular case.

Leadership in action: some initial hypotheses

Clarifying the distinctions among forms of leadership is an objective worthy of pursuit in its own right. But this is not sufficient to account for the role of leadership as a determinant of success or failure in the processes of institutional bargaining that dominate efforts to form regimes or, more broadly, institutional arrangements in international society. For this, we must consider leadership in action and, in the process, formulate a set of propositions about the linkages between leadership and regime formation. This section tackles this task in a preliminary fashion, laying out for further consideration several specific propositions regarding relationships between leadership and regime formation. The basic message I seek to communicate is a simple one: the establishment of effective international institutions ordinarily requires the interplay of at least two forms of leadership, and it is not uncommon for all three forms of leadership to come into play in the effort to form specific institutional arrangements.

1. Institutional bargaining cannot yield agreement concerning the provisions of constitutional contracts in the absence of leadership.

This is a strong proposition in the sense that it states a necessary condition. It says, in effect, that whenever we observe success in institutional bargaining at the international level, we can expect to encounter leadership in action. Failure to achieve success, on the other hand, may result from a number of factors other than an absence of leadership. Thus, the presence of leadership is a necessary condition, but not a sufficient one, for success in reaching agreement on the terms of constitutional contracts in international society.

The reasoning underlying this proposition is straightforward; it flows directly from an examination of the attributes of institutional bargaining. Even in the fully specified and drastically simplified world of formal models of interactive decision making, bargainers frequently fail to reach mutually beneficial agreements despite the presence of a sizable contract zone.[47] While studies of the game-theoretic construct known as prisoners' dilemma have come to symbolize this phenomenon,[48] analyses of a number of other prototypical cases

47. Raiffa, *The Art and Science of Negotiation,* especially pp. 6–9.
48. Axelrod's work, based on an analysis of prisoners' dilemma, suggests that large numbers of actors can develop cooperative practices in the absence of leadership. Whatever the merits of this

of interactive decision making yield the same conclusion.[49] To this we must add the considerable complications characteristic of actual processes of institutional bargaining in international society. Issues are seldom well specified at the outset, so that it is ordinarily necessary to engage in one or more rounds of preliminary negotiations simply to determine the content of the issues to be covered and the identity of the parties that will participate in processes of regime formation. There are normally a number of actors who operate under a rule of unanimity in their efforts to reach agreement on the terms of a constitutional contract. The parties are complex collective entities, a fact that ensures the occurrence of extensive and sometimes crippling intraparty bargaining. And regime formation in international society does not occur in a vacuum; one or another of the parties will often be preoccupied with other issues to the point that it has difficulty focusing on the issue at hand.

In combination, these complications present those endeavoring to form institutional arrangements with formidable obstacles. In the absence of countervailing forces, in fact, complications of this sort would doom institutional bargaining to failure. The existence of opportunities for integrative bargaining in the presence of a (more or less thick) veil of uncertainty is surely helpful in this regard. But it does not solve all the complications afflicting institutional bargaining and, in any case, these opportunities must be taken up and used by actors capable of devising innovative options and inducing other participants to buy into them. This is where leadership comes to the fore. It is the task of leaders to solve or circumvent the formidable obstacles to success that arise in institutional bargaining at the international level.

2. No one form of leadership is adequate by itself to produce constitutional contracts in institutional bargaining at the international level.

This proposition carries the argument a step further. Not only is leadership, in some general sense, necessary to produce agreement on the terms of constitutional contracts in international society, but success in such endeavors also requires the operation of more than one form of leadership. Again, this is not an argument about sufficiency. Institutional bargaining may fail to yield new institutional arrangements, even with the active efforts of more than one type of leader. The point is that success in efforts to form regimes cannot occur without the contributions of several forms of leadership. To see this, consider the circumstances that arise when only one form of leadership is present.

---

argument (a matter that is far from settled), however, it deals with spontaneous interactions and not with institutional bargaining. See Robert Axelrod, *The Evolution of Cooperation* (New York: Basic Books, 1984).

49. Russell Hardin, *Collective Action* (Baltimore, Md.: Johns Hopkins University Press, 1982).

There is, to begin with, the case in which bargaining leverage is present but negotiating skill and appropriate intellectual capital are lacking. Those who describe Great Britain in the second half of the nineteenth century and the United States in the postwar era as hegemons often overlook the fact that, in each case, the structural power of these states was accompanied not only by considerable diplomatic finesse but also by the existence of a coherent program for a preferred set of international institutions or an international order. In both cases, as it happens, this program centered on the liberal ideal of free trade and mutually beneficial economic intercourse. It is instructive as well to consider what happens when structural power is not accompanied by intellectual leadership. By the late 1920s, the United States was already in possession of extraordinary material resources, but the absence of intellectual leadership paralyzed American efforts with regard to the international economy, resulting in the failure of the United States to assume an effective role in avoiding or coping with the Great Depression that Kindleberger has described so well.[50] As for Great Britain, its gradual abandonment of the liberal ideal of free trade in the waning years of the nineteenth century clearly helped bring on the erosion of the British position of leadership in international society which became apparent during the first decade of this century. By itself, therefore, structural power is not capable of producing positive results in institutional bargaining. Bargaining leverage in the absence of programmatic leadership or diplomatic finesse leads either to paralysis or to illegitimacy.

The activities of clever entrepreneurs who are not backed by intellectual capital or by bargaining leverage yield equally unimpressive results. Given sufficiently high levels of negotiating skill, entrepreneurs sometimes work wonders in persuading the principals in institutional bargaining to accede in some superficial sense to the terms of constitutional contracts. But this is no guarantee of success in more substantive terms. Because the results are either hideously complex or mere facades that paper over continuing conflicts of interest, institutional arrangements that rest on nothing more than clever entrepreneurship ordinarily end up as dead letters. In other words, they typically fail to become operative institutions that are effective in the sense of playing a significant role as determinants of individual and collective behavior in international society. And in those atypical cases in which they do become operative, institutional arrangements that are the product of entrepreneurship alone are apt to be regarded as illegitimate, with the result that key players defect from the arrangements at the first opportunity.

The effort of the 1970s to work out an international regime to govern deep seabed mining is rich in examples of these problems.[51] The defection of the United States, which refused to sign the 1982 Convention on the Law of the Sea

---

50. Kindleberger, *The World in Depression*.

51. Bernard H. Oxman, David D. Caron, and Charles L. O. Buderi, eds., *Law of the Sea: U.S. Policy Dilemma* (San Francisco: ICS Press, 1983).

largely because of unhappiness with the deep seabed mining provisions set forth in Part XI and which brought considerable pressure to bear on several other important states to follow its example, threw the effort to reach agreement on an international regime in this area into disarray. But in any case, the provisions relating to deep seabed mining ultimately incorporated into the convention are so complex that it is questionable whether they could have been activated successfully under the best of circumstances. Today, it seems clear that the constitutional contract outlined in Part XI is a dead letter. Because the economics of deep seabed mining are not encouraging at this stage, it may be some time before a serious effort is made to devise a more workable regime covering this activity. But for the moment, the effort that eventuated in the regime set forth in Part XI of the 1982 convention stands as a symbol of what happens when entrepreneurial leadership is not backed by structural or intellectual leadership in the processes of institutional bargaining at the international level.

Similar observations are in order when we turn to the case of intellectual leadership unaccompanied by structural or entrepreneurial leadership. Curiously, innovative thinkers do sometimes succeed in getting their ideas incorporated into documents that purport to establish institutional arrangements in international society. The raft of arbitration and conciliation treaties signed early in this century as well as the 1928 Pact of Paris (the Kellogg-Briand Pact) claiming to outlaw war through a renunciation of organized violence "as an instrument of national policy" come to mind as cases in point.[52] But as these examples also suggest, it takes more than intellectual capital to produce institutions that have some real bearing on the behavior of the participants.

More often, the efforts of intellectual leaders that are not buttressed by bargaining leverage or negotiating skill are lost in the shuffle or simply ignored. A classic example is the vision of international society featuring republican forms of government coupled with self-determination for distinct ethnic groups or nationalities, a vision that Woodrow Wilson articulated (perhaps most memorably in his Fourteen Points) toward the end of World War I. Attractive as this program may seem in the abstract, it did not fare well in the negotiations that took place in Paris in 1919. The United States, which had entered the war only in 1917, was not yet in possession of the structural power we associate with the American position following World War II. And it seems clear that Wilson lacked negotiating skill, despite his facility in articulating attractive principles.[53] In fact, this example serves to reinforce the basic distinction between intellectual leadership and entrepreneurial leadership. With rare exceptions, the personality traits and skills that mark intellectual leadership are not compatible with those that give rise to entrepreneurial leadership.

---

52. Morton A. Kaplan and Nicholas Katzenbach, *The Political Foundations of International Law* (New York: Wiley, 1961), chap. 8.
53. Inis L. Claude, Jr., *Power and International Relations* (New York: Random House, 1962).

*3. Much of the real work of regime formation in
international society occurs in the interplay of bargaining
leverage, negotiating skill, and intellectual innovation.*

There is an understandable and healthy tendency among students of international affairs to search for explanations of international phenomena that are parsimonious. This is surely a major source of the appeal of the arguments of the hegemonists or, for that matter, of structuralists more generally.[54] The sheer simplicity of ideas such as the notion that the presence of a dominant power is necessary for the emergence or survival of institutionalized cooperation in international society is appealing to all those who value parsimony. Unfortunately, however, such ideas frequently fly in the face of reality. Nowhere is this more clearly illustrated than in the case of the role of leadership in international regime formation.

To be sure, the mix of structural, entrepreneurial, and intellectual leadership can and does vary considerably from one case of regime formation to another. Sometimes this is a consequence of the character of the overall relationship among the parties involved or of the nature of the issue-area under consideration. Structural leadership is apt to loom large, for instance, in settings featuring a highly asymmetrical distribution of power among participating actors. Intellectual leadership, on the other hand, can be expected to take on particular importance with regard to issue-areas in which major gaps in understanding are coupled with the prospect of dramatic and possibly irreversible changes—issues such as those now coming into focus in the area of global environmental change. In other cases, the balance is closely tied to relationships that develop among the specific individuals engaged in leadership activities. The emergence of a particularly adept structural leader, for instance, reduces the need for entrepreneurial leadership. Similar observations are in order with regard to the role of particularly persuasive intellectual innovators in reducing the need for structural leadership.

Nonetheless, it is easy to carry this line of reasoning too far. Despite the acknowledged dominance of the United States in the aftermath of World War II and the presence of individuals prepared to act as structural leaders, for example, American negotiators found it difficult to devise an international trade regime that was acceptable, at one and the same time, to domestic interests and to the other members of international society; they quickly came to appreciate the value of entrepreneurial skills in working out the terms of what became the GATT. Much the same can be said of today's rising concern about international cooperation to solve large-scale environmental problems. While those thinking systematically about global environmental change are adding rapidly to our stock of intellectual capital in this area, it seems apparent that both bargaining leverage and negotiating skill of a high order will be

54. For a particularly influential case in point, see Kenneth Waltz, *Theory of International Relations* (Reading, Mass.: Addison-Wesley, 1979).

required to translate the resultant intellectual capital into international institutions capable of harnessing the array of relevant interests and interest groups to cope effectively with issues such as climate change and the loss of biodiversity.

Because those who act as structural leaders, entrepreneurial leaders, and intellectual leaders are typically (though not always) different individuals, it is also pertinent to consider relations among those who assume leadership roles in thinking about the development of international institutions. Richardson and Koh, for instance, appear to have interacted constructively in the context of the law of the sea negotiations. And there is every indication that Benedick and Tolba got on well in the context of the negotiations resulting in the 1987 Montreal protocol on ozone depletion. Yet there is no basis for assuming that relations among leaders will always, or even ordinarily, be trouble-free. The personality traits and skills associated with the three forms of leadership are so different that we should not be surprised to encounter problems of communication in this area. The gulf between entrepreneurs, who sell themselves as well-informed and hard-headed practitioners, and intellectuals, who portray themselves as disciplined and principled thinkers, for example, is legendary. And while the gap between structural leaders and entrepreneurs may not be quite as wide, the difficulties that agents of powerful states have in comprehending the sources of the influence wielded by those associated with nongovernmental organizations are well known.

Conclusion

To deepen our understanding of the roles that leaders play in the formation of international institutions, we need to clarify the concept of leadership itself, eliminating sources of confusion in current thinking and then proceeding to draw distinctions among structural leadership, entrepreneurial leadership, and intellectual leadership. The structural leader translates power resources into bargaining leverage in an effort to bring pressure to bear on others to assent to the terms of proposed constitutional contracts. The entrepreneurial leader makes use of negotiating skill to frame the issues at stake, devise mutually acceptable formulas, and broker the interests of key players in building support for these formulas. The intellectual leader, by contrast, relies on the power of ideas to shape the thinking of the principals in processes of institutional bargaining. Drawing on this multidimensional conception of leadership, I have argued that the emergence of leadership is a necessary (but not sufficient) condition for success in efforts to reach agreement on constitutional contracts at the international level. In fact, the real work of regime formation in international society generally occurs in the interplay among those representing the different forms of leadership.

To the extent that the argument of this article is persuasive, leadership emerges as an important research frontier for students of international affairs. We need to sharpen our understanding of the contributions leaders make to regime formation and to examine alternative leadership styles and strategies. We need to inquire whether the types of leadership needed to produce successful outcomes in institutional bargaining depend on the attributes of the issue-areas under consideration. We need to improve our understanding of the relations between leaders and the organizations they represent along with the problems that arise when different types of leaders interact. Above all, we need to ask what steps can and should be taken to prepare future leaders in order to enhance the quality of leadership available to deal with emerging international concerns. Given the growing pluralism of international society, the rise of complex interdependencies, and the increasing significance of global change issues, it is hard to avoid the conclusion that the role of leadership in devising effective international institutions will become even more important during the foreseeable future. It follows that those who have something to say about leadership in institutional bargaining will be able to make a significant contribution not only to our general understanding of international affairs but also to our ability to act on our own behalf in solving international problems that are with us already and are destined to become increasingly urgent with the passage of time.

Interests, Power, and Multilateralism
Lisa L. Martin

Within the European Community (EC), member states increasingly accept the results of majoritarian voting procedures as constraints on their foreign policies, particularly on economic issues. At the same time, the United States is turning more frequently to bilateral negotiations to solve its international trade dilemmas. Some international organizations involve all members in important decisions through regularized, weighted voting mechanisms; others—for example, the United Nations (UN)—delegate some decision-making powers to a subset of actors (such as the UN Security Council). Some organizations have gained widespread monitoring powers and have developed dispute resolution mechanisms; others are primarily talking shops or negotiating arenas. This article considers the functional imperatives that contribute to such variance in patterns of international cooperation and uses the concept of multilateralism as a metric with which to characterize the patterns thus observed.

States can choose from a wide array of organizing forms on which to base their interactions; among these is multilateralism. A number of recent works have explored situations in which states have used varying degrees of multilateralism to structure their relations.[1] This article argues that studies of

This article was originally prepared for the Ford Foundation West Coast Workshop on Multilateralism, organized by John Gerard Ruggie. The author gratefully acknowledges the Ford Foundation's financial support for this project. My thanks also to Robert Keohane and Stephen Krasner, as well as to the participants in this project, for their valuable comments on this research.

1. See Geoffrey Garrett, "International Cooperation and Institutional Choice: The European Community's Internal Market," *International Organization* 46 (Spring 1992), pp. 533–60; John Gerard Ruggie, "Multilateralism: The Anatomy of an Institution," *International Organization* 46 (Summer 1992), pp. 561–98; James A. Caporaso, "International Relations Theory and Multilateralism: The Search for Foundations," *International Organization* 46 (Summer 1992), pp. 599–632; Steve Weber, "Shaping the Postwar Balance of Power: Multilateralism in NATO," *International Organization* 46 (Summer 1992), pp. 633–80; Miles Kahler, "Multilateralism with Small and Large Numbers," *International Organization* 46 (Summer 1992), pp. 681–708; and John Gerard Ruggie, ed., *Multilateralism Matters: The Theory and Praxis of an Institutional Form* (New York: Columbia University Press, forthcoming). See also *International Journal* 45 (Autumn 1990), which is a special issue on multilateralism.

International Organization 46, 4, Autumn 1992, pp. 765–792

state choice can achieve high payoffs by giving serious consideration to functional arguments that view institutions as a solution to dilemmas of strategic interaction.[2] Consideration of the power and interests of state actors in different situations leads to hypotheses about the modal tendencies in the types of norms and organizations that states create to facilitate pursuit of their interests—what Beth Yarbrough and Robert Yarbrough term the "form of successful cooperation."[3]

The first section of this article briefly defines multilateralism as used throughout. The second section discusses a typology of cooperation problems and the potential roles of the institution of multilateralism (IM) and multilateral organizations (MOs) in helping states to overcome these problems. Each of four ideal types of cooperation problems—collaboration, coordination, suasion, and assurance—presents states with unique challenges. In some, the functions performed by formal organizations, such as monitoring and enforcement, will be essential to the achievement of cooperation. In others, multilateral norms, such as nondiscrimination, will be more efficient. The functional considerations behind alternative institutional solutions for different types of games will be illuminated. To structure this analysis, I have treated multilateralism as a strict, ideal type and will consider whether multilateral norms will facilitate cooperation. Thus, a claim that states may choose to compromise multilateral norms does not imply any normative judgment; it is only a statement about the likely form of cooperation.

However, at this abstract, functional level of analysis, outcomes remain indeterminate. Multiple feasible solutions exist for each problem. Therefore, the third section takes into consideration two key elements of international structure in the postwar era: U.S. hegemony within the Western subsystem and the bipolar distribution of power in the international system as a whole. These factors lead us to consider the strengths and weaknesses of multilateralism from the hegemon's point of view and the impact of a bipolar security structure. Considerations of power and time horizons suggest likely choices among functional solutions.

The final section turns from comparative statics and introduces a dynamic element to the analysis by inquiring about changes in institutions in the face of changing distributions of power and other exogenous changes. Some solutions to cooperation problems are preferable to others because certain structures can adapt to changes in relative power; this feature is one of the main advantages of a multilateral architecture. Other forms of cooperation will be brittle and susceptible to challenge as the hegemon declines relative to other members. Changes in the distribution of power can lead to shifts in the kind of game being played, in addition to affecting the outcome within specified games.

2. Robert O. Keohane, "Multilateralism: An Agenda for Research," *International Journal* 45 (Autumn 1990), pp. 731–64.

3. Beth V. Yarbrough and Robert M. Yarbrough, "Cooperation in the Liberalization of International Trade: After Hegemony, What?" *International Organization* 41 (Winter 1987), p. 4.

The concept of multilateralism

John Gerard Ruggie presents a precise and useful definition of the "institution of multilateralism" in his recent article entitled "Multilateralism: The Anatomy of an Institution." According to this definition, IM consists of three principles: (1) indivisibility, (2) nondiscrimination, or generalized organizing principles, and (3) diffuse reciprocity.[4] Indivisibility is illustrated by collective security arrangements wherein an attack on one is considered an attack on all. Nondiscrimination implies that all parties be treated similarly, as in the use of most-favored nation (MFN) status in trade agreements. Diffuse reciprocity implies that states do not rely on specific, quid-pro-quo exchanges, but on longer-term assurances of balance in their relations.

In this article, I inquire into the instrumental value of multilateral norms under different configurations of state interests, i.e., in different types of "cooperation problems." By treating multilateralism as a means rather than a goal, we open the possibility that alternative organizing devices will be equal to or superior to IM in their utility for reaching higher-level ends, such as liberalization. The choice of tools depends, at least in part, on the configuration of state power and interests in particular issue-areas. Thus, I assume that states are self-interested and turn to multilateralism only if it serves their purposes, whatever those may be.

A belief in the utility of multilateralism was expressed after World War II in a drive to create many international organizations. MOs must be distinguished from IM: MOs are formal organizations with more than two members. However, we see a great deal of variation in the degree to which actual organizations conform to the norms of multilateralism. This article attempts to explain variation in the organizing principles and strength of these organizations on the basis of the strategic problems facing states. In addition, it suggests hypotheses about relationships among norms, formal organizations, and behavioral outcomes.

Multilateralism is used here as a metric by which to gauge patterns of interaction, not as a normative standard. Thus, claims that multilateralism is not efficient under some conditions are not meant to imply that states will refuse to cooperate; rather, such claims imply only that alternative architectures will promote international cooperation more efficiently under those conditions. The concept of multilateralism provides a language with which to describe variation in the character of the norms governing international cooperation and the formal organizations in which it occurs. Thus, this article is less about whether multilateralism "matters" than an exploration of the comparative utility of multilateralism and alternative organizational forms.

In the following analysis, I find it useful to differentiate among the roles of multilateralism at three separate points in the cooperation process. The first

4. Ruggie, "Multilateralism," pp. 569–74.

stage is that of arriving at decisions. States can reach decisions through genuinely multilateral discussions, a series of bilateral agreements, or the imposition of decisions on a unilateral basis. Second, we need to specify the scope of state decisions. Decisions may only apply to those directly involved in their negotiation, or they may be extended to a broader range of actors. Finally, norms of multilateralism may apply at the stage of implementation. Central problems at that stage involve the monitoring and enforcement of agreements. States may utilize mechanisms ranging from the highly centralized to the completely decentralized to solve such problems. Multilateral norms, for example, may apply to the scope of agreements but not to their negotiation or enforcement. The questions I address are about the utility of multilateral norms and organizations (which need to be carefully distinguished from one another) at each stage, and thus about expectations for the multilateral character of the forums within which specific instances of cooperation are embedded. The conclusions I draw should be seen as hypotheses for the purpose of future empirical examination.

Strategic interaction and multilateralism

Multilateralism, as defined by Ruggie, requires that states sacrifice substantial levels of flexibility in decision making and resist short-term temptations in favor of long-term benefits. Therefore, it is unrealistic to expect state behavior to conform to pure multilateralism. Instead, we need to ask about the role IM and MOs can play under specified conditions. Here, I suggest that focusing on the fundamental problem of strategic interaction within an issue-area provides answers to questions about the likelihood of successful use of IM and MOs.

Drawing on the work of Duncan Snidal, Arthur Stein, and others, I present a simple four-category typology of cooperation problems. Each of these problems—collaboration, coordination, suasion, and assurance—uniquely challenges states considering cooperation. Thus, the problems lead to expectations about variance in the roles of norms and organizations. Consideration of the strategic dilemmas underlying particular issue-areas in their simplest forms suggests particular relationships between IM and MOs. In addition, each situation leads to different relations between IM or MOs and behavioral outcomes. Snidal and Stein differentiate between two prototypical cooperation problems.[5] Snidal refers to these as "coordination" and "prisoners' dilemma," while Stein discusses "coordination games" and "collaboration games." In this article, I use Stein's terminology, as it is more general than Snidal's. I also argue

---

5. See Duncan Snidal, "Coordination Versus Prisoners' Dilemma: Implications for International Cooperation and Regimes," *American Political Science Review* 79 (December 1985), pp. 923–42; and Arthur A. Stein, "Coordination and Collaboration: Regimes in an Anarchic World," in Stephen D. Krasner, ed., *International Regimes* (Ithaca, N.Y.: Cornell University Press, 1983), pp. 115–40.

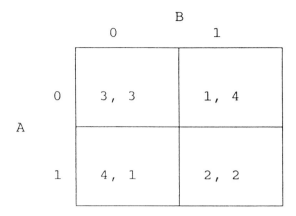

FIGURE 1. *A collaboration game (prisoners' dilemma)*

that two additional game types require consideration. Coordination and collaboration both assume symmetrical interests. In a "suasion game," defined below, states have asymmetrical interests, so the equilibrium outcome leaves one of them dissatisfied. Although analysts have downplayed the significance of regimes or institutions in such asymmetrical situations, I argue that the postwar distribution of power often created precisely this kind of problem and that institutions could, nevertheless, facilitate cooperation. In "assurance games," institutions have little to contribute to cooperation under conditions of complete information. However, given the structural uncertainty of international relations, states may find some modest level of institutionalization in these situations conducive to their ability to achieve mutual gains.

Collaboration problems

Collaboration games are characterized by situations in which equilibrium outcomes are suboptimal. These games, and the nature of potential solutions to them, have been the subject of extensive discussion among economists and political scientists, who often consider them "the" collective action problem.[6] Prisoners' dilemma, as shown in Figure 1, is the most thoroughly studied collaboration game in the international relations literature.[7]

Resolving the dilemma of collaboration games is a matter of mutual policy adjustment, since both players must agree to move away from the suboptimal equilibrium, thus rejecting their dominant strategy. Many authors have identified factors that allow states to overcome collaboration problems. Such

6. Michael Laver, "Political Solutions to the Collective Action Problem," *Political Studies* 28 (June 1980), pp. 195–209.

7. I illustrate only two-person games here. Obviously, situations of multilateralism involve more players. However, many of the fundamental dilemmas of cooperation appear in these simple two-person illustrations.

factors focus on (1) using the proper strategy, (2) extending the shadow of the future, and (3) reliance on centralized mechanisms, such as formal international organizations. MOs can play a role in facilitating cooperation in the above types of problems. However, the norms of multilateralism do not meet the functional demands of collaboration games, in that they do not overcome state incentives to defect. This leads us to expect divergence between IM and MOs in such cases. The remainder of this section identifies those functional demands and the ways in which multilateral norms fail to resolve, or may even exacerbate, collaboration dilemmas.

Collaboration problems contain strong incentives to defect from established cooperative patterns of behavior, since defection results in immediate payoffs. Therefore, mechanisms to promote cooperation must focus on *maintenance* of agreements. As Snidal argues, the need for maintenance mechanisms suggests that solutions to collaboration problems will be centralized, creating a significant role for formal organizations.

Two factors in particular promote cooperation in collaboration games. First, states will demand extensive information on others' behavior, since undetected defection will be costly for those who continue to cooperate and will complicate attempts at retaliation. Thus, we should expect extensive monitoring and assessment of compliance in successfully resolved collaboration problems. Such activity contrasts to that of coordination games, in which exchange of information should take the form of notification of intentions in order to avoid a mutually disliked outcome. According to the logic of strategic interaction, in collaboration, states will exchange information retrospectively; in coordination, prospectively.

Second, in collaboration problems, states should search for mechanisms to increase the shadow of the future in order to assure that the immediate costs associated with cooperation will be offset by the long-term benefits of mutual assistance.[8] Formal organizations can perform such functions.[9] Conventions alone, without monitoring or enforcement, cannot ensure cooperation. The solution to collaboration problems in the absence of a state acting as an entrepreneur and in the presence of large numbers of players requires centralization, leading to expectations of relatively strong formal organizations.

Research on current problems of international cooperation supports the plausibility of this argument. Analyses have suggested that the completion of

8. The folk theorem demonstrates that cooperation can be maintained as an equilibrium in repeated prisoners' dilemmas, conditional on a low discount rate (i.e., the future is valued highly) and credible retaliatory threats. See Dilip Abreu, "On the Theory of Infinitely Repeated Games with Discounting," *Econometrica* 56 (March 1988), pp. 383–96; James Friedman, "A Noncooperative Equilibrium for Supergames," *Review of Economic Studies* 38 (January 1971), pp. 1–12; and Robert Axelrod, *The Evolution of Cooperation* (New York: Basic Books, 1984).

9. For an example, see Paul Milgrom, Douglass North, and Barry Weingast, "The Role of Institutions in the Revival of Trade: The Medieval Law Merchant, Private Judges, and the Champagne Fairs," *Economics and Politics* 1 (Spring 1989), pp. 1–23.

the internal market in the EC can be understood in these terms.[10] The removal of internal trade barriers presents a typical collaboration problem. EC members have responded by replacing their previous pattern of bilateral, self-enforcing trade arrangements with a pattern of third-party enforcement mechanisms on an increasingly large range of issues. As expected, the liberalizing process involves a higher degree of both centralization and surrender of individual states' decision-making power than is often found in international relations. In fact, the necessary surrender of sovereignty by EC member states has been a significant impediment to even more rapid movement toward a unified economic region.

This finding about the important role of MOs, however, does not extend to the norms of multilateralism. In collaboration problems, multilateral norms may complicate attempts to cooperate. The norms of diffuse reciprocity and indivisibility, in particular, are not conducive to the solution of collaboration problems. Theoretical and experimental studies of repeated prisoners' dilemmas show the value of strategies of specific reciprocity, such as tit-for-tat and trigger strategies, for maintaining cooperation. Diffuse reciprocity, with its lack of direct retaliation for defections, is unlikely to maintain cooperation in demanding collaboration problems effectively, although it may be efficient in less demanding situations.[11] Under diffuse reciprocity, members rely on generalized norms of obligation to promote cooperation. However, if cheating is not punished, states will face short-term incentives to do so in spite of a longer-term sense of obligation. Although ongoing mutual cooperation provides benefits over mutual defection, without the threat of specific retaliation, the temptation to cheat in order to maximize immediate payoffs rises substantially. Strict adherence to the norm of diffuse reciprocity, particularly at the enforcement stage, would encourage free riding in collaboration situations. Therefore, beyond mechanisms to increase the sense of obligation among states caught in such a dilemma, we might expect to find some compromise of diffuse reciprocity to allow issue-specific sanctioning of egregious free riders. The General Agreement on Tariffs and Trade (GATT), for example, provides for direct retaliation for unfair trading practices, a clear example of specific reciprocity at the enforcement stage.

Similarly, the multilateral norm of indivisibility, taken in its strictest sense, is antithetical to the solution of collaboration dilemmas. Indivisibility, when combined with diffuse reciprocity, implies nonexclusion and creates publicness. If all threats and decisions apply equally to all members of the regime, and all members must be treated equally, the regime will create public goods where

---

10. Beth V. Yarbrough and Robert M. Yarbrough, "International Institutions and the New Economics of Organization," paper delivered to the University of California, Berkeley, Institutional Analysis Workshop, May 1990; and Garrett, "International Cooperation and Institutional Choice."

11. Robert O. Keohane, "Reciprocity in International Relations," *International Organization* 40 (Winter 1986), pp. 1–27.

private goods existed previously. Multilateral security arrangements, for example, make exclusion from protection extremely difficult, since states view a threat to one as a threat to all. Dilemmas of collective choice arise when dealing with public goods. Strict adherence to multilateral principles, rather than solving such dilemmas, would create public goods from private ones. Regime members, under a strict interpretation of such norms, could not be excluded from benefits created by the regime without compromising the indivisibility and diffuse reciprocity principles. Thus, multilateralism creates huge incentives to free ride.

One way around the dilemma of public goods would involve sacrificing some indivisibility and diffuse reciprocity, making regime benefits excludable. Organizations could sanction states that free ride by denying them "entitlements" according to the norms of the regime. One example of such a compromise occurred during the Tokyo Round in the GATT: states that refused to sign the government procurement and other protocols were denied the benefits provided to the signatory states.[12] The previous GATT practice of multilateralism in the scope of agreements was modified, making some regime benefits excludable and contingent on policy commitments. In general, we should expect formal organizations to reflect compromises of the indivisibility and diffuse reciprocity norms to allow for privatization of benefits and sanctioning of free riders in collaboration games. As Snidal argues, "The possibility of exclusion will be especially important in mitigating the adverse effects of increased numbers of states on the prospects for international cooperation."[13] Thus, regimes in issue-areas characterized by collaboration will likely depart significantly from the norms of indivisibility and diffuse reciprocity at the scope and implementation stages, allowing for specific reciprocity and exclusion. IM will appear weak in collaboration cases, while MOs should be strong.

Thus far, the logic of collaboration has suggested a limited role for multilateralism at the scope and implementation stages. I turn now to the decision-making stage. Making decisions on a multilateral basis may save transaction costs during periods of "normal politics," when a group of states is faced with only routine decisions. However, open, egalitarian processes will become cumbersome when a group confronts major decisions. For example, multilateral decision making will create problems for an organization attempting to determine members' budget contributions or to respond quickly to some exogenous crisis. In a distributive or crisis situation, multilateral decision making will entail higher transaction costs than centralized mechanisms. In addition, the collective choice literature points to the problem of cycling. When confronted with a set of choices, majoritarian voting procedures may not lead

---

12. John H. Jackson, "GATT Machinery and the Tokyo Round Agreements," in William R. Cline, ed., *Trade Policy in the 1980s* (Washington, D.C.: Institute for International Economics, 1983), pp. 159–87.

13. Snidal, "Coordination Versus Prisoners' Dilemma," pp. 929–30.

to a conclusive outcome, as each new option receives majority approval.[14] An organization may find itself unable to settle on any specific proposal unless some form of agenda control is imposed, again suggesting a role for centralized or hierarchical decision making.

Groups can overcome the difficulties of multilateral decision making by delegating urgent issues to a smaller group of actors or by allowing such a subset to exercise agenda control under certain conditions. The UN Security Council is one such example. It is a compromise of pure multilateralism that fulfills the above functions and helps account for the UN's ability to act quickly and decisively, as in the Iraqi invasion of Kuwait. Without such delegation, it is difficult to imagine swift, successful cooperation in crises. By delegating difficult decisions and agenda control to smaller groups of states, organizations can avoid some of the transaction-cost problems caused by multilateral decision making. The logic of delegation in international organizations mirrors that in legislatures, which develop systems such as committees to overcome the problems of multilateralism.[15]

MOs typically have a large number of members. As many authors have pointed out, large numbers create problems for states attempting to cooperate.[16] Having many players can increase the conflicts of interest among them, uncertainty about others' preferences, and opportunities for undetected free riding. An MO could deal with some of these difficulties by devoting substantial resources to surveillance and sanctioning of free riders, as discussed above. However, a less expensive tactic might be to sacrifice some degree of multilateralism by decomposing conflictual issues. For example, the GATT has adopted strategies of allowing major trading powers to negotiate agreements rather than mandating negotiations with the entire membership.[17] By focusing on just a few important actors for specific issues, members avoid some of the problems of numerous participants. Negotiations on arms control have followed a similar pattern of decomposition and de facto delegation to those with the most at stake.[18]

This discussion has so far stressed the role that MOs can play in solving collaboration problems, although these MOs will be weak on IM; i.e., they will not strictly reflect the principles of multilateralism. However, analysts have

---

14. See Kenneth J. Arrow, *Social Choice and Individual Values,* 2d ed. (New Haven, Conn.: Yale University Press, 1963), pp. 2–3; and Richard P. McKelvey, "Intransitivities in Multidimensional Voting: Models and Some Implications for Agenda Control," *Journal of Economic Theory* 12 (June 1976), pp. 472–82.

15. Barry R. Weingast and William J. Marshall, "The Industrial Organization of Congress; or, Why Legislatures, Like Firms, Are Not Organized as Markets," *Journal of Political Economy* 96 (February 1988), pp. 132–63.

16. For example, see Kenneth A. Oye, "Explaining Cooperation Under Anarchy: Hypotheses and Strategies," in Oye, ed., *Cooperation Under Anarchy* (Princeton, N.J.: Princeton University Press, 1986), pp. 18–22.

17. Jock A. Finlayson and Mark W. Zacher, "The GATT and the Regulation of Trade Barriers: Regime Dynamics and Functions," in Krasner, ed., *International Regimes,* pp. 273–314.

18. I am grateful to Patrick Morgan for suggesting this example.

noted that at least two other solutions to collaboration problems exist: hegemony and self-enforcing agreements among smaller numbers of players. The argument about the possibility for a single, dominant state to provide public goods and to thus enforce a solution to collaboration problems has been thoroughly explored under the rubric of hegemonic stability theory.[19] The logical and empirical weaknesses of this theory have also been subject to extensive discussion.[20] For the purposes of this article, I will simply note that if a hegemon has incentives to provide a public good and/or undertake the costs of enforcement, the strategic situation has changed from one of collaboration to one of suasion. The hegemon's size creates the incentives to provide public goods, thus changing the player's preference ordering and creating a new type of cooperation problem (one which is discussed below). Also, the hegemonic solution to collaboration problems is available only when a specific configuration of state power obtains. Thus, insofar as no single state is dominant or makes up a "uniquely privileged group," the hegemonic solution is not available.

Another potential response to collaboration problems involves the use of bilateralism at the stage of decision making but multilateralism in the scope of those decisions. In other words, states reach bilateral agreements and then, through application of the norm of nondiscrimination, extend these agreements to other members of the system. In contrast, use of IM at the negotiation stage would imply participation of far more members of the regime. The bilateral negotiating solution has been used in international trade, in both the nineteenth and twentieth centuries, through the application of unconditional MFN treatment.[21]

However, the temptation to cheat on these agreements still exists, suggesting that multilateral norms will not extend to implementation. States could perhaps make such agreements self-enforcing, for example through an "exchange of hostages" in the form of asset-specific investments.[22] If such a solution is to work, the calculation that continued cooperation is more profitable than cheating must hold for every state to which MFN treatment is extended, creating complications when large numbers of states are involved. Another numbers problem arises simply through the high transaction costs of negotiating a series of bilateral treaties, which a self-enforcing agreements

19. See Charles P. Kindleberger, *The World in Depression* (Berkeley: University of California Press, 1973); Steven D. Krasner, "State Power and the Structure of International Trade," *World Politics* 38 (April 1976), pp. 317–43; and Robert O. Keohane, "The Theory of Hegemonic Stability and Changes in International Regimes, 1967–1977," in Ole Holsti, ed., *Change in the International System* (Boulder, Colo.: Westview Press, 1980), pp. 131–62.

20. For example, see John A. C. Conybeare, *Trade Wars: The Theory and Practice of International Commercial Rivalry* (New York: Columbia University Press, 1987), pp. 55–72.

21. Arthur A. Stein, "The Hegemon's Dilemma: Great Britain, the United States, and the International Economic Order," *International Organization* 38 (Spring 1984), pp. 355–86.

22. Beth V. Yarbrough and Robert M. Yarbrough, "Reciprocity, Bilateralism, and Economic 'Hostages': Self-enforcing Agreements in International Trade," *International Studies Quarterly* 30 (March 1986), pp. 7–21.

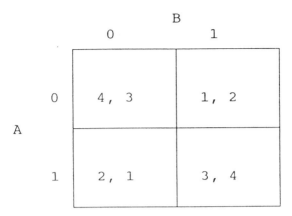

FIGURE 2. *A coordination game with divergent interests (battle of the sexes)*

model for collaboration requires.[23] Thus, if the MFN-type of solution is to lead to stable cooperation without the use of international organizations that have enforcement power, we should expect to find it only on a regional or subregional basis.[24] As GATT membership and the complexity of issues with which GATT deals grow, we find increasing use of centralized mechanisms for dispute resolution and of specific reciprocity. Thus, the ghost of collaboration dilemmas increasingly haunts the multilateral trading regime.[25]

Coordination problems

Figure 2 shows a typical coordination problem, the battle of the sexes. This game has two possible equilibrium outcomes, one of which is preferred by each of the players. Neither has a dominant strategy, so the best course of action is dependent on how the other player behaves. The central dilemma in this situation is deciding which of the two equilibria will prevail. The two players disagree on this and bargaining over the outcome might be quite intense, especially if players expect the result to hold far into the future. Coordination games can have major distributional implications, which sometimes make cooperative solutions difficult to achieve.[26] However, once an equilibrium has been established either by convention or by agreement, neither player has an incentive to defect from it.

23. Conybeare, *Trade Wars,* p. 278.
24. See Yarbrough and Yarbrough, "Cooperation in the Liberalization of International Trade."
25. The strategic problems states confront in international monetary affairs differ substantially from those in commercial activities. Under the Bretton Woods regime, for example, the central role of the United States prevented the cooperation problem from being one of collaboration. Instead, we saw a significant asymmetry of interests, perhaps creating a suasion game as discussed below.
26. See Stephen D. Krasner, "Global Communications and National Power: Life on the Pareto Frontier," *World Politics* 43 (April 1991), pp. 336–66.

Thus, coordination games do not require institutions with strong mechanisms for surveillance and enforcement. Since no state would gain by deviating from the established outcome, each need devote little attention to the prevention of cheating. However, structures that facilitate bargaining and allow states to identify a focal point will contribute to cooperative outcomes.[27] General multilateral principles (namely, IM) may play a central role in allowing states to settle on a particular outcome. In such cases, the benefits of multilateralism in reducing the costs of arriving at an agreement suggest that IM will contribute to cooperative outcomes if used at the negotiation stage. The logic of coordination suggests that a series of bilateral negotiations would be highly inefficient. Thus, in coordination situations (in contrast to collaboration situations) IM may be quite strong.

There is, however, no reason to expect that the strength of multilateral norms will be reflected in strong formal organizations. The roles such organizations can play (e.g., providing information about others' actions and sanctioning free-riders) are not essential to the maintenance of cooperation in coordination games. We have little reason to expect that states will choose to devote scarce resources to formal organizations that will be superfluous. Thus, while IM may be most efficacious in coordination games, MOs will not have strong enforcement powers.

Why might states create formal organizations at all under these conditions? The answer lies in transaction-cost savings on the prospective collection of information about state intentions. Consider a case in which players are choosing frequencies for radio transmissions. As long as a sufficient number of frequencies exist to satisfy everyone, the case represents a pure coordination problem. To avoid confusion and the mutually disliked outcome of two players attempting to use the same frequency, players will likely set up a centralized system of notification to advise each how the others plan to behave. Nevertheless, this system will only be an efficient means of distributing information, and states will not delegate to it unnecessary monitoring powers since no player has an incentive to cheat by deviating from his or her announced intention.[28] Although information is important to the solution of coordination games, it is signaling information about future plans, rather than retrospective information about compliance, that states need. In coordination problems, there is no incentive for surreptitious cheating. Since the point of diverging from an established equilibrium is to force joint movement to a new one, defection must be public. Under these conditions, secret defection makes as little sense as

27. See Geoffrey Garrett and Barry Weingast, "Ideas, Interests, and Institutions: Constructing the EC's Internal Market," presented at the annual meeting of the American Political Science Association, Washington, D.C., 28 August–1 September, 1991.

28. For another perspective on the functions regimes can perform in coordination games under conditions of imperfect information, see James D. Morrow, "Modelling International Regimes," paper presented at the annual meeting of the Public Choice Society, New Orleans, La., 20–22 March 1991.

undertaking terrorist operations while attempting to prevent publicity about them. In both cases, the point is to impose high costs on others in order to force them to change their policies in a specified manner—which requires publicity about the reasons for and nature of defection.

In coordination games, the primary instrumental value of multilateral norms appears during the negotiation stage, when states are attempting to reach agreements and set conventions. As in collaboration cases, however, alternative solutions exist. A primary one is action by a dominant player to establish a focal point. If a single, powerful state can commit itself to a particular equilibrium, others will find it in their interest simply to go along with this decision. Such a solution obviates the need for extensive discussions. It may have occurred, for example, during the transition from an allocative to a market-based regime in telecommunications, when the United States forced others to move to a new basis for regulation.[29] U.S. actions in the establishment of the postwar monetary order could be interpreted in a similar manner.[30]

In problems of standardization, such as transborder data flows, state preferences approach the ideal type of coordination problem. Although each actor has a preferred standard, there is a strong common interest in avoiding the use of conflicting standards. In such cases, the major analytical puzzle is the establishment of a convention, which typically follows extensive multilateral discussions. Negotiations focus on the creation of new standards rather than on arguments about whether members are violating old ones, since there is nothing to gain from concealed deviation from the focal point. States will find it easier to maintain cooperation, once established, in coordination games than in collaboration or suasion games, although some actors will inevitably have preferred a different outcome. Thus, in issues that reflect coordination preferences, IM will contribute more to cooperative outcomes than will the more formal MOs.

Suasion problems

Both coordination and collaboration problems embody a symmetry of interests among states. However, in reality, many multilateral institutions have been established under conditions of significant asymmetry. Because the United States far exceeded others in power and wealth, it frequently formed a "privileged group" of one, willing unilaterally to supply public goods. The control of technology sales to the Soviet bloc through the Coordinating Committee on Export Controls (COCOM) illustrates just such a situation, inasmuch as the United States often had a dominant strategy to control

29. Peter F. Cowhey, "The International Telecommunications Regime: The Political Roots of Regimes for High Technology," *International Organization* 44 (Spring 1990), pp. 169–99.

30. Barry Eichengreen, "Hegemonic Stability Theories of the International Monetary System," in Richard N. Cooper et al., *Can Nations Agree? Issues in International Economic Cooperation* (Washington, D.C.: The Brookings Institution, 1989), pp. 255–98.

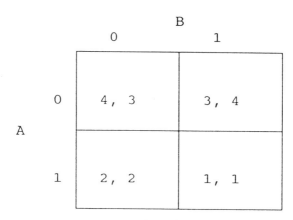

FIGURE 3. *A suasion game*

technology regardless of the policies of other states.[31] In this situation, smaller states have a strong incentive to free ride, knowing that public goods, such as control of significant technologies, will nevertheless be provided. In the COCOM case, while the United States controlled most production of high-technology goods, Europeans could reap the benefits of exports while being assured that their sales were insufficient in quantity and quality to change the overall balance of power. Such a situation presents the United States, or any hegemon, with a dilemma. The hegemon would prefer others' cooperation and is dissatisfied with the equilibrium outcome of unilateral action. I call this kind of asymmetric situation a "suasion" game, since the dilemma facing the hegemon is to persuade or coerce others to cooperate. Figure 3 shows a typical suasion game.

Suasion problems have equilibrium outcomes that leave one actor dissatisfied. In the situation shown in Figure 3, player A (perhaps the United States) has a dominant strategy to cooperate. Knowing this, player B can achieve its most favored outcome by defecting. Faced with this situation, the United States has, in the abstract, two ways to convince the other to cooperate, both of which go beyond the confines of the game illustrated here. First, it could threaten to act irrationally in the short term, defecting if player B does. This would lead to player B's least favored outcome, and, if credible, convince him to cooperate. The problem with such a strategy, of course, is establishing credibility. The United States would have to be willing to bear high short-term costs if player B did not respond to that threat. To make the threat credible, a mechanism to make U.S. defection automatic would be needed. This would involve a

31. See Michael Mastanduno, "Trade as a Strategic Weapon: American and Alliance Export Control Policy in the Early Postwar Period," *International Organization* 42 (Winter 1988), pp. 121–50; and Lisa L. Martin, *Coercive Cooperation: Explaining Multilateral Economic Sanctions* (Princeton, N.J.: Princeton University Press, 1992).

significant surrender of control over decision making and seems an unlikely course of action.

More frequently, the aggrieved actor will choose the second path—tactical issue linkage.[32] This linkage could take the form of either threats or promises (e.g., side-payments). By linking issues, the hegemon can either decrease player B's payoff associated with unilateral defection (threats) or increase the payoff for mutual cooperation (side payments). In either case, understanding the emergence of cooperation requires that we look beyond the single issue supposedly at stake. In the nuclear nonproliferation regime, for example, the goal of nonproliferation has been pursued by offering various forms of technical assistance to those who comply with regime rules.[33] Private, linked benefits contribute to the supply of a public good (nonproliferation) in suasion games.[34]

What role can multilateralism play? For the smaller states (those being either bribed or threatened into submission), maintaining the appearance of multilateralism may be quite important. Governments that give in to U.S. pressure, for example, may need to conceal this behind a veil of "multilateral agreement," for domestic purposes. Thus, we should expect that actual decision making processes in these situations are obscured, i.e., not transparent to the public. In fact, COCOM was the most secretive of international organizations; its very existence was concealed in many countries. At least prior to the Korean War, and for some period thereafter, U.S.–European efforts to control technology exports fit the suasion pattern.

While smaller states may benefit from a velvet glove of multilateralism in the above situations, there is little reason to expect that multilateral norms will play a significant role in constraining state behavior. Actual control over the agenda and decisions will likely be maintained by the hegemonic state, with face-saving arrangements to isolate others from domestic pressure. Strong asymmetries of interests and power may lead to widespread disregard of the nondiscrimination norm, since the functions performed by the hegemonic state will differ significantly from those of the smaller members. In addition, the threats or promises that lead to mutual cooperation will need to be implemented on a basis of specific reciprocity. For example, threats to retaliate against all due to

32. For discussions of this strategy, see James K. Sebenius, "Negotiation Arithmetic: Adding and Subtracting Issues and Parties," *International Organization* 37 (Spring 1983), pp. 281–316; Arthur A. Stein, "The Politics of Linkage," *World Politics* 33 (October 1980), pp. 62–81; and Michael D. McGinnis, "Issue Linkage and the Evolution of Cooperation," *Journal of Conflict Resolution* 30 (March 1986), pp. 141–70.

33. Benjamin N. Schiff, "Dominance Without Hegemony: U.S. Relations with the International Atomic Energy Agency," in Margaret P. Karns and Karen A. Mingst, eds., *The United States and Multilateral Institutions: Patterns of Changing Instrumentality and Influence*, Mershon Center Series on International Security and Foreign Policy, vol. 5 (Boston, Mass.: Unwin Hyman, 1990), pp. 57–89.

34. Mancur Olson, *The Logic of Collective Action* (Cambridge, Mass.: Harvard University Press, 1965).

the defection of individuals will be costly and lack credibility. Thus, IM—the embodiment of multilateral principles—suffers in suasion situations.

Even if the dominant state adopts a linkage strategy, it faces a credibility problem. Carrying out either threats or promises is costly. Thus, the hegemonic actor needs to establish a credible commitment to linkage. For the United States, making tactical linkages credible presents the major challenge in suasion situations. In the COCOM case, for example, a linkage between control of technology and Marshall Plan aid was established by Congress, thus improving the administration's bargaining position within the regime. The United States also looked to MOs to make its threats or promises credible.[35] From this perspective, one role of formal organizations in suasion games is to tie together issues that have no substantive rationale for linkage.[36] In addition to their role in tactical linkage, organizations can provide the hegemon with information on others' behavior, allowing it to respond quickly to defections.

A useful typology of cooperation problems must include suasion games if only because the conditions of the early postwar period made this asymmetric type of strategic interaction common. The asymmetry of suasion games suggests that IM may provide cover for smaller states but will have little impact on actual decision making. Formal organizations, on the other hand, may facilitate the dominant state's attempts at issue linkage. There is no reason to expect, however, that the organizations thus formed will operate on the basis of multilateral principles.

Assurance problems

For the sake of completeness, I include a fourth type of cooperation problem in this typology: the assurance game, as shown in Figure 4. In an assurance game, the sole preferred outcome is mutual cooperation. Thus, in equilibrium, rational states with complete information will cooperate within the confines of this single issue-area, one-time game. As long as all players cooperate, there are no gains to be derived from cheating; hence, there are no incentives to defect. Although mutual defection is also an equilibrium in this game, mutual cooperation is Pareto-superior and so should quite easily become a focal point—differentiating assurance from the coordination problem discussed above. On this basis, studies of regimes have concluded that institutions have little role to play in assurance games; states will therefore not waste resources to construct them.[37]

---

35. Domestic strategies can also influence the credibility of commitments to international agreements. See Peter Cowhey's chapter in Ruggie, *Multilateralism Matters.*

36. See Robert O. Keohane, *After Hegemony: Cooperation and Discord in the World Political Economy* (Princeton, N.J.: Princeton University Press, 1984), pp. 91–92, for a general discussion of the role of institutions in issue linkage.

37. Stein, "Coordination and Collaboration," p. 119.

B

0   1

	0	1
0	4 , 4	1 , 3
1	3 , 1	2 , 2

A

FIGURE 4. *An assurance game (stag hunt)*

The above conclusion, however, is sensitive to changes in assumptions about the information available to states and about the ability of states to behave as unitary actors. Although mutual cooperation makes all players happy, unilateral cooperation is disastrous in assurance games. Thus, two kinds of problems could cause states to fail to reach their preferred outcome: (1) uncertainty about others' payoffs and (2) suspicion that others may not actually be rational, unitary actors.

If country A has assurance preferences but believes that there is some probability that country B has collaboration preferences, for example, country A will be reluctant to take the risk of cooperation. If country B did, in fact, see benefits from unilateral defection, country A may need to protect itself by preemptive defection. Similar concerns by country B could lead to mutual defection in spite of the fact that mutual cooperation is a Pareto-superior equilibrium. This is Robert Jervis's analysis of the security dilemma, suggesting why defensive, rational states in a world of uncertainty may behave in a manner that appears quite irrational.[38]

A second problem involves the question of whether the other player is, in fact, acting as a rational, unitary actor. Although the story underlying this concern differs from the previous scenario, its formal expression is equivalent: a probability distribution over the type of game being played. Here, state A's concern is that state B is not in control of its actions. One explanation may simply be a lack of rationality on B's part, leading to some probability that B will defect regardless of its preferences.[39] A second, perhaps more plausible,

38. Robert Jervis, "Cooperation Under the Security Dilemma," *World Politics* 30 (January 1978), pp. 58–79.
39. The impact of small deviations from intended strategies has led to the concept of trembling-hand equilibria. See Reinhard Selten, "Re-examination of the Perfectness Concept for Equilibrium Points in Extensive Games," *International Journal of Game Theory,* vol. 4, no. 1, 1975, pp. 25–55.

rendering is that B's policies are the result of a domestic game being played out between factions with different preference orderings. Perhaps the chief executive has assurance preferences, for example, while the legislative branch sees immediate benefits from cheating. In that case, if the outcome of the domestic struggle is unclear, state A will want to protect itself against the possibility that the legislature will prevail in the domestic game. The outcome here is the same as in the case of uncertainty about preferences. Suboptimal, mutual defection can result and will be an equilibrium since neither player has an incentive unilaterally to change strategies.

Admitting uncertainty into the assurance problem may have, at first glance, created a situation analogous to that of a collaboration game, in which rational, self-interested behavior leads to a suboptimal outcome. However, the solution to the problem of suboptimal, mutual defection is much less demanding in the assurance than in the collaboration case. In collaboration, stringent systems of monitoring and enforcement are required to prevent cheating. In assurance games, the problem is simply one of assuring all players that each sees no benefits from unilateral defection and is in control of domestic policymaking processes. An efficient solution in this case is provided by transparency in domestic arrangements: open democratic governments may see little need for complex international arrangements to solve assurance problems.

Democracies, however, are also especially subject to the problem of divided control over policymaking. Analysts often explain U.S. problems with foreign policy, for instance, by reference to the weaknesses of divided control. Thus, governments may choose to bolster their commitment to cooperation through the use of international arrangements. The primary function of these arrangements under assurance conditions would be exchange of information about the preferences of various domestic groups with access to the decision-making process. Multilateral norms—with their emphasis on collective decision making and extensive consultation and with their transaction-cost savings—will enhance governments' knowledge about one anothers' preferences. States may even centralize information exchange to economize further on transaction costs, as in coordination cases. However, the logic of the assurance situation does not suggest a need for centralized enforcement mechanisms. Although we should expect to see extensive cooperation in assurance games when information is not scarce, it would be a mistake to credit strong organizations or regimes with this success.

In sum, different cooperation problems lead us to expect different solutions. While there is no unique solution to any problem, a functional analysis does suggest that certain norms or types of formal organizations will be either dysfunctional or inefficient under specified conditions. In collaboration games with many actors, high incentives to engage in undetected cheating lead us to expect the emergence of strong organizations, unless enforcement and monitoring are taken over by a hegemon. Thus, in collaboration games, multilateral norms cannot promote cooperation except under the restricted circumstances of self-enforcing agreements among a small number of states (minilateralism).[40] Coordination problems, on the other hand, do present room for the use of multilateral norms, since states see no advantages in concealed defection from established conventions. In suasion games, cooperation is achieved through issue linkages. MOs can play some role in this process through committing the dominant power and making agreements easier to sell domestically for smaller states; however, these MOs are unlikely to embody IM to any extensive degree. Finally, assurance games, like coordination games, lead us to expect that IM will encourage transparency. However, also as in coordination cases, the role of formal organizations will be limited to exchange of information.

The effects of state power

Thus far, this article has employed a functional approach as it has inquired into the effects of potential solutions to a variety of cooperation problems. The analysis has adopted a systemic perspective, asking about the "correct" solutions to problems on a macro level. However, more than one solution exists for each type of problem. In addition to the problem of multiple equilibria, we have yet to address the micro-level foundations of various solutions to ask why individual states would choose to adopt them. To address these concerns, in this section I examine cooperation problems from the perspective of a hegemon, relying on a fundamental characteristic of the period in which postwar institutions were established. Bipolarity in the security realm also distinguished this period. The benefits of various solutions from the perspective of a hegemon in a bipolar system provide further insight into the types of solutions states prefer to adopt, and can be generalized to develop propositions about the form of cooperation in other systems.

Hegemonic interests

As Ruggie points out, the United States played a leading role in establishing multilateral institutions after World War II.[41] For this historical reason, the potential benefits of multilateral institutions for a dominant state, such as the United States, deserve attention. These benefits fall primarily into three categories: (1) lower transaction costs, (2) the deflection of challenges to the institution by its weaker members, and (3) increased stability under conditions of changes in relative power. These are benefits from the perspective of any type of hegemon, liberal or illiberal, although different types of regimes may put different weights on these benefits relative to the costs associated with

---

40. See Kahler, "Multilateralism with Small and Large Numbers."
41. Ruggie, "Multilateralism," p. 586.

cooperation. Any type of state gains from either reducing its costs of interacting with other countries or preventing challenges to the regimes it establishes.

Multilateralism can lower the transaction costs of interaction among states, particularly when they are attempting to overcome coordination problems. Ruggie uses the example of the International Telegraph Union to illustrate this dynamic.[42] When the distributional implications of agreements are minimal and the major problem is standardization, the transaction cost savings of multilateral institutions may be sufficient to explain why a hegemon would choose the multilateral form. Because a hegemonic power would face higher costs in negotiating a series of bilateral agreements than in negotiating a single, multilateral agreement, it should prefer multilateralism. However, the hegemon may be able to choose a particular equilibrium in coordination games simply through unilateral action.[43] If so, there are few short-term gains from multilateralism. Only a long-term, risk-averse perspective, anticipating future challenges to unilateral action, could explain hegemonic reliance on multilateralism in such a situation. These incentives are discussed below.

Multilateralism may also have advantages when greater conflicts of interest arise. From the hegemon's perspective, the maintenance costs of IM will be lower than those of an organizational form with more concentrated decision-making power. As long as patterns of state interests and power do not change abruptly, a hegemon can expect fewer challenges to an institution in which smaller states have a say in joint decisions than to a unilaterally imposed arrangement. As Miles Kahler has argued regarding the early years of the International Monetary Fund (IMF), "Even in these years of American predominance, the United States found it valuable to veil its power through conventions that convinced other countries that the rules of the game were reasonably fair or at least better than no rules at all."[44]

We could consider the establishment of IM as a transfer of resources in the form of decision-making power from the hegemon to other actors.[45] This transfer legitimates the organization's decisions in the eyes of weaker states, thus reducing the chance that they will continually challenge the regime.[46] As Margaret Levi has argued in a domestic context, institutionalized bargaining under conditions of asymmetry of power is less costly and risky for the dominant actor than constant expenditure of resources to quell rebellions.[47]

---

42. Ibid., p. 577.

43. See Krasner, "Global Communications and National Power."

44. Miles Kahler, "The United States and the International Monetary Fund: Declining Influence or Declining Interest?" in Karns and Mingst, *The United States and Multilateral Institutions,* p. 97.

45. Giulio M. Gallarotti, "Revisions in Realism: The Political Economy of Domination," paper presented at the Annual Meeting of the American Political Science Association, Atlanta, Georgia, September 1989.

46. Stephen D. Krasner, *Structural Conflict: The Third World Against Global Liberalism* (Berkeley: University of California Press, 1985), p. 62.

47. Margaret Levi, *Of Rule and Revenue* (Berkeley: University of California Press, 1988), p. 28.

Careful institutional design can create "quasi-voluntary compliance," reducing the transaction costs embodied in bargaining, monitoring, and enforcement.

Uncertainty about the actual distribution of benefits will also help to make a multilateral institution resistant to challenges from below. All else being equal, we should expect multilateral decision making to result in a more egalitarian distribution of benefits than decision making in a regime dominated by one or a few powers. Thus, smaller states should more willingly comply with multilateral decisions than commands from above, reducing the need for the hegemon to expend resources policing behavior and enforcing rules. By investing in MOs, the United States could expect fewer challenges to its activities and thus lower maintenance costs. As discussed above, a multilateral institution does create incentives to free ride in some situations. However, from the perspective of smaller states, taking advantage of such opportunities might threaten the institution as a whole, leading to the creation of one more detrimental to their interests. When asymmetry of interests and power allow for the possibility of decision making dominated by a hegemon, others may rationally comply with a more egalitarian, though demanding, arrangement.

On a related note, MOs with some IM may be more resistant to shifts in the balance of power than forums with concentrated decision-making powers. Because the major power is not overtly privileged in multilateral structures, diffusion of power will not necessarily lead to a challenge to the organization's structure. Crises resulting from changes in the distribution of power that might destroy other types of institutions can be weathered by multilateral arrangements. In this sense, multilateralism makes sense from the perspective of a far-sighted hegemon. It requires short-term sacrifices of control over decision making but can result in more stable arrangements over the long term.

As studies of U.S. foreign policy in the 1940s have shown, many key officials adopted a long-term perspective. They saw themselves engaged in the construction of a world order that they wanted to last for more than a few years and were willing to bear short-term costs in pursuit of long-term goals.[48] In addition, there was a widespread belief that U.S. hegemony was an ephemeral situation, and there were even efforts to speed up the inevitable diffusion of power.[49] Under these conditions, when a multilateral solution was a feasible option, the United States could rationally prefer it to more brittle solutions, such as overt coercion. For a far-sighted actor, attempts to exploit power in the short run could be more costly than the design of a durable decision-making structure.[50] Overall, multilateralism provides a relatively inexpensive and

---

48. Robert A. Pollard, *Economic Security and the Origins of the Cold War, 1945–1950* (New York: Columbia University Press, 1985).

49. Weber, "Shaping the Postwar Balance of Power."

50. Joanne Gowa, "Rational Hegemons, Excludable Goods, and Small Groups: An Epitaph for Hegemonic Stability Theory?" *World Politics* 41 (April 1989), pp. 307–24. Gowa also emphasizes the point made earlier in this article that the excludibility of free trade is an essential element of its maintenance.

stable organizational form. In exchange for a loss of some power over decision making and probably some decrease in distributional benefits, the hegemon gains a stable decision-making forum. The choice between unilateral action—a feasible solution—and multilateralism depends heavily on the hegemon's discount rate. The longer the time horizon, the more attractive multilateralism.

The effects of bipolarity.

While the United States was the dominant economic and security power within the Western subsystem in the 1950s, that grouping was nested in a larger, bipolar security structure. Examination of the effects of bipolarity gives further insight into the kinds of choices a rational hegemon might make when confronted with a range of feasible solutions to cooperation problems.

Neorealist analyses of the effects of bipolarity agree on one central point: a bipolar distribution of power makes exit from cooperative arrangements a less credible threat than it is in multipolar systems.[51] Given the power and threat of the Soviet Union, neither the United States nor Western Europe could credibly threaten to realign and thus destroy the Western alliance. Although within the bipolar alliance structure numerous conflicts of interest arose, the fundamental stability of alignment was guaranteed by bipolarity. In fact, the very publicity of policy differences between Western alliance members likely resulted from the understanding that such differences could not lead to defections to the Soviet bloc.[52]

The central question, in both security and economics issue-areas, is why the United States did not take advantage of its unique position to exploit the other members of these regimes. Above, I argued that the more far-sighted the hegemon, the less attractive that option becomes. One of the most important impacts of bipolarity is to encourage far-sighted behavior on the part of the hegemon toward its allies. Joanne Gowa argues that in a bipolar system the security externalities of exploitation decrease the utility of exploitation among allies: "The discount factors of allies in a bipolar system, in contrast [to a multipolar system], are not subject to the same downward bias: the greater stability of bipolar coalitions allows the value of future to approximate present benefits more closely."[53]

---

51. See Glenn H. Snyder, "The Security Dilemma in Alliance Politics," *World Politics* 36 (July 1984), pp. 461–95; Joanne Gowa, "Bipolarity, Multipolarity, and Free Trade," *American Political Science Review* 83 (December 1989), pp. 1245–56; and Kenneth N. Waltz, *Theory of International Politics* (Reading, Mass.: Addison-Wesley, 1979).

52. Snyder, "The Security Dilemma in Alliance Politics," p. 473. The question of burden sharing within the alliance, however, is an entirely different issue. Here, the asymmetry of power within the alliance put the United States into a suasion game whereby it contributed a disproportionately high level of resources to the alliance. See also Mancur Olson and Richard Zeckhauser, "An Economic Theory of Alliances," *Review of Economics and Statistics* 48 (August 1966), pp. 266–79; and John R. Oneal, "Testing the Theory of Collective Action: NATO Defense Burdens, 1950–1984," *Journal of Conflict Resolution* 34 (September 1990), pp. 426–48.

53. Gowa, "Bipolarity, Multipolarity, and Free Trade," p. 1250.

Thus, within both international economic regimes and the North Atlantic Treaty Organization (NATO), the United States was unlikely to prefer solutions that sacrificed long-term aggregate benefits for short-term relative gains at the expense of its allies. This tradeoff is the heart of the hegemon's dilemma, namely, whether to pursue its own immediate gains at the expense of its allies, or to accept a smaller share of the benefits in exchange for long-term growth and stability. A bipolar system creates incentives to pursue the latter solution, pushing a hegemon toward a multilateral rather than discriminatory solution to cooperation problems.

Although exit is a less attractive option in bipolar than in multipolar systems, significant variations in the credibility of the exit option remain even within bipolar systems. Within the bipolar structure of the cold war, in particular, exit from the Soviet bloc was a credible threat. While Western European states had no credible exit option, creating U.S. incentives as just described, Eastern European countries could credibly threaten to leave the sphere of Soviet dominance, since the alternative was attractive to them. This variation within the bipolar structure can only be explained by domestic differences between the United States and the Soviet Union, not by power differentials. Bipolarity thus creates the possibility of multilateralism but does not require it.

In the aggregate, structural approaches lead us to expect observable differences between the behavior of hegemons in bipolar and multipolar systems; bipolarity favors multilateralist policies on the part of a hegemon. However, it is not a sufficient condition. If allies have a credible exit option, as Eastern European states did, the hegemon rationally will avoid the sharing of decision-making power and benefits implied by multilateralism. The credibility of threats to exit determine the long-term costs and benefits of multilateralism. Credibility depends in the first instance on structural considerations, as threats to exit are typically quite credible in multipolarity. Bipolarity creates the possibility that such threats will become incredible, but does not assure it.[54]

According to this logic, the current movement toward multipolarity should lead powerful states to favor solutions other than multilateralism. For example, we might expect to see greater use of self-enforcing agreements among smaller numbers of players, as those who see a move toward regionalism in the global economy argue is happening. Note, however, that changing preferences over organizational form do not imply that the goal of liberalization will disappear but simply that solutions other than multilateralism will become more important for its realization. The clearest example of this trend seems to be in U.S. trade policy. The increasing reliance on retaliatory bilateral threats and negotiation of bilateral free trade agreements signal a significant change in

---

54. Current changes in the structure of security arrangements in Europe bear out this logic. East European states are turning to NATO for security. However, NATO, wary of the reliability and stability of the new East European regimes, is insisting on a series of bilateral arrangements rather than formal incorporation into the multilateral framework.

U.S. tactics to pursue the goal of freer trade.[55] While the goals espoused in the GATT remain firmly embedded, the structure used to further them appears to be in transformation, largely due to U.S. initiatives.[56]

The discussion in this section has assumed a powerful state making choices in the absence of pre-existing institutional constraints, in the sort of "blank slate" condition that confronted the United States in the early postwar era. However, ongoing events in Europe should caution us against applying these hypotheses without modification to more highly institutionalized settings. Two fundamental sets of decisions by powerful actors will provide grist for future analysts' mills: (1) Germany's dealings with the rest of Europe, and (2) Russia's dealings with the other former Soviet republics. Both are, in a highly simplified sense, situations of powerful states making decisions about institutional design. However, the context in which each is making such decisions varies greatly, creating different incentives.

Germany, as the most powerful economic actor in Europe, faces two general sets of decisions about the form of relations with its neighbors. To the west, Germany is involved in restructuring the EC. These negotiations are taking place within an unusually well-developed institutional framework. By 1991, the scope and depth of the benefits provided by the EC established it as a central piece of German foreign policy. These benefits and the dense network of relationships built within the EC over the last few decades encourage long-term thinking with respect to dealings with other EC members. Thus, in spite of the end of the cold war, Germany continues to pursue multilateral arrangements within this context.

However, bargains within the EC contrast sharply to those between Germany and Eastern European states. While the new democracies of Eastern Europe struggle to present a common front to the West in hopes of gaining political and economic support, and are searching for access to MOs—including the EC, the GATT, the IMF, and others—bargains have thus far taken on primarily bilateral forms. High levels of uncertainty and constant change contribute to reluctance to rely on multilateral forums.[57] Within the former Soviet Union, the collapse of Soviet institutions has created opportunities and demands for new arrangements. Russia, in its dealings with the other republics, confronts a situation of even more uncertainty than that in Eastern Europe, but also one of relatively high levels of interdependence. No clear pattern has yet emerged, since attempts to organize multilateral arrangements

55. For an example, see Rudiger W. Dornbusch, "Policy Options for Freer Trade: The Case for Bilateralism," in Robert Z. Lawrence and Charles L. Schultze, eds., *An American Trade Strategy* (Washington, D.C.: The Brookings Institution, 1990), pp. 106–34.

56. For a discussion of embedded goals, see John Gerard Ruggie, "International Regimes, Transactions, and Change: Embedded Liberalism in the Postwar Economic Order," in Krasner, ed., *International Regimes,* pp. 195–231.

57. For an example, see Debora L. Spar, "The Political Economy of Foreign Direct Investment in Eastern Europe," prepared for the Center for International Affairs project on International Institutions after the Cold War, Harvard University, Cambridge, Mass., November 1991.

coexist with both reliance on bilateral mechanisms to meet immediate and pressing needs and unilateral Russian actions.

Overall, consideration of the incentives and constraints created by hegemony and bipolarity gives greater precision to the earlier functional analysis, suggesting how a hegemonic state might choose from among a set of feasible solutions. From a hegemon's perspective, the primary choice is from among discriminatory bilateralism, unilateral dominance, and the use of institutions that cede greater decision-making power to other states.

Multilateralism provides benefits of transaction-cost savings and greater stability. However, these advantages are offset by the loss of short-term direct benefits, since a greater share of the immediate gains of cooperation will accrue to states other than the hegemon. The discount rate of the hegemon, therefore, influences the choice among these options: a far-sighted state will value the benefits of multilateralism more highly than a short-sighted one. It might be that bipolarity creates stability and thus encourages far-sighted behavior.

Institutional change

The previous sections of this article adopted a comparative statical approach to institutional choice, asking about the likelihood of finding different patterns of norms and organizations under certain configurations of interests and power. This section turns to the question of change. I do not attempt to develop a fully dynamic theory of change, which would require endogenizing the factors that lead to observable changes in institutions. Instead, I treat the causes of change as exogenous. Thus, this discussion does not address the possibility that participation in a multilateral regime may itself change states' conceptions of their interests. The explanatory puzzle addressed here involves the most likely causes of change in each type of cooperation problem discussed above. Assuming that a pattern of cooperation has been established in an issue-area, what factors are likely to upset it?

In collaboration situations, crises will result from constant temptations to defect in order to reap short-term benefits. Two factors in particular can lead to crises in collaboration: (1) developments that decrease the shadow of the future for individual states, and (2) changes that decrease states' ability to remain informed about the behavior of others. Numerous factors—impending change of government, threats to national security, domestic strife, increasing multipolarity—can lead to a shrinking of states' relevant time horizons. Any of these could increase states' temptation to defect sufficiently to lead to crisis within an issue-area. Similarly, if institutions' ability to provide information is threatened—for example, by technical innovations that make verification of agreements more difficult—the likelihood of defection will increase. Relative to coordination cases, crises are likely to occur frequently in collaboration situations.

In coordination cases, crises will arise when one state whose actions matter to other participants develops a particularly strong interest in changing the established equilibrium. This may occur for a number of reasons, such as domestic political change or a change in technology that makes maintenance of the existing equilibrium more costly. It is interesting to note that changes that give rise to a *longer* time horizon will likely lead to attempts to change the regime. As states value the future more highly, the short-term costs of forcing movement to a new equilibrium may be outweighed by the long-term benefits of a new outcome. Thus, in contrast to collaboration cases, cooperation is threatened rather than enhanced by a longer shadow of the future.

The state desiring change, if it believes its participation is important enough to other actors that they can be influenced by its actions, may challenge the existing equilibrium. If this state is a major player, the challenge could eventually succeed in spite of the short-term costs in deviating from the established standard. U.S. actions in challenging the telecommunications regime could be interpreted this way, as changes in technology and domestic politics led the U.S. government to challenge the existing regime, looking for an outcome more conducive to its interests in the long run.[58] Because the United States was an important player in the regime, its defection was costly to other states and eventually forced them to a new outcome, one based more on market principles.

In sum, crises arise in coordination games when some exogenous force leads an important state to challenge the existing conventions, even though this challenge will be costly in the short term. An important difference from collaboration cases lies in the fact that such challenges will be public. Since there is nothing to gain from unilaterally moving to a different standard, any challenge will be a public attempt to force others to accommodate. Thus, technological developments that threaten cooperation in coordination problems are not those that decrease transparency, but those that change the costs and benefits of specific outcomes for key members of the regime.

Regimes that rely on tactical issue linkage to foster cooperation in suasion games will face crises as the power of the hegemon declines. In this situation, the threats and promises that maintain cooperation will become less credible, increasing others' temptation to defect. This effect may be offset, however, by changing patterns of interests that result directly from changes in power relationships. A declining hegemon may no longer find it worthwhile unilaterally to provide any public goods, thus changing the cooperation problem from one of suasion to one of collaboration.[59] We should expect a fundamental shift in the nature of the regime under these conditions, although we may not see a significant decline in overall cooperation. As asymmetries of power and interest

58. See Cowhey, "The International Telecommunications Regime."

59. Duncan Snidal, "The Limits of Hegemonic Stability Theory," *International Organization* 39 (Autumn 1985), pp. 579–614.

decline, the de facto monopoly of decision making by the hegemon should give way to more genuinely multilateral behavior. Organizations that merely collected information may gain monitoring and enforcement powers. The International Atomic Energy Agency seems to illustrate this pattern, since it has continued to function even as U.S. power has declined.[60] Overall, crises in suasion situations will typically arise from changes in the distribution of power.

Assurance problems, in spite of their high degree of common interest, are not immune from crises. Changes in the domestic political arrangements of key actors or technological innovations that create uncertainty about preference orderings will create a desire to protect oneself from the defection of others. Thus, the kinds of factors that threaten collaboration also challenge cooperation in assurance games. Such threats to stable cooperation, however, will be moderated by the existence of viable multilateral institutions. If states have created international arrangements for the exchange of information, whether formal or informal, they will ease the adjustment process to exogenous changes in assurance games.

Conclusion

Will rational, self-interested states ever see instrumental value in multilateral norms? Consideration of the functional demands of various cooperation problems and the benefits of various patterns of cooperation for powerful states leads to a mixed answer. On the one hand, there is never an absolute need for IM, nor for formal MOs. A hegemonic actor could feasibly construct a series of bilateral arrangements, or assert its own preferences as the prerogatives of power, thus avoiding the use of IM or MOs. On the other hand, while such behavior may bring a powerful state immediate benefits, it is likely to prove highly inefficient and difficult to sustain in the long term. Thus, a far-sighted actor may choose to rely on IM or MOs in specified circumstances, rather than simply using its power to enforce a solution to cooperation problems. The extent to which a powerful state will sacrifice control over international decision making in exchange for stability depends on the degree to which conditions allow it to value future interactions as highly as it values today's. Conditions of instability and uncertainty may impair a powerful state's ability to adopt a multilateral approach to international cooperation.

This article has outlined a rational-choice approach to the relationships among IM, MOs, and international cooperation. The analysis here developed expectations about institutional and state behavior by focusing on specific cooperation problems and considering functional constraints. I argued that the relationships between principles, formal organizations, and behavior depend on the nature of strategic interaction in particular issue-areas. The next step in

60. Schiff, "Dominance without Hegemony," p. 78.

this research program should involve similar development of hypotheses from competing perspectives and systematic collection of empirical evidence that will allow us to evaluate their respective explanatory power.

Collaboration should lead to relatively strong organizations but also to the disregard of multilateral principles, particularly diffuse reciprocity and indivisibility. In coordination situations, on the other hand, IM may be strong but formal organizations are hardly necessary and will be quite weak. IM will be weak in suasion situations. In suasion games, formal organizations will probably play a larger role than they play in coordination games but less so than in collaboration games. The potential role of IM and MOs in assurance games is similar to that in coordination. The central problem in both is provision of information about preferences and intentions, and multilateral norms provide an efficient means of information exchange. However, there is no reason to expect strong organizations with enforcement power, and unilateral action by a hegemon may constitute a functional substitute for multilateralism.

Although we can rule out certain kinds of solutions for each type of cooperation problem with such functional analysis, more than one potential solution usually remains. Analysis can further narrow the range of feasible solutions, however, by considering the structural characteristics of the international system. The third section of this article examined preferred solutions from the perspective of a hegemon, asking why multilateralism might ever be preferred to an architecture where the hegemon could more directly exercise dominance. The stability of the Western alliance under conditions of bipolarity led the United States to behave as a far-sighted hegemon, often willing to bypass exploitative solutions in favor of long-term benefits and stability.

In the final section I argued that any "crisis of multilateralism" will result from different factors in each of the four situations. Changes in the distribution of power will be most threatening to cooperation in suasion games. Factors that reduce transparency will challenge both assurance and collaboration games, while increasing discount rates will be most troubling for collaboration. Coordination games are most likely to be upset by technological innovations that alter the cost-benefit calculus of existing conventions for key players. Given the urgency of decisions about institutional design in the post–cold war world, an understanding of the incentives underlying the use or non-use of multilateral norms and/or organizations has both historical and practical significance.

International Organizations as Teachers of Norms: The United Nations' Educational, Scientific, and Cutural Organization and Science Policy
Martha Finnemore

The structure of states is continually evolving. Since their establishment in Europe some five hundred years ago and particularly since World War I, states have grown in terms of both the variety of tasks they perform and the organizational apparatuses with which they perform these tasks.

The research outlined below investigates the causes underlying this process of state change in the case of one recently adopted set of state bureaucracies, those designed to coordinate scientific research. In the last fifty years science policymaking organizations have sprung up in virtually all developed countries and in most developing ones. Most explanations for the appearance of these new pieces of state machinery found in the political science or economics literatures describe this development as demand-driven, that is, some domestic group perceives a problem to which a science policy bureaucracy is the solution. Social groups such as producers of science (e.g., scientists) or consumers of science (e.g., technology-intensive businesses) may come to perceive that state coordination and direction of a growing science establishment are in their interest. State officials may come to perceive that the intimate relationship between science and security makes control of science in the national interest. Depending on the perspective adopted, one would predict different configurations of science bureaucracies serving different interests, but in all cases, the impetus for creating those organizations would be a demand by state or societal actors that the government should direct and control science.

This study quantitatively tests these demand-driven hypotheses by comparing a variety of indicators of state conditions that have been argued to prompt demand with the timing of adoption of science policy bureaucracies. The

I am grateful to Laura Helvey, Peter Katzenstein, Steve Krasner, Forrest Maltzman, Rose McDermott, John Meyer, John Odell, Francisco Ramirez, Nina Tannenwald, Kurt Weyland, and two anonymous reviewers for helpful comments on earlier drafts.

International Organization 47, 4, Autumn 1993, pp. 565–597

results provide little support for any of the demand-driven hypotheses. Consequently, an alternative explanation is investigated. Early in the diffusion of this bureaucratic innovation, several international organizations took up science policy as a cause and promoted it among member states. The article traces the process whereby one of these international organizations, the United Nations Educational, Scientific, and Cultural Organization (UNESCO), "taught" states the value and utility of science policy organizations.

I argue that the creation of this teaching mission, whereby UNESCO would supply the organizational innovation to states, was a reflection of a new norm elaborated within the international community.[1] This norm held that coordination and direction of science are necessary tasks of the modern state and that a science policy bureaucracy having certain well-specified characteristics was the appropriate means to fulfill those tasks. States created science bureaucracies, with UNESCO's help, to comply with the new norm about states' responsibility for science. Thus, the organizational innovation was supplied to states from outside, from an international organization, rather than being the product of any characteristics internal to or inherent in the state itself.

The article makes contributions to three different theoretical debates ongoing in the field. First, the findings outlined above lend support to constructivist or reflective theoretical approaches that treat states as social entities, shaped in part by international social action. State policies and structures in this case are influenced by changing intersubjective understandings about the appropriate role of the modern state.

However, in most cases the causes of those changed understandings lie not at the national level but at the systemic level: it is an international organization that persuades states to adopt these changes. Thus, a second contribution of this article is to demonstrate the role of international organizations as principals, rather than agents, in international politics.

Finally, the article raises questions about the nature and role of epistemic communities. While many of the UNESCO officials involved in this reorganization of international science had scientific credentials, their reasons for acting had more to do with their status as international bureaucrats than with their professional socialization or principled beliefs about science. This suggests that the "epistemic" aspect of groups may not always be their most important feature and that caution is warranted in ascribing causal status to specialized knowledge when explaining political behavior.

---

1. For purposes of this article a "norm" is defined as a rulelike prescription which is both clearly perceptible to a community of actors and which makes behavioral claims upon those actors. Although comments of McElroy were influential in formulating this definition, McElroy's own definition differs significantly from mine; see Robert McElroy, *Morality and American Foreign Policy: The Role of Moral Norms in International Affairs* (Princeton, N.J.: Princeton University Press, 1992).

The development of science policy

The relationship between states and science by no means begins with the establishment of formal state science policy bureaucracies.[2] National academies and royal societies of science, many of which enjoyed some amount of state sponsorship and whose members were in frequent contact with government officials, date back to the seventeenth century. Similarly, state-sponsored universities often housed scientists and their activities. However, state sponsorship of the sciences in this early period was understood to be analogous to state sponsorship of the arts; greatness and accomplishment in arts and sciences reflected state power rather than being a means to achieve power. Further, patronage of this kind usually entailed minimal direction and control. Academies and universities may (or may not) have benefited from state funding, but they were not part of the state apparatus and were left free to pursue their work with a minimum of state interference.

The modern concept of science policy differs on both these issues. It understands science as a means to national power and consequently seeks to bring science activity under the control of the state. Most often this has entailed the creation of a new piece of state apparatus dedicated explicitly to this task. The first effort to do this was made by the British in 1915 when they established the Department of Scientific and Industrial Research to wean British science and industry from continental, especially German, innovations, expertise, and technical equipment during World War I.[3] A few Commonwealth members mimicked the British lead and established similar organizations, but it was not until after World War II that science policy bureaucracies became widespread. Before 1955 only a handful of countries (fourteen) had such entities; by 1975 eighty-nine countries did. This research seeks to explain how and why the state interest in and use of science changed in this way.

2. The history of states' changing attitudes toward science obviously is much more complex than the overview presented here. For more on this subject, see Joseph Ben David, "The Scientific Role: The Conditions of Its Establishment in Europe," *Minerva* 4 (Autumn 1965), pp. 15–54; A. Hunter Dupre, *Science in the Federal Government: A History of Policies and Activities to 1940* (Cambridge, Mass.: Harvard University Press, 1957); Philip Gummett, *Scientists in Whitehall* (Manchester, England: Manchester University Press, 1980); Ros Herman, *The European Scientific Community* (Harlow, England: Longman Press, 1986); Eric Hutchinson, "Scientists as an Inferior Class: The Early Years of the DSIR," *Minerva* 8 (July 1970), pp. 396–411; Daniel Kevels, *The Physicists: The History of a Scientific Community in Modern America* (New York: Alfred A. Knopf, 1978); Frank Pfetsch, "Scientific Organization and Science Policy in Imperial Germany, 1871–1914: The Founding of the Imperial Institute of Physics and Technology," *Minerva* 8 (October 1970), pp. 557–80; Jarlath Royane, *Science in Government* (London: Edward Arnold, 1984); Ian Varcoe, "Scientists, Government, and Organized Research in Great Britain, 1914–1916: The Early History of the DSIR," *Minerva* 8 (April 1970), pp. 192–216; and Robert Wuthnow, "The World Economy and the Institutionalization of Science in Seventeenth Century Europe," in Albert Bergesen, ed., *Studies of the Modern World-System* (New York: Academic Press, 1980), pp. 57–76.

3. Peter Alter, *The Reluctant Patron: Science and the State in Britain, 1850–1920* (Oxford: Berg, 1987), pp. 201ff.

For purposes of this study I define science policy bureaucracies as organs of the state that have as their primary mission the tasks of coordinating, organizing, and planning scientific and technological activities at a national level. I exclude from my definition the following types of organizations: (1) nonstate organizations (such as scientists' professional societies); (2) organizations dealing with only one branch of science (such as the National Weather Service or medical and health organizations); (3) educational organizations whose primary mission is to train scientific and technical personnel rather than coordinate activities broadly; and (4) research organizations whose primary mission is to conduct research rather than to make policy. This definition is based on UNESCO's definition used in compiling its world directories of national science policymaking bodies and so ensures that the UNESCO activities chronicled below and my analysis concern the same phenomena.[4]

Demand-driven explanations for science policy organizations

Most explanations for the creation of new state bureaucracies trace the cause to some change in material conditions that reconfigures the interests of actors within the state. Functionalists might regard such an objective change to be sufficient as well as necessary for the new bureaucracy to appear. Others less sanguine about the efficacy of political systems in meeting all needs or fulfilling all functions would regard change in material conditions only as a necessary condition and look to the process by which demands are voiced and, once voiced, are realized for sufficient conditions. Even in this latter set of explanations, however, some material change must prompt the demand-making process.

Thus in most explanations there is some prerequisite condition associated with the creation of new state bureaucracies.[5] Three kinds of prerequisites have been argued to be relevant. The first are what I call *issue-specific* conditions. Here, it is the situation in the issue-area particularly relevant to the new

4. The first of these directories appeared during the 1960s. See United Nations Educational, Scientific, and Cultural Organization (UNESCO), *World Directory of National Science Policy-making Bodies,* 3 vols. (Paris: UNESCO, 1966–68). Volume 1 covered Europe and North America; volume 2, Asia and Oceania; and volume 3, Latin America. A second directory was published in 1984. See UNESCO, *World Directory of National Science Policy-making Bodies,* Science Policy Studies and Documents Series, vol. 59 (UNESCO: Paris, 1984). A second edition of this 1984 directory was published in 1990. See UNESCO, *World Directory of National Science Policy-making Bodies,* Science Policy Studies and Documents Series, vol. 71 (Paris: UNESCO, 1990). I have made several refinements to the UNESCO definitions. For further explanation, see the appendix.

5. I have borrowed the term "prerequisite" from Collier and Messick's analysis of the spread of social security across states. See David Collier and Richard Messick, "Prerequisites versus Diffusion: Testing Alternative Explanations of Social Security Adoption," *American Political Science Review* 69 (December 1975), pp. 1299–315.

organization that prompts its creation. Applied to science, this argument links the creation of a state science policymaking apparatus to the growth and strength of the domestic science community. An argument of just this type has been made by David Dickson to explain the origins of science policymaking in the United States.[6] In Dickson's view the growth of the domestic science establishment prompted the creation of a state science policy apparatus in two ways. On the one hand state actors saw a science policy bureaucracy as an opportunity to direct and control this new activity. On the other hand scientists saw such an organization as a potential conduit for state aid and coordination. This thesis would predict adoption of science policy organizations to be highly correlated with domestic levels of science activity, for example, with the number of scientists in the country and the amount of research and development (R&D) spending.

The next two types of conditions apply to consumers rather than producers of science. *Development or modernization* levels are argued to prompt the creation of science policy entities through the actions of the economic consumers of science, particularly industry. The idea here is that as a state's economy develops, it will become more technology-intensive and so require more scientific support. Economic actors therefore put pressure on the state to organize and supply this support; a new science policy organization is the result. In many mixed economies, these actors may be state economic actors; what is important for this analysis is that the purpose of demand-making is economic. According to this thesis, indicators of economic development, such as per capita gross domestic product (GDP), should predict the creation of a science policy organization.

Security conditions are argued to prompt the creation of science policy bureaucracies through the actions of military consumers of science. In the modern era of warfare, scientific prowess has been clearly linked to technological and hence to military success. Thus states perceiving threats to their power and/or security will be pushed to find new and more effective technologies to meet those threats. Militaries in these states will demand that the state organize and support the scientific establishment for reasons of national defense.

The timing of science bureaucracy creation in Britain (during World War I) and in the United States (immediately following World War II) has led a number of scholars to draw causal connections between security concerns and science policy. Sanford Lakoff, Jean-Jacques Salomon, and Harvey Sapolsky all point to these wars as well as to another perceived security threat—the launching of Sputnik—as the catalysts for government interest in harnessing science to achieve national objectives in the United States and Europe. Having organized science to meet security threats during wartime with apparent

6. David Dickson, *The New Politics of Science* (New York: Pantheon, 1984), pp. 25ff.

success, these wartime institutions were then redeployed by states to meet peacetime objectives.[7]

Robert Gilpin makes a more detailed and broader security argument based on his investigations of French science.[8] He argues that France's creation of science policy organizations was the direct result of a perceived threat to French influence and independence from a preponderance of U.S. power immediately following World War II. At one level, this threat was understood militarily and led the French to use their science community to upgrade their defense establishment, notably to establish a separate nuclear strike force. But threats to influence and security in the French view were not limited to the military sphere. The French were also concerned about loss of economic dominance. U.S. economic strength following World War II was viewed with trepidation, and direct U.S. investment in France was viewed as a form of imperialism by a foreign power. During that time the French spoke of a "technology gap" that they must bridge by harnessing French science in the service of French industry to protect French economic independence and integrity.[9]

Security understood in this sweeping way, as any threat to influence and independence, could operate in so many arenas that developing tidy objective indicators to test for its presence is probably impossible.[10] The narrower arguments about security threats understood in a military context are some-what easier to uncover. If armed conflict or the threat of armed conflict is critical, indicators of perceived military threat, such as defense spending as a percentage of GNP, should be correlated with the creation of science policy organizations. States perceiving military threats should be among the first to adopt science policy; conversely, relatively secure states should be clustered among the late adopters.

Testing the demand-driven explanations

Each of these explanations posits a material condition that then sparks a demand for the state to adopt new tasks and to create new bureaucracies to carry out those tasks. While it would be impractical to investigate the actual

---

7. See the following chapters in Ina Spiegel-Rosing and Derek de Solla Price, eds., *Science, Technology and Society: A Cross-disciplinary Perspective* (London: Sage, 1977): Jean-Jacques Salomon, "Science Policy Studies and the Development of Science Policy," pp. 43–70; Sanford Lakoff, "Scientists, Technologists, and Political Power," pp. 355–92; and Harvey Sapolsky, "Science, Technology, and Military Policy," pp. 443–72.

8. Robert Gilpin, *France in the Age of the Scientific State* (Princeton, N.J.: Princeton University Press, 1968).

9. Ibid.

10. For example, in the French case, threats to influence and independence extended to cultural matters and led France to pursue a number of foreign policy initiatives aimed at preserving and extending French language and culture in other states.

demand-making process over a large number of countries having very different political systems, it is quite simple to check for the existence of conditions said to be prerequisite to those demands. The test reported here compiled and analyzed quantitative indicators of domestic conditions that might prompt creation of a science policy bureaucracy in a sample of forty-four countries chosen to be globally representative in terms of both geography and development levels. As suggested in the foregoing discussion, these were percentage of GDP spent on R&D; proportion of scientists and engineers in the population; per capita GDP; and percentage of gross national product (GNP) spent on defense. A complete description of the indicators used and the method of compiling them can be found in the appendix.

Testing a global sample of states raises issues about comparability among the units of analysis, particularly comparability of developing and industrialized states. Cameroon and the United States, for example, are so different on so many measures that one may question whether the units of analysis are sufficiently alike to make comparison appropriate and meaningful.

In this case, comparability of the units is ensured by the research questions being asked. The hypotheses being tested concern the behavior of states as a political and organizational form: What prompts states to adopt new tasks and construct new apparatuses to carry out those tasks? The hypotheses do not carry with them caveats about degrees of stateness, state capacity, or other potentially limiting characteristics. Instead they make arguments about the behavior of states qua states. Cameroon and the United States may be very different states, but they are both states nonetheless. In fact the article will suggest that what is going on in this case is a redefinition of the state as a political and organizational form; that is, a redefinition of what is necessary and appropriate behavior for a state.

Figures 1–4 show the distribution of values for each of the indicators of state conditions at the time science policy bureaucracies were created in the countries studied. A quick look at figures reveals that none of the patterns corresponds to the expected patterns described above. If any of these conditions were both necessary and sufficient, there would be a large cluster of adoptions on the histogram at that necessary and sufficient value. Instead, the adoptions appear to occur at a very wide range of values for all four of the variables. No single value of any variable appears likely as a necessary and sufficient condition for adoption.

In fact, countries adopted these science bureaucracies at wildly different levels of each of these domestic conditions. Some elaboration from the raw data will make the extremely wide range of variation in values even clearer:

(1) Countries created these bureaucracies when they had as few as nine scientists employed in R&D (e.g., Congo) or as many as half a million (e.g., the United States and the Soviet Union).

(2) R&D spending as a percentage of GDP ranged from 0.01 percent at the time of adoption (Bangladesh) to 1.5 percent (France).

(3) Per capita GDP in constant U.S. dollars ranged from a low of $118/year

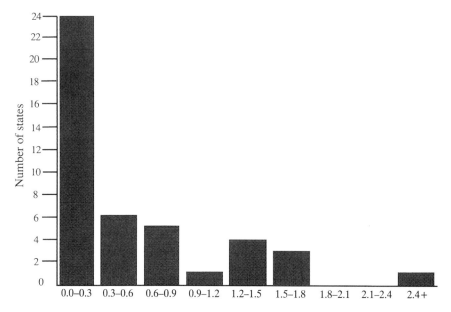

Percentage of gross domestic product spent on R&D

FIGURE 1. *Research and development (R&D) spending at the time of science policy adoption*

(Pakistan) to a high of more than $9,000/year (Denmark) at the time these bureaucracies were created.

(4) Defense spending as a percentage of GNP ranged from 0.7 percent (Mexico, Sri Lanka) to more than 10 percent at the time of adoption (France, Iraq, Jordan, and the Soviet Union).

The range of variation on the defense variable is more than a factor of ten; the range of variation on all of the other variables is a factor of one hundred or more. Ranges of variation this large do not readily suggest any causal connection between sufficient state conditions and the adoption of science bureaucracies.

Similarly, Figures 1–4 provide little support for the necessary condition hypothesis, that is, that there is some minimum threshold value of these variables that triggers demand for the bureaucracy. If such a value existed, we should see very few (or no) adoptions at the low end of the value range for one or more of these variables; all values would be spread across the upper end of the range at or above the necessary condition level.

Again, the far-flung distribution of values revealed in these figures and elaborated in the text above does not readily support this proposition. Rather than clustering at the upper end of the value ranges, there seems to be a concentration of values at the low end, particularly on the science variables. This is clearly not a bunching that would support the existence of a necessary

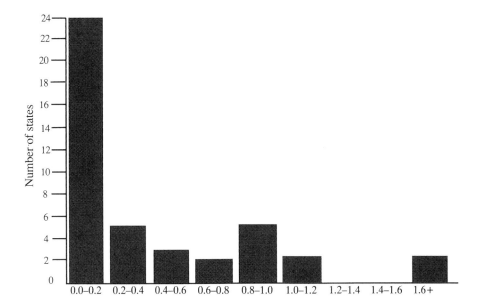

Scientists and engineers per 1,000 population

FIGURE 2. *Proportion of scientists and engineers in the population at the time of science policy adoption*

and sufficient condition, since the bunching in each case is accompanied by a large number of data points at the high end of each scale. Instead, it appears to be a strong negation of any necessary-but-not-sufficient-condition argument. If arriving at some minimum threshold level of these variables is supposed to trigger demand for a science policy bureaucracy, that threshold must be so low as to have very little explanatory power.

In fact a large number of small, poor, technologically unsophisticated, and militarily unthreatened countries created these bureaucracies in the 1950s and 1960s. It is this group that accounts for the clustering of data points at the low end of Figures 1–4. Guatemala, for example, created its Consejo Nacional de Investigacionnes Científicas y Técnicas in 1966 when it reported having only fourteen scientists employed in R&D jobs, spent only 0.01 percent of GDP on research, had a GDP per capita of $806, and, since it faced no serious military threats, spent only 1.07 percent of GNP on defense. Cameroon and the Congo were equally unlikely candidates for a science bureaucracy.[11]

11. The Congo created its Conseil National de la Recherche Scientifique in 1963 when it reported having only nine scientists engaged in R&D jobs and when spending on R&D was only 0.11 percent of GDP. Measured in U.S. dollars, GDP per capita was only $253 that year, and military spending accounted for only 2.04 percent of GNP. Cameroon created its Office National de la Recherche Scientifique et Technique in 1965 when it reported employing only eighty scientists in research jobs and spending only 0.16 percent of its GDP on research. Per capita GDP was $334 for that year, and the country spent only 2.3 percent of its GNP on defense.

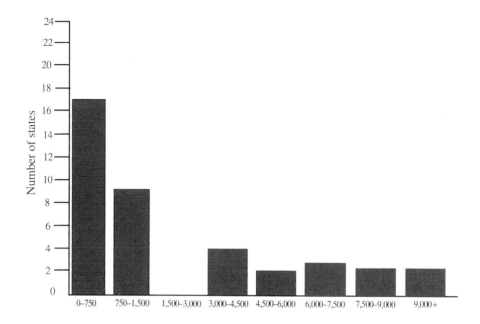

GDP per capita in constant $US (1980)

FIGURE 3. *Gross domestic product (GDP) per capita at the time of science policy adoption*

At the same time, the histograms do show that some countries create science bureaucracies at reasonably high levels of all the indicator variables. Significantly, the first instances of this science bureaucracy creation occur among this group, suggesting that demand-driven explanations may fit some of the earliest adopters of science policy. Britain, the first adopter, clearly created its Department of Science and Industrial Research in 1915 for security reasons to counter German advances in chemicals and machinery that were directly supporting the German war effort.[12] The establishment of the National Science Foundation in the United States in 1950 was explicitly related to concerns about military and industrial competitiveness and was strongly influenced by the creation of the atom bomb.[13] French science policymaking, as chronicled by

12. Alter, *The Reluctant Patron.* See also Roy McLeod and E. Kay Andrews, "The Origins of the D.S.I.R.: Reflections on Ideas and Men, 1915–1916," *Public Administration,* vol. 48, no. 1, 1970, pp. 23–48; and Ian Varcoe, "Scientists, Government, and Organized Research in Great Britain 1914–1916," pp. 192–216. The United Kingdom is not included in the quantitative analysis above because science data for that country for 1915 are unavailable.

13. Dickson, *The New Politics of Science.* See also J. Merton England, *A Patron for Pure Science: The National Science Foundation's Formative Years, 1945–1957* (Washington, D.C.: National Science Foundation, 1982); N. Dupree, *Science in the Federal Government;* Bruce Smith, *American Science Policy Since World War II* (Washington, D.C.: Brookings Institution, 1990); and U.S. Congress, House Committee on Science and Technology, Task Force on Science Policy, *A History of Science Policy in the United States, 1940–1985,* Science Policy Study Background Report, no. 1, 99th Congress, 2d sess., 1986, serial R.

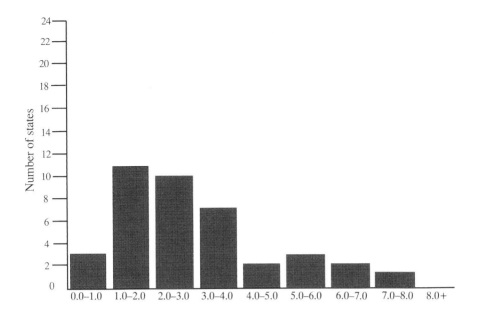

Percentage GNP spent on defense

FIGURE 4. *Defense spending as a percentage of gross national product (GNP) at the time of science policy adoption*

Gilpin, seems also to have been prompted by security and competitiveness concerns, albeit of a more general nature since the French were concerned about a general loss of influence in the world, especially vis-à-vis the United States.[14]

But how do we explain the creation of science policy organizations in more than a hundred other states covering the extremes of science capacity, development levels, and military situations in the subsequent twenty years? Countries as dissimilar as Bulgaria, Czechoslovakia, El Salvador, the Federal Republic of Germany, Indonesia, Italy, Lebanon, Mali, Pakistan, and Sweden all created their first science policy bureaucracy during the peak adoption year of 1962.[15]

It will be argued below that these two phenomena, the apparent responsiveness to state conditions in a few early-adopting states followed by a pattern of adoption unrelated to state conditions, can be reconciled in the following way: science policy bureaucracies appeared as an innovation in the international system in response to clear domestic demands in a few prominent developed countries. The innovation was then picked up and popularized by an international organization, UNESCO, for reasons of its own and spread by that

14. Gilpin, *France in the Age of the Scientific State.*
15. "Peak adoption year" in this case means the single year in which the largest number of states created these science policy bureaucracies.

organization to other states in which the conditions that ordinarily would prompt such demands did not exist.

A supply-driven explanation

Since demand-side explanations for the creation of science policy organizations appear to be on weak ground for most states, the next logical question is, what if these bureaucratic innovations are not demanded inside the state but supplied from outside? In fact, most (roughly 70 percent) of these science policy organizations were created between 1955 and 1975.[16] Beginning in the early 1950s two international organizations, UNESCO and the Organization for Economic Cooperation and Development (OECD), began actively to promote this science policy innovation among their member states.[17] In this section I describe the promotion activities of one of these organizations, UNESCO, and present evidence that its activities were the impetus for widespread adoption of science policy. Such an explanation allows us to make sense of the data presented earlier since it is consistent with both (1) the low-end clustering on the histograms, indicating that many countries adopted these bureaucracies at very low levels of the indicator variables, and (2) the timing of adoption across states, specifically the rapid increase immediately after the international organizations begin to promote the science policy innovation.

Specifically, I will argue that from its inception UNESCO as an organization has had to address two constituencies—the states comprising its membership and the professional experts in its substantive areas of concern. As will be described below, the relationship between these two constituencies within the organization has changed over time. These shifts in turn have been responsible for changes in UNESCO's programs, particularly the rise of science policy as an area of concern.[18]

Origins of UNESCO's interest in science

As originally conceived, UNESCO was to be named the United Nations Educational and Cultural Organization. Science was understood to be part of culture. The notion that science was qualitatively different from other aspects

16. By extending the period by five years to include the years 1976–80, the percentage of adopting states rises to 84.4.

17. For more on the science policy promotion activities of the OECD see Martha Finnemore, "Science, the State, and International Society," Ph.D. diss., Stanford University, 1991, chap. 3.

18. The following account of UNESCO activities is based on research done at the library and archives of UNESCO's Paris headquarters. While these contain a wide variety of documents authored by national governments, it must be acknowledged that carrying out the research at the international organization's headquarters does run the risk of bias in favor of an international organization-driven explanation at the expense of a national one. A research design in which the science policy archives were consulted at a variety of national capitals in countries of different regions and development levels and facing different security situations would be superior. However, such a design was not feasible in this case.

of culture and therefore merited special recognition in the organization's mission and title had to be fought for by scientists and science promoters in government during the preliminary meetings and negotiations that took place in 1942–45. The fact that they succeeded in getting a piece of the new organization to serve their own interests was due in part to the organizational strength and coherence of the international science community and in part to their ability to influence world affairs, as had been demonstrated at Hiroshima.[19] The combination of these two convinced the president of the conference charged with establishing the new organization to support addition of the word "Scientific" to the title with the following remarks: "In these days, when we are all wondering, perhaps apprehensively, what the scientists will do to us next, it is important that they should be linked closely with the humanities and should feel that they have a responsibility to mankind for the result of their labours."[20]

UNESCO's early science programs and organizational structure

Giving science a titular role in the new interstate organization was a way of recognizing the importance of science to the state but did not, in those early years, entail state direction or control of scientific research. UNESCO's early science programs were designed to serve science and scientists rather than states. They aimed to increase the world sum of scientific knowledge and access to that knowledge without regard to national boundaries. The notion implicit in science policy, that science is a national resource to be developed by individual states, is very different from UNESCO's original notions of science as a transnational enterprise. Indeed, the principal rationale for internationalizing science and for bringing it under the auspices of the United Nations in the first place was to free it from the meddling of self-interested (and presumably self-aggrandizing) states.

Apart from the dangers of states exploiting scientific discoveries for military gain, state interference in science had long been understood to stifle scientific progress. Science was believed to proceed most efficiently and productively when left to scientists. Certainly this was the attitude of the League of Nations' International Institute for Intellectual Cooperation in the interwar period, and it continued to be the attitude of most scientists' professional organizations and of individual scientists active in international affairs.[21]

19. Details on the lobbying efforts of scientists for special recognition in the embryonic UNESCO can be found in James Sewell, *UNESCO and World Politics* (Princeton, N.J.: Princeton University Press, 1975).

20. Conference for the Establishment of UNESCO, "Opening Address by the President of the Conference, the Rt. Honorable Ellen Wilkinson, MP," *Conference for the Establishment of UNESCO, London, 1–16 November 1945* (Paris: UNESCO, 1946), p. 24.

21. Julian Huxley, the first executive director of UNESCO, and Joseph Needham, the first director of UNESCO's Natural Sciences Department, were instrumental in the founding of that organization and wrote extensively on their views of science as a transnational activity. See, for example, Julian Huxley, *Unesco: Its Purpose and Its Philosophy* (Washington, D.C.: Public Affairs

Early statements of UNESCO's purpose with regard to science reflect this view. At the first session of the General Conference in November 1946, the Subcommission of the General Conference for Natural Sciences summed up the aims of UNESCO's Department of Natural Sciences in the field of science as follows:

1. to establish a world-wide network of field science cooperation offices;
2. to support the scientific unions, add to their number and assist them in their work;[22]
3. to organize and operate an international clearing house for scientific information;
4. to support the work of the United Nations and its specialized services;
5. to inform the general public in all countries of the international implications of scientific discoveries;
6. to create new forms of international scientific cooperation (international observatories and laboratories, etc.).[23]

Science policy and promoting science capabilities of member states were not even mentioned.

Early UNESCO science programs conformed very much to these aims.[24] Science cooperation field offices were set up in Cairo, Nanking, New Delhi, and Rio de Janeiro to facilitate the movement of scientists and information around the globe.[25] Financial support was extended to nongovernmental organizations, particularly the International Council of Scientific Unions, as a means of promoting cooperation among scientists, and more of these unions were established.[26] Research institutes were established, such as the Institute of the Hylean Amazon, the Institute of the Arid Zone, and an International Computation Center, to bring scientists from different countries together to

Press, 1947). Sir Henry Dale, who persuaded the establishing conference to accept science as a distinct part of the embryonic UNESCO and who had been part of the League of Nations' International Institute for Intellectual Cooperation, held similar views. See Sewell, *UNESCO and World Politics.*

22. "Scientific unions" are scientists' professional organizations, such as the International Astronomical Union and the International Geodesy and Geophysical Union. Their umbrella organization is the International Council of Scientific Unions.

23. This summary is from Marcel Florkin, "Ten Years of Science at UNESCO," *Impact of Science on Society* 7 (September 1956), pp. 123–24.

24. See, for example, "Activities of Unesco in the Natural Sciences During 1948," 14 February 1949, Natural Sciences (NS)/67, UNESCO Archives, Paris.

25. The Rio de Janeiro office was moved to Montevideo in 1949, and in 1951 the Nanking office was relocated to Djakarta in the wake of the Chinese revolution. In creating these field offices Joseph Needham (head of UNESCO's Natural Sciences Department) was realizing the International Science Cooperation Service he had proposed during the war. See Joseph Needham, "An International Science Cooperation Service," *Nature* 154 (25 November 1944), pp. 657–59. For original plans for the field offices, see "UNESCO Science Cooperation Offices," 12 June 1947 Nat Sci/28/1947, UNESCO Archives, Paris. For a brief history of early field office program see Florkin, "Ten Years of Science at UNESCO."

26. Specifically, UNESCO helped found the Union of International Engineering Associations and the Council of International Organizations of Medical Sciences. See Florkin, "Ten Years of Science at UNESCO."

work on problems of mutual interest. All of these activities provided services directly to scientists rather than states.

The early organizational structure of UNESCO also reflected this understanding of science and culture as transnational and often nongovernmental activities. While the General Conference was composed of equal member states, UNESCO's executive board was to be composed of eighteen individuals, elected by General Conference delegates for their distinction in the organization's substantive fields. Board members were to serve on behalf of the conference as a whole and not as representatives of their respective governments.[27]

Change

The principle of nongovernmentalism enshrined in the composition of UNESCO's executive board soon came under attack. While board members were to be elected as individuals, the original UNESCO constitution provided that no state could supply more than one of its nationals to the board. In practice this focused pressure on board members when their governments wanted to pursue particular policies through the organization. (James Sewell cites one high American official's description of the U.S. government bringing its board member back to Washington to "brief the hell out of [him] to try to get [him] to see things the State Department way."[28]) Accounts of UNESCO conference delegates from the period describe the decline of participation by scientists, scholars, educators, and writers and the increased presence of "government technicians" who viewed themselves as government spokespersons.[29]

In 1954 UNESCO members voted to amend the constitution and reorganize the executive board into a body of twenty-two governmental representatives. The shift toward a governmentalized secretariat was justified on several grounds. The reason cited most often was a financial one; since states were footing the bill for UNESCO's operations, the organization should serve states. In the words of one official who left the organization about that time, the shift was "the price for financial support." A cynical French delegate, Roger Seydoux, predicted that with this change "the Finance Ministries . . . would become masters of UNESCO and its programme."[30]

However, participants also understood the shift to be in keeping with a larger shift in the international climate from postwar Kantian transnationalism to

---

27. Note that this was a deliberate shift from the way in which the Conference of Allied Ministers of Education's executive bureau and UNESCO's preparatory commission executive committee were constituted. Both of these were composed of national representatives. See Sewell, *UNESCO and World Politics.*

28. As quoted in Sewell, *UNESCO and World Politics,* p. 169.

29. Ibid., pp. 168–69.

30. Both quotations are from ibid., p. 169.

cold war Hobbesian nationalism. The original nongovernmental structure was a reflection of 1940s beliefs (or at least hopes) that ideas were a unifying force in the world. Education, science, and culture could weave a web that would draw a divided world of nation-states together. If "wars begin in the minds of men," then the UNESCO solution follows logically, namely, that "it is in the minds of men that the defences of peace must be constructed."[31] Harry Truman voiced similar beliefs in his appeal to the 1945 United Nations founding conference in San Francisco to "set up an effective agency for consistent and thorough interchange of thought and ideas, for there lies the road to a better and more tolerant understanding among nations and among peoples."[32]

By the mid-1950s this view had been eclipsed. At best, ideas were irrelevant to the intense power struggle raging in the world; at worst, ideas were viewed as divisive and dangerous, in which case states could not afford to leave them to a collection of unaccountable individuals. As realpolitik replaced Kantian liberalism, states were reintegrated as major players in determining UNESCO policies.

Not surprisingly, the United States, then in the grip of anticommunist fervor, was the standard-bearer for this new attitude. UNESCO came to be viewed as a political instrument in the cold war; its purpose was to be a "Marshall Plan for ideas," which would block the expansion of "intolerant" communism. Failure to convert UNESCO wholeheartedly to its own foreign policy agenda led U.S. officials to erect organizational barriers to contain and control its influence. Chief among these was the International Organizations Employment Loyalty Board, established in early 1953 to oversee the employment of U.S. representatives to all United Nations agencies. Such screening ensured that American executive board members would be sympathetic to their government's views. This screening clearly flew in the face of the nongovernmental principles under which UNESCO was formed.

While the Americans succeeded in replacing intellectuals of dubious leanings with patriots and loyalists, they failed in their ultimate goal of making the organization a tool of U.S. foreign policy. Just as their governmentalist reforms were enacted in 1954, the Soviet Union and several of its Eastern bloc allies finally agreed to join UNESCO. Shortly thereafter came the influx of newly independent developing states with an agenda of their own, effectively blocking control by the United States or by any other great power.

The shift from nongovernmentalism to governmentalism represented a shift in the balance of power among UNESCO's two constituencies. As the international climate changed and optimism about the utility of transnational

---

31. Constitution of the United Nations Educational, Scientific, and Cultural Organization as reprinted in William Preston, Edward S. Herman, and Herbert I. Schiller, *Hope and Folly: The United States and UNESCO, 1945–1985* (Minneapolis: University of Minnesota Press, 1989), p. 315. The original phrase, "war begins in the minds of men," was coined by Clement Atlee. See ibid., p. 33.
32. Truman is quoted in Preston, Herman, and Schiller, *Hope and Folly,* p. 33.

activities declined, the champions of those activities—scientists, scholars, artists, and educators—lost ground. Their rhetoric about building bridges to all humankind became less and less appealing to UNESCO's member states, each of whom increasingly viewed the world as hostile and much of the rest of humanity with suspicion. Thus, during the cold war states reasserted themselves as UNESCO's chief constituents, and UNESCO officials reshaped their programs to accommodate them.

Effects of organizational change on science programs

UNESCO's science activities soon reflected the shift in worldview and the organization's rediscovered constituency of states. While international scientific projects begun previously had continued, UNESCO also became concerned with promoting science at the national level. UNESCO began to focus its attention on helping states to organize, direct, and expand their own domestic science establishments. Its preferred method of doing this was to help states to create a new state agency to take care of these tasks.

As a first step in this direction, UNESCO conducted a survey of the national research councils of member states in 1953.[33] The stated purpose was twofold. The first purpose was to collect reference material for anyone asking advice on how to set up a research council. The second purpose was to provide background material for the establishment within UNESCO of an advisory committee (the International Advisory Committee on Scientific Research) whose role would be to provide assistance to states seeking science policy advice.[34]

At this stage, UNESCO still viewed its role in science policy promotion as a relatively passive one; it waited for states to ask for advice and assistance. Following the 1954 reforms, the organization became more activist and science policy activities grew by leaps and bounds. In 1955, partly as an outgrowth of the 1953 survey, UNESCO convened a meeting of directors of national research centers in Milan at which thirty countries were represented.[35] The first agenda item for this meeting was discussion of "the role of national plans for the development of scientific research."[36] At the conference UNESCO staff members outlined the virtues of nationally directed science activity, discussed different models for such direction, and emphasized the role UNESCO could

33. The original survey analysis is contained in UNESCO Archives, document NS/107. Survey results were also published as "Reports and Documents: Survey of National Research Councils for Pure and Applied Science in the Member States of UNESCO," *Impact of Science on Society* 4 (Winter 1953), pp. 231–55.
34. "Reports and Documents," p. 231. See also Pierre Auger, "UNESCO and the Development of Research in the Field of Natural Sciences," *UNESCO Chronicle* 1 (July 1955), p. 5.
35. See UNESCO/NS/124, UNESCO Archives, Paris, for the final report of this meeting. See also Auger, "UNESCO and the Development of Research in the Field of Natural Sciences," p. 5.
36. *UNESCO Chronicle* 1 (July 1955), p. 26.

play in providing assistance to governments wishing to pursue the outlined objectives.[37]

By the late 1950s UNESCO had begun actively to assist countries in setting up science policy organizations: in 1957 when the Belgian government asked for help in setting up its National Science Policy Council, UNESCO sent the chief of its Science Policy Division to direct those activities.[38] UNESCO also provided assistance to the Lebanese government in creating a National Council for Scientific Research.[39]

These activities received a boost in 1960 when Pierre Auger, then acting as a special consultant to the United Nations as a whole,[40] issued a report recommending that national scientific policy be one of the "foremost preoccupations of governments":

> States should make it their business to ensure [that] interaction between the encouragement of scientific research, on the one hand, and economic and social progress, on the other, operates smoothly to the advantage of both. It is, at the same time, the duty of organizations in the United Nations family to assist States in this matter.[41]

Auger's detailed report, requested and approved by the larger United Nations, validated the science policy activities in which UNESCO had been engaged over the last five years and provided a basis for formalizing what had been an ad hoc collection of activities.[42] Beginning in 1960, UNESCO General Conference resolutions included instructions that the Director-General "collect, analyse and disseminate information concerning the organization of scientific research in Member States and the policies of Member States in this respect."[43] By 1963 the General Conference resolutions were more explicit. The Director-General was authorized to assist member states "in the establishment or improvement of science policy planning and research organization,

37. Several of the presented papers were later published in the journal *Impact of Science on Society.* Most relevant is Werner Moller's "National Research Councils and Science Policy," *Impact of Science on Society* 6 (September 1955), pp. 155–68. Moller was a member of the Department of Natural Sciences at UNESCO.

38. The Belgian National Science Policy Council was established in 1959. UNESCO Archives, NS/(Research Organization Unit)ROU/100, UNESCO Archives, Paris.

39. See NS/ROU/Lebanon (LEB) 1–23; and NS/ROU/100, UNESCO Archives, Paris.

40. Auger had been the second head of the Natural Sciences Department after Joseph Needham and had recently retired from the Secretariat.

41. Pierre Auger, *Current Trends in Scientific Research* (Paris: UNESCO, 1961), p. 220.

42. This report is routinely cited as the basis for UNESCO's science policy activities. See, for example, Y. de Hemptinne, "UNESCO's Role in the Organization of Scientific Research," *UNESCO Chronicle* 9 (July 1963), p. 245; and Alexi Matveyev opening speech to the meeting of the Coordinators of Science Policy Studies, Karlovy Vary, Czechoslovakia, June 1966. Matveyev was UNESCO's Assistant Director-General for Science. His speech is reprinted in *Principles and Problems of National Science Policies,* Science Policy Studies and Documents Series, vol. 5 (Paris: UNESCO, 1967), p. 12. Also see, "Survey of UNESCO's activities and achievements with regard to science policy," NS/ROU/100, UNESCO archives, Paris, p. 3.

43. UNESCO, General Conference, 11th sess., 1960, *Resolutions,* 2.1131 (Paris: UNESCO, 1960).

through sending advisory missions, conducting scientific and technological potential surveys, with particular regard to human resources and budgets, or organizing training seminars and, to this end, to participate in their activities in the field."[44] From this point on the goal of spreading and improving science policy organizations was firmly entrenched in UNESCO's official science program.

The new norm

What is interesting about UNESCO's program in terms of the questions raised in this article is that the language used is prescriptive not evaluative, and in this sense it is normative. UNESCO officials simply declared science policymaking to be necessary and good; there was no serious attempt to prove that that was so: "States *should* make it their business" to coordinate and direct science,[45] or, "The development of science policy should be the responsibility of an organization at the highest level of government in the country."[46] Also "the Science Policy Programme of UNESCO is formulated on the basis of *the principle* that the planning of science policy is indispensable" for the coordination and promotion of scientific research.[47] These assertions are not coupled with any evidence that such bureaucratic entities enhance science capabilities. This is surprising given that until only a few years earlier, conventional wisdom had held exactly the opposite—that government involvement stifled scientific creativity.

In addition the language is universal; it promotes these bureaucracies as good for all states and at all levels of scientific capability. This ignores an obvious potential strategy for many countries, particularly less developed countries (LDCs)—free-riding. Science, with its imperatives to disseminate results widely and immediately, has many properties of a collective good. The economic advantages of being a follower rather than a leader in technological innovation have been widely discussed in other contexts.

Thus, from a functional standpoint, it is not obvious why all states suddenly "needed" a science policy bureaucracy at that particular point in time. In fact, it appears that these events were not related to functional need in any strict sense. Rather, they constitute a redefinition of the norms and expectations of state roles with regard to science. Initially scientists sought to harness state resources to further their own scientific projects by claiming a piece of an interstate organization. To do so they had to proclaim science an appropriate

---

44. UNESCO, General Conference, 13th sess., 1964, *Resolutions,* 2.112(d) (Paris: UNESCO, 1964), p. 32.

45. Pierre Auger, *Current Trends in Scientific Research,* p. 220, emphasis added.

46. UNESCO, *Principles and Problems of Science Policy,* Science Policy Studies and Documents Series, vol. 5 (Paris: UNESCO, 1966), p. 87.

47. "The Proposed Science Policy Programme of UNESCO for 1967–68," NS/ROU/117, UNESCO Archives, Paris, p. 1, emphasis added.

concern of governments. The debate over the *S* in *UNESCO* and Wilkinson's comments in prompting it reveal the scientists' success in this. However, when scientists and the other epistemic communities lost control of UNESCO to the member states, the situation did not simply revert to the status quo ante.[48] The norm that science was now an appropriate concern of states remained firmly entrenched, but the relationship between science and states was redefined to reflect the new world climate and UNESCO's new dominant constituency. Rather than states *collectively* within an international organization promoting and directing science as a transnational enterprise, Natural Sciences Department officials in UNESCO now argued that states *individually* should take responsibility for promoting and directing science within their own borders. By proclaiming science policymaking to be an appropriate and necessary function of states qua states and by offering themselves as a source of knowledge about this new function, UNESCO science officials successfully redefined their role in a way that was neither irrelevant nor dangerous to their new clients.

The interest in and success of UNESCO's efforts is not unrelated to the fact that during this period large numbers of new states were being created, virtually all of which were LDCs. While it was developed countries such as the United States and the United Kingdom that initially had pushed for the reorganization of UNESCO's executive board to favor states for cold war-related reasons in the 1950s, UNESCO's reorientation toward states fit well with the climate of national self-determination in the 1960s. Among the large and growing membership of newly independent LDCs, the notion that states should and could promote and direct science, with all its economic and military applications, was popular. At the 1963 United Nations Conference on Science and Technology for the Benefit of Less Developed Areas, the agenda item on organizing and planning scientific and technological policies was reported to yield "one of the most fruitful discussions in the whole conference."[49] In addition to lauding science policy as an activity, conference delegates stressed the importance of building up in the developing countries indigenous programs of research. They argued that "just as no country could develop economically on imported goods, so none could develop intellectually on imported ideas alone."[50] For these states, science as a transnational activity spelled continued dependence. Science had to be a national pursuit to be normatively compatible

48. The term "epistemic community" refers to "a community of experts sharing a belief in a common set of cause-and-effect relationships as well as common values to which policies governing these relationships will be applied." See Peter Haas, "Do Regimes Matter? Epistemic Communities and Mediterranean Pollution Control," *International Organization* 43 (Summer 1989), pp. 377–403; the quotation is drawn from footnote 20, p. 384. Haas provides a more extensive discussion of this definition on page 3 of Peter Haas, "Introduction: Epistemic Communities and International Policy Coordination," *International Organization* 46 (Winter 1992), pp. 1–35.

49. United Nations, Secretariat, Economic and Social Council, 36th sess., *Report to the Secretary-General on the Results of the United Nations Conference on Science and Technology for the Benefit of Less Developed Areas,* 1963, E/3772, annexes, agenda item 15.

50. Ibid., section 181, p. 24.

with the nationalism of the newly created state and provide it with the means of resisting encroachments from outside.[51]

This national or statist conception is distinct from the understanding of science that prevailed in UNESCO's early years. States were now understood to be the primary purveyors of development and progress. Thus it was states, not scientists, who could best bring the fruits of science and technology to their citizens. Scientific knowledge could be translated into increased wealth and security or improved standards of living only if it was harnessed by states and integrated into their larger economic and military establishments. Scientific capacity or "scientific potential" was viewed as a national resource, not as a branch of some larger collectively held international resource.

The redefinition of science as a state concern did not necessarily have negative implications for the independence or productivity of the scientific community. In fact the establishment of national science bureaucracies very often had the effect of giving scientists more power at the national level and access to more resources. The argument here is not that states would now run and control scientists and science but that science would be organized nationally, for national benefit, rather than internationally, for overall benefit.

Spreading science policy

Teaching states to fulfill their new role quickly became UNESCO's principal science mission; by 1960 a special Research Organization Unit of the Natural Sciences Department had been established to deal with these tasks.[52] Efforts to establish and expand science policy organizations were undertaken on several fronts. First, following instructions from the executive board, UNESCO field offices organized a series of meetings to promote the idea of science policy and disseminate information about establishing the necessary policy machinery.[53] At the time these meetings took place (1959–60) in Latin America, the Middle East, and Southeast Asia very few of the attending countries had science bureaucracies. Only three of the eleven countries at the Latin American regional meeting did; only one of the Middle Eastern countries at the Cairo meeting had such a body.[54] In all three cases, these regional conferences were

51. This interpretation is compatible with the conclusions of Stephen D. Krasner in *Structural Conflict: The Third World Against Global Liberalism* (Berkeley: University of California Press, 1985).

52. The Research Organization Unit was subsequently renamed the Science Policy Division. For more on the early activities of the Research Organization Unit, see de Hemptinne, "UNESCO's Role in the Organization of Scientific Research," pp. 244–48.

53. "UNESCO Science Cooperation Offices," *UNESCO Chronicle* 7 (December 1961), pp. 433–435.

54. See Guy B. Grestford, "The Development of Science in South-east Asia," *Nature* 186 (11 June 1960), pp. 859–60; and B. A. Houssay, "Organization of Scientific Research in Latin America," *Nature* 188 (31 December 1960), pp. 1157–58. The three Latin American countries having science bureaucracies were Argentina, Brazil, and Mexico. Resolutions and declarations from this seminar are found in NS/ROU/36, UNESCO Archives, Paris. On the Middle East

only the first of what became a series of meetings on science policy, for once all states in the region had created the policy machinery, talks continued on how this machinery could be refined and improved.[55]

In addition, UNESCO undertook a series of studies on science policy issues.[56] Many of these works examined the science policy establishments of individual states and were designed to provide ideas and models to others seeking to establish and improve science policymaking in their own countries. Others examined general issues of science policymaking. Studies often were coupled with meetings of government science officials from member states.[57] Governmental participation in producing the recommendations of the studies ensured that these recommendations were reaching the desired audience.

Perhaps most interesting, UNESCO officials would, if requested, come into a country and provide on-site consulting services about how a science policy program might be established. By early 1966 UNESCO had science policy promotion programs of this kind either completed or under way in fifteen countries plus programs to revise existing state science policy bureaucracies along preferred UNESCO lines in several others.[58]

The preferred UNESCO form for a science bureaucracy had two key features. First, the entity making policy about science could not also *do* science; that is, it could not also be a research organization. The new science organization could not objectively assess national research priorities when it also had a vested interest in certain lines of research being done in its own laboratories. (The science policy body had to be liberated from any possible conflicts of interest.) Second, the science policy body was to have access to the highest levels of government. It was either to be a ministerial-level body or be located close to the seat of power, for example in the President's office. It was thought that it should not be subservient to any other ministry (for example, education or planning), since such an arrangement would seriously limit the organization's independence and prevent the nationwide coordination across all aspects of science that was required.

---

conference, see UNESCO, *Structural and Operation Schemes of National Science Policy,* Science Policy Studies and Documents Series, vol. 6 (Paris: UNESCO, 1967); and "Science Planning, Development and Co-operation in the Countries of the Middle East and North Africa," *Nature* 189 (4 February 1961), pp. 362–63.

55. Results of some of the later meetings were subsequently published as part of the Science Policy Studies and Documents Series.

56. These were published in the (ongoing) book series UNESCO, *Science Policy and Documents Series* (UNESCO: Paris). The studies to which I refer here were published during the period 1965–90.

57. This was true for two of the volumes in particular. See UNESCO, *Principles and Problems of National Science Policies,* Science Policy and Documents Series, vol. 5, and UNESCO, *Structural and Operational Schemes of National Science Policy,* Science Policy and Documents Series, vol. 6 (UNESCO: Paris, 1966 and 1967, respectively).

58. Science policy establishment missions were complete or under way in Algeria, Congo (Leopoldville), Ethiopia, Guinea, Iran, Iraq, Kenya, Lebanon, Madagascar, Morocco, Senegal, Sudan, Tanzania, Venezuela, and Zambia. Science policy modification or reorganization programs were undertaken in Indonesia, Nepal, the Philippines, and the United Arab Republic, among others.

UNESCO consultants' insistence on these two features guided its science policy promotion efforts in member states. The organization's commitment to this particular form of the bureaucracy shows up consistently in its on-site "teaching" activities in member states. The following examples illustrate the ways in which UNESCO succeeded in persuading states to set up science bureaucracies and, more specifically, science bureaucracies of the kind UNESCO preferred.

Examples of UNESCO's promotion of science policy

Lebanon

One of the first places UNESCO officials undertook this kind of science policy consulting was in Lebanon. Because it was one of the first, the Lebanese case became a prototype for UNESCO consultants on later missions. A more detailed examination of the Lebanese case reveals the extent of UNESCO's influence on the construction of a science bureaucracy there. UNESCO officials did not just sit on the sidelines and make suggestions; the head of the UNESCO Natural Sciences Department actually drafted the enabling legislation for the new bureaucracy, while other members of the secretariat staff lobbied relevant Lebanese politicians to get it passed. In so doing they squelched a conflicting Lebanese proposal for the new bureaucracy which they considered inappropriate and inadequate.

The starting point for UNESCO's involvement in Lebanon was the December 1960 regional conference on science planning organized by the UNESCO Middle Eastern field office in Cairo. At that conference field office staff members presented reports on the organization of science in various countries of the region. The report on science and technology in Lebanon revealed that Lebanese research lacked any practical orientation and that coordination of research was almost nonexistent.[59] However, the report did not have precisely the intended effect. Rather than prompting the Lebanese government to begin organizing and coordinating scientific research, as the Cairo conference had recommended, it prompted the Lebanese Foreign Affairs Ministry to request UNESCO's help in setting up a scientific research *center,* to be part of the University of Lebanon, which could carry out (rather than coordinate) scientific research in Lebanon in an efficient and effective way.[60]

This request was channeled to Yvan de Hemptinne, then scientific secretary to the director of the Natural Sciences Department at UNESCO. After

---

59. Unless otherwise indicated, citations of letters and memoranda below are from UNESCO Secretariat Registry files, UNESCO Archives, Paris. Where documents were assigned file numbers, these are so noted. For a description of the report on Lebanese science and technology, see memorandum by Yvan de Hemptinne, scientific secretary to the director of the Department of Natural Sciences, to Malcolm S. Adiseshiah, UNESCO Assistant Director-General, May 1961, NS memo 50.085.

60. This proposal is described in a letter from Lebanese Director General of National Education Fouad Sawaya to UNESCO Assistant Director-General Adiseshiah, 23 May 1961.

reviewing the request, de Hemptinne responded that a country like Lebanon did not need more laboratories or research centers; instead it needed coordination of its existing research efforts. He proposed that rather than sending an expert to set up a research center, UNESCO should send an expert to set up a coordinative science policy body in Lebanon.[61] Negotiations over which project UNESCO would support, the center to carry out research or the science policy body to coordinate research, were eventually resolved when the Director-General of UNESCO, René Maheu, intervened with the President of Lebanon.[62] The new body was to be a national research council that would organize research and make policy about science rather than a research center that would do research.

On Maheu's instructions, de Hemptinne spent several weeks during the summer of 1961 in Lebanon drafting enabling legislation for this council.[63] Key features of de Hemptinne's proposal were: (1) that coordination of research in all scientific disciplines were to be centralized under the council and (2) that the council was under no circumstances to operate any type of laboratory or research facility itself. The next stage of UNESCO's work involved sending a second science policy expert, Charles Boschloos, to Lebanon to work with the Lebanese to refine and revise the proposed legislation drafted by de Hemptinne. By this time the Lebanese had formed a national scientific commission of their own whose purpose was to work with UNESCO specialists in designing the new council. In December, Boschloos and the Lebanese commission circulated their revised draft of the enabling legislation. It differed in several ways from de Hemptinne's draft, notably by weakening both of what de Hemptinne had considered to be the key provisions of the legislation—that all scientific disciplines were to be brought under council jurisdiction and that no direct involvement in research activities would be permitted.

De Hemptinne and other secretariat members were furious.[64] Boschloos's contract was terminated and elaborate negotiations were undertaken with the Lebanese National Scientific Commission to push the legislation back onto what secretariat members considered to be the right track. UNESCO submit-

61. Memorandum from de Hemptinne to Adiseshiah, May 1961, NS memo 50.085. De Hemptinne also proposed an elaborate three-tiered structure for this coordinative bureaucracy. These proposals were greatly simplified under pressure from F. Karam at the Bureau of Member States (BMS) and from the Director-General of UNESCO himself. See memorandum from F. Karam, BMS, to José Correa, director of BMS, 5 May 1961, BMS 80/memo 100; and memorandum from UNESCO Director-General René Maheu to M. V. Kovda, director of UNESCO Department of Natural Sciences, n.d. (possibly June or July 1961).

62. Memorandum from Maheu to Kovda, n.d. (possibly June or July 1961). The fact that the Director-General of UNESCO and the President of Lebanon both were involved in these negotiations indicates the importance attached to them by both parties. Maheu, in fact, goes on to say in the above-cited memo: "For many reasons, I attach the utmost importance to this project which, in my view, has great value as an example"; translation mine.

63. This proposed legislation comprises NS/ROU/7, 8 February 1962, UNESCO Archives, Paris.

64. See memorandum from F. Karam, BMS, to A. K. Kinany, chief, Unit of Arabic-speaking Countries, BMS, 15 December 1961; and letter from de Hemptinne to T.O.P. Lilliefelt, permanent resident, Technical Assistance Bureau, Beirut, 20 December 1961, NS 801/226(40).

ted formal comments to the commission on the revised draft, arguing for changes back to the original proposals on these important issues.[65] After several weeks of negotiation, de Hemptinne was permitted to compile a synthesis of the two existing drafts for consideration by the Lebanese Parliament.[66] In it de Hemptinne included strong statements about both of his chief concerns while making concessions to the commission's draft on issues of less consequence.

The synthesis proposal was submitted to the Lebanese Parliament in February 1962. Now the Parliament had two alternatives to consider: the Lebanese scientific commission's proposal and de Hemptinne's revised proposal. To promote his alternative, de Hemptinne traveled to Beirut that spring to answer questions and speak with members of Parliament about the new council proposals. He feared that the commission would produce some new counterproposal and derail his efforts. To offset this possibility he enlisted the help of the National Scientific Commission's new president, Joseph Najjar, to keep him informed of any new developments.[67] In the end, the lobbying efforts by Maheu, de Hemptinne, F. Karam, Malcolm Adiseshiah, and others at UNESCO paid off. On 28 August 1962 the Lebanese Parliament approved without discussion de Hemptinne's synthesis proposal for a National Scientific Research Council.[68]

UNESCO's activities in Lebanon did not stop with the creation of the council. Following passage of the enabling legislation, UNESCO immediately plunged into the task of helping the Lebanese set up the new bureaucracy and ensuring that that bureaucracy headed in the desired direction. Before the end of 1962, UNESCO was recruiting two "experts in the organization of scientific research" to go to Lebanon and draft operating regulations, budgets, and an organizational chart for the new Scientific Research Council.[69] UNESCO also

65. These comments are contained in "Commentaires de l'UNESCO sûr l'avant-projet de loi portant création d'un 'Conseil National de la Recherche Scientifique' redige en novembre 1961 pare la Commission Scientifique National du Liban," (Comments by UNESCO on the proposed legislation concerning the creation of a "National Council for Scientific Research" drafted in November 1961 by the National Scientific Commission of Lebanon), 8 February 1962, NS/ROU/9, UNESCO Archives, Paris.

66. "Avant-projet de loi portant création d'un conseil national de la recherche scientifique au Liban: Synthèse des avant projets de loi établis par M. Y. de Hemptinne, Chef du Groupe d'organisation de la recherche scientifique de l'UNESCO et par la Commission Scientifique Nationale du Liban" (Proposed legislation concerning the creation of a National Council for Scientific Research for Lebanon: synthesis of proposed legislation drawn up by M. Y. de Hemptinne, group leader of UNESCO's Research Organization Unit, and by the National Scientific Commission of Lebanon), 8 February 1962, NS/ROU/10, UNESCO Archives, Paris.

67. Letter from de Hemptinne to Joseph Najjar, National Scientific Commission President, 20 February 1962. De Hemptinne was then head of the new Research Organization Unit at UNESCO's Natural Sciences Department.

68. Letter from Chafic Moharram, technical counselor to the President of Lebanon, to de Hemptinne, 3 October 1962. De Hemptinne's enabling legislation specified that the council's budget was not to be less than 1 percent of the state's budget.

69. See, for example, B. K. Blount, "Report to the National Research Council of Lebanon," compiled 10 March–7 April 1964, Lebanon file, Secretariat Registry Files, UNESCO Archives, Paris. Blount was deputy director of the British Department of Scientific and Industrial Research and was a temporary consultant to UNESCO.

conducted external reviews of Lebanese science policymaking at frequent intervals over the next decade and offered suggestions for improvements.[70]

East Africa

Obviously UNESCO's experiences in promoting science policy bodies among its members differed from country to country. Records from one of UNESCO's large subsequent science policy campaigns in East Africa during 1967 and 1968 provides some insight into the range of experience encountered by UNESCO consultants.

First, UNESCO consultants did not always spoon-feed the structure of the new science policy bureaucracy to countries as they did in Lebanon. Sometimes the original draft of enabling legislation for the new bureaucracy came from some group within the country, often a Ministry of Education or a Ministry of Planning, and was then sent either to UNESCO's headquarters or to its regional office for comments and suggestions.[71] However as discussed earlier, UNESCO officials had some firm notions about what these science policy bureaucracies should look like and did not let opportunities to impose their views escape. Most often the drafts were returned not just with extensive comments but also with a visit by a UNESCO expert who would meet with relevant local officials about what UNESCO perceived as shortcomings of the country's plan and UNESCO's proposed remedies.

For example, in 1966 the Ethiopian government sent a draft of their order on the establishment of a national research council to UNESCO's regional office, which forwarded it along with suggested revisions to the Science Policy Division staff at UNESCO headquarters in Paris. Headquarters then sent one of their science policy experts out to Addis Ababa to attend meetings of the drafting committee for the research council order and to provide information regarding certain aspects of the proposed council's potential activities.[72] A similar course of events took place in Tanzania.[73]

Zambian officials on the other hand were making good progress toward

70. See, for example, P. Piganiol, "Organisation de la politique scientifique au Liban" (Organization of science policy in Lebanon), 1967–68; and M. Steyaert, "Liban: politique scientifique national et organisation des recherches oceanographiques" (Lebanon: national science policy and the organization of oceanographic research), 1968, Lebanon file, Secretariat Registry Files, UNESCO Archives, Paris.

71. It should be noted that even where enabling legislation originated in the countries themselves, UNESCO still provided some of the impetus for creating the new bureaucracy. Virtually all locally drafted enabling documents cite UNESCO regional science policy conferences (for example, the 1964 Lagos conference among African countries) as prompting local activity, and most follow conference recommendations to a large extent.

72. Memorandum from I. C. Koupalov-Yaropolk to A. Matveyev, 13 April 1967, science policy memo 541, Secretariat Registry Files, UNESCO Archives, Paris. Koupalov-Yaropolk was a UNESCO policy consultant and Matveyev, UNESCO Assistant Director-General. In particular, see confidential annex I, "Ethiopia."

73. Ibid., annex V, "Tanzania."

creating a national science policy board without UNESCO intervention when UNESCO staff officials discovered their activity. UNESCO consultants immediately inserted themselves into the process, offering advice and suggestions without any direct appeal from the Zambian government.[74]

The obstacles encountered by UNESCO officials in setting up these science bureaucracies also varied from country to country. In Ethiopia, UNESCO experts complained that creation of the research council was "not very popular" and that those working on the project "seem to be interested in safeguarding those rights and privileges of their institutions that might be delegated to the N.R.C. [National Research Council]. Hence they try to reduce the would-be powers of the N.R.C."[75] In Sudan, UNESCO officials had trouble finding enough qualified scientists to draft a proposal for the new science policy body, let alone staff it once it was created.[76] In Tanzania, UNESCO officials complained that a general apathy about the entire project prevailed.[77] In Kenya consultants complained of attempts to subordinate the science policy body to the Ministry of Economic Planning rather than making it part of the President's office and giving it direct access to the highest levels of government.[78]

One feature of all of UNESCO consultants' experience was the lack of familiarity with the notion of a science policy bureaucracy in member states, even in the highest government and science circles, and the "necessity" for UNESCO officials to spread the word. For example, in Ethiopia UNESCO consultants were astonished to find that they were the first people to present the idea of a national research council to the deans of the medical, engineering and building colleges at Haile Selassie I University, despite the fact that the vice-chairman of the committee drafting the enabling legislation for the council was the dean of the Faculty of Sciences at the university.[79]

Despite these difficulties, all of the above-mentioned East African states had installed science policy bureaucracies of a type in keeping with UNESCO's guidelines by 1970—within three years of the UNESCO consultants' initial visits.[80]

---

74. Ibid., annex VIII, "Zambia."

75. Ibid., confidential annex I, "Ethiopia."

76. Ibid., annex VII, "Sudan."

77. UNESCO consultant Koupalov-Yaropolk described the situation as follows: "The draft Constitution of the National Research Council has been lying for some 14 months in the Ministry of Agriculture. [This] indicates that there are few people really interested in the establishment of N.R.C. or that they do not have influence enough to push this matter forward." See ibid., annex V, "Tanzania."

78. See discussion of two key features of UNESCO's preferred form of a science policymaking body, above.

79. "Ethiopia," confidential annex I to science policy memo 541.

80. Kenya is the only exception, since it did not create its own national science policy bureaucracy until 1977. The Kenyan rationale for not creating such a bureaucracy earlier was that the nation could derive the necessary benefits from an existing East African regional science policy bureaucracy.

The relationship between demand and supply

When initially analyzing the data on creation of science policy organizations, I noted that for the earliest innovators in this area such as the United States and the United Kingdom, demand-driven explanations may be sufficient. UNESCO did not after all invent science policy. Rather, it picked up the notion from successful and powerful states and popularized it. Thus, while the first science policy organizations may have been created in response to domestic demand, subsequent adoptions were strongly influenced by systemic norms promoted by UNESCO.

This kind of systemic supply operation differs from simple imitation or mimetic explanations—the more common explanation for diffusion patterns in the organization theory literature—on two counts. First, mimesis is an unmediated process; it locates the impetus for imitative actions in the imitator. In this case mimesis would claim that each state, looking out at the world of states, decided it wanted a science bureaucracy like the ones created by these few prominent trendsetters. As the foregoing analysis makes clear, this is not what happened. Knowledge of these innovations and assertions of the value of these innovations were supplied to states by a third party, UNESCO.

Second, mimesis is a process, not a cause. It says nothing about why countries would choose to imitate one particular innovation and not others. I have argued that in this case the driving force behind adoption of this innovation is normative. Positive evidence for the effects of norms is always difficult to provide, which is one reason such explanations are often treated as residuals. Here I cite rhetorical shifts in discourse about the organization of science both within UNESCO and among member states that coincide with the behaviors described. This positive evidence, coupled with the failure of alternative explanations, provides a strong case for the role of norms.[81]

Conclusions and implications

The analysis offered here is suggestive in several ways. First and most obviously, it shows how forces external to states can shape choices about internal state structure. This in itself is noteworthy since, as was discussed earlier, the literature on state structure has little to say about international-level causes of state structural change.

---

81. In their analysis of the spread of municipal reforms across U.S. cities at the turn of the century, Tolbert and Zucker provide a similar explanation of a diffusion process. Their interpretation is as follows: "As an increasing number of organizations adopt a program or policy, it becomes progressively institutionalized, or widely understood to be a necessary component of rational organizational structure. The legitimacy of the procedures themselves serves as the impetus for the later adopters." See Pamela Tolbert and Lynne Zucker, "Institutional Sources of Change in the Formal Structure of Organizations: The Diffusion of Civil Service Reform, 1880–1935," *Administrative Science Quarterly* 28 (March 1983), p. 35.

In addition, the UNESCO story reveals a relationship between the international system and states that is not easily accommodated within traditional state-centric neorealist analysis. In neorealism, the force exercised by the international system on states is constraint; the system is passive or at best reactive. The system prevents states from pursuing certain policies that they may want to pursue, but the identification and definition of preferred policies come from states. In this case, the system-level actors were *pro*active; identification and definition of the policy options were supplied by an international-level actor, UNESCO.

Interest in international-level sources of state policy has been growing in recent years. The literatures on epistemic communities, ideas, and transnational relations all deal in one way or another with international sources of state policy in which system-level actors contribute to state policy debates in a positive rather than merely a negative and constraining way. Surprisingly little attention has been paid to international organizations in this research; the analysis here suggests that international organizations have an important role to play.

Third, the analysis presented here suggests that states are more socially responsive entities than is recognized by traditional international relations theory. State policies and structures are influenced by intersubjective systemic factors, specifically by norms promulgated within the international system. In this case, states were socialized by international organizations and an international community of experts—in this case scientists—to accept the promotion and direction of science as a necessary and appropriate role.[82] Before 1955 most states had no perception that a science policy bureaucracy was in their interest; it was not part of their utility function. Actions by UNESCO and examples of a few prominent developed states persuaded states that making science policy was an appropriate and necessary task of states, regardless of objective science, developmental, or security conditions. Thus, the empirical anomaly identified at the beginning of this research—that states have coordinative science bureaucracies regardless of whether they have any science to coordinate—is the result of a behavioral norm (that states should direct science) making similar claims on dissimilar state actors.

This finding is more compatible with constructivist or "reflective" theoretical approaches than it is with the more conventional approaches to international relations.[83] The fact that states adopt policies not as an outgrowth of their individual characteristics or conditions but in response to socially constructed norms and understandings held by the wider international community demon-

---

82. For an alternative perspective on socialization of states in which hegemons rather than international organizations are the socializing force, see G. John Ikenberry and Charles A. Kupchan, "Socialization and Hegemonic Power," *International Organization* 44 (Summer 1990), pp. 283–315.

83. Robert Keohane, "International Institutions: Two Approaches," *International Studies Quarterly* 32 (December 1988), pp. 379–96.

strates an embeddedness of states in an international social system that conventional approaches ignore.

In concrete terms, this research suggests at least three avenues for further research. First, it indicates a largely unexplored role for international organizations, namely, their role as an arena in which norms and convergent expectations about international behavior are developed. The regimes literature correlates norms and convergent expectations with regimes that often have affiliated international organizations, but it understands the norms and convergent expectations to produce the international organizations.[84] It does not focus on the reverse process documented here in which international organizations, once established, produce their own new convergent expectations and norms. Thus, the regimes literature has continued to treat international organizations as agents only; it also has had little to say about these organizations as principals and the active role played by these organizations in promoting new norms.

Second, this research builds on the growing literature on epistemic communities by showing how international communities of experts may use international organizations as a base from which to wield influence. However, this case does raise questions for epistemic communities scholars. While most of the people involved in UNESCO teaching activities had scientific credentials, their motivations for acting derived from their status as international bureaucrats rather than from professional norms in the science community or principled beliefs about science. In fact, these scientists were challenging existing norms in the science community, norms about state-science relations.

The case here suggests that specialized knowledge may not provide compelling principles for political action; those principles came from understandings about appropriate political organization that were developed in UNESCO. Further work on the conditions under which "epistemic" characteristics are determinative and the ways these interact with political and organizational variables might strengthen and clarify the epistemic communities framework.

Third, this research underscores the now widely recognized need for more theoretical work to address the increasingly well-documented feedback effects of social structures such as norms, shared expectations, and even international organizations on actors such as states.[85] Neorealist theory takes preferences as given and understands them to drive international interaction. To the extent

84. Stephen D. Krasner, ed., *International Regimes* (Ithaca, N.Y.: Cornell University Press, 1983).

85. Krasner, in the conclusion of *International Regimes,* raised this issue as did Keohane in his more recent address to the International Studies Association. Implications of the structure–actor relationship have been explored by Ashley and by Kratchowil and Ruggie, among others. See Krasner, *International Regimes;* Keohane, "International Institutions: Two Approaches"; Richard Ashley, "The Poverty of Neorealism," in Robert Keohane, ed., *Neorealism and Its Critics* (New York: Columbia University Press, 1986), pp. 255–300; and Friedrich Kratchowil and John Gerard Ruggie, "International Organization: A State of the Art on an Art of the State," *International Organization* 40 (Autumn 1986), pp. 753–75.

that preferences are shown to be the product rather than the producer of international interaction, a new theoretical apparatus to guide research in these areas is needed.

Appendix: data and sources

Science policy organizations

Definition. UNESCO has defined science policy organizations as organizations whose

> central policy making function [is] . . . national level . . . planning, organization, or co-ordination of scientific and technological activities. Organizations such as Ministries or Departments of Science and Technology, National Research Councils, and Academies of Science, as well as other bodies with similar overall responsibilities, have thus been included in the new UNESCO directory; bodies whose responsibilities are limited to specific sectors of the economy or particular fields of science and technology have, on the contrary, not been included.[86]

Two ambiguities arose in coding. The first concerns generalized state planning agencies whose responsibility is to plan all aspects of the economy. If these plans include science, do they qualify as science policymaking bodies? The 1984 directory is silent on this point, but the earlier 1960s directories specifically exclude entities with such general responsibilities.[87] I have done the same in requiring that science policy organizations have science as their central concern.

The second ambiguity concerns the status of national academies of science. For theoretical reasons made clear in the article, I am interested only in state organizations. However, not all academies are part of the state apparatus. (In the United States, for example, the National Academy of Sciences is a private professional society.) However, in many countries academies enjoy some amount of state support; in the former Soviet Union and Soviet-style states, academies are constituted in such a way as to make them difficult to distinguish from the state apparatus. In such cases, the active policymaking and advising role played by academies might very well be considered the first state science policymaking organization.

To determine whether or not academies should be counted as state science policy bureaucracies, I deferred to the UNESCO Science Policy Studies and Documents Series. These documents were authored by officials of the countries under study. If they presented their academy as their first science policy organization, as Cuba does, then it was coded as such. If they treated the academy as a forerunner of the "real" science policymaking apparatus, as the former Soviet Union did, then it was not coded as a science policy organization.

---

86. UNESCO, *World Directory of National Science Policy-making Bodies,* Science Policy Studies and Documents Series, vol. 59 (Paris: UNESCO, 1984); p. viii. See also the definitions in the earlier directories, listed in the textual notes above.

87. See UNESCO, *World Directory of National Science Policy-making Bodies,* 3 vols. (Paris: UNESCO, 1966–68).

Date of creation of initial science policy organizations. Data on creation dates were obtained from UNESCO's Science Policy Studies and Documents Series. Most items in that series are analyses of science policy activity in a region or UNESCO member country and usually include a brief history of science policy activity in member countries. Often countries have formed a series of science policymaking organizations as different governments reorganized their bureaucracies. Ambiguity about which of these might be the first science policymaking organization was resolved by deferring to the nationals of the country or region in question who had authored these studies. This is clearly preferable to coding that would have allowed UNESCO designation of the first organization that qualifies as a science policy body.

Science data

Data on the number of scientists and engineers involved in R&D and the amount of spending on R&D as a percentage of GDP in the year science policy organizations were created were obtained from the UNESCO *Statistical Yearbook*.[88] Not all countries collect science data in all years. Data collection by developing countries in particular is sporadic. Where figures were not available for the year of creation, the figure for the closest year available was used. In two cases (Chile and Tanzania), R&D spending figures were unavailable; thus the analysis of R&D as a percentage of GDP has been done for a sample of forty-two rather than forty-four countries.

The yearbooks contain extensive definitions of "scientist," "engineer," and "research and development" used in compiling their data. For purposes here it is worth noting that all of these figures, including R&D spending, are for both public and private sectors.

Development data

GDP per capita in constant 1980 U.S. dollars was used as a rough measure of development. These data were not available in constant dollars of the same base year for the relatively large span of years under study here; they were calculated based on data published by the International Monetary Fund (IMF).[89] Where necessary, conversions from one base year of U.S. dollars to 1980 dollars was made using producer price indexes found in the *Statistical Abstract of the United States*.[90] Populations figures were taken from the UNESCO *Statistical Yearbooks.* For countries not members of the IMF, figures for per capita GNP were substituted.[91]

88. UNESCO, *Statistical Yearbook* (Paris: UNESCO, various years).
89. International Monetary Fund (IMF), *International Financial Statistics Yearbook* (City of publication: IMF, various years).
90. U.S. Department of Commerce, Bureau of the Census, *Statistical Abstract of the United States* (Washington, D.C.: U.S. Government Printing Office, 1992).
91. U.S. Arms Control and Disarmament Agency, *World Expenditures and Arms Trade, 1963–1973* (Washington, D.C.: U.S. Government Printing Office, 1975).

Security data

Defense spending as a percentage of GNP in the year of science policy creation was used as a measure of perceived security threat. These figures were obtained when available for the necessary years.[92] In cases where science policy organizations were created prior to 1963 (when the U.S. Arms Control Agency began collecting these data), the figures were obtained from national statistical abstracts.

Defense spending is only a rough measure of perceived security threat since there are a host of domestic reasons why states may spend on defense having to do with maintaining stability of governments. However, since these distortions generally increase rather than decrease defense spending, they should make us suspicious of false-positive findings rather than false-negative ones. Thus, if the data revealed a correlation between high defense spending and creation of science policy institutions, we would want to look more closely at our defense figures. The fact that even with these distortions states create science institutions at consistently low levels of defense spending supports rather than undermines my hypotheses.

92. U.S. Arms Control and Disarmament Agency, *World Military Expenditures and Arms Trade, 1963–1973* (Washington, D.C.: U.S. Government Printing Office, 1975).

II.
Empirical Studies

W hile much of the modern literature on international institutions has been highly theoretical in nature, untested theories obviously have limited influence. This section focuses on empirical studies that begin to test some of the central theoretical arguments in the literature. These arguments are about both the causes and consequences of institutions. One of the biggest questions concerns the effect of institutions on actors' behavior. Other questions involve the design of specific institutions and the factors to which institutional design responds. To what degree can IOs act autonomously from their supposed governmental masters? What role do IOs play in international politics? The four articles included in this section tackle all of these issues.

Ronald Mitchell (Chapter 4) tests the proposition that specific aspects of regime design change the likelihood that actors will comply with regime rules. He considers the problem of intentional oil discharge at sea, where the economic incentives for discharging oil in violation of international rules are high. Over time, the regime changed as governments searched for more effective mechanisms to limit oil discharge. In spite of the presence of sanctions, rules that directly limited the amount ships could discharge were not initially effective because it was difficult to monitor ships' behavior. An innovative move in regime design required ships to install new technology that dramatically increased the transparency of their activities. In combination with provisions for sanctions and attention to minimizing the costs of compliance by building on existing infrastructure, new rules led to a substantial decrease in the amount of oil intentionally discharged. Mitchell thus demonstrates, by examining variation in outcomes and its correlation with variation in regime provisions, that the specific rules and norms of a regime can significantly influence outcomes.

Cheryl Shanks, Harold Jacobson, and Jeffrey Kaplan (Chapter 5) move away from the focus on individual IOs that characterizes most work in this area to consider the changing population of IOs. Drawing generally from an organizational behavior perspective, they note that organizations tend to persist over time rather than to disappear, even if their initial justification has faded away. Inertia characterizes most organizations—indeed, persistence is a defining feature of institutions more generally. The authors undertake the equivalent of a census for the population *of IOs and find surprising patterns of rapid change, including institutional death. A single decade (1981–92) saw the disappearance of one-third of the IOs that had initially existed. However, their disappearance did not lead to a decline in the population, since even more new IOs were created during the same period. One of the most novel findings of this study concerns the origins of new IOs. During this period, they were most often created not by new intergovernmental agreements but by preexisting IOs. The authors also identify patterns in population change that merit further study: that many IOs became defunct because of tumultuous political change; that wealthy democratic countries belong to more IOs over time, while poor and unstable countries have fewer memberships; and that a few core institutions that reflect Western values are becoming increasingly important.*

International institutions seem to have reached the greatest degree of significance and influence in the process of European integration. While earlier studies of integration focused on the European Commission and Council as the major institutional actors in the process of integration, attention more recently has turned to the European Court of Justice (ECJ). Through mechanisms not always antici-pated by national governments, but difficult to overturn, the ECJ has produced major steps toward European integration, such as promulgating the doctrine of mutual recognition. International Organization *has published numerous analyses of the ECJ.[1] We reproduce here the work of Karen Alter (Chapter 6), who examines the interaction between national governments and the ECJ. Bringing to bear both political analysis of institutions and concepts developed by legal scholars, Alter asks about the extent to which the ECJ can take steps that member governments do not see as being in their own immediate self-interest. Other accounts attribute the ECJ with either extreme autonomy or absolute submission to the wishes of national governments. Alter, in contrast, shows that the autonomy of the ECJ has shifted in fairly dramatic ways over time. It has moved away from its submissive beginnings to an ability and willingness to take bold steps that might provoke negative reactions from governments. Alter identifies factors on the domestic and international level within Europe that account for this change. Justices with longer time horizons than political actors can act boldly, and national judiciaries have become more actively supportive of the ECJ over time. In addition, supranational procedures for making decisions in practice put heavy constraints on governments' ability to control the ECJ. Thus the evolution of the ECJ has brought it to a point of significant autonomy, which it is not afraid to exercise.*

One of the striking features of IOs at the turn of the century is the extent to which many of them are becoming legalized.[2] Legalization is especially prominent in trade organizations and in dispute-resolution procedures. James McCall Smith (Chapter 7) develops a dataset on dispute-resolution mechanisms in regional trade agree-ments. He ranks these mechanisms according to how "legalistic" they are—for

---

1. See Burley and Mattli 1993; Garrett, Kelemen, and Schulz 1998; and Mattli and Slaughter 1998.
2. See Goldstein et al. 2000.

example, whether they involve binding decisions by supposedly neutral actors. He develops hypotheses about the degree of legalism from two perspectives. The first is a functional perspective that sees the design of mechanisms as a direct response to collective-action problems, such as transaction costs or the need to prevent states from reneging when attempting "deep cooperation." The second is a more power-oriented approach, in which the degree of economic asymmetry between parties to a pact determines the level of legalism. Regional hegemons will resist legalism as it limits their discretion and as they have the power to impose their preferred institutional form. Smith finds the evidence weighted in favor of the effect of economic asymmetry in interaction with the depth of cooperation proposed in the agreement.

References

Burley, Anne-Marie, and Walter Mattli. 1993. Europe Before the Court: A Political Theory of Legal Integration. *International Organization* 47 (1):41–76.

Garrett, Geoffrey, R. Daniel Kelemen, and Heiner Schulz. 1998. The European Court of Justice, National Governments, and Legal Integration in the European Union. *International Organization* 52 (1):149–76.

Goldstein, Judith, Miles Kahler, Robert O. Keohane, and Anne-Marie Slaughter, eds. 2000. Legalization and World Politics. *International Organization* 54 (3). Special issue.

Mattli, Walter, and Anne-Marie Slaughter. 1998. Revisiting the European Court of Justice. *International Organization* 52 (1):177–209.

Regime Design Matters: Intentional Oil Pollution and Treaty Compliance
Ronald B. Mitchell

Too many people assume, generally without having given any serious thought to its character or its history, that international law is and always has been a sham. Others seem to think that it is a force with inherent strength of its own. . . . Whether the cynic or sciolist is the less helpful is hard to say, but both of them make the same mistake. They both assume that international law is a subject on which anyone can form his opinions intuitively, without taking the trouble, as one has to do with other subjects, to inquire into the relevant facts.
—J. L. Brierly

Regime design matters.[1] International treaties and regimes have value if and only if they cause people to do things they would not otherwise do. Governments spend considerable resources and effort drafting and refining treaty language with the (at least nominal) aim of making treaty compliance and effectiveness more likely. This article demonstrates that whether a treaty elicits compliance or other desired behavioral changes depends upon identifiable characteristics of the regime's compliance systems.[2] As negotiators incorporate certain rules into a regime and exclude others, they are making choices that have crucial implications for whether or not actors will comply.

For decades, nations have negotiated treaties with simultaneous hope that those treaties would produce better collective outcomes and skepticism about

The research reported herein was conducted with support from the University of Oregon and the Center for Science and International Affairs of Harvard University. Invaluable data were generously provided by Clarkson Research Studies, Ltd. The article has benefited greatly from discussions with Abram Chayes, Antonia Chayes, William Clark, and Robert Keohane and from collaboration with Moira McConnell and Alexei Roginko as part of a project on regime effectiveness based at Dartmouth College and directed by Oran Young and Marc Levy. John Odell, Miranda Schreurs, David Weil, and two anonymous reviewers provided invaluable comments on earlier drafts of this article. The epigraph is from J. L. Brierly, *The Outlook for International Law* (Oxford: Clarendon Press, 1944), pp. 1–2.

1. This article summarizes the arguments made in Ronald B. Mitchell, *Intentional Oil Pollution at Sea: Environmental Policy and Treaty Compliance* (Cambridge, Mass.: MIT Press, forthcoming).

2. The term "compliance system" comes from Oran Young, *Compliance and Public Authority: A Theory with International Applications* (Baltimore, Md.: Johns Hopkins University Press, 1979), p. 3.

International Organization 48, 3, Summer 1994, pp. 425–58
© 1994 by The IO Foundation and the Massachusetts Institute of Technology

the ability to influence the way governments or individuals act. Both lawyers and political scientists have theorized about how international legal regimes can influence behavior and why they often do not.[3] Interest in issues of compliance and verification has a long history in the field of nuclear arms control.[4] More recently, this interest in empirically evaluating how international institutions, regimes, and treaties induce compliance and influence behavior has broadened to include other security areas as well as international trade and finance.[5] Concern over the fate of the earth's environment recently has prompted a further extension into questions of whether and how environmental treaties can be made more effective at eliciting compliance and achieving their goals.[6]

Researchers in all these issue-areas face two critical questions. First, given that power and interests play important roles in determining behavior at the international level, is any of the compliance we observe with international treaties the result of the treaty's influence? Second, if treaties and regimes can alter behavior, what strategies can those who negotiate and design regimes use to elicit the greatest possible compliance? This article addresses both these questions by empirically evaluating the international regime controlling intentional oil pollution. Numerous efforts to increase the regime's initially low levels of compliance provide data for comparing the different strategies for eliciting compliance within a common context that holds many important

3. See, for example, Abram Chayes and Antonia Handler Chayes, "On Compliance," *International Organization* 47 (Spring 1993), pp. 175–205; Young, *Compliance and Public Authority;* Roger Fisher, *Improving Compliance with International Law* (Charlottesville: University Press of Virginia, 1981); and W. E. Butler, ed., *Control over Compliance with International Law* (Boston: Kluwer Academic Publishers, 1991).

4. See, for example, Abram Chayes, "An Inquiry into the Workings of Arms Control Agreements," *Harvard Law Review* 85 (March 1972), pp. 905–69; Coit D. Blacker and Gloria Duffy, eds., *International Arms Control: Issues and Agreements,* 2d ed. (Stanford, Calif.: Stanford University Press, 1984); and Antonia Handler Chayes and Paul Doty, *Defending Deterrence: Managing the ABM Treaty into the Twenty-first Century* (Washington, D.C.: Pergamon-Brassey's International Defense Publishers, 1989).

5. See, for example, John S. Duffield, "International Regimes and Alliance Behavior: Explaining NATO Conventional Force Levels," *International Organization* 46 (Autumn 1992), pp. 819–55; Ethan Kapstein, *Governing the Global Economy: International Finance and the State* (Cambridge, Mass.: Harvard University Press, 1994); and Joseph M. Grieco, *Cooperation Among Nations: Europe, America, and Non-tariff Barriers to Trade* (Ithaca, N.Y.: Cornell University Press, 1990).

6. For example, see Peter Haas, Robert Keohane, and Marc Levy, eds., *Institutions for the Earth: Sources of Effective International Environmental Protection* (Cambridge, Mass.: MIT Press, 1993); Peter H. Sand, *Lessons Learned in Global Environmental Governance* (Washington, D.C.: World Resources Institute, 1990); and Peter M. Haas, "Do Regimes Matter? Epistemic Communities and Mediterranean Pollution Control," *International Organization* 43 (Summer 1989), pp. 377–403. Current projects that deal with questions of regime compliance and effectiveness (and their principal investigators) include those being conducted at, or with funding from, Dartmouth College (Oran Young and Marc Levy); the European Science Foundation (Kenneth Hanf and Arild Underdal); the Foundation for International Environmental Law and Diplomacy (James Cameron); the Fridtjof Nansen Institute (Steinar Andresen); Harvard University (Abram Chayes and Antonia Chayes); Harvard University (William Clark, Robert Keohane, and Marc Levy); the International Institute for Applied Systems Analysis (David Victor and Eugene Skolnikoff); and the Social Science Research Council (Edith Brown Weiss and Harold Jacobson).

explanatory variables constant. The goal of the treaties underlying this regime has been to reduce intentional discharges of waste oil by tankers after they deliver their cargoes. Since the late 1970s, these treaties have established two quite different compliance systems, or "subregimes," to accomplish this goal. One has prohibited tanker operators from discharging oil in excess of specified limits. The other has required tanker owners to install expensive pollution-reduction equipment by specified dates. Treaty parties viewed both subregimes as equally legitimate and equally binding.[7] The two subregimes regulated similar behavior by the same nations and tankers over the same time period. The absence of differences in power and interests would suggest that compliance levels with the two subregimes would be quite similar.[8] According to collective action theory, these cases are among the least likely to provide support for the hypothesis that regime design matters: subregime provisions required the powerful and concentrated oil industry to incur large pollution control costs to provide diffuse benefits to the public at large.[9] Indeed, the lower cost of complying with discharge limits would suggest that compliance would be higher with those limits than with equipment requirements.

Not surprisingly, violations of the limits on discharges have occurred frequently, attesting to the ongoing incentives to violate the agreement and confirming the characterization of oil pollution as a difficult collaboration problem.[10] A puzzle arises, however, from the fact that contrary to expectation compliance has been all but universal with requirements to install expensive equipment that provided no economic benefits. The following analysis clearly demonstrates that the significant variance across subregimes can only be explained by specific differences in subregime design. Comparing the two compliance systems shows that the equipment subregime succeeded by ensuring that actors with incentives to comply with, monitor, and enforce the treaty were provided with the practical ability and legal authority to conduct

7. Thomas M. Franck, *The Power of Legitimacy Among Nations* (New York: Oxford University Press, 1990).

8. Case selection that holds these other factors constant avoids the notorious difficulties of measuring power and interests and allows us to "attribute variance in collective outcomes to the impact of institutional arrangements with some degree of confidence"; see Oran Young, *International Cooperation: Building Regimes for Natural Resources and the Environment* (Ithaca, N.Y.: Cornell University Press, 1989), p. 208. On difficulties in measuring power, see David A. Baldwin, "Power Analysis and World Politics: New Trends Versus Old Tendencies," *World Politics* 31 (January 1979), pp. 161–93.

9. Michael McGinnis and Elinor Ostrom, "Design Principles for Local and Global Commons," Workshop in Political Theory and Policy Analysis, Bloomington, Ind., March 1992, p. 21. Olson's argument that small groups supply public goods more often than large groups assumes that group members benefit from providing the good, which is not true in the oil pollution case; see Mancur Olson, *The Logic of Collective Action: Public Goods and the Theory of Groups* (Cambridge, Mass.: Harvard University Press, 1965), p. 34.

10. See Arthur A. Stein, *Why Nations Cooperate: Circumstance and Choice in International Relations* (Ithaca, N.Y.: Cornell University Press, 1990); and Robert Axelrod and Robert O. Keohane, "Achieving Cooperation Under Anarchy: Strategies and Institutions," in Kenneth Oye, ed., *Cooperation Under Anarchy* (Princeton, N.J.: Princeton University Press, 1986).

those key implementation tasks. Specifically, the regime elicited compliance when it developed integrated compliance systems that succeeded in increasing transparency, providing for potent and credible sanctions, reducing implementation costs to governments by building on existing infrastructures, and preventing violations rather than merely deterring them.

Compliance theory and definitions

Explaining the puzzle of greater compliance with a more expensive and economically inefficient international regulation demands an understanding of existing theories about the sources of compliance in international affairs. Realists have inferred a general inability of international regimes to influence behavior from the fact that the international system is characterized by anarchy and an inability to organize centralized enforcement. In what has been the dominant theoretical view, "considerations of power rather than of law determine compliance."[11] To explain variance in treaty compliance, look for variance in the power of those with incentives to violate it or in the interests of those with the power to violate it. Treaties are epiphenomenal: they reflect power and interests but do not shape behavior.

This view does not imply that noncompliance is rare in international affairs. Although nations will violate rules whenever they have both the incentives and ability to do so, as Hans Morgenthau notes, "the great majority of the rules of international law are generally observed by all nations."[12] For the realist, behavior frequently conforms to treaty rules because both the behavior and the rules reflect the interests of powerful states. More specifically, compliance is an artifact of one of three situations: (1) a hegemonic state forces or induces other states to comply; (2) the treaty rules merely codify the parties' existing behavior or expected future behavior; or (3) the treaty resolves a coordination game in which no party has any incentive to violate the rules once a stable equilibrium has been achieved.[13]

Treaty rules correlate with but do not cause compliance. Therefore, efforts to improve treaty rules to increase compliance reflect either the changed interests of powerful states or are misguided exercises in futility. The strength of this view has led to considerable attention being paid to whether rules influence behavior and far less being paid to design features that explain why one rule influences behavior and another does not.

11. The quotation is from Hans Joachim Morgenthau, *Politics Among Nations: The Struggle for Power and Peace,* 5th ed. (New York: Alfred A. Knopf, 1978), p. 299. See also Kenneth Waltz, *Theory of International Politics* (Reading, Mass.: Addison-Wesley Publishing Co., 1979), p. 204; and Susan Strange, "Cave! Hic Dragones: A Critique of Regime Analysis," in Stephen D. Krasner, ed., *International Regimes* (Ithaca, N.Y.: Cornell University Press, 1983), pp. 337–54 at p. 338. For a contrasting view, see Young, *International Cooperation,* p. 62.

12. Morgenthau, *Politics Among Nations,* p. 267.

13. On this distinction, see Stein, *Why Nations Cooperate.*

In contrast, international lawyers and institutionalists contend that the anarchic international order need not lead inexorably to nations violating agreements whenever doing so suits them. Other forces—such as transparency, reciprocity, accountability, and regime-mindedness—allow regimes to impose significant constraints on international behavior under the right conditions.[14] Implicit in the institutionalist view is the assumption that power and interests alone cannot explain behavior: a given constellation of power and interests leaves room for nations to choose among treaty rules that will elicit significantly different levels of compliance. High compliance levels can be achieved even in difficult collaboration problems in which incentives to violate are large and ongoing. Treaties can become more effective over time, and regimes may even learn.[15] Agreeing with Morgenthau that compliance will be quite common, institutionalists do not exclude the possibility that the regime, rather than mere considerations of power, causes some of that compliance.[16]

In essence, this debate revolves around whether in a realm of behavior covered by an international agreement, that behavior is ever any different than it would have been without the agreement. If we define "treaty-induced compliance" as behavior that conforms to a treaty's rules because of the treaty's compliance system, institutionalists view treaty-induced compliance as possible. In contrast, realists see all compliance as "coincidental compliance," that is, behavior that would have occurred even without the treaty rules.

The debate between these theories highlights the demands placed on research that seeks to identify those design characteristics of a regime, if any, that are responsible for observed levels of compliance. I define compliance, the dependent variable, as an actor's behavior that conforms with an explicit treaty provision. Speaking of compliance with treaty provisions rather than with a treaty captures the fact that parties may well comply with some treaty provisions while violating others. A study of "treaty compliance" would aggregate violation of one provision with compliance with another, losing valuable empirical information.[17] Restricting study to the explicit rules in a treaty-based regime allows the analyst to distinguish compliance from noncompliance in clear and replicable ways. Obviously, a focus on explicit rules ignores other potential mechanisms of regime influence, such as norms, principles, and

---

14. See, for example, Abram Chayes and Antonia Chayes, "Compliance Without Enforcement: State Behavior Under Regulatory Treaties," *Negotiation Journal* 7 (July 1991), pp. 311–30; Young, *International Cooperation;* Robert O. Keohane, "Reciprocity in International Relations," *International Organization* 40 (Winter 1986), pp. 1–27; and Krasner, *International Regimes.*

15. Joseph S. Nye, Jr., "Nuclear Learning and U.S.–Soviet Security Regimes," *International Organization* 41 (Summer 1987), pp. 371–402.

16. See, for example, Louis Henkin, *How Nations Behave: Law and Foreign Policy* (New York: Columbia University Press, 1979), p. 47; Young, *International Cooperation,* p. 62; and Chayes and Chayes, "Compliance Without Enforcement," p. 31.

17. At the extreme, if all parties violated treaty provision A and complied with treaty provision B, they could all be classified as in partial compliance, ignoring the important variance in compliance rates.

processes of knowledge creation.[18] However, this restrictive definition has the virtue of bringing the debate to a level at which research on actual treaties and actual compliance can contribute to the intellectual and policy debates.

This article evaluates the features of a regime that may determine compliance by differentiating among three parts of any compliance system: a primary rule system, a compliance information system, and a noncompliance response system. The primary rule system consists of the actors, rules, and processes related to the behavior that is the substantive target of the regime. In the choice of who gets regulated and how, the primary rule system determines the pressures and incentives for compliance and violation. The compliance information system consists of the actors, rules, and processes that collect, analyze, and disseminate information on instances of violations and compliance. Self-reporting, independent monitoring, data analysis, and publishing comprise the compliance information system that determines the amount, quality, and uses made of data on compliance and enforcement. The noncompliance response system consists of the actors, rules, and processes governing the formal and informal responses—the inducements and sanctions— employed to induce those in noncompliance to comply. The noncompliance response system determines the type, likelihood, magnitude, and appropriateness of responses to noncompliance. These categories provide the framework used in the remainder of this article to evaluate the oil pollution regime's sources of success and failure in its attempt to elicit compliance.

Two subregimes for international oil pollution control

For most people, oil pollution conjures up images of tanker accidents such as that of the *Exxon Valdez*.[19] While oil from such accidents poses a concentrated but localized hazard to the marine environment, the waste oil traditionally generated during normal oil transport has posed a more diffuse but ubiquitous threat. After a tanker delivers its cargo, a small fraction of oil remains onboard, adhering to cargo tank walls. Ballasting and tank-cleaning procedures mixed this oil—averaging about 300 tons per voyage—with seawater, creating slops. These in turn were most easily and cheaply disposed of by discharging them overboard while at sea.[20] By the 1970s, the intentional discharges made on thousands of tanker voyages were putting an estimated million tons of oil into the oceans annually.[21] While scientific uncertainty remains regarding the extent

18. See Haas, Keohane, and Levy, *Institutions for the Earth;* George W. Downs and David M. Rocke, *Tacit Bargaining, Arms Races, and Arms Control* (Ann Arbor: University of Michigan Press, 1990); Charles Lipson, "Why Are Some International Agreements Informal?" *International Organization* 45 (Autumn 1991), pp. 495–538; and Chayes and Chayes, "On Compliance," pp. 188–92.
19. The *Exxon Valdez* wrecked in Prince William Sound, Alaska, on 24 March 1989.
20. For comparison, the *Exxon Valdez* spilled thirty-five thousand tons.
21. National Academy of Sciences, *Petroleum in the Marine Environment* (Washington, D.C.: National Academy of Sciences, 1975). See also National Academy of Sciences and National Research Council, *Oil in the Sea: Inputs, Fates, and Effects* (Washington, D.C.: National Academy Press, 1985).

of damage to marine life caused by such chronic but low-concentration discharges, their impact and that of accidents on seabirds and resort beaches have produced regular international efforts at regulation.[22]

Intentional oil discharges were one of the first pollutants to become the subject of an international regulatory regime.[23] In the International Convention for the Prevention of Pollution of the Seas by Oil (OILPOL) of 1954, nations addressed the coastal oil pollution problem by limiting the oil content of discharges made near shore.[24] In what has been a regime largely focused on regulation,[25] numerous revisions were negotiated within diplomatic conferences sponsored by the Intergovernmental Maritime Consultative Organization (IMCO) or within its committees and those of its successor, the International Maritime Organization (IMO). By the late 1970s, the regime's major provisions, now contained in the International Convention for the Prevention of Pollution from Ships (MARPOL), consisted of restrictions on both tanker operations and tanker equipment that relied on quite different compliance systems.[26] Although rule-making has remained consistently international, governments and nonstate actors have played crucial roles in the implementation and enforcement of the regime: tanker owners and operators have been the targets of the regulations while maritime authorities, classification societies, insurers, and shipbuilders have monitored and enforced the regulations.

The discharge subregime

The discharge subregime of the last fifteen years evolved from the initial regulations of 1954. That agreement constituted a compromise between the United Kingdom—which wielded strong power in oil markets but had strong

22. See, for example, National Academy of Sciences and National Research Council, *Oil in the Sea;* and Joint Group of Experts on the Scientific Aspects of Marine Pollution (GESAMP), *The State of the Marine Environment,* Reports and Studies no. 39 (New York: United Nations, 1990).

23. For the history of oil pollution control from the 1920s through the 1970s, see Sonia Zaide Pritchard, *Oil Pollution Control* (London: Croom Helm, 1987); for a history from the 1950s through the 1970s, see R. Michael M'Gonigle and Mark W. Zacher, *Pollution, Politics, and International Law: Tankers at Sea* (Berkeley: University of California Press, 1979).

24. "International Convention for the Prevention of Pollution of the Sea by Oil," 12 May 1954, *Treaties and Other International Agreements Series (TIAS),* no. 4900 (Washington, D.C.: U.S. Department of State, 1954).

25. For an excellent description of a regime more focused on developing scientific understanding of an environmental problem, see Levy's description of the regime on European acid precipitation in Marc Levy, "European Acid Rain: The Power of Tote-board Diplomacy," in Haas, Keohane, and Levy, *Institutions for the Earth,* pp. 75–132.

26. See *International Convention for the Prevention of Pollution from Ships (MARPOL),* 2 November 1973, reprinted in *International Legal Materials (ILM),* vol. 12 (Washington, D.C.: American Society of International Law, 1973), p. 1319 (hereafter cited by abbreviation, volume, and year); and *Protocol of 1978 Relating to the International Convention for the Prevention of Pollution from Ships,* 17 February 1978, reprinted in *ILM,* vol. 17, 1978, p. 1546 (hereafter cited together as *MARPOL 73/78*).

environmental nongovernmental organizations pushing it to reduce coastal pollution—and Germany, the Netherlands, the United States, and other major states that viewed any regulation as either environmentally unnecessary or as harmful to their own shipping interests. Although the United Kingdom had sought to restrict tanker discharges throughout the ocean, the final agreement limited the oil content of discharges made within fifty miles of any coastline to 100 parts oil per million parts water (100 ppm). In 1962, the British pushed through an amendment applying this 100 ppm standard to discharges made by new tankers regardless of their distance from shore.

The principle underlying the 1962 amendment—that crude oil could float far enough that discharge zones would not effectively protect coastlines—had gained sufficient support by 1969 that nations agreed to limit discharges by all tankers throughout the ocean. The pressure to amend the 1954/62 agreement came from two different sources. On one side, the thirty-five million gallons of oil spilled by the grounding of the *Torrey Canyon* off Britain and France on 18 March 1967 and growing environmentalism, especially in the United States, supported a push for stronger regulations.[27] The previously resistant United States replaced the United Kingdom as the leading activist state and especially sought to ensure that amendments would address the growing evidence of enforcement problems with existing regulations.

On the other side, oil companies rightly interpreted the 1962 amendments as a wake-up call that discharge standards would soon be replaced by expensive equipment requirements. In response, Shell Marine International developed and promoted an operational means by which tankers could reduce oil discharges without any new equipment.[28] The load-on-top procedure (LOT) involved consolidating ballast and cleaning slops in a single tank, letting gravity separate out the water so it could be decanted from beneath the oil, and loading the next cargo on top of the remaining slops. The beauty of LOT was that it ensured that less cargo was wasted, thereby advancing both the environmental goal of reducing intentional oil pollution and the economic goal of reducing the amount of valuable oil discharged overboard. LOT even improved on the regime's existing standards, since its use reduced rather than merely redistributed intentional discharges. The problem was that normal operation of LOT produced discharges that exceeded the 100 ppm standard. If this criterion had remained in effect, tankers would have had to install expensive new equipment to comply with OILPOL, defeating LOT's major economic virtue. With the support of France, the Netherlands, Norway, and the now less-activist United Kingdom, oil and shipping companies therefore also sought to amend the treaty. Oil companies considered LOT so effective that they wanted diplomats to scrap the 1954/62 zonal approach altogether.

27. M'Gonigle and Zacher, *Pollution, Politics, and International Law,* p. 100.
28. J. H. Kirby, "The Clean Seas Code: A Practical Cure of Operation Pollution," in *Third International Conference on Oil Pollution of the Sea: Report of Proceedings, Rome 7–9 October 1968* (Winchester, England: Warren and Son, 1968), pp. 201–19.

The pressures for greater environmental protection, however, led them to support the more limited objective of redefining the limits on discharges from the 100 ppm "content" criterion to one that could be monitored using existing on-board equipment.[29]

In a unanimously accepted compromise in 1969, more stringent and enforceable regulations were framed in terms that averted equipment requirements. Within the fifty-mile near-shore zones, discharges could now only involve "clean ballast" that left no visible trace; outside the fifty-mile zones, discharges could not exceed 60 liters of oil per mile (60 l/m). Proponents argued that the clean ballast provision would improve enforcement by transforming any sighting of a discharge into evidence of a violation.[30] The more crucial change involved a new limit that total discharges not exceed one fifteen-thousandth of a tanker's capacity.[31] Although compliance with this standard required a tanker to reduce its average discharges by almost 98 percent, Shell's J. H. Kirby claimed that "any responsibly run ship, no matter how big, could operate" within these standards if it used LOT.[32] The low total discharge limit also allowed port authorities to assume that any tanker with completely clean tanks had blatantly violated the agreement.[33] These standards took effect in 1978 and remain in force today through their incorporation into the 1973 MARPOL agreement.

The equipment subregime

By the early 1970s, public concern was pushing environmental issues onto the international political scene with increasing frequency. The United Nations Conference on the Human Environment and negotiation of the London Dumping Convention in 1972 set the stage for a major overhaul of the OILPOL agreement. IMCO hosted a major conference in 1973 to negotiate the MARPOL treaty. Its goal was the replacement of OILPOL's rules with rules that would cover all major types of vessel-source marine pollution.

---

29. Kirby, "The Clean Seas Code," p. 206.

30. Assembly resolution 391, IMCO/IMO doc. resolution A.391(X), 1 December 1977, Annex, par. 5. All document citations herein refer to IMCO/IMO documents housed in the IMO Secretariat library. They are numbered similarly: according to issuing committee (abbreviated), meeting number, agenda item, and document number. Information documents are designated by "Inf." prior to the document number. Circulars are designated by "Circ.," issuing committee, and circular number only. Resolutions are designated by adopting body, resolution number, and meeting number. Conference documents are cited by abbreviated conference title, preparatory meeting number, agenda item, and document number. Hence the above resolution citation would be interpreted as the 391st resolution adopted by the 10th meeting of the (IMCO) assembly.

31. *1969 Amendments to the International Convention for the Prevention of Pollution of the Sea by Oil*, 21 October 1969, reprinted in Bernd Ruster and Bruno Simma, eds., *International Protection of the Environment: Treaties and Related Documents* (Dobbs Ferry, N.Y.: Oceana Publications, 1975).

32. Kirby, "The Clean Seas Code," p. 208.

33. See Kirby, "The Clean Seas Code," pp. 200 and 209; and William T. Burke, Richard Legatski, and William W. Woodhead, *National and International Law Enforcement in the Ocean* (Seattle: University of Washington Press, 1975), p. 129.

The U.S. government had become increasingly concerned that the ease with which tanker crews could violate discharge standards and the massive resources and diligence needed to detect violations were preventing effective mitigation of the growing oil pollution problem.[34] By 1972, Congress had adopted legislation that threatened to require all American tankers as well as all tankers entering U.S. ports to install expensive pollution-reducing equipment. The legislation included a proposal to require all large tankers to install double hulls to address accidental spills and segregated ballast tanks (SBT) to address intentional discharges. The SBT system involved arranging ballast tanks and associated piping such that ballast water could not come into contact with oil being carried as cargo. The system was expensive both in terms of capital and the reduction to cargo-carrying capacity. The United States sought international agreement to require SBT but threatened to require it unilaterally if necessary. Discharge requirements clearly were cheaper, more economically efficient, and "in theory . . . a good idea."[35] However, environmental pressures and growing evidence that LOT was neither as widespread nor as effective as had been hoped led the United States and the United Kingdom to support rules that offered easier and more effective enforcement.

The largely U.S.-based oil companies initially opposed SBT requirements but eventually supported them as preferable to threatened U.S. unilateral rules. Many shipping states also reluctantly supported SBT requirements. They believed such requirements would avert an even more costly double bottom requirement. It was also fiscally acceptable: the combination of a recent building boom and the proposed language of the requirements meant that tanker owners would only have to incur the additional costs of SBT many years in the future and then only for large tankers. However, governments representing shipbuilding interests (France and Japan) and those representing independent tanker owners (Denmark, Germany, Greece, Norway, and Sweden) opposed the requirement.[36] By a vote of thirty to seven, the conference adopted a requirement for tankers over 70,000 tons built in 1980 and later to install SBT.

By 1977, a spate of accidents in the United States and continuing enforcement concerns led President Jimmy Carter to propose that SBT requirements be applied to all tankers, not just large new tankers.[37] Given (1) that the United States was again explicitly threatening unilateral action and (2) that the 1973

---

34. M'Gonigle and Zacher, *Pollution, Politics, and International Law,* p. 108.

35. See statements submitted by the U.S. delegation to the 13th Preparatory Session for an International Conference on Marine Pollution in 1973: IMCO/IMO doc. MP XIII/2(c)/5, 23 May 1972. (Using note 30 as a guide, this would be the 5th document issued relating to agenda item 2[c]). See also doc. MP XIII/2(a)/5, 1 June 1972; G. Victory, "Avoidance of Accidental and Deliberate Pollution," in *Coastal Water Pollution: Pollution of the Sea by Oil Spills* (Brussels: North Atlantic Treaty Organization [NATO], 2–6 November 1970), p. 2.3.

36. M'Gonigle and Zacher, *Pollution, Politics, and International Law,* p. 114.

37. Jacob W. Ulvila, "Decisions with Multiple Objectives in Integrative Bargaining," Ph.D. diss., Harvard University, 1979, appendix A1.1.

MARPOL agreement still had been ratified by only three states, IMCO called a second major conference in 1978.[38] State positions reflected the fact that retrofitting existing tankers with SBT would reduce each tanker's (and the fleet's) cargo capacity by some 15 percent.[39] Greece, Norway, and Sweden saw this as a means to put scores of their laid up independent tankers back to work. However, most states saw SBT retrofitting as extremely expensive.[40] Just as the 1962 amendments had prompted LOT development, the 1973 MARPOL agreement prompted oil companies to perfect a technique known as crude oil washing (COW), which entailed spraying down cargo tanks with the cargo itself rather than with seawater. Operating COW equipment during cargo delivery transformed oil that otherwise would have been discharged as slops into usable delivered cargo, simultaneously reducing oil pollution and increasing cargo owner revenues. The industry proposal for COW as an alternative to SBT produced a compromise in which tankers built after 1982 had to install both SBT and COW, while existing tankers had to be retrofitted with either SBT or COW by 1985. The 1978 Protocol Relating to the International Convention for the Prevention of Pollution from ships was made an integral part of the 1973 MARPOL agreement. While MARPOL and its protocol, known collectively as MARPOL 73/78, did not enter into force until 1983, their standards regulated all new construction after 1979.

Observed compliance levels

Available evidence demonstrates a wide divergence in levels of compliance under these two subregimes. During the same time period in which almost every tanker owner was retrofitting existing tankers and buying new tankers to conform with MARPOL's requirements for SBT and COW, large numbers of tanker operators continued to discharge oil well in excess of legal limits. The variance between the observed compliance rates with the two subregimes is quite marked.

Violations of the clean ballast, 60 l/m, and total discharge standards in place since 1978 have been common. Oil company surveys from the 1970s show that neither oil company nor independent tankers reduced average discharge levels to the one fifteen-thousandth limit in any year between 1972 and 1977 (see Figure 1). Although oil company tankers dramatically reduced average discharges in the early 1970s, discharges remained at three times the legal limit. The two-thirds of the fleet operated by independent oil transporters did far worse, with discharges that were thirty times the legal limit and that were not

---

38. M'Gonigle and Zacher, *Pollution, Politics, and International Law,* pp. 122 and 130.

39. See Sonia Z. Pritchard, "Load on Top: From the Sublime to the Absurd," *Journal of Maritime Law and Commerce* 9 (April 1978), pp. 185–224 at p. 194.

40. For an excellent discussion of state positions during both the 1973 and 1978 conferences, see M'Gonigle and Zacher, *Pollution, Politics, and International Law,* pp. 107–42.

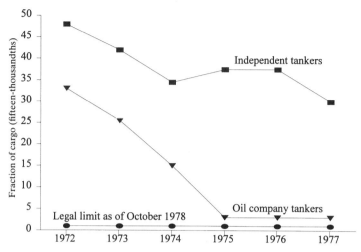

FIGURE 1. *Average tanker discharges, 1972–77*

Source. U.S. Congress, House Committee on Government Operations, *Oil Tanker Pollution: Hearings Before the Subcommittee on Government Activities and Transportation, 18 and 19 July 1978,* 95th Congress, 2d sess., p. 322.

much below levels that a tanker practicing no pollution control would have produced.[41] The trends in these discharges suggest that few tankers complied with the limit after it took legal effect in 1978.[42]

Other evidence confirms the frequency of discharge violations. A 1981 National Academy of Sciences estimate of oil pollution relied on an assumption that 50 percent of the world's tanker fleet was violating the total discharge limit.[43] A 1989 revision of that study assumed 15–20 percent of tankers were still violating this limit, although it provided no evidence to support the dramatic improvement.[44] Representatives of independent transporters admit that tankers often violate discharge limits to comply with their contracts: some charter arrangements require ships to arrive with clean tanks but many ports lack facilities to receive the slops they generate by cleaning.[45] Studies of

41. See, for example, the estimate of 0.3 percent in James E. Moss, *Character and Control of Sea Pollution by Oil* (Washington, D.C.: American Petroleum Institute, 1963), p. 47, and the estimate of 0.4 percent in IMCO/IMO doc. OP I/21, 15 January 1965, of the Oil Pollution subcommittee. (Using note 30 as a guide, this indicates the only document issued relating to agenda item 21 at the 1st meeting of the subcommittee.)

42. Unfortunately, oil companies discontinued the surveys after 1977. Personal communication from Arthur McKenzie, Tanker Advisory Center, New York, 1992.

43. Informational document of the Marine Environment Protection Committee: IMCO/IMO doc. MEPC XVI/Inf.2, 4 November 1981.

44. IMCO/IMO doc. MEPC 30/Inf.13, 19 September 1990, p. 15.

45. For example, "IMO, Tanker Owners Urge Increase in Facilities Accepting Oily Wastes," *International Environment Reporter,* 8 March 1989, p. 130.

detected oil slicks and dead seabirds as well as violation reports provided to IMO confirm that many tankers continue to discharge their slops at sea.[46]

The variety of sources pointing to violation of the discharge standards contrasts sharply with the uniformity of evidence that compliance with the equipment standards has been exceptionally high. By 1981, one shipping research firm already had evidence that new tankers were being built with SBT and existing tankers were being retrofitted with SBT and/or COW.[47] Recent national and international studies as well as industry experts reveal a common assumption that all tankers comply with the equipment standards although none provides empirical support for this assumption.[48]

Analysis of previously unavailable data on equipment installed on large tankers supports these perceptions (see Table 1).[49] Among large tankers in the fleet at the end of 1991, 94 percent of tankers built in 1979 or earlier had installed SBT or COW as required, 98 percent of those built between 1980 and 1982 had installed SBT as required, and 98 percent of those built after 1982 had installed both SBT and COW as required. The figures not only confirm remarkably high compliance rates but also document that tankers of all nations, not merely those that supported the equipment requirements during negotiation, have complied.

The variance between the subregimes is more remarkable when one considers that both international politics and private economics would lead us to expect higher compliance with the discharge standards, not the equipment standards. The discharge standards had been adopted unanimously. In contrast, several powerful nations opposed the equipment standards in both 1973 and 1978. Tankers seeking the economic benefits of conserving oil could have done so most cheaply by using the equipment-free option of LOT, not by installing COW or the even more expensive SBT. Indeed, in 1978, one

46. See, for example, C. J. Camphuysen, *Beached Bird Surveys in the Netherlands 1915–1988: Seabird Mortality in the Southern North Sea Since the Early Days of Oil Pollution* (Amsterdam: Werkgroep Noordzee, 1989); United States Coast Guard, *Polluting Incidents In and Around U.S. Waters* (Washington, D.C.: U.S. Department of Commerce, 1973 and 1975–86); N. Smit-Kroes, *Harmonisatie Noordzeebeleid: Brief van de Minister van Verkeer en Waterstaat* (Tweede Kamer der Staten-Generaal: 17-408) (Harmonization of North Sea policy: Letter from the Minister of Transport and Waterways; Lower House of Parliament) (The Hague: Government Printing Office of the Netherlands, 1988); IMCO/IMO doc. MEPC 21/Inf. 8, 21 March 1985; and Second International Conference on the Protection of the North Sea, *Quality Status of the North Sea: A Report by the Scientific and Technical Working Group* (London: Her Majesty's Stationery Office, 1987), p. 14.

47. Drewry Shipping Consultants, Ltd., *The Impact of New Tanker Regulations,* Drewry publication no. 94 (London: Drewry Shipping Consultants, Ltd., 1981), p. 25.

48. See IMCO/IMO doc. MEPC 30/Inf.13, 19 September 1990, p. 8; Second International Conference on the Protection of the North Sea, *Quality Status of the North Sea,* p. 57; Pieter Bergmeijer, "The International Convention for the Prevention of Pollution from Ships," paper presented at the 17th Pacem in Maribus conference, Rotterdam, August 1990, p. 12; and personal interview with E. J. M. Ball, Oil Companies International Marine Forum, London, 26 June 1991;

49. The detailed statistics in Table 1 and Figure 2 were developed from an electronic version of Clarkson Research Studies, Ltd., *The Tanker Register* (London: Clarkson Research Studies, Ltd., 1991) generously provided by Clarkson Research Studies, Ltd.

TABLE 1. *Percentage of crude oil tankers weighing over 70,000 deadweight tons with segregated ballast tanks (SBT) and/or crude oil washing equipment (COW) onboard*[a]

	Tanker construction date (and MARPOL requirement)[b]		
Equipment onboard	1979 and earlier (SBT or COW)	1980–82 (SBT only)	Post 1982 (SBT and COW)
SBT and COW	32%	94%	98%
SBT or COW	94%	99%	100%
Total SBT (alone and with COW)	36%	98%	99%
Total COW (alone and with SBT)	89%	95%	99%
SBT alone	4%	4%	1%
COW alone	58%	1%	1%
Neither SBT nor COW	6%	1%	0%
MARPOL compliance level	94%	98%	98%

[a]Data reflect tankers in the fleet as of 31 December 1991.
[b]MARPOL = International Convention for the Prevention of Pollution from Ships.

Source. Electronic version of Clarkson Research Studies, Ltd., *The Tanker Register* (London: Clarkson Research Studies, Ltd., 1991).

academic analyst, Charles Okidi, predicted that the enormous costs of SBT would make compliance "negligible."[50]

In short, the empirical evidence of higher compliance levels with the equipment subregime runs contrary to predictions based on a simple analysis of exogenous power and interests. How do we explain what appears to be a significant divergence between theory and observed outcomes? Was any of the observed compliance treaty-induced? If so, what elements of the equipment standards compliance system explain its greater success at eliciting compliance? The rest of this article answers these questions.

Was compliance treaty-induced?

Before we can explain how one subregime produced such dramatically higher compliance levels than another within the same issue-area, we need to assure ourselves that we can accurately attribute this variance to features of the

50. Charles Odidi Okidi, *Regional Control of Ocean Pollution: Legal and Institutional Problems and Prospects* (Alphen aan den Rijn, The Netherlands: Sijthoff and Noordhoff, 1978), p. 34.

regime. Taking realist analysis seriously requires that we avoid attributing causation where only spurious correlation exists. Factors other than variation in the compliance systems of the two subregimes may explain the observed behaviors. Did tanker owners and operators act any differently than they would have in the absence of international regulations? The following accounting of incentives to comply with regulations from both within and outside of the regime strongly suggests (1) that increased use of LOT owes more to economics than to international law, (2) that increased installation of COW equipment owes much to economics but also reflects the MARPOL regime's influences, and (3) that increased installation of SBT largely is due to MARPOL influences.

LOT

Several pieces of evidence indicate that the 1969 rules had little to do with the observed increase in the use of LOT by tanker operators. A large share of tankers simply did not use LOT or comply with the discharge standards. The continuing noncompliance with discharge standards did not result from an inability to use LOT—a noncomplex procedure that required no new equipment—but from insufficient incentives to use it.

The subregime itself produced few effective mechanisms for inducing operators to adopt LOT. While I discuss these failures more fully below, the discharge subregime's compliance system failed to induce the monitoring and enforcement necessary to deter violations. The subregime's failure effectively to detect, identify, prosecute, and penalize violators left tanker operators' incentives to comply with it largely uninfluenced. As the official IMO newsletter put it, "Little has changed in the three decades since [1962]. The problem is detecting a violation in the first place (which is difficult) and then collecting sufficient evidence to prove the case in court (which has all too often proved to be impossible)."[51]

Given the absence of these pathways for regime influence, it is not surprising to find that economic influences readily explain the pattern of LOT usage. A tanker operator's first-order incentives to use LOT depended on the costs of recovering waste oil, the value of that oil, and the ownership of the oil being transported. This last factor meant that oil companies had far greater incentives to adopt LOT than did independent transporters. The latter carry oil on charter to cargo owners and are paid for the amount of oil initially loaded, known as the bill-of-lading weight, not for the amount delivered. Therefore, discharging waste oil at sea costs the independent transporter nothing. Indeed, using LOT reduces the bill-of-lading weight in subsequent cargo by the amount of remaining slops, thereby reducing the payment that the independent transporter receives. In contrast, operators that own their cargoes, as oil

51. See p. 9 of "Cleaner Oceans: The Role of the IMO in the 1990s," *IMO News,* no. 3, 1990, pp. 6–12.

companies usually do, can offset a LOT tanker's slightly smaller cargo capacity with the benefit of having all the oil it paid for delivered. At 1976 prices, the lower bill-of-lading weight cost the tanker owner some $700, while the value of oil recovered benefited the cargo owner some $16,000.[52]

The decrease in average discharges of oil company tankers in the 1970s and the absence of a similar decrease in discharges of independent tankers correlate more with these divergent incentives and with rising oil prices than with any treaty proscription. Oil companies' greater incentives to conserve oil explain why their average discharges were lower than those of independent tankers in 1972 and why they decreased discharges more rapidly after the 1973 oil price hikes (see Figure 1). If the regime, rather than economics, were influencing oil company behavior, these decreases should have occurred only after the total discharge limits took legal effect in 1978, not after 1973. The far smaller decrease in average discharge among independents reflects the fact that conserved oil had little value to them.

Nevertheless, the OILPOL regime does appear to have been responsible for the timing of LOT development in the early 1960s and to have at least contributed to some adoption of LOT. Oil company representatives noted at the time that they had developed LOT in response to the increasing pressures for equipment requirements that were evident at the 1962 conference. The facts that (1) oil prices remained constant throughout the 1960s and (2) LOT involved a procedural—not a technological—breakthrough support this more limited claim of regime influence. Declines in discharges by both oil company and independent tankers before the oil price increases of 1973 and declines in independent tankers' discharges after 1973 also prove difficult to attribute exclusively to economic factors. Having said this, however, it remains clear that economic factors rather than the features of the subregime were the dominant factors influencing tanker operators' behavior.

COW

The almost universal installation of COW equipment initially tempts one to conclude that compliance was treaty-induced. The contrast in rates of use of LOT and COW suggest that differences in the designs of the corresponding subregimes may be responsible, given that both methods allowed a tanker operator to reduce waste oil. However, closer evaluation reveals that here, too, economic factors played an important role, although not an exclusive one.

Like LOT, COW has economic as well as environmental benefits. COW's costs include those for the washing machines and the additional time and labor needed to wash tanks in port during delivery rather than during the ballast

---

52. The following discussion of the costs of LOT, COW, and SBT draws heavily on William G. Waters, Trevor D. Heaver, and T. Verrier, *Oil Pollution from Tanker Operations: Causes, Costs, Controls* (Vancouver, B.C.: Center for Transportation Studies, 1980).

voyage.[53] As with LOT, the offsetting benefit of more delivered cargo accrues to the cargo owner. However, the tanker operator also benefits: the decrease in oil left on board increases the tanker's effective cargo capacity and reduces sludge buildup, which can lead to large repair and maintenance costs. Compared with a tanker that was not practicing pollution control, using COW produced a net savings per voyage of $9,000.

These economic incentives to adopt COW are borne out by the evidence of the timing of its adoption. In many instances, tankers adopted COW before required to do so by MARPOL. Recall that negotiators only incorporated COW requirements into MARPOL in 1978 and only made them applicable to tankers built after 1982. Yet by the mid-1970s, many oil companies had already incorporated COW as a standard operational procedure.[54] This timing does not correspond with the development of COW technology in the late 1960s or with the deadline set by MARPOL. Instead, like LOT, it corresponds with the rising oil prices of the 1970s.

The contrast to the SBT requirements also confirms the role of economics. The higher capital costs of SBT and the significant reduction to cargo-carrying capacity that SBT involved imposed a net cost per voyage on a tanker with SBT of $1,500 relative to a tanker with no pollution-control equipment. A new tanker installing both COW and SBT, as required by MARPOL, faced costs of almost $8,000 per voyage. Owners of large tankers built before 1980, who were allowed to choose between SBT and COW, installed COW equipment on 89 percent of their tankers and SBT on only 36 percent (see Table 1). Owners also installed COW equipment on 95 percent of large tankers built between 1980 and 1982, even though MARPOL only required them to install SBT. COW's economic benefits certainly appear to be a major influence on COW installations.

Several details suggest that economics were not the sole influence on behavior, however. If they were, we should expect companies to achieve the economic goal of conserving oil by the cheapest and most cost-effective means possible, that is, by LOT, not COW. We should also expect to see the same divergence between the behavior of independent carriers and oil companies as we observed in the LOT case. Yet the 99 percent compliance rate attests to the fact that all tanker owners were installing COW. The adoption of COW more frequently than SBT does not imply that the subregime was ineffective, only that when the subregime left owners with alternatives, their choices were driven by costs. In contrast to clear flaws in the compliance system supporting

53. Drewry Shipping Consultants, Ltd., *Tanker Regulations: Enforcement and Effect,* Drewry publication no. 135 (London: Drewry Shipping Consultants, Ltd., 1985), p. 25.

54. See M. G. Osborne and J. M. Ferguson, "Technology, MARPOL, and Tankers: Successes and Failures," *IMAS 90: Maritime Technology and the Environment* (London: Institute of Marine Engineers, 1990), p. 6–2; Testimony of William Gray, in U.S. Congress, House Committee on Government Operations, *Oil Tanker Pollution: Hearings Before the Subcommittee on Government Activities and Transportation, 18 and 19 July 1978,* 95th Congress, 2d sess., 1978, p. 92; and IMCO/IMO doc. MEPC V/Inf.A, 27 April 1976.

discharge standards, as I detail below, the design of the compliance system supporting equipment requirements provided several means of successfully reducing both the incentives and ability of tanker owners to violate COW requirements. Thus, an interplay among economics and subregime characteristics appears to have been the source of widespread COW adoption.

SBT

Adoption of the SBT standard provides an unambiguous example of subregime influence on behavior. Unlike COW or LOT, tanker owners had no economic incentives to install this technology. SBT's additional piping and equipment added several million dollars to the cost of a new tanker, representing almost 5 percent of total cost.[55] Installing SBT also reduced cargo capacity, especially when installed on an existing tanker. Yet these costs provided no offsetting benefits in the form of reduced cargo wastage. Even those governments that had supported the 1978 proposal that all tankers be retrofitted with SBT admitted that SBT would increase the cost of carrying oil by 15 percent; some oil company estimates ran up to 50 percent.[56] As late as 1991, oil and shipping interests opposed mandatory SBT retrofitting as being too expensive.[57]

The pattern of observed SBT installation follows that which one would predict for behavior driven by effective treaty rules rather than economics. Among tankers currently in the fleet, more than 98 percent of those required to install SBT have done so despite the significant costs involved. Compliance has been elicited even among those required to install both SBT and COW. Rates of SBT installation among older tankers bolster the argument: among tankers built before 1980, which MARPOL allowed to choose between SBT and COW, only 36 percent have installed SBT. Indeed, owners installed SBT alone on only 4 percent of older tankers but installed COW alone on 58 percent, suggesting that owners installed SBT only when a tanker was already in dock to be retrofitted with COW. Figure 2 graphs the percentages of current tankers using SBT and COW by year of construction. The timing of the increase in the number of tankers installing SBT seen in the figure reinforces the conclusion that owners installed SBT only under the regulatory threat posed by the subregime's compliance system. In short, owners have installed SBT only when MARPOL required them to do so. As one analyst noted, "If there were not a

---

55. See Philip A. Cummins, Dennis E. Logue, Robert D. Tollison, and Thomas D. Willett, "Oil Tanker Pollution Control: Design Criteria Versus Effective Liability Assessment," *Journal of Maritime Law and Commerce* 7 (October 1975), pp. 181–82; and Charles S. Pearson, *International Marine Environmental Policy: The Economic Dimension* (Baltimore, Md.: The Johns Hopkins University Press, 1975), p. 98.

56. See IMCO/IMO doc. MEPC V/Inf. 4, 8 March 1976, p. A18; and M'Gonigle and Zacher, *Pollution, Politics, and International Law*, p. 134.

57. See IMCO/IMO doc. MEPC 31/8/5, 4 April 1991; and Osborne and Ferguson, "Technology, MARPOL, and Tankers," p. 6-2.

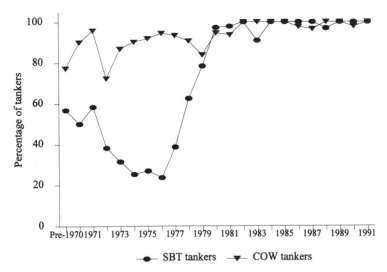

FIGURE 2. *Percentage of tankers with segregated ballast tanks (SBT) and/or crude oil washing equipment (COW) on board in 1991, by year of tanker construction*

Source. Electronic version of Clarkson Research Studies, Ltd., *The Tanker Register* (London: Clarkson Research Studies, Ltd., 1991), provided to the author.

regulatory requirement, there would not be SBT."[58] Within several years, the subregime had caused a radical change in tanker owner behavior.

One alternative explanation of SBT adoption deserves special attention. At least one analyst has claimed that hegemonic pressures exerted by the United States explain the success of MARPOL.[59] Certainly the negotiation history demonstrates that the SBT requirements of 1973 and 1978 resulted directly from threats of unilateral U.S. regulation. Indeed, the United States is the only state that adopted national legislation containing a faster schedule and broader application of equipment requirements than MARPOL.[60] Admitting that MARPOL's rules resulted from hegemonic pressures, however, does not imply that subsequent behaviors result from that same pressure. As international diplomats arc all too well aware, resources adequate to elicit votes for a resolution during a conference may prove inadequate to cause corresponding changes in behavior. The relevant question is, "Could the United States,

58. Personal interview with Sean Connaughton, marine transportation analyst, American Petroleum Institute, Washington, D.C., 8 April 1992.

59. Jesper Grolin, "Environmental Hegemony, Maritime Community, and the Problem of Oil Tanker Pollution," in Michael A. Morris, ed., *North–South Perspectives on Marine Policy* (Boulder, Colo.: Westview Press, 1988).

60. Drewry Shipping Consultants, Ltd., *Tanker Regulations,* p. 11.

through unilateral measures, have induced so many tanker owners to install SBT?" Available evidence suggests not.

While the United States wields tremendous diplomatic leverage, it wields nothing near hegemonic power in oil transportation markets. Since the United States became concerned about oil pollution in the late 1960s, it has been responsible for less than 5 percent of new tankers built, less than 7 percent of tanker registrations, and less than 20 percent of world oil imports.[61] Given SBT's high costs, oil transportation companies would have been more likely to respond to unilateral U.S. equipment requirements by installing SBT on a sufficient number of tankers to service the U.S. market than by installing it on all tankers. Nor has the United States sought to link MARPOL enforcement with other issues through threats of sanctions or through side-payments.[62] Indeed, in terms of power to control oil tankers, Japan—which opposed SBT requirements in both 1973 and 1978—consistently has controlled larger shares of tanker construction, tanker registration, and oil imports than the United States. Thus, while the nation most strongly supporting universal installation of SBT could not have imposed its preferences on its own, the nation most capable of doing so consistently opposed such measures.

Mechanisms of influence

Compliance with discharge standards via the use of LOT was largely an artifact of economic factors. Compliance with requirements for SBT and COW has been both higher and more clearly the result of the treaty. Rival explanations of economic influences and international political hegemony prove incapable of adequately explaining the observed outcomes and behaviors. The equipment subregime succeeded at inducing reluctant tanker owners to spend considerable money on additional equipment that provided them with no economic benefit. The following assessment of the exact means by which it did so simultaneously reinforces the conclusion that the regime caused the change in behavior and identifies design features that might be used to improve the effectiveness of other regimes.

Which of the many differences between the two subregimes best explain the different levels of observed compliance? In what ways did the equipment subregime "get it right" where the discharge standards failed? In subsequent portions of this article, I shall show how the design of the equipment regime

61. See Lloyd's Register of Shipping, *Annual Summary of Merchant Ships Completed* (London: Lloyd's Register of Shipping, various years); Lloyd's Register of Shipping, *Statistical Tables* (London: Lloyd's Register of Shipping, various years); and United Nations, *Statistical Yearbook* (New York: United Nations, various years).

62. For examples of U.S. sanctions to enforce the International Convention for the Regulation of Whaling, see Gene S. Martin, Jr., and James W. Brennan, "Enforcing the International Convention for the Regulation of Whaling: The Pelly and Packwood–Magnuson Amendments," *Denver Journal of International Law and Policy* 17 (Winter 1989), pp. 271–92.

induced compliance by (1) eliciting monitoring and enforcement and (2) reducing opportunities for violation.

Enhancing transparency

The equipment subregime had one major advantage over the discharge subregime in its significantly higher transparency level. Violations of the SBT and COW requirements simply were far easier to observe than violations of any discharge standard.

Consider the two compliance information systems. Both OILPOL and MARPOL required tanker captains to note discharges in record books and to make those books available to port authorities for inspection. This obvious reliance on self-incrimination made naval and aerial surveillance programs the more common means of detecting illegal discharges. The total discharge standard of one fifteen-thousandth of cargo capacity improved on this system by providing a criterion that could be monitored by tank inspections in port without relying on information supplied by the tanker captain. Practically speaking, these inspections were restricted to ports in oil-exporting states, since discharges occurred after delivery, on a tanker's return to port to load more cargo.

In contrast, the compliance information system for equipment standards relied on the fact that buying or retrofitting a tanker requires the knowledge and consent of at least three other actors: a builder, a classification society, and an insurance company. Agents in each of these industries would know of a violation even before it was committed. MARPOL also required flag state governments, or classification societies nominated by them, to survey all tankers to ensure compliance before issuing the required International Oil Pollution Prevention (IOPP) certificate and to conduct periodic inspections thereafter.[63] As part of the process of evaluating tankers to provide insurers with the information needed to set rates, classification societies regularly monitor compliance with international construction requirements through representatives stationed in shipyards.[64] Finally, MARPOL gave all port states the legal authority to inspect a tanker's IOPP certificate and its equipment to ensure compliance with the equipment requirements.

The equipment standards subregime made violations more transparent than violations in the discharge standards subregime in several ways. To begin with, regulating the tanker builder–tanker buyer transaction yielded a drastically reduced number of events to be monitored. While several thousand tankers ply the world's oceans, they are owned, built, and classified by only a few owners, shipyards, and classification societies. A tanker making ten trips per year could

---

63. *MARPOL 73/78*, Annex I, Regulations 4 and 5.
64. Personal interview with John Foxwell, Shell International Marine, London, 27 June 1991.

violate the total discharge standard three hundred times in its thirty-year life but could only violate the equipment requirements once.

Equipment standards also required authorities to monitor far fewer locations to detect violations. The discharge process standards—100 ppm, clean ballast, and 60 l/m—required patrols of wide areas of ocean to detect slicks that often could not be linked with the responsible tanker. As early as the 1920s, experts had noted the difficulties of such a monitoring system.[65] The addition of total discharge limits allowed detection of violations while a tanker was in an oil port, a procedure involving far fewer resources. Unfortunately, most oil-exporting states had exhibited little interest in preventing marine pollution; many such states were not even parties to MARPOL.[66] Inspections to verify compliance with equipment standards could occur in developed oil-importing states, which had shown far more interest in enforcement. The shift from the 100 ppm and 60 l/m limits to total discharge limits improved dramatically the practical ability to detect violations. The shift from total discharge ·limits to equipment standards improved the regime further by increasing incentives for monitoring among those who already had the practical ability to monitor.

Equipment standards dramatically eased the problem of obtaining evidence needed to sanction a violator. The standards eliminated any reliance on self-incrimination by the perpetrator of a violation. Detecting an equipment violation and identifying its perpetrator also were not time-sensitive. Successful detection and identification of a violation had to occur within hours for violations of the initial standards and within days for total discharge violations but could wait for years for equipment violations. Authorities also faced several difficulties in transforming detection of a discharge at sea into a case worthy of prosecution. In what can be called "passive voice" violations, often a tanker could not be identified as responsible for a detected slick: authorities could only say a violation "had been committed." Even if a responsible tanker could be identified, determining whether the 100 ppm or 60 l/m criterion had been exceeded generally was difficult. The total discharge standard could have eliminated this problem, but oil-exporting states never established inspection programs. These flaws in the design of the discharge standards compliance system were not necessarily inherent or insurmountable. For example, some analysts proposed placing observers on all tankers to verify compliance with discharge standards.[67] Even without such a system, governments could have established enough ocean patrol and in-port inspection programs to make detection of discharge violations likely. However, such programs would have

---

65. Charles Hipwood, United Kingdom Marine Department, cited in Pritchard, *Oil Pollution Control,* p. 23.

66. While Iran and Iraq never have signed either agreement, Kuwait, Libya, Nigeria, Qatar, Saudi Arabia, the United Arab Emirates, and Venezuela have never signed MARPOL.

67. Cummins et al., "Oil Tanker Pollution Control," p. 171.

involved huge expenditures of resources to produce only a low probability of successful deterrence.

In the first years after OILPOL was signed, evidence quickly demonstrated that only the Federal Republic of Germany and the United Kingdom were making any significant efforts to monitor compliance with discharge standards.[68] By the late 1970s, the Americans, British, Dutch, and French had instituted aerial surveillance programs.[69] Many other countries used aerial surveillance during the 1980s.[70] However, these programs were most often small and nonsystematic. The Dutch program flew more surveillance flights per year in the late 1970s than at any time in the 1980s, and the United States discontinued its program in the 1980s due to budgetary pressures.[71] Reports to IMO from 1983 to 1990 show that only one-quarter of the sixty-seven MARPOL signatories had any programs to detect discharges at sea.[72] British and Dutch data confirm the problems of identifying perpetrators: the British could link detected spills to tankers in only 22 percent of cases and the Dutch, in only 14 percent.[73]

The entry into force of total discharge standards in 1978 allowed inspectors in oil-loading ports to assume that any incoming tanker with all tanks free of slops had violated the very low limit placed on total discharges. However, even those oil-exporting states that were party to MARPOL had strong disincentives to inspect ships in their ports: ports that were conducting inspections were less attractive loading sites than neighboring ports that were not conducting inspections. Not surprisingly, most governments did not alter their enforcement strategies in response to the greater potential for enforcement provided by the promulgation of total discharge standards. In contrast, considerable evidence confirms that the equipment regime significantly changed the ways in which nations and classification societies conducted tanker inspections. Many of the states that originally had opposed the 1973 and 1978 U.S. proposals for equipment regulations subsequently have conducted the in-port inspections needed to detect violations. In 1982, the maritime authorities of fourteen European states signed a Memorandum of Understanding on Port State Control, committing themselves annually to inspect 25 percent of ships

---

68. IMCO/IMO doc. OP/CONF/2, 1 September 1961.

69. See James Cowley, "IMO and National Administrations," *IMO News,* no. 4, 1988, pp. 6–11; Smit-Kroes, *Harmonisatie Noordzeebeleid;* and IMCO/IMO doc. MEPC 21/Inf.9, 25 March 1985.

70. James McLoughlin and M. J. Forster, *The Law and Practice Relating to Pollution Control in the Member States of the European Communities: A Comparative Survey* (London: Graham and Trotman, 1982).

71. Personal interview with Daniel Sheehan, U.S. Coast Guard, Washington, D.C., 9 April 1992.

72. Gerard Peet, *Operational Discharges from Ships: An Evaluation of the Application of the Discharge Provisions of the MARPOL Convention by Its Contracting Parties* (Amsterdam: AIDEnvironment, 1992), annexes 5 and 10.

73. See United Kingdom Royal Commission on Environmental Pollution, *Eighth Report: Oil Pollution of the Sea* (London: Her Majesty's Stationery Office, 1981), p. 195; and Smit-Kroes, *Harmonisatie Noordzeebeleid.*

entering their ports for violations of maritime treaties, including MARPOL.[74] Notably, until 1992, the memorandum of understanding explicitly excluded inspections for discharge violations from its mandate, limiting cooperation to inspection for equipment violations. Even though several member states had voted against SBT, all fourteen have included checks of IOPP certificates in the thousands of inspections they conduct each year. In reports to the IMO secretariat, five additional countries and the United States have reported finding discrepancies in tankers' oil pollution certificates. Canada, Japan, Poland, and Russia have major port inspection programs, and ten Latin American states have recently signed an agreement similar to the European memorandum.[75] While these countries undoubtedly vary widely in how frequently and carefully they conduct inspections, all have made inspections for MARPOL-required equipment a standard element of their inspection programs.

The effectiveness of these governmental inspections depends at least in part on the initial issue of accurate IOPP certificates by flag states or classification societies designated by them. Reports to IMO for 1984 to 1990 show that missing and inaccurate pollution certificates declined steadily from 9 percent to 1 percent; the memorandum of understanding secretariat reports similar declines—from 11 percent to 3 percent.[76] These trends suggest that after an initial period of learning how to issue and inspect certificates, classification societies and governments both now issue thorough and accurate certifications. Like port state governments, flag states and classification societies appear to have altered their behavior to become active participants in the equipment subregime's compliance information system. It would seem unlikely that classification societies and flag states would have responded in the same fashion to U.S.-only legislation.

The greater transparency of violations of equipment requirements served perhaps most importantly to reassure other tanker owners that their own compliance would not place them at a competitive disadvantage in the marketplace. An environmentally concerned tanker operator inclined to comply with the discharge standards could not escape the knowledge that others probably would not comply. The economic incentives to discharge oil at sea, the absence of transparency about who was and who was not complying, and the attendant inability of enforcement efforts to effectively deter dis-

---

74. "Memorandum of Understanding on Port State Control," reprinted in *ILM,* vol. 21, 1982, p. 1.

75. *Acuerdo de Viña del Mar: Acuerdo Latinoamericano Sobre Control de Buques por el Estado Rector Del Puerto* (Viña del Mar Accord: Latin American Accord on Port State Control of Vessels), 5 November 1992. The text of the agreement is almost identical to the text of the "Memorandum of Understanding on Port State Control," cited above. Reference to the agreement can be found in Secretariat of the Memorandum of Understanding on Port State Control, *Annual Report* (The Hague: The Netherlands Government Printing Office, 1992).

76. Secretariat of the Memorandum of Understanding on Port State Control, *Annual Report* (The Hague: The Netherlands Government Printing Office, various years).

charges precluded any assumption other than that many competitors would violate the discharge standards to reduce their costs. The greater transparency of equipment requirements assured a tanker owner installing SBT and COW that all other owners also were doing so. Each company could rest assured that its competitors also would have to incur equipment costs or be sanctioned for not doing so.

The equipment standards provided the foundation for a compliance information system far more transparent than was possible under the discharge subregime. In response, even governments that had opposed the adoption of the requirements conducted inspections for compliance. The subregime's compliance information system channeled the behavior of both governments and classification societies into monitoring activities that supported the regime. It did so by ensuring that those actors with incentives to monitor compliance also had the practical ability and legal authority to do so. The transparency of the system improved the ability to deter violations and simultaneously reassured tanker owners that their own compliance would not place them at a competitive disadvantage with respect to other owners.

Facilitating potent but low-cost sanctions

Greater transparency translated into higher levels of compliance with equipment standards only because the compliance system also induced likely and potent sanctions. The noncompliance response system of the discharge subregime failed to do the same. Even after a violation was detected, tanker operators were unlikely to be successfully prosecuted and equally unlikely to receive a stiff penalty. In contrast, the equipment subregime authorized governments to use the administrative sanction of detention, which made both the likelihood and the cost of being penalized far higher for the equipment standards than for discharge standards. The incentives and abilities of governments to prosecute and to impose large penalties for violation were far lower under the discharge standards than under the equipment standards.

Detected discharge violations frequently remained unprosecuted because the subregime relied on customary international law with its deference to enforcement by flag states. Both OILPOL and MARPOL required a government that detected a discharge violation at sea to forward all evidence to the flag state for prosecution. Only if a tanker discharged illegally within a state's twelve-mile territorial sea and then entered a port of that state could that state prosecute a tanker registered elsewhere. Flag states have generally been less than aggressive in following up on evidence referred to them.[77] Flag states often lack the ability to prosecute, since tankers flying their flag may rarely enter their ports. They also have few incentives to prosecute because vigorous enforcement on their part would induce owners to take their registrations, and the

---

77. See Organization for Economic Cooperation and Development (OECD), "OECD Study on Flags of Convenience," *Journal of Maritime Law and Commerce* 4 (January 1973), pp. 231–54.

large associated fees, to a less scrupulous state.[78] The fact that pollution occurred off another state's coastline and that many developing flag states lack vocal environmental constituencies only reinforced these disincentives to prosecute. In short, the flag states with the authority to prosecute lacked incentives to do so, and the coastal states with the incentives to prosecute lacked the authority to do so.

Under the discharge standards, even states sincerely seeking to prosecute and convict a violator faced major obstacles to success. As already noted, evidence of a violation often failed to produce a violator, and otherwise convincing evidence often failed to meet the legal standards of proof needed for conviction. Evidentiary hurdles should have decreased with the prohibition of discharges that produced visible traces. However, even with aerial photographs of discharges, tankers frequently avoid conviction.[79] Between 1983 and 1990, port and coastal states discarded for lack of evidence an average of 36 percent of cases occurring in territorial seas and successfully convicted and fined less than 33 percent of all detected violators.[80] An additional 20 percent of high-seas cases referred to flag states were not prosecuted for the same reason, and less than 15 percent of all referrals resulted in fines being imposed.[81] Indeed, according to Paul Dempsey, from 1975 through 1982 "ninety-two percent of all fines were imposed through port state enforcement."[82] Many experts had hoped that the clearer evidence from inspections for total discharge violations would overcome these problems, but, according to E. J. M. Ball, there is no record "of a single case where the one fifteen-thousandth rule was used for prosecution."[83]

When conviction was successful, governments rarely imposed penalties adequate to deter future discharge violations as required by MARPOL.[84] Although governments have the ability and legal authority to impose high fines, the conflicting goals of the judiciary often inhibit them from doing so. Most states' courts are reluctant to impose fines disproportionate to the offense to compensate for low detection and conviction rates. The principle that "the punishment should fit the crime" places an upper bound on fines that may be too low to successfully deter violation, if detection and prosecution is difficult.

---

78. Paul Stephen Dempsey, "Compliance and Enforcement in International Law—Oil Pollution of the Marine Environment by Ocean Vessels," *Northwestern Journal of International Law and Business* 6 (Summer 1984), pp. 459–561 and p. 576 in particular.

79. See ibid., p. 526; and personal interview with Ronald Carly, Ministry of Transportation, Brussels, 10 June 1991.

80. Peet, *Operational Discharges from Ships,* pp. 17–18, Tables 11 and 12; and Marie-Jose Stoop, *Olieverontreiniging door schepen op de noordzee over de periode 1982–1987: opsporing en vervolging* (Oil pollution by ships on the North Sea 1982–1987: Investigations and prosecution) (Amsterdam: Werkgroep Noordzee, July 1989).

81. Ronald Bruce Mitchell, "From Paper to Practice: Improving Environmental Treaty Compliance," Ph.D. diss., Harvard University, Cambridge, Mass., 1992, Table 5-1.

82. Dempsey, "Compliance and Enforcement in International Law," p. 537.

83. Personal interview with E. J. M. Ball.

84. *MARPOL 73/78,* Article 4(4).

Since 1975, the average fine imposed by states never has exceeded $7,000 and actually has decreased over time.[85] A Friends of the Earth International study concluded that fines have remained "very low in comparison to the price the vessel would have to pay for using port reception facilities."[86] Even when a large penalty is assessed, the delays between initial violation and final sentencing and the reluctance of most states to detain tankers for minor discharge violations often mean that the responsible tanker and crew have long since left the state's jurisdiction, making fine collection difficult. Owen Lomas points out that the problem is further exacerbated by the fact that "shipowners and their insurers routinely indemnify the masters of their ships against fines imposed upon them for oil pollution."[87]

In place of the discharge subregime's legal system of prosecution, conviction, and fines, the equipment subregime relied on quite different responses to noncompliance. The most immediate sanctions involved the ability of classification societies, insurers, and flag state governments to withhold the classification, insurance, and pollution prevention certificates that a tanker needed to conduct international trade. As John Foxwell put it, tankers "cannot get insurance without certification, and can't get certification without compliance."[88] These sanctions amounted to preventing any illegally equipped tanker from doing business. Even if an owner could devise a means to avoid these direct economic effects, a noncompliant tanker that could not trade to all ports would still bring a far lower price in the large tanker resale market.[89]

Besides these market-based sanctions, the equipment subregime obligated port states either to detain tankers with false pollution prevention certificates or inadequate equipment or to bar them from port.[90] As administrative sanctions, these responses skirted both flag state and port state legal systems—and the associated sensitivities regarding legal sovereignty. Paradoxically, this strategy made port states more likely to use detention and flag states more willing to accept it. Detention also had the virtue that even low usage by a few major oil-importing states forced tanker owners to choose between risking detention and the more costly option of not trading to those lucrative markets. Authorizing developed states to detain violating tankers effectively moved the right to sanction to countries that had far greater domestic political pressures to use it.

Coupling the equipment requirements themselves with these administrative sanctions completely eliminated the legal and evidentiary problems that make

85. Mitchell, "From Paper to Practice," Table 4–5.

86. IMCO/IMO doc. MEPC 29/10/3, 15 January 1990.

87. Owen Lomas, "The Prosecution of Marine Oil Pollution Offences and the Practice of Insuring Against Fines," *Journal of Environmental Law,* vol. 1, no. 1, 1989, p. 54. See also IMCO/IMO doc. MEPC 32/14/3, 17 January 1992.

88. Personal interview with John Foxwell, Shell International Marine, London, 27 June 1991.

89. Bergmeijer, "The International Convention for the Prevention of Pollution from Ships," p. 12.

90. *MARPOL 73/78,* Articles 5(2) and 5(3).

even clear violations of discharge standards difficult to prosecute successfully. Detention imposed opportunity costs on a tanker operator of several thousand dollars per day, and forced retrofitting could cost millions of dollars—far exceeding the fines for discharge violations.[91] Detention had the positive quality that it was not so costly as to be considered a disproportionate response to the crime but was costly enough to deter other violations. In short, detention was simultaneously more likely and more costly.

While many states inspected tankers for compliance with equipment requirements, most have not detained noncompliant ships frequently. IMO records from 1984 to 1990 reveal that seven of fifteen states, including Japan, have detained ships at least once. Only Germany, the United Kingdom, and the United States have detained ships often. This undoubtedly reflects a reluctance on the parts of some states to detain foreign tankers as well as the fact that most tankers were equipped appropriately in the first place.

Although few states detained ships, available evidence supports the conclusion that the subregime altered enforcement behavior. Not one of the states that detained ships began to do so until after MARPOL took effect in 1983.[92] Even the United States waited until that year—ten years after the detention provision had been accepted. Consider the counterfactual: it is unlikely that the United States would have detained tankers for breaching U.S.-only requirements for SBT, even though it had the practical ability to do so. Without MARPOL, such detentions would have constituted a major infringement of flag state sovereignty. If the use of the more costly detention sanction had reflected an exogenous increase in the interests of states in environmental enforcement, fines for discharge violations should have increased at the same time. Yet, as states began to use detention, fines did not increase dramatically.[93] Finally, public goods theory predicts that actors will tend not to enforce rules that supply benefits to other parties.[94] Contrary to theory, however, European states and the United States spend far more on enforcing equipment standards—a public good that improves the global ocean environment—than on enforcing discharge standards off their own coastlines—the benefits of which would be more "private."

The equipment subregime operated not by convincing reluctant actors to enforce rules with which they disagreed but by removing the legal barriers that inhibited effective enforcement by those states and nonstate actors willing to enforce them. Classification societies had interests in ensuring that the tankers they classified were able to trade without fear of detention. The incorporation of equipment requirements into their classification criteria provided the

---

91. Personal interviews with John Foxwell; and with Richard Schiferli, Memorandum of Understanding Secretariat, Rijswijk, The Netherlands, 17 July 1991.

92. Personal interview with Daniel Sheehan.

93. See Peet, *Operational Discharges from Ships,* annex 15; and Dempsey, "Compliance and Enforcement in International Law."

94. Axelrod and Keohane, "Achieving Cooperation Under Anarchy."

foundation for insurers to penalize noncompliant tankers. The willingness of a few environmentally concerned oil-importing states to inhibit tankers that lacked the required equipment from trading freely posed an extremely potent threat to a tanker owner. However, the ability and willingness of these states to threaten this sanction depended on removing international legal barriers to its use. Once these barriers were removed, imposing sanctions involved few costs to those imposing them, whether classification societies, insurers, or port state authorities. It thereby made detention more likely, even though it created no new incentives for states to impose sanctions. In a case of "nothing succeeds like success," the various threats of the equipment subregime's noncompliance system led to initial compliance by almost all tankers, making it rare that sanctions ever needed to be imposed.

Building on existing institutions

The oil pollution control regime induced implementation of those provisions that involved few direct costs to governments. Monitoring and enforcement proved especially likely when their costs were pushed "off-budget" by deputizing private, nonstate actors to issue certificates and conduct inspections. Piggy backing monitoring and enforcement efforts onto existing government programs also has been successful in accomplishing the regime's objectives with only minor program modifications and minimal cost. Governments have tended to ignore or put little effort into those stipulations that require significant new expenditure of government resources.

MARPOL's equipment subregime fostered monitoring by allowing governments to delegate responsibility for surveys to classification societies. This in turn increased the likelihood that tankers would be initially surveyed and subsequently inspected; additionally, the quality of inspections increased. Delegation also helps developing flag states, many of which lack the resources, the practical ability, and the incentives to conduct such inspections. MARPOL allowed such states to fulfill their treaty commitments by assigning classification and inspection responsibilities to actors who often had greater access to and more resources with which to conduct such inspections. Classification societies also had strong incentives to conduct accurate surveys as a means of protecting their business reputations and avoiding problems with insurance companies. The strategy thus simultaneously removed these tasks and the resources they required from the hands of governments and placed them in the hands of actors who could more easily accomplish them. Classification societies already had infrastructures to monitor tanker purchases for safety, financing, and insurance purposes. Adding pollution control to their long inspection checklists required only marginal changes to existing procedures.

The many inspection programs operated by developed port states parallel this pattern. Like classification societies, the maritime authorities of the European memorandum of understanding states, the United States, and other states interested in enforcing the equipment requirements could make simple, low-cost alterations to port state inspections already being conducted for safety, customs, and other purposes. The recent establishment of a Latin American memorandum and current negotiations for an Asian-Pacific memorandum suggest that the equipment subregime has provided states with a low-cost means to implement their international commitments as their interests in enforcement increase. In contrast, where states have had to incur significant new costs to implement treaty provisions, they have proved highly unlikely to do so. Detection of discharge violations required development of completely new surveillance programs. Most developed states have not established large, ongoing surveillance programs. Even in environmentally concerned states, aerial surveillance programs have tended to be relatively small and subject to the vagaries of domestic budget battles.

In the realm of compliance, the tendency for governments to push implementation costs onto nonstate actors is obvious. Compliance with the equipment standards has involved significant costs to tanker owners and no direct costs to governments. Yet, the treaty also required member states to ensure that their ports had facilities to receive the slops that tankers traditionally had discharged overboard. Although developed states have built more reception facilities, ports in the oil-loading states where they are most needed still largely lack any facilities. IMO participants consistently have failed to adopt proposals for developed states to fund reception facilities in developing states. Even in many developed states, facilities are sorely inadequate relative to the demands of their tanker traffic.[95] Additionally, the task of determining which ports have adequate facilities and which do not largely has fallen on the shoulders of nonstate actors.[96] National governments consistently have argued that providing reception facilities is the responsibility of either the ports themselves or of the oil industry.

Coercing compliance rather than deterring violation

The compliance systems of the two subregimes differ most strikingly in the fundamental model underlying their regulatory strategies. The equipment standards subregime relied on a "coerced compliance" strategy, which sought to monitor behavior to prevent violations from occurring in the first place. The discharge standards subregime was deterrence-oriented, attempting to detect, prosecute, and sanction violations after they occurred to deter future violations.[97] This basic difference in orientation made the compliance task facing the

---

95. IMCO/IMO doc. MEPC 30/Inf.32, 12 October 1990.

96. See IMCO/IMO docs. MEPC 19/5/2, 21 October 1983; MEPC 22/8/2, 8 October 1985; and MEPC 30/Inf.30, 15 October 1990.

97. Neither strategy was incentive-based, as was the funding of compliance under the Montreal Protocol and Framework Convention on Climate Change. For development of the distinction between these three strategies, see Albert J. Reiss, Jr., "Consequences of Compliance and Deterrence Models of Law Enforcement for the Exercise of Police Discretion," *Law and Contemporary Problems* 47 (Fall 1984), pp. 83–122; and Keith Hawkins, *Environment and Enforcement: Regulation and the Social Definition of Pollution* (Oxford: Clarendon Press, 1984).

equipment standards subregime more manageable than that facing the discharge standards subregime. The underlying strategy choice had important consequences for the level of compliance achieved: inhibiting the ability to violate treaty provisions proved far more effective than increasing the disincentives for violating them.

MARPOL's equipment standards created a remarkably effective system for detecting and sanctioning violations. Even if this compliance system had relied exclusively on the threat of oil-importing states detecting and detaining noncompliant tankers, most tankers would have installed COW and SBT. However, the equipment subregime's strength really came from the fact that it rarely had to use the more potent sanctions it made possible. Involving shipbuilders, classification societies, and insurers in the regulatory process could well have produced the same outcome even without the additional threat of detention. The subregime relied on surveying behavior and preventing violations rather than detecting and investigating them afterwards.[98] By regulating the business transaction of a tanker purchase rather than the autonomous action of a discharge, the equipment rules allowed identification of potential violators and made it harder to actually commit a violation. Tanker captains faced many regular autonomous decisions about whether to violate discharge standards. In contrast, tanker owners only had to decide once between violating or complying with equipment standards, and their decision required cooperation from other actors and involved major economic consequences. Even before construction began, classification societies and insurance companies were pressing for and monitoring compliance with international standards, helping avert violations before they occurred. Classification societies, insurance companies, and flag state inspectors could withhold the papers necessary to conduct business in international oil markets, thereby frustrating any tanker owner's attempt to reap the benefits of sidestepping these standards.

Experience with the discharge standards had shown that many states would not enforce pollution standards; indeed, even detention was used regularly by only a few states. Given the costs of SBT, if deterrence had been the major source of compliance, one would expect some tankers initially to have violated the equipment standards in an attempt to identify which and how many states actually would enforce the rules. Especially in light of their votes against the requirements, owners might well have assumed less than rigorous enforcement in places like France and Japan. Yet, compliance levels did not follow a pattern of initial noncompliance followed by stiff sanctions and subsequent compliance. The compliance system of the equipment subregime succeeded by effectively restricting the opportunities to violate it rather than making the

---

98. Reiss, "Consequences of Compliance and Deterrence Models of Law Enforcement for the Exercise of Police Discretion."

choice of violation less attractive. The very low noncompliance levels suggest that in most cases an owner simply decided it would be impossible to convince a tanker builder, a classification society, and an insurer to allow the purchase of a tanker without COW and SBT. Likewise, tankers coming in for repairs and maintenance undoubtedly would have found it difficult to explain why they were not planning on installing SBT or COW, as required. The low levels of detected violations of the equipment standards reveal that obstacles to committing a violation played a major role in preventing such violations. New tankers have been built initially to MARPOL standards, not retrofitted later in response to deterrence threats. Even before MARPOL's equipment deadlines passed, owners were building new and retrofitting older tankers to meet the requirements.

The equipment subregime may have been as successful as it was precisely because it produced a redundant regulatory system. It established compliance information and noncompliance response systems that prevented most violations but could successfully deter any actors who might otherwise have considered violating it. As the experience with discharge standards clarifies, deterrence-based strategies often require the successful completion of a complex chain of actions to be effective. The initial discharge standards subregime faced problems at almost every step of the process: detecting violations, identifying violators, prosecuting violators, and imposing potent sanctions. The shift to total discharge standards eliminated or mitigated some of these problems, but the problems remaining left overall deterrent levels essentially unchanged. A tanker captain evaluating the expected costs of violating OILPOL's or MARPOL's discharge standards could only conclude that the magnitude and likelihood of a penalty were quite small. Successful deterrence strategies must ensure that the whole legal chain operates smoothly, since the breakdown of any link can significantly impair its effectiveness.

Conclusions

Nations can design regime rules to improve compliance. This article has demonstrated that, even within a single issue-area, reference to design features of compliance systems surrounding particular provisions is necessary to explain observed variance in compliance. In the regime regulating intentional oil pollution, the same governments and corporations with the same interests during the same time period complied far more frequently with rules requiring installation of expensive equipment than they did with rules limiting total discharges of oil. Where theories of hegemonic power and economic interests fail to explain this variance, differences in the subregime's compliance systems readily explain why the former subregime led powerful actors to comply with it while the latter did not.

The equipment standards elicited significantly higher compliance because they selected a point for regulatory intervention that allowed for greater transparency, increased the likelihood of forceful responses to detected violations, built on existing institutions, and coerced compliance by preventing actors from violating them rather than merely deterring actors from doing so. In any regime, the distribution of state power and interests and the traits of relevant economic sectors constrain, but fail to fully explain, the regulations to which states will agree and the degree of possible compliance. By acknowledging these limits and realizing that the same goal often may be achieved by regulating quite different activities, policymakers can improve compliance by regulating those sectors more vulnerable to pressures for compliance and by facilitating the efforts of those governments and nonstate actors more likely to implement and enforce such regulations. This matching of regulatory burdens to expected behavior places the careful choice of the regime's primary rules at the center of any effective compliance system.

Once such primary rules have been established, careful crafting of the compliance information system and the noncompliance response system can further increase the likelihood of compliance. Oil pollution regulations succeeded by facilitating the goals of, placing responsibilities on, and removing the legal and practical barriers limiting those governments and private actors predisposed to monitor and enforce agreements, not by imposing obligations on recalcitrant actors. Inducing compliance required an integrated system of rules and processes that placed actors within a strategic triangle of compliance so that they had the political and economic incentives, practical ability, and legal authority to perform the tasks necessary to implement the treaty.[99] When such efforts succeeded, governments and private actors acted differently than they would have in the absence of the regime. When such efforts failed, opportunities to increase compliance were missed. We should not expect treaties to achieve perfect compliance.[100] Nevertheless, negotiators can and should design and redesign them to maximize compliance within the constraints that power and interests impose.

Eliciting compliance is only one of the criteria on which we would want to judge a regime's rules. Indeed, the value of compliance itself rests on the assumption that more compliance makes the treaty itself more effective. In the oil pollution case, compliance with the equipment rules involved at least as great a reduction in intentional discharges as did compliance with the discharge standards. Thus, we can safely infer that the higher compliance levels under the former rules also led to increased treaty effectiveness, a fact confirmed by a consensus among most experts that intentional oil discharges have declined since MARPOL took effect.[101] However, I am not arguing here for "command and control" regulations but for considering compliance levels—along with efficiency, cost, and equity—as an important evaluative criteria in regime design. The cheaper, more flexible, and more efficient discharge standards simply failed to induce the level of compliance needed to achieve a socially

99. I am indebted to Robert O. Keohane for the notion of a strategic triangle of compliance.
100. Chayes and Chayes, "On Compliance."
101. See Ronald B. Mitchell, "Intentional Oil Pollution of the Oceans," in Haas, Keohane, and Levy, *Institutions for the Earth,* pp. 183–248.

desired outcome; yet the costs of the equipment standards may have exceeded the benefits of that outcome. In cases in which more efficient solutions elicit compliance sufficient to achieve a policy goal, they are clearly preferable. If expected compliance with such solutions appears low, effective regime design requires evaluating whether the benefits of higher compliance outweigh the expense and inefficiency of alternative solutions.

Can we apply the findings developed from studying these two oil pollution cases to other issue-areas? Initial selection of a difficult collaborative problem with characteristics common to many international collaboration problems provides some confidence that we can do so. Other treaties provide anecdotal support for some of the findings reported herein. Nuclear powers consistently have sought to increase the transparency of arms control treaties through progressively tighter provisions for data exchange and on-site inspections. Although the experience with Iraq provides a dramatic example of failure, the nuclear materials and missile technology control regimes rely primarily on coerced compliance models of regulation, seeking to prevent countries from violation in the first instance. Human rights regimes frequently have used information from nongovernmental organizations to monitor compliance with their provisions. These design features seem likely to be the source of some regime compliance, but confirming that conclusion requires considerably more research. The solutions adopted in the oil pollution regime also undoubtedly cannot be applied to all regimes or even to all environmental regimes. Wildlife and habitat protection, for example, can rarely be achieved through technological solutions or quantitative requirements that can be easily monitored. In other instances, the solutions to new problems will not be able to build on existing infrastructures and institutions. The strategies available to international regulators will depend at least in part on features unique to the problem being addressed. Analysts have already shown how regimes influence behavior in realms involving security.[102] How the impacts of similar compliance systems vary across security, economic, human rights, or environmental regimes remains one of many important future questions.

Whether the nations of the world can collaborate to resolve the many international problems, both environmental and otherwise, that face them will depend not on merely negotiating agreements requiring new behaviors but on ensuring that those agreements succeed in inducing governments, industry, and individuals to adopt those new behaviors. We can hope and work for a day when all nations and their citizens are sufficiently concerned about peace, economic well-being, human rights, and the environment that we will not need international law to criminalize the behavior threatening those values and to dictate more benign behaviors. Until then, however, careful crafting and recrafting of international treaties provides one valuable means of managing the various problems facing the nations of the world.

---

102. See Robert Jervis, "Security Regimes," in Krasner, *International Regimes,* pp. 173–94; and Duffield, "International Regimes and Alliance Behavior."

Inertia and Change in the Constellation of International Governmental Organizations, 1981–1992
Cheryl Shanks, Harold K. Jacobson, and Jeffrey H. Kaplan

No one expects public institutions to die. Max Weber described bureaucracies as "practically indestructible," contending that "History shows that wherever bureaucracy gained the upper hand, as in China, Egypt and, to a lesser extent, in the Roman empire and Byzantium, it did not disappear again unless in the course of the total collapse of the supporting culture."[1] Whereas private organizations, such as charitable institutions and firms, might collapse from apathy or competition, many suppose public bureaucracies to endure indefinitely. An organization's presence itself creates a constituency, and even if institutions' creators no longer need them, they would let the institutions slide into obscurity rather than expend resources in a battle to kill them. As Herbert Kaufman pointed out with regard to U.S. bureaucracies, "Even with an extremely low birth rate, a population of immortals would gradually attain immense proportions."[2] Once established, a governmental organization should cling like a barnacle to its niche.

If this were true, international governmental organizations (IGOs)—metabureaucracies even further removed from citizens' calls for accountability and efficiency—should be even more impervious to change. IGOs are those associations established by governments or their representatives that are sufficiently institutionalized to require regular meetings, rules governing decision making, a permanent staff, and a headquarters. From the Congress of Vienna through the 1990s, the population of IGOs has added new members steadily, occasionally plateauing following periodic organizing bursts. In 1981, there were 1,063 IGOs. In 1992, there were 1,147. Since common wisdom holds

For their helpful comments and criticisms, we thank Christopher Achen, Lars-Erik Cederman, Martha Feldman, Isebill Gruhn, Paul Huth, M. Kent Jennings, A.F.K. Organski, Richard Rockwell, Edith Brown Weiss, and William Zimmerman, and the reviewers for *International Organization*. We thank Elisabeth Bennion for her research assistance.
    1. Weber 1978, 988, 1401.
    2. Kaufman 1976, 1. Kaufman is here characterizing, not advocating, this view.

International Organization 50, 4, Autumn 1996, pp. 593–627
© 1996 by The IO Foundation and the Massachusetts Institute of Technology

that organizations do not die, and the scholarship addressing IGOs shares this assumption, one would conclude that countries created 84 new IGOs in this decade.[3] In fact, however, hundreds of IGOs were born and died during this period. Five main dimensions of change have transformed the web of IGOs—the organizations themselves and states' memberships in them—over the last decade.

First, although the total number of organizations grew and many new organizations were created, a significant number were formally set aside. Many others in effect vanished. Only two-thirds of the IGOs that existed in 1981 were still active in 1992. Although slightly more IGOs were created than were cast off (84 more), both sets of organizations number in the hundreds. IGOs, like the domestic bureaucracies that Kaufman studied, do have a mortality rate, and it can be surprisingly high.

Second, not governments but other IGOs created a huge proportion of these new organizations. Emanations—second-order IGOs created through actions of other IGOs—and traditionally created IGOs are not always of equal weight, but both connect states through an overlay of institutional rules and a commitment to shared goals; and both indicate the same sort of assumed obligation. For this reason, we make no judgments about IGOs' relative importance. The number of traditional IGOs, those established through formal international treaties, decreased in absolute as well as relative terms, declining from 394 in 1981 to 339 in 1992. Emanations increased from 669 to 808, jumping from 64 percent of the IGO population to more than 70 percent. This increase in emanations accounts for the apparent growth at the aggregate level.

Third, organizations created during this decade do not mirror the character-istics of the older organizations. IGOs can be classified along two dimensions: membership criteria and mandated function. Membership in some organiza-tions is open to all states, whereas others limit membership according to criteria such as geography, historical association, or shared purpose. Some organizations have broad general mandates, while others limit themselves to specific functions. The new organizations allocate membership differently from those that were abandoned; as a result, the distribution of organizations by type changed fundamentally, although the proportions of IGOs dedicated to a variety of functions did not.

Fourth, states have changed their connections to IGOs. While some have increased the number of their IGO memberships, for others, memberships in IGOs actually declined. The result is a growing polarization between powerful countries—dominated by the literate, wealthy, and democratic—that establish and control IGOs and countries whose populations and governments are badly off and increasingly disengaged from international organizations.

---

3. For examples of studies that incorporate this assumption (but that fail to note the mortality rate of IGOs), see Wallace and Singer 1970; Russett and Starr 1985; Hughes 1993; and Jacobson, Reisinger, and Mathers 1986.

Fifth, IGOs are no longer found primarily in competitive sets, with each geopolitical bloc having its own institutions. The end of the cold war explains part of this change, accounting for about one-eighth of IGO deaths, but it does not explain the changing distribution of organizations by mode of creation, membership, or function. Developing countries' regional strategies also have largely failed. This factor, combined with the end of the cold war, has meant the elimination of a set of IGOs that existed as an alternative to the West. States' resource capacities now better explain the pattern of countries' memberships in IGOs; in addition, more recently formed IGOs are more likely to have purposes that most countries could share.

In order to understand what these changes mean and who or what drives them, we first must describe what the IGO world looked like in 1981 and in 1992 and then assess possible sources of any changes we see. At issue is who determines which institutions will tie governments and their populations together. One source is the IGO population itself. Like biological populations, organizational populations acquire dynamic properties affecting their development; these are related to, but not entirely dependent on, their environments.[4] Another possible source of change lies within the group of states that funds and officially directs the IGOs. Following the series of descriptions, we turn to what influences countries' membership levels in IGOs and assess the degree to which changes in membership account for the different number and types of IGOs present in 1981 and 1992. The analysis concludes by considering two distinct but related questions about the relation between states and IGOs: we examine how countries affect the IGO population and how the IGO population in turn affects the choices that countries make about institutionalizing cooperation. The web of international organizations maps areas in which governments are committed to take others' interests into account. Changes in the web of IGOs reflect struggles about what sorts of governmental decisions will be limited in this way and which states will be bound to such limitations. We concentrate solely on whether IGOs and state memberships exist or do not exist. In this way the picture we present below is less a survey of public opinion, which asks what people think, than a census, which asks how many people are alive to form opinions in the first place. Like a census, we do not differentiate between the weak and the strong.

Data collection and coding rules

The Union of International Associations (UIA) tracks IGOs annually, relying on a variety of reporting mechanisms to create the most comprehensive and reliable catalog of the world's international organizations. Our data set de-

---

4. The organizational ecology literature on which we have depended most heavily includes Hannan and Freeman 1989; Pfeffer 1982; and Scott 1992.

TABLE 1. *Comparison of the UIA data set with our own (SJK) data set, by alphabetic code*

	A	B	C	D	E	F	G	Missing[a]	Total
1981									
UIA	1	31	50	255	384	278	40	0	1,039
SJK	1	35	51	267	359	227	28	95	1,063
1992									
UIA	1	34	36	215	719	633	52	0	1,690
SJK	1	35	48	245	440	315	4	59	1,147

[a]Missing codes are those for which the Union of International Associations (UIA) did not supply a category between A and G.
Source. UIA data are based on UIA 1982; and 1993.

rives from the UIA's *Yearbook of International Organizations.*[5] Because the presence or absence of an IGO's necessary characteristics is not always clear—for example, the Group of 7 meets regularly to discuss common problems researched by large staffs but does not have a headquarters—and an organization's autonomy is also at times ambiguous, rather than define and hold to an intricate rule of inclusion, the UIA's policy has been to include "many bodies which may be perceived, according to narrower definitions, as not being fully international or as not being of sufficient significance to merit inclusion. Such bodies are nevertheless included, so as to enable users to make their own evaluation in the light of their own criteria."[6] Because the UIA has become more inclusive over the past decade, the number of IGOs it lists in its 1992 yearbook deviates noticeably from our more conservative estimate.

Our rules for inclusion are more restrictive than those of the UIA. This usually results in smaller IGO totals, though for two categories our figures exceed those of the UIA. Information about the IGOs listed in the yearbooks was coded into exhaustive and mutually exclusive categories. An IGO was either traditional or an emanation; allocated membership either universally or by geography or function; and saw its purpose either as general or as primarily political/military, economic, or social. As Table 1 shows, the degree to which our data depart from the comprehensive list offered by the UIA increases as the organizations in question become further removed from the states that establish them. Traditional organizations, those established by governments

5. The four data sets that we created for this analysis have been deposited with the Inter-university Consortium for Political and Social Research, Institute for Social Research, University of Michigan 48106–1248. They are entitled "International Governmental Organizations 1981: Memberships and Characteristics," "International Governmental Organizations 1992: Memberships and Characteristics," "Countries and Territories 1981: IGO Memberships and Characteristics," and "Countries and Territories 1992: IGO Memberships and Characteristics."
6. UIA 1993, viii.

through treaties, have UIA alphabetic codes A through D, and G. Type A organizations are federations of international organizations, of which the only IGO is the United Nations (UN). Type B have "widespread, geographically balanced membership and management."[7] Examples include the World Health Organization and Interpol. Type C organizations include countries in more than one geographical area but concentrate their membership in one area. Type D organizations are clearly regional IGOs. The UIA lists type G organizations as "internationally oriented national organizations as well as bilateral intergovernmental bodies."[8] We include only bilateral IGOs, thus reducing drastically the number of type G IGOs in our data set. The number of IGOs in this set of classifications departs substantially from the first UIA count only in the case of this last set of organizations. The four that we included are bilateral IGOs, such as the Mano River Union.

More ambiguity lies in the case of emanations' autonomous existence, so it is not surprising that here we have selected a more limited set of IGOs than the UIA offered for inspection. Eligible were those that the UIA categorized as type E or type F. The UIA lists organizations as type E if they can "be considered an 'emanation' of a particular organization, place, or person." Indications of this criterion include having another IGO's name in its title, having been created by a provision in another IGO's charter, being a joint- or inter-IGO committee, or being an "international centre or institute." Type F organizations are those of special form, including foundations, funds, news agencies, laboratories, libraries, banks, and courts.[9] Our coding rule in all cases was to include an organization only if its members were listed as governments. The effect was to eliminate the many organizations whose members are state banks, public libraries, hospitals, or other nongovernmental entities.

Data on organizational deaths are also derived from the UIA yearbook, which indicates in small type which organizations are defunct or inactive. Because the UIA assigns each organization a unique code number (beginning with the alphabetic code described above, followed by a four-digit identity tag), we were able to follow organizations that changed their names from one year to the next. These codes, rather than English alphabetical listings, were our main form of identification.

Since we used the same coding rules (and coders) to create the 1981 and 1992 data sets, bias appears not in interyear comparisons but in our tendency to understate the number and proportion of emanations relative to traditional IGOs. We have not systematically analyzed the borderline organizations we have excluded, but they most probably are not randomly distributed. Instead they are likely to be associated with one or another parent IGO or regional grouping. For example, European Community organizations are unlikely to

---

7. The definition is quoted from UIA 1981, title page to section B.
8. The type G definition is quoted from ibid., title page to section G.
9. Ibid., title pages to sections E and F, respectively.

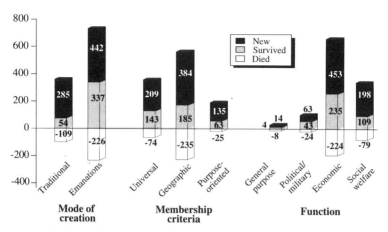

FIGURE 1. *The fate of international governmental organizations by type, 1981–92*

present the UIA with unclear descriptions and so are unlikely to be inaccurately represented in our data set.

Four snapshots of the IGO population

Aggregate change over time within the IGO population, and between states and this population, results from several trends that occur at different rates and sometimes even move in different directions. To understand the dynamics within the population, we must first disentangle the individual trends that produced the aggregate results sketched above. Figure 1 illustrates the fate of IGOs by type from 1981 to 1992. In the figure, the bars above the *x*-axis represent the IGO population in 1992. This includes those IGOs that survived from 1981 and those that were created between 1981 and 1992. The bars below the *x*-axis show those IGOs that ceased activity during the decade. Below, we examine the trends depicted in the figure.

Number and turnover

From the early 1800s until the late 1970s, the number of IGOs increased regularly. For example, from approximately 30 in 1910, the population grew to almost 70 in 1940 and then expanded to the more than 1,000 we saw in 1980. The birthrate peaked in the mid-1970s, remained high until the early 1980s, and has steadily declined since. A declining birthrate itself will not decrease the population but will simply slow its growth; it is in combination with the decade's mortality rate that this slowing birthrate allows overall stability in the size of the IGO population.

Although more IGOs existed in 1992 than in 1981, this stability of the IGO population hides turbulence and fluidity. Of the 1981 population of 1,063 IGOs, only 728 (or 68 percent) survived, while 335 (or 32 percent) died—they either disappeared, were reabsorbed by their parent bodies as committees, or ceased to be active. By 1992, another 391 IGOs had been created (that is, were made autonomous by IGOs or were established by states), bringing the population total back up to 1,147.[10] Given bureaucracies' reputation for permanence, the death rate during this decade is striking. In his study of American federal bureaucracies, Kaufman found that 62 percent of agencies in existence in 1923 were still present in 1973; 38 percent had died.[11] Since his study covered half a century, the population of IGOs appears to be more fluid than that of national bureaucracies.

If births and deaths were distributed evenly across population categories, mortality would not affect the balance among types of IGOs. From 1981 to 1992, however, various categories of organizations had different fates. The following sections elaborate the impact of birth- and death rates on the proportions of organizations along three dimensions: mode of creation, membership criteria, and function.

Mode of creation

Most international organizations are no longer created by states. In fact, those that governments establish by treaty have been in the minority since sometime before World War I.[12] Currently, most IGOs are created by other IGOs. The Food and Agriculture Organization, for example, spawned the European Commission on Agriculture as well as about twenty other agencies; the European Commission on Agriculture then created its own spin-off IGOs. In 1992, emanations comprised more than 70 percent of the IGO population; of these, almost 25 percent were third-, fourth-, or fifth-generation IGOs; that is, they were themselves created by emanations or even emanations of emana-tions. States become members of such organizations by passive assent simply by virtue of their membership in the parent organization.

Traditional organizations are difficult to create but once established, are tenacious; emanations, in contrast, are much easier to create and somewhat easier to kill off. In the 1980s, traditional IGOs died at a lower rate than did emanations (28 versus 34 percent), and traditional IGOs comprised a smaller proportion of newly created organizations than did emanations (14 versus 86 percent). Emanations, at the outset more numerous than traditional organiza-tions (63 versus 37 percent), became an even larger component of the IGO web

10. We have assumed that the 29 IGOs for which no information about creation was available were founded between 1981 and 1992, bringing the number of new IGOs to 420.

11. Kaufman 1976, 34.

12. The UIA did not characterize IGOs as traditional versus emanations before the 1920s. We guess that emanations exceeded traditional IGOs at about the turn of the century.

(70 percent). In statistical terms, these trends are unlikely to be due to chance.[13] Traditional IGOs had more staying power than did emanations but were relatively rare among the batch of new IGOs. They died at a lower rate than did emanations and were born at about one-fifth the emanation birthrate.[14] Traditional organizations constitute a relatively stable core within the IGO population, while emanations come and go rapidly, comprising a fluid and rapidly enlarging periphery.

The numerical dominance of emanations has consequences for member states. First, since emanations emerge from decisions that IGOs take via their normal decision-making channels rather than through the classic procedures of international treaty making, the most powerful states wield less influence over the evolution of IGOs than they would were all IGOs created by traditional means. Because their assent can be crucial to a treaty's creation, powerful states have greater influence in the treaty-making process than they do within international institutions, where they are subject to procedural rules that can limit their influence. Second, although decisions made within IGOs involve government representatives, they also grant a voice to international administrative staff and nongovernmental organizations, thus giving new and different actors a role. Through a web of emanations a country can represent its interests broadly and become eligible for an array of institutional resources, but individually it has little control over the package of subsidiary agencies to which it belongs and what those agencies do. The United States, for example, argued against the creation of the United Nations Industrial Development Organization (UNIDO). When that organization was launched anyway, the United States had to decide how best to manage it. Secretariats and representative staffs, often those of the most powerful states, now create new IGOs; home governments then decide whether to refuse membership.

Membership criteria and function

Organizational membership and function are interrelated. All IGOs can be separated into three categories: those whose membership is open to all (i.e., is potentially universal), those that limit membership to countries of a given region (or history), and those that restrict membership to states sharing a narrow purpose. In the universal category are the UN and the agencies that comprise the UN system. The highest-profile regional organizations are the European Union, the Organization of American States, and the Organization of African Unity; the best-known historical associations are those of the Commonwealth and the Francophone countries. Organizations limiting membership to those sharing a purpose include the Organization of Coffee-

---

13. Comparing the survival rates of 1981 IGOs generates a chi-square of 4.4 ($p = 0.036$); comparing the creation rates by 1992 yields a chi-square of 77.6 ($p = 0.000$).
14. Based on data from UIA 1993, appendix 6, 1668–72.

Exporting Countries and the Secretariat of the Convention on International Trade in Endangered Species. An IGO's membership criteria therefore reflect both what the IGO wants to do and whom it wants to involve or exclude. Functions to which IGOs devote their primary energies fall into four categories: political/military; economic; social welfare and human rights; or general purpose. Some parts of the population are reproducing at high rates while others reproduce at or below replacement levels.

Membership criteria. The distribution of IGOs among the three types of memberships shifted during the 1980s. In 1981, almost 60 percent of IGOs limited membership according to geography, while slightly more than 20 percent were open to all and 15 percent limited membership by purpose. While geographically defined IGOs still comprised the largest category in 1992, constituting 51 percent of the total, both universal and purpose-based IGOs had grown at their expense. Universal organizations accounted for 32 percent of the total and organizations defined by purpose, 18 percent. (Although traditional organizations survived at a higher rate than did emanations, their distribution among these membership categories is similar to that of emanations.) This shift in the balance among membership types is a consequence of two mutually reinforcing trends: survival and birthrate.

During the 1980s, 84 percent of organizations that restricted their membership by purpose survived as did 74 percent of universal organizations, but only 62 percent of IGOs restricting membership by geography survived. New organizations continued to favor geography, but they did so at a lower rate than in the past. Of the 391 new organizations, less than half were geographically defined, while 37 percent were universal and 16 percent were defined by purpose.[15]

This produced an IGO population more evenly distributed across membership categories. Geography has weakened as a basis for institutional collaboration, while shared purpose (whether of inherently limited appeal or not) has strengthened. A common goal has apparently become a stronger force for institutional collaboration than a common border.

Function. In contrast, the distribution according to mandated function barely changed during the decade. In 1981, 64 percent of IGOs were dedicated to economic tasks, with 26 percent engaged in social welfare activities and only 8 percent committed to political and military functions; general-purpose organizations made up 2 percent of the total. Organizations in all categories died at about the same rate, one-third. New organizations also grew at about the same rate across the four categories. The result is a slight change in the distribution by 1992: 61 percent of IGOs were economic, 28 percent social, 10

---

15. Comparing the survival rates of 1981 IGOs generates a chi-square of 34.4 ($p = 0.000$), while comparing rates of creation by membership generates a chi-square of 7.5 ($p = 0.023$).

percent political, and 2 percent general purpose. The change is without significance statistically, although the lack of decrease in political and military institutions runs counter to post–cold war expectations.

Bloc politics and IGO families

While quite a few IGOs are loners, having no constitutional or historical ties to any other organization, most belong to one of several prominent organizational families. The UN family includes its major organs, its specialized agencies, and their emanations, all with historical and legal ties to the UN; the Atlantic alliance includes the North Atlantic Treaty Organization (NATO) and the Organization for Economic Cooperation and Development; the regional families include all those IGOs that set membership criteria within continental limits. The African family, for example, includes the Organization for African Unity and its subsidiaries as well as the Economic Community for West African States, and so on. Fourteen major families encompassed 86 percent of IGOs in 1981 and 82 percent in 1992.

Table 2 lists the major IGO families in 1981 and 1992 and traces each family's birth-, death-, and survival rates between these two points in time. The classifications are strictly for IGOs, not for states. For example, "Arab" includes the League of Arab States and Islamic cultural organizations as well as regional Middle East IGOs; any given Arab country might belong to none or all of these institutions. In other words, the membership of individual states cannot be deduced from these family patterns.

Table 2 reveals a few important patterns. The two IGO families with notably higher survival rates than others, the Commonwealth and the American IGOs, are those organized around a single powerful state. Both discarded few of their components and replaced them with at least as many. Because these families grew very little, they comprised a slightly smaller proportion of the total IGO population at the end of the decade under study, but they demonstrated an organizational conservatism and tenacity unmatched by other sets of IGOs.

Combining a tenacity close to this with a more energetic approach to organizational change is the UN family. This family's powerful and dramatic increase is another striking change among IGO families during the 1980s. Although it discarded or demoted a quarter of its affiliates in the decade after 1981, it added more than twice this many. As a result, the UN family was one hundred members—one-third—larger by 1991. This increase also boosted the degree to which the UN dominated the IGO population as a whole. Its share of all international governmental organizations climbed from 27 to 35 percent in these eleven years.

Organizations without any family identification comprise not only the next-largest share of the IGO population but also the only other segment to increase. Loner organizations often dedicate themselves to accomplishing narrow tasks. For example, the International Tin Council, established in 1956,

TABLE 2. *Fate of IGOs by family, 1981 to 1992*[a]

Family	1981	Died (percentage of 1981 total)	Survived	New (percentage of 1992 total)	1992
Atlantic alliance	26	7 (26.9)	19	5 (20.8)	24
Benelux	4	1 (25.0)	3	0 (0.0)	3
Council of Europe	18	7 (38.9)	11	5 (31.3)	16
European Union	41	10 (24.4)	31	11 (26.2)	42
Nordic Council	63	24 (38.1)	39	13 (25.0)	52
Eastern bloc	56	48 (85.7)	8	1 (11.1)	9
American regional	119	25 (21.0)	94	32 (25.4)	126
Commonweath	30	6 (20.0)	24	6 (20.0)	30
African regional	109	32 (29.4)	77	16 (17.2)	93
Arab regional[b]	87	44 (50.6)	43	34 (44.2)	77
Asian regional	46	19 (41.3)	27	18 (40.0)	45
Nonaligned	6	2 (33.3)	4	3 (42.8)	7
United Nations	282	73 (25.9)	209	173 (45.3)	382
Bretton Woods	15	3 (20.0)	12	3 (20.0)	15
Independent	147	31 (21.1)	116	88 (43.1)	204
Missing data	14	4	10	12	22
Total	1,063	336 (31.6)	727	420 (35.6)	1,147

[a]The death rate from 1981 to 1992 (comparing columns 2 and 3) generates a chi-square of 116.3 ($p = 0.0$); the creation rate to 1992 (comparing columns 3 and 4) generates a chi-square of 56.93 ($p < .001$).
[b]These figures include Islamic cultural and political organizations.

represents government interests in the tin market. Such unaffiliated IGOs numbered 57 more in 1992 than they did in 1981; like the UN, this is a full third larger than earlier, an increase that brings it from 14 to 18 percent of the population. By 1992, the UN and the unaffiliated organizations together accounted for over half of all IGOs.

A final major development among IGO families during this decade is the decreasing number as well as proportion of organizations dedicated to regional integration. Whether this is due to increasing efficiency resulting in consolidation or to apathy and abandonment, the numbers have decreased across the board.

As a set, the Western IGO families have consolidated. By 1992, the total number of organizations linked with the Atlantic alliance, the European Union, and the Council of Europe had contracted less than 4 percent. The organizations that each family shed were replaced with others. In contrast, the Nordic Council family declined by 17 percent prior to the Nordic states' votes on membership in the European Union.

Organizations devoted to sparking and maintaining regional cooperation among developing countries have not fared as well over the past decade. Deep differences in capacity among the regional groupings explain their different fates. The decline in the Asian family of IGOs was almost imperceptible; Asian organizations are more like European IGOs than like those of the developing world. Asian IGOs help to integrate a region with the two largest and most steadily growing developing countries, China and India. The region also contains Indonesia, Pakistan, and the "Four Tigers," as well as Japan. Each of these countries has combined a regional trading strategy with integration into the global system.

By contrast, Africa is home to the poorest and politically least stable countries. From 1980 to 1992, 20 of the 29 African countries for which the World Bank had economic data had negative per capita gross national product (GNP) growth rates, and an additional three were at zero.[16] The African IGO family, at one time the most extensive and ambitious, shed 32 and added only 16 organizations, reducing its total by 15 percent, from 109 to 93.

Political rather than economic problems plague the Arab countries. Many are struggling against severe political and religious challenges that have polarized society. This family of organizations is in turmoil, having lost over half its members in this decade. By 1992 it gained back 34 additional organizations, for a net decrease of 10 percent. Unlike other IGO families, the losses as well as increases were high. Taken together, southern regional IGO families fell from 23 to 19 percent of all IGOs, with the entire drop coming from the African and Arab organizational families.

Most dramatically, the Eastern bloc dis-organized with no intention of resuscitating itself. Over the last two or three years of the decade under study, five out of every six Eastern bloc IGOs had vanished. Alone, this family had constituted 5 percent of all IGOs; by 1992 the remnants accounted for under 1 percent.

The ensemble of changes in the IGO population: summary

The typical international governmental organization in 1992 was, like its predecessor in 1981, either an emanation or geographically based or economic

---

16. World Bank 1994, 162–63.

in function—or all three. Yet only emanations grew proportionately, while geographical and economic organizations shrank as a percentage of IGOs, due to the collapse of the Eastern bloc and to economic and political disorganization in much of the developing world.

Five snapshots of countries' memberships in IGOs

During the 1980s, not only did the IGO population change but also countries altered their involvements with international organizations. This change is both conceptually and practically distinct from that within the IGO population. Countries can join or leave IGOs without causing organizations' demise or changing the IGO population in any way. Some countries joined many more organizations, while others not only refrained from accepting membership in new IGOs but also disengaged themselves from many of those to which they had belonged.

While dramatic divorces from an international organization, such as the departures of the United Kingdom, the United States, and Singapore from the UN Educational, Scientific, and Cultural Organization or New Zealand's termination of its connection to the ANZUS alliance, remain rare, countries often alter their connections to IGOs. Countries acquire, and can slough, memberships actively; they can also increase or decrease IGO memberships passively by remaining in an organization that creates its own IGOs or by allowing organizations to which they belong to cease functioning altogether.

Number and turnover

Statistics on membership present a paradox. The number of traditional organizations declined and emanations grew, but, on average, memberships in traditional organizations actually rose, from 33.4 per country in 1981 to 44.2 in 1992. This is true even while overall memberships declined by 12 percent, from 199.5 to 187.9 per country. Fewer traditional organizations each had more members, and more emanations each had fewer members.

Memberships in IGOs changed during this decade for various categories of states, defined by simple economic and political characteristics.[17] Literacy, too, should be related to a country's propensity to join IGOs. Literacy rates directly measure the proportion of the population that has reached a threshold level allowing it knowledge of state policy and thus potential access to the political system. According to some variants of functionalist theory, an activist population helps to drive governments toward membership in IGOs. Literacy can, moreover, be a proxy for educational socialization and hence for the distribu-

---

17. Jacobson, Reisinger, and Mathers 1986.

tion of values within a country. We examine literacy first and then assess the influence of economic and political characteristics.

Literacy

We can examine the relation between literacy and the level of (and change in) IGO memberships by dividing established states into three categories, defined modally with respect to their levels of adult literacy: high (approximately the top 20 percent of states), low (approximately the bottom 20 percent of states), and medium (the 60 percent of states in the middle).[18] The top 26 states clustered above the 99 percent level for adult literacy, while the lowest 34 states had literacy levels ranging from 18 to 49 percent. The majority of states, the 102 countries that make up the intermediate category, had literacy levels of 50 to 98 percent. In 1992, the average state's literacy level was 71.5 percent.

Literacy affects IGO memberships only at the highest level. States with the most literate populations held memberships in 254.3 IGOs; states with moderate levels, 200.1 IGOs; and states with the lowest levels, 201.0 IGOs. More impressively, between 1981 and 1992 the average IGO memberships of states in the highest category increased by 18.6, while those of states in the medium and lowest categories decreased by 3.3 and 5.7, respectively.

Aggregate and per capita income

Countries were grouped into income categories by both their aggregate and their per capita gross domestic product (GDP). With respect to each dimension, we again divided states into three categories: high and low, defined as the upper and lower 20 percent, respectively; and medium, defined as the middle 60 percent. Table 3 shows the average number of IGO memberships for states in our six categories. Column (1) shows states classified by their 1981 ranking. Columns (2) through (4) show states classified by their 1992 rankings. As can be seen from columns (1) and (4), in both years states in the higher-income categories had more IGO memberships than those in the lower categories, and they increased their average number of memberships. States in the lower categories had fewer memberships in both years, and these states decreased their average number of memberships during the decade. Column (2), which lists the average number of IGO memberships in 1992 and in 1981 held by the same states, demonstrates that these changes are not artifacts of states moving among the three categories or of the merger and birth of states. Column (3)

18. When the number of countries in the top 20 and bottom 20 percent do not match, this is because a large number of states clump at an identical level. For example, if ten countries were at 99 percent literacy and thirty countries were at 98 percent literacy, a line separating 98 percent countries into different categories would be pointless. The line has therefore been set as close to the 20 percent figure as possible without arbitrarily dividing states. This is true for income and freedom levels as well as for literacy.

TABLE 3. *Mean level of intergovernmental organization (IGO) membership by income category in 1981 and 1992*

	(1) 1981 mean of all states (N)	*(2)* 1992 mean of established states[a] (N)	*(3)* 1992 mean of new states (N)	*(4)* 1992 mean of all states (N)
Aggregate GDP				
High	251.5 (26)[b]	1992: 283.8 1981: 251.6 (24)	204.0 (1)	280.6 (25)
Medium	220.0 (106)	1992: 207.2 1981: 214.5 (119)	76.8 (12)	195.3 (131)
Low	158.9 (26)	1992: 114.1 1981: 110.1 (16)	85.7 (3)	109.6 (19)
GDP per capita				
High	259.3 (24)	1992: 291.9 1981: 270.3 (23)	—	291.9 (23)
Medium	210.8 (111)	1992: 198.5 1981: 200.0 (110)	86.4 (16)	184.0 (124)
Low	190.4 (23)	1992: 189.5 1981: 203.6 (27)	—	189.5 (27)

[a]1981 membership information provides a way to determine how much of the difference between the 1981 and 1992 figures is due to the population change in each category as states' income changed and how much to individual states adding or dropping their IGO memberships. The 1981 figure is for the states that were in a given category in 1992.

Sources. Gross domestic product (GDP) categories are based on absolute figures in *World Almanac and Book of Facts* for 1982 and 1993 (New York: Ballantine, 1981 and 1992, respectively). We defined high and low modally, as the endmost (approximately) 20 percent, and medium as the middle 60 percent.

lists the average number of IGO memberships in 1992 of states created between 1981 and 1992.

Between 1981 and 1992, states with the largest aggregate GDP and the highest per capita GDP became more enmeshed in the IGO network, while those with a smaller aggregate GDP and lower per capita GDP drifted toward the network's periphery. Although countries in the different income categories behaved differently with respect to their total IGO memberships, they were fairly similar in their relationships to traditional IGOs, with states in each category increasing their average memberships in them. The numbers reported in Table 3 include this increase, so the decreases are entirely within the population of emanations. The pattern of change by per capita income category is, however, the same for traditional and emanating IGOs.

TABLE 4. *Mean level of state memberships in intergovernmental organizations (IGOs) by level of political and civil freedom in 1981 and 1992*[a]

	(1) 1981 mean of all states *(N)*	*(2)* 1992 mean of established states[b] *(N)*	*(3)* 1992 mean of new states *(N)*	*(4)* 1992 mean of all states *(N)*
Level of openness				
Free	220.8 (54)	1992: 228.7 1981: 220.6 (66)	99.3 (8)	214.7 (74)
Partly	205.0 (47)	1992: 202.1 1981: 202.2 (59)	46.3 (13)	174.0 (72)
Unfree	199.9 (60)	1992: 188.7 1981: 193.2 (33)	41.2 (5)	169.3 (38)
Change in openness				
Improve	—	1992: 187.9 1981: 199.2 (44)	47.2 (15)	152.2 (59)
No change	—	1992: 221.1 1981: 216.4 (99)	51.9 (7)	210.0 (106)
Worsen	—	1992: 214.6 1981: 206.4 (44)	160.0 (1)	211.0 (15)

[a]Numbers of old and new states do not add across categories because some states unified and others switched categories. When the numbers add to less than the number of sovereign countries (172 in 1981 and 186 in 1992), this is due to missing data.

[b]1981 membership information provides a way to determine how much of the difference between 1981 and 1992 is due to a shift in the population of states in each category as states' freedom categories changed, and how much to individual states adding or dropping their IGO memberships. The 1981 figure is for the states that were in a given category in 1992.

Sources. The classification of degrees of freedom and descriptions of each state's level of openness are from Freedom House's annual survey, *Freedom at Issue* (January/February) 1982 and 1993.

Democracy and democratization

Freedom House describes itself as "a nonpartisan national organization devoted to the strengthening of free societies."[19] It classifies states as "free," "partly free," and "unfree," providing a convenient mechanism for examining the relationship between political openness and IGO memberships. Columns (1) and (4) in Table 4 show average number of IGO memberships for states in each category in 1981 and 1992. Column (2) shows the 1981 average for states that were still in existence in 1992, and column (3), the average for new states.

19. Freedom House, New York, N.Y.

In both years free states belonged on average to more IGOs than those that were partly free or unfree. Controlling for the dampening effect that new states have on the average, free and partly free states belonged to more IGOs and unfree states to fewer than they had a decade earlier. By 1992, unfree states held significantly fewer IGO memberships than those in the other two categories. Since some states switched categories, these data do not allow us to draw conclusions about any single state's memberships.

The distribution across categories for traditional IGOs is consistent with what we see for all IGOs, though the differences among free, partly free, and unfree states' memberships in traditional organizations are more pronounced. Not shown in the table is free countries' extraordinary propensity to join traditional IGOs. The new, free countries joined traditional IGOs at three times the rate of other countries, although older countries' memberships in all IGOs was higher by an order of two. The difference indicates the buffer effect that emanations have on all states' memberships.

Given that free countries have higher IGO membership levels, one might expect democratizing countries to increase their IGO memberships. The table divides states into three categories: those that became more democratic, such as Brazil and Czechoslovakia; those that remained what they were, whether democratic or not, such as France and Cambodia; and those that became less democratic, such as Colombia and India. (The set of countries considered here excludes those that became independent during the 1980s and hence have no clear starting point.) Democratizing entails moving to a higher Freedom House category and therefore captures only major changes. In 1981, those that were to become clearly more democratic belonged to an average of 199.2 IGOs; this declined to 187.9 by 1992. Those whose status did not change belonged to 216.4 IGOs in 1981 and 221.1 in 1992. Countries that worsened throughout this decade started with an average of 206.4 memberships but by 1992 belonged on average to 214.6. Democratization decreased membership by 11.2 percent; states whose status did not change increased their memberships by 3.4 percent. Those whose status worsened increased memberships by 8.3 percent. This pattern holds whether considering traditional IGOs or emanations. The lower portion of Table 4 outlines the relation between democratization and change in IGO memberships.

Contrary to liberal expectations, democratizing countries reduced their memberships—but contrary to the assumptions underlying the liberal view, many of the IGOs to which these countries had been committed were elite alliances rather than institutions tying together populations. Of the 44 states that became more democratic, 16 were involved in one way or another in the former Eastern bloc. For the rest, democratization in the short run indicated fundamental instability. During the transition when countries must concentrate on their internal problems, IGOs may not be of central concern. Among the more established countries that moved toward democracy, such as Argentina, Bolivia, Brazil, Chile, the Republic of Korea, Pakistan, and

TABLE 5. *Polarization of memberships in intergovernmental organizations, 1981 to 1982*

Enthusiasts	Change	Dropouts	Change
St. Kitts and Nevis (1983)	+135	Cambodia	−76
Spain	+104	Albania	−74
France	+80	Mongolia	−70
Egypt	+68	Laos	−63
South Korea·	+66	Romania	−59
Lithuania (1990)	+61	Afghanistan	−48
China	+53	Singapore	−43
Japan	+51	Vietnam	−33
Switzerland	+51	South Africa	−30
Portugal	+46	Myanmar	−30

Uruguay, an increase in IGO memberships accompanied the transition. Russia and several of the former Soviet republics also moved quickly to join IGOs. Worsening states, which should have experienced instability similar to that of the democratizing countries, also joined IGOs.

Because we have not made judgments about which IGOs serve the populations' goals and which have only elite support, we are unable to do more than speculate about reasons for this increasing membership. Apparently, nondemocratic countries that join IGOs do so when IGO goals coincide with those of the regime; when they no longer do, the government sheds its membership by withdrawing or, more likely, by refusing money and personnel. Democratization has meant the ability to shed memberships in bloc alliances, to distance one's country from those IGOs that had upheld an unpopular order. Some states may have deferred the decision to join alternative organizations, thus explaining lost memberships.

Pariahs and the powerful

To this point we have considered countries as if the number of IGOs to which they belonged were susceptible only to their capacities and wills. In fact, countries are pressured into and out of joining international organizations by allies and enemies. Tables 5 and 6 illustrate this most clearly. Table 5 lists the most and least involved countries by the extent of change in their IGO memberships; Table 6 lists countries by the number of IGOs to which each belongs.

The ten countries that dropped out of the most IGOs isolated themselves or were isolated by others. Among these ten are countries that are or were engaged in frighteningly successful or harshly unsuccessful attempts to impose an ideologically or racially pure social order on a predominantly rural agricultural population. The end of the cold war created pariahs of the

TABLE 6. *Gap between intergovernmental organization (IGO) membership among countries in 1992*[a]

Most integrated	No. of IGO memberships	Least integrated	No. of IGO memberships
France	441	Taiwan	14
United Kingdom	396	Liechtenstein	81
Germany	392	North Korea	100
Netherlands	375	Maldives	125
Denmark	373	Mozambique	146
Italy	371	Angola	147
Spain	360	Nepal	147
Belgium	351	Swaziland	156
Sweden	344	Israel	159
Norway	340	Rwanda	166

[a]None of the countries is either very tiny or very new.

communist states that did not follow the others in reform. Indigenous communist ruling parties such as the Khmer Rouge steadily disengaged from the IGO web throughout the 1980s, as they sought to distance themselves both from the West and from the reformers of the old Eastern bloc. Some countries sustained by the East–West rivalry have in addition been thrown into domestic turmoil and find themselves unable to maintain connections to IGOs.

Some of the countries that withdrew from international organizations chose to do so, while others were pushed to withdraw. If not so consumed by war or famine that they were incapable of formulating any policy toward IGOs, they were excluded from the system—boycotted unilaterally or sanctioned through the UN. Their reduced memberships signal both their failure to support IGOs and IGOs' failure to work for them. In early 1994, Freedom House noted "a new polarization" between the free regimes and those repressive regimes that withdrew from international networks prior to 1992.[20]

States that increased their memberships during the 1980s were typically either the most powerful or those pointedly seeking inclusion in international society.[21] These memberships were votes in favor of the IGOs and what they represent. The gaps are somewhat wider for traditional memberships (not indicated in Table 5) than for emanations, so we can hypothesize both that the better off a country is, the more likely it is to acquiesce in organizational extensions and the more likely it is to take action to tie its fate, in some institutional area, to that of others.

The second part of Table 5 presents a familiar pattern. Those states that have the densest connections with IGOs are all in Western Europe, where the

20. Karatnycky 1994.
21. This obviously excludes the newly independent, which, since they had no memberships before, automatically increased their participation at a high rate.

Westphalian system began. They are all prosperous and democratic. None has a population of more than one hundred million. Least involved in the IGO web are states that have for one reason or another suffered the opprobrium of the international community (Israel, North Korea, Taiwan); five African states that are newer and economically and politically troubled (Angola, the Maldives, Mozambique, Rwanda, and Swaziland); an isolated Asian state (Nepal); and a European principality (Liechtenstein). Were this polarization to continue for another decade, IGOs would institutionalize differences among states' capacities to sustain life as well as to defend or even to articulate particular visions of political, economic, and social order.

The ensemble of changes in memberships: summary

These data on literacy, on aggregate and per capita income, and on freedom together suggest a developing polarization between the industrial democracies and the worst-off countries. By 1992, the Western democratic and relatively rich countries with highly literate populations had increased their involvement with a variety of IGOs, while poor and unfree countries, whose populations were barely literate, and some of which were immersed in chronic civil wars, dropped out of the IGO network. During the 1980s, while the IGO population shifted toward emanations and away from geographical organizations, differences among states' connections with these institutions widened.

Balancing the factors that explain IGO membership

Three types of influences largely determine the number of IGOs to which a country belongs. The first set of factors, already discussed, includes characteristics commonly thought to be sources of state power and affluence, such as a skilled and literate population, broad economic capacity, and political openness. It also includes the number of years a state has been independent, which ought to predict its membership level, since the newer a state, the less opportunity it has had to join IGOs. However, these measures are related and might be capturing indirectly the same phenomena. To estimate their relative contributions, we have used multiple regression analysis. (We have not reported results for any variable with missing data.) Two other main influences, government type and region, have deeper historical roots and help to capture the profound influence of cultural and historical context on a government's decisions.[22]

Table 7 reports the ordinary least squares regression results. The first column's results describe the relative importance of aggregate and per capita GDP; level and change in freedom; literacy; and years since independence in

22. March and Olsen 1989.

TABLE 7. *Factors explaining states' memberships in international governmental organizations, 1992: results of ordinary least squares regression analysis*[a]

	Equation (1)	Equation (2)	Equation (3)	Equation (4)
Constant	252.8**	−345.4**	15.8	−579.0**
	(23.7)	(109.7)	(61.4)	(117.8)
1992 GDP[b]	0.01	0.01	0.02	0.02*
	(0.01)	(0.01)	(0.01)	(0.01)
1992 GDP per capita[c]	0.004**	0.002*	0.003	0.001
	(0.001)	(0.001)	(0.001)	(0.001)
1992 level of freedom[d]	17.9**	11.3	19.6*	11.7
	(7.9)	(8.6)	(7.9)	(8.6)
Change in freedom 1981–92[e]	−29.5**	−19.7*	−35.5**	−27.2**
	(9.0)	(8.8)	(8.6)*	(9.3)
Years since independence[f]	0.35**	0.25**	0.31**	0.20**
	(0.06)	(0.05)	(0.06)	(0.05)
1992 literacy[g]	−91.3*	−34.1	−78.8*	−41.0
	(23.5)	(24.2)	(29.2)	(28.3)
Government type, 1981				
Newly chaotic countries (*n* = 14)	—	Base = 0[h]	—	Base = 0
Communist (*n* = 17)	—	76.9**	—	86.5**
		(21.0)		(20.1)
Dictatorship (*n* = 59)	—	105.4**	—	106.6*
		(19.8)		(19.3)
Unstable democracy (*n* = 16)	—	95.8**	—	98.4
		(22.2)		(22.0)
One-party democracy (*n* = 29)	—	77.0**	—	91.5**
		(19.5)		(19.8)
Multiparty democracy (*n* = 34)	—	115.6*	—	119.8**
		(21.7)		(21.3)
Region				
Africa (*n* = 45)	—	—	47.9**	36.7*
			(15.7)	(14.8)
Americas (*n* = 33)	—	—	54.1*	47.0*
			(14.9)	(14.1)
Asia (*n* = 37)	—	—	Base = 0	Base = 0
Europe (*n* = 35)	—	—	47.5**	64.5**
			(17.3)	(16.6)
Middle East (n = 19)	—	—	53.8**	40.5*
			(17.9)	(17.2)
N	169	169	169	169
R^2	0.42	0.53	0.44	0.58

*p < 0.05.
**p < 0.01.
[a]Standard errors are reported in parentheses below each coefficient.
[b]In millions of U.S. dollars.
[c]In U.S. dollars.
[d]Ordinal 1, 2, 3.
[e]Ordinal 1(−), 2(0), 3(+).
[f]In years.
[g]In percentages.
[h]For an explanation of bases, see the text.

predicting the number of IGOs to which countries belong. Per capita GDP, level of freedom, change in freedom, and the number of years a country has been independent emerge as strong predictors, while literacy also has a significant effect. The measure of overall power, GDP, drops away as an independent predictor; other measures cancel out what it contributed. Together, these variables account for more than two-fifths of the variance among countries' IGO membership levels.

Both literacy and democratization matter in predicting states' membership levels, but in a way opposite what one would expect. States whose populations are uneducated, and those moving away from democracy, belong to more IGOs on average than do their literate and democratizing peers. As noted earlier, since democratization indicates a change in the holders of power, it signals a move from one foreign policy agenda to another. Memberships could go down as the new power holders detach themselves from their predecessors' institutional ties. We can speculate that literacy measures popular access to information and to political institutions; like democratization, increasing literacy follows broad social reforms that are tied to regime change and can signal a shift from one set of social goals to another. Dictatorships depend on thwarting participation; when they begin to fail, the ties they forged to other countries and to IGOs also falter.

Basic measures of power and of political and civil rights capture important influences on countries' propensities to belong to IGOs. Institutional and historical characteristics constitute additional influences. We divided countries into six groups according to their government structures: communist one-party states; noncommunist dictatorships, which include military and other undemocratic rule; unstable democracies, which include countries that tilt regularly between elections and coups; one-party democracies, which comprise open electoral democracies in which the same party is victorious at least 90 percent of the time; two- or multiparty democracies, in which party control regularly changes; and the newly chaotic countries—those emerging from subjugation to independence, though of what sort is not yet clear.

Government structure's importance to IGO memberships lies mainly in three areas. First, domestic institutions reflect the direction of social influence: from the bottom up in democracies and from the top down in dictatorships, with variants in between. In this way, a government structure can amplify or mute a population's, or a regime's, attitude toward IGOs. Second, some institutional types are more stable than others. Communist countries are more stable than their former relations, the newly chaotic countries; this is also true of dictatorships when compared with unstable democracies, and of one-party when compared with multiparty democracies. Since predictability is thought to be both a prerequisite for IGO membership and a consequence of it, the more stable countries should belong to more IGOs than their peers. Third, government structure reflects both ideology and the degree to which a particular sort of ideology pervades a country's politics. Since many of the post–World War II institutions were associated with the West, those countries opposed to the Western system and whose government institutions reflect this ought to belong to fewer IGOs than do the other countries. Column (2) in Table 6 lists the results of a statistical analysis in which government structure is added to the power variables.

Government structure significantly affects the likelihood that countries belong to many IGOs, even when the other economic and political indicators are taken into account. Because they had the lowest IGO membership level, the newly chaotic countries were set equal to zero as a way to provide a base from which to gauge other groups' membership levels. Relative to these countries, communist countries and one-party democracies belonged to an additional 76.9 and 77.0 IGOs, respectively, and unstable democracies to an additional 95.8. Dictatorships had 105.4 and multiparty democracies 115.6 more memberships.

In the case of all six categories of countries, these figures represent additional memberships, everything else being equal. That is, if two countries had been independent the same number of years and had identical GDPs, per capita GDPs, literacy levels, and the like, the fact that one was a two-party democracy and the other was a dictatorship would by itself explain a membership gap of 10.2 IGOs. Adding information about government type changes the relative weight of the other variables, indicating that government type is independent of per capita GDP, years since independence, and even democratization but that it is tied to level of freedom and literacy. Adding information about government type increases the predictive power of the regression equation, bringing the explained variance to more than half.

How much weight ought to be given to government type cannot be known reliably until a potentially confounding factor is separated. For historical reasons, government types vary across regions. Geography presents countries with a fait accompli, determining their neighbors and their resources. Government type can vary over the long run. The spread of commerce and development—as well as capitalism, imperial conquest, and invasion—mean that geography can serve as a proxy for government institutions, for culture, and for economic base as well as provide information about cultural and geographical distance from other countries. If where a country is determines what it is, location would subsume in importance those characteristics that a country could control, such as economic performance or electoral patterns. Since most IGOs are regional, location also can indicate how often a country will be invited to join IGOs. For these reasons, geography ought to be substituted for, and then added to, the variables describing government type.

When the five main geographical regions are substituted for the six government types, the explanatory power of the regression equation falls almost to the same level as that of the original equation but does so by replacing the initially significant aggregate variables rather than by failing to capture anything. For historical reasons, government type, GDP, and social affluence vary across regions. Column (3) in Table 6 indicates the results of this statistical analysis. Asia, which contains the countries with the lowest average number of IGO memberships, is set as base. Just as government type eliminated level of freedom as a significant factor, geographical region eliminates per capita GDP as a significant factor. Where a country is located predicts the degree to which it has institutionalized its connections to others, even when all other character-istics are held constant.

To understand the factors that contribute to a country's propensity to join IGOs, all of these variables have been analyzed simultaneously. Column (4) of Table 6 lists the results of doing this. Most important, the table demonstrates that when both government type and region are added to the basic equation in column (1), they increase the equation's explanatory power 16 percent. Aggregate GDP becomes a significant factor, while per capita GDP, level of freedom, and literacy drop out. This suggests that our earlier speculations are true: namely, states with a vast amount of power, made possible by minimal popular participation, join IGOs at a high rate. Government type captures level of freedom, while region eliminates the effects of per capita GDP. Almost three-fifths of the variation among countries' membership levels in IGOs can be explained the following way: a country's base membership level depends on its location and government type. An Asian one-party democracy, for example, would hold 77 memberships, while a multiparty European democracy would hold 163. Once these are taken into account, aggregate GDP, age, and instability due to democratization provide important information about whether such a base should be raised or lowered.

This approach to predicting the number of IGOs to which a country belongs asks the question, What is the consequence of being (for example) African, or being communist, for IGO membership? A separate sort of question is, For African (or communist) countries, what sort of factors influence membership levels? The first question deals with the importance of region, the second with influences within a particular region. To answer the second question, it is appropriate to perform regressions using each subset of countries separately. By examining the motives that affect the propensity of states with particular government types or in particular regions alone to join IGOs, one can sort the factors affecting different types of countries. Below we discuss the results of regressions, each of which takes as its population countries of the same government type or the same region. Because the numbers in some of the categories are small, these results should be taken as suggestive.

The IGO memberships of the 17 countries that remained communist and of the 14 newly chaotic countries are not systematically related to any of the above variables. For the other four categories, different factors account for each group's IGO memberships. For the 59 dictatorships, the only factor to be significant is aggregate GDP; i.e., the larger a dictatorship's GDP, the more IGO memberships it will hold. Age is a significant factor for the countries in the other three categories. Democratization is significant for the 16 unstable democracies—countries moving toward democracy drop out of IGOs—and both age and literacy matter for the 29 one-party democracies.

The effects of region parallel government type. None of the factors in the basic regression equation helps to explain the 19 Middle Eastern states' memberships. Age makes a significant difference for the 37 Asian and 33 American states. African states in transition to democracy disengage from IGOs. This is true as well in Europe, where aggregate GDP and level of freedom are also significant. The greater a European state's GDP and the more democratic it is, the higher will be its level of IGO memberships.

If countries were similarly motivated, all would respond to a declining economy or an upsurge in political participation or the benefits of geographical contiguity in the same way. Instead, different constellations of forces motivate different groups of states. It is not only that the rich behave differently from the poor or that the powerful behave differently from the powerless but that the dominant, stable states have a set of motivations wholly different from those of the weak and unstable. Groups of states seem to be operating in different worlds and according to different logics.

Explanations and implications

Although no theory at hand is sufficient to explain the changes that we see, two theoretical perspectives illuminate parts of the puzzle. From them we can begin to piece together an understanding of what propels change in the IGO web. Functionalism, like international relations theory generally, views states as units of analysis. Because functionalism offers an explanation of what motivates states to join and maintain international organizations, we can apply it to changes in states' connections to IGOs. Government type, income level, and ideology, all are embedded in the functionalist explanation of why states pursue interdependence. Functionalism helps to illuminate why some countries have thrown themselves into the IGO web while others have been extricating themselves from it. After reviewing functionalism's contributions, we examine another perspective, organizational ecology, that addresses change within an organizational population.

Functionalism

Functionalist theory treats two important aspects of the relationship between states and IGOs, one of which directly relates to the question of membership. Classical functionalists argue that governments join international organizations as a way to provide their constituencies with the goods they demand but that the government on its own cannot provide. (Because neofunctionalism addresses how IGOs grow stronger, it does not apply to the question of increases and decreases in states' memberships.) David Mitrany contends that advances in communications and transportation technologies lead to two developments that, when combined, pressure governments to cooperate with each other.[23] As technology develops, goods can be produced most efficiently by relying on specialization and trade and by taking advantage of economies of scale. National borders become too small for the optimal organization of production, and this stalls growth. At the same time, technology fosters links among greater numbers of people. People have access to each other and to markets; they also have access to their governments. The result is more people pressuring the government to raise living standards, which can come about only through transnationalizing production and markets. In order to stay in power, a government must help industries to transcend national barriers. This requires cooperating with other governments. By helping them to accomplish this, IGOs serve as lifeboats for national political elites.

To a classical functionalist, pressure to perform economically propels governments into IGOs. A functionalist would, therefore, expect countries whose populations already have reached a high standard of living to belong to more organizations than those whose populations have not begun to reap the benefits of the home market. Per capita income and literacy levels would predict IGO membership, with some threshold figure below which a country would belong to very few. Government type would also predict IGO membership, as some institutional forms are designed to amplify popular desires and others to mute them. Electoral democracies should belong to the most IGOs, military dictatorships to the least.

Because economic desires motivate countries, IGOs should devote themselves to economic tasks. States should organize around standardization, trade rules, infrastructure creation, and perhaps research and development. The more technical or economic the task, the more likely that states would institutionalize cooperation on it. Once a task has been synchronized effectively, an organization could be abandoned. The IGO population would consolidate as it moved on to harder tasks. Organizational death would be a sign of success, just as organizational creation was a sign of intent.

Many of the patterns we saw can be explained by reference to such processes. Clearly, the wealthiest states belong to more organizations than do the poorer, the democracies to more than the dictatorships, and those moving from democracy or keeping still to more than those moving toward it. Many of the snapshots of memberships displayed earlier would not surprise a functionalist. Nor would many of the changes; for example, the richest countries did increase their IGO memberships while others saw their memberships drop. A functionalist would also argue that we should not be surprised that the end of the cold war resulted in the former Eastern bloc countries clamoring for membership, since they were well-off, with high literacy rates and access to communications

---

23. Mitrany 1966.

technology. This would signal the end of a temporary and inefficient obsession with ideology.

Also as functionalists would expect, more than three-fifths of all IGOs devoted themselves to economic tasks. Organizations committed to a specific purpose increased their share of the IGO population, indicating a growth in cooperation on narrower, more technical matters. Emanations, moreover, which indicate increasing organizational complexity, suggest a functional intensification and specialization. Finally, regionalism has no special place in functionalist theory; no reason besides transportation costs would lead contiguous countries to cooperate more than those at a distance. For this reason, the decreasing proportion of geographical IGOs is consistent with functionalist expectations, while the increasing number of universal-membership organizations might signal broader acceptance of liberal norms.

States without wealthy, literate, and participatory populations, however, not only join IGOs but serve at times as their linchpins. Brazil, India, Mexico, and Turkey are all in the top 20 percent in terms of IGO memberships, along with Canada, Spain, Switzerland, and others of the industrialized West. China, too, is in this quintile, as is Japan. The intensive joiners are as likely to be states with great aggregate wealth but low per capita income as they are to be those with the wealthiest citizens. Since functionalism locates government motives at the level of citizen wealth, it cannot account for the equal propensity of governments whose economies have not yet produced great individual wealth to join IGOs. That powerful states lacking pressure from their citizens also join IGOs suggests that governments are more than conduits translating citizen preferences into foreign policy, as functionalism assumes.

Organizational ecology

Organizational ecology takes private and public organizations—unions, shops, universities, charitable institutions, and the like—as the center of study. Organizations operate in an environment composed of similar organizations; dissimilar or hostile ones, such as regulatory agencies and competitors; and an organization's membership or constituency. Clientele influence organizations, but they develop a character and perhaps goals of their own. This refusal to reduce an organization to its constituent parts distinguishes organizational ecology from the perspectives central to international relations theory.

In arguing that students of international organizations should pay greater attention to organizational sociology, Gayl Ness and Steven Brechen note that whereas conventionally, "The organizations of the international scene are . . . seen merely as creatures of the dominant actors, with little initiative, power, or effectiveness," in the sociological view organizations "are not simple mechanical tools obediently doing the work of their creators. They are live collectivities interacting with their environments, and they contain members who seek to use the organization for their own ends, often struggling with others over the content and allocation of the product. These dynamics produce a distinctive organizational character over time."[24] Organizations act in part according to an internal and external logic that is independent of their creators and develop personalities and unique strategies for interacting with their environments.

Organizations compete directly, each trying to maintain a hold on key economic and political resources. Others, to survive, forgo mass competition and stake out a niche for themselves.[25] Different types of organizations face different sorts of threats. The more general organizations will be threatened by the growing efficiency of those with which they compete or by a general reduction in the resource base that supports all of these organizations. Specialized organizations, by contrast, are unaffected by other organizations' efficiency and can be protected from financial drought if they provide a service that is or can be successfully characterized as essential. Their main threat is intellectual or political rather than financial; they are more vulnerable to their constituency changing its mind and altering its goals than to a short-term loss of money.

General organizations are less efficient, though more flexible, than specialized ones.[26] Organizational ecology anticipates that generalized institutions will have higher survival rates than specialized ones during times of environmental uncertainty. Because they are more flexible, a generalized organization will be able to meet new demands, whereas a more specialized organization is likely to find tasks newly asked of it beyond its capabilities. Organizations need not just a large but also a stable supply of support.

One way of becoming general is to master a variety of specialties. Organizations can maximize their flexibility by fashioning an assortment of specialized subsidiaries. Organizational ecology labels these "loosely coupled organizations"; the looseness "allows portions of the organization to persist and evolve independently of other parts."[27] Each part can test whether the new environment will be hospitable and to whom. Larger organizations have the financial and administrative resources to conduct such tests and to absorb the costs of failure necessary to locate areas of success.

Many of the changes within the IGO population during the 1980s are consistent with organizational ecology's expectations. First, the simple fact of death and birth in the organizational population both is consistent with organizational ecology and runs counter to the view that organizations once created might adapt themselves indefinitely but do not die. At the same time, organizational ecology expects that older organizations, which have proved their seaworthiness, will survive at higher rates, with most of the deaths coming from the younger, untested IGO population. As a consequence, the population

---

24. Ness and Brechen 1988, 246–47.
25. Pfeffer 1982, 180–83.
26. Ibid., 182.
27. Aldrich 1979, 83.

will age. Indeed, the average age of IGOs did increase, from 18.4 years in 1981 to 25.4 years in 1992.

Even if the new organizations in important ways mimic the old, the volume of births and deaths tells us that many organizations do not adapt. The institution as institution has to be abandoned. At the level of individual organizations, adapting to external change involves creating emanations. At the level of the organizational population, deaths are an important mechanism of adaptation. Individual deaths demonstrate, paradoxically, the ability of a population to adapt to changes in its environment.

New organizations within the IGO population resembled neither the abandoned nor the surviving organizations. They were more likely to be emanations and, moreover, emanations of universal-membership organizations. The largest organizations spun off subsidiary agencies, giving them a way to hedge their bets. The trend away from geographically limited IGOs and toward those having potential for universal membership is consistent with the notion that times of uncertainty favor general, flexible organizations. The increase in the proportion of organizations defining their membership by purpose is likewise consistent with that notion. Task-specific IGOs with a niche shield themselves from uncertainty by perfecting the service they provide.

Taken together, these changes are consistent with those that organizational ecology expects in reaction to an unstable, though resource-rich, environment. Insofar as the 1980s were both unstable—witnessing a decisive shift in the distribution of power among states—and resource-rich—marking a period of extraordinary growth among the already wealthy states—organizational ecology's tools help illuminate trends in the IGO population during this period.

Alone, however, its explanatory capacities are insufficient. First, organizational ecology's expectations are not entirely fulfilled. Organizational ecology leads one to expect that organizations' purposes would have changed, perhaps even more than membership rules. This is not borne out in the 1980s. Organizations have adapted by manipulating membership criteria rather than by redefining their functions.

Of course, organizational ecology cannot be brought to bear on areas that it does not attempt to address, such as change in the behavior of its constituents. For this reason, it cannot be applied to the broad changes in countries' involvement with IGOs. From the ecological perspective, states are important to IGOs as components of the environment, especially as providers of resources, but they are not the object of study. Organizational ecology provides no way to explain why a particular actor in the environment would increase or shut off its support for particular institutions. Functionalism complements organizational ecology in this way, offering hypotheses about such motives.

Spinning the web: sources of change

States clearly pursue membership in international institutions before they have exhausted the benefits they can reap from their home markets. To gain political influence is the most obvious motive for doing so. Large and small states seek alliances, some of which become permanent features of the organizational landscape. NATO, for example, is more than a rapid response force with a complex command structure; it has research facilities, multiple offices, a large staff, and an executive to handle its intricate routine. Countries seek intellectual or normative alliances as well as military ones. As a way to gain domestic legitimacy, to pressure another country to change, or to gain respect and power internationally, governments propose and IGOs adopt resolutions and conventions in which are proclaimed standards for state and individual behavior.[28] Many norms acquire their own organizations. Machinery to monitor progress under the Declaration on the Granting of Independence to Colonial Countries and Peoples, for instance, achieved autonomous status.

At any point in time, the activities of IGOs as well as of citizens will affect a country's membership strategy. As Robert Keohane demonstrated, the convenience and predictability of an IGO's way of accomplishing some task argue for continuing to rely on that IGO.[29] Even if an alternative structure would be more efficient, the cost of dismantling the old organization and establishing the new discourages such overhauls. Institutional stability can have both economic and political benefits, imposing costs on anything more than an incremental move toward efficiency.

But more than money is involved. IGOs at a minimum register member countries' belief that a particular sort of cooperation not only is beneficial but ought to be made permanent. At a maximum, when they succeed, international organizations both provide the benefits for which they were designed and act as magnets, drawing nonmembers toward their own beliefs about how best to act internationally. International organizations always say something about how some countries want the international system to function. Sometimes they do so powerfully enough that their prophecies become self-fulfilling.

In fact, organizations would be failures if they did not permanently affect their environments. Continuing to support an organization means at least accepting, and maybe approving, the values on which it is based. Negotiations over the composition of the UN Security Council, conflict over the World Bank's goals and voting rules, worry over whether to consider Turkey European—all of these are political rather than simply financial questions, and they resonate widely. Even the World Trade Organization is more than "just" an economic organization, as it is the standard-bearer for the liberal trading system and all that that implies.

Organizational ecology and functionalism each provide part, but only part, of the answer to the central issue: who determines which institutions will tie governments, and their populations, together. Organizational ecology points out that organizations' internal structures, constitutions, and mandates affect

28. Claude 1966.
29. Keohane 1984.

their capacities to survive and explains why the organizations themselves make most of the life and death decisions that so dramatically transform the IGO population. Functionalism helps to explain why it is the rich, free states—those that are presumably least in need of outside help—that not only are engaged in massive cooperative efforts but also are so eager to institutionalize these efforts, effectively circumscribing their own future options.

A full explanation must also take into account motives and perceptions usually associated with realist analysis, such as the intangible geopolitical costs and benefits of IGO entanglement, which derive from the fundamentally political nature of international "cooperative" networks. IGOs play an important role as partial codifications of "the rules," as manifestations of the political culture that dominant states want to transmit and that member states must at least accept. Only when this is fully taken into account does the temptation that IGOs present to elites of countries whose people are poor and unmobilized become clear. Acknowledging this also helps to explain why these countries are apparently more susceptible than functionally driven countries to dropping out of the web.

The microcosm of the 1980s

Unlike the periods after World Wars I and II or following decolonization, the period following the end of the cold war has not seen states articulating new goals or establishing institutions better suited to a new distribution of power. In fact, the cold war's end has strengthened, not weakened, the organizations associated with the resolution of World War II. Voting and membership rules amplify the voice of the dominant countries in the UN and Bretton Woods institutions, and insofar as specialized IGOs rely on the resources of their members to accomplish organizational goals, the powerful have more sway.

The cold war's end had a politically but not statistically important impact on the IGO population for three reasons. First, IGOs whose raison d'être was the East–West conflict constituted a very small portion of the IGO population. As noted, the Eastern bloc at its peak represented only 5 percent of the total. Second, the IGOs that were dependent on the cold war were no different, in cross-section, than the ones that were not; this is true even when considering whether the IGO was devoted to military, social, or economic activities. Their failure therefore did not disadvantage any one category. Third, the presence of alternative organizations allowed countries that shed Eastern bloc memberships to move toward the world that the central, powerful states created. Rather than create new organizations, as happened at the conclusion of other wars, countries have joined existing IGOs.

The UN system and the Bretton Woods organizations have drawn new members, which as yet show little sign of dissent from the organizations' implicit values and explicit goals. These IGOs arguably helped to fight and/or to end the cold war; they definitely provided a safety net for the newly independent Eastern bloc countries, making available a highly developed set of rules and resources with which these countries could integrate themselves into the international system. The International Atomic Energy Agency, for example, guided Kazakhstan's decision to disarm and provided a framework within which to organize weapons disposal and to discuss compensation. It is difficult to imagine a non-IGO world in which any newly independent and fairly poor country could be convinced that such a decision was sane, let alone beneficial.

As important, countries that once staunchly proclaimed their nonaligned/ Third World status turned toward these central institutions and away from independent regional efforts. Whether enthusiastically or reluctantly, many poorer and troubled states chose to abandon the go-it-alone strategy begun in the 1960s and 1970s and to throw in their lot with the powerful. This phenomenon should not be overstated—many geographical organizations remain, and some are growing stronger—yet the decision to turn toward universal efforts must be seen as significant. Values other than independence from the dominant military, economic, and cultural centers have become more important to many developing countries. In addition, these two shifts mean that the number of IGOs to which a state belongs depends more on material resources than on ideological convictions. With a greater consensus on the rules, countries are separated by their power to succeed within the rules.

These changes were made possible by this IGO population, but they also affected it. A move toward consensus on institutions eliminated duplication both among sets of IGOs and within IGO families. Such streamlining makes it possible to use saved energy for new tasks. Emanations result from IGOs having more decision-making authority as well as more resources to devote to specialized projects. It is convergence—or acquiescence—on the dimension of values that has thrown into sharp relief the importance that relative wealth or poverty has in determining countries' abilities to participate in IGOs.

By the end of the 1980s, the number of IGOs had stabilized while many countries' memberships declined, indicating that, for some countries, involvement leveled or reversed after reaching a ceiling. The IGO population might finally have come to a point at which it can grow marginally only if the resources devoted to international institutions grow substantially. Institutional death indicates that member states are unwilling or unable to continue cooperation in some area; this can be a general refusal to engage with others on the issue or a narrower renunciation of a particular organization's goals and methods. It also might indicate that countries have reached saturation points beyond which they find additional memberships pointless or too expensive for the returns they promise.

Countries' involvements in IGOs might continue to diverge, even were the poorer countries' economies to grow at a faster rate than the rich. Since the powerful countries are all wealthy in aggregate terms, they set the limits of IGO growth. If a country's resource level is low, its economy would have had at least to triple each decade to fund the number of IGOs that it could join. A country with a hundred thousand people having an average income of U.S.$1,000 could perhaps afford one ambassador to the United States, one to the Vatican, and one to the UN. It could not send two hundred representatives to the IGOs that suddenly sought its support in the 1960s and 1970s, nor could it send money in lieu of ambassadors, even if it supported the IGOs' goals.

The institutions that died at the highest rate in the 1980s were those central to the cold war or to furthering developing countries' goals. The Arab organizations, which accounted for much of the 1970s expansion, failed at a high rate, as did the other regional organizations that sprang up after decolonization. Rather than imply geopolitical doom, the regional differences in IGO deaths might partly be due to their earlier overrepresentation in IGO births. Bursts of enthusiasm for IGOs that erupt after independence or sudden wealth might become more tempered after decades have indicated what life will be like for the new states. Like a technical correction in the stock market, the population of IGOs might adjust to a common interpretation of what the market will bear.

While states in this sense can fail IGOs, the IGOs can also fail states. Adrian Karatnycky argued that "the decline in freedom can . . . be attributed in part to the failure of the democratic nations to promote a new, compelling international structure to create stability, economic growth and respect for human rights."[30] IGOs exert influence on states through their programs, but also—and perhaps most important—they represent to the international community the extent of normative consensus and the degree of its implementation.

The potential to alienate countries carries with it the potential to integrate them. Although IGOs reflect countries' polarization, they also can mute its effect. If countries' well-being continues to diverge, then international organizations can provide the few lifelines available to them. International organizations can provide information and other resources enabling countries to achieve welfare goals and can help to boost them into the order in which the better-off states live. They can in that way provide an institutional connection able to prevent reversals.

Conclusion

Anticipating the future based on these trends would be justified if the 1980s had been similar to previous decades, but it was not. Third World debt, a massive bipolar defense buildup, the disintegration of the Eastern bloc—all unique events—had noticeable effects on the connections between states and IGOs, as did periodic events such as a wave of independence and democratiza-

30. Karatnycky 1994, p. 4.

tion, European unification, and bitter proxy wars. Even using the entire period from 1900 to 1980 would have failed to predict what actually happened in the 1980s. A prediction based on changes up to 1980 would have estimated the 1992 population at triple its true size, with most organizations created and funded by the same Third World countries that disengaged from regional IGOs in the 1980s.

What is certain is that change within the IGO population, and between states and the organizations to which they belong, has multiple and complicated causes with roots both within the IGO population and within states. IGOs are neither autonomous nor immune from state policies. In turn, states, even powerful states, do not dictate change in the numbers and types of institutions organizing international cooperation. On one hand we have the IGOs themselves, which tend toward a task-oriented universalism consistent with what one might expect from an organizational population that was self-propelled rather than from a population sensitive to countries' changing goals. On the other we have the states, whose different capabilities and government structures prompt them in different directions, even when they are faced with similar circumstances. IGOs have institutionalized the growing polarization between wealthy, liberal countries and those facing chronic problems of poverty and repression. Whether the quality of life in the world's countries continues to diverge or begins to improve, the population of international organizations will continue to define as well as to serve states' goals.

References

Aldrich, Howard E. 1979. *Organizations and environments.* Englewood Cliffs, N.J.: Prentice-Hall.

Claude, Inis L., Jr. 1966. Collective legitimization as a political function of the United Nations. *International Organization* 20:367–79.

Hannan, Michael T., and John Freeman. 1989. *Organizational ecology.* Cambridge, Mass.: Harvard University Press.

Hughes, Barry B. 1993. *International futures.* Boulder, Colo.: Westview. Cited in Bruce Russett and Harvey Starr, *World politics: The menu for choice,* 5th ed. New York: W.H. Freeman, 1995.

Jacobson, Harold K., William Reisinger, and Todd Mathers. 1986. National entanglements in international governmental organizations. *American Political Science Review* 80:141–59.

Karatnycky, Adrian. 1994. Freedom in retreat. *Freedom Review* 25(6): 4–9.

Kaufman, Herbert. 1976. *Are government organizations immortal?* Washington, D.C.: Brookings Institution.

Keohane, Robert O. 1984. *After hegemony: Cooperation and discord in the world political economy.* Princeton, N.J.: Princeton University Press.

March, James G., and Johan P. Olsen. 1989. *Rediscovering institutions: The organizational basis of politics.* New York: Free Press.

Mitrany, David. 1966. *A working peace system.* Chicago, Ill.: Quandrangle.

Ness, Gayl D., and Steven R. Brechen. 1988. IOs as organizations. *International Organization* 42:245–73.

Pfeffer, Jeffrey. 1982. *Organizations and organization theory.* Boston: Pitman.

Russett, Bruce, and Harvey Starr. 1985. *World politics: The menu for choice.* 2d ed. New York: W.H. Freeman.

Scott, W. Richard. 1992. *Organizations: Rational, natural, and open systems.* 3d. ed. Englewood Cliffs, N.J.: Prentice-Hall.

Union of International Associations. 1982. *Yearbook of international organizations 1981.* New York: K.G. Saur.

————. 1993. *Yearbook of international organizations 1992/93.* Vol. 1. New York: K.G. Saur.

Wallace, Michael, and J.D. Singer. 1970. Intergovernmental organization in the global system, 1816–1964: A quantitative description. *International Organization* 24:239–87.

Weber, Max. 1978. *Economy and society.* Vol. 2. Edited by Guenther Roth and Claus Wittich. Berkeley: University of California Press.

World Bank. 1982, 1993, and 1994. *World development report.* Washington, D.C.: World Bank.

Who Are the "Masters of the Treaty"? European Governments and the European Court of Justice

Karen J. Alter

Few contest that the European Court of Justice (ECJ) is an unusually influential international court.[1] The Court can declare illegal European Union (EU) laws and national laws that violate the Treaty of Rome in areas traditionally considered to be purely the prerogative of national governments, including social policy, gender equality, industrial relations, and competition policy, and its decisions are respected. Nevertheless, there is significant disagreement about the extent of the Court's political autonomy from member states and the extent to which it can decide cases against their interests.

Legal and neofunctionalist scholars have asserted that the ECJ has significant autonomy by virtue of the separation of law and politics and the inherent legitimacy of courts as legal actors, and that it can use this autonomy to rule against the interests of member states.[2] Such an analysis implies that virtually any court, international or national, can decide against a government's interests because it is a legal body.[3] Neorealist analysts have argued that member states have sufficient control over the Court so that it lacks the autonomy to decide against the interests of powerful member states.[4] This implies that the ECJ, as an international court, is particularly dependent on national governments and must bend to their interests.

Research for this article was funded by the Program for the Study of Germany and Europe at the Center for European Studies, Harvard University. I would like to thank the anonymous reviewers of this article, and Suzanne Berger, Brian Hanson, Ken Oye, Paul Pierson, Mark Pollack, and Anne-Marie Slaughter for their helpful comments on earlier drafts.

1. This article discusses the European Court of Justice, the supreme court of the European Union located in Luxembourg. The European Union was known as the European Community during most of the period discussed in this article.

The law of the European Union was and usually is still considered European Community (EC) law. I will refer to the European Union and its legal system by its current title, but retain the reference to its law as EC law.

2. See Weiler 1991; and Burley and Mattli 1993.

3. This generalization follows from the logic of the argument, with an important caveat that this argument applies to liberal democracies where the rule of law is a political reality. If domestic courts in general lack political authority, an international court is also likely to lack political authority; Burley 1993.

4. Garrett and Weingast 1993.

International Organization 52, 1, Winter 1998, pp. 121–147

© 1998 by The IO Foundation and the Massachusetts Institute of Technology

Both accounts contain significant elements of truth. The legal nature of ECJ decisions affords the Court some protection against political attacks, but member states have significant tools to influence it. Neither theory, however, can explain why the Court, which was once politically weak and did not stray far from the interests of the European governments, now has significant political authority and boldly rules against their interests. The nature of the ECJ as a court has not changed, nor have the tools the member states have to influence judicial politics. This article is an attempt to move beyond the categories of legalism, neofunctionalism, and neorealism, drawing on theories from comparative politics literature to explain the nature of ECJ–member state relations.

Member states intended to create a court that could not significantly compromise national sovereignty or national interest, but the ECJ changed the EU legal system, fundamentally undermining member state control over the Court. A significant part of the "transformation" of the EU legal system has been explained by legal scholars who have shown how the Court turned the "preliminary ruling system" of the EU from a mechanism to allow individuals to challenge *EC law* in national courts into a mechanism to allow individuals to challenge *national law* in national courts.[5] But important questions remain. How could the Court expand the EU legal system so far from the desire of the member states and beyond their control? Once the ECJ had transformed the EU legal system, why did member states not reassert control and return the system to the one they had designed and intended? If member states failed to control the transformation of the EU legal system or the bold application of EC law by the ECJ, what does this mean about the ability of national governments to control legal integration in the future?

Through an investigation of how the ECJ escaped member state control, I develop a general argument about ECJ–member state relations. The argument has three components. First, I argue that judges and politicians have fundamentally different time horizons, which translates into different preferences for judges and politicians regarding the outcome of individual cases. By playing off the shorter time horizons of politicians, the ECJ developed legal doctrine and thus constructed the institutional building blocks of its own power and authority without provoking a political response.

Second, I argue that the transformation of the European legal system by the ECJ limited the possible responses of national governments to its decisions within the domestic political realm. In the early years of the EU legal system, national politicians turned to extralegal means to circumvent unwanted decisions; they asserted the illegitimacy of the decisions in a battle for political legitimacy at home, instructed national administrations to ignore ECJ jurisprudence, or interpreted away any difference between EC law and national policy. The threat that national governments might turn to these extralegal means, disobeying an ECJ decision, helped contain ECJ activism. With national courts enforcing ECJ jurisprudence against their own governments, however, many of these extralegal avenues no longer worked. Because of

5. See Rasmussen 1986; and Weiler 1991.

national judicial support for ECJ jurisprudence, national governments were forced to frame their response in terms that could persuade a legal audience, and thus they became constrained by the legal rules of the game.

Third, national court enforcement of ECJ jurisprudence also changed the types of policy responses available to national governments at the EU level. Member states traditionally relied on their veto power to ensure that EU policy did not go against strongly held interests. The ECJ, however, interpreted existing EC laws in ways that member states had not intended and in ways that compromised strongly held interests and beliefs. As member states began to object to ECJ jurisprudence, they found it difficult to change EU legislation to reverse court decisions or to attack the jurisdiction and authority of the ECJ. Because there was no consensus among states to attack the authority of the ECJ, member states lacked a credible threat that could cow the Court into quiescence. Instead, the institutional rules combined with the lack of political consensus gave the ECJ significant room to maneuver.

In the first section I identify the functional roles the ECJ was designed to serve in the process of European integration and show how the Court's transformation of the preliminary ruling process went beyond what member states had intended, significantly compromising national sovereignty. In the second section I explain how the ECJ was able to transform the EU legal system during a period when the system was inherently weak, developing the time horizons argument and the argument about how national court enforcement of ECJ jurisprudence changed the policy options of national governments at the national level. In the third section I explain why member states were not able to reform the EU legal system once it was clear that the Court was going beyond the narrow functional interests of the member states, developing the third argument about the changes within the EU political process. In the conclusion I develop a series of hypotheses about the institutional constraints on ECJ autonomy and discuss the generalizability of the EU legal experience to other international contexts.

The ECJ as the Agent of Member States

Before looking at how the ECJ escaped member state control, I first consider the role the ECJ was created to play in the EU political system. Geoffrey Garrett and Barry Weingast use principal-agent analysis to explain how the ECJ is an agent of the member states, serving important yet limited functional roles in the EU political process and politically constrained by the member states. The principal-agent framework is useful in identifying the interests of national governments in having an EU legal system at all. But the emphasis of Garret and Weingast on the Court's role in enforcing contracts and dispute resolution is historically misleading. It attributes to the ECJ certain roles that rightfully belong to the European Commission, and it misses the main role the member states wanted the ECJ to play in the EU political system: keeping the Commission from exceeding its authority. Why is Garrett and

Weingast's historical inaccuracy important? It overlooks entirely the role of the courts in a democratic system of government where courts provide checks and balances against abuse of executive authority and thus overlooks a whole area for judicial influence in the political process. And, importantly for this article, focusing on enforcing contracts and dispute resolution misrepresents the interests of the member states in the EU legal system and misrepresents the role the preliminary ruling system was intended to play in the EU legal process, thereby giving the impression that the preliminary ruling system existed to help enforce EC law. This impression is wrong, and it leads one to overlook the importance and the meaning of the transformation of the preliminary ruling system, missing the essence of the Court's political power.

The ECJ was created to fill three limited roles for the member states: ensuring that the Commission and the Council of Ministers did not exceed their authority, filling in vague aspects of EC laws through dispute resolution, and deciding on charges of noncompliance raised by the Commission or by member states. None of these roles required national courts to funnel individual challenges to national policy to the ECJ or to enforce EC law against their governments. Indeed, negotiators envisioned a limited role for national courts in the EU legal system.

The ECJ was created as part of the European Coal and Steel Community in order to protect member states and firms by ensuring that the supranational high authority did not exceed its authority.[6] When the EU was founded, the Court's mandate was changed, but its primary function remained to keep the Commission and the Council in check. Indeed, most of the Treaty of Rome's articles regarding the Court's mandate deal with this "checking" role, and access to the ECJ is the widest for this function: individuals can bring challenges to Commission and Council acts directly to the ECJ, and the preliminary ruling system (Article 177 §2) allowed individuals to raise challenges to EU policy in national courts.[7] The most significant expansion of the Court's authority by national governments since the Treaty of Rome has also been in this area. The creation of a Tribunal of First Instance, which was long opposed because it was seen as a steppingstone to a federal system of courts, was finally accepted so that the ECJ could better review the Commission's decisions in the area of competition policy.

A second role of the Court is dispute resolution when EC laws are vague (or, in the language of Garrett and Weingast, filling in incomplete contracts). In the EU, the Commission is primarily responsible for filling in contracts in areas delegated to it (competition law, agricultural markets, and much of the internal market), and national administrations fill in the principles in EU regulations and directives they

6. The ECJ was modeled after the French Conseil d'État, which controls government abuses of authority. In France individuals can bring charges against the government to the Conseil d'État. They cannot challenge the validity of a national law, but if they think that the law was implemented incorrectly, or that a government official exceeded their authority under the law, they can challenge the government action in front of the Conseil. For more on the history of the ECJ, see Kari 1979, chap. III; Rasmussen 1986, 201–12; and Robertson 1966, 150–80.

7. Articles 173–176, 177 §2, 178–179, 181, and 183–184 of the Treaty of Rome pertain to the checking function of the ECJ.

administer. The ECJ may be seized in the event of a disagreement between member states or firms on the one hand, and the Commission or national governments on the other, about how the treaty or other provisions of EC law should be interpreted.[8] The ECJ resolves the disagreement by interpreting the disputed EC legal clause and thus by filling in the contract through its legal decision. The preliminary ruling procedure (Article 177 §1 and 3) allowed individuals to challenge in national courts EC law interpretations of the Commission or of national administrations (for example, an individual could challenge the government's administration of EU agricultural subsidies.) Article 177 challenges were to pertain only to questions of European law, not to the interpretation of national law or to the compatibility of national law with EC law.

The ECJ was not designed to monitor infringements of EU agreements (in Garrett and Weingast's terms, monitoring defection), which has always been the Commission's responsibility.[9] In the Coal and Steel Community, the Commission monitored compliance with ECSC policies on its own, and the ECJ was an appellate body hearing challenges to Commission decisions. Under the Treaty of Rome, the ECJ was designed to play a co-role in the enforcement process. The Commission was still the primary monitor, but the ECJ mediated Commission charges and member state defenses regarding alleged treaty breaches. The ECJ was to play this role, however, only if diplomatic efforts to secure compliance failed. The preliminary ruling system was *not* designed to be a "decentralized" mechanism to facilitate more monitoring of member state compliance with the treaty.[10] Indeed, the ECJ clearly lacks the authority to review the compatibility of national law with EC law in preliminary ruling cases.[11]

---

8. Articles 183 and 177 §1 and 3 of the Treaty of Rome pertain to the filing in incomplete contracting role of the ECJ.

9. The Commission's first task, as enumerated in Article 155 EEC, is "to ensure that the provisions of [the] Treaty and the measures taken by the institutions pursuant thereto are applied."

10. Negotiators of the treaty confirm that member states intended only the Commission or member states to raise infringement charges, through Article 169 EEC and Article 170 EEC infringement cases, based on interviews with the Luxembourg negotiator of the Treaty of Rome (Luxembourg, 3 November 1992), a commissioner in the 1960s and 1970s (Paris, 9 June 1994), and a director of the Commission's legal services in the 1960s who also negotiated the treaty for France (Paris, 7 July 1994). National ratification debates for the Treaty of Rome also reveal that member states believed that only the Commission or other member states could raise infringement charges; document 5266, annex to the verbal procedures of 26 March 1957 of the debates of the French National Assembly, prepared by the Commission of the Foreign Ministry; "Entwurf eines Gesetzes zu den Verträgen vom 25 März 1957 zur Gründung der Europäischen Wirtschaftsgemeinschaft und der Europäischen Atomgemeinschaft" Anlage C; report of representative Dr. Mommer from the Bundestag debates of Friday, 5 July 1957, p. 13391; Atti Parlamentari, Senato della Repubblica; Legislatura II 1953–57, disegni di legge e relazioni-document, N. 2107-A, and Camera dei deputati document N. 2814 seduta del 26 marzo 1957.

11. The preliminary ruling system is designed to allow questions of the interpretation of EC law to be sent to the ECJ. The original idea was that if a national court was having difficulty interpreting an EC regulation, it could ask the ECJ what the regulation meant. It was not designed to allow individuals to challenge national laws in national courts or to have national courts ask if national law is compatible with EC law.

*The Transformation of the Preliminary Ruling Procedure into an
Enforcement Mechanism*

Member states continue to want the ECJ to keep EU bodies in check, fill in contracts, and mediate oversight, which is why they have expanded the resources of the ECJ with respect to these narrow functional roles.[12] But none of these roles requires or implies that EC law is supreme to national law, that individuals should help monitor member state compliance with EC law through cases raised in national courts, or that national courts should enforce EC law instead of national law and national policy. These aspects of the Court's jurisdiction were not part of the Treaty of Rome; rather, they were created by the ECJ, which transformed the preliminary ruling system from a mechanism to allow individuals to question *EC law* into a mechanism to allow individuals to question *national law*.

The Court's doctrine of direct effect declared that EC law created legally enforceable rights for individuals, allowing individuals to draw on EC law directly in national courts to challenge national law and policy. The doctrine of EC law supremacy made it the responsibility of national courts to ensure that EC law was applied over conflicting national laws.[13] In using the direct effect and supremacy of EC law as its legal crutches, the ECJ does not itself exceed its authority by reviewing the compatibility of national law with EU law in preliminary ruling cases. Indeed, the ECJ usually tells national courts that it cannot consider the compatibility of national laws with EC law but can only clarify the meaning of EC law. But it intentionally encourages national courts to use the preliminary ruling mechanism (Article 177) to do this job for it, by indicating in its decision whether or not certain types of national law would be in compliance with EC law and encouraging the national court to set aside incompatible national policies. ECJ Justice Federico Mancini candidly acknowledged the Court's complicity in this jurisdictional transgression:

> It bears repeating that under Article 177 national judges can only request the Court of Justice to interpret a Community measure. The Court never told them they were entitled to overstep that bound: in fact, whenever they did so—for example, whenever they asked if national rule A is in violation of Community Regulation B or Directive C—, the Court answered that its only power is to explain what B or C actually mean. But having paid this lip service to the language of the Treaty and having clarified the meaning of the relevant Community measure, the court usually went on to indicate to what extent a certain type of na-

12. As already mentioned, in 1986 the Treaty of Rome was amended to allow for the creation of a Court of First Instance to allow the ECJ to examine in more detail competition policy decisions of the Commission. In 1989 the role of the ECJ in checking the Commission and the Council was expanded by allowing Parliament to also challenge Commission and Council acts. Also in 1989 the Commission was given the authority to request a lump sum penalty from states that had willfully violated EC law and ignored an ECJ decision.

13. For more on the doctrines of direct effect and EU law supremacy, see Weiler 1991; Mancini 1989; and Stein 1981.

tional legislation can be regarded as compatible with that measure. The national judge is thus led hand in hand as far as the door; crossing the threshold is his job, but now a job no harder than child's play.[14]

Having national courts monitor Treaty of Rome compliance and enforce EC law was not part of the original design of the EU legal system. The transformation of the preliminary ruling system significantly undermined the member states' ability to control the ECJ.[15] It allowed individuals to raise cases in national courts that were then referred to the ECJ, undermining national governments' ability to control which cases made it to the ECJ. Individuals raised cases involving issues that member states considered to be the exclusive domain of national policy, such as the availability of educational grants to nonnationals, the publication by Irish student groups of a how-to guide to get an abortion in Britain, and the dismissal of employees by recently privatized firms. The extension of direct effects to EC treaty articles also made the treaty's common market provisions enforceable despite the lack of implementing legislation, so that EC law created constraints member states had not agreed to. Finally, the transformed preliminary ruling system made ECJ decisions enforceable, undermining the ability of member states to ignore unwanted ECJ decisions.[16]

One might think that member states would welcome any innovation that strengthened the monitoring and enforcement mechanisms of the EU legal system, but national governments were not willing to trade encroachments in national sovereignty for ensuring treaty compliance. Negotiators of the Treaty of Rome had actually weakened its enforcement mechanisms compared to what they were in the European Coal and Steel Community (ECSC) Treaty in order to protect national sovereignty, stripping the sanctioning power from European institutions.[17] In most of the original member states, ordinary courts lacked the authority to invalidate national law for any reason. It is unlikely that politicians would give national courts a new power that could only be applied to EC law simply to ensure better treaty compliance, especially because in some countries it would mean that the EU treaty would be better protected from political transgression than the national constitution! Indeed, if monitoring defection were such a high priority for member states, it might have served their interests better to have made ECJ decisions enforceable by attaching financial sanctions to ECJ decisions (as was done in 1989) to have made transfer payments from the EU contingent on compliance with common market rules, or to have given the Commis-

---

14. Mancini 1989, 606. The ECJ has been known to go beyond this trick and on occasion to tell the national court exactly what to do. In 1994 Mancini acknowledged that the ECJ "enters the heart of the conflict . . . but it takes the precaution of rendering it abstract, that is to say it presents it as a conflict between Community law and a hypothetical national provision having the nature of the provision at issue before the national court." The fiction is necessary to avoid the charge that the ECJ is exceeding its authority. Mancini 1994, 184–85.

15. Alter 1996a.

16. Alter 1996a.

17. In the Coal and Steel Community, the Commission and the ECJ could issue fines and extract payments by withholding transfer payments. In the Treaty of Rome ECJ decisions were purely declaratory.

sion more monitoring resources.[18] This would have given member states the benefits of a court that could coerce compliance, and they would not have had to risk having the ECJ delve so far into issues of national policy and national sovereignty.

Most evidence indicates that politicians did not support the transformation of the EU legal system, and that legal integration proceeded despite the intention and desire of national politicians. As Joseph Weiler has pointed out, the largest advances in EU legal doctrine at both the national and the EU level occurred at the same time that member states were scaling back the supranational pretensions of the Treaty of Rome and reasserting national prerogatives.[19] When the issue of the national courts enforcing EC law first emerged in front of the ECJ, representatives of member states argued strongly against any interpretation that would allow national courts to evaluate the compatibility of EC law with national law.[20] In the 1970s, while politicians were blocking attempts to create a common market, the doctrine of EC law supremacy was making significant advances within national legal systems. With politicians actively rejecting supranationalism, one can hardly argue that they actually supported an institutional transformation that greatly empowered a supranational EU institution at the expense of national sovereignty.

The preliminary ruling system (Article 177), the direct effect, and the supremacy of EC law continue to be polemic. The Council has refused attempts to formally enshrine the supremacy of EC law in a treaty revision or to formally give national courts a role in enforcing EC law supremacy.[21] Numerous battles have ensued over extending the preliminary ruling process to "intergovernmental" agreements. It took nearly three years after the signing of the 1968 Brussels convention on the mutual recognition of national court decisions for member states to reach a compromise regarding preliminary ruling authority for the ECJ. For the Brussels convention, member states restricted the right of reference of national courts to a narrow list of high courts[22]—courts that are known to be reticent to refer cases to the ECJ.[23] In the late 1970s negotiations over intergovernmental conventions to deal with fraud against the EU and crimes committed by EU employees broke down altogether over the issue of an Article 177 role for the ECJ. The terms of the conventions had been agreed to, and little national sovereignty was at stake. Nevertheless, France refused to extend Article 177 authority for the ECJ at all, and the Benelux countries refused to ratify the agreements without an Article 177 role for the ECJ.[24] This conflict over extending preliminary ruling jurisdiction played itself out again regarding the 1992

18. Frustrated that certain member states (especially Italy and Greece) repeatedly violate EC law and ignore ECJ decisions, in 1989 member states returned to the ECJ some of the sanctioning power it had in the ECSC Treaty granting it authority order lump sum payments.

19. Weiler 1981.

20. Stein 1981.

21. Based on an interview with a member of the German negotiating team who put forward the proposal at the Maastricht negotiations for the Treaty on a European Union, 17 February 1994 (Bonn).

22. Protocol regarding the interpretation of the Brussels Convention of 27 September 1968, adopted 3 June 1971.

23. Alter 1996a.

24. Based on interviews with French, German, and Dutch negotiators for these agreements: 27 October 1995 (Brussels), 30 October 1995 (Paris), and 2 November 1995 (Bonn).

Cannes conventions on Europol, the Customs Information System, and the resurrected conventions regarding fraud in the EU.[25] And it was an issue again in negotiations for the Treaty of Amsterdam where national governments could not agree on the desirability of preliminary ruling powers for the ECJ in Justice and Home Affairs.

Transforming the preliminary ruling system was not necessary for the ECJ to serve the member states' limited functional interests, and it brought a loss of national sovereignty that the Council would not have agreed to then and still would not agree to today. Member states had significant political oversight mechanisms to control the ECJ. As Garrett and Weingast have pointed out,

> Embedding a legal system in a broader political structure places direct constraints on the discretion of a court, even one with as much constitutional independence as the United States Supreme Court. This conclusion holds even if the constitution makes no explicit provisions for altering a court's role. The reason is that political actors have a range of avenues through which they may alter or limit the role of courts. Sometimes such changes require amendment of the constitution, but usually the appropriate alterations may be accomplished more directly through statute, as by alteration of the court's jurisdiction in a way that makes it clear that continued undesired behavior will result in more radical changes.[26]

Member states controlled the legislative process and could legislate over unwanted ECJ decisions or change the role or mandate of the ECJ. They could also manipulate the appointments process and threaten the professional future of activist judges.[27] How could the ECJ construct such a fundamental transformation of the EU legal system against the will of member states?

Escaping Member State Control

> Although the Court likes to pose modestly as "the guardian of the Treaties" it is in fact an uncontrolled authority generating law directly applicable in Common Market member states and applying not only to EEC enterprises but also to those established outside the Community, as long as they have business interests within it.[28]

Principal-agent theory tells us that agents have interests that are inherently different than principals; principals want to control the agent, but the agent wants as much authority and autonomy from the principals as possible.[29] The ECJ preferred the transformed preliminary ruling system for the same reason that member states did

25. This time Britain has refused to extend Article 177 authority, and Germany, Italy, and the Benelux parliaments have refused to ratify the agreement without Article 177 authority for the ECJ. According to sources within the Legal Services of the Council, France and perhaps Spain are hiding behind the British position, laying low so that the British take the political heat for a position they too support.

26. Garrett and Weingast 1993, 200–201.

27. Ibid.

28. From "More Powerful Than Intended," *Financial Times*, 22 August 1974.

29. See Garrett and Weingast 1993; Pollack 1995; and Moravcsik 1995. See also Burley and Mattli 1993; and Pierson 1996.

not want it: it decreased the Court's dependence on member states and the Commission to raise infringement cases by allowing individuals to raise challenges to national law, and it decreased the Court's need to craft decisions to elicit voluntary compliance by making ECJ decisions enforceable.[30] In other words, it enhanced the power of the ECJ. This inherent difference of interests explains *why* the ECJ would want to expand its authority, but not *how* it was able to expand its authority. If member states had political oversight controls, how could the agent escape the principals' control?

The answer lies in the different time horizons of politicians and judges and the lack of a credible political threat that was a direct result of the transformation of the preliminary ruling system. With national courts enforcing EC law against their governments, politicians could not simply ignore unwanted ECJ decisions. They were forced to respond to the issues raised by the ECJ in a way that would be legally acceptable both to the ECJ and to national courts.

Different Time Horizons of Courts and Politicians

Legalist and neofunctionalist scholars have argued that politicians were simply not paying attention to what the ECJ was doing, or that they were compelled into acquiescence by the apolitical legal language or by their reverence of legal authority.[31] A different explanation is that politicians and judges have different time horizons, a difference that manifests itself in terms of differing interests for politicians and judges in each court decision. Because of these different time horizons, the ECJ was able to be doctrinally activist, building legal doctrine based on unconventional legal interpretations and expanding its own authority, without provoking a political response.

Politicians have shorter time horizons because they must deliver the goods to the electorate in order to stay in office. The focus on staying in office makes politicians discount the long-term effects of their actions or, in this case, inaction.[32] Member states were most concerned with protecting national interests in the process of integration, while avoiding serious conflicts that could derail the common market effort. As far as the Court's decisions were concerned, member states wanted to avoid decisions that could upset public policies or create a significant material impact (be it political or financial).[33] The strategy of relying on "fire alarms" to be set off by ECJ decisions before politicians actually act has advantages. Politicians do not have to expend political energy fighting every court decision that could potentially create

30. See Burley and Mattli 1993; and Alter 1996a.

31. Joseph Weiler implied that being a supreme court, the ECJ had an inherent legitimacy that was difficult to politically contest; Weiler 1991, 2428. Burley and Mattli argued that it was the nonpolitical veneer of judicial decisions that made them hard for politicians to contest. They acknowledge that this veneer is more myth than reality, but the judicial use of nominally neutral legal principles "masks" the politics of judicial decisions, gives judges legitimacy, and "shields" judges from political criticism; Burley and Mattli 1993, 72–73.

32. Pierson 1996, 135–36.

33. Rasmussen also observed that states' short-term interests influenced their participation in EU legal proceedings. States tended to participate in cases in which their own national laws were at stake, not paying attention to other countries' cases; Rasmussen 1986, 287.

political problems in the future, and they can take credit and win public support for addressing the public and political concerns raised by adverse ECJ decisions.[34] But such an approach leads to a focus that prioritizes the material impact of legal decisions over the long-term effects of ECJ doctrine. The short-term focus of politicians explains why they often fail to act decisively when doctrine that is counter to their long-term interest is first established.

The ECJ took advantage of this political fixation on the material consequences of cases to construct legal precedent without arousing political concern. Following a well-known judicial practice, the ECJ expanded its jurisdictional authority by establishing legal principles but not applying the principles to the cases at hand. For example, the ECJ declared the supremacy of EC law in the *Costa* case, but it found that the Italian law privatizing the electric company did not violate EC law.[35] Given that the privatization was legal, what was there for politicians to protest, not comply with, or overturn? Trevor Hartley noted that the ECJ repeatedly used this practice:

> A common tactic is to introduce a new doctrine gradually: in the first case that comes before it, the Court will establish the doctrine as a general principle but suggest that it is subject to various qualifications; the Court may even find some reason why it should not be applied to the particular facts of the case. The principle, however, is now established. If there are not too many protests, it will be re-affirmed in later cases; the qualifications can then be whittled away and the full extent of the doctrine revealed.[36]

The Commission was an accomplice in the efforts of the ECJ to build doctrinal precedent without arousing political concerns. In an interview the original director of the Commission's legal services argued that legal means—with or without sanctions— would not have worked to enforce the treaty if there was no political will to proceed with integration. He argued that the Commission adopted the "less worse" solution of compromising on principles but worked to help the ECJ develop its doctrine. The Commission selected infringement cases to bring that were important in terms of building doctrine, especially doctrine that national courts could apply, and avoided cases that would have undermined the integration process by arousing political passions.[37] By making sure that ECJ decisions did not compromise short-term political interests, the judges and the Commission could build a legal edifice without serious political challenges.

Indeed, the early jurisprudence of the ECJ shows clear signs of caution. Although bold in doctrinal rhetoric, the ECJ made sure that the political impact was minimal in terms of both financial consequences and political consequences. Clarence Mann commented on the early jurisprudence of the ECJ in politically contentious cases,

34. In their work on the U.S. Congress McCubbins and Schwartz develop the notion of "fire alarms" as a form of political oversight and identify the many benefits for politicians of such an approach; McCubbins and Schwartz 1987.

35. *Costa v. Ente Nazionale per L'Energia Elettrica (ENEL)*, ECJ Case 6/64 (1964) ECR 583.

36. Hartley 1988, 78–79.

37. A former commissioner called the Commission's strategy "informal complicity." Interview with the former director of the Commission's Legal Services, 7 July 1994 (Paris), and with a former commissioner, 9 June 1994 (Paris).

saying that "by narrowly restricting the scope of its reasoning, [the ECJ] manages to avoid almost every question in issue."[38] Stuart Scheingold observed that, in Article 173 cases, "the ECJ used procedural rules to avoid decisions of substance."[39] A French legal advisor at the Secretariat General de Coordination Interministerial des Affaires Européen argued that the ECJ did not matter until the 1980s because the decisions were principles without any reality. Since there was not much EC law to enforce in the 1960s and 1970s, and since national courts did not accept that they should implement European law over national law, ECJ jurisprudence was simply marginal.[40]

Politicians may have been myopic in their focus on material consequences, but this does not mean that they did not realize that their long-term interest in protecting national sovereignty might be compromised by the doctrinal developments. The Court's *Van Gend* and *Costa* decisions were filled with rhetoric to make politicians uneasy, and lawyers from member states had argued strongly against the interpretations the ECJ eventually endorsed.[41] Indeed, some politicians were clearly unsettled by the legal precedents the ECJ was establishing in the 1960s. According to former Prime Minister Michel Debré, General de Gaulle *did* ask for revisions of the Court's power and competences in 1968.[42] But other member states were unwilling to renegotiate the Treaty of Rome, especially at a French request, so the political threat to the ECJ was not credible.

In the 1960s the risk of the ECJ running amok was still fairly low given the inherent weakness of the EU legal system. Most national legal systems did not allow for international law supremacy over subsequent national law (indeed, the Italian Constitutional Court and the French Conseil d'État rejected a role enforcing EC law supremacy in the 1960s), and there were relatively few national court references to the ECJ. Until the ECJ began applying the doctrine in unacceptable ways, politicians lacked a compelling interest in mobilizing an attack on the Court's authority. In

38. Mann 1972, 413.
39. Scheingold 1971, 21.
40. Based on an interview in Paris, 31 October 1995.
41. The *Van Gend* decision declared that

> the Community constitutes a new legal order of international law for the benefit of which the states have limited their sovereign rights, albeit within limited fields, and the subjects of which comprise not only member states but also their nationals. Independently of the legislation of member states, Community law therefore not only imposes obligations on individuals but is also intended to confer upon them rights which become part of their legal heritage.

And the *Costa* decision added that

> the transfer by the States from their domestic legal system to the Community legal system of the rights and obligations arising under the Treaty carries with it a permanent limitation of their sovereign rights, against which subsequent unilateral acts incompatible with the concept of the Community cannot prevail.

It does not take a legal expert to recognize the potential threat to national sovereignty inherent in this rhetoric. *Van Gend en Loos v. Nederlandse Administratie Belastingen,* ECJ. 26/62 (1963) ECR 1, p. 12. *Costa v. Ente Nazionale per L'Energia Elettrica (ENEL),* ECJ Case 6/64 (1964) ECR 583.
42. Debré mentioned this in the discussion of the Foyer-Debré's Propositions de Loi, cited in Rasmussen 1986, 351.

retrospect political nonaction seems quite shortsighted. But predicting what would happen in light of the Court's declarations was difficult, and the strategy of holding off an attack on the ECJ was not stupid. EC law supremacy was at that time only a *potential* problem. Member states thought that controlling the legislative process would be enough to ensure that no objectionable laws were passed.[43] In any event, the problem was for another elected official to face.

Transformation of the Preliminary Ruling Procedure

By limiting the material impact of its decisions, the ECJ could minimize political focus on the Court and build doctrine without provoking a political response, creating the opportunity for it to escape member state oversight. What were marginal legal decisions from a political perspective, were revolutionary decisions from a legal perspective. They created standing for individuals to draw on EC law and a role for national courts enforcing EC law supremacy against national governments. Once national courts became involved in the application of EC law, it was harder for politicians to appeal to extralegal means to avoid complying with EC law. Instead, politicians had to follow the legal rules of the game.

Through the doctrines of direct effect and EC law supremacy, the ECJ harnessed what became an independent base of political leverage for itself—the national judiciaries. With national courts sending cases to the ECJ and applying ECJ jurisprudence, interpretive disputes were not so easily kept out of the legal realm. National courts would not let politicians ignore or cast aside as invalid unwanted decisions. Nor could politicians veto ECJ decisions through a national political vote, because EC law was supreme to national law. Indeed, national courts have refused political attempts to circumvent ECJ jurisprudence by passing new laws at the national level, applying the supreme EC law instead. National courts created both financial and political costs for ignoring ECJ decisions.

I have explained elsewhere why national courts took on a role enforcing EC law against their own governments.[44] What is important is that because of national court support of ECJ jurisprudence, extralegal means to avoid ECJ decisions were harder to use, forcing governments to find legally defensible solutions to their EU legal problems. In the EU legal arena, however, member states were at an inherent disadvantage vis-à-vis the ECJ. As Joseph Weiler has argued,

> by the fact of their own national courts making a preliminary reference to the ECJ, governments are forced to juridify their argument and shift to the judicial arena in which the ECJ is preeminent (so long as it can carry with it the national judiciary). . . . when governments are pulled into court and required to explain, justify, and defend their decision, they are in a forum where diplomatic license is far more restricted, where good faith is a presumptive principle, and where states

---

43. See Moravcsik 1995; and Weiler 1981.
44. Alter 1996a. For more on the motivations of national courts in the EU legal process, see Alter 1997; Golub 1996; Mattli and Slaughter 1998; and Weiler 1994.

are meant to live by their statements. The legal arena imposes different rules of discourse.[45]

The turnover tax struggle of 1966 offers a clear example of how the ECJ could rely on governments' fixations with the short-term impact of its decisions to diffuse political protests. It also shows how national judicial support shifted the types of responses available to governments to the advantage of the ECJ. When the Court's 1966 *Lütticke* decision created hundreds of thousands of refund claims for "illegally" collected German turnover equalization taxes, the German Finance Ministry issued a statement, saying "We hold the decision of the European Court as invalid. It conflicts with the well reasoned arguments of the Federal Government, and with the opinion of the affected member states of the EC," and it instructed German customs officials and tax courts to ignore the ECJ decision in question.[46] The decree would have worked if it were not for the national courts that refused to be told by the government that they could not apply a legally valid ECJ decision. Lower tax courts insisted on examining case-by-case whether or not a given German turnover tax was discriminatory. With national courts refusing to follow this decree, with lawyers publishing articles about the government's attempts to intimidate plaintiffs and order national courts to ignore a valid EC legal judgment,[47] with legal cases clogging the tax branch and creating the possibility that nearly all German turnover taxes might be illegal, and with members of the Bundestag questioning a Ministry of Finance official on how the decree was compatible with the principles of a Rechtsstaat[48]—a state ruled by law—the German government turned to its lawyers to find a solution to the problem.

The lawyers for the Ministry of Economics constructed a test case strategy, suggesting that the wrong legal question had been asked in the 1966 case, that really Article 97 EEC was the relevant EC legal text, not Article 95 EEC, and that Article 97 did not create direct effects, so that individuals did not have legal standing to challenge German turnover taxes in national courts.[49] The ECJ accepted the legal argument, and all of the plaintiffs lost legal standing, thus the government won in its efforts to minimize the material impact of the Court's decision. But the strategy implicitly left the Court's precedence established in the *Lütticke* case intact. Article 95 remained directly effective, and, even more importantly, member states became obliged to remove national laws that created tariff and nontariff barriers to trade even though no new EC-level policies had been adopted to replace the national policies. The government was quieted because its problem (the numerous pending cases) was gone. But the precedent came back to haunt the German government and other member states in subsequent cases.

Because of national court support, politicians were forced to play by the legal rules of the game, where precedence (legal doctrine) matters, and any position must be

---

45. Weiler 1994, 519. Burley and Mattli make a similar point; Burley and Mattli 1993.
46. 7 July 1966 (IIIB.4-V8534-1/66), republished in *der Betrieb* (1966), 1160.
47. See Meier 1967a; Stöcker 1967; and Wendt 1967a,b.
48. See Meier 1967b; and Meier 1994.
49. See Meier 1994; and Everling 1967.

justified in legal terms in a way that is credible within the legal community.[50] Most importantly, in the legal sphere judges—not politicians—are in the power position of deciding what to do.

The doctrinal precedents stuck into the Court's benign legal decisions were in fact formidable institutional building blocks that would be applied in the future to more polemic cases. Once national courts had accepted EC law supremacy, they became supporters and advocates of the ECJ in the national legal realm, using their judicial position to limit the types of responses politicians could use to avoid unwanted ECJ decisions. Indeed, once the important legal precedents of direct effect and supremacy of EC law were established, judges were loath *not* to apply them or to reverse them fearing that frequent reversals would undermine the appearance of judicial neutrality, which is the basis for parties accepting the legitimacy of their decisions.[51] If legal arguments cannot persuade either the national court or the ECJ, in the end politicians can do little to influence the legal outcome. The ECJ is after all the highest authority on the meaning of EC law, and national courts will defer to the ECJ for this reason. The only choice left for politicians is to rewrite the EU legislation itself.

The legal rules of the game limited political responses to ECJ jurisprudence, but national governments still had significant means to influence the EU legal process. Member states could influence the interpretation of the law through legally persuasive arguments, mobilization of public opinion, or political threats. They could rewrite the contested legislation and even rewrite the mandate of the ECJ, limiting access to it and cutting back its jurisdictional authority without violating the legal rules of the game. The next section considers why member states have not exercised these options.

Could Member States Regain Control? Why Did Member States Accept Unwanted ECJ Jurisprudence?

> Our sovereignty has been taken away by the European Court of Justice. It has made many decisions impinging on our statute law and says that we are to obey its decisions instead of our own statute law. . . . Our courts must no longer enforce our national laws. They must enforce Community law. . . . No longer is European law an incoming tide flowing up the estuaries of England. It is now like a tidal wave bringing down our sea walls and flowing inland over our fields and houses—to the dismay of all.[52]

Some scholars have argued that the fact that member states did not reverse the direct effect and supremacy declarations of the ECJ shows that the Court had not deviated significantly from member state interests. The strongest argument of the strongest proponent of this view, Garrett, comes down to a tautology. He argues that, "If member governments have neither changed nor evaded the European legal system,

---

50. See Weiler 1994; and Mattli and Slaughter 1995.

51. Shapiro has argued that judges search for legitimacy by applying legal principles across cases; Shapiro 1981, chap. 1.

52. Lord Denning, judicial branch of the House of Lords, in Denning 1990.

then from a 'rational government' perspective, it must be the case that the existing legal order furthers the interests of national governments," and thus reflects the interests of national governments.[53] But the failure to act against judicial activism cannot be assumed to mean political support for the transformation of the preliminary ruling system. It is equally plausible, and more consistent with the evidence,[54] that national leaders disagreed with the Court's activist jurisprudence but were institutionally unable to reverse it.[55]

Institutional Constraints: The Joint-Decision Trap

EC law based on regulations or directives can be rewritten by a simple statute that, depending on the nature of the statute, requires unanimity or qualified majority consent. A few of the Court's interpretations have been rewritten in light of their decisions, though surprisingly few. This is because ECJ decisions usually affect member states differently, so there is not a coalition of support to change the disputed legislation. Also, it takes political capital to mobilize the Commission and other states to legislate over a decision. If a member state can accommodate the decision of the ECJ on its own, by interpreting it narrowly or by buying off the people the decision affects, such an approach is easier than mobilizing other member states to relegislate. Such actions can reverse the substance of the decisions, allowing the specific policies affected by the Court's interpretation to remain unchanged. But they do not affect the Court's legal doctrine or the EU legal system as an institution. Nor do they undermine the doctrines that form the foundation of ECJ authority: the supremacy or the direct effect of EC law, or the "four freedoms" (the free movement of goods, capital, labor, and services). Reversing these core institutional foundations or any ECJ decision based on the EU treaty would require a treaty amendment, a threshold that is even harder to reach under the policymaking rules of the EU.

In order to change the treaty, member states need unanimous agreement plus ratification of the changes by all national parliaments. Obtaining unanimous agreement about a new policy is hard enough. But creating a unanimous consensus to change an existing policy is even more difficult. Fritz Scharpf calls the difficulty of changing entrenched policies in the EU context the "joint-decision trap."[56] According to

53. Garrett 1995. Rasmussen also implies that states "tacitly welcomed" ECJ expansions through the in-court behavior of their council and by their willingness to accept ECJ legal interpretations; Rasmussen 1986, 291.

54. As mentioned earlier, EU authority expanded at a time when member states were contesting the Court's supranational powers, making it unlikely that they would support a significant aggrandizement of the Court's authority at the cost of national sovereignty. Lawyers for the national governments argued strongly against the Court's eventual interpretations on the grounds that they would compromise national sovereignty. Evidence indicates that De Gaulle protested the growing powers of the ECJ and tried to organize an attack on it. See Weiler 1981; and Stein 1981.

55. This finding is consistent with Brian Marks, who shows how legislators may be hamstrung to reverse a legal decision. Marks argues that "inaction is neither a sufficient nor necessary condition for acceptability [of a legal decision] by a majority of legislators. Nor can we conclude that the absence of legislative reaction implies that the Court's policy choice leads to a 'better' policy in the view of the legislature." Marks 1989, 6.

56. Scharpf 1988.

Scharpf, a joint-decision trap emerges when (1) the decision making of the central government (the Council in the case of the EU) is directly dependent on the agreement of constituent parts (the member states), (2) when the agreement of the constituent parts must be unanimous or nearly unanimous, and (3) when the default outcome of no agreement is that the status quo policy continues. The default outcome is the critical factor hindering changes in existing polices. As Scharpf notes,

> What public choice theorists have generally neglected . . . is the importance of the "default condition" or "reversion rule.". . . The implications of unanimity (or of any other decision rule) are crucially dependent upon what will be the case if agreement is not achieved. The implicit assumption is usually that in the absence of a decision there will be no collective rule at all, and that individuals will remain free to pursue their own goals with their own means. Unfortunately, these benign assumptions are applicable to joint decision systems only at the formative stage of the "constitutional contract," when the system is first established. Here, indeed, agreement is unlikely unless each of the parties involved expects joint solutions to be more advantageous than the status quo of separate decisions. . . . The "default condition" changes, however, when we move from single-shot decisions to an ongoing joint-decision system in which the exit option is foreclosed. Now nonagreement is likely to assure the *continuation* of existing common policies, rather than reversion to the "zero base" of individual action. In a dynamic environment . . . when circumstances change, existing policies are likely to become sub-optimal even by their own original criteria. Under the unanimity rule, however, they cannot be abolished or changed as long as they are still preferred by even a single member.[57]

States can block the attribution of new powers to the ECJ until their concerns are met. But the joint-decision trap makes reversing the Court's key doctrinal advances virtually impossible. Small states have an interest in a strong EU legal system. In front of the ECJ, political power is equalized, and within the ECJ, small states have disproportionate voice, since each judge has one vote, and decisions are taken by simple majority. The Benelux states are unlikely to agree to anything they perceive will weaken the legal system's foundations and thus compromise their own interests. The small states are not alone in their defense of the ECJ. The Germans from the outset wanted a "United States of Europe," and considered a more federal-looking EU legal system a step in the right direction. Although sometimes critical of the ECJ, the German government is also a supporter of a European Rechtstaat. Germany and the Benelux countries tend to block attempts to weaken ECJ authority, and they try to extend its authority as the EU expands into new legal areas whenever the political possibility exists. Britain and France, on the other hand, block attempts to expand EU legal authority.

The need to call an Intergovernmental Conference (IGC) to amend the treaty is an additional institutional impediment to member state attacks on the ECJ. Any member state can add an item to the agenda of the IGC, making member states hesitant to call for an IGC lest the agenda get out of control.

57. Ibid., 257.

The reality of the joint-decision trap fundamentally changes the assumptions of Garrett and Weingast regarding member states' ability to control the ECJ through political oversight mechanisms. Recall Garrett and Weingast's argument:

> Embedding a legal system in a broader political structure places direct constraints on the discretion of a court, even one with as much constitutional independence as the United States Supreme Court. This conclusion holds even if the constitution makes no explicit provisions for altering a court's role. The reason is that political actors have a range of avenues through which they may alter or limit the role of courts. Sometimes such changes require amendment of the constitution, but usually the appropriate alterations may be accomplished more directly through statute, as by alteration of the court's jurisdiction in a way that makes it clear that continued undesired behavior will result in more radical changes . . . *the possibility of such a reaction drives a court that wishes to preserve its independence and legitimacy to remain in the area of acceptable latitude.*[58]

Certainly, courts have political limits, some area of "acceptable latitude," beyond which they cannot stray. Indeed, *all* political actors are ultimately constrained to stay within an "acceptable latitude." But Garrett and Weingast imply that the political latitude of the ECJ is very limited—so limited that the ECJ has to base its individual decisions directly on the economic and political interests of the dominant member states.[59] They compare the institutional authority of the ECJ to that of the U.S. Supreme Court to highlight what they see as the inherent political vulnerability of the ECJ and of ECJ justices, arguing

> The autonomy of the ECJ is clearly less entrenched than that of the Supreme Court of the United States. Its position is not explicitly supported by a constitution. One of the thirteen judges is selected by each of the twelve member states, and their terms are renewable every six years. Many are likely to seek government employment in their home countries after they leave the ECJ. Moreover, there is no guarantee that the trend to ever greater European integration—legal or otherwise—will continue. At any moment, the opposition of a few states will be enough to derail the whole process.[60]

The difficulty of changing the Court's mandate given the requirement of unanimity and given the lack of political consensus implies that the Court's room for maneuver may be, in some respects, even greater than that of the U.S. Supreme Court or other constitutional courts. Changing the authority of the ECJ requires a treaty amendment, not a simple statute. Securing an agreement on a treaty amendment from all member states could be even harder than convincing a national parliament to agree on a statute amending jurisdictional authority, especially if the parliament were dominated by one party. Because of the decision-making rules of the EU, the political threat to alter the Court's role is usually not credible. The ECJ can safely calculate that political controversy will not translate into an attack on its institutional standing,

---

58. Garrett and Weingast 1993, 200–201 (emphasis in original).
59. Garrett has made this argument more clearly elsewhere; see Garrett 1992, 1995.
60. Garrett and Weingast 1993, 201.

thus it will not need to reconcile its behavior with a country's political preferences. For these reasons, Mark Pollack calls amending the treaty the "nuclear option— exceedingly effective, but difficult to use—and is therefore a relatively ineffective and noncredible means of member state control."[61]

The joint-decision trap also affects the ability of member states to control the ECJ through the appointment process. The relevant EU institutional feature is that decision making takes place in the subunit of the member state. Using appointments to influence judicial positions is never a sure thing, but without a concerted appointment strategy on the part of a majority of member states, such a strategy is extremely unlikely to succeed. Each state has its own selection criteria for EU justices, and high-level political appointments are governed by a variety of political considerations, including party affiliation and political connections. A judge's opinion on EU legal matters is seldom the determining factor, and only a few member states have even attempted to use a judge's views regarding European integration as a factor in the selection process.[62] The individual threat to the judge's professional future may also be more hypothetical than real. Because ECJ decisions are issued unanimously, knowing if a given justice is ignoring its state's wishes is impossible. And in most European member states the judiciary is a civil bureaucracy, and judges have all the job protection of civil servants. If an ECJ judicial appointee came from the judiciary (or academia), which many do, they are virtually guaranteed that a job will be awaiting them on their return.

Garrett and Weingast raise another potential political tool of control over the ECJ— the threat of noncompliance—arguing that the ECJ must fear that a failure to implement its jurisprudence will undermine its legitimacy and thus its influence in the political process.[63] Although courts do not like flagrant flaunting of their authority, as Walter Mattli and Anne-Marie Slaughter have argued, it could hurt a court's legitimacy even more to disregard legal precedent and bend to political pressure than to make a legally sound decision that politicians will contest or ignore.[64] Indeed, in most legal systems a significant level of noncompliance remains: think of the many states in the United States where unconstitutional law and policy exist despite U.S. Supreme Court rulings. Does this mean that the U.S. Supreme Court curbs its jurisprudence to avoid noncompliance? It is hard to sustain the argument that in most cases or even in the most political of cases the fear of noncompliance shapes the jurisprudence of the ECJ.

The key to member states' ability to cow the ECJ into political subservience is the credibility of their threat. If a political threat is not credible, politicians can protest all they want without influencing judicial decisions. That being said, the ECJ is more

61. Pollack 1997, 118–19.

62. I have explored this issue in interviews with the Italian, Greek, Dutch, Belgian, French, German, British, and Irish judges at the ECJ and with legal scholars and government officials in France, Germany, and the United Kingdom. The criteria for ECJ judicial selection varied across countries but included factors such as party affiliation, ethnicity, legal background, ability to speak French, familiarity with EC law, and domestic party politics. Only in France and Germany could appointments designed to limit judicial activism be identified.

63. Garrett and Weingast 1993, 200. See also Garrett, Kelemen, and Schulz 1996, 9.

64. Mattli and Slaughter 1995.

interested in shaping future behavior than exacting revenge for past digressions, especially if the past digression was not intentional (which is usually the case). Neither politicians, nor the public, nor the ECJ has an interest in a judicial decision that would cripple a government bureaucracy by filling it with thousands of claims, bankrupt a public pensions system, or force a significant redistribution of gross national product to pay back a group of citizens for past wrongs. That the ECJ takes these political considerations into account is not a sign of politicians dominating the ECJ. Rather, it is a sign that the ECJ shares a commitment to serving the public interest.

Overcoming the Joint-Decision Trap? The 1996–97 IGC and the Treaty of Amsterdam

I have argued that decision-making rules significantly undermine the ability of national governments to control the ECJ. Although reforming existing policies is made difficult by the joint-decision trap, this does not mean that policies can never be reformed. Scharpf argues that the joint-decision trap can be overcome in a given policy debate if a member state adopts a confrontational bargaining style, such as threatening exit or holding hostage something that other member states want. Thus intensely held interests by one state can lead to hard bargaining and reform of entrenched policies if the state will subjugate other issues to a single goal.

British Euro-skeptics had a very intense interest in weakening the powers of EU institutions, especially the ECJ. In the Maastricht Treaty negotiations the British demanded the scheduling of an intergovernmental conference to discuss the roles and powers of EU institutions, and the British made it part of their list of demands that the Court's powers be addressed. Euro-skeptics wanted to make the ECJ directly accountable to political bodies and leaked to the press a proposal to allow a political body to veto or delay the effect of ECJ decisions.[65] They forced the British government to put into the negotiating process of the IGC a series of proposals to make the ECJ more politically accountable and to limit the cost of its decisions. British officials hoped to elicit German support for their proposals. There had been rumors about a potential German proposal to limit preliminary ruling reference rights to high courts. And Chancellor Helmut Kohl had become increasingly critical of the ECJ. The British challenge to the ECJ was the most serious to date because it went beyond rhetoric to articulate and specify an anti-ECJ policy.

In interviews during the fall of 1995, while meetings of the planning group for the 1996 IGC were being held, Dutch, German, and French legal advisors and members of the Council's legal services all agreed that the mandate of the ECJ, as it stood in the Treaty of Rome, was not up for renegotiation.[66] Because the other member states were unwilling to renegotiate the *aquis communautaire,* the British put forward pro-

---

65. Brown 1995.

66. Based on interviews in the British Foreign and Commonwealth Office (10 November 1995), the Tribunal of First Instance (2 November 1995), and the German Economics Ministry (correspondence from 6 January 1996). The desire to "clip the Court's wings" was also announced in an article in the *Financial Times* and in an academic article written by a civil servant, Mr. Clever, in the Bundesministerium für Arbeit und Sozialordnung; Brown 1995; and Clever 1995.

posals to the IGC planning group that did not directly attack the authority or autonomy of the ECJ or attempt to dismantle the preliminary ruling procedure or the supremacy of EC law. The British suggested creating an ECJ appeals procedure that would give the Court a second chance to reflect on its decisions in light of political displeasure, but according to the proposal it would still ultimately be the ECJ that executed the appeal! The British also suggested a treaty amendment to limit liability damages *in cases where the member state acted in good faith,* as well as an amendment that explicitly allowed the Court to limit the retrospective effect of its judgments. Nothing in the current text of the Treaty of Rome denies the authority of the ECJ to limit the liability of member states if they have acted in good faith or to limit the retrospective effect of its decisions. Nevertheless, the British hoped that having these texts in the treaty would encourage the ECJ to use them and open the possibility that governments could appeal ECJ findings using good faith and retrospective effects arguments. Being forced to put its ideas in legally acceptable terms that other member states might accept stripped most of the political force from the British government's proposals.

The British proposals were rejected entirely by the other member states. The existing jurisdiction of the ECJ for common market issues was not altered in the new Treaty of Amsterdam, thus the British threats never materialized. But in the new areas of jurisdiction given to the Court, the ECJ was significantly restricted. In the Maastricht Treaty, the ECJ had been excluded from the new areas of EU authority: the Common Foreign and Security Policy, and Justice and Home Affairs (so-called pillars 2 and 3, respectively). This exclusion showed that member states had learned from the past, and that they were unwilling to allow the ECJ to meddle in these important policy areas. As usual, the small states were especially unhappy that the ECJ was excluded from Justice and Home Affairs. In the Treaty of Amsterdam, formally concluded in October 1997, the small states managed to have aspects of Justice and Home Affairs transferred into the realm of the ECJ, but in a restricted way. For issues of asylum law, migration policy, border controls, and the Schengen Agreement, the preliminary ruling system was extended only to the courts of last instance, which are less likely to send controversial issues of national policy to the ECJ. Officially, the explanation for excluding lower courts from sending references is that states were worried about a flood of asylum appeals to the ECJ, but EU officials admit that behind this official stance is a fear of ECJ activism on lower court references. The ECJ was also explicitly denied jurisdiction over domestic issues concerning internal order and security, including assesments of the proportionality of state security actions (Article K.5 and K.7 §5). For issues of policing and judicial cooperation (that is, fighting terrorism and drug trafficking), each government is allowed to chose if its courts will be able to make preliminary ruling references; thus national governments can keep the ECJ out of domestic issues by denying the right of reference to national courts (Article K.6 §2). More easily overlooked is the provision stating that policies adopted under the EU framework with respect to Article K will not create direct effects, that is, individual rights that can be claimed in national courts (Article K.6 §2). Thus no individual or group will be able to draw on these EU rules to challenge national policy. This restriction will make it possible for individuals to challenge the EU agreements themselves but not national implementation of the agreements.

This outcome accords exactly with the expectations of the joint-decision trap. For existent ECJ jurisprudence and for areas of the Court's established jurisdiction, the ECJ remained virtually immune from political sanction. But in areas of new legislation and new authority for the ECJ, member states were able to block changes that they feared would undermine their sovereignty.

The ECJ has survived the most serious attack on its authority in its history. The ECJ may have retreated in some of its jurisprudence, but it has still shown a willingness to make bold decisions even at the height of the political threats against it.[67] The ECJ knew that the British government was angry over the cost of ECJ decisions, yet in March 1996, while the IGC was still underway, the ECJ ordered the British government to pay Spanish fishermen a fine for violating European law. It also ordered the German government—the British government's desired ally—to compensate a French brewery prevented from exporting to Germany.[68] Even under the most concrete and direct political attacks to date, the ECJ continued its doctrine building—and in an area of significant concern to the attacking member states. This experience shows yet again that the ECJ continues to have the institutional and political capacity and the will to make decisions that go against member state interests.

Conclusion: A New Framework for Understanding ECJ–Member State Interactions

In this article I have offered an account of how ECJ–member state relations are embedded in and constrained by institutions. I have argued that these institutional links, both at the national and supranational levels, directly shape the maneuverability of the ECJ so that its decisions do not have to be simple reflections of national interests. The account is self-consciously historical, focusing on understanding the evolution of the EU legal system over time as a window into how the present system operates.[69] Only when one considers that the current EU legal system was not intended to function as it does can we understand why member states that have an interest in maximizing national sovereignty have ended up with a legal system that greatly compromises national sovereignty. To say that this outcome was unintended is not to say that it happened by chance. The ECJ was very conscious in its strategy,

67. In an article entitled "Language, Culture, and Politics in the Life of the European Court of Justice," Justice Mancini of the ECJ argued that there had been a "retreat from activism," citing three reasons for this retreat: (1) the change in public opinion signaled by the debates of the Maastricht Treaty, which identified the ECJ as one of the chief EU villains; (2) two protocols in the Maastricht Treaty designed to circumvent potential ECJ decisions regarding awarding retrospective benefits for pension discrimination and German house ownership in Denmark; and (3) recent criticism from Germany—one of the Court's historic allies—especially in light of the IGC; Mancini 1995, 12.

68. Rice, Harding, and Hargreaves 1996.

69. A similar general account of this nature has been developed by Pierson 1996. I am indebted to Pierson for helping crystallize many of the ideas with which I have been working.

as were the member states. But their different time horizons combined with a national judicial dynamic that propelled legal integration forward created a situation that national governments had not agreed to and, collectively, would not agree to today. Only by knowing this evolution of the Court's political power can we understand why these same countries are still very reluctant to extend the jurisdictional authority of the ECJ even in very limited areas, such as the Cannes conventions for Europol and a common customs information system. Because we know the history of the European legal system, we can understand why European states, committed to a rule of law and benefiting from increased compliance with EU law, are also reluctant to agree to replicate the successful EU legal system in other international contexts or even in other areas of European integration.

The arguments advanced in this article are built on many important insights from the early literature on the ECJ. Like the neofunctionalist and legalist literature, this article stresses the important difference between the legal and the political rules of the game. Like the neorealist literature, it examines the ECJ as an agent of the member states and identifies important political constraints created by the control of the decision-making process by member states. This article goes beyond these accounts, however, offering a different and even competing conception of the interests of the ECJ and member states and of the relationship between the ECJ and the member states. By moving beyond international relations approaches, I hope to widen the variables considered in evaluating EU–member state relations and contribute to the growing debate on how domestic politics influences European integration, and vice versa.

Many of the arguments raised in this article can be stated as more general hypotheses about ECJ–member state relations and about national government–judicial relations. If these hypotheses hold, there are also significant reasons to question how generalizable the experience of the ECJ is to other international legal contexts.

Different Time Horizons for Different Political Actors

One of the reasons why the ECJ could develop legal doctrine that went against the long-term interests of the member states is that politicians focused on the short-term material and political impact of the decisions rather than the long-term doctrinal implications of the decisions. Member states *understood* that the legal precedent established might create political costs in the future, and thus they were not fooled by seemingly apolitical legalese or by the technical nature of law. But national governments were willing to trade off potential long-term costs so long as they could escape the political and financial costs of judicial decisions in the present. From this experience, one could hypothesize that legislators are more likely to act against judicial activism when it creates significant financial and political consequences and less likely to act against judicial activism that does not upset current policy.[70] In other words, the doctrinal significance matters less to national governments than the impact of decisions. If, however, the doctrine itself created a political impact by mobi-

---

70. For similar arguments, see Alter 1996a; and Garrett, Kelemen, and Schulz 1996.

lizing groups, as many U.S. Supreme Court decisions do, the doctrine alone might be enough to upset member states.

This time horizons argument comes from rational choice and historical institutional analysis and is, of course, generalizable beyond the ECJ or EU case.[71]

Importance of National Judicial Support

National judicial support was critical in limiting the ability of national governments to simply ignore unwanted legal decisions from the international ECJ. In other words, where the inherent legitimacy of the ECJ or the compelling nature of the legal argumentation did not convince member states to accept ECJ decisions, national court legitimacy forced the government to find legally acceptable solutions to accommodate the jurisprudence of the ECJ.[72] This implies that in areas where national courts cannot be invoked, either because EC law does not create direct effects or the ECJ does not have jurisdictional authority to be seized by national courts, politicians would more likely ignore unwanted ECJ decisions or adopt extralegal means to mitigate the effects of ECJ decisions. Consequently, the ECJ would be more careful to take member state interests into account. The critical role of national courts as enforcers of ECJ decisions also implies that in countries where national courts are less legitimate, less vigilant, and a rule of law ideology is not a significant domestic political factor, politicians would be more likely to use extralegal means to circumvent ECJ jurisprudence.[73]

The EU experience highlights the importance of having domestic interlocutors to make adherence to international institutions politically constraining at home. One could hypothesize that international norms will most influence national politics when they are drawn on or pulled into the domestic political realm by domestic actors.[74]

Creating a Credible Threat

If courts should start deciding against national interests, what can national governments do? In the European Union, where governments cannot selectively opt out of the European legal system, the only solution available to member states is to rewrite EU legislation or renegotiate the jurisdictional authority of the ECJ. For the many reasons discussed, doing this is not so easy. This is not to say that states can never overcome the institutional constraints. Germany and the Netherlands are pivotal countries in the coalition protecting the ECJ. If these countries turned, and all other countries agreed to go along, a credible threat could be mustered. One could hypothesize that when political support for the ECJ is waning in the key states blocking jurisdictional change, we can expect the ECJ to moderate its jurisprudence to avoid the emergence of a consensus to attack its prerogatives. But when a clear blocking con-

---

71. Pierson 1996.
72. This argument is supported in survey research on ECJ legitimacy by Caldeira and Gibson; Caldeira and Gibson 1995.
73. This hypothesis follows from Slaughter 1995.
74. Alter and Vargas 1997.

tingent exists, the ECJ can be expected to decide against the interests of powerful member states.

In international contexts where states can opt out of legal mechanisms or keep disputes from even getting to an international body, it will be easier for governments to credibly threaten international tribunals to moderate their jurisprudence. Whether these threats will be enough to cow the tribunal into quiescence is another story. As mentioned earlier, in some circumstances the legitimacy of a legal body could be hurt more by caving in to political pressure than by making a legally sound decision that the court knows politicians will ignore.[75]

The ECJ: A Model for Other International Legal Systems?

The ECJ began as a fairly weak international tribunal, suffering from many of the problems faced by international courts. It lacked cases to adjudicate. No enforcement mechanism was in place, so ECJ decisions were easy to ignore. The neutrality of the ECJ and its reputation for high-quality decisions and sound legal reasoning was not enough to make member states use the legal mechanism to resolve disputes or to force member states to adhere to decisions that went against important interests. The ECJ has changed the weak foundations of the EU legal system, with the help of national judiciaries. If the ECJ, by building legal doctrine, created a base of political leverage for itself, could other international legal bodies not do the same?

If national courts are the main reason why European governments adhere to ECJ decisions in cases that go against national interests, one must question how generalizable the EU experience is to other international contexts. In the EU the preliminary ruling mechanism serves as a direct link coordinating interpretation of national courts with the ECJ. As I have argued elsewhere, the preliminary ruling system also serves a political function, pressuring national high courts to bring their jurisprudence into agreement with the ECJ.[76] In most other international judicial or quasi-judicial systems, there is no direct link between the international court and national courts, making it much more difficult to coordinate legal interpretation across boundaries. Although it is always possible that national courts could look to jurisprudence generated from international bodies and thus enhance the enforceability of international law, without the preliminary ruling mechanism one must wonder if independent-minded national judges with different legal traditions and much legal hubris will turn for guidance to international bodies whose jurisprudence goes against strong political interests.

Given that unintended consequences almost always accrue when institutions are created, it should not surprise us if politicians wake up at some other time to find their sovereignty constrained in unintended ways in other international contexts. At the same time, it could be that member states are now wise to the benefits and costs of the EU legal system, and that they will not make such a mistake in the future. Although great strides have been made in the development of international dispute resolution

75. Mattli and Slaughter 1995.
76. Alter 1996b.

mechanisms, none of the new systems includes a preliminary ruling mechanism. These systems still have significant political controls for the member states that allow them to avoid the costs of an international judicial decision that greatly compromises national interests. Whether the success of the EU legal system is a prototype for other international legal systems is still open for debate.

References

Alter, Karen. 1996a. The European Court's Political Power. *West European Politics* 19 (3):458–87.

———. 1996b. The Making of a Rule of Law: The European Court and the National Judiciaries. Ph.D. diss., Massachusetts Institute of Technology.

———. 1997. Why, Where, and When National Courts Enforce European Law Against Their Governments. Paper presented at Domestic Policy and International Law Conference, 4–8 June, St. Helena, California.

Alter, Karen, and Jeannette Vargas. 1997. Shifting the Domestic Balance of Power in Europe: European Law and UK Social Policy. Paper presented at 93d American Political Science Association Meeting, 28–31 August, Washington D.C.

Brown, Kevin. 1995. Government to Demand Curb on European Court. *Financial Times*, 2 February, 9.

Burley, Anne-Marie Slaughter. 1993. International Law and International Relations Theory: A Dual Agenda. *The American Journal of International Law* 87:205–39.

Burley, Anne-Marie, and Walter Mattli. 1993. Europe Before the Court. *International Organization* 47 (1):41–76.

Caldeira, Gregory, and James Gibson. 1995. The Legitimacy of the Court of Justice in the European Union: Models of Institutional Support. *American Political Science Review* 89 (2):356–76.

Clever, Peter. 1995. EuGH-Rechtsprechung im Sozialbereich-Kritik, aber auch hoffnungsvolle Zuversicht. *Zeitschrift für Sozialhilfe und Sozialgesetzbuch* (1):1–14.

Denning, Lord. 1990. Introduction to "The European Court of Justice: Judges or Policy Makers?" London: The Bruge Group.

Everling, Ulrich. 1967. Sprachliche Mißverständnisse beim Urteil des Gerichtshofes der Europäischen Gemeinschaften zur Umsatzausgleichsteuer. *Außenwirtschaftsdiensts des Betriebs-Beraters* 5 (15 May): 182–84.

Garrett, Geoffrey. 1992. The European Community's Internal Market. *International Organization* 46 (2): 533–60.

———. 1995. The Politics of Legal Integration in the European Union. *International Organization* 49 (1):171–81.

Garrett, Geoffrey, and Barry Weingast. 1993. Ideas, Interests, and Institutions: Constructing the EC's Internal Market. In *Ideas and Foreign Policy*, edited by Judith Goldstein and Robert Keohane, 173–206. Ithaca, N.Y.: Cornell University Press.

Geoffrey Garrett, R. Daniel Kelemen, and Heiner Schulz. 1998. The European Court of Justice, National Governments, and Legal Integration in the European Union. *International Organization* 52 (1): 149–76.

Golub, Jonathan. 1996. The Politics of Judicial Discretion: Rethinking the Interaction Between National Courts and the European Court of Justice. *West European Politics* 2:360–85.

Hartley, Trevor. 1988. *The Foundations of European Community Law*. Oxford: Clarendon Press.

Kari, Jutsamo. 1979. *The Role of Preliminary Rulings in the European Community, Dissertations Humanarum Litterarum 16*. Helsinki: Suomalainen Tiedeakatemia.

Mancini, Federico. 1989. The Making of a Constitution for Europe. *Common Market Law Review* 24:595–614.

Mancini, Federico, with David Keeling. 1994. Democracy and the European Court of Justice. *Modern Law Review* 57 (2):175–90.

————. 1995. Language, Culture, and Politics in the Life of the European Court of Justice. *Columbia Journal of European Law* 1 (2):397–413.

Mann, Clarence J. 1972. *The Function of Judicial Decision in European Economic Integration*. The Hague: Martinus Nijhoff Press.

Marks, Brian A. 1989. A Model of Judicial Influence on Congressional Policy Making: *Grove City College v. Bell* (1984). Ph.D. diss., University of Washington.

Mattli, Walter, and Anne-Marie Slaughter. 1995. Law and Politics in the European Union: A Reply to Garrett. *International Organization* 49 (1):183–90.

————. 1998. Revisiting the European Court of Justice. *International Organization* 52 (1):177–209.

McCubbins, Mathew, and Thomas Schwartz. 1987. Congressional Oversight Overlooked: Police Patrols Versus Fire Alarms. In *Congress: Structure and Policy*, edited by Matthew McCubbins and Terry Sullivan, 409–25. Cambridge: Cambridge University Press.

Meier, Gert. 1967a. Aktuelle Fragen zur Umsatzausgleichsteuer. *Außenwirtschaftsdienst des Betriebs-Beraters* Heft 3 (15 March):97–101.

————. 1967b. Zur Aussetzung der Einsprüche gegen Umsatzausgleichsteuerbescheide. *Außenwirtschaftsdienst des Betriebs-Beraters* Heft 2 (15 February):75–77.

————. 1994. Der Streit um die Umsatzausgleichsteuer aus integrationspolitischer Sicht. *Recht der Internationalen Wirtschaft* 3.

Moravcsik, Andrew. 1995. Liberal Intergovernmentalism and Integration: A Rejoinder. *Journal of Common Market Studies* 33 (4):611–28.

Pierson, Paul. 1996. The Path to European Integration: A Historical Institutionalist Perspective. *Comparative Political Studies* 29 (2):123–63.

Pollack, Mark. 1997. Delegation, Agency, and Agenda Setting in the EC. *International Organization* 51 (1):99–134.

Rasmussen, Hjalte. 1986. *On Law and Policy in the European Court of Justice*. Dordrecht: Martinus Nijhoff Publishers.

Rice, Robert, James Harding, and Deborah Hargreaves. 1996. EU States Ordered to Pay for Breaches of European Law. *Financial Times*, 6 March, 12.

Robertson, A. H. 1966. *European Institutions—Cooperation, Integration, Unification*. 2d ed. New York: Frederick A. Praeger.

Scharpf, Fritz. 1988. The Joint-Decision Trap: Lessons from German Federalism and European Integration. *Public Administration* 66 (Autumn):239–78.

Scheingold, Stuart. 1971. The Law in Political Integration: The Evolution and Integrative Implications of Regional Legal Processes in the European Community. Occasional Paper in International Affairs, 27. Cambridge, Mass.: Harvard University Center for International Affairs.

Shapiro, Martin. 1981. *Courts: A Comparative Political Analysis*. Chicago: University of Chicago Press.

Slaughter, Anne-Marie. 1995. International Law in a World of Liberal States. *European Journal of International Law* 6:503–38.

Stein, Eric. 1981. Lawyers, Judges, and the Making of a Transnational Constitution. *American Journal of International Law* 75 (1):1–27.

Stöcker, Hans A. 1967. Einzelklagebefugnis und EWG-Kommissionsentscheidung: Alternative oder kumulierter Rechtsschutz in Umsatzausgleichsteuersachen. *Der Betrieb* (40):1690–92.

Weiler, Joseph. 1981. The Community System: The Dual Character of Supranationalism. *Yearbook of European Law* 1:257–306.

————. 1991. The Transformation of Europe. *Yale Law Journal* 100:2403–83.

————. 1994. A Quiet Revolution—The European Court of Justice and Its Interlocutors. *Comparative Political Studies* 26 (4):510–34.

Wendt, Peter. 1967a. Kein Rechtsschutz im Umsatzausgleichsteuer-Sachen? *Der Betrieb* (48):2047–48.

————. 1967b. Ungeklärte Fragen im Streit um die Unmsatzausgleichsteuer. *Außenwirtschaftsdienst des Betriebs-Beraters* Heft 9 (September):348–54.

The Politics of Dispute Settlement Design: Explaining Legalism in Regional Trade Pacts

James McCall Smith

In recent years two parallel trends have emerged in the organization of international trade. The first development is the rise of regionalism, with a host of new integration initiatives drawn along geographical lines. More than thirty regional accords were officially notified to the General Agreement on Tariffs and Trade (GATT) between 1990 and 1994 alone, a total exceeding that of any previous five-year period.[1] The second is a distinct but less widespread move toward legalism in the enforcement of trade agreements. To an unusual extent trading states have delegated to impartial third parties the authority to review and issue binding rulings on alleged treaty violations, at times based on complaints filed by nonstate or supranational actors. Separately, the two trends have garnered scholarly attention, sparking comparative analysis of regional versus multilateral arrangements and debates regarding the political dynamics of judicialization within individual pacts, especially in Europe.[2] The intersection of these two trends, however, remains little examined.

Few comparative studies of institutional form, across different trade accords, have been undertaken. This is curious, for regional trade pacts exhibit considerable variation in governance structures. Moreover, questions of institutional design—which constitute a dimension of bargaining distinct from the substantive terms of liberalization—have proven contentious in recent trade negotiations, underscoring their political salience.[3] The creation of supranational institutions in regional trade accords has direct implications for academic debates regarding sovereignty, globalization, and interdependence. Nevertheless, research on this particular issue remains scarce. Schol-

For helpful comments I would like to thank the editors of *IO*, three anonymous reviewers, John Barton, Martha Finnemore, James Foster, Geoffrey Garrett, Kurt Gaubatz, Judith Goldstein, Miles Kahler, Stephen Krasner, Derek Scissors, Susan Sell, Lee Sigelman, Paul Wahlbeck, and Beth Yarbrough.

1. WTO 1995, 25.
2. On multilateralism, see Ruggie 1993. On judicialization in Europe, see Burley and Mattli 1993; Garrett 1995; and Mattli and Slaughter 1995 and 1998.
3. Mexico threatened to walk away from the North American Free Trade Agreement (NAFTA) over the inclusion of sanctions in the side accords. See *International Trade Reporter*, 18 August 1993, 1352. Canada risked its 1988 pact with the United States through its insistence on "binding" dispute settlement. See Hart 1994, 260–63, 301–302.

International Organization 54, 1, Winter 2000, pp. 137–180

ars have examined the strategic behavior of disputing states and judges within isolated agreements, but few have aimed to account for variation in the organizational details of international trade.[4]

Addressing this gap, I focus on a specific aspect of governance in international trade: the design of dispute settlement procedures. In particular, I investigate the conditions under which member states adopt legalistic mechanisms for resolving disputes and enforcing compliance in regional trade accords. Some pacts are diplomatic, requiring only consultations between disputing states, but others invest standing judicial tribunals with the authority to issue prompt, impartial, and enforceable third-party rulings on any and all alleged treaty violations. To account for these variable levels of legalism, I offer a theory of trade dispute settlement design based on the domestic political trade-off between treaty compliance and policy discretion. The chief implication of this theory highlights the importance of economic asymmetry, in interaction' with the proposed depth of integration, as a robust predictor of dispute settlement design. This framework helps explain otherwise puzzling delegations of authority by sovereign states to supranational judiciaries, linking variation in institutional design to domestic political factors conventionally ignored by traditional systemic theories of international relations. It also complements recent work combining elements of international law and international relations theory.[5]

At issue in this study is the nature of *ex ante* institutional design, not the record of *ex post* state behavior. During trade negotiations, governments stand, in part, behind a veil of ignorance with regard to future implementation of the treaty and future disputes. The question I investigate involves the type of dispute settlement mechanism, given this uncertainty, the signatory states agree to establish. In advance of actual integration, it is difficult to distinguish sincere commitments from symbolic ones. Even the most successful regional initiative, the European Union, has weathered crises of confidence in its uneven movement toward a single market.[6] Without evaluating the extent to which integration has proceeded, I seek to explain the design of the institutions within which that process unfolds. I examine the institutional structure of the general game, not the outcome of specific disputes, which depend on strategic interactions and highly contextual international and domestic political variables. Multiple policy outcomes and compliance rates may function as equilibria under a single dispute settlement mechanism, and this study remains for the most part neutral with respect to subsequent use of a particular procedure.

Nevertheless, I do assert that legalism tends to improve compliance by increasing the costs of opportunism. Legalistic mechanisms alter the cost-benefit calculus of cheating by increasing the probability of detection, resolving conflicts of interpretation, and endorsing commensurate sanctions or making rulings directly applicable in

---

4. Yarbrough and Yarbrough concur that regional trade dispute settlement is "underexplored" in comparative terms. Yarbrough and Yarbrough 1997, 134, 139, 160. Their research on institutions for governance in international trade is a welcome exception; see, among others, Yarbrough and Yarbrough 1997, 1994, and 1992. Another significant work comparing institutions for integration is Kahler 1995.

5. For a survey, see Slaughter, Tulumello, and Wood 1998.

6. Tsoukalis 1993, 14–45.

domestic law. As the debate over the role of the European Court of Justice suggests, even the most legalistic of mechanisms may not guarantee treaty compliance by sovereign states willing to defy its rulings.[7] Likewise, the least legalistic of pacts may give rise to highly successful integration.[8] Legalism is thus neither a necessary nor a sufficient condition for full compliance. Without determining it, legalism does influence compliance by providing rulings of violation that are viewed as credible and legitimate by the community of member states. This information at a minimum increases the reputational costs of noncompliance, potentially jeopardizing opportunities for future international cooperation on issues of relevance to the domestic economy.[9]

In the first section of the article I introduce the dependent variable, levels of legalism, by identifying specific institutional features that render one dispute settlement mechanism more or less legalistic than another. Next I sketch the elements of a theory of dispute settlement design, defining the basic trade-off and how it varies. Subsequent sections delimit the data set of regional trade agreements and summarize the principal characteristics of their dispute settlement mechanisms. Finally, after defining an index of economic asymmetry and indicators of depth of integration, I evaluate the explanatory leverage of my analytical framework, comparing it briefly to alternative approaches that emphasize the transaction costs of collective action or the functional requirements of deep integration.

Defining the Spectrum: From Diplomacy to Legalism

Discussions of dispute settlement in international and comparative law texts present the universe of institutional options as a standard set that ranges from direct negotiation at one extreme to third-party adjudication at the other.[10] Which features of institutional design determine the level of legalism along this spectrum? The first question is whether there is an explicit right to third-party review of complaints regarding treaty application and interpretation. A handful of agreements provide only for consultations and perhaps mediation or conciliation, which implies a very low level of legalism in that the disputing parties retain the right to reject any proposed settlement lawfully—the hallmark of a diplomatic system.[11] These pacts are identical in effect to treaties that offer an arbitral process but require explicit consent from all parties to the dispute, including the defendant, before the arbitration proceeds. In either situation, disputes will be addressed exclusively through bilateral negotiation and self-help measures if one disputant is averse to scrutiny from a third party. In other agreements, such as the 1981 Gulf Cooperation Council (GCC), member countries

---

7. See Garrett 1995; and Garrett, Kelemen, and Schulz 1998.

8. For example, Kahler notes the effectiveness of the Australia–New Zealand Closer Economic Relations Trade Agreement (ANZCERTA) in the absence of formal governance structures. Kahler 1995, 110–11.

9. Maggi 1996.

10. See Malanczuk 1997, 273–305; Merrills 1991; and Shapiro 1981.

11. Diverse examples include the 1969 Southern African Customs Union; the 1983 ANZCERTA; and the 1992 Central European Free Trade Agreement.

that are not directly involved in the dispute may control access to the arbitration process. They play the role of political gatekeeper, ensuring that only cases deemed worthy by the community reach the dispute settlement process. The chance of a political veto of third-party review renders such mechanisms less legalistic than others in which complaints automatically qualify for arbitration.

Where there is an automatic right to third-party review, the second issue concerns the status in international law of rulings that result from the dispute settlement process. The question is whether arbitral or judicial rulings and reports are formally binding in international legal terms. Many treaties stipulate that disputants have an international legal obligation to comply with rulings. The 1985 U.S.–Israel Free Trade Agreement, by contrast, treats third-party decisions as mere recommendations in the form of a conciliation report. Other treaties give legal force to arbitral rulings only after they have been officially adopted, and perhaps substantially revised, by political representatives of the member governments acting through one of the pact's governing institutions.[12] If the disputants can lawfully ignore panel recommendations or sabotage panel reports by lobbying political allies, the system is less legalistic than mechanisms whose third-party rulings directly and irreversibly create an international legal obligation.

The next question concerns third parties—in particular, the number, term, and method of selecting arbitrators or judges in each treaty. At the diplomatic end of the spectrum are mechanisms that call for the appointment of ad hoc arbitrators to address a particular dispute. In the event that the disputing parties cannot agree on the composition of the arbitral panel, most agreements designate a neutral third party to appoint the remaining members. Having delivered its arbitral report, the panel disbands. At the legalistic end of the spectrum are treaties that create a standing tribunal of justices who rule collectively on any and all disputes during extended terms of service. Even in the absence of explicit stare decisis, decisions made by a standing tribunal are likely to be more consistent over time—and thus more legalistic—than rulings by ad hoc panels whose membership changes with each dispute. On the selection of third parties, most agreements lie between these two poles. What varies is the extent to which disputants are able to angle strategically for sympathetic or biased judges. With a standing tribunal, the parties have little if any influence over the composition of the court after its initial establishment. With arbitrators selected ad hoc by the disputants, however, each party may be free to name nearly half the panel. Some arbitration mechanisms include innovative procedures that help enhance the impartiality of the panel; for example, many agreements require the formation of a roster of potential panelists in advance of any disputes.[13]

---

12. Prominent examples of this type of political oversight are the 1973 Caribbean Community (CARICOM) and the recent dispute settlement protocol of the 1992 Association of Southeast Asian Nations Free Trade Area.

13. Rosters formed by consensus give member governments a veto over each other's nominees, restricting the potential for strategic appointments. Rosters that are small in number tend to do the same, since disputants have fewer candidates to consider. And mechanisms that require cross-selection—where each disputant must select arbitrators named to the roster by the other or of foreign nationality—also tend to improve impartiality.

A fourth question is which actors have standing to file complaints and obtain rulings. The tradition in international law has long been that only sovereign states have full international legal personality, according states an almost exclusive right to conclude international agreements and to bring claims regarding treaty violations. Most trade accords reflect this tradition by allowing only member states to initiate disputes. In some instances, however, standing is defined more expansively to allow treaty organizations—such as a secretariat or commission, which may have a bureaucratic interest in the treaty's effective implementation—to file official complaints against member countries for some failure to comply.[14] In other agreements even private individuals or firms, whose economic interests are most directly at stake in the context of trade policy, have standing to file complaints and require a ruling. Rather like private attorneys general, individuals with access to dispute settlement are able to generate information about compliance at minimal cost to member states. Where individuals have standing, they can bring cases in one of two ways: directly, by filing a complaint with the tribunal; or indirectly, by requesting a domestic court to seek a preliminary ruling from the tribunal on any issue of relevance to the treaty. As long as national courts are willing to request preliminary rulings, the indirect route offers individuals a meaningful way to obtain supranational review of government policy. This procedure has been central to the prominent role of the European Court of Justice, as Alec Stone Sweet and Thomas Brunell demonstrate, and several other pacts—including the Central American Common Market and the Common Market of Eastern and Southern Africa—provide for preliminary references.[15] In general, the more expansive the definition of standing, the more legalistic the dispute settlement mechanism. When treaty organizations and private parties can file complaints, alleged violations are likely to be more frequent than if standing is accorded only to states, whose multiple diplomatic considerations make them reluctant to pursue certain cases.

Finally, there is the question of remedies in cases of treaty violation. The most legalistic alternative is to give direct effect in domestic law to dispute settlement rulings made at the international level.[16] Where rulings are directly applicable, government agencies and courts have a binding obligation under national law to abide by

14. In the Andean Pact, the Junta—a panel of three technocrats who administer the treaty—has standing to file complaints of noncompliance against member states. The European Union Commission enjoys similar powers.

15. Stone Sweet and Brunell 1998.

16. The question of direct effect may depend as much on domestic constitutional norms as on the terms of the treaty. There is a vast literature on the differences between "dualist" states where international laws must undergo acts of transformation before having domestic legal force and "monist" states where treaties are directly applied. I confine my analysis to explicit treaty provisions, assuming that reciprocal treaties should not provide for direct effect where domestic constitutional norms preclude it. In any event, national courts can interpret constitutional law creatively to minimize its conflict with international treaty commitments. For example, the often "dualist" United States has been able to give direct effect to Chapter 19 rulings on antidumping and countervailing duty determinations under NAFTA essentially by regarding the international arbitral panel as if it were a federal court enforcing U.S. law. Constitutional challenges to this process have been rejected by U.S. courts. See "Court Rejects Constitutional Challenge to NAFTA Dispute Settlement," *Inside U.S. Trade*, 21 November 1997.

and enforce their terms. In most instances direct effect creates a right of action in national courts, allowing individuals to invoke the treaty and file suit against the government for disregarding its international commitments.[17] Different levels or units of government may also have a similar right of action against one another.[18] Only a handful of agreements give direct effect to third-party rulings. The most prominent example is the European Union, where scholars attribute the development of the doctrine as much to a series of rulings by the European Court of Justice as to the 1957 Treaty of Rome, whose provisions on direct applicability the Court has extended incrementally through case law.[19]

Among treaties in which rulings have no direct effect, another remedy is the authorization of retaliatory trade sanctions. Permission to impose sanctions is granted only to the complaining state, not to the community of member states for collective action. This type of decentralized enforcement system has deep roots in international law and resembles the concept of retorsion.[20] For several reasons, sanctions are not always viewed as an effective remedy in international trade,[21] but other things being equal treaties that provide for sanctions are more legalistic than those with no remedy at all, like the Organization of East Caribbean States (OECS). The specific way in which sanctions are authorized is relevant. Some accords, such as the original European Free Trade Association, require approval from a political body—usually the council of ministers—before sanctions are authorized. Depending on the decision rule in the governing body, it may be possible for the defendant to block or delay sanctions at this stage. Agreements that empower the arbitral panel or tribunal to authorize or prescribe sanctions directly are less subject to political interference and thus more legalistic. Also relevant is whether the treaty provides any guidelines or potential limits on the level of sanctions that is approved. Mechanisms that offer a blanket authorization are less legalistic than those that apply certain norms regarding the appropriate level and sectoral composition of sanctions. Because unilateral measures are always an option in the self-help international system, however, the distinction between treaties that provide for sanctions and those that do not is far less significant than the question of direct effect.

Table 1 summarizes the key features of institutional design that make a dispute settlement system more or less legalistic. This list is not comprehensive, since other

---

17. The existence of a private right of action may also depend as much on domestic law as on specific treaty provisions. Again I restrict my analysis to the terms of the treaty. Some agreements ignore or confuse the issue, but others are clear. For example, Article 2021 of NAFTA explicitly prohibits the signatory states from allowing any private right of action under the treaty in national courts. Chapter 19 panel rulings in NAFTA are an extremely unusual exception to this rule, possible only because they enforce existing U.S. unfair trade laws.

18. Jackson 1992, 318, 327–28.

19. Weiler 1991.

20. Retorsion refers to lawful acts designed to injure a state that has acted illegally. See von Glahn 1996, 533–36.

21. Even if carefully designed, sanctions impose costs on the sanctioning country as well as on the defendant. Moreover, a system of sanctions systematically favors larger, less trade-dependent states, which are able to implement and withstand retaliatory measures with less economic dislocation than smaller, more open countries. For a general critique of sanctions, see Chayes and Chayes 1995.

TABLE 1. *Institutional options in dispute settlement design*

Treaty provision	Spectrum of legalism		
	More diplomatic <———————————> More legalistic		
Third-party review	None	Access controlled by political body	Automatic right to review
Third-party ruling	Recommendation	Binding if approved by political body	Directly binding obligation
Judges	Ad hoc arbitrators	Ad hoc panelists drawn from roster	Standing tribunal of justices
Standing	States only	States and treaty organs	States, treaty organs, and individuals
Remedy	None	Retaliatory sanctions	Direct effect in domestic law

issues—such as the presence or absence of deadlines or the extent to which arbitrators and judges have relevant legal expertise—can push an agreement toward one end of the spectrum or the other.[22] With these basic indicators, however, it is possible to categorize individual pacts. Even though the features in Table 1 are in theory independent of one another, they tend to cluster in practice, suggesting a hierarchical ordering of four dimensions: third-party review, third-party ruling, judges, and standing. The first question is whether the treaty provides for independent third-party review. Among pacts with some system of review, the next issue is whether rulings are directly binding in international law. Among pacts with binding rulings, those with standing tribunals are more legalistic than those with ad hoc arbitrators. Finally, tribunals with jurisdiction over claims by individuals, treaty organs, and states alike are more legalistic than those accessible only by states. In terms of remedy, the most legalistic pacts provide rulings with direct effect in national law, but the presence or absence of sanctions—though still significant—is a less meaningful indicator of legalism, with unilateral measures always available to states seeking to enforce third-party rulings in the decentralized international system. The basic issue is how effectively a given dispute settlement mechanism is able to produce impartial, consistent, and legally binding third-party rulings on any and all alleged treaty violations.

The Argument

When negotiating a trade pact, governments must decide how legalistic its dispute settlement mechanism will be. In making this choice, political leaders confront a

---

22. The GATT panel system, for example, became more legalistic over time as disputing states appointed arbitrators with greater legal expertise and imposed certain deadlines on the review process. For an account of the system's development, see Hudec 1993.

trade-off between mutually exclusive goals. On the one hand, they care about compliance with the agreement, the value of which depends on the extent to which other parties honor their commitments. The more legalistic the dispute settlement mechanism they design, the higher the likely level of compliance. On the other hand, they also care about their own policy discretion—and the less legalistic the mechanism, the greater their discretion to craft policies that solidify domestic support.[23] This section briefly examines each objective, assesses how the trade-off between them varies, and identifies the conditions under which legalistic dispute settlement is a likely institutional outcome.

Policy Discretion

International trade agreements pose a familiar dilemma for national political leaders motivated to remain in power.[24] Among the principal determinants of any executive's or ruling party's popularity is the state of the economy.[25] One way political leaders seek to increase growth and create jobs is to negotiate reciprocal trade agreements, which almost as a rule produce net welfare benefits.[26] The political dilemma lies in the distribution of costs and benefits. Although benefits outweigh costs in the aggregate, for consumers and producers they are diffuse, or shared in small amounts by numerous individuals, whereas costs are concentrated. In political terms, concentrated costs imply organized opposition from adversely affected groups in import-competing sectors.

Political leaders, anticipating this opposition, may use a range of strategies to facilitate reciprocal trade liberalization. They can encourage exporting firms to organize on behalf of liberalization; delegate trade policy authority to relatively insulated parts of the government; or, most important, offer compensation to groups that will bear a disproportionate share of the costs of adjustment.[27] Compensation may come in the form of side payments, special exemptions, or gradual liberalization. Such arrangements allow political leaders to reap the general benefits of liberalization while dampening the specific opposition of vulnerable domestic groups.

This generic problem of trade liberalization—diffuse net benefits, concentrated costs—is a factor in the political calculus of dispute settlement design. Political leaders cannot perfectly anticipate which groups will bear the heaviest costs of adjustment. During the negotiations, they propose specific exemptions or side payments for sectors that are clearly vulnerable to import competition. The substantive terms of a treaty, which establish the depth and pace of liberalization, usually reflect such concerns. But political leaders realize that liberalization will impose concentrated

---

23. Yarbrough and Yarbrough pose a trade-off between rigor and the opportunity for derogations that parallels the one I have drawn between treaty value and policy discretion; See Yarbrough and Yarbrough 1997, 148–49; and Smith 1995.

24. On the political economy of trade, see Schattschneider 1935; Pastor 1980; and Magee, Brock, and Young 1989.

25. See Kieweit and Rivers 1984; and Alesina and Rosenthal 1995.

26. Wolf 1987.

27. See Destler 1986; Destler and Odell 1987; Goldstein 1993; and Pastor 1980.

costs they cannot foresee. As a result, they want to retain the discretion to respond in the future to uncertain demands for relief from injured groups.[28] Under a legalistic dispute settlement system, political leaders who provide import protection *ex post* run the risk of provoking complaints from foreign trade partners that could lead to rulings of violation, with attendant reputational costs and perhaps sanctions.

In disputes over nontariff barriers, legalistic dispute settlement also threatens to compromise the autonomy of domestic officials across a range of general regulations, from health and safety standards to environmental, antitrust, and procurement policies. Historically, trading states negotiated reciprocal tariff reductions, achieving dramatic success in early GATT rounds. In recent decades, however, the principal obstacles to open trade have been nontariff barriers, domestic regulations that discriminate against foreign producers. The agendas of contemporary trade negotiations reflect this shift in the form of protection. The politics of regulation is not unlike the political economy of trade: the marginal impact of regulatory policy on small, organized groups is often disproportionately large compared to its impact on the general, unorganized public. This characteristic increases its salience to officials seeking to remain in power. With the shift to nontariff trade pacts, political leaders may now face unprecedented complaints from foreign governments alleging unfair regulatory barriers to trade. If the merits of these complaints are judged in legalistic dispute settlement procedures, the policy discretion of political leaders may be constrained—and in areas where the domestic political stakes, given mobilized interest groups, are high.

The threat that legalistic trade dispute settlement poses to the discretion of political leaders is threefold. First, it may constrain their ability to manage the unforeseen costs of adjustment, making it more costly to provide relief or protection to specific groups injured by trade liberalization. Second, it may limit their general policy autonomy across a range of domestic regulations, which it judges against treaty commitments to eliminate nontariff barriers to trade. A third and final consideration is that the delegation of authority to third parties may constrain their ability to pursue trade policy bilaterally, a strategy with distinct political advantages. On all three counts, political leaders in trading states are risk-averse regarding the impact of dispute settlement on policy discretion. Other things being equal, they do not want to cede veto power over domestic policies to appointed trade law experts or judges, because the political price of doing so may be high.

Treaty Compliance

If legalistic trade dispute settlement poses such a clear domestic political threat, why would trade negotiators ever consider, much less adopt, any binding procedures? The answer lies in the benefits generated by dispute settlement mechanisms that improve government compliance and instill business confidence. The very procedures that constrain the policy autonomy of public officials, giving rise to political risks, also

---

28. Downs and Rocke 1995, 77.

improve the economic value of the treaty, yielding domestic political benefits. If those benefits are sufficiently large, they may offset the potential costs of policy constraints, making legalistic dispute settlement an attractive institutional option.

There are several ways in which legalistic dispute settlement is likely to enhance the level of compliance with international trade agreements. When implementing reciprocal liberalization, trading states confront what theorists of the new economics of organization describe as problems of motivation and information.[29] Each state knows its partners may be motivated at times to violate their treaty commitments in order to provide protection to domestic groups. Each state also knows that with the prevalence and complexity of nontariff barriers, it may be difficult to generate information about every instance of defection by its partners. These transactions costs may prevent states from achieving mutually beneficial gains from exchange. As neoliberal institutionalists emphasize, international institutions arise in part to mitigate such costs by providing information about violations and in some instances by enforcing commitments.[30]

Formal dispute settlement procedures serve these very functions. As official forums where complaints are filed and judged, dispute settlement mechanisms play an important role in monitoring treaty violations, helping to offset problems of information. As independent bodies with the authority to endorse sanctions against offenders, dispute settlement mechanisms also help enforce treaty commitments, mitigating problems of motivation. Trading states realize that agreements are valuable only if compliance with their terms is high. Cheating, in the form of *ex post* protectionism, undermines the expected benefits of free trade accords. One way to discourage defection is to craft dispute settlement mechanisms that monitor and enforce compliance. The more legalistic the mechanism—in other words, the more effectively and impartially it identifies violations and enforces third-party rulings—the higher the likely level of government compliance.[31]

In addition to monitoring and enforcing compliance, dispute settlement procedures also serve to define compliance, clarifying the meaning of the treaty in disputes over how to interpret its terms. In new economics of organization terminology, dispute settlement operates in this respect as a type of relational contract.[32] Because the parties to a trade agreement cannot foresee all possible contingencies, they find it very difficult *ex ante* to define compliance. The accord they negotiate is inevitably incomplete; it does not specify how the parties are to behave under all possible circumstances. As circumstances change, conflicts of interpretation may arise, potentially jeopardizing the treaty. To avoid such conflicts, parties agree in relational contracts to assign rights and responsibilities to define compliance, a role that trade accords often confer on impartial third parties.[33]

---

29. See Yarbrough and Yarbrough 1990; and Milgrom and Roberts 1992.
30. Keohane 1984.
31. Economists have sought to demonstrate the benefits of third-party trade dispute settlement with formal models. See Maggi 1996; and Kovenock and Thursby 1994.
32. Milgrom and Roberts 1992, chap. 5.
33. See Garrett and Weingast 1993; and Weingast 1995.

Finally, legalistic dispute settlement also improves the expected value of reciprocal trade pacts through its impact on the behavior of private traders and investors. For political leaders to realize fully the benefits of liberalization, private sector actors must believe that having committed specific assets to production for (or sales in) foreign markets, they will not be denied access to that market by new protectionist policies. Traders and investors are risk-averse with respect to decisions about investment, production, and distribution involving assets that are highly specific—in other words, assets that are costly to convert to other uses.[34] Other things being equal, they prefer minimum uncertainty, prizing a stable policy environment in which to assess alternative business strategies.[35] Legalistic dispute settlement serves as an institutional commitment to trade liberalization that bolsters the confidence of the private sector, reducing one source of risk. The private sector thus increases the volume of trade and investment among the parties, amplifying the macroeconomic—and, in turn, political—benefits of liberalization.

To summarize, legalistic dispute settlement improves the value of trade agreements through two principal channels. First, by defining, monitoring, and enforcing compliance, it constrains the opportunistic behavior of foreign governments that are tempted to provide protection to their constituents. Second, as an institutional commitment to policy stability, it promotes the confidence of the private sector, inducing traders and investors to take risks that increase the aggregate benefits of liberalization. With reduced foreign cheating and increased private sector activity, trade accords have a larger positive effect on economic factors that influence domestic political support. If legalistic dispute settlement promises to improve rates of unemployment, inflation, and growth, political leaders may very well choose to forgo policy discretion, despite the obvious risks.

Assessing the Trade-off

Political leaders negotiating the design of dispute settlement always confront this tension between policy discretion and treaty compliance. The trade-off between these objectives is universal, but not uniform. Different governments assess it in dissimilar ways. And the weight a specific government assigns to each objective changes in different settings, as does the probability that its preferred mechanism will be adopted. In specifying the dimensions of variance, it is helpful to distinguish two stages in the process of dispute settlement design. The first is national preference formation; the second, international bargaining.[36]

The level of legalism preferred by a particular government in a specific trade negotiation depends on several factors. The first is the extent to which its economy

---

34. Not all assets, obviously, are specific. For a discussion, see Frieden 1991, 434–40, who builds on the pioneering work of Oliver Williamson. Williamson 1985.

35. Not all firms prefer the certainty of stable, liberal trade policy to the prospect of future protection. Firms close to insolvency or in sectors with low productivity are likely to prefer trade policy discretion—and the increased probability of protection—to the constraints of legalistic dispute settlement.

36. This distinction follows Moravcsik 1993, 480–82.

depends on trade with other signatories to the accord. The more trade-dependent the economy, measured as the ratio of intrapact exports to gross domestic product (GDP), the more legalistic the dispute settlement mechanism its government will tend to favor. Legalistic dispute settlement is more valuable politically where trade with prospective partner countries accounts for a larger share of the domestic economy.

A second source of dispute settlement preferences is relative economic power. The more powerful the country in relative terms, the less legalistic the dispute settlement mechanism its government will favor. This hypothesis derives from the distinction legal scholars have made between rule-oriented and power-oriented dispute settlement.[37] Rule-oriented systems resolve conflicts by developing and applying consistent rules to comparable disputes, enabling less powerful parties to win independent legal rulings that may be costly for more powerful parties to ignore. For small countries, the benefits of such rulings may outweigh the costs of diminished policy discretion. In power-oriented systems, parties resolve disputes through traditional diplomatic means of self-help, such as issue-linkage, hostage taking, and in particular the threat of retaliatory sanctions.[38] These strategies systematically favor more powerful countries, which tend to favor pragmatism over legalism. A telling measure of relative economic power within regional trade accords is each country's share of total pact GDP. The larger the country's economy in relative terms, the more influence it is likely to wield as the destination of imports from other signatories. Larger economies also tend to be less dependent on exports, giving their leaders diplomatic leverage in trade disputes.[39]

A third factor shaping dispute settlement preferences is the proposed depth of liberalization. Trade agreements come in a variety of forms, and the type of agreement at hand influences the type of dispute settlement system favored by member governments. In particular, the more ambitious the level of proposed integration, the more willing political leaders should be to endorse legalistic dispute settlement. One reason is that deeper integration promises to generate larger net economic gains.[40] A second consideration is that legalism, viewed from a functional perspective, may be the most appropriate institutional design for the resolution of disputes in the process of deep integration, which includes coverage of complex nontariff barriers to trade and common regulatory regimes.[41]

Together these simple measures—intrapact trade dependence, relative economic power, and depth of liberalization—provide a way of specifying dispute settlement preferences *ex ante*. To specify outcomes, one must also identify which country's preferences—given divergent ideal points on the Pareto frontier of trade coopera-

37. For discussions of this distinction, which is also cast as "pragmatism" versus "legalism," see Dam 1970, 3–5; Hudec 1971, 1299–1300, 1304; and Jackson 1979.
38. Yarbrough and Yarbrough 1986.
39. Alesina and Wacziarg 1997.
40. The same logic applies to the breadth of trade pacts: where coverage is comprehensive, excluding no major export sectors, political leaders are more likely to endorse legalism than in pacts that exempt significant sectors.
41. For diverse studies of deep integration, see the Brookings Institution series entitled "Integrating National Economies: Promise and Pitfalls."

tion[42]—should prevail at the bargaining stage. Like most international treaty negotiations, trade talks require consensus. In the presence of a unanimity rule, the design of dispute settlement is likely to be only as legalistic as the signatory that most values policy discretion and least values treaty compliance will allow. The lowest common denominator drives the institutional outcome when all parties have a unit veto.

In trade negotiations, one proxy for legalism's lowest common denominator is intrapact economic asymmetry. Its utility lies in the fact that larger economies stand to gain less, in proportional terms, from regional liberalization than smaller economies. Within a given agreement, the largest economies—defined in terms of aggregate GDP—traditionally represent the most valuable potential markets for intrapact exports.[43] Larger economies also are less dependent on and less open to trade—with openness measured either in terms of policy measures or as the ratio of trade to GDP—than smaller economies.[44] In an econometric analysis Alberto Alesina, Enrico Spolaore, and Romain Wacziarg report that the benefits of openness to trade, measured in terms of the impact on per capita GDP growth rates, diminish as aggregate GDP increases.[45] Such observations suggest that the relative value of liberalization—and, by implication, of legalistic dispute settlement—is usually lower to larger economies than to smaller economies. The signatory state with the largest economy, therefore, is most likely to wield the unit veto that determines the level of legalism in a given agreement.

This analysis leads one to expect less legalistic dispute settlement in accords between parties whose relative economic size and bargaining leverage are highly unequal. In pacts where a single member country is much larger than its partners—in other words, where intrapact economic asymmetry is high—the regional hegemon, whose economy stands to gain least from trade liberalization, has little incentive to risk its policy discretion on behalf of improved treaty compliance. Moreover, this hegemon also has the bargaining leverage to impose its preference for a pragmatic, power-oriented system, under which it can more effectively use unilateral trade measures. In other words, size matters—and significant disparities in relative economic position augur poorly for legalism. Legalistic dispute settlement is expected only in accords among parties whose relative size and bargaining leverage are more symmetric. In settings of low economic asymmetry—provided the proposed liberalization is sufficiently deep—all member governments have an incentive to improve treaty compliance through the use of impartial third parties. Given their comparable economic power *ex ante*, no signatory stands to lose bargaining leverage *ex post* from the transition to a legalistic system. The projected gains from liberalization must be significant, however, if political leaders are to compromise their policy discretion. If

42. Krasner 1991.
43. For this observation to hold, per capita income levels should be comparable across member countries. Most regional trade pacts between 1957 and 1995 have been exclusively among either developed or developing countries, with NAFTA as the first of few exceptions.
44. Alesina and Wacziarg report a strong negative correlation between country size and openness to trade. Alesina and Wacziarg 1997. This finding is robust across multiple measures of both variables, but of particular relevance to this study is their analysis of size based on the log of aggregate GDP.
45. Alesina, Spolaore, and Wacziarg 1997.

the level of integration is not ambitious—or if the pact exempts crucial export sectors—officials may very well reject legalism even in settings of low asymmetry.

Behind my argument are several simplifying assumptions. First, the model takes as unproblematic the motivation and capacity of domestic political leaders to negotiate a trade pact. My question is not why or when nations cooperate in reciprocal trade accords, but how they do so. Second, the model also takes as exogenous the substantive terms of a trade agreement. Given a set of reciprocal concessions, it focuses on the procedures chosen by the parties to enforce those commitments.[46] This division between substance and procedure may be misguided if some systematic relationship between the two goes beyond my expectations regarding the proposed depth and relative value of liberalization. Third, the model assumes a single bargaining forum, examining the negotiation of dispute settlement procedures in isolated trade agreements. It ignores the fact that as a party to multiple accords a given country may define its preferences in one setting strategically to influence the outcome of other dispute settlement negotiations. Fourth, the model does not address the potential impact of regime type on preferences, as democratic governments may prize policy discretion more than relatively insulated authoritarian leaders. Finally, the model does not incorporate the internal logic of incremental judicialization that scholars have highlighted in cases such as the European Union.[47] Although it allows for change over time, given shifts in asymmetry or the proposed depth of integration, these factors are external to the strategic interaction of disputants and independent third parties.

The Data Set

Among advanced industrial and developing countries alike, regional trade integration has been a persistent feature of the world economy in recent decades. Counts vary, but no fewer than sixty regional trade arrangements, established through formal treaties, have come into being since 1957.[48] As the international economy began to recover from the inflationary shocks of the 1970s and debt crises of the early 1980s, the number of pacts began to increase sharply from the late 1980s onward. No continent has been spared its share of the resultant alphabet soup of acronyms, from AFTA (ASEAN Free Trade Area) in Southeast Asia to COMESA (Common Market for Eastern and Southern Africa) in Africa (see Appendix A for a list of acronyms and their definitions).

---

46. This assumption of a two-stage process, with negotiations on substance preceding procedural talks, is consistent with what one observer of the Canada–U.S. pact called the "conventional trade policy view" in 1986, which was "that little could be done on dispute settlement until the shape of the agreement as a whole had become clearer." Dispute settlement without substantive rules, Canadian officials told the private sector, "was a fool's paradise." See Hart 1994, 207.

47. Stone Sweet 1999.

48. In 1994 the International Monetary Fund compiled a list of more than sixty-eight regional agreements. An earlier study listed thirty-four existing and nineteen prospective arrangements. See IMF 1994; and de la Torre and Kelly 1992.

Despite the general trend toward formal economic integration, these trade pacts differ on many dimensions, the first of which is size. In terms of the number of signatories, they range from bilateral and trilateral agreements to much larger panregional accords such as the Caribbean Community (CARICOM). Second, they vary according to their members' level of economic development. Many pacts tend to fall into one of two exclusive categories: most include either industrial countries or developing countries. A third variable is the scope or depth of liberalization to which the signatories aspire. Some agreements call for little more than reduced tariffs on selected merchandise trade, whereas others aim to establish full-blown common markets or economic unions. Fourth, these accords differ widely in terms of compliance and durability. Several pacts, especially among developing countries, have collapsed or never been implemented.

With such a diverse set of possible cases, it has been necessary to apply certain criteria to ensure comparability. In this study there are no restrictions on the number of signatories, though I do exclude GATT and the World Trade Organization—which stand alone as the world's only multilateral trade institutions—from this overview of regional accords. Similarly, there are no categorical restrictions on the type of agreement, with free trade areas, customs unions, common markets, and economic unions all represented. Finally, to minimize selection bias, the data set includes both successful and failed pacts. My focus is treaty design, not implementation, and among the covered agreements are a handful of largely inoperative pacts, such as the Commonwealth of Independent States, as well as two treaties that were formally dissolved: the 1967 East African Community and the 1973 West African Economic Community. Despite these inclusive rules, trade agreements that failed to meet one or more of the following requirements did not qualify for this study.

First, liberalization must be reciprocal. Concessions need not be strictly equivalent or simultaneous. Many of the agreements listed in Table 2 give less developed members sectoral exemptions or additional time to comply. But at least among some core signatories, reciprocal market access must be the rule. Pacts that provide for unilateral liberalization, such as the U.S. Caribbean Basin Initiative or the Australia–Papua New Guinea pact, are excluded. Where concessions are unilateral, dispute settlement is likely be driven by a logic distinct from that offered in this study of the trade-off between compliance and discretion.

Second, liberalization must be relatively comprehensive in scope. Universal free trade, with no sectoral exceptions at all, is by no means required. Still, coverage of at least merchandise trade must in principle be broad. Narrow sectoral initiatives, such as the 1951 European Coal and Steel Community or the later U.S.–Canada Automotive Agreement, fall short of this standard. Economic cooperation agreements that do not aim to achieve trade liberalization, such as the 1992 Black Sea Economic Cooperation Project, are also excluded, as are framework agreements—like the Latin American Integration Association or African Economic Community—within which specific trade pacts are negotiated. Where liberalization commitments are narrow in scope or vague and distant in time, the basic trade-off is inoperative, since domestic political leaders have little to risk and little to gain.

TABLE 2. *Data set of selected regional trade agreements, 1957–95*

Pact	Year signed	Members[a]
AFTA (ASEAN Free Trade Area)	1992	Indonesia, Malaysia, Philippines, Singapore, Thailand, Brunei, Vietnam (1995), Laos (1997), Burma (1997)
Andean Pact	1969	Bolivia, Colombia, Ecuador, Peru, Venezuela (1973) (Chile withdrew in 1976)
ANZCERTA (Australia–New Zealand Closer Economic Relations Trade Agreement)	1983	Australia, New Zealand
Baltic Free Trade Agreement	1993	Estonia, Latvia, Lithuania
CACM (Central American Common Market)	1960	El Salvador, Guatemala, Honduras, Nicaragua, Costa Rica (1963) (Honduras withdrew in 1970 but rejoined in 1990)
CARICOM (Caribbean Community)	1973	Antigua and Bermuda, Barbados, Belize, Dominica, Grenada, Guyana, Jamaica, Montserrat, Saint Kitts and Nevis, Saint Lucia, Saint Vincent and the Grenadines, Suriname (1995), Trinidad and Tobago (Bahamas is a member of the Community but not of the Common Market)
CEAO (West African Economic Community) (dissolved in 1994)	1973	Benin, Burkina Faso, Ivory Coast, Mali, Mauritania, Niger, Senegal
CEEC (Central and East European Country) Pacts (5)		
Bulgaria–Czech Republic Free Trade Agreement	1995	Bulgaria, Czech Republic
Bulgaria–Slovak Republic Free Trade Agreement	1995	Bulgaria, Slovak Republic
Hungary–Slovenia Free Trade Agreement	1994	Hungary, Slovenia
Romania–Czech Republic Free Trade Agreement	1994	Romania, Czech Republic
Romania–Slovak Republic Free Trade Agreement	1994	Romania, Slovak Republic
CEFTA (Central European Free Trade Agreement)	1992	Czech Republic, Hungary, Poland, Slovakia, Slovenia (1996), Romania (1997)
Chile and Mexico Pacts (9)		
Chile–Bolivia Free Trade Agreement	1993	Chile, Bolivia
Chile–Canada Free Trade Agreement	1995	Chile, Canada
Chile–Colombia Free Trade Agreement	1993	Chile, Colombia
Chile–Ecuador Free Trade Agreement	1994	Chile, Ecuador
Chile–Venezuela Free Trade Agreement	1991	Chile, Venezuela
Mexico–Bolivia Free Trade Agreement	1994	Mexico, Bolivia
Mexico–Chile Free Trade Agreement	1991	Mexico, Chile
Mexico–Costa Rica Free Trade Agreement	1994	Mexico, Costa Rica
Group of Three Free Trade Agreement	1994	Colombia, Mexico, Venezuela
CIS (Commonwealth of Independent States)	1993	Russia, Armenia, Azerbaijan, Armenia, Belarus, Georgia, Kazakhstan, Kyrgyzstan, Moldova, Tajikistan, Turkmenistan, Uzbekistan (Ukraine is a full member of the CIS but an associate member of the Economic Union)

TABLE 2. *continued*

Pact	Year signed	Members[a]
COMESA (Common Market for Eastern and Southern Africa)	1993	Angola, Burundi, Comoros, Djibouti, Eritrea, Ethiopia, Kenya, Lesotho, Madagascar, Malawi, Mauritius, Mozambique, Namibia, Rwanda, Somalia, Sudan, Swaziland, Tanzania, Uganda, Zaire (1994), Zambia, Zimbabwe (Seychelles signed the treaty but does not participate)
EAC (East African Community) (collapsed in 1977; dissolved in 1984)	1967	Kenya, Tanzania, Uganda
EC (European Community)	1957	Austria (1995), Belgium, Denmark (1973), Finland (1995), France, Germany, Greece (1981), Ireland (1973), Italy, Luxembourg, Netherlands, Portugal (1986), Spain (1986), Sweden (1995), United Kingdom (1973)
EC Associations (12)		
EC–Bulgaria Association Agreement	1993	EC, Bulgaria
EC–Cyprus Association Agreement	1972	EC, Cyprus
EC–Czech Republic Association Agreement	1991	EC, Czech Republic
EC–Estonia Free Trade Agreement	1994	EC, Estonia
EC–Hungary Association Agreement	1991	EC, Hungary
EC–Poland Association Agreement	1991	EC, Poland
EC–Romania Association Agreement	1993	EC, Romania
EC–Slovak Republic Association Agreement	1991	EC, Slovak Republic
EC–Turkey Customs Union	1963	EC, Turkey
EC–Latvia Free Trade Agreement	1994	EC, Latvia
EC–Lithuania Free Trade Agreement	1994	EC, Lithuania
EC–Malta Association Agreement	1970	EC, Malta
EC–Israel Free Trade Agreement	1995	EC, Israel
ECOWAS (Economic Community of West African States) (revised in 1993)	1975	Benin, Burkina Faso, Cape Verde, Gambia, Ghana, Guinea, Guinea-Bissau, Ivory Coast, Liberia, Mali, Mauritania, Niger, Nigeria, Senegal, Sierra Leone, Togo
EEA (European Economic Area)	1992	EC, Iceland, Liechtenstein, Norway (Swiss voters rejected the EEA in 1992; Austria, Finland, and Sweden joined EC in 1995)
EFTA (European Free Trade Association)	1960	Iceland (1970), Liechtenstein (1991), Norway, Switzerland (United Kingdom and Denmark withdrew in 1973; Portugal in 1986; Austria, Finland (1986), and Sweden in 1994)
EFTA Agreements (12)		
EFTA–Bulgaria Agreement	1993	EFTA, Bulgaria
EFTA–Czech Republic Agreement	1992	EFTA, Czech Republic
EFTA–Estonia Agreement	1995	EFTA, Estonia
EFTA–Hungary Agreement	1993	EFTA, Hungary
EFTA–Israel Agreement	1992	EFTA, Israel
EFTA–Latvia Agreement	1995	EFTA, Latvia

TABLE 2. *continued*

Pact	Year signed	Members[a]
EFTA Agreements (12) *(continued)*		
EFTA Lithuania Agreement	1995	EFTA, Lithuania
EFTA–Poland Agreement	1992	EFTA, Poland
EFTA–Romania Agreement	1992	EFTA, Romania
EFTA–Slovak Republic Agreement	1992	EFTA, Slovak Republic
EFTA–Slovenia Agreement	1995	EFTA, Slovenia
EFTA–Turkey Agreement	1991	EFTA, Turkey
GCC (Gulf Cooperation Council)	1981	Bahrain, Kuwait, Oman, Qatar, Saudi Arabia, United Arab Emirates
Mano River Union	1973	Liberia, Sierra Leone, Guinea (joined after 1974)
MERCOSUR (Common Market of the South)	1991	Argentina, Brazil, Paraguay, Uruguay (Chile and Bolivia are associate members)
NAFTA (North American Free Trade Agreement)	1992	Canada, Mexico, United States
OECS (Organization of East Caribbean States)	1981	Antigua and Bermuda, Dominica, Grenada, Montserrat, Saint Kitts and Nevis, Saint Lucia, Saint Vincent and the Grenadines
SACU (Southern African Customs Union)	1969	Botswana, Lesotho, Namibia, South Africa, Swaziland
U.S.–Israel Free Trade Agreement	1985	Israel, United States
UDEAC (Central African Customs and Economic Union)	1964	Cameroon, Central African Republic, Chad, Republic of Congo, Gabon, Equatorial Guinea

[a]Dates in parentheses indicate years of accession for member states that were not among the original signatories. Countries that signed but later withdrew from the agreement are also noted, as are their years of departure.

Third, the trade pacts must have been signed between January 1957 and December 1995. Negotiations that did not produce specific liberalization commitments by the end of 1995 are excluded. Pacts in which implementation was at that point incomplete but in which liberalization had begun are incorporated. This time frame, which opens with the creation of the European Community (EC) and closes in the first year of the World Trade Organization, covers all but the most recent agreements since World War II. The postwar era has witnessed two distinct waves of regional integration, the first in the 1960s and early 1970s and the second in the early 1990s, both of which the data set includes.

Table 2 lists the sixty-two trade agreements that met these criteria. It also lists the year in which each treaty was signed and all member governments, identifying those governments that were not among the original signatories by indicating their years of accession in parentheses. Countries that signed but later withdrew from the agreement are noted, as are their years of departure. Appendix B lists the treaties from the relevant time period that failed to meet one of the first two criteria listed earlier, as well as those whose texts were for various reasons unavailable. As Table 2 suggests, one potential problem in the data set is a lack of independence among certain cases. There are four clusters of agreements, one in the Americas and three in Europe, within which the timing and terms of the accords are rather similar. So as not to exacerbate this problem, I exclude treaties that were later encompassed or superceded by subsequent agreements; examples include the Canada–U.S. Free Trade Agreement, which the North American Free Trade Agreement (NAFTA) supplanted, and various bilateral pacts between the EC and individual European Free Trade Association (EFTA) countries, almost all of which were replaced either by accession to the EC or by membership in the European Economic Area (EEA).

Overview of Regional Dispute Settlement

In this segment I summarize the level of legalism in each of the regional trade pacts in the data set. The basic features of dispute settlement in each pact are highlighted in Table 3, which draws on the treaty texts listed in Appendix A. Related agreements in Europe and the Americas are aggregated; within each group, dispute settlement provisions are identical in every important respect. I include two observations for EFTA, whose membership changed significantly over time (see Table 2) and whose 1960 dispute settlement system was transformed with the creation of the EEA in 1992. On all three key variables—asymmetry, proposed level of integration, and legalism—the two EFTA cases, from 1960 and 1992, differ sharply and thereby warrant separate treatment. In this respect, EFTA is an exception to the rule. There are a handful of other agreements whose dispute settlement procedures changed over time—namely the Andean Pact, Central American Common Market (CACM), Common Market of the South (MERCOSUR), AFTA, and a few bilateral EFTA agreements. Unlike EFTA, however, these cases have not undergone radical changes in membership or in other variables of interest to this study. As a result, I report and evaluate their most recent dispute settlement design (citations for the relevant agreements are listed in Appendix A).

Table 3 underscores the dramatic extent of institutional variation in the data set. Its final column organizes the agreements into five clusters that capture basic differences in the level of legalism. To define these categories, I start with the most basic question: whether a treaty provides any system of independent third-party review of disputes. For eighteen treaties, the answer is no, and they thus constitute the lowest level of legalism: none.[49] At the next level, with low legalism, are five agreements with

---

49. Inclusion of the EEA in this category may be controversial. Technically, all member states of both EFTA and the EC have access to highly legalistic tribunals for the resolution of disputes regarding issues of EC law, which the EEA extends to EFTA. Nevertheless, this option applies only to disputes among EFTA states before the EFTA Court or among EC states before the European Court of Justice. For disputes *between* the EC and EFTA, neither group has automatic access to third-party review. By common consent, questions of interpretation of EC law may be referred to the European Court of Justice, but EFTA states have no direct access. Their complaints go instead to the EEA Joint Committee for bilateral consultations between the EC Commission and the EFTA states "speaking with one voice." The original EEA draft proposed an EEA Court, but the European Court of Justice struck it down as an usurpation of its exclusive authority over EC law. See Bierwagen and Hull 1993, 119–24.

TABLE 3. *Levels of legalism in dispute settlement design*[a]

Pact	Treaty provision					Level of legalism
	Third-party review	Third-party ruling	Judges	Standing	Remedy	
ANZCERTA	None	—	—	—	—	None
Baltic FTA	None	—	—	—	—	None
CEEC Pacts (5)	None	—	—	—	—	None
CEFTA	None	—	—	—	—	None
EEA	None—unless by mutual consent to ECJ on EC law	—	—	—	—	None
EFTA agreements with Czech Republic, Hungary, Poland, Romania, Slovak Republic, and Turkey	None	—	—	—	—	None
Mano River Union	None	—	—	—	—	None
SACU	None	—	—	—	—	None
UDEAC	None	—	—	—	—	None
AFTA	Yes—automatic	Not binding (ministers "consider" report in vote)	Ad hoc—roster	States only	Compensation, sanctions (only by vote of Council)	Low
CARICOM	Yes—automatic	Not binding (Council "may" vote to recommend)	Ad hoc—roster	States only	Sanctions (only by vote of Council)	Low
EFTA 1960	Yes—but only by majority vote of Council	Not binding (Council "may" vote to recommend)	Ad hoc	States only	Sanctions (only by vote of Council)	Low
GCC	Yes—but only by vote of Council	Not binding (panel issues recommendation to Supreme Council)	Ad hoc—roster	States only	None	Low
U.S.–Israel Pact	Yes—automatic	Not binding (merely a conciliation report)	Ad hoc	States only	Sanctions ("any appropriate measure")	Low
Chile and Mexico Pacts[b] (9)	Yes—automatic	Binding	Ad hoc—roster	States only	Sanctions (if prescribed or authorized)	Medium
EC associations (12)	Yes—but risk of deadlock at panel formation	Binding	Ad hoc	States and EC	None	Medium

EC–Israel Pact	Yes—but risk of deadlock at panel formation	Binding	Ad hoc	States and EC	None	Medium
EFTA agreements with Bulgaria, Israel, Estonia, Latvia, Lithuania, and Slovenia	Yes—automatic	Binding	Ad hoc	States only	None	Medium
MERCOSUR	Yes—but only after three preliminary reviews	Binding	Ad hoc—roster	States only	Sanctions	Medium
NAFTA	Yes—automatic (except in side accords, where two of three states must approve review)	Chap. 20 general disputes: not binding (contrary settlement or compensation allowed) Chap. 19 unfair trade law and Chap. 11 investment disputes: binding Side accords on labor and environment: binding	Ad hoc—roster	Chap. 20: states only Chap. 11: individuals only Chap. 19 and side accords: states and individuals	Chap. 20: sanctions Chap. 11 and Chap. 19: direct effect Side accords: fines (direct effect for Canada)	Medium
OECS	Yes—automatic	Binding	Ad hoc—roster	States only	None	Medium
CEAO	Yes—automatic	Binding	**Standing tribunal**	States only	None	High
CIS	Yes—but jurisdiction limited	Binding	**Standing tribunal**	States only	None	High
EAC	Yes—automatic	Binding	**Standing tribunal**	States only	None	High
ECOWAS	Yes—automatic	Binding	**Standing tribunal**	States and treaty organs	Sanctions (imposed by heads of state)	High
Andean Pact	Yes—automatic	Binding	Standing tribunal	**States, treaty organs, and individuals**	Direct effect, sanctions (prescribed by tribunal)	Very High
CACM	Yes—automatic	Binding	Standing tribunal	**States, treaty organs, and individuals**	Direct effect	Very High
COMESA	Yes—automatic	Binding	Standing tribunal	**States, treaty organs, and individuals**	Sanctions (prescribed by tribunal)	Very High
EC	Yes—automatic	Binding	Standing tribunal	**States, treaty organs, and individuals**	Direct effect	Very High
EFTA 1992	Yes—automatic	Binding	Standing tribunal	**States, treaty organs, and individuals**	Direct effect	Very High

Sources: See Appendix A.

[a] Boldface indicates the distinguishing features of cases at levels above and below medium legalism.

[b] Several of the Chilean and Mexican pacts also include investor-state dispute mechanisms, rather like Chapter 11 of NAFTA.

dispute settlement mechanisms whose rulings are not binding in international law. These pacts nominally provide a system of third-party review but hold it hostage to decisions by political bodies, often a council of ministers, or in the case of the U.S.–Israel accord treat its rulings as mere recommendations.[50]

The midpoint of the sample—medium legalism—includes a diverse set of thirty-one agreements that provide for some version of standard international arbitration, offering states an automatic right to binding rulings by ad hoc arbitrators. Within this category there is variation regarding remedies, since a few pacts provide for sanctions. The only agreements with multiple dispute settlement procedures—NAFTA and several pacts signed by Chile and Mexico—also fall into this category. NAFTA includes at least five distinct mechanisms for different issue areas: general disputes (Chapter 20), unfair trade laws (Chapter 19), investment (Chapter 11), and the side accords on labor and the environment.[51] The mechanism most relevant to this study, Chapter 20 for general disputes, might qualify NAFTA at the level of low legalism because its rulings are not legally binding: compensatory payments can substitute for compliance, and disputants can reach a settlement contrary to the terms of a panel ruling after it has been issued. However, NAFTA's innovative procedures for unfair trade law and investment disputes—which include binding rulings and standing for individuals—push the agreement in the direction of legalism. Without any standing tribunal, the combination of these mechanisms arguably leaves NAFTA at the level of medium legalism. Many of the Chilean and Mexican pacts incorporate a version of NAFTA's mechanism for investment disputes. Although this procedure grants standing to individuals, it is limited in scope to rules on investment and relies on ad hoc arbitrators, which keep the Chilean and Mexican pacts within this category.

At the level of high legalism are four agreements that establish a standing tribunal to issue binding rulings on cases brought by states. Although in other respects these pacts resemble standard arbitration, the appointment of judges to a permanent court implies a significant step in the direction of legalism. These agreements create supranational institutions whose judges are likely to issue consistent legal rulings in developing their treaty jurisprudence. In practice, these four accords are among the most poorly implemented in the data set. Both the East African Community (EAC) and the West African Economic Community (CEAO), in fact, have been formally dissolved. The Economic Community of West African States (ECOWAS) Community Court of Justice awaits the realization of trade commitments in that largely dormant economic area, while the jurisdiction of the Commonwealth of Independent States (CIS) Economic Court appears to be severely restricted even among the CIS signatories that have endorsed it.[52]

---

50. Azrieli 1993, 203–205.

51. For details on NAFTA's different mechanisms, see Smith 1995.

52. Very little information is available, but reports suggest that the jurisdiction of the CIS Economic Court has lawfully been refused by Kazakhstan. Three CIS members have not recognized it, and others have ignored its rulings. See "CIS Court Dismisses Moldova Claim for Kazakh Grain," *Reuter European Business Report*, 6 February 1997; and "CIS Economic Court to Be in Session," *TASS*, 7 July 1997.

There is a sizable leap toward legalism at the final level. All five agreements with very high legalism expand the definition of standing beyond member states to include both treaty organs and private individuals. With the exception of COMESA, they also give the rulings of standing tribunals direct effect in national law. To a significant extent, the judicial bodies envisaged for the CACM, Andean Pact, EFTA 1992, and COMESA draw on the model of the European Court of Justice. For example, all five tribunals have the authority, on request, to issue preliminary rulings to national courts, which can serve to broaden the access of individuals to supranational judicial review. On encountering questions of treaty interpretation, domestic judges may or may not exercise this option, but the preliminary question procedure has helped forge important links between the European Court of Justice and national judiciaries in Europe.[53]

In summary, Table 3 locates individual treaties along the spectrum from diplomacy to legalism. Within each level of legalism, there is some variation in the details of dispute settlement procedures—for example, with regard to remedy or selecting arbitrators. Of course, there are also differences in the extent to which states have used and complied with the mechanisms in each category. Whatever the equilibrium of *ex post* implementation, however, Table 3 captures fundamental distinctions in *ex ante* institutional design that require analysis.

Measuring Asymmetry and Proposed Integration

To test my argument on the trade-off between treaty compliance and policy discretion, I must find summary statistics that describe the level of economic asymmetry and proposed depth of integration within each regional trade arrangement. Measuring GDP asymmetry in trade pacts is not unlike measuring the level of industry concentration—or market share asymmetry—in different sectors of the economy. A standard measure for industrial concentration in economics is the Herfindahl-Hirschman index (HH), which equals the sum of the squared market shares of the firms in a given industry. In a situation of pure monopoly, the index is $(1.0)^2 = 1.00$. Where two firms divide the market evenly, $HH = (0.5)^2 + (0.5)^2 = 0.50$.

In its traditional form, this index is not an ideal measure of intrapact GDP asymmetry. In the two-firm example, a score of 0.50—which is very high by antitrust standards—for me represents a situation of perfect symmetry if derived from a bilateral pact where the two countries have identical GDP shares. Yet the same index score could reflect a situation of high asymmetry in a pact with six signatories where the GDP shares are as follows: $HH = (0.68)^2 + (0.17)^2 + (0.10)^2 + (0.02)^2 + (0.02)^2 + (0.01)^2 = 0.50$. To correct for this problem, I subtract from the Herfindahl-Hirschman index what the index would be in a situation of perfect economic symmetry, where all signatories to a trade accord have identical shares of the total pact GDP. Given the nature of summed squares, this baseline of perfect symmetry always equals

53. See Stone Sweet and Brunell 1998; and Mattli and Slaughter 1996.

1 divided by the number of signatories (N). By subtracting it, I obtain a new measure (P) that describes the proportional asymmetry of each pact. It captures the distance of each pact from symmetry: the further a pact is from that baseline, the higher the index. In the two-signatory example P would be zero, indicating perfect symmetry, but in the six-signatory example it would be much higher: $P = 0.50 - (1/6) = 0.33$.

To define this proportional asymmetry index in more formal terms,

$$P = \Sigma x_i^2 - 1 / N \text{ for all } i$$

where x_i = each member's share of total pact GDP, such that $\Sigma x_i = 1$

Among alternative indicators of inequality, P is related to variance measures. In fact, P is formally equivalent to N times the variance of income shares.[54] In other words, P represents the sum of the squared deviation of individual GDP shares from their sample mean. One disadvantage is that the upper bound (MAX) of P, which is equivalent to $1 - 1/N$, varies with the number of signatories. To control for differences in the maximum value of P, I use the ratio of the proportional asymmetry index to its range (P/MAX).

This measure, P/MAX, manages to account for differences in the number of signatories and to provide a meaningful summary statistic without compromising certain useful properties of the Herfindahl-Hirschman index. Like the Herfindahl-Hirschman index, it increases as asymmetry grows, bounded by zero at one end of its range and approaching 1 at the other, and it meets many of the criteria sought by economists for inequality measures.[55] It is invariant with respect to scale: were all individual country GDP totals to double, it would not change. It meets standard transfer tests: if some amount of GDP were transferred from a larger country to a smaller one without altering the total, it would decrease. It is not translation invariant, which is appropriate in this context: if the GDP of all countries were increased by a fixed sum, it would decrease (if nonzero) to reflect the proportionately larger gains of smaller countries. And in contrast to several measures, it is not at all invariant with respect to sample replication: if each country were to be cloned, thereby producing two identical data points for each original GDP observation, it would decrease by roughly half.[56]

To estimate the level of asymmetry within each accord, I use aggregate GDP figures denominated in U.S. dollars at current exchange rates. Where possible the index uses data from the year in which the treaty was signed.[57] For all cases, the index incorporates only countries that signed the accord at the time of its creation or

54. The variance of a given sample (Var) is the average squared deviation of data points from their sample mean, which for income shares that sum to one is by definition $1/N$: Var $(x) = (1/N) \cdot \Sigma (x_i - 1/N)^2$.
55. See Sen and Foster 1997; Cowell 1995; or Young 1985.
56. This attribute is helpful, for if a hegemon were matched by a rival clone, the index should fall. With a new partner of comparable size, the hegemon's cost-benefit analysis would change: it would have more to gain from secure access to a significant new market and less to lose in any move toward legalism, since its twin should be able to avail itself of power politics tactics with similar effect.
57. The two exceptions are the 1973 CARICOM and the 1969 SACU, both of which reflect GDP data from 1970.

reinvigoration; it excludes member states that later acceded and includes any that later withdrew. As in the summary of legalism, EFTA is the only pact to have duplicate entries, one from 1960 and the other from 1992. During this time period, thanks to the departure of the United Kingdom, the level of asymmetry in EFTA fell sharply. Other agreements that underwent various changes over time—such as the EC, which doubled in size, or the Andean Pact and CACM, which fell dormant but were later revived—hardly shifted in terms of asymmetry and thus have one entry from the year of their establishment.[58]

Using these guidelines, Table 4 ranks and organizes the sixty-three data points into two categories, low and high, based on the level of economic asymmetry within each pact. The rank order of the pacts derives from their *P*/MAX scores, which are listed from low to high. To facilitate comparisons, Table 4 reports the underlying GDP shares of signatories to each agreement in descending order, omitting only shares of *de minimis* value. These GDP shares make evident the intuitive appeal of this ordering, but with a small sample size and categorical dependent variable it is also necessary to draw a line between low and high asymmetry. Although this *P*/MAX index captures the level of asymmetry across all signatories, my theoretical approach suggests that the relative size of the largest members may be more important than the distribution of shares among smaller economies. The reason is that two or three symmetrically positioned regional powers that depend heavily on access to each others' markets may endorse a legalistic system even if the gap in size between them and their neighbors is substantial.[59] By focusing on the relative size of the largest signatories, one can define a threshold between high and low asymmetry that conforms to the rank order in Table 4. For bilateral pacts, if the larger country's share of GDP exceeds 70 percent, asymmetry is high, as it is in multilateral pacts where the GDP share of the largest signatory is more than twice that of the next largest. Using these criteria to supplement the index, the line between low and high stands at a *P*/MAX score of.140, which separates the Romania–Slovak Republic pact from the Central African Customs and Economic Union (UDEAC). Only two cases are borderline—and in the event of conflict between the rank order and my criteria for dividing high from low asymmetry, I defer to the index.[60]

Like asymmetry, the proposed level of integration is a key variable that requires a metric. An adapted version of the traditional concept of stages of integration seems best able to capture the basic differences between shallow and deep initiatives. In a study of regional trade pacts, the International Monetary Fund labeled agreements as

---

58. The twelve EC signatories of the Single European Act in 1987 had a *P*/MAX of.098, and the fifteen European Union members in 1995 had a *P*/MAX of .100. The index score of the CACM was .068 when the Tegucigalpa Protocol was signed in 1991, and that of the Andean Pact was .108 when the Quito Protocol was signed in 1987.

59. For an argument along these lines regarding the critical role of the United States and the European Union in the legalistic dispute settlement reforms of the Uruguay Round of GATT, see Smith 1998.

60. CARICOM is coded as high asymmetry despite the fact that the difference between Jamaica (.48) and Trinidad and Tobago (.31) in 1970 was less than a multiple of two. And the CEAO is coded as low asymmetry despite the fact that in 1973 Ivory Coast (.38) had exactly twice the GDP share of Senegal (.19).

TABLE 4. *The proportional asymmetry index of intrapact GDP shares*

Asymmetry	Pact	Year	GDP shares (x)	N	P	P/MAX
Low	Mano River Union	1973	.52, .48	2	.0007	.001
	EAC	1967	.38, .34, .28	3	.005	.007
	Romania–Czech Republic	1994	.545, .455	2	.004	.008
	Chile–Colombia	1993	.55, .45	2	.005	.010
	Bulgaria–Slovak Republic	1995	.57, .43	2	.011	.021
	COMESA	1993	.11, .10, .10, .08, .07, .07, .06, .06, .06, .05, .05, .04 and below	22	.023	.024
	Baltic FTA	1993	.45, .31, .23	3	.025	.037
	OECS	1981	.26, .22, .14, .12, .12, .10, .05	7	.032	.037
	Chile—Venezuela	1991	.61, .39	2	.024	.048
	CACM	1960	.38, .23, .19, .12, .08	5	.053	.067
	AFTA	1992	.34, .27, .14, .13, .12, .01	6	.068	.082
	EFTA 1992	1992	.27, .26, .20, .14, .12, .01, .002	7	.073	.085
	Andean Pact	1969	.34, .28, .27, .07, .04	5	.072	.089
	CEAO	1973	.38, .19, .14, .09, .08, .08, .05	7	.076	.089
	EC	1957	.36, .33, .18, .07, .06, .003	6	.113	.136
	Romania–Slovak Republic	1994	.69, .31	2	.069	.138
High	UDEAC	1964	.47, .16, .14, .13, .09, .01	6	.124	.149
	CEFTA	1992	.53, .23, .17, .07	4	.112	.149
	Hungary–Slovenia	1994	.74, .26	2	.118	.235
	Chile–Ecuador	1994	.77, .23	2	.134	.268
	CARICOM	1970	.48, .31, .09, .05, .02, .01 and below	12	.252	.275
	Bulgaria–Czech Republic	1995	.79, .21	2	.162	.325
	EFTA 1960	1960	.63, .12, .07, .05, .05, .04, .02	7	.281	.328
	MERCOSUR	1991	.65, .32, .02, .01	4	.278	.371
	GCC	1981	.67, .14, .11, .04, .03, .01	6	.313	.376
	Group of Three	1994	.75, .13, .12	3	.261	.392
	ECOWAS	1975	.72, .07, .05, .04, .02 and below	15[a]	.458	.491
	ANZCERTA	1983	.88, .12	2	.293	.586
	CIS	1993	.79, .06, .05, .04, .01 and below	11	.540	.594
	Mexico–Chile	1991	.89, .11	2	.311	.622
	Chile–Canada	1995	.89, .11	2	.311	.622
	Chile–Bolivia	1993	.89, .11	2	.311	.622
	NAFTA	1992	.87, .08, .05	3	.430	.645
	EEA	1992	.91, .09	2[b]	.338	.676
	EFTA Agreements (mean)	Various	.96, .04	2[b]	.421	.841
	Mexico–Costa Rica	1994	.98, .02	2	.458	.916
	Mexico–Bolivia	1994	.99, .01	2	.472	.944
	SACU	1970	.984, .007, .005, .004	4	.718	.957
	EC–Israel	1995	.99, .01	2[b]	.479	.958
	U.S.–Israel	1985	.99, .01	2	.487	.974
	EC Associations (mean)	Various	.99, .01	2[b]	.490	.980

Sources: World Bank (various years); OECD (various years); and *UN Statistical Yearbook* (various years).
Note: Shares of GDP may not sum to 1 or match the index scores exactly because of rounding.
GDP shares = members' GDP shares (x_i) (in current $US) in reported year.
$P = \Sigma\, x_i^2 - 1/N$ for all i where x_i is member i's share of total pact GDP such that $\Sigma\, x_i = 1$.
MAX $= 1 - 1/N$, the upper bound of P for each pact.
N = number of members at the time the agreement was signed.
[a]GDP data for Guinea were unavailable.
[b]Member states of the EC and/or EFTA act collectively as a unit in a bilateral governance structure.

belonging to one of four categories.[61] At the shallow end of integration arrangements are free trade areas, which remove tariff and certain nontariff barriers to cross-border trade in goods and perhaps services. More ambitious are customs unions, which in addition to free trade aim to establish harmonized external tariffs vis-à-vis nonmember countries. Common markets go a significant step beyond customs unions by guaranteeing freedom of movement not only for goods and services but also for factors of production such as capital and labor. And at the deepest level of liberalization are economic unions, which are common markets whose member states harmonize certain macroeconomic and regulatory policies.

Along the continuum of these four stages of integration, there is a fundamental break between customs unions and common markets. Free trade areas and customs unions focus on removing barriers to the cross-border movement of goods (and, at times, services), with an emphasis on tariffs and quantitative restrictions. Common markets and economic unions aim for a much higher level of integration, including the free movement of labor and capital and the harmonization of economic policies. Although certain free trade areas and customs unions may cover a range of nontariff barriers, thereby including elements of deep integration, the line between customs unions and common markets captures significant variation between low and high integration. Table 5 presents a complete list of the cases, grouped by level of legalism, with regard to treaty type. Free trade areas and customs unions indicate low integration, whereas common markets and economic unions signify high integration. This typology reflects the proposed level of integration in each agreement, not the extent of actual policy implementation.

With indicators for both asymmetry and integration, it is possible to generate a third independent variable that represents their interaction. This interaction term, of course, reflects my principal hypothesis—which is that legalism is most likely where asymmetry is low and proposed integration is high. By defining the level of proposed integration as a dummy variable, with zero for low and 1 for high, the product of the asymmetry index and integration yields a continuous interaction term. Wherever proposed integration is low, with a free trade area or customs union, the interaction term is zero. Where proposed integration is high, with a common market or economic union, the multiplicative interaction term equals the level of asymmetry, be it low or high. Table 5 below summarizes all three variables for each agreement.

Asymmetry, Proposed Integration, and Legalism

Tables 6, 7, and 8 summarize the relationship between legalism and each of the three independent variables in turn: asymmetry, proposed integration, and their interaction. To facilitate analysis of the small sample in this study, I collapse the five levels of legalism into three rows. Treaties coded as none or low legalism, none of which generate binding third-party rulings, appear together. Similarly, I combine agree-

---

61. IMF 1994, 90.

TABLE 5. *Legalism, asymmetry, and proposed level of integration*

Legalism	Pact	Asymmetry	Integration	Interaction
None or low	SACU	High	High—common market	High
	UDEAC	High	High—economic union	High
	ANZCERTA	High	High—common market[a]	High
	EEA	High	High—common market	High
	CARICOM	High	High—common market	High
	GCC	High	High—common market	High
	EFTA–Israel	High	Low—free trade area	Zero
	EFTA–Bulgaria	High	Low—free trade area	Zero
	EFTA–Estonia	High	Low—free trade area	Zero
	EFTA–Latvia	High	Low—free trade area	Zero
	EFTA–Lithuania	High	Low—free trade area	Zero
	EFTA–Slovenia	High	Low—free trade area	Zero
	Hungary–Slovenia	High	Low—free trade area	Zero
	Bulgaria–Czech Republic	High	Low—free trade area	Zero
	U.S.–Israel	High	Low—free trade area	Zero
	EFTA 1960	High	Low—free trade area	Zero
	Baltic FTA	Low	Low—free trade area	Zero
	CEFTA	Low	Low—free trade area	Zero
	Romania–Czech Republic	Low	Low—free trade area	Zero
	Bulgaria–Slovak Republic	Low	Low—free trade area	Zero
	Romania–Slovak Republic	Low	Low—free trade area	Zero
	Mano River Union	Low	Low—customs union	Zero
	AFTA	Low	Low—free trade area	Zero
Medium	MERCOSUR	High	High—common market	High
	EC–Israel	High	Low—free trade area	Zero
	EC Associations (12)	High	Low—free trade areas[b]	Zero
	EFTA–Czech Republic	High	Low—free trade area	Zero
	EFTA–Poland	High	Low—free trade area	Zero
	EFTA–Hungary	High	Low—free trade area	Zero
	EFTA–Romania	High	Low—free trade area	Zero
	EFTA–Slovak Republic	High	Low—free trade area	Zero
	EFTA–Turkey	High	Low—free trade area	Zero
	NAFTA	High	Low—free trade area	Zero
	Chile–Ecuador	High	Low—free trade area	Zero
	Group of Three	High	Low—free trade area	Zero
	Mexico–Chile	High	Low—free trade area	Zero
	Chile–Canada	High	Low—free trade area	Zero
	Chile–Bolivia	High	Low—free trade area	Zero
	Mexico–Costa Rica	High	Low—free trade area	Zero
	Mexico–Bolivia	High	Low—free trade area	Zero
	OECS	Low	Low—customs union	Zero
	Chile–Colombia	Low	Low—free trade area	Zero
	Chile–Venezuela	Low	Low—free trade area	Zero
High or very high	CIS	High	High—economic union	High
	ECOWAS	High	High—common market	High
	CEAO	Low	High—economic union	Low
	COMESA	Low	High—common market	Low
	EAC	Low	High—common market	Low
	CACM	Low	High—common market[c]	Low
	Andean Pact	Low	High—common market	Low
	EC	Low	High—economic union	Low
	EFTA 1992	Low	High—common market	Low

Sources: For treaty type, see IMF 1994, app. I; and WTO 1995.

[a]IMF (1994) codes ANZCERTA as a free trade area, but because it has achieved labor mobility, full coverage of services, and a competition policy, it is much more like a common market—or, given the extent of legal harmonization, an economic union. See Kahler 1995, 109–11.

[b]The EC–Turkey agreement is a customs union.

[c]IMF (1994) codes the CACM as a customs union. The members had accomplished little more than a customs union at that point, but the aim of the treaty—as the name implies—is clearly to establish a common market.

ments with high or very high legalism, all of which endorse the creation of a permanent court. At the level of medium legalism are treaties with binding rulings issued by ad hoc arbitrators.

With a simplified dependent variable, it is possible to use chi-squared tests of statistical significance. For all three independent variables, the null hypothesis of independence can be rejected with very high levels of confidence ($p < .01$), suggesting a significant relationship to legalism.[62] To estimate the strength of that relationship, I also report Cramer's V, which for all three tables is relatively large ($V > .5$). The direction of each variable's effect on legalism is as expected: negative for asymmetry, positive for proposed integration, and negative for their interaction, reflecting the impact of asymmetry where proposed integration is high. Nevertheless, the results suggest that these variables are better predictors of legalism at its extreme values, none/low and high/very high, than at the medium level of traditional international arbitration. Even excluding the category of medium legalism, several potentially anomalous cases lie off the predicted diagonals and are shown in italics in Tables 6, 7, and 8. These cases require analysis, as do my specific hypotheses.

The first hypothesis to evaluate is whether levels of asymmetry and legalism are inversely related, given the preferences and negotiating leverage of regional hegemons. In its strongest form, the implication is that highly legalistic forms of dispute settlement should not occur in highly asymmetric settings. The evidence supports this claim, as shown in Table 6. Among the forty-seven cases of high asymmetry, there are only two examples of highly legalistic dispute settlement: the CIS and ECOWAS. Strikingly, not a single treaty in this large and diverse subset of cases has established the most legalistic form of dispute settlement, a standing tribunal to which individuals have access. All five pacts with very high legalism—the CACM, Andean Pact, EC, EFTA 1992, and COMESA—are also cases of low asymmetry. And both anomalies with high legalism, the CIS and ECOWAS—within which Russia and Nigeria, respectively, are dominant—at this point remain far from effective implementation, suggesting potential tension between the structure of political power in these accords and their institutional design.[63]

Where asymmetry is low, high levels of legalism are expected only where the proposed level of integration is high. The evidence supports this claim as well. Six potentially anomalous cases shown in Table 6 combine low asymmetry with low or no legalism, but all six treaties—four of which are among formerly socialist countries in Europe—aim to establish no more than a free trade area or customs union. Despite conditions of symmetry that might permit the adoption of rule-oriented dis-

---

62. Given a sample size of sixty-three cases, the low expected frequencies of certain cells imply that the use of Pearson's chi-squared may be inappropriate. The reduced sample in Table 8 is especially problematic. For this reason I also report Fisher's exact, a more conservative test designed for small samples.

63. The CIS Economic Court, for example, has yet to be given effective powers. President Lukashenka of Belarus has proposed reforming the CIS tribunal on the model of the European Court of Justice. See *BBC Summary of World Broadcasts* SU/D3168/D, 6 March 1998. In ECOWAS, very little progress has been made on liberalization. See "Ecobank Boss Deplores Rivalry in ECOWAS," *Panafrican News Agency*, 6 March 1999.

TABLE 6. *Legalism and asymmetry*[a]

Level of legalism	Level of economic asymmetry		Total
	Low	*High*	
High or very high			9
	CACM	*CIS*	
	Andean Pact	*ECOWAS*	
	EC		
	EFTA 1992		
	COMESA		
	CEAO		
	EAC		
Medium			31
	OECS	MERCOSUR	
	Chile–Colombia	Mexico Pacts (4)	
	Chile–Venezuela	Chile–Bolivia	
		Chile–Canada	
		Chile–Ecuador	
		NAFTA	
		EC–Israel	
		EC Associations (12)	
		EFTA–Czech Republic	
		EFTA–Poland	
		EFTA–Hungary	
		EFTA–Romania	
		EFTA–Slovak Republic	
		EFTA–Turkey	
Low or none			23
	Baltic FTA	CARICOM	
	Romania—Czech Republic	U.S.–Israel	
	Bulgaria—Slovak Republic	EFTA 1960	
	Romania—Slovak Republic	EFTA–Israel	
	AFTA	EFTA–Bulgaria	
	Mano River Union	EFTA–Estonia	
		EFTA–Latvia	
		EFTA–Lithuania	
		EFTA–Slovenia	
		EEA	
		CEFTA	
		Hungary–Slovenia	
		Bulgaria–Czech Republic	
		SACU	
		UDEAC	
		ANZCERTA	
		GCC	
Total	16	47	63

Note: $P (\chi^2[2] > 17.08) = 0.000$.
Fisher's exact $= 0.000$.
Cramer's $V = .52$.
[a]Cases that lie off the predicted diagonal at high and low levels of legalism are shown in italics.

TABLE 7. *Legalism and integration*[a]

	Level of proposed integration		
Level of legalism	*Low*	*High*	*Total*
High or very high	None	CACM Andean Pact EC EFTA 1992 CIS COMESA CEAO EAC ECOWAS	9
Medium	OECS Chile and Mexico Pacts (9) NAFTA EC–Israel EC Associations (12) EFTA–Czech Republic EFTA–Poland EFTA–Hungary EFTA–Romania EFTA–Slovak Republic EFTA–Turkey	MERCOSUR	31
Low or none	U.S.–Israel AFTA Mano River Union Romania–Czech Republic Bulgaria–Czech Republic Romania–Slovak Republic Bulgaria–Slovak Republic Hungary–Slovenia EFTA 1960 EFTA–Israel EFTA–Bulgaria EFTA–Estonia EFTA–Latvia EFTA–Lithuania EFTA–Slovenia CEFTA Baltic FTA	*CARICOM* *EEA* *SACU* *ANZCERTA* *GCC* *UDEAC*	23
Total	47	16	63

Note: $P (\chi^2[2] > 34.49) = 0.000$.
    Fisher's exact $= 0.000$.
    Cramer's $V = 0.74$.
[a]Cases that lie off the predicted diagonal at high and low levels of legalism are shown in italics.

TABLE 8. *Legalism and the interaction of asymmetry and integration*[a]

| Level of legalism | Interaction of economic asymmetry and proposed integration | | Total |
	Low	*High*	*Total*
High or very high			9
	CACM	*CIS*	
	Andean Pact	*ECOWAS*	
	EC		
	EFTA 1992		
	COMESA		
	CEAO		
	EAC		
Medium	None	MERCOSUR	1
Low or none	None		6
		CARICOM	
		EEA	
		SACU	
		UDEAC	
		ANZCERTA	
		GCC	
Total	7	9	16

Note: $P(\chi^2[2] > 9.68) = 0.008$.
  Fisher's exact $= 0.004$.
  Cramer's V $= 0.78$.
[a]Cases where the interaction term is zero have been omitted to capture the impact of asymmetry where proposed integration is high. Cases that lie off the predicted diagonal at high and low levels of legalism are shown in italics.

pute settlement, in these pacts governments have opted for relatively diplomatic systems. If they commit to deeper liberalization in the future, member states might endorse more legalistic dispute settlement. The adoption of a limited system of third-party review in AFTA, for example, came only after member states promised deeper cuts in tariff and nontariff barriers. Even then, political leaders in the Association of Southeast Asian Nations (ASEAN) discussed the reforms with some reluctance but reached an accord thanks in large part to active pressure from industry representatives eager to gain secure market access.[64]

64. A senior official reported that "strong requests" for formal dispute settlement "had come mainly from the private sector," apparently in an attempt to improve implementation. See *Singapore Straits Times*, 21 November 1996, 3.

A second test is for a positive relationship between the level of proposed integration and legalism, which the evidence generally confirms, as shown in Table 7. The majority of cases with low or high legalism fall on the predicted diagonal. No mere free trade agreements or customs unions have embraced the concept of binding rulings by a standing tribunal of justices. Only where the level of proposed integration is high, in the form of a common market or economic union, have highly legalistic mechanisms been endorsed. Nevertheless, no fewer than six cases lie at the intersection of ambitious integration and low or no legalism. In all six agreements, the signatories have embraced the prospect of deep integration but rejected binding third-party review. In the EEA, Southern African Customs Union (SACU), Australia–New Zealand Closer Economic Relations Trade Agreement (ANZCERTA), and Gulf Cooperation Council (GCC), member states have even managed to achieve considerable market integration in the absence of highly legalistic institutions—in three of these cases without any system of third-party review at all.

These anomalous combinations of high integration and low legalism share one telling attribute: all six treaties shown in italics in Table 6 are cases of high asymmetry. This structural attribute—through its impact on the domestic political economy of trade—appears to be one of the principal reasons these deep integration initiatives have not adopted correspondingly legalistic dispute settlement mechanisms. This contrast between ambitious liberalization objectives and modest institutional structure has not gone unnoticed. Scholars have explored the surprising effectiveness of ANZCERTA's thin institutional framework and criticized the arbitration procedure of MERCOSUR for being less legalistic than the aims of the treaty require.[65] An exclusive focus on the relationship between treaty type and institutional design, however, obscures the implications of the trade-off between treaty compliance and policy discretion across agreements at different levels of asymmetry.

The most robust predictor of dispute settlement design seems to be the interaction of asymmetry and proposed integration. Where the level of proposed integration is relatively low—implying a value of zero for the interaction term—not a single treaty has approved a permanent court, as noted in Table 7. By excluding those cases, Table 8 highlights the impact of asymmetry where proposed integration is high. In this subset of sixteen common markets and economic unions, the multiplicative interaction term assumes the value of the asymmetry index. Where asymmetry is high, legalism is unlikely to be high even in cases where the proposed integration is deep. At high values of the interaction term, as Table 8 indicates, very few treaties endorse binding third-party review. The CIS and ECOWAS again stand out as exceptions. Among cases with low asymmetry, legalism is likely to be high only where policy goals are ambitious and the potential value of liberalization is considerable. As Table 8 reveals, where the interaction term is low—the most favorable conditions for legalism, according to this framework—all seven treaties have endorsed standing tribunals.

---

65. On ANZCERTA, see Kahler 1995, 110–11; for MERCOSUR, see O'Neal Taylor 1996, 870. Predictably, the main obstacle to institutional reform in MERCOSUR is Brazil, by far the largest signatory. During negotiations for a permanent dispute settlement mechanism, Brazil rejected proposals by Uruguay and Argentina for a more legalistic system. See Pastori 1994, 4–7; and O'Neal Taylor 1996, 874–75.

TABLE 9. *Ordered probit regression of legalism*

Variable	Coefficient	Standard error
Proposed integration	3.203**	0.682
Economic asymmetry	1.067*	0.484
Interaction	−5.604**	1.483
Number of observations	63	
Log likelihood	−49.59	
Chi-squared	26.16	
Significance	0.000	

*p < .01, two-tailed test.
*p < .05, two-tailed test.

The dramatic impact of this interaction appears also in an ordered probit regression of legalism. Table 9 summarizes the results of this statistical test, which uses asymmetry and the interaction term as continuous variables that range from zero to 1, capturing more variation than the preceding tabular analysis. Proposed integration (low = 0; high = 1) and legalism (none or low = 0; medium = 1; high or very high = 2) remain categorical variables. Despite the small sample size, which is not ideal for maximum likelihood estimation,[66] both integration and the multiplicative interaction term exhibit highly significant and strong effects on legalism.[67] These effects, moreover, are in the predicted direction. The coefficient of the interaction term is the largest in magnitude, indicating the decisively negative relationship of asymmetry to legalism where the level of proposed integration is high.[68]

This simple analytical framework, tested with basic indicators of GDP concentration and treaty type, successfully accounts for thirty of the thirty-two cases at the more extreme levels of legalism, where the implications of the theory are clearest. Where treaties have endorsed standard interstate arbitration, however, it performs less well. Almost all of the cases of medium legalism (twenty-seven of thirty-one) are instances of high asymmetry and shallow integration, both of which weigh against establishing a standing tribunal. With the exception of MERCOSUR, these pacts all

66. Firm guidelines on sample size for maximum likelihood estimation do not exist, but this data set is at best borderline. Eliason notes that with fewer than five parameters to estimate, "a sample size of more than 60 is usually large enough," but Long suggests a minimum of one hundred observations. See Eliason 1993, fn. 2; and Long 1997, 54.

67. In maximum likelihood analysis of small samples, positive findings of significance may be more reliable than negative results. Hart and Clark report that in probit models of binary dependent variables, the risk of false positive findings does not change appreciably as sample size decreases. Hart and Clark 1999. They conclude that "the likelihood that small samples will induce Type I errors is small," in contrast to the substantial risk of false negative findings.

68. The analysis of interactions in maximum likelihood estimation is a topic of debate. Berry contends that when the dependent variable is latent, unbounded, and continuous—as legalism is here—interactions should be tested by directly examining the estimated coefficients of multiplicative terms. Berry 1999.

envision no more than free trade or a customs union, rendering the potential value of liberalization too low in the pacts with low asymmetry (OECS, Chile–Columbia, and Chile–Venezuela) to encourage highly legalistic dispute settlement. Those conditions, however, also hold for a majority of the cases with no or low legalism, making it difficult to account for that variation within the scope of my argument. Among potential explanations, one might point to the tremendous levels of asymmetry in many cases with standard arbitration mechanisms, especially the bilateral agreements negotiated by the EC and EFTA. Commitments to abide by arbitral rulings backed only by the threat of sanctions arguably mean little when EC or EFTA members account for more than 95 percent of intrapact GDP. In the Americas, the institutional homogeneity of the nine Chilean and Mexican pacts may be driven by expectations of a hemispheric free trade agreement modeled on NAFTA, whose dispute settlement provisions the Chilean and Mexican agreements resemble in several respects.[69] The prospect of accession to larger regional accords is also a factor in Europe, and it is beyond the scope of my theory.

Given the failure of my framework to account for this variation, it seems useful to assess other approaches. One alternative emphasizes the transactions costs of collective action, and in particular the variable difficulties of monitoring and enforcing compliance in trade pacts of different sizes. From this perspective, the number of signatories is a meaningful predictor of institutional form. Beth V. Yarbrough and Robert M. Yarbrough, for example, pose a distinction between self-help and third-party enforcement in international trade.[70] They contend that self-help enforcement ("bilateralism") should appear within very small groups or pairs, where continuity is valued and the strategic use of hostages might be effective. Because the efficiency costs of self-enforcement increase with the number of signatories, third-party enforcement ("minilateralism") is more likely in somewhat larger pacts, though not in multilateral agreements such as GATT. Yarbrough and Yarbrough do not restrict their analysis to the details of dispute settlement design; nor do they emphasize the number of signatories alone. Nevertheless, a transactions costs approach seems to account well for the pacts at the legalistic end of the spectrum. All nine highly legalistic treaties have between three and twenty-two signatories. Unfortunately, there are an equal number of comparably sized accords at the opposite end of the spectrum. No fewer than nine pacts with low or no legalism have between three and twelve signatories, which this framework would not predict. Nor can this approach account for the presence of bilateral pacts across multiple levels of legalism. Whatever the logic, there seems to be no systematic relationship in this data set between the number of signatories and legalism.

For another approach one might consider a functional account that focuses on the depth of liberalization as a rival explanation in and of itself. Where the proposed

---

69. There are also notable differences: unlike Chapter 20 of NAFTA, for example, the general dispute mechanisms of the Chile and Mexico pacts provide for unambiguously binding rulings.

70. Yarbrough and Yarbrough 1994 and 1992.

level of integration is deep, in other words, legalism may be far more likely than where integration is shallow. Variants of this functional argument are not uncommon among legal scholars who have examined the design of dispute settlement mechanisms.[71] The claim is that deep integration encourages—and may in fact require—legalistic dispute settlement, given the technical complexity of the regulatory and other nontariff barriers to trade that are the focus of recent agreements. Evaluating and interpreting arcane health, safety, and competition policies in light of treaty commitments, in this view, is an inherently legal enterprise that is best assigned to legal institutions. Moreover, the sectoral scope of liberalization in many agreements has broadened to cover new areas such as services, intellectual property, and investment. Opening markets in these areas usually involves crafting legal standards against which domestic regulations must be weighed. The implication of this functional line of reasoning is that where treaty commitments are most ambitious, legalism is most likely. In other words, as I contend, legalism and the level of proposed integration should be positively related. Preliminary evidence for this hypothesis appears in Table 7, but the functional argument by itself cannot easily account for the six anomalous cases of deep integration and low or no legalism.

Among possible explanations of these anomalies, defenders of the functional approach might point to the fact that in CARICOM and UDEAC, to name the clearest examples, integration has remained shallow in practice despite the ambitious treaty goals. Without the credible prospect of real integration, they might ask, why invest resources in a standing tribunal? The political will or capacity to achieve deep liberalization does seem to be lacking in these pacts. It is crucial to note, however, that implementation has also been problematic in many of the common markets—such as COMESA, CEAO, EAC, and ECOWAS—whose member states did elect to establish highly legalistic judicial systems for the resolution of disputes in advance of actual integration. Moreover, the European Court of Justice was in place before the 1957 Treaty of Rome and long before the vision of a European Economic Community approached reality in the last decade.[72]

This exchange points to the considerable differences in implementation between agreements with similar institutional designs. To place both the European Court of Justice and the COMESA Court of Justice at the level of very high legalism, for example, invites questions regarding what critics might term naïve institutionalism.[73] My definition of legalism, in other words, might itself seem excessively legalistic in the sense that it focuses on formal procedures, not policy outcomes. The actual operation of regional pacts, however, is beyond the scope of my theory. Unlike neoliberal institutionalists, my objective in this study is not to demonstrate how institutions

---

71. See Reisman and Wiedman 1995, 10–11; and O'Neal Taylor 1996, 851, 870.

72. The European Court of Justice originally began its work in December 1952 as part of the European Coal and Steel Community. Pescatore 1992, 853. Many of its landmark decisions preceded the 1987 Single European Act. Alter 1998.

73. Comments of Robert O. Keohane in Kahler 1995, 135–44.

influence the process of regional integration. It is to highlight the political factors that account for significant variation in institutional design.

Conclusion

In this article I offer a political theory of dispute settlement design in international trade. My aim is to demonstrate and account for significant variation in the level of legalism across different regional accords. With a dual emphasis on economic asymmetry and the proposed depth of integration, I predict the extent to which trading states will delegate judicial review authority to impartial third parties. My central assertion is that in drafting governance structures for international trade, political leaders weigh the benefits of improved treaty compliance against the costs of diminished policy discretion. To make this judgment, they assess their economic stake in intrapact trade; their relative economic power vis-à-vis other parties to the accord; and the depth or intensity of the proposed liberalization. Thanks to their market size and lesser dependence on trade, relatively large countries tend to prefer less legalism than their smaller counterparts. Because treaties require unanimity, the institutional preferences of larger countries tend to prevail in negotiations, defining the lowest common denominator.

The implications of this approach—chief among which is that legalistic mechanisms are unlikely where asymmetry is high or integration is shallow—stand up to empirical scrutiny against a sizable set of more than sixty regional trade agreements. In almost every pact with high asymmetry, legalism is absent—even, in contrast to functional accounts, where integration is deep. Where asymmetry is low, legalism occurs only where at least a common market, and not just free trade or a uniform external tariff, is the ultimate policy objective. Despite these encouraging results, the empirical test of this theory could be improved. Case studies that trace the process and political dynamics of dispute settlement design within individual pacts would usefully supplement the cross-tabulations of this article. Moreover, the use of country- and sector-specific data regarding intrapact trade flows and barriers in case studies would allow for more refined testing.

Seen from a broad perspective, this theory of trade dispute settlement design ostensibly relies on a hybrid of neoliberal institutionalist logic and structural realist indicators of relative economic power. Unlike those systemic approaches, however, it is grounded in a political calculation of costs and benefits in the domestic arena, not in expectations about absolute or relative gains internationally. Political leaders in this model are not primarily focused on overcoming market failures or improving their defensive positions in an anarchic international system, however germane such considerations may be to the decision to pursue economic integration in the first instance. Given a regional trade initiative, negotiations over dispute settlement design in my view are driven by domestic political concerns. Without delving into the particulars of comparative politics, my analytical framework connects generic domestic political incentives to issues of international institutional design. Like recent work by

Judith Goldstein and George Downs and David Rocke on international trade governance, it bridges the steadily receding divide between comparative and international political economy.[74]

My emphasis on the details of trade dispute settlement design enables me to define specific features of procedural legalism, with potential relevance to institutional innovations in a wider set of international agreements. I neglect other governance structures—such as secretariats, commissions, and surveillance authorities—that may also help monitor and enforce compliance with trade pacts. But my exclusive focus on third-party review seems to complement recent studies of judicialization that chronicle the development of supranational legal systems over time, especially in Europe.[75] Despite their divergent conclusions regarding the extent of judicial autonomy, these investigations of the European Court of Justice all confront issues that I ignore: namely the strategic incentives and actual behavior of judges, disputing states, and nonstate litigants within particular mechanisms after their establishment.

In contrast to their focus on incremental change, my account privileges the moment of institutional creation, when member states negotiate and establish a system for the resolution of disputes. This moment need not coincide with the signing of the initial treaty. In a few pacts, such as the CACM, MERCOSUR, and AFTA, member states adopted or amended their permanent dispute settlement mechanisms well after their commitments to liberalize trade. Like asymmetry and the depth of integration, dispute settlement designs may change over time, with one blueprint substituted for another as in EFTA. Within the parameters of that design, at every level of legalism, a range of behavioral outcomes—from frequent use to utter irrelevance—are possible. Nevertheless, outcomes still remain subject to boundary conditions established by the institutional blueprint of each treaty, rendering the basic design itself worthy of investigation.

Appendix A: Sources for Treaty Texts

The date following the treaty title indicates the year the treaty was published. The original signing date for each treaty can be found in Table 2.

AFTA (ASEAN Free Trade Area). 1992. *International Legal Materials* 31:506.
Protocol on Dispute Settlement Mechanism, available from the ASEAN Secretariat or online at <http://www. asean.or.id/economic/dsm.htm>.
Andean Pact. 1979. Treaty Creating the Court of Justice of the Cartagena Agreement. *International Legal Materials* 18:1203.
Statute of the Court of Justice of the Cartagena Agreement, available from the Organization of American States or online at <http://www.sice.oas.org/trade/junac/tribunal/cartage2.stm>.
ANZCERTA (Australia–New Zealand Closer Economic Relations Trade Agreement). 1983. *International Legal Materials* 22:945.

---

74. See Goldstein 1996; and Downs and Rocke 1995.
75. See Alter 1998; Garrett, Kelemen, and Schulz 1998; Mattli and Slaughter 1998; and Stone Sweet and Brunell 1998.

Baltic Free Trade Agreement. Available from the foreign ministries of member states.

CACM (Central American Common Market). 1994. *Basic Documents of International Economic Law* 2:529.

Statute of the Central American Court of Justice. 1995. *International Legal Materials* 34:921.

CARICOM (Caribbean Community). 1974. *United Nations Treaty Series* 946:17. New York: UN.

CEAO (West African Economic Community). 1981. *United Nations Treaty Series* 1257:362. New York: UN.

CEEC (Central and East European Country) Pacts. Available online at <http://www.wto.org/wto/online/ddf.htm>.

CEFTA (Central European Free Trade Agreement). 1995. *International Legal Materials* 34:3.

Chile and Mexico Pacts. Available from the Organization of American States or online at <http://www.sice.oas.org/trade.stm>.

CIS (Commonwealth of Independent States). 1995. *International Legal Materials* 34:1279.

COMESA (Common Market for Eastern and Southern Africa). 1994. *International Legal Materials* 33: 1067.

EAC (East African Community). 1967. *International Legal Materials* 6:932.

EC (European Community). Agreement Establishing the European Economic Community and Protocol on the Statute of the Court of Justice of the EEC. 1958. *United Nations Treaty Series* 298:11, 147. New York: UN.

EC Associations. Available in *Official Journal of the European Communities,* or online at <http://europa.eu.int/eur-lex/en/>.

EC–Israel. 1996. *Official Journal of the European Communities* 39:1–11.

ECOWAS (Economic Community of West African States). 1975. *International Legal Materials* 14:1200.

Revised Treaty. 1996. *International Legal Materials* 35:660.

Protocol A/P.1/7/91 on the Community Court of Justice. 1996. *Revue Africaine de Droit International et Compare* 8:228.

EEA (European Economic Area). 1993. *Common Market Law Reports* 29:1247.

EFTA (European Free Trade Association). 1960. *United Nations Treaty Series* 370:5. New York: UN.

EFTA. 1994. *Official Journal of the European Communities* 37:1–83.

EFTA Associations. Available online at <http://www.efta.int/docs/EFTA/LegalTexts/FTAs/FTAdefault.htm>.

GCC (Gulf Cooperation Council). 1987. *International Legal Materials* 26:1131.

Mano River Union. 1974. *United Nations Treaty Series* 952:264. New York: UN.

MERCOSUR (Common Market of the South). 1991. *International Legal Materials* 30:1041.

Protocol of Brasilia for the Settlement of Disputes. 1997. *International Legal Materials* 36:691.

Ouro Preto Protocol, available from the Organization of American States or online at <http://www.sice.oas.org/trade/mrcsr/ourop/index.stm>.

NAFTA (North American Free Trade Agreement). 1993. *International Legal Materials* 32:605.

OECS (Organization of East Caribbean States). 1981. *International Legal Materials* 20:1166.

SACU (Southern African Customs Union). 1973. *United Nations Treaty Series* 860:69. New York: UN.

U.S.–Israel. 1985. *International Legal Materials* 24:654.

UDEAC (Central African Customs and Economic Union). 1964. *International Legal Materials* 4:699.

Appendix B: Excluded Regional Economic Agreements, 1957–95

This list draws largely on de la Torre and Kelly 1992; IMF 1994; and WTO 1995. These sources also include pacts that were superceded by subsequent agreements included in Table 2 or listed here.

Nonreciprocal Agreements

U.S. Caribbean Basin Initiative
EC Lomé Conventions with African, Caribbean, and Pacific States
EC Cooperation Agreements with Algeria, Egypt, Jordan, Lebanon, Morocco, Syria, and Tunisia
EFTA Cooperation Agreements with Albania, Egypt, and Tunisia
1976 Australia–Papua New Guinea Trade and Commercial Relations Agreement
1980 South Pacific Regional Trade and Economic Agreement
1991 CARICOM–Venezuela Agreement
1991 CARICOM–Colombia Agreement

Cooperation or Framework Agreements

1976 Economic Community of the Great Lakes Countries
1980 Latin American Integration Association
1983 Economic Community of Central African States
1984 Indian Ocean Commission
1985 Economic Cooperation Organization
1985 South Asian Association for Regional Cooperation (signed limited preferential trade pact in 1993)
1989 Asia Pacific Economic Cooperation Forum
1991 African Economic Community
1992 Southern African Development Community (signed free trade agreement in 1996)
1992 Black Sea Economic Cooperation Project
1994 Association of Caribbean States
1994 Free Trade Area of the Americas

Unavailable Agreements

1961 Borneo Free Trade Area
1962 African Common Market
1964 Arab Common Market
1975 Bangkok Agreement
1989 Arab Maghreb Union
1991 Thailand–Lao People's Democratic Republic Trade Agreement
1992 Slovak Republic–Czech Republic Customs Union
1993 Slovenia–Czech Republic Free Trade Agreement
1993 Slovenia–Slovak Republic Free Trade Agreement
1994 Kazakhstan–Kyrgyz Republic–Uzbekistan Customs Union
1994 Economic and Monetary Community of Central Africa (renewal of moribund 1964 UDEAC)
1994 West African Economic and Monetary Union (successor to dissolved 1973 CEAO)

References

Alesina, Alberto, and Howard Rosenthal. 1995. *Partisan Politics, Divided Government, and the Economy.* Cambridge: Cambridge University Press.

Alesina, Alberto, and Romain Wacziarg. 1997. Openness, Country Size, and the Government. NBER Working Paper 6024. Cambridge, Mass.: National Bureau of Economic Research.

Alesina, Alberto, Enrico Spolaore, and Romain Wacziarg. 1997. Economic Integration and Political Disintegration. NBER Working Paper 6163. Cambridge, Mass.: National Bureau of Economic Research.

Alter, Karen J. 1998. Who Are the "Masters of the Treaty"?: European Governments and the European Court of Justice. *International Organization* 52 (1):121–47.

Azrieli, Avraham. 1993. Improving Arbitration Under the U.S.–Israel Free Trade Agreement: A Framework for a Middle East Free Trade Zone. *St. John's Law Review* 67 (2):187–263.

Berry, William D. 1999. Testing for Interaction in Models with Binary Dependent Variables. Society for Political Methodology Working Paper. San Luis Obispo, Calif.: California Polytechnic State University.

Bierwagen, Rainer M., and David W. Hull. 1993. Decisions of Regional and Foreign Courts. *American Journal of International Law* 87:117–37.

Burley, Anne-Marie, and Walter Mattli. 1993. Europe Before the Court: A Political Theory of Legal Integration. *International Organization* 47 (1):41–76.

Chayes, Abram, and Antonia Handler Chayes. 1995. *The New Sovereignty: Compliance with International Regulatory Agreements.* Cambridge, Mass.: Harvard University Press.

Cowell, Frank A. 1995. *Measuring Inequality.* 2d ed. New York: Prentice Hall.

Dam, Kenneth W. 1970. *The GATT: Law and International Economic Organization.* Chicago: University of Chicago Press.

de la Torre, Augusto, and Margaret R. Kelly. 1992. Regional Trade Arrangements. International Monetary Fund Occasional Paper 93. Washington, D.C.: IMF.

Destler, I. M. 1986. *American Trade Politics: System under Stress.* Washington, D.C.: Institute for International Economics.

Destler, I. M., and John S. Odell. 1987. *Anti-protection: Changing Forces in United States Trade Politics.* Washington, D.C.: Institute for International Economics.

Downs, George W., and David M. Rocke. 1995. *Optimal Imperfection? Domestic Uncertainty and Institutions in International Relations.* Princeton, N.J.: Princeton University Press.

Eliason, Scott R. 1993. *Maximum Likelihood Estimation: Logic and Practice.* Thousand Oaks, Calif.: Sage.

Foroutan, Faezeh. 1993. Regional Integration in Sub-Saharan Africa: Past Experience and Future Prospects. In *New Dimensions in Regional Integration*, edited by Jaime de Melo and Arvind Panagariya, 234–71. Cambridge: Cambridge University Press.

Sen, Amartya Kumar, and James E. Foster. 1997. On Economic Inequality After a Quarter Century. In Sen, *On Economic Inequality.* New York: Oxford University Press.

Frieden, Jeffry A. 1991. Invested Interests: The Politics of National Economic Policies in a World of Global Finance. *International Organization* 45 (4):425–51.

Garrett, Geoffrey. 1995. The Politics of Legal Integration in the European Union. *International Organization* 49 (1):171–81.

Garrett, Geoffrey, and Barry R. Weingast. 1993. Ideas, Interests, and Institutions: Constructing the European Community's Internal Market. In *Ideas and Foreign Policy: Beliefs, Institutions, and Policy Change*, edited by Judith Goldstein and Robert O. Keohane, 173–206. Ithaca, N.Y.: Cornell University Press.

Garrett, Geoffrey, R. Daniel Kelemen, and Heiner Schulz. 1998. The European Court of Justice, National Governments, and Legal Integration in the European Union. *International Organization* 52 (1):149–76.

Goldstein, Judith. 1993. *Ideas, Interests, and American Trade Policy*. Ithaca, N.Y.: Cornell University Press.

———. 1996. International Law and Domestic Institutions: Reconciling North American "Unfair" Trade Laws. *International Organization* 50 (4):541–64.

Hart, Michael. 1994. *Decision at Midnight: Inside the Canada–U.S. Free Trade Negotiations*. Vancouver, B.C.: UBC Press.

Hart, Robert A., and David H. Clark. 1999. Does Size Matter? Exploring the Small Sample Properties of Maximum Likelihood Estimation. Society for Political Methodology Working Paper. San Luis Obispo, Calif.: California Polytechnic State University.

Hudec, Robert E. 1971. GATT or GABB? The Future Design of the General Agreement on Tariffs and Trade. *Yale Law Journal* 80 (7):1299–1386.

———. 1993. *Enforcing International Trade Law: The Evolution of the Modern GATT Legal System*. Salem, N.H.: Butterworth.

International Monetary Fund (IMF). 1994. *International Trade Policies: The Uruguay Round and Beyond*. Vol. 2, *Background Papers*. Washington, D.C.: IMF.

Jackson, John H. 1979. Governmental Disputes in International Trade Relations: A Proposal in the Context of GATT. *Journal of World Trade Law* 13:1–21.

———. 1992. Status of Treaties in Domestic Legal Systems: A Policy Analysis. *American Journal of International Law* 86:310–40.

Kahler, Miles. 1995. *International Institutions and the Political Economy of Integration*. Washington, D.C.: Brookings Institution.

Keohane, Robert O. 1984. *After Hegemony: Cooperation and Discord in the World Political Economy*. Princeton, N.J.: Princeton University Press.

Kiewiet, D. Roderick, and Douglas Rivers. 1984. A Retrospective on Retrospective Voting. *Political Behavior* 6 (4):369–93.

Kovenock, Dan, and Marie Thursby. 1994. GATT, Dispute Settlement, and Cooperation. In *Analytical and Negotiating Issues in the Global Trading System*, edited by Alan V. Deardorff and Robert M. Stern, 361–98. Ann Arbor: University of Michigan Press.

Krasner, Stephen D. 1991. Global Communications and National Power: Life on the Pareto Frontier. *World Politics* 43 (3):336–66.

Long, J. Scott. 1997. *Regression Models for Categorical and Limited Dependent Variables*. Thousand Oaks, Calif.: Sage.

Magee, Stephen P., William A. Brock, and Leslie Young. 1989. *Black Hole Tariffs and Endogenous Policy Theory: Political Economy in General Equilibrium*. London: Cambridge University Press.

Maggi, Giovanni. 1996. The Role of Multilateral Institutions in International Trade Cooperation. *American Economic Review* 89 (1):190–214.

Malanczuk, Peter. 1997. *Akehurst's Modern Introduction to International Law*. 7th ed. New York: Routledge.

Mattli, Walter, and Anne-Marie Slaughter. 1995. Law and Politics in the European Union: A Reply to Garrett. *International Organization* 49 (1):183–90.

———. 1996. Constructing the European Community Legal System from the Ground Up: The Role of Individual Litigants and National Courts. Jean Monnet Chair Working Paper 6/96. Cambridge, Mass.: Harvard Law School.

———. 1998. Revisiting the European Court of Justice. *International Organization* 52 (1):177–209.

Merrills, J. G. 1991. *International Dispute Settlement*. 2d ed. Cambridge: Grotius.

Milgrom, Paul, and John Roberts. 1992. *Economics, Organization, and Management*. Englewood Cliffs, N.J.: Prentice-Hall.

Moravcsik, Andrew. 1993. Preferences and Power in the European Community: A Liberal Intergovernmentalist Approach. *Journal of Common Market Studies* 31 (4):473–524.

O'Neal Taylor, Cherie. 1996. Dispute Resolution as a Catalyst for Economic Integration and an Agent for Deepening Integration: NAFTA and MERCOSUR. *Northwestern Journal of International Law and Business* 17 (2/3):850–99.

Organization for Economic Co-operation and Development (OECD). Various years. *National Accounts Statistics*. Paris: OECD.

Pastor, Robert A. 1980. *Congress and the Politics of U.S. Foreign Economic Policy*. Berkeley: University of California Press.

Pastori, Alejandro. 1994. The Institutions of MERCOSUR: From the Treaty of Asuncion to the Protocol of Ouro Preto. *Inter-American Legal Materials* 6 (3/4):1–31.

Pescatore, Pierre. 1992. Court of Justice of the European Communities. In *Encyclopedia of Public International Law*, vol. 1., edited by Rudolf Bernhardt, 852–67. New York: North-Holland.

Reisman, Michael, and Mark Wiedman. 1995. Contextual Imperatives of Dispute Resolution Mechanisms: Some Hypotheses and their Applications in the Uruguay Round and NAFTA. *Journal of World Trade* 29 (3):5–38.

Ruggie, John Gerard, ed. 1993. *Multilateralism Matters: The Theory and Praxis of an Institutional Form*. New York: Columbia University Press.

Schattschneider, E. E. 1935. *Politics, Pressures, and the Tariff: A Study of Free Private Enterprise in Pressure Politics, as Shown in the 1929–30 Revision of the Tariff*. Englewood Cliffs, N.J.: Prentice-Hall.

Shapiro, Martin M. 1981. *Courts: A Comparative and Political Analysis*. Chicago: University of Chicago Press.

Slaughter, Anne-Marie, Andrew S. Tulumello, and Stepan Wood. 1998. International Law and International Relations Theory: A New Generation of Interdisciplinary Scholarship. *American Journal of International Law* 92 (3):367–97.

Smith, James McCall. 1995. The Limits of Legalization: Dispute Settlement in NAFTA. Stanford Center on Conflict and Negotiation Working Paper 49. Stanford, Calif.: Stanford Law School.

————. 1998. Policing International Trade: The Politics of Dispute Settlement Design. Ph.D. diss., Stanford University, Stanford, Calif.

Stone Sweet, Alec. 1999. Judicialization and the Construction of Governance. *Comparative Political Studies* 32 (2):147–84.

Stone Sweet, Alec, and Thomas L. Brunell. 1998. Constructing a Supranational Constitution: Dispute Resolution and Governance in the European Community. *American Political Science Review* 92:63–81.

Tsoukalis, Loukas. 1993. *The New European Economy: The Politics and Economics of Integration*. 2d ed. New York: Oxford University Press.

United Nations (UN). Various years. *Statistical Yearbook*. New York: UN.

von Glahn, Gerhard. 1996. *Law Among Nations: An Introduction to Public International Law*. 7th ed. Boston: Allyn and Bacon.

Weiler, Joseph H. H. 1991. The Transformation of Europe. *Yale Law Journal* 100 (8):2403–83.

Weingast, Barry R. 1995. A Rational Choice Perspective on the Role of Ideas: Shared Belief Systems and State Sovereignty in International Cooperation. *Politics and Society* 23 (4):449–64.

Williamson, Oliver E. 1985. *The Economic Institutions of Capitalism: Firms, Markets, Relational Contracting*. New York: Free Press.

Wolf, Martin. 1987. Why Trade Liberalization Is a Good Idea. In *The Uruguay Round: A Handbook on the Multilateral Trade Negotiations*, edited by J. Michael Finger and Andrzej Olechowski, 14–21. Washington, D.C.: World Bank.

World Bank. Various years. *World Development Indicators*. CD-ROM. Washington, D.C.: World Bank.

World Trade Organization (WTO). 1995. *Regionalism and the World Trading System*. Geneva: WTO.

Yarbrough, Beth V., and Robert M. Yarbrough. 1986. Reciprocity, Bilateralism, and Economic "Hostages": Self-enforcing Agreements in International Trade. *International Studies Quarterly* 30 (1):7–21.

————. 1990. International Institutions and the New Economics of Organization. *International Organization* 44 (2):235–59.

————. 1992. *Cooperation and Governance in International Trade: The Strategic Organizational Approach*. Princeton, N.J.: Princeton University Press.

————. 1994. Regionalism and Layered Governance: The Choice of Trade Institutions. *Journal of International Affairs* 48 (1):95–117.

————. 1997. Dispute Settlement in International Trade: Regionalism and Procedural Coordination. In *The Political Economy of Regionalism*, edited by Edward D. Mansfield and Helen V. Milner, 134–63. New York: Columbia University Press.

Young, H. Peyton, ed. 1985. *Fair Allocation*. Providence, R.I.: American Mathematical Society.

III.
The Compliance Debate

W hen and to what degree do states comply with the provisions of international agreements? This question is central to any understanding of the effectiveness of institutions. Theoretical and empirical studies of compliance issues have thus become prominent in the institutional literature. The articles included in this section illustrate the vastly different approaches to compliance taken by legal scholars and political scientists. Legal scholars, like constructivists, concentrate on issues of interpretation and intersubjective agreement on what constitutes compliance and acceptable reasons to deviate from the letter of the law. Because such interpretation is the essence of state interaction in institutions, they reject attempts to quantify compliance and explain variation in its degree. In contrast, political scientists see compliance as an empirical, measurable phenomenon and are focused on explaining variations in patterns of compliance. Compliance with difficult agreements is the most interesting and consequential aspect of international institutions, and it often requires strong enforcement provisions. States make conscious decisions about whether to comply, taking into account not only the immediate consequences of noncompliance but also its effect on their reputations in the international arena.

The examination of compliance issues has its roots in legal scholarship, and Abram Chayes and Antonia Handler Chayes (Chapter 8) bring the perspective of legal scholars to bear. While identifying the potential for a new, fruitful dialogue between legal scholars and political scientists, Chayes and Chayes pose a number of arguments that should be highly provocative to political scientists. First, they argue that the degree of compliance with international agreements is not an empirical issue. Due to the difficulties of interpreting and classifying actions as "in compliance" or "not in compliance" with specific treaties, it would be folly to attempt to develop a statistical protocol for measuring rates of compliance and their variation. Therefore, they argue for the utility of beginning from the assumption that most states comply with most of their commitments, most of the time. Second, and following a similar logic about the difficulty of measuring "interests," they argue that one cannot sensibly test hypotheses about whether states comply to the degree that compliance is in their self-interest. States offer numerous justifications for their apparent deviation from the requirements of agreements, and other states routinely *accept these justifications as reasonable. Decisions to deviate are rarely conscious and explicit. Building on these assumptions, the authors make the normative argument that judging the effects of agreements using standards of strict compliance is inappropriate. Instead, in different regimes different rates of compliance are seen by members as "acceptable." International agreements thus change the behavior and expectations of states, but not in a way that a strict calculation of costs and benefits, and a strict interpretation of the letter of the law, would suggest.*

George Downs, David Rocke, and Peter Barsoom (Chapter 9) challenge Chayes and Chayes' "managerial" view of international agreements by drawing a distinction between compliance and cooperation. They accept the descriptive assessment that rates of compliance with agreements are generally high. However, they challenge the implications that Chayes and Chayes draw from this observation by pointing to severe problems of selection bias and endogeneity. In many cases, rates of compliance are high simply because treaties do not call on states to do very much; they simply ratify preexisting patterns of behavior. When this is true, compliance has little to do with genuine international cooperation. The authors conclude that once these inferential problems are taken into account, Chayes and Chayes' argument that enforcement mechanisms are not very important in international agreements cannot be supported. Indeed, noncompliance does sometimes occur, and it is examples of noncompliance that allow us to evaluate the importance of enforcement in supporting international cooperation. Downs, Rocke, and Barsoom thus argue that when strategic action by states is taken into account, both expectations about enforcement and calculations of self-interest are necessary to understand patterns of compliance and cooperation.

Beth Simmons (Chapter 10) contributes a careful empirical study to the debate on compliance by examining the increasing use of legalistic principles and procedures in the international monetary system. She concentrates on the provisions of the Articles of Agreement of the International Monetary Fund (IMF) for liberalization of states' current accounts and adoption of unified exchange-rate systems. Prior to World War II, little "hard law" existed relevant to international monetary affairs. The lack of legalism contributed to an inability of governments to make credible commitments to market actors about their economic policies. Thus when the IMF was established during the war, governments chose to integrate legal standards into its provisions. They believed that such provisions would increase the credibility of their commitments to liberalize. However, the IMF has little direct enforcement power; therefore, the mechanism that would lead to compliance with rules requires elaboration. Simmons argues that reputational concerns explain why states comply with legal rules. If states have a good reputation for compliance, a decision to deviate from the rules could have devastating implications for their reputation in the market, leading directly to negative economic outcomes. Simmons thus supports arguments about the central importance of credibility, reputation, and calculations about costs and benefits of compliance in the context of legalized international institutions.

On Compliance

Abram Chayes and
Antonia Handler Chayes

In an increasingly complex and interdependent world, negotiation, adoption, and implementation of international agreements is a major component of the foreign policy activity of every state.[1] International agreements come in a variety of shapes and sizes—formal and informal, bilateral and multiparty, universal and regional. Our concern is with contemporary agreements of relatively high political salience in fields such as security, economics, and environment, where the treaty is a central structural element in a broader international regulatory regime.[2] Some of these agreements are little more

This is an introductory chapter to a more extended study of compliance with international treaty obligations. The research has been supported by grants from the Pew Charitable Trust and the Carnegie Corporation of New York, for which we wish to express our gratitude. Earlier versions of this article were presented at seminars at the Kennedy School of Government, Harvard University, and at the University of Chicago Law School. Robert Keohane has been particularly helpful in commenting on the earlier efforts. Our thanks are also due to our many student research assistants and especially to Sean Cote, Fred Jacobs, and Jan Martinez, who labored on the references.

1. Barry E. Carter and Phillip R. Trimble, *International Law* (Boston: Little, Brown, 1991), pp. 133–252, cite a statistical study showing that of 10,189 U.S. treaties and international agreements made between 1789 and 1979, 8,955 were concluded between 1933 and 1979 (see p. 169). In the U.S. lexicon, the term "treaty" is reserved for international agreements ratified with the advice and consent of the Senate in accordance with Article 2, cl. 2 of the Constitution. Other international agreements are concluded by the President, in the great majority of cases with the authorization of Congress and less frequently on his or her own responsibility. All of these are "treaties" according to international usage, which defines a treaty as "an international agreement, concluded between states in written form and governed by international law." See Vienna Convention on the Law of Treaties (entered into force on 27 January 1980) Article 2(1)(a), in *International Legal Materials,* vol. 8 (Washington, D.C.: The American Society of International Law, July 1969), pp. 679–735 (hereafter cited as Vienna Convention on the Law of Treaties). The quotation is found on p. 701. The computer bank of the United Nations (UN) Treaty Office shows treaty growth, including multilateral and bilateral treaties and amendments, as follows: 373 treaties were entered into during the ten-year period ending in 1955; 498 in the period ending in 1965; 808 in the period ending in 1975; 461 in the period ending in 1985; and 915 in the period ending in 1991.

2. Treaty law, based on nineteenth-century practice, adopts, implicitly or explicitly, a contractual model of bilateral relationships (or, at most, agreements among a few parties), and a good deal of contemporary work in international relations reflects this same framework. Although nineteenth-century legal thought was hospitable to conceptions based on contract, they do not fit comfortably with regulatory lawmaking.

International Organization 47, 2, Spring 1993, pp. 175–205

than statements of general principle, while others contain detailed prescriptions for a defined field of interaction. Still others may be umbrella agreements for consensus building in preparation for more specific regulation. Most of the agreements of concern are multilateral, except in the field of nuclear arms control, in which the cold war generated a series of bilateral negotiations and agreements between the United States and the Soviet Union.

We believe that when nations enter into an international agreement of this kind, they alter their behavior, their relationships, and their expectations of one another over time in accordance with its terms. That is, they will to some extent comply with the undertakings they have made.[3] How or why this should be so is the subject of a burgeoning literature and debate in which, for the first time in half a century, the possibility of fruitful dialogue between international lawyers and students of international relations has emerged. This article explores some basic propositions we think should frame this discussion.

First, the general level of compliance with international agreements cannot be empirically verified. That nations generally comply with their international agreements, on the one hand, and that they violate them whenever it is "in their interests to do so" are not statements of fact or even hypotheses to be tested, but assumptions. We give some reasons why we think the background assumption of a propensity to comply is plausible and useful.

Second, compliance problems often do not reflect a deliberate decision to violate an international undertaking on the basis of a calculation of interests. We propose a variety of other (and in our view more usual) reasons why states may deviate from treaty obligations and why, in particular circumstances, these reasons are accepted by the parties as justifying such departures.

Third, the treaty regime as a whole need not and should not be held to a standard of strict compliance but to a level of overall compliance that is "acceptable" in the light of the interests and concerns the treaty is designed to safeguard. We consider how the "acceptable level" is determined and adjusted.

---

3. We are mindful of the distinction between treaty compliance and regime effectiveness. See Oran Young, "The Effectiveness of International Institutions: Hard Cases and Critical Variables," in James N. Rosenau and Ernst-Otto Czempiel, eds., *Governance Without Government: Order and Change in World Politics* (Cambridge: Cambridge University Press, 1992), pp. 160–92; and Jesse Ausubel and David Victor, "Verification of International Environmental Agreements," *Annual Review of Energy and Environment,* vol. 17, 1992, pp. 1–43. The parties to the International Whaling Convention, for example, complied fully with the quotas set by its commission, but the whale population crashed because the quotas were too high. Nevertheless, we think the observance (or not) of treaty commitments by the parties is a subject worth studying in its own right. Moreover, treaties are ordinarily intended to induce behavior that is expected to ameliorate the problem to which they are directed, so that, if Young's warning is kept in mind, compliance may be a fair first approximation surrogate for effectiveness.

Background assumption

According to Louis Henkin, *"almost all nations observe almost all principles of international law and almost all of their obligations almost all of the time."*[4] The observation is frequently repeated without anyone, so far as we know, supplying any empirical evidence to support it. A moment's reflection shows that it would not be easy to devise a statistical protocol that would generate such evidence. For example, how would Iraq's unbroken respect for the borders of Turkey, Jordan, and Saudi Arabia count in the reckoning against the invasions of Iran and Kuwait?

Equally, and for much the same reasons, there is no way to validate empirically the position of mainstream realist international relations theory going back to Machiavelli, that "a prudent ruler cannot keep his word, nor should he, where such fidelity would damage him, and when the reasons that made him promise are no longer relevant."[5] Contemporary realists accept that the interest in reciprocal observation of treaty norms by other parties or a more general interest in the state's reputation as a reliable contractual partner should be counted in the trade-off of costs and benefits on which a decision is based (an extension that detracts considerably from the power and elegance of the realist formula).[6] No calculus, however, will supply a rigorous, nontautological answer to the question whether a state observed a particular treaty obligation, much less its treaty obligations generally, only when it was in its interest to do so. Anecdotal evidence abounds for both the normative and the realist propositions, but neither of them, in their general form, is subject to statistical or empirical proof. The difference between the two schools is not one of fact but of the background assumption that informs their approach to the subject.

A critical question for any study of compliance, then, is which background assumption to adopt, and that question is to be resolved not on the basis of whether the assumption is "true" or "false" but whether or not it is helpful for the particular inquiry. Thus, for game-theoretic approaches that focus on the abstract structure of the relationship between states, the realist assumption of a unitary rational actor optimizing utilities distributed along smooth preference curves may have value. As Thomas Schelling said at the beginning of his classic

---

4. See Louis Henkin, *How Nations Behave,* 2d ed. (New York: Columbia University Press, 1979), p. 47; and p. 69 of Louis Henkin, "International Law: Politics, Values, and Functions: General Course on Public International Law," *Recueil Des Cours,* vol. 216, 1989, pp. 1–416, emphasis original.

5. Niccolò Machiavelli, *The Prince,* eds. Quentin Skinner and Russell Price (Cambridge: Cambridge University Press, 1988), pp. 61–62. For a modern instance, see Hans J. Morgenthau, *Politics Among Nations: The Struggle for Power and Peace,* 5th ed. (New York: Alfred A. Knopf, 1978), p. 560: "In my experience [states] will keep their bargains as long as it is in their interest."

6. See, for example, James A. Caporaso, "International Relations Theory and Multilateralism: The Search for Foundations," *International Organization* 46 (Summer 1992), pp. 599–632.

work, "The premise of 'rational behavior' is a potent one for the production of theory. Whether the resulting theory provides good or poor insight into actual behavior is . . . a matter for subsequent judgment."[7]

Our interest in this work is in improving the prospects for compliance with treaties, both at the drafting stage and later as the parties live and operate under them. From this perspective, the realist analysis, focusing on a narrow set of externally defined "interests"—primarily, in the classical version, the maintenance or enhancement of state military and economic power—is not very helpful. Improving compliance becomes a matter of the manipulation of burdens and benefits defined in terms of those interests, which translates into the application of military or economic sanctions. Because these are costly, difficult to mobilize, and of doubtful efficacy, they are infrequently used in practice. Meanwhile, analytic attention is diverted from a wide range of institutional and political mechanisms that in practice bear the burden of efforts to enhance treaty compliance.

For a study of the methods by which compliance can be improved, the background assumption of a general propensity of states to comply with international obligations, which is the basis on which most practitioners carry out their work, seems more illuminating.[8] We note here some of the chief considerations that lend plausibility to such an assumption. We do not suggest that these factors, singly or in combination, will lead to compliance in every case or even in any particular instance. Our claim is only that these considerations support the background assumption of a general propensity for states to comply with their treaty obligations.

Efficiency

Decisions are not a free good. Governmental resources for policy analysis and decision making are costly and in short supply. Individuals and organizations seek to conserve those resources for the most urgent and pressing matters.[9] In these circumstances, standard economic analysis argues against the continuous recalculation of costs and benefits in the absence of convincing evidence that circumstances have changed since the original decision. Efficiency dictates considerable policy continuity. In areas of activity covered by

---

7. Thomas C. Schelling, *The Strategy of Conflict* (Cambridge, Mass.: Harvard University Press, 1980), p. 4.

8. Oran R. Young, *Compliance and Public Authority: A Theory with International Applications* (Baltimore, Md.: Johns Hopkins University Press, 1979), pp. 31–34.

9. See George Stigler, "The Economics of Information," *Journal of Political Economy* 69 (June 1961), pp. 213–25; G. J. Stigler and G. S. Becker, "De Gustibus non Est Disputandum" (There is no disputing taste), in Karen S. Cook and Margaret Levi, eds., *The Limits of Rationality* (Chicago: University of Chicago Press, 1990), pp. 191–216; Charles E. Lindblom, *The Policy Making Process* (Englewood Cliffs, N.J.: Prentice-Hall, 1968), p. 14; and Young, *Compliance and Public Authority,* pp. 16–17.

treaty obligations, the alternative to recalculation is to follow the established rule.

Organization theory would reach the same result as economic analysis, but by a different route. In place of the continuously calculating, maximizing rational actor, it substitutes a "satisficing" model of bounded rationality that reacts to problems as they arise and searches for solutions within a familiar and accustomed repertoire.[10] In this analysis, bureaucratic organizations are viewed as functioning according to routines and standard operating procedures, often specified by authoritative rules and regulations. For Max Weber, this was the defining characteristic of bureaucracy.[11] The adoption of a treaty, like the enactment of any other law, establishes an authoritative rule system. Compliance is the normal organizational presumption.

The bureaucracy is not monolithic, of course, and it will likely contain opponents of the treaty regime as well as supporters. When there is an applicable rule in a treaty or otherwise, opposition ordinarily surfaces in the course of rule implementation and takes the form of argument over interpretation of language and definition of the exact content of the obligation. Such controversies are settled in accordance with normal bureaucratic procedures in which, again, the presumption is in favor of "following" the rule. Casuistry is admissible, though sometimes suspect. An advocate of outright violation bears a heavy burden of persuasion.

Interests

The assertion that states carry out treaty commitments only when it is in their interest to do so seems to imply that commitments are somehow unrelated to interests. In fact, the opposite is true. The most basic principle of international law is that states cannot be legally bound except with their own consent. So, in the first instance, the state need not enter into a treaty that does not conform to its interests.[12]

---

10. Herbert Simon, *Models of Man: Social and Rational—Mathematical Essays on Rational Human Behavior in a Social Setting* (New York: John Wiley & Sons, 1957), pp. 200–204. See also James G. March and Herbert A. Simon, *Organizations* (New York: John Wiley & Sons, 1958), p. 169. For an example of this model of organizational behavior applied to the analysis of international affairs, see Graham T. Allison, *The Essence of Decision: Explaining the Cuban Missile Crisis* (Glenview, Ill.: Scott, Foresman, 1971), chaps. 3 and 4.

11. M. Rheinstein, ed., *Max Weber on Law in Economy and Society* (New York: Simon and Schuster, 1954), p. 350: "For modern bureaucracy, the element of 'calculability of its rules' has really been of decisive significance."

12. Even in the case of peace treaties, the victor seems to attach importance to the signature of the vanquished on the document. After the Persian Gulf War, for example, the UN Security Council insisted that Iraq accept the terms of Resolution 687 establishing a cease-fire. See Sean Cote, *A Narrative of the Implementation of Section C of UN Security Council Resolution 687,* Occasional Paper, Center for Science and International Affairs, Harvard University, Cambridge, Mass., forthcoming; and Morgenthau, *Politics Among Nations,* p. 282.

More important, a treaty does not present the state with a simple binary alternative, to sign or not to sign. Treaties, like other legal arrangements, are artifacts of political choice and social existence. The process by which they are formulated and concluded is designed to ensure that the final result will represent, to some degree, an accommodation of the interests of the negotiating states. Of course, if state interests are taken to be fixed and given, the assertion that states do not conclude treaties except as they embody those interests would add little to the realist position. But modern treaty making, like legislation in a democratic polity, can be seen as a creative enterprise through which the parties not only weigh the benefits and burdens of commitment but explore, redefine, and sometimes discover their interests. It is at its best a learning process in which not only national positions but also conceptions of national interest evolve.

This process goes on both within each state and at the international level. In a state with a well-developed bureaucracy, the elaboration of national positions in preparation for treaty negotiations requires extensive interagency vetting. Different officials with different responsibilities and objectives engage in what amounts to a sustained internal negotiation. Phillip Trimble's list of the U.S. groups normally involved in arms control negotiations includes the national security staff, the Departments of State and Defense, the Arms Control and Disarmament Agency, the Joint Chiefs of Staff, the Central Intelligence Agency, and sometimes the Department of Energy or the National Aeronautics and Space Administration (NASA).[13] These organizations themselves are not unitary actors. Numerous subordinate units of the major departments have quasi-independent positions at the table. Much of the extensive literature on U.S.–Soviet arms control negotiations is devoted to analysis of the almost byzantine complexity of these internal interactions.[14]

The process is not confined to arms control but can be seen in every major U.S. international negotiation. For example, at the end of what Ambassador Richard Benedick calls "the interagency minuet" in preparation for the Vienna Convention for the Protection of the Ozone Layer, the final U.S. position "was drafted by the State Department and was formally cleared by the Departments of Commerce and Energy, The Council on Environmental Quality, EPA

13. Phillip R. Trimble, "Arms Control and International Negotiation Theory," *Stanford Journal of International Law* 25 (Spring 1989), pp. 543–74, especially p. 549.

14. See John Newhouse, *Cold Dawn: The Story of SALT* (New York: Holt, Rinehart and Winston, 1973); Gerard C. Smith, *Doubletalk: The Story of SALT I* (Lanham, Md.: University Press of America, 1985); Strobe Talbott, *Endgame: The Inside Story of SALT II* (New York: Harper & Row, 1979); Strobe Talbott, *Deadly Gambits: The Reagan Administration and the Stalemate in Nuclear Arms Control* (New York: Knopf, 1984); Raymond L. Garthoff, *Detente and Confrontation: American–Soviet Relations from Nixon to Reagan* (Washington, D.C.: Brookings Institution, 1985); and J. McNeill, "U.S.–U.S.S.R. Arms Negotiations: The Process and the Lawyer," *American Journal of International Law* 79 (January 1985), pp. 52–67. Although knowledge of the process in the former Soviet Union is less detailed, the sources cited above, among others, suggest that (making allowances for a more compartmentalized bureaucratic structure) the process was not fundamentally dissimilar.

[Environmental Protection Agency], NASA, NOAA [National Oceanographic and Atmospheric Administration], OMB [Office of Management and Budget], USTR [U.S. Trade Representative], and the Domestic Policy Council (representing all other interested agencies)."[15] In addition to this formidable alphabet soup, White House units, like the Office of Science and Technology Policy, the Office of Policy Development, and the Council of Economic Advisers, also got into the act. According to Trimble, "each agency has a distinctive perspective from which it views the process and which influences the position it advocates. . . . All these interests must be accommodated, compromised or overridden by the President before a position can even be put on the table."[16]

In the United States in recent years, increasing involvement of Congress—and with it nongovernmental organizations (NGOs) and the broader public—has introduced a new range of interests that must ultimately be reflected in the national position.[17] Similar developments seem to be occurring in other democratic countries.

In contrast to day-to-day foreign policy decision making that is oriented toward current political exigencies and imminent deadlines and is focused heavily on short-term costs and benefits, the more deliberate process employed in treaty making may serve to identify and reinforce longer range interests and values. Officials engaged in developing the negotiating position often have an additional reason to take a long-range view, since they may have operational responsibility under any agreement that is reached.[18] What they say and how they conduct themselves at the negotiating table may return to haunt them

---

15. Richard Elliot Benedick, *Ozone Diplomacy: New Directions in Safeguarding the Planet* (Cambridge, Mass: Harvard University Press, 1991), pp. 51–53. The Domestic Policy Council, which established a special senior-level working group to ride herd on the process, consists of nine Cabinet secretaries, the director for the OMB, and the USTR. At the time of the ozone negotiations, the council was chaired by Attorney General Edwin Meese. Other states, at least in advanced industrialized societies, exhibit similar, if perhaps not quite as baroque, internal practices in preparation for negotiations. Developing countries, with small resources to commit to bureaucratic coordination, may rely more on the judgment and inspiration of representatives on the scene.

16. Trimble, "Arms Control and International Negotiation Theory," p. 550.

17. See Benedick, *Ozone Diplomacy,* p. 57, for a description of the emphasis on Congress, industry, and environmental groups in the development of the U.S. strategy to build support for the Protocol on Substances that Deplete the Ozone Layer. For a discussion of how governments "organize themselves to cope with the flow of business generated by international organizations" in an international political system of "complex interdependence," see Robert O. Keohane and Joseph S. Nye, *Power and Interdependence,* 2d ed. (Glenview, Ill.: Scott, Foresman, 1989), p. 35.

18. Hudec uses the examples of the General Agreement on Tariffs and Trade (GATT) and the International Trade Organization (ITO): "For the better part of the first decade, GATT meetings resembled a reunion of the GATT/ITO draftsmen themselves. Failure of the code would have meant a personal failure to many of these officials, and violation of rules they had helped to write could not help being personally embarrassing." See p. 1365 of Robert E. Hudec, "GATT or GABB? The Future Design of the General Agreement of Tariffs and Trade," *Yale Law Journal* 80 (June 1971), pp. 1299–386. See also Robert E. Hudec, *The GATT Legal System and World Trade Diplomacy,* 2d ed. (Salem, N. H.: Butterworth Legal Publishers, 1990), p. 54.

once the treaty has gone into effect.[19] Moreover, they are likely to attach considerable importance to the development of governing norms that will operate predictably when applied to the behavior of the parties over time. All these convergent elements tend to influence national positions in the direction of broad-based conceptions of the national interest that, if adequately reflected in the treaty, will help to induce compliance.

The internal analysis, negotiation, and calculation of the benefits, burdens, and impacts are repeated, for contemporary regulatory treaties, at the international level.[20] In anticipation of negotiations, the issues are reviewed in international forums long before formal negotiation begins. The negotiating process itself characteristically involves intergovernmental debate often lasting years and involving not only other national governments but also international bureaucracies and NGOs. The most notable case is the UN Conference on the Law of the Sea, in which that process lasted for more than ten years, spawning innumerable committees, subcommittees, and working groups, only to be torpedoed in the end by the United States, which had sponsored the negotiations in the first place.[21] Bilateral arms control negotiations between the United States and the Soviet Union were similarly extended, and although only the two superpowers were directly involved, each felt a measure of responsibility to bring along the members of its alliance. Current environmental negotiations on ozone and on global warming follow very much the Law of the Sea pattern. The first conference on stratospheric ozone was convoked by the UN Environment Program (UNEP) in 1977, eight years before the adoption of the Vienna Convention on the Protection of the Ozone Layer.[22] The formal beginning of the climate change negotiations in February 1991 was preceded by two years of work by the Intergovernmental Panel on Climate Change, convened by the World Meteorological Organization and the UNEP to consider scientific, technological, and policy response questions.[23]

19. The Vienna Convention on the Law of Treaties permits limited recourse to the negotiating history when the treaty text is ambiguous, though the emphasis given to such history differs in various tribunals and national courts. See Vienna Convention on the Law of Treaties, Article 32. In the United States, resort to the negotiating history is much freer. See *United States v. Stuart,* 489 U.S. 353–377 (1989); and Detlev F. Vagts "Senate Materials and Treaty Interpretation: Some Research Hints for the Supreme Court," *American Journal of International Law* 83 (July 1989), pp. 546–50.

20. Robert D. Putnam, "Diplomacy and Domestic Politics: The Logic of Two-Level Games," *International Organization* 42 (Summer 1988), pp. 427–60.

21. See James K. Sebenius, *Negotiating the Law of the Sea* (Cambridge, Mass.: Harvard University Press, 1984); and William Wertenbaker, "The Law of the Sea," parts 1 and 2, *The New Yorker,* 1 August 1983, pp. 38–65, and 8 August 1983, pp. 56–83, respectively.

22. As early as 1975, the UNEP funded a World Meteorological Organization (WMO) technical conference on implications of U.S. ozone layer research. But the immediate precursor of the negotiating conference in Vienna came in March 1977, when the UNEP sponsored a policy meeting of governments and international agencies in Washington, D.C., that drafted a "World Plan of Action on the Ozone Layer." See Benedick, *Ozone Diplomacy,* p. 40.

23. The Intergovernmental Panel of Climate Change was set up by the UNEP and WMO after the passage of UN General Assembly Resolution 43/53, A/RES/43/53, 27 January 1989, "Resolution on the Protection of the Global Climate."

Much of this negotiating activity is open to some form of public scrutiny, triggering repeated rounds of national bureaucratic and political review and revision of tentative accommodations among affected interests. The treaty as finally signed and presented for ratification is therefore likely to be based on considered and well-developed conceptions of national interest that have themselves been shaped to some extent by the preparatory and negotiating process.

Treaty making is not purely consensual, of course. Negotiations are heavily affected by the structure of the international system, in which some states are much more powerful than others. As noted, the Convention of the Law of the Sea, the product of more than a decade of international negotiations, was ultimately derailed when a new U.S. administration found it unacceptable.

On the other hand, a multilateral negotiating forum provides opportunities for weaker states to form coalitions and exploit blocking positions. In the same UN Conference on the Law of the Sea, the caucus of what were known as "land-locked and geographically disadvantaged states," which included such unlikely colleagues as Hungary, Switzerland, Austria, Uganda, Nepal, and Bolivia, had a crucial strategic position. The Association of Small Island States, chaired by Vanuatu, played a similar role in the global climate negotiations. Like domestic legislation, the international treaty-making process leaves a good deal of room for accommodating divergent interests. In such a setting, not even the strongest state will be able to achieve all of its objectives, and some participants may have to settle for much less. The treaty is necessarily a compromise, "a bargain that [has] been made."[24] From the point of view of the particular interests of any state, the outcome may fall short of the ideal. But if the agreement is well-designed—sensible, comprehensible, and with a practical eye to probable patterns of conduct and interaction—compliance problems and enforcement issues are likely to be manageable. If issues of noncompliance and enforcement are endemic, the real problem is likely to be that the original bargain did not adequately reflect the interests of those that would be living under it, rather than mere disobedience.[25]

It is true that a state's incentives at the treaty-negotiating stage may be different from those it faces when the time for compliance rolls around. Parties on the giving end of the compromise, especially, might have reason to seek to escape the obligations they have undertaken. Nevertheless, the very act of making commitments embodied in an international agreement changes the

---

24. Susan Strange, "Cave! Hic Dragones: A Critique of Regime Analysis," in Stephen D. Krasner, ed., *International Regimes* (Ithaca, N.Y.: Cornell University Press, 1983), pp. 337–54; the quotation is on p. 353.

25. Systems in which compliance can only be achieved through extensive use of coercion are rightly regarded as authoritarian and unjust. See Michael Barkun, *Law Without Sanctions: Order in Primitive Societies and the World Community* (New Haven, Conn.: Yale University Press, 1968), p. 62.

calculus at the compliance stage, if only because it generates expectations of compliance in others that must enter into the equation.

Moreover, although states may know they can violate their treaty commitments in a crunch, they do not negotiate agreements with the idea that they can do so in routine situations. Thus, the shape of the substantive bargain will itself be affected by the parties' estimates of the costs and risks of their own compliance and expectations about the compliance of others. Essential parties may be unwilling to accept or impose stringent regulations if the prospects for compliance are doubtful. The negotiation will not necessarily collapse on that account, however. The result may be a looser, more general engagement. Such an outcome is often deprecated as a lowest-common-denominator outcome, with what is really important left on the cutting room floor. But it may be the beginning of increasingly serious and concerted attention to the problem.

Finally, the treaty that comes into force does not remain static and unchanging. Treaties that last must be able to adapt to inevitable changes in the economic, technological, social, and political setting. Treaties may be formally amended, of course, or modified by the addition of a protocol, but these methods are slow and cumbersome. Since they are subject to the same ratification process as the original treaty, they can be blocked or avoided by a dissatisfied party. As a result, treaty lawyers have devised a number of ways to deal with the problem of adaptation without seeking formal amendment. The simplest is the device of vesting the power to "interpret" the agreement in some organ established by the treaty. The U.S. Constitution, after all, has kept up with the times not primarily by the amending process but by the Supreme Court's interpretation of its broad clauses. The International Monetary Fund (IMF) Agreement gives such power to the Governing Board, and numerous key questions—including the crucial issue of "conditionality," whether drawings against the fund's resources may be conditioned on the economic performance of the drawing member—have been resolved by this means.[26]

A number of treaties establish authority to make regulations on technical matters by vote of the parties (usually by a special majority), which are then binding on all, though often with the right to opt out. The International Civil Aeronautics Organization has such power with respect to operational and safety matters in international air transport.[27] In many regulatory treaties, "technical" matters may be relegated to an annex that can be altered by vote of the parties.[28] In sum, treaties characteristically contain self-adjusting mecha-

26. Articles of Agreement of the IMF, 27 December 1945, as amended, Article 8, sec. 5, in *United Nations Treaty Series (UNTS),* vol. 2, Treaty no. 20 (New York: United Nations, 1947), p. 39. For the conditionality decision, see decision no. 102-(52/11) 13 February 1952, "Selected Decisions of the Executive Directors and Selected Documents," p. 16.

27. Convention on International Civil Aviation, 7 December 1944, Article 90, in *UNTS,* vol. 15, Treaty no. 102, 1948, p. 295.

28. Montreal Protocol on Substances that Deplete the Ozone Layer, in *International Legal Materials,* vol. 26, 1987, p. 1541, Article 2(9) (signed 16 September 1987 and entered into force 1 January 1989; hereafter cited as Montreal Protocol) as amended, London Adjustment and

nisms by which, over a significant range, they can be and in practice are commonly adapted to respond to shifting interests of the parties.

Norms

Treaties are acknowledged to be legally binding on the states that ratify them.[29] In common experience, people, whether as a result of socialization or otherwise, accept that they are obligated to obey the law.[30] So it is with states. It is often said that the fundamental norm[31] of international law is *pacta sunt servanda* (treaties are to be obeyed).[32] In the United States and many other countries, they become a part of the law of the land. Thus, a provision contained in an agreement to which a state has formally assented entails a legal obligation to obey and is presumptively a guide to action.

It seems almost superfluous to adduce evidence or authority for a proposition that is so deeply ingrained in common understanding and so often reflected in the speech of national leaders. Yet the realist argument that national actions are governed entirely by calculation of interests (including the interest in stability and predictability served by a system of rules) is essentially a denial of the operation of normative obligation in international affairs. This position has held the field for some time in mainstream international relations theory (as have closely related postulates in other positivist social science

---

Amendments to the Montreal Protocol on Substances that Deplete the Ozone Layer, in *International Legal Materials,* vol. 30, 1991, p. 537 (signed 29 June 1990 and entered into force 7 March 1991; hereafter cited as London Amendments).

29. The Vienna Convention on the Law of Treaties, signed 23 May 1969 (entered into force on 27 January 1980), Article 2(1)(a), states that " 'treaty' means an international agreement concluded between States in written form and governed by international law, whether embodied in a single instrument or in two or more related instruments and whatever its particular designation." See UN Doc. A/CONF. 39/27.

30. According to Young, " 'obligation' encompasses incentives to comply with behavioral prescriptions which stem from a general sense of duty and which do not rest on explicit calculations of costs and benefits. . . . Feelings of obligation often play a significant role in compliance choices." Moreover, "rules constitute an essential feature of bureaucracies and . . . routinized compliance with rules is a deeply ingrained norm among bureaucrats." See Young, *Compliance and Public Authority,* pp. 23 and 39. See also R. H. Fallon, "Reflections on Dworkin and the Two Faces of Law," *Notre Dame Law Review,* vol. 67, no. 3, 1992, pp. 553–85, summarizing H. L. A. Hart's concept of a law as a social rule: "From an internal point of view—that of an unalienated participant of the social life of the community—a social rule is a standard that is accepted as a guide to conduct and a basis for criticism, including self-criticism" (p. 556); Rheinstein, *Max Weber on Law in Economy and Society,* pp. 349–56; and Friedrich V. Kratochwil, *Rules, Norms, and Decisions: On the Conditions of Practical and Legal Reasoning in International Relations and Domestic Affairs* (Cambridge: Cambridge University Press, 1989), pp. 15 and 95–129.

31. We use "norm" as a generic term including principles, precepts, standards, rules, and the like. For present purposes, it is adequate to think of legal norms as norms generated by processes recognized as authoritative by a legal system. Compare H. L. A. Hart, *The Concept of Law* (Oxford: Oxford University Press, 1961).

32. The Vienna Convention on the Law of Treaties, Article 26, specifies that "every treaty in force is binding upon the parties to it and must be performed in good faith." See also chap. 30 of Arnold Duncan McNair, *The Law of Treaties* (Oxford: Clarendon Press, 1961), pp. 493–505.

disciplines).[33] But it is increasingly being challenged by a growing body of empirical study and academic analysis.

Such scholars as Elinor Ostrom and Robert Ellickson show how relatively small communities in contained circumstances generate and secure compliance with norms, even without the intervention of a supervening sovereign authority.[34] Others, like Frederick Schauer and Friedrich Kratochwil, analyze how norms operate in decision-making processes, whether as "reasons for action" or in defining the methods and terms of discourse.[35] Jon Elster, often regarded as one of the most powerful scholars of the "rational actor" school, says in his most recent book, "I have come to believe that social norms provide an important kind of motivation for action that is irreducible to rationality or indeed to any other form of optimizing mechanism."[36]

As applied to treaty obligations, this proposition seems almost self-evident. For example: in the absence of the antiballistic missile (ABM) treaty, the Soviet Union would have been legally free to build an ABM system. The exercise of this freedom would surely have posed serious military and political issues for U.S. analysts, diplomats, and intelligence officers. In due course, the United States would have responded, with either its own ABM system or some other suitable military or political move. The same act, the construction of an ABM system, would be qualitatively different, however, if it were done in violation of the specific stipulations of the ABM treaty. Transgression of such a fundamental engagement would trigger not a limited response, but a hostile reaction across the board, jeopardizing the possibility of cooperative relations between the parties for a long time to come. Outrage when solemn commitments are treated as "scraps of paper" is rooted in U.S. history.[37] It is unlikely that this kind of reaction is unique to the United States.

The strongest circumstantial evidence for the sense of an obligation to comply with treaties is the care that states take in negotiating and entering into them. It is not conceivable that foreign ministries and government leaders could devote time and energy on the scale they do to preparing, drafting,

33. William Eskridge, Jr., and G. Peller, "The New Public Law: Moderation as a Postmodern Cultural Form," *Michigan Law Review* 89 (February 1991), pp. 707–91.

34. See Elinor Ostrom, *Governing the Commons: The Evolution of Institutions for Collective Action* (Cambridge: Cambridge University Press, 1990); and Robert C. Ellickson, *Order Without Law: How Neighbors Settle Disputes* (Cambridge, Mass.: Harvard University Press, 1991).

35. See Frederick F. Schauer, *Playing by the Rules: A Philosophical Examination of Rule-based Decision-making in Law and Life* (Oxford: Clarendon Press, 1991); Kratochwil, *Rules, Norms and Decisions;* and Sally Falk Moore, *Law as Process* (London: Routledge & Kegan Paul, 1978).

36. Jon Elster, *The Cement of Society: A Study of Social Order* (Cambridge: Cambridge University Press, 1989), p. 15. See also Margaret Levi, Karen S. Cook, Jodi A. O'Brien, and Howard Fay, "Introduction: The Limits of Rationality," in Cook and Levi, *The Limits of Rationality,* pp. 1–16.

37. The quotation is from German Chancellor Theobald von Bethman-Hollweg's remark to the British ambassador about the treaty guaranteeing Belgian neutrality when Germany invaded in 1914. See *Encyclopedia Britannica,* 14th ed., s.v. Bethman-Hollweg, Theobald von. For an example of the U.S. response, see the letter of ex-President Theodore Roosevelt to British Foreign Secretary Sir Edward Grey dated 22 January 1915, quoted in Hans J. Morgenthau, *Politics Among Nations: The Struggle for Power and Peace,* 4th ed. (New York: Knopf, 1967).

negotiating, and monitoring treaty obligations unless there is an assumption that entering into a treaty commitment ought to and does constrain the state's own freedom of action and an expectation that the other parties to the agreement will feel similarly constrained. The care devoted to fashioning a treaty provision no doubt reflects the desire to limit the state's own commitment as much as to make evasion by others more difficult. In either case, the enterprise makes sense only on the assumption that, as a general rule, states acknowledge an obligation to comply with agreements they have signed.

These attitudes are not confined to foreign offices. U.S. Department of Defense testimony during the cold war repeatedly sounded the theme that arms control treaties with the Soviet Union were important in providing the stability of expectations and predictability the Pentagon needed for sound strategic planning.[38] In the United States and other Western countries, the principle that the exercise of governmental power in general is subject to law lends additional force to an ethos of national compliance with international undertakings.[39] And, of course, appeals to legal obligations are a staple of foreign policy debate and of the continuous critique and defense of foreign policy actions that account for so much of diplomatic interchange and international political commentary.

All this argues that states, like other subjects of legal rules, operate under a sense of obligation to conform their conduct to governing norms.

Varieties of noncomplying behavior

If the state's decision whether or not to comply with a treaty is the result of a calculation of costs and benefits, as the realists assert, the implication is that noncompliance is the premeditated and deliberate violation of a treaty obligation. Our background assumption does not exclude that such decisions may occur from time to time, especially when the circumstances underlying the original bargain have changed significantly.[40] Or, as in the area of international human rights, it may happen that a state will enter into an international agreement to appease a domestic or international constituency but have little

---

38. See, for example, the testimony of General David C. Jones, chairman of the Joint Chiefs of Staff, before the U.S. Senate Committee on Foreign Relations on the Strategic Arms Limitation Talks (SALT) II treaty, Congressional Information Service, S381-24 79, 9 July 1979.

39. It is not clear, however, that democracies are more law-abiding. See *Diggs v. Shultz,* 470 F. 2d 461 (D.C. Cir. 1972): "Under our constitutional scheme, Congress can denounce treaties if it sees fit to do so, and there is nothing the other branches of the government can do about it. We consider that is precisely what Congress has done in this case" (pp. 466–67).

40. International law recognizes a limited scope for abrogation of an agreement in such a case. See the Vienna Convention on the Law of Treaties, Article 62. Generally, however, the possibility of change is accommodated by provisions for amendment, authoritative interpretation, or even withdrawal from the agreement. See, for example, the withdrawal provision of the ABM Treaty, Article 25(2), or the Limited Test Ban Treaty, Article 4. None of these actions poses an issue of violation of legal obligations, though they may weaken the regime of which the treaty is a part.

intention of carrying it out. A passing familiarity with foreign affairs, however, suggests that only infrequently does a treaty violation fall into the category of a willful flouting of legal obligation.[41]

At the same time, general observation as well as detailed studies often reveal what appear or are alleged to be significant departures from established treaty norms. If these are not deliberate violations, what explains this behavior? We discuss three circumstances, infrequently recognized in discussions of compliance, that in our view often lie at the root of behavior that may seem prima facie to violate treaty requirements: (1) ambiguity and indeterminacy of treaty language, (2) limitations on the capacity of parties to carry out their undertakings, and (3) the temporal dimension of the social and economic changes contemplated by regulatory treaties.

These factors might be considered "causes" of noncompliance. But from a lawyer's perspective, it is illuminating to think of them as "defenses"—matters put forth to excuse or justify or extenuate a prima facie case of breach. A defense, like all other issues of compliance, is subject to the overriding obligation of good faith in the performance of treaty obligations.[42] If the plea is accepted, the conduct is not a violation, strictly speaking. Of course, in the international sphere, these charges and defenses are rarely made or determined in a judicial tribunal. However, diplomatic practice in other forums can be understood in terms of the same basic structure, reflecting, perhaps, the pervasiveness of the underlying legal framework.

Ambiguity

Treaties, like other canonical statements of legal rules, frequently do not provide determinate answers to specific disputed questions.[43] Language often is unable to capture meaning with precision. Treaty drafters do not foresee many of the possible applications—let alone their contextual settings. Issues that are foreseen often cannot be resolved at the time of treaty negotiation and are swept under the rug with a formula that can mean what each party wants it

---

41. Keohane surveyed two hundred years of U.S. foreign relations history and identified only forty "theoretically interesting" cases of "inconvenient" commitments in which there was a serious issue of whether or not to comply. See the chapter entitled "Commitments and Compromise," in Robert O. Keohane, "The Impact of Commitments on American Foreign Policy," manuscript, 1993, pp. 1–49.

42. See Vienna Convention on the Law of Treaties, Article 26; Lassa Oppenheim, *International Law: A Treatise,* 8th ed., ed. H. Lauterpacht (London: Longmans, 1955), p. 956; and McNair, *The Law of Treaties,* p. 465.

43. See Abram Chayes and Antonia Handler Chayes, "Living Under a Treaty Regime: Compliance, Interpretation, and Adaptation," in Antonia Handler Chayes and Paul Doty, eds., *Defending Deterrence: Managing the ABM Treaty Regime into the 21st Century* (Washington, D.C.: Pergamon-Brassey's International Defense Publishers, 1989), chap. 11. See also Young, *Compliance and Public Authority,* pp. 106–8, which discusses issues of interpretation in the context of deliberate attempts at "evasion" of obligation. We argue that alternative interpretations are frequently invoked in good faith. No doubt in practice there is often some of both.

to mean. Economic, technological, scientific, and even political circumstances change. All these inescapable incidents of the effort to formulate rules to govern future conduct frequently produce a zone of ambiguity within which it is difficult to say with precision what is permitted and what is forbidden.

Of course, treaty language, like other legal language, comes in varying degrees of specificity.[44] The broader and more general the language, the wider the ambit of permissible interpretations to which it gives rise. Yet there are frequently reasons for choosing a more general formulation of the obligation: the political consensus may not support more precision, or, as with certain provisions of the U.S. Constitution, it may be wiser to define a general direction, to try to inform a process, rather than seek to foresee in detail the circumstances in which the words will be brought to bear. If there is some confidence in those who are to apply the rules, a broader standard defining the general policy behind the law may be more effective in realizing it than a series of detailed regulations. The North Atlantic Treaty has proved remarkably durable, though its language is remarkably general: "In order more effectively to achieve the objectives of this Treaty, the Parties, separately and jointly, by means of continuous and effective self-help and mutual aid, will maintain and develop their individual and collective capacity to resist armed attack."[45]

In the arms control field, the United States has opted for increasingly detailed agreements on the ground that they reduce interpretative leeways. The 1963 Limited Test Ban Treaty (LTBT), the first bilateral arms control agreement between the United States and the Soviet Union, consisted of five articles covering two or three pages. The Strategic Arms Reduction Treaty (START) signed in 1989 is the size of a telephone book.

Detail also has its difficulties. It is vulnerable to the maxim *expressio unius est exclusio alterius* (to express one thing is to exclude the other). As in the U.S. Internal Revenue Code, precision generates loopholes, necessitating some procedure for continuous revision and authoritative interpretation. The corpus of the law may become so complex and unwieldy as to be understandable (and manipulable) by only a small coterie of experts. The complexities of the rule system may give rise to shortcuts that reduce inefficiencies when things are going well but may lead to friction when the political atmosphere darkens.

In short, more often than not there will be a considerable range within which parties may reasonably adopt differing positions as to the meaning of the obligation. In domestic legal systems, courts or other authoritative institutions are empowered to resolve such disputes about meaning as between parties in a

---

44. See Duncan Kennedy, "Form and Substance in Private Law Adjudication," *Harvard Law Review* 89 (June 1976), pp. 1685–788; Ronald Dworkin, "The Model of Rules," *University of Chicago Law Review* 35 (Autumn 1967), pp. 14–16; Louis Kaplow, *Rules Versus Standards: An Economic Analysis,* Discussion Paper no. 108, Program in Law and Economics, Harvard Law School, April 1992.

45. North Atlantic Treaty, Article 3, 63 stat. 2241 (signed 4 April 1949 and entered into force 24 August 1949), in *UNTS,* vol. 34, no. 541, 1949, p. 243.

particular case. The international legal system can provide tribunals to settle such questions if the parties consent. But compulsory means of authoritative dispute resolution—by adjudication or otherwise—are not generally available at the international level.[46] Moreover, the issue of interpretation may not arise in the context of an adversarial two-party dispute. In such cases, it remains open to a state, in the absence of bad faith, to maintain its position and try to convince the others.

In many such disputes, a consensus may exist or emerge among knowledgeable professionals about the legal rights and wrongs.[47] In many others, however, the issue will remain contestable. Although one party may charge another with violation and deploy legions of international lawyers in its support, a detached observer often cannot readily conclude that there is indeed a case of noncompliance, at least in the absence of "bad faith." The numerous alleged violations of arms control treaties with which the Soviet Union was annually charged were, with the exception of the radar at Krasnoyarsk in Siberia, contestable in that sense.[48] In fact, it can be argued that if there is no authoritative arbiter (and even sometimes when there is), discourse among the parties, often in the hearing of a wider public audience, is an important way of clarifying the meaning of the rules.

In the face of treaty norms that are indeterminate over a considerable range, even conscientious legal advice may not avoid issues of compliance. At the extreme, a state may consciously seek to discover the limits of its obligation by testing its treaty partners' responses. There was speculation that the pattern of Soviet deployment of Pechora-type radars prior to the construction of the phased array radar at Krasnoyarsk was an attempt to test the limits of the radar deployment provision of the ABM treaty. The Pechora sites were located as far as four hundred kilometers from the border, arguably "on the periphery of the national territory," as required by the treaty—but also arguably not.[49] The failure of the United States to react was thought by some to have contributed to the decision to site Krasnoyarsk even further from the nearest border—some seven hundred kilometers.

---

46. Abram Chayes and Antonia Handler Chayes, "Compliance Without Enforcement: State Behavior Under Regulatory Treaties," *Negotiation Journal* 7 (July 1991), pp. 311–31. See also Louis B. Sohn, "Peaceful Settlement of Disputes in Ocean Conflicts: Does UN Clause 3 Point the Way?" *Law and Contemporary Problems* 46 (Spring 1983), pp. 195–200. Our work-in-progress examines signs of a recent trend toward more formal dispute resolution procedures in such areas as trade, the law of the sea, and others. The current emphasis in the United States on alternative dispute resolution suggests that international judicial settlement may not be an entirely unmixed blessing, however.

47. Oscar Schachter, "The Invisible College of International Lawyers," *Northwestern University Law Review,* vol. 72, no. 2, 1977, pp. 217–26.

48. Gloria Duffy, *Compliance and the Future of Arms Control: Report of a Project Sponsored by the Center for International Security and Arms Control* (Cambridge, Mass: Ballinger, 1988), pp. 31–60.

49. See Antonia Handler Chayes and Abram Chayes, "From Law Enforcement to Dispute Settlement: A New Approach to Arms Control Verification and Compliance," *International Security* 14 (Spring 1990), pp. 147–64; and Duffy, *Compliance and the Future of Arms Control,* p. 107.

Justice Oliver Wendell Holmes said, "The very meaning of a line in the law is that you intentionally may come as close to it as you can if you do not pass it."[50] Nevertheless, deliberate testing of the kind described above might in ordinary circumstances be thought to be inconsistent with good faith observation of the treaty obligation. On the other hand, in the early years of the Interim Agreement on Limitation of Strategic Arms (SALT I) the United States played a similar game by erecting opaque environmental shelters over missile silos during modification work, despite the treaty undertaking "not to use deliberate concealment measures which impede verification by national technical means."[51] In the context of the long cold war confrontation between the United States and the Soviet Union, a certain amount of such probing seems to have been within the expectations of the parties.[52]

Perhaps a more usual way of operating in the zone of ambiguity is to design the activity to comply with the letter of the obligation, leaving others to argue about the spirit. The General Agreement on Tarrifs and Trade (GATT) prohibits a party from imposing quotas on imports. When Japanese exports of steel to the United States generated pressures from U.S. domestic producers that the Nixon administration could no longer contain, U.S. trade lawyers invented the "voluntary restraint agreement," under which private Japanese producers agreed to limit their U.S. sales.[53] The United States imposed no official quota, although the Japanese producers might well have anticipated some such action had they not "volunteered." Did the arrangement violate GATT obligations?

Questions of compliance with treaty obligations ordinarily arise as an adjunct to activity designed to achieve an objective that the actor regards as important.[54] Lawyers may be consulted or may intervene. Decisions about how the desired program is to be carried out emerge from a complex interaction of legal and policy analysis that generates its own subrules and precedents. The process is reminiscent of that in a classic U.S. bureaucracy or corporation.

50. *Superior Oil Co. v. Mississippi,* 280 U.S. 390 (1920), p. 395.

51. Interim Agreement of Limitation of Strategic Arms (SALT I), Article 5(3). See also *Compliance with SALT I Agreements,* Special Report no. 55, Bureau of Public Affairs, U.S. Department of State, July 1979, p. 4. The issue was finally resolved by Article 15(3) of the SALT II treaty, prohibiting the use over intercontinental ballistic missile silo launchers of shelters that impede verification by national technical means.

52. Unilateral assertion is a traditional way of vindicating claimed "rights" in international law. In the spring of 1986, U.S. forces engaged in two such exercises, one off the Soviet Black Sea coast in the "exercise of the right of innocent passage" (*The New York Times,* 19 March 1986, p. A1) and the other in the airspace over the Gulf of Sidra, which Libya considers its territorial waters and the United States does not. The Black Sea maneuver was concluded with nothing more than some bumping between U.S. and Soviet ships, but in the Gulf of Sidra, U.S. aircraft sank two Libyan patrol vessels that had fired antiaircraft missiles. See *Chicago Tribune,* 19 March 1986, sec. 1, p. 10; *Los Angeles Times,* 26 March 1986, p. I1; and *Los Angeles Times,* 27 March 1986, p. I1.

53. *Consumers Union v. Kissinger,* 506 F2d 136 (D.C. Cir. 1974).

54. Chayes and Chayes, "Living Under a Treaty Regime," pp. 197 and 200.

For example, the Reagan administration was bent on developing a space-based ABM system. Congress insisted that research and testing should conform to the "traditional" interpretation of the ABM treaty, which prohibited the testing of ABM "components," rather than the administration's "broad interpretation," which would have permitted full development and testing of a space-based ABM system. To ensure that it remained within the treaty constraint, the administration established a special legal unit in the Defense Department, nominally independent of the Strategic Defense Initiative (SDI) organization, to review each proposed test against an intricate set of internal rules. The unit satisfied itself that the items as tested would not be capable of performing as ABM "components," usually because of power limitations or other design characteristics known to the testers but not necessarily observable by outsiders. These rules were conscientiously applied to the testing program, and on that basis the administration maintained that it had stayed within the bounds of the traditional interpretation of the treaty.[55] No Soviet lawyer had seen or approved the rules, however (indeed, they were classified), and it is not likely that the United States would have accepted Soviet tests as compliant if the limiting design elements were not externally observable.

Even in the stark, high politics of the Cuban Missile Crisis, State Department lawyers argued that the United States could not lawfully react unilaterally, since the Soviet emplacement of missiles in Cuba did not amount to an "armed attack" sufficient to trigger the right of self-defense in Article 51 of the UN Charter. Use of force in response to the missiles would only be lawful if approved by the Organization of American States (OAS). Though it would be foolish to contend that the legal position determined President John Kennedy's decision, there is little doubt that the asserted need for advance OAS authorization for any use of force contributed to the mosaic of argumentation that led to the decision to respond initially by means of the quarantine rather than an air strike. Robert Kennedy said later, "It was the vote of the Organization of American States that gave a legal basis for the quarantine . . . and changed our position from that of an outlaw acting in violation of international law into a country acting in accordance with twenty allies legally protecting their position."[56] This was the advice he had heard from his lawyers, and it was a thoroughly defensible position. Nevertheless, many international lawyers in the United States and elsewhere disagreed because they thought the action was inconsistent with the UN Charter.[57]

---

55. For example, the so-called Foster box rules serve to distinguish between strategic missile reentry vehicles, which are prohibited by the ABM treaty, and tactical missile reentry vehicles, which are not, on the basis of performance characteristics such as velocity and reentry angle not mentioned anywhere in the ABM treaty. See Ashton B. Carter, "Limitations and Allowances for Space Based Weapons," in Chayes and Doty, *Defending Deterrence,* pp. 132–37.

56. Robert Kennedy, *Thirteen Days* (New York: W. M. Norton, 1971), p. 99.

57. See, for example, Quincy Wright, "The Cuban Quarantine," *American Journal of International Law* 57 (July 1963), pp. 546–65; James S. Campbell, "The Cuban Crisis and the UN Charter: An Analysis of the United States Position" *Stanford Law Review* 16 (December 1963), pp. 160–76;

Capability

According to classical international law, legal rights and obligations run between states. A treaty is an agreement among states[58] and is an undertaking by them as to their future conduct. The object of the agreement is to affect state behavior. This simple relationship between agreement and relevant behavior continues to exist for many treaties. The LTBT is such a treaty. It prohibits nuclear testing in the atmosphere, in outer space, or underwater. Only states conduct nuclear weapons tests, so only state behavior is implicated in the undertaking. The state, by governing its own actions, without more, determines whether it will comply with the undertaking or not. Moreover, there is no doubt about the state's capacity to do what it has undertaken. Every state, no matter how primitive its structure or limited its resources, can refrain from conducting atmospheric nuclear tests.

Even when only state behavior is at stake, the issue of capacity may arise when the treaty involves an affirmative obligation. In the 1980s it may have been a fair assumption that the Soviet Union had the capability to carry out its undertaking to destroy certain nuclear weapons as required by the START agreement. In the 1990s, that assumption was threatened by the emergence of a congeries of successor states in place of the Soviet Union, many of which may not have the necessary technical knowledge or material resources to do the job.[59]

The problem is pervasive in contemporary regulatory treaties. Much of the work of the International Labor Organization (ILO) from the beginning has been devoted to improving its members' domestic labor legislation and enforcement. The current spate of environmental agreements poses the difficulty in acute form. Such treaties formally are among states, and the obligations are cast as state obligations—for example, to reduce sulfur dioxide (SO_2) emissions by 30 percent against a certain baseline. Here, however, the real object of the treaty is not to affect state behavior but to regulate the behavior of nonstate actors carrying out activities that produce SO_2—generating power, driving automobiles, and the like. The ultimate impact on the relevant private behavior depends on a complex series of intermediate steps. It will normally require an implementing decree or legislation followed by detailed administrative regulations. In essence, the state will have to establish and enforce a full-blown domestic regime designed to secure the necessary reduction in emissions.

---

and William L. Standard, "The United States Quarantine of Cuba and the Rule of Law," *American Bar Association Journal* 49 (August 1963), pp. 744–48.

58. Vienna Convention on the Law of Treaties, Article 2(1)(a).

59. Kurt M. Campbell, Ashton B. Carter, Steven E. Miller, and Charles A. Zraket, *Soviet Nuclear Fission: Control of the Nuclear Arsenal in a Disintegrating Soviet Union,* CSIA Studies in International Security, no. 1, Harvard University, Cambridge, Mass., November 1991, pp. 24, 25, and 108.

The state may be "in compliance" when it has taken the formal legislative and administrative steps, and, despite the vagaries of legislative and domestic politics, it is perhaps appropriate to hold it accountable for failure to do so. Quite apart from political will, however, the construction of an effective domestic regulatory apparatus is not a simple or mechanical task. It entails choices and requires scientific and technical judgment, bureaucratic capability, and fiscal resources. Even developed Western states have not been able to construct such systems with confidence that they will achieve the desired objective.[60]

The deficit in domestic regulatory capacity is not limited to environmental agreements. The nonproliferation treaty (NPT) is supported by a side-agreement among nuclear-capable states not to export sensitive technology to nonweapons states.[61] The agreement is implemented by national export control regulations. The UN–International Atomic Energy Agency (IAEA) inspections in Iraq, however, revealed that the Iraqi nuclear weapons program was able to draw on suppliers in the United States and West Germany, among others, where governmental will and ability to control such exports are presumably at their highest.

Although there are surely differences among developing countries, the characteristic situation is a severe dearth of the requisite scientific, technical, bureaucratic, and financial wherewithal to build effective domestic enforcement systems. Four years after the Montreal Protocol was signed, only about half the member states had complied fully with the requirement of the treaty that they report annual chlorofluorocarbon (CFC) consumption.[62] The Conference of the Parties promptly established an Ad Hoc Group of Experts on Reporting, which recognized that the great majority of the nonreporting states were developing countries that for the most part were simply unable to comply without technical assistance from the treaty organization.[63]

The Montreal Protocol is the first treaty under which the parties undertake to provide significant financial assistance to defray the incremental costs of compliance for developing countries. The same issue figured on a much larger

60. Kenneth Hanf, "Domesticating International Commitments: Linking National and International Decision-making," prepared for a meeting entitled Managing Foreign Policy Issues Under Conditions of Change, Helsinki, July 1992.

61. Treaty on the Non-proliferation of Nuclear Weapons, 21 U.S.T. 483 (1970) (signed 1 July 1968 and entered into force 5 March 1970), in *International Legal Materials,* vol. 7, 1968, p. 809.

62. See Report of the Secretariat on the Reporting of Data by the Parties in Accordance with Article 7 of the Montreal Protocol, UNEP/OzL.Pro.3/5, 23 May 1991, pp. 6–12 and 22–24; and Addendum, UNEP/OzL.Pro3/5/Add.1, 19 June 1991.

63. For the establishment of the Ad Hoc Group of Experts, see Report of the Second Meeting of the Parties to the Montreal Protocol on Substances that Deplete the Ozone Layer, UNEP/OzL.Pro.2/3, Decision 2/9, 29 June 1990, p. 15. At its first meeting in December 1990, the Ad Hoc Group of Experts concluded that countries "lack knowledge and technical expertise necessary to provide or collect" the relevant data and made a detailed series of recommendations for addressing the problem. See Report of the First Meeting of the Ad Hoc Group of Experts on the Reporting of Data, UNEP/OzL.Pro/WG.2/1/4, 7 December 1990.

scale in the negotiations for a global climate change convention and in the UN Conference on Environment and Development, held in Brazil in June 1992. The last word has surely not been spoken in these forums, and the problem is not confined to environmental agreements.

The temporal dimension

The regulatory treaties that are our major concern are, characteristically, legal instruments of a regime for managing a major international problem area over time.[64] Significant changes in social or economic systems mandated by regulatory treaties take time to accomplish. Thus, a cross section at any particular moment in time may give a misleading picture of the state of compliance. Wise treaty drafters recognize at the negotiating stage that there will be a considerable time lag after the treaty is concluded before some or all of the parties can bring themselves into compliance. Thus modern treaties, from the IMF Agreement in 1945 to the Montreal Protocol in 1987, have provided for transitional arrangements and made allowances for special circumstances.[65] Nevertheless, whether or not the treaty provides for it, a period of transition will be necessary.

Similarly, if the regime is to persist over time, adaptation to changing conditions and underlying circumstances will require a shifting mix of regulatory instruments to which state and individual behavior cannot instantaneously respond. Often the original treaty is only the first in a series of agreements addressed to the issue-area. Even the START agreement to reduce nuclear arsenals contemplates a process extending over seven years, by which time it is expected that new and further reductions will have been mandated.[66]

Activists in all fields lament that the treaty process tends to settle on a least-common-denominator basis. But the drive for universality (or universal membership in the particular region of concern) may necessitate accommodation to the response capability of states with large deficits in financial, technical, or bureaucratic resources. A common solution is to start with a low obligational ante and increase the level of regulation as experience with the regime grows.

---

64. The now-classical definition of an international regime appears in Krasner, "Structural Causes and Regime Consequences," p. 2: "Regimes are sets of implicit or explicit principles, norms, rules, and decision-making procedures around which actors' expectations converge in a given area of international relations." Regime theorists find it hard to say the "L-word" but "principles, norms, rules, and decision-making procedures" are what international law is all about, and it is apparent from their work that formal legal norms, most often embodied in treaties, are an important structural element in most of the phenomena of interest to them.

65. See Articles of Agreement of the International Monetary Fund, Article 14, in *UNTS*, vol. 2, 1945, p. 1501; and Montreal Protocol, Article 5.

66. Under START, the agreed reductions in strategic nuclear weapons are to take place over a seven-year period divided into three phases of three, two, and two years. See U.S. Congress, Senate, *Treaty Between the United States and the Union of Soviet Socialist Republics on the Reduction and Limitation of Strategic Offensive Arms,* 102d Cong., 1st sess., 1991, S. Treaty Doc. 102-20, Article 2.

The convention-protocol strategy adopted in a number of contemporary environmental regimes exemplifies this conception.

The Vienna Convention on the Protection of the Ozone Layer, signed in 1985, contained no substantive obligations but required only that the parties "in accordance with the means at their disposal and their capabilities" cooperate in research and information exchange and in harmonizing domestic policies on activities likely to have an adverse effect on the ozone layer.[67] Two years later, as scientific consensus jelled on the destructive effect of CFCs on the ozone layer, the Montreal Protocol was negotiated, providing for a 50 percent reduction from 1986 levels of CFC consumption by the year 2000.[68] By June 1990, the parties agreed to a complete phaseout by the above date and to regulate a number of other ozone-destroying chemical compounds.[69]

A similar sequence marks the Convention on Long-Range Transboundary Air Pollution (LRTAP).[70] It began with a general agreement to cooperate signed in 1979, was followed by a protocol imposing limits on SO_2 emissions in 1985,[71] and then by another imposing limits on nitrogen oxides, which was signed at Sofia in October 1988.[72] The pattern has a long pedigree, extending back to the ILO, the first of the modern international regulatory agencies, whose members agreed in 1921 only to "bring the recommendation[s] or draft

67. Vienna Convention for the Protection of the Ozone Layer (signed 22 March 1985 and entered into force 22 September 1988; hereafter cited as Vienna Ozone Convention), Article 2(2), in *International Legal Materials,* vol. 26, 1986, p. 1529.

68. Montreal Protocol, Article 2(4).

69. London Amendments, Annex 1, Articles 2A(5) and 2B(3).

70. Convention on Long-Range Transboundary Air Pollution (signed 13 November 1979 and entered into force 16 March 1983), in *International Legal Materials,* vol. 18, 1979, p. 1442.

71. Protocol to the 1979 Convention on Long-Range Transboundary Air Pollution on the Reduction of Sulphur Emissions or Their Transboundary Fluxes by at Least 30 Percent (signed 8 July 1985), UN Doc. ECE/EB.AIR/12, reproduced in *International Legal Materials,* vol. 27, May 1988, pp. 698–714; see especially p. 707.

72. Protocol to the 1979 Convention on Long-Range Transboundary Air Pollution Concerning the Control of Emissions of Nitrogen Oxides or Their Transboundary Fluxes (signed 31 October 1988 and entered into force 14 February 1991), UNEP/GC.16/Inf.4, p. 169. Additional protocols to the original convention are the Protocol to the 1979 Convention on Long-Range Transboundary Air Pollution on Long-Term Financing of the Co-operative Program for Monitoring and Evaluation of the Long-Range Transmission of Air Pollutants in Europe (signed 28 September 1984), UN Doc. EB.AIR/AC.1/4, reproduced in *International Legal Materials,* vol. 27, March 1988, pp. 698–714 (see especially p. 701); and the Protocol Concerning the Control of Emissions of Volatile Organic Compounds or Their Transboundary Fluxes (signed November 1991), reproduced in *International Legal Materials,* vol. 31, May 1992, pp. 568–611. See also the Barcelona Convention for the Protection of the Mediterranean Sea Against Pollution, in *International Legal Materials,* vol. 15, 1976, p. 290, which was accompanied by the Protocol for the Prevention of Pollution of the Mediterranean Sea by Dumping from Ships and Aircraft, UNEP/GC.16.Inf.4, p. 130, and the Protocol Concerning Co-operation in Combating Pollution of the Mediterranean Sea by Oil and Other Harmful Substances in Cases of Emergency, UNEP/GC.16/Inf.4, p. 132. The Protocol for the Protection of the Mediterranean Sea Against Pollution for Land-based Sources, UNEP/GC.16/Inf.4, p. 134, followed in 1980; the land-based sources protocol contemplates that pollution will be eliminated in accordance with "standards and timetables" to be agreed to by the parties in the future (see Article 5[2]). The Protocol Concerning Mediterranean Specially Protected Areas (UNEP/GC.16/Inf.4, p. 136) was signed at Geneva in 1982.

convention[s] [prepared by the organization] before the authority or authorities within whose competence the matter lies, for the enactment of legislation or other action."[73] The ILO then became the forum for drafting and propagating a series of specific conventions and recommendations on the rights of labor and conditions of employment for adoption by the parties.

The effort to protect human rights by international agreement may be seen as an extreme case of time lag between undertaking and performance. Although the major human rights conventions have been widely ratified, compliance leaves much to be desired. It is apparent that some states adhered without any serious intention of abiding by them. But it is also true that even parties committed to the treaties had different expectations about compliance than with most other regulatory treaties. Indeed, the Helsinki Final Act, containing important human rights provisions applicable to Eastern Europe, is by its terms not legally binding.[74]

Even so, it is a mistake to call these treaties merely "aspirational" or "hortatory." To be sure, they embody "ideals" of the international system, but like other regulatory treaties, they were designed to initiate a process that over time, perhaps a long time, would bring behavior into greater congruence with those ideals. These expectations have not been wholly disappointed. The vast amount of public and private effort devoted to enforcing these agreements— not always in vain—evinces their obligational content. Moreover, the legitimating authority of these instruments was an important catalyst of the revolutions of the 1980s against authoritarian regimes in Latin America and Eastern Europe and continues to spark demands for democratic politics elsewhere in the world.

Acceptable levels of compliance

The foregoing section identified and advanced a range of matters that might be put forward by the individual actor in defense or excuse of a particular instance of deviant conduct. From the perspective of the system as a whole, however, the central issue is different. For a simple prohibitory norm like a highway speed limit, it is in principle a simple matter to determine whether any particular driver is in compliance. Yet most communities and law enforcement organizations in the United States seem to be perfectly comfortable with a situation in which the average speed on interstate highways is perhaps ten miles above the limit. Even in individual cases, the enforcing officer is not likely to pursue a driver operating within that zone. The fundamental problem for the

73. Constitution of the International Labor Organization, 11 April 1919, Article 405, 49 stat. 2722.
74. Conference on Security and Cooperation in Europe, Final Act (1 August 1975), Article 10, in *International Legal Materials,* vol. 14, 1975, p. 1292.

system is not how to induce all drivers to obey the speed limit but how to contain deviance within acceptable levels.[75] So, too, it is for international treaty obligations.

"An acceptable level of compliance" is not an invariant standard. The matter is further complicated because many legal norms are not like the speed limit that permits an on–off judgment as to whether an actor is in compliance. As noted above, questions of compliance are often contestable and call for complex, subtle, and frequently subjective evaluation. What is an acceptable level of compliance will shift according to the type of treaty, the context, the exact behavior involved, and over time.

It would seem, for example, that the acceptable level of compliance would vary with the significance and cost of the reliance that parties place on the others' performance.[76] On this basis, treaties implicating national security would demand strict compliance because the stakes are so high, and to some extent that prediction is borne out by experience. Yet even in this area, some departures seem to be tolerable.

In the case of the NPT, indications of deviant behavior by parties have been dealt with severely. In the 1970s, U.S. pressures resulted in the termination of programs to construct reprocessing facilities in South Korea and Taiwan.[77] Recently, a menu of even more stringent pressures was mounted against North Korea, which ultimately signed an IAEA safeguard agreement and submitted to inspection.[78] The inspection and destruction requirements placed on Iraq under UN Security Council resolution 687 are, in one sense, an extreme case of this severity toward deviation by NPT parties.

Although over 130 states are parties to the NPT, the treaty is not universal, and some nonparties have acquired or are seeking nuclear weapons capability.[79] Despite these important holdouts, compliance with the NPT by the parties remains high. In fact, in recent years prominent nonparties—including Argentina, Brazil, and South Africa—have either adhered to the treaty or announced that they will comply with its norms.[80] Even the recalcitrant nonparties have not

75. Young, *Compliance and Public Authority,* p. 109.

76. Charles Lipson, "Why Are Some International Agreements Informal," *International Organization* 45 (Autumn 1991), pp. 495–538.

77. See Joseph A. Yager, "The Republic of Korea," and "Taiwan," in Joseph A. Yager, ed., *Nonproliferation and U.S. Foreign Policy* (Washington, D.C.: Brookings Institution, 1980), pp. 44–65 and 66–81, respectively.

78. See David Sanger, "North Korea Assembly Backs Atom Pact," *The New York Times,* 10 April 1992, p. A3; and David Sanger, "North Korea Reveals Nuclear Sites to Atomic Agency, *The New York Times,* 7 May 1992, p. A4. The initial U.S. response included behind-the-scenes diplomatic pressure and encouraging supportive statements by concerned states at IAEA meetings. See L. Spector, *Nuclear Ambitions: The Spread of Nuclear Weapons, 1989–1990* (Boulder, Colo.: Westview Press, 1990), pp. 127–30. Japan apparently has refused to consider economic assistance or investment in North Korea until the nuclear issue is cleared up.

79. Countries that have not ratified the NPT include Argentina, Brazil, China, France, India, Israel, and Pakistan. See Spector, *Nuclear Ambitions,* p. 430.

80. Reuters News Service, "Argentina and Brazil Sign Nuclear Accord," *The New York Times,* 14 December 1991, p. 7; "Brazil and Argentina: IAEA Safeguard Accord," U.S. Department of State

openly tested or acknowledged the possession of nuclear weapons. Thus, despite some significant departure from its norms, the NPT and the nonproliferation regime built around it have survived.

The U.S. emphasis on the importance of verification of arms control agreements seems to portend the application of a strict compliance standard.[81] However, at least since the Reagan administration, presidential reports to Congress, mandated by the Arms Control and Disarmament Act, listed a long series of alleged Soviet violations without igniting any serious move to withdraw from the applicable treaties.[82]

One of these violations, the phased array radar constructed at Krasnoyarsk, was widely regarded as a deliberate and egregious breach of the ABM treaty. Article 6 requires that early-warning radars be sited "along the periphery of [the] national territory and oriented outward." Krasnoyarsk was seven hundred kilometers from the Mongolian border and pointed northeast over Siberia. The issue was repeatedly thrashed out between the two governments over a period of years, sometimes at the highest levels. The United States linked its resolution to progress on future arms control agreements. The Soviets maintained that the installation was a space-tracking radar system and thus not subject to the prohibition, but ultimately they acknowledged the breach and agreed to eliminate the offending installation. Nevertheless, throughout this entire period the ABM treaty regime continued in full force and effect, and the U.S. administration never seriously pursued the option of withdrawal or abrogation.[83] Even in connection with its cherished SDI, the Reagan administration preferred to attempt to "reinterpret" the treaty rather than accept the more serious domestic political costs of abrogation.

Dispatch, 23 December 1991, p. 907; Reuters News Service, "South Africa Signs a Treaty Allowing Nuclear Inspection," *The New York Times,* 9 July 1991, p. A11; and "Fact Sheet: Nuclear Non-proliferation Treaty," U.S. Department of State Dispatch, 8 July 1991, p. 491.

81. The 1977 Congress enacted a requirement for "adequate verification" of arms control agreements. This was described by Carter administration officials as a "practical standard" under which the United States would be able to identify significant attempted evasions in time to respond effectively. See Chayes and Chayes, "From Law Enforcement to Dispute Settlement," pp. 147–48. It should be noted that when the Soviet Union in 1987 finally agreed to substantially unlimited on-site inspection, the United States drew back from its earlier insistence on that requirement, as it has in chemical warfare negotiations.

82. Withdrawal from all U.S.–Soviet arms control agreements is permitted on short notice if "extraordinary events related to the subject matter of the treaty jeopardize the supreme interests" of the withdrawing party. See, for example, Treaty Between the United States and the Soviet Union on the Limitation of Antiballistic Missile Systems, 26 May 1972, Article 15(2), 23 U.S.T. 3435 (1972). The law of treaties also permits the suspension of a treaty in whole or in part if the other party has committed a material breach. See the Vienna Convention on the Law of Treaties, Article 60(1),(2).

83. The closest approach to such an initiative was the mildly comic bureaucratic squabble in the closing years of the Reagan administration about whether the Krasnoyarsk radar should be denominated a material breach of the ABM treaty. See Paul Lewis, "Soviets Warn U.S. Against Abandoning ABM Pact," *The New York Times,* 2 September 1988, p. A9; and Michael R. Gordon, "Minor Violations of Arms Pact Seen," *The New York Times,* 3 December 1988, p. 5.

In the last analysis, the long list of asserted "violations" presented no threat either to the U.S. security interests that the treaties were designed to safeguard or to the basic bargain that neither side would deploy ABM systems. American political and military leaders were more than willing to tolerate nonperformance at the margin as the price of continuing constraint on a meaningful Soviet attempt to shift the strategic balance.

If national security regimes have not collapsed in the face of significant perceived violation, it should be no surprise that economic and environmental treaties can tolerate a good deal of noncompliance. Such regimes are in fact relatively forgiving of violations plausibly justified by extenuating circumstances in the foreign or domestic life of the offending state, provided the action does not threaten the survival of the regime. As noted above, a considerable amount of deviance from strict treaty norms may be anticipated from the beginning and accepted, whether in the form of transitional periods, special exemptions, limited substantive obligations, or informal expectations of the parties.

The generally disappointing performance of states in fulfilling reporting requirements is consistent with this analysis.[84] It is widely accepted that failure to file reports reflects a low domestic priority or deficient bureaucratic capacity in the reporting state. Since the reporting is not central to the treaty bargain, the lapse can be viewed as "technical." When, as in the Montreal Protocol, accurate reporting was essential to the functioning of the regime, the parties and the secretariat made strenuous efforts to overcome the deficiency, and with some success.[85]

The Convention on International Trade in Endangered Species (CITES) ordinarily displays some tolerance for noncompliance, but the alarming and widely publicized decline in the elephant population in East African habitats in the 1980s galvanized the treaty regime. The parties took a decision to list the elephant in Appendix A of the treaty (shifting it from Appendix B, where it had previously been listed), with the effect of banning all commercial trade in ivory. The treaty permits any party to enter a reservation to such an action, in which case the reserving party is not bound by it. Nevertheless, through a variety of pressures, the United States together with a group of European countries insisted on universal adherence to the ban, bringing such major traders as Japan and Hong Kong to heel.[86] The head of the Japanese Environment

84. U.S. General Accounting Office, *International Environment: International Agreements Are Not Well-Monitored,* GAO, RCED-92-43, January 1992.

85. See Report of the Secretariat on the Reporting of Data by the Parties in Accordance with Article 7 of the Montreal Protocol, UNEP/OzL.Pro.3/5, 23 May 1991, pp. 6–12 and 22–24; and Addendum, UNEP/OzL.Pro.3/5/Add.1, 19 June 1991.

86. For a report of Japan's announcement of its intention not to enter a reservation on the last day of the conference, see United Press International, "Tokyo Agrees to Join Ivory Import Ban," *Boston Globe,* 21 October 1989, p. 6. Japan stated that it was "respecting the overwhelming sentiment of the international community." As to Hong Kong, see Jane Perlez, "Ivory Ban Said to Force Factories Shut," *The New York Times,* 22 May 1990, p. A14. The Hong Kong reservation was

Agency supported the Japanese move in order "to avoid isolation in the international community."[87] It was freely suggested that Japan's offer to host the next meeting of the conference of parties, which was accepted on the last day of the conference after Japan announced its changed position, would have been rejected had it reserved on the ivory ban.

The meaning of the background assumption of general compliance is that most states will continue to comply, even in the face of considerable deviant behavior by other parties. In other words, the free-rider problem has been overestimated. The treaty will not necessarily unravel in the face of defections. As Mancur Olson recognized, if the benefits of the collective good to one or a group of parties outweigh the costs to them of providing the good, they will continue to bear the costs regardless of the defections of others.[88]

It seems plausible that treaty regimes are subject to a kind of critical-mass phenomenon, so that once defection reaches a certain level, or in the face of particularly egregious violation by a major player, the regime might collapse.[89] Thus, either the particular character of a violation or the identity of the violator may pose a threat to the regime and evoke a higher demand for compliance. This analysis would account for both the similarities and differences between the Krasnoyarsk and CITES cases. In the first case, although core security values were at stake and the violation was egregious, it did not threaten the basic treaty bargain. The United States responded with a significant enforcement effort but did not itself destroy the basic bargain by abrogating the treaty. In the second case, involving relatively peripheral national interests from the realist perspective, a reservation permitted under the treaty threatened the collapse of the regime. A concerted and energetic defense resulted.

Determining the acceptable compliance level

If, as we argue above, the "acceptable level of compliance" is subject to broad variance across regimes, times, and occasions, how is what is "acceptable" to be determined in any particular instance? The economists have a straightforward answer: invest additional resources in enforcement (or other measures to

---

not renewed after the initial six-month period. Five African producer states with effective management programs did enter reservations but agreed not to engage in trade until at least the next conference of the parties. See Michael J. Glennon, "Has International Law Failed the Elephant," *American Journal of International Law* 84 (January 1990), pp. 1–43, especially p. 17. At the 1992 meeting they ended their opposition. See "Five African Nations Abandon Effort to Resume Elephant Trade in CITES Talks," *Bureau of National Affairs Environment Daily,* electronic news service, 12 March 1992.

87. United Press International, "Tokyo Agrees to Join Ivory Import Ban," *Boston Globe,* 21 October 1989.

88. Mancur Olson, *The Logic of Collective Action* (Cambridge, Mass.: Harvard University Press, 1971), pp. 33–36.

89. For a discussion of critical-mass behavior models, see Thomas Schelling, *Micromotives and Macrobehavior* (New York: Norton, 1978), pp. 91–110.

induce compliance) up to the point at which the value of the incremental benefit from an additional unit of compliance exactly equals the cost of the last unit of additional enforcement resources.[90] Unfortunately, the usefulness of this approach is limited by the impossibility of quantifying or even approximating, let alone monetizing, any of the relevant factors in the equation—and markets are not normally available to help.

In such circumstances, as Charles Lindblom has told us, the process by which preferences are aggregated is necessarily a political one.[91] It follows that the choice whether to intensify (or slacken) the international enforcement effort is necessarily a political decision. It implicates all the same interests pro and con that were involved in the initial formulation of the treaty norm, as modified by intervening changes of circumstances. Although the balance will to some degree reflect the expectations of compliance that the parties entertained at that time, it is by no means rare, in international as in domestic politics, to find that what the lawmaker has given in the form of substantive regulation is taken away in the implementation. What is "acceptable" in terms of compliance will reflect the perspectives and interests of participants in the ongoing political process rather than some external scientific or market-validated standard.

If the treaty establishes a formal organization, that body may serve as a focus for mobilizing the political impetus for a higher level of compliance. A strong secretariat can sometimes exert compliance pressure, as in the IMF or ILO. The organization may serve as a forum for continuing negotiation among the parties about the level of compliance. An example of these possibilities is the effort of the International Maritime Consultative Organization (IMCO)—and after 1982 its successor, the International Maritime Organization (IMO)—to control pollution of the sea by tanker discharges of oil mixed with ballast water.[92] IMCO's regulatory approach was to impose performance standards limiting the amount of oil that could be discharged on any voyage. From 1954, when the first oil pollution treaty was signed, until the 1978 revisions, there was continuous dissatisfaction with the level of compliance. IMCO responded by imposing increasingly strict limits, but these produced only modest results because of the difficulty of monitoring and verifying the amount of oil discharged by tanker captains at sea. Finally, in 1978 IMO adopted a new regulatory strategy and imposed an equipment standard requiring all new

90. See Gary Becker, "Crime and Punishment: An Economic Approach," *Journal of Political Economy* 76 (March/April 1968), pp. 169–217; and Stigler, *"The Optimum Enforcement of Laws,"* p. 526. Also see Young, *Compliance and Public Authority,* pp. 7–8 and 111–27.

91. Charles E. Lindblom, *Politics and Markets* (New York: Basic Books, 1977), pp. 254–55. At the domestic level, the decision whether to intensify enforcement of the treaty implicates a similar political process, as the continuous debates in the United States over GATT enforcement testify. Our work-in-progress includes a consideration of second-level enforcement.

92. Ronald Mitchell, "Intentional Oil Pollution of the Oceans: Crises, Public Pressure, and Equipment Standards," in Peter M. Haas, Robert O. Keohane, and Mark A. Levy, eds., *Institutions for the Earth: Sources of Effective International Environmental Protection* (Cambridge, Mass.: MIT Press, forthcoming).

tankers to have separate ballast tanks that physically prevent the intermixture of oil with the discharged ballast water. The new requirement was costly to tanker operators but easily monitored by shipping authorities. Compliance with the equipment standard has been close to 100 percent, and discharge of oil from the new ships is substantially nil. The sequence reflects the changing configuration of political strength between domestic environmental and shipping constituencies in the members of IMO (and IMCO) which was originally referred to as a "shipping industry club." At the same time, the major oil companies, which in the earlier period were shipping industry allies, shifted political allegiance under environmentalist pressures.

Since the international system is horizontal rather than hierarchical, if one state or a group of states is willing to commit enforcement resources, it may be able to short-circuit cumbersome organizational procedures and pursue improved levels of compliance by its own decision. The U.S. deployment of trade sanctions under Section 301 of the Tariff Act against violators of GATT obligations reflects a unilateral political decision (1) that existing levels of compliance were not acceptable and (2) to pay the costs of additional enforcement.[93] In that case, however, gains in compliance with substantive obligations must be weighed against losses attendant on departure from the procedural norms mandating multilateral dispute settlement.[94]

Again, after a considerable period of fruitless exhortation in the International Whaling Commission, Japan finally agreed to participate in a temporary moratorium on whaling that had been proclaimed by the organization when the United States threatened trade sanctions under the Marine Mammal Protection Act.[95] The Japanese ban on ivory imports shows a mixture of economic and reputational threats. The United States hinted at trade sanctions, and the conference of the parties of CITES threatened not to schedule its next meeting in Kyoto if Japan remained out of compliance.

If there are no objective standards by which to recognize an "acceptable level of compliance," it may be possible at least to identify some general types of situations that might actuate the deployment of political power in the interest of greater compliance. First, states committed to the treaty regime may sense that a tipping point is close, so that enhanced compliance would be necessary for regime preservation. As noted above, the actions against Japan on the ivory

93. *United States Code,* Title 19, Section 2411. Section 301, however, has been widely criticized as itself a violation of GATT. See A. O. Sykes, "Constructive Unilateral Threats in International Commercial Relations: The Limited Case for Section 301," *Law and Policy in International Business* 23 (Spring 1992), pp. 263–330; and Thomas O. Bayard and Kimberly A. Elliott, "Aggressive Unilateralism and Section 301: Market Opening or Market Closing," *The World Economy* 15 (November 1992), pp. 685–706.

94. GATT, Articles 22 and 23, 30 October 1947, as amended. See "GATT Basic Instruments and Selected Documents," in *UNTS,* vol. 55, no. 814, 1950, p. 194.

95. See Steinar Andresen, "Science and Politics in the International Management of Whales," *Marine Policy,* vol. 13, no. 2, 1989, p. 99; and Patricia Birnie, *International Regulation of Whaling* (New York: Oceana, 1985).

import ban may have been of this character. After the high visibility given to the CITES moves to ban the ivory trade, there would not have been much left of the regime if Japan had been permitted to import with impunity.

Second, states committed to a level of compliance higher than that acceptable to the generality of the parties may seek to ratchet up the standard. The Netherlands often seems to play the role of "leader" in European environmental affairs both in the North Sea and Baltic Sea regimes and in LRTAP.[96] Similarly, the United States may be a "leader" for improving compliance with the NPT, where its position is far stronger than that of its allies.

Finally, campaigning to improve a compliance level that states concerned would just as soon leave alone is a characteristic activity for NGOs, especially in the fields of the environment and of human rights. NGOs increasingly have direct access to the political process both within the treaty organizations and in the societies of which they are a part. Their technical, organizational, and lobbying skills are an independent resource for enhanced compliance at both levels of the two-level game.

Conclusion

The foregoing discussion reflects a view of noncompliance as a deviant rather than an expected behavior, and as endemic rather than deliberate. This in turn leads to de-emphasis of formal enforcement measures and even, to a degree, of coercive informal sanctions, except in egregious cases. It shifts attention to sources of noncompliance that can be managed by routine international political processes. Thus, the improvement of dispute resolution procedures goes to the problem of ambiguity; technical and financial assistance may help cure the capacity deficit; and transparency will make it likelier that, over time, national policy decisions are brought increasingly into line with agreed international standards.

These approaches merge in the process of jawboning—an effort to persuade the miscreant to change its ways—that is the characteristic form of international enforcement activity. This process exploits the practical necessity for the putative offender to give reasons and justifications for suspect conduct. These reasons and justifications are reviewed and critiqued in a variety of venues, public and private, formal and informal. The tendency is to winnow out reasonably justifiable or unintended failures to fulfill commitments—those that comport with a good-faith compliance standard—and to identify and isolate the few cases of egregious and willful violation. By systematically addressing and eliminating all mitigating circumstances that might possibly be advanced,

---

96. See Peter M. Haas, "Protecting the Baltic and North Seas," in Haas, Keohane, and Levy, *Institutions for the Earth.*

this process can ultimately demonstrate that what may at first have seemed like ambiguous conduct is a black-and-white case of deliberate violation. The offending state is left with a stark choice between conforming to the rule as defined and applied in the particular circumstances or openly flouting its obligation. This turns out to be a very uncomfortable position for even a powerful state. The Krasnoyarsk story represents an example of this process in action. Perhaps another is the repeated Iraqi retreat in showdowns with the UN–IAEA inspection teams.[97]

Enforcement through these interacting measures of assistance and persuasion is less costly and intrusive and is certainly less dramatic than coercive sanctions, the easy and usual policy elixir for noncompliance. It has the further virtue that it is adapted to the needs and capacities of the contemporary international system.

---

97. For an account of the Iraqi response, see Sean Cote, *A Narrative of the Implementation of Section C of UN Security Council Resolution 687.*

Is the Good News About Compliance Good News About Cooperation?

George W. Downs, David M. Rocke, and Peter N. Barsoom

In the past few years many social scientists interested in cooperation have turned their attention to the problem of compliance in international regulatory regimes. Much of the empirical research in this area has been conducted by a group composed mainly of qualitative political scientists and scholars interested in international law.[1] Its message is that (1) compliance is generally quite good; (2) this high level of compliance has been achieved with little attention to enforcement; (3) those compliance problems that do exist are best addressed as management rather than enforcement problems; and (4) the management rather than the enforcement approach holds the key to the evolution of future regulatory cooperation in the international system. As Oran Young notes, "A new understanding of the bases of compliance—one that treats compliance as a management problem rather than an enforcement problem and that has profound practical as well as theoretical implications—is making itself felt among students of international relations."[2] In short, not only are the dreary expectations born of factors such as relative gains concerns, collective action problems, anarchy, and fears of self-interested exploitation incorrect but also the enforcement limitations that always have appeared to sharply bound the contributions of international law and many international institutions now appear to have been exaggerated.

In this essay we will argue that the empirical findings of this group, which we refer to as the "managerial" school, are interesting and important but that its

An earlier version of this article was presented at the annual meeting of the International Studies Association, Chicago, February 1994. The authors thank Abram Chayes, Robert Keohane, Marc Levy, Ron Mitchell, Ken Oye, Michael Ross, the editor of *International Organization,* and the anonymous referees for their helpful comments. The authors also acknowledge the support of the John D. and Catherine T. MacArthur Foundation to the Center of International Studies, Princeton University.

1. For example, see Arora and Cason 1995; Chayes and Chayes 1990; 1991; 1993a; 1993b; Duffy 1988; Haas, Keohane, and Levy 1993; Hawkins 1984; Mitchell 1993; 1994a; 1994b; 1995; Scholz 1984; Sparrow 1994; Young 1989; and 1994.
2. Young's quotation is taken from the dust jacket of Mitchell 1994a.

International Organization 50, 3, Summer 1996, pp. 379–406
© 1996 by The IO Foundation and the Massachusetts Institute of Technology

policy inferences are dangerously contaminated by selection problems. If we restrict our attention to those regulatory treaties that prescribe reductions in a collectively dysfunctional behavior (e.g., tariffs, arms increases), evidence suggests that the high level of compliance and the marginality of enforcement result from the fact that most treaties require states to make only modest departures from what they would have done in the absence of an agreement. This creates a situation where states often are presented with negligible benefits for even unpunished defections; hence the amount of enforcement needed to maintain cooperation is modest. Nothing is wrong with this situation in itself, but it is unlikely to provide the model for the future that the managerialists claim. Even if we assume that the absolute value of the benefits generated by this small amount of regulation is relatively large, further progress in international regulatory cooperation will almost certainly require the creation of agreements that present far greater incentives to defect than those currently in place (e.g., more demanding environmental standards, fewer nontariff barriers, steeper arms reductions). We have precious little evidence that such progress can be obtained in the absence of better enforcement.

After discussing the problems posed by endogeneity and selection, we present the theoretical argument for linking enforcement level to what we call "depth of cooperation" and examine the extent to which deep cooperation has been achieved without enforcement. We then present a number of prominent exceptions to the managerial school's unqualified generalizations about the causes and cures of noncompliance. Finally, we discuss the strategic implications of the evolution of increasingly cooperative regimes.

The managerial thesis

The bedrock of the managerial school is the finding that state compliance with international agreements is generally quite good and that enforcement has played little or no role in achieving and maintaining that record. In Abram Chayes and Antonia Chayes's words, what ensures compliance is not the threat of punishment but "a plastic process of interaction among the parties concerned in which the effort is to reestablish, in the microcontext of the particular dispute, the balance of advantage that brought the agreement into existence."[3] For the members of the managerial school, "noncompliance is not necessarily, perhaps not even usually, the result of deliberate defiance of the legal standard."[4] On those rare occasions when compliance problems do occur they should not be viewed as violations or self-interested attempts at exploitation, but as isolated administrative breakdowns. The causes of noncompliance are to be found in (1) the ambiguity and indeterminacy of treaties, (2) the

3. Chayes and Chayes 1991, 303.
4. Ibid., 301.

capacity limitations of states, and (3) uncontrollable social or economic changes.[5]

Not surprisingly, the managerial school takes a dim view of formal and even informal enforcement measures. Punishment not only is inappropriate given the absence of any exploitative intent but it is too costly, too political, and too coercive. As Ronald Mitchell notes, "Retaliatory non-compliance often proves unlikely because the costs of any individual violation may not warrant a response and it cannot be specifically targeted, imposing costs on those that have consistently complied without hurting the targeted violator enough to change its behavior."[6] As a result, according to Young, "arrangements featuring enforcement as a means of eliciting compliance are not of much use in international society."[7] Since sanctions usually are more successful against economically vulnerable and politically weak countries and "unilateral sanctions can be imposed only by the major powers, their legitimacy as a device for treaty enforcement is deeply suspect," as Chayes and Chayes point out.[8] Moreover, retaliation for violating a treaty may risk the breakdown of current and future cooperation:

> the actor considering *retaliation* must also think of the possible future costs. It may be dangerous to prejudice the possibility of support from the violator at some point in time in the future when it may be needed. . . . [T]he risk of setting off "a long echo of alternating retaliations" will often dwarf the consequences of overlooking what are arguably relatively minor or "technical" violations.[9]

Instances of apparent noncompliance are problems to be solved, rather than violations that have to be punished. According to Chayes and Chayes, "As in other managerial situations, the dominant atmosphere is that of actors engaged in a cooperative venture, in which performance that seems for some reason unsatisfactory represents a problem to be solved by mutual consultation and analysis, rather than an offense to be punished. Persuasion and argument are the principal motors of this process."[10] The strategies necessary to induce compliance and maintain cooperation involve: (1) improving dispute resolution procedures, (2) technical and financial assistance, and (3) increasing transparency. The last is especially important: "For a party deliberately contemplating violation, the high probability of discovery reduces the expected benefits rather than increasing the costs and would thus deter violation regardless of the prospect of sanctions."[11]

---

5. Chayes and Chayes 1993b, 188.
6. Mitchell 1993, 330.
7. Young 1994, 74 and 134.
8. Chayes and Chayes 1993a, 29.
9. Ibid. The authors quote Robert Axelrod, *The Evolution of Cooperation* (New York: Basic Books, 1984), emphasis original.
10. Chayes and Chayes 1991, 303.
11. Chayes and Chayes 1993a, 18.

The endogeneity and selection problems

It is not difficult to appreciate why the findings of the managerial school suggest that both international institutions and even international law have a far brighter future than most international relations specialists have believed for the past fifty years. Apart from sharply contradicting the pessimistic expectations of many realists and neorealists about the inability of cooperation and self-regulation to flourish in an anarchic world, they also run counter to the claims of cooperation researchers in the rational-choice tradition. Such researchers emphasize the centrality of enforcement concerns in regulatory environments and characterize them as mixed-motive games, where the danger of self-interested exploitation is significant, as opposed to coordination games, where it is not.[12] Such findings certainly add credibility to the frequent speculation that the rational-choice tradition's affection for the repeated prisoners' dilemma has led it to overemphasize enforcement and underemphasize the potential for voluntary compliance and noncoercive dispute resolution.

In trying to understand the prescriptive significance of the managerialists' compliance findings, it is useful to consider the following hypothetical story. An article has recently appeared in an education journal criticizing the state of musical education in an age of funding cutbacks. The author, a longtime music teacher, argues that such cutbacks inevitably have dire consequences for the quality of school music programs. A member of the school board who has aggressively supported the elimination of frivolous expenditures is skeptical of what she believes to be characteristically self-interested reasoning. In an effort to get to the bottom of the issue, she attends fifteen concerts in her district and fifteen concerts in a rival district that has not reduced its support of music education or extracurricular activities. She finds that the quality of the two orchestras as measured by the number of mistakes they made to be pretty much the same and quite low in both cases. Noting that the orchestras in her district have achieved this high level of performance despite a 75 percent reduction in the number of rehearsals, she is delighted. Not only has she demonstrated that the cutbacks have had no effect on school orchestras but she believes that she has confirmed her long-held suspicion that rehearsals do not make school orchestras better, they simply line the pockets of music teachers eager to buy hot tubs and Steinway pianos.

These conclusions may, however, be invalid. It is likely that orchestras in her district may have adapted to the decrease in resources by playing less demanding pieces. No orchestra is eager to embarrass itself, and one of the most effective ways to avoid doing so is to play Haydn rather than Mahler or Stravinsky. Unless the school board member counting mistakes figures out a way to control for the difficulty of repertoire, we do not really know what her

---

12. See, for example, Abreu 1988; Abreu, Pearce, and Stacchetti 1986; 1989; Bayard and Elliott 1994; Downs and Rocke 1995; Hungerford 1991; Martin 1992; Staiger 1995; and Sykes 1990.

findings tell us about the impact of the budget cuts. A treaty, like the selection of an orchestra's repertoire, is also an endogenous strategy. States choose the treaties they make from an infinitely large set of possible treaties. If some treaties are more likely to be complied with than others or require more enforcement than others, this will almost certainly affect the choices states make. Just as orchestras will usually avoid music that they cannot play fairly well, states will rarely spend a great deal of time and effort negotiating agreements that will continually be violated. This inevitably places limitations on the inferences we can make from compliance data alone. As in the case of the orchestra's mistakes, we do not know what a high compliance rate really implies. Does it mean that even in the absence of enforcement states will comply with any agreement from the set of all possible agreements, or does it mean that states only make agreements that do not require much enforcement? If the latter is the case, what are the implications for the future of regulatory cooperation?

To even begin to overcome the problems that endogeneity poses for understanding the role of enforcement in regulatory compliance, we need to control for the basis of state selection; that is, those characteristics of international agreements that play the same role for states as musical difficulty does for the school orchestras. One likely candidate is what we have termed the depth of cooperation. International political economists define the depth of an agreement by the extent to which it requires behind-the-border integration with regard to social and environmental standards as well as with regard to the reduction of barriers to trade. Here, however, the depth of an agreement refers to the extent to which it captures the collective benefits that are available through perfect cooperation in one particular policy area. Given the difficulties involved in identifying the cooperative potential of an ideal treaty, it is most useful to think of a treaty's depth of cooperation as the extent to which it requires states to depart from what they would have done in its absence. If we are examining the critical subset of regulatory treaties that require states to reduce some collectively dysfunctional behavior like tariffs or pollution, a treaty's theoretical depth of cooperation would refer to the reduction it required relative to a counterfactual estimate of the tariff or pollution level that would exist in the absence of a treaty. Of course, the depth of cooperation that a treaty actually achieved might be quite different than this figure. Here we measure depth of cooperation by the treaty level because that is the figure which serves as the basis for judging the level of compliance. In the absence of a trustworthy theoretical estimate of this counterfactual, it could be based on the status quo at the time an agreement was signed or on a prediction derived from the year-to-year change rate prior to that time.

Either estimate of depth of cooperation is obviously quite crude. There are doubtless policy areas in which, for any number of reasons, the potential for cooperation is much smaller than others. In such cases our depth measure will make cooperation in these areas appear shallower than it really is. Yet if one is willing to concede, as both managerialists and more conventional institutional-ists argue, that there are substantial cooperative benefits that are as yet unrealized in the areas of arms control, trade, and environmental regulation, this depth of cooperation measure provides a rough idea of what states have accomplished. We can in turn use it to interpret compliance data and help assess the role of enforcement. While this measure of depth is hardly perfect, there is no reason to expect that it is biased in such a way as to distort the relationship between the depth of cooperation represented by a given treaty, the nature of the game that underlies it, and the amount of enforcement needed to maintain it.

Depth of cooperation is important to track because just as the role of enforcement differs in mixed-motive and coordination games, it also varies within mixed-motive games according to depth. To appreciate the connection, consider the following model. States A and B are playing a repeated bilateral trade game in which each state in each period chooses a level of protection $P \in [0, \infty)$ that influences the level of trade. The utility of state A is denoted as $U_A(P^A, P^B)$, and the utility of state B is denoted as $U_B(P^A, P^B)$. We do not specify the functional form of these utilities but instead adopt a series of plausible assumptions detailed in Appendix A.[13]

We will adopt the convention of representing the trade game as a prisoners' dilemma. While some have argued that this pattern of incentives emerges from a variety of plausible circumstances, we assume it has emerged from electoral and financial incentives provided by interest groups working to protect domestic products from foreign competition.[14] If we consider only two particular levels of tariffs $P^A < P_0^A$ and $P^B < P_0^B$, then the four outcomes represented by each side choosing P or P_0 form a payoff matrix of the prisoners' dilemma type. In this case, each side prefers higher tariffs regardless of the choice of the other side, but both sides prefer mutual cooperation to mutual defection. Unlike the repeated prisoners' dilemma, the choices defined by the present model are continuous rather than discrete. Treaties can be set at any level below the noncooperative tariff rates. Cheating can be limited or flagrant. And punishments can range from a barely perceptible increase in tariffs that lasts for one period to a multiple of current tariffs that lasts indefinitely.

Under the assumptions of our model, if tariff levels are high, both states have an opportunity to benefit by devising an agreement to lower them. Neverthe-less, there is an incentive to exploit the other party's trust; that is, A's optimal one-period response to side B's cooperative tariff level will always be to raise tariffs. Self-interest will prevent such cheating only if the consequences of cheating are greater than the benefits. To achieve a situation where this

13. These assumptions also contain conditions on the response functions $R_A(P_B)$ and $R_B(P_A)$, which denote the optimal single-period response of one state to a particular level of protection (e.g., tariff) chosen by the other state.

14. For the former argument, see Staiger 1995, 27. For the latter, see Grossman and Helpman 1994.

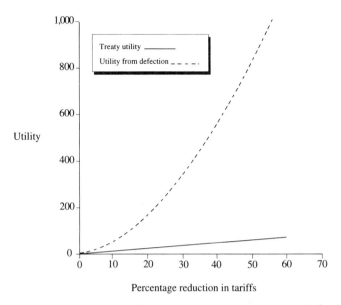

FIGURE 1. *One-period utility of treaty compliance versus defection*

disincentive exists, states must resort to a punishment for defection. In this case, one punishment strategy prescribes that state A begin by observing the treaty, but if B violates it, even modestly, state A should respond by abrogating the agreement (or otherwise reducing its level of compliance) for some specified period of time. During cooperative periods each side's tariff is supposed to be limited to $\bar{P}^A < P_0^A$ and $\bar{P}^B < P_0^B$, while in the punishment periods both sides raise tariffs to some noncooperative level. The most extreme punishment strategy, often called the "grim strategy," occurs when the response to any violation is permanent reversion to the noncooperative Nash equilibrium. A punishment strategy is sufficient to enforce a treaty when each side knows that if it cheats it will suffer enough from the punishment that the net benefit will not be positive.

To make this more concrete, consider an example where the noncooperative tariff is at a level of 100 percent for each side, and plausible treaties would provide for symmetric reductions in tariffs for each side.[15] Figure 1 compares the one-period utility of both sides observing the treaty with the temptation to defect. The temptation to cheat in this model rises rapidly with the cooperativeness of the treaty, while the treaty benefits rise less rapidly. This is what imposes a limit on which treaties can be supported. Figure 2 shows the punishment periods necessary to support treaties of various sizes. A shorter

---

15. Of course, in the multiperiod model, the feasibility of maintaining this treaty depends on the discount factor, δ, as well as on the previous parameters. In this case, we use a discount factor of $\delta = .95$, corresponding to an interest rate of 5 percent.

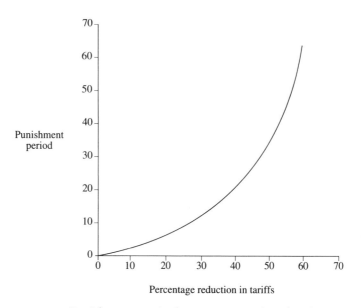

FIGURE 2. *Punishment required to support treaties of various sizes*

period would make the treaty vulnerable to cheating because it would be insufficient to remove all of the gains from violating the treaty. For example, a treaty that specifies a 5 percent reduction in tariffs only requires a punishment of two periods; the best treaty that can be supported with the maximal punishment of infinite duration is 37.19 percent. The increase in the ratio of the benefit of cheating to the benefit of cooperating means that increasingly severe punishments are necessary to deter defection—here severity means length of punishment—as the benefits of the treaty and corresponding restrictiveness of its requirements increase. Although the rate of increase in utility with the increase in punishment length decreases, the utility obtainable by very long punishments is still many times that of the utility obtainable with punishment lengths of one or two periods. The essential point the graph demonstrates is the deeper the agreement is, the greater the punishments required to support it.

The only relevant criterion is that the punishment must hurt the transgressor state at least as much as that state could gain by the violation. This does not imply that, say, a certain amount of trade restriction should be punished by an equal trade restriction (tit-for-tat); nor does it mean that the transgressor be punished at least as much as the transgressor's violation hurt the other party. Although both of these standards possess aspects of fairness, neither is relevant to supporting the treaty equilibrium. Fairness and justice must take a back seat to the correct disincentive.

The specific mechanism by which states punish violations is less relevant to the relationship between depth of cooperation and enforcement than is the magnitude of enforcement. Although we motivate the model by using a case of centralized enforcement for convenience, nothing in the analysis precludes effective decentralized enforcement schemes. Enforcement can occur through linkages, as in the case of the Soviet Union and United States during the Kissinger years; through formal institutions such as the General Agreement on Tariffs and Trade (GATT) Dispute Settlement Procedure; through unilateral actions, as in the U.S. enforcement of fishery and wildlife agreements under the Pelly and Packwood–Magnuson amendments; or by domestic law as in the European Union and environmental treaties. Given the weakness of current international institutions and the relative difficulty in mobilizing formal sanctions, we suspect—like the majority of managerialists—that the most effective enforcement schemes may well be decentralized and not involve perfectly coordinated action by every signatory of a multilateral agreement.[16] This, however, does not negate the connection between depth of cooperation and the magnitude of the punishment necessary to maintain compliance in mixed-motive games.

Discussion

This logical connection between the depth of cooperation represented by a given treaty and the amount of enforcement that is needed in mixed-motive games suggests that evaluating the importance of enforcement by examining how high compliance is when it is low or absent might be misleading. We need to worry about the possibility that both the high rate of compliance and relative absence of enforcement threats are due not so much to the irrelevance of enforcement as to the fact that states are avoiding deep cooperation—and the benefits it holds whenever a prisoners' dilemma situation exists—because they are unwilling or unable to pay the costs of enforcement. If this were true, prescribing that states ignore enforcement in favor of other compliance strategies would be equivalent to telling the school orchestras to avoid wasting their time rehearsing. Just as the latter would condemn the orchestras to a repertoire of simple compositions, the prescriptions of the managerial school would condemn states to making agreements that represent solutions to coordination games and shallow prisoners' dilemmas.

Of course, knowing that statistics about the role of enforcement might be misleading is hardly equivalent to establishing its importance as a compliance strategy. If members of the managerial school are correct in believing in their (usually implicit) assumption that mixed-motive games and prisoners' dilemmas play a much smaller role in critical regulatory arenas than game theorists assume, the argument fizzles. Unfortunately, settling this controversy is no easy matter. Utility functions are notoriously difficult to access directly and any attempt to cope with selection by estimating the character of the set of

---

16. On the role of decentralized enforcement schemes, see Ostrom 1990; and Kandori 1992.

regulatory agreements that are potentially possible would be hopelessly circular.

Given the circumstances, it seems advisable to sidestep any attempt to inventory the nature of the underlying game and to evaluate some of the implications of the rival theories. We examine two. First, we will assess the depth of cooperation and the level of enforcement connected with prominent regulatory agreements that involve the reduction of behaviors that states have concluded are collectively counterproductive but that contain few enforcement provisions. Ideally, one would like to examine the correlation between enforcement and depth of cooperation, but as we noted above, we agree with the managerial school's observation that such strongly enforced regulatory agreements are relatively rare. If the managerial school is correct, the absence of strong enforcement provisions or the informal threat of enforcement should have no bearing on the depth of cooperation. There should be numerous examples of states agreeing to alter dramatically the trajectory that they were following at the time a treaty was signed while paying little attention to enforcement. If the game theorists are correct that most important regulatory agreements are mixed-motive games of some variety, any tendency of states to avoid committing themselves to punishing noncompliance is likely to be associated with either a world in which there are relatively few deeply cooperative agreements or in which violations run rampant. Since we agree that while regulatory violations exist they are not frequent, we expect the former to be true.

Second, we will examine the managerial school's claim that self-interest rarely plays a conspicuous role in the treaty violations that do take place and that violations are driven instead solely by a combination of the ambiguity of treaties, the capacity limitations of states, and uncontrollable social and economic changes. We are skeptical of this assertion because the set of violations should be less distorted by selection than the set of treaties. This is true because we expect that, ceteris paribus, the rate of violation connected with mixed-motive game treaties should in the absence of perfect information and appropriate enforcement be much higher than the rate of violation connected with coordination game treaties. Hence, even if there are fewer such treaties they would be overrepresented relative to coordination game based-treaties in any sample of violations.

The rarity of deep cooperation

Are we correct in our suspicion that inferences about the importance of enforcement are likely to be contaminated by selection? That is, does evidence show that there is little need for enforcement because there is little deep cooperation? Let us begin by considering the set of arms agreements that the United States has made since 1945 (see appendix B). We note at the outset that, however valuable, a number of the treaties such as the "Hot Line" agreement and the United States–Union of Soviet Socialist Republics Ballistic Missile Launch Notification Agreements do not directly regulate an arms output such as the number and/or location of a weapons system. Of those that do, a significant subset such as the Outer Space Treaty, the Seabed Arms Control Treaty, and the Antarctic Treaty involve agreements to maintain the status quo trajectory rather than to alter it significantly. At the time the treaties were signed, neither the Soviet Union nor the United States had cost-effective plans for major weapons systems in these areas or possessed a strategic mission for which such a system was believed necessary. The fact that this situation has basically continued is the reason Chayes and Chayes can report that "there has been no reported deviation from the requirements of these treaties over a period of four decades."[17] That there was more enforcement in this case than officially is embodied in these agreements might also play a role. Both the Soviet Union and the United States likely knew that if one broke an agreement in a dramatic fashion, the other probably would retaliate in kind. Even though these expectations were established tacitly, they are no less real than expectations described formally in the treaty.[18] While we are not denying that obtaining tangible reassurance of a rival's intentions through a treaty is valuable, it is difficult to argue that these treaties exhibit the deep cooperation that would have taken place if the superpowers had each agreed to terminate major modernization programs or dramatically reduce their defense budgets. Much the same argument can be made in connection with the Anti-Ballistic Missiles (ABM) Treaty. While the treaty may have provided a significant benchmark that helped prevent both states from exploiting the technological gains that were made during the period since the treaty was signed, neither side had the technology or the budget to deploy a major system when the treaty was signed in 1972. In 1967 when President Johnson and Premier Kosygin first began to move toward discussion, Soviet ABM efforts were limited to a spare system around Moscow and the United States announced that it would begin deployment of a "thin" system to guard against Chinese attack and possible accidental launches.[19] As the technology of these antiballistic systems gradually has advanced and attention has shifted away from defense against a terrorist state, the depth of the original agreement in terms of today's "counterfactual" (i.e., the ABM system that the United States would construct today in the absence of an agreement) probably has increased. Given a constant or decreasing level of enforcement because of the weakness of the former Soviet Union and increasing depth, the game theorist would expect the agreement to come under increasing pressure in the form of violations on the part of the most powerful state. This appears to have occurred.

17. Chayes and Chayes 1993a, chap. 7, p. 9.
18. Downs and Rocke 1990.
19. Arms Control and Disarmament Agency 1990, 150.

Neither the initial Strategic Arms Limitation Talks (SALT) Interim Agreement nor SALT II was characterized by much depth. The interim agreement froze the number of intercontinental ballistic missile (ICBM) launchers at the status quo level (the United States had none under construction at the time and the Soviet Union was permitted to complete those it was building), but it allowed increases in the number of submarine-launched ballistic missiles (SLBMs) on both sides and failed significantly to restrict qualitative improvements in launchers, missiles, or a host of systems that allowed both sides to increase their nuclear capabilities.[20] SALT II required significant reductions in each side's number of operational launchers or bombers but permitted the number of ICBMs equipped with multiple independently targeted reentry vehicles (MIRVed ICBMs) to increase by forty percent between the time of signing and 1985. When this figure is added to the number of cruise missiles permitted each bomber, the total number of nuclear weapons was allowed to increase 50–70 percent. As Jozef Goldblat notes, "There is a remarkable compatibility between the Treaty limitations and the projected strategic nuclear weapons programs of both sides."[21]

Intermediate-range nuclear forces (INF), conventional forces in Europe (CFE), and the strategic arms reduction talks (START) agreements are deeper, of course. The first prescribes the elimination of intermediate- and shorter-range missiles in Europe; the second dramatically reduced conventional forces; and the third cuts the arsenals of strategic nuclear delivery vehicles that come under the agreement by about 30 percent and cuts warheads by 40 percent.[22] While one can argue in connection with START that the number of accountable weapons is smaller than the actual number of weapons, the cuts are significant in terms of either the status quo at the time of signing and each state's trajectory. Do these suggest that deep agreements that make no provisions for enforcement play an important role in arms control?

There is no easy answer. On the one hand, we are inclined to simply include these agreements in the set of deep regulatory agreements that seem to require little enforcement. We do not claim that such agreements do not exist—they clearly do—simply that many important prospective agreements require enforcement. Yet, it is not clear that these agreements are as deep as they appear to be. After all, the counterfactual—whether estimated on the basis of the status quo or the trajectory of year to year differences in arms production— represents the behavior of a political system that no longer exists. No one would gauge the depth of cooperation represented by the North Atlantic Treaty Organization (NATO) by comparing German behavior during wartime with German behavior after the war.

---

20. Ibid., 168.
21. Goldblat 1993, 35.
22. Arms Control and Disarmament Agency 1991.

Managerialists might respond to this analysis by arguing that there are good reasons for believing that the connection between enforcement and depth of cooperation in the areas of international trade and the environment is different from that connection in security. Not only are many of the actors obviously different but security historically has been dominated by the realist logic that managerialists find so inadequate. We are not unsympathetic to this argument. The dynamics of cooperation may indeed differ across policy areas, just as they may vary within the same policy area over time. Nonetheless, at least with respect to the relationship between enforcement and depth of cooperation, the areas are not as different as one might imagine or as some might hope.

Recent environmental agreements to control transboundary pollution, for instance, exhibit a similar lack of depth. Despite the apparently large cutbacks in chlorofluorocarbon (CFC) emissions, the Montreal Protocol provided few benefits to cooperation and little incentive to defect from the agreement. Scott Barrett has argued that "the Montreal Protocol may not have increased global net benefits substantially compared with the noncooperative outcome."[23] In their extensive empirical analysis, James Murdoch and Todd Sandler have similarly concluded that "the Montreal Protocol was enacted because it codified reductions in CFC emissions that polluters were voluntarily prepared to accomplish. . . . [T]he Montreal Protocol may be more symbolic than a true instance of a cooperative equilibrium."[24] In fact, most of the cutbacks in emissions preceded the ratification of the Montreal Protocol.

Perhaps the best test of the relationship between the depth of cooperation and enforcement can be found when we examine the history of a specific policy area in which regulations have become increasingly strict over time. The game theorist would predict that as regulatory rules tighten, the magnitude of the punishment needed to deter defection would also have to increase. Even if the system achieves some dynamic equilibrium, there should be some tangible sign of this under imperfect information.

If we discount the events that occurred in arms control after the downfall of the Soviet empire, the best examples of steadily increasing depth of coopera-tion are to be found in the areas of trade and European integration. In each case the role of enforcement has increased accordingly. Thomas Bayard and Kimberly Elliott, for example, conclude that the Uruguay Round has "substan-tially reduced many of the most egregious trade barriers around the world," but they also emphasize the enhanced ability of the World Trade Organization (WTO) to respond to and punish trade violations.[25] The WTO's procedures for dealing with violations are now more automatic and less manipulable by individual parties. Time limits on the establishment of panels have now been

---

23. Barrett 1994, 892.
24. Murdoch and Sandler 1994, 2.
25. The quotation is from Bayard and Elliott 1994, 336.

set to nine months with the conclusion of panels within eighteen months, eliminating the inexorable delays under GATT. The principle of consensus voting in the adoption of panel reports has been reversed; previously, both parties to a dispute had an automatic veto on panel recommendations and retaliation. The new system provides for automatic adoption of panel reports, including approval for retaliation, unless a unanimous consensus rejects it. Previously, sanctions were utilized only once in GATT's history. Now, retaliation will be authorized automatically in the absence of a withdrawal of the offending practice or compensation to the defendant. We believe that the negotiating history of the WTO demonstrates that the more demanding levels of cooperation achieved by the Uruguay Round would not have been possible without its having reduced the likelihood of self-interested exploitation by member states.

The deepening of European integration exhibits a similar pattern. Simultaneous with the increased cooperation embodied in the Maastricht Treaty, Anne-Marie Burley and Walter Mattli point out with regard to the European Court of Justice that "the member states chose to strengthen the Court's power to monitor and punish defections."[26] In the European case, enforcement took the form of penetration of European Community (EC) law into the domestic law of its members states.[27] It is difficult to believe that this increased enforcement represents nothing more than an attempt to pacify the few naive realists who remain influential in member states.

The causes and cures of noncompliance

The principal goal of the managerial school's investigation of compliance is to design more effective strategies for overcoming compliance problems in regulatory regimes. It is thus useful to shift our attention away from the likelihood of selection and the relationship between depth of cooperation and enforcement to why those compliance problems that do exist have occurred and how they might be remedied.

As noted above, selection bias should affect an examination of the reasons that compliance problems arise and their solutions less than it would an analysis of which type of cooperative agreements exist. We will briefly consider, first, the extent to which compliance problems appear to be caused by the ambiguity of treaties, the capacity limitations of states, and uncontrollable social and economic changes rather than the calculation of states bent on exploiting other states, as the managerial school alleges; and, second, extent to which compliance problems appear to be solved by improving dispute resolution procedures, technical and financial assistance, and transparency without any attention to increased enforcement.

---

26. Burley and Mattli 1993, 74.
27. Ibid., 43.

Scholars in the field of arms control agree that the Washington Naval Treaty of 1923 not only was the most pathbreaking and ambitious arms control agreement ever formulated but also experienced the most compliance problems. For example, the treaty permitted the conversion of battle cruisers into aircraft carriers up to a maximum of 33,000 tons, yet both the U.S.S. *Lexington* and *Saratoga* were closer to 36,000 tons. For their part as Robert Kaufman notes, the Japanese "broke the rules seriously, systematically, and often clandestinely."[28] Emily Goldman reports that its cruiser *Atago* exceeded its announced size by 20 percent, and its *Yamato* was 95 percent heavier than announced and carried eighteen-inch rather than sixteen-inch guns. Italy's *Gloriza* exceeded its announced size by 20 percent.[29] To what extent were these problems attributable to the ambiguity of the treaty, the capacity limitations of the states, or uncontrollable social and economic changes?

Ambiguity was certainly a problem, especially with regard to the extent to which the Japanese violated their commitment not to build fortifications on the Mandates. The treaty left terms like "naval base" and "fortification" undefined. However, ambiguity in some areas does not detract from the purposefulness and exploitative character of the violations in other areas, such as shipbuilding. Both Kaufman and Goldman provide overwhelming evidence that more than confusion over treaty parameters was behind the treaty violations on the part of all parties during the interwar years. It would be even more implausible to attribute the myriad violations to capacity limitations or the sort of uncontrollable social and economic changes that are usually covered by the *rebus sic stantibus* standard.

Since the pattern of violations that plagued the Washington Treaty never was brought under control, any analysis of how control might have been achieved is entirely speculative. It is difficult to imagine, however, that it could have occurred purely through dispute resolution; and technical and financial assistance to the violator is not relevant. Mechanisms to increase transparency certainly could have played a more active and important role. Kaufman argues that the United States failed to detect most of Japan's violations. He goes on to say that "Domestic politics inhibited effective response to those violations about which the American public officials had full knowledge or at least some suspicions."[30] Kaufman is not specific about the response he has in mind, but it appears likely that he is referring to the administration's lack of appetite for retaliation rather than the mere initiation of some dispute settlement procedure. This is hardly surprising. As Fred Ikle pointed out in his classic article, "After Detection—What?" the importance of transparency almost inevitably lies in the reaction that it provokes.[31] This reaction is, of course, the substance of enforcement.

28. Kaufman 1990.
29. Goldman 1994.
30. Kaufman 1990, 102.
31. Ikle 1961.

As the centerpiece of a sometimes problematic postwar trade regime, the GATT provides researchers with a wealth of material about the sources of noncompliance and the ability of its signatories to deal with them. Typical examples of GATT violations include EC payments and subsidies to oilseed producers, U.S. quantitative restrictions on sugar, Japanese import restrictions on beef and citrus, and Canadian export restrictions on unprocessed salmon and herring.[32] This is just a sample of the long list of commonly employed discriminatory techniques states have used to satisfy protectionist political elements in contravention of the GATT's rules and norms.

Ambiguity about what constitutes noncompliance is a source of some of these problems, but no one denies a considerable number of violations indeed has occurred. The framers of the GATT were careful not to limit its policing or dispute settlement procedures to actions that were prohibited explicitly. Instead, they based enforcement provisions on the nullification or impairment of benefits that countries might expect. Indeed, Article 23 permits that settlement procedures be initiated

> If any contracting party should consider that any benefit accruing to it directly or indirectly under this agreement is being nullified or impaired or that the attainment of any objective of the agreement is being impeded as the result of (a) the failure of another contracting party to carry out its obligations under this Agreement, or (b) the application by another contracting party of any measure, whether or not it conflicts with the provisions of this Agreement, or (c) the existence of any other situation.[33]

Although variation in expectations doubtless exists, few parties—including the states responsible—have argued that the EC subsidies of wheat flour or pasta or the Multifiber Agreement, which clearly violated the most-favored nation (MFN) principle, were based on confusion about the expectations of other trading partners.

Capacity limitations and uncontrollable social and economic changes rarely are cited as major determinants of violations. This is not so much because they are never present but because their effect is dwarfed by the most conspicuous cause of GATT noncompliance: the demands of domestic interest groups and the significant political benefits often associated with protection. Though GATT supporters would argue that any ill effects have been overshadowed by the GATT's positive achievement of reducing tariffs, the demand for protection is not being entirely ignored.

If the managerialists are wrong about the source of the GATT's problems, are they correct about the steps that appear to have reduced the rate of violations? The GATT provides a better laboratory for evaluating the managerialist claims about how compliance can best be improved than the Washington

---

32. See, respectively, Hudec 1993, 559 and 568; Bayard and Elliott 1994, 233; and Hudec 1993, 217–19.

33. The article is quoted in Bhagwati 1990, 105–6.

Treaty because unlike the latter, the GATT has evolved. Dispute resolution in the form of GATT panels undoubtedly has played some role, but certainly not an overwhelming one. Until recently, the panels moved at a ponderous pace and could easily be frustrated, especially by large states.[34] Far more successful have been the rounds of multilateral negotiations that have operated over time to ensure that certain categories of disputes would reappear less often and that have extended the boundaries of the regime.

Nevertheless, enforcement also has played an important, if controversial, role in the operation and evolution of the GATT. Between 1974 and 1994, the United States imposed or publicly threatened retaliation in 50 percent of the cases that it took to the GATT. It did so independent of any GATT action and indeed even in five cases that Bayard and Elliott believe would have fallen under GATT jurisdiction.[35] Observers such as Robert Hudec credit increased enforcement and such "justified disobedience" of the GATT's dispute resolution process with being an important element in the process of GATT legal reform.[36] Others, like Alan Sykes, credit Section 301 and Super 301 unilateralism with having inspired—ironically given the claims of the managerial school—the enhanced dispute settlement procedures of the WTO.[37] As Bayard and Elliott conclude in their recent study, the "USTR [U.S. Trade Representative] generally wielded the section 301 crowbar deftly and constructively, employing an aggressive unilateral strategy to induce support abroad for strengthening of the multilateral trade system."[38]

Even in the case of environmental regimes, the source of many of the managerialist examples, enforcement plays a greater role in successes than one is led to believe and its absence is conspicuous in some notable failures. For example, until very recently compliance with the weakly enforced agreements issued under eleven international fisheries commissions was highly problematic. Agreement ambiguity and social and economic changes were not a major source of these compliance problems. State capacity was more relevant since monitoring catches is costly, but scholars agree that the developed states that were often the principal violators could have coped with the monitoring issue if they believe it was in their interest to do so. The crux of the problem was the paradox of collective action: states saw little reason to pressure their fishermen to obey rules that other states were likely to flout.[39] The creation of the 200-mile exclusive economic zones was a dramatic improvement because it made enforcement much easier. Consequently, the role of enforcement is growing. For instance, in April 1995 a long-simmering dispute over fishing rights in the North Atlantic among Canada, the EC, and the United States was

34. Bayard and Elliott 1994, chaps. 3 and 4.
35. Ibid., 70.
36. Hudec 1990, 116.
37. Sykes 1992.
38. Bayard and Elliott 1994, 350.
39. Peterson 1993, 280.

resolved by an agreement that the *New York Times* reported, "could serve as a model for preserving endangered fish stocks throughout the world." The key to the accord, says the article, is "enforcement." The deal provides for elaborate verification measures and "imposes stiff fines and other penalties for violations."[40] The elaborate verification measures testify to the importance of transparency, but to believe that they would be effective in the absence of sanctions is naive. The benefits of cheating are too great to be offset by transparency alone.

The cost of ignoring the connection between enforcement and compliance when there is a substantial incentive to defect is well-illustrated by the Mediterranean Plan, considered by many to be an example of how epistemic communities have been able to play a significant role in effecting international cooperation. The Mediterranean Plan achieved consensus by eliminating any meaningful restrictions on dumping and providing no enforcement mechanism for those minimal targets and restrictions that were agreed to. As a result, it has been an embarrassing failure. Pollution has increased, dolphin hunting continues, and despite a European Union ban on drift nets longer than 2.5 kilometers, the rules are widely flouted.[41] The result has been a collapsing ecosystem in the Mediterranean.

The complementary relationship between transparency and enforcement is exemplified by a case that the managerialists believe to be an archetype of their approach. The case, described by Mitchell, involves the attempt by the International Maritime Consultative Organization (IMCO) and its successor, the International Maritime Organization (IMO), to regulate intentional oil pollution by oil tankers. From 1954 until 1978, the regime had little success and oil discharges were over three to thirty times the legal limit.[42] In 1978 the IMO switched strategies and with the negotiation of the International Convention for the Prevention of Pollution from Ships (MARPOL) began to regulate oil pollution by requiring tankers to be equipped with segregated ballast tanks (SBT). Despite the reduced cargo capacity and increased costs of equipping new and old oil tankers with the new equipment, and "despite strong incentives not to install SBT, tanker owners have done so as required. . . . Compliance is almost perfect."[43]

Why was the equipment regime so much more effective at inducing compliance? It is not difficult to argue that increased enforcement was anything but irrelevant. We learn for example, that "the [equipment violations regime] provided the foundation for a noncompliance response system involving far more potent sanctions than those available for discharge violations."[44] State-

---

40. *New York Times,* 17 April 1995, A2.
41. "Dead in the Water," *New Scientist,* 4 February 1995.
42. Mitchell 1994b, 439 in particular.
43. Mitchell 1994a, 291.
44. Ibid., 289.

ments such as these suggest that while increased transparency was critical to the success of MARPOL, it was also critical that tankers lacking the International Oil Pollution Prevention (IOPP) certificate could be barred from doing business or detained in port.

> The huge opportunity costs of having a ship barred from port or detained would force a tanker owner to think twice. . . . A single day of detention cost a tanker operator some $20,000 in opportunity costs, far higher than typical fines being imposed. . . . Detention provisions have altered behavior because they have had the virtue of imposing . . . high costs on the violator, making their use more credible and more potent . . . detention is a large enough penalty to deter a ship from committing future violations.[45]

Enforcement and the future of cooperation

The significance of the cases discussed above lies not in their representing typical cases of noncompliance but in their salience and role as counterexamples to the unqualified prescriptions of the managerial theory. They should also make us skeptical of any contention that mixed-motive game-based cooperation (with its incentive for one or both sides to defect if they can get away with it) plays only an insignificant role in regulatory regimes. If some persistently have underestimated the value of interstate coordination vis-à-vis the solution of mixed-motive games, others should not commit the opposite error of pretending that the latter—and enforcement—is irrelevant. This is especially true in light of the likely evolution of regulatory cooperation.

Cooperation in arms, trade, and environmental regulation may begin with agreements that require little enforcement, but continued progress seems likely to depend on coping with an environment where defection presents significant benefits. It is not appropriate to counter skepticism about the success of treaties that require steep cuts in nontariff barriers, arms, or air pollution but that contain no enforcement provision with statistics about the average rate of compliance with international agreements that require states to depart only slightly from what they would have done in the absence of an agreement. Techniques used to ensure compliance with an agreement covering interstate bank transfers cannot be counted on to ensure the success of the WTO's new rules governing intellectual property.

It is possible, of course, that deeper cooperation (e.g., stricter arms control or environmental regulation) can be ensured without much enforcement. This can occur whenever the underlying game changes in such a way that there is less incentive to defect from a given agreement. One of the points too rarely made by either the managerial or political economy (i.e., enforcement) school

---

45. Ibid., 266 and 182–85.

is that changes in technology, relative prices, domestic transitions, and ideas have inspired more international cooperation and regulatory compliance than have all efforts at dispute resolution and enforcement combined. This is particularly true in the area of trade liberalization. As Kenneth Oye recently has noted, "Over the long term, the diffusion of ideas, the impact of market-driven shifts in exchange rates, and fundamental concerns over productivity and growth are more consequential sources of pressure for reducing protection."[46] Yet, while we agree that ideas and relative prices are important determinants of compliance, they are not well-specified strategies that instruct policymakers how they can increase the rate of compliance.[47] We know relatively little about how to use ideas to change preferences about discount rates, consumption versus savings, or the environment and still less about the endogenous manipulation of relative prices for policy aims such as arms control. We know much more, as crude as our knowledge may be, about the impact of enforcement coupled with managerial variables such as transparency.

If the managerialists want to hope (like most of us) that ideas or relative prices will inspire states to value the environment more or to be more energetic in controlling arms, this is understandable. It is nevertheless different from the prescriptions that they are currently emphasizing and may also prove overly optimistic. While some regimes appear over the years to have been strengthened by the changes in relative prices, the dissemination of progressive ideas about the potential of cooperation, and the weakening of parochial domestic interests, others have shown signs of weakening because of these same factors. The nonproliferation regime, for example, has shown signs of fraying because the relative cost of nuclear weaponry has declined.

We do not mean to imply that the managerial model and the failure to embrace the idea that enforcement is often necessary are the only things preventing deeper cooperation. Obviously, states have reasons to refrain from vigorous enforcement. The question is whether it is better to cope with such reluctance by declaring that its importance has been vastly exaggerated or by trying to remedy matters.

We obviously prefer the second course of action, and we believe that the managerialists' vision of cooperation and compliance distracts political scientists from a host of problems that lie squarely within their area of expertise. For example, the vast majority of political economists would argue that the reason the GATT has encountered compliance problems and the reason why states have not obtained the cooperative benefits that would be possible through the use of more aggressive enforcement strategies involves an agency problem.

---

46. Oye 1994, 161.
47. For discussions of the impact of ideas on cooperation and compliance, see Goldstein and Keohane 1993; P. Haas 1992; and E. Haas 1990.

Political leaders, if not the consumers who make up their constituencies, are left better off if they acquiesce to protectionist demands during those periods (e.g., recessions, following a technological breakthrough by foreign competition) when interest groups are likely to pay a premium that is greater than the electoral punishment they are likely to receive. Because the timing of such events is uncertain and most leaders are similarly vulnerable to such events, they deal with this situation by creating penalties for violations that are high enough to prevent constant defection but low enough to allow self-interested defection when circumstances demand it. Even leaders of states that are, for whatever reason, more committed to free trade are reluctant to increase the penalty for violations to a very high level because they suspect (probably correctly) that the "protectionist premium" is at times far greater than the cost of any credible punishment for violations. Thus, their hand is stayed not by any appreciation for the accidental nature of defection but by an appreciation for just how unaccidental it is.[48]

This is a dimension of political capacity that the managerial school rarely discusses and that is unlikely to be exorcized by technical assistance. It is, however, intimately connected to the design of both domestic political institutions and international regimes. One possible strategy is to restrict regime membership to states that will not have to defect very often. The idea is that whatever benefit is lost by excluding such states from the regime will be more than made up by permitting those that are included to set and also enforce a deeper level of cooperation—in this case a higher standard of free trade. This may be a reason, quite different from the large-*n* coordination concerns of collective action theory, why many deeply cooperative regimes have a limited number of members and why regimes with a large number of members tend to engage in only shallow cooperation. Is this trade-off real? Must states sometimes choose between aggressively addressing an environmental or trade problem and trying to create a community of states? We do not know. What we do know is that to ignore the issue on the basis of high compliance rates and the relative absence of enforcement is dangerously premature.

Appendix A

This appendix gives the assumptions of the model we use and some propositions derived from these assumptions. Proofs are omitted.

ASSUMPTION 1. *The utilities of states A and B, U_A and U_B, have two continuous partial derivatives.*

48. Downs and Rocke 1995.

ASSUMPTION 2. *It is never in A's interest for B to have a greater amount of protection; that is*

$$\frac{\partial U_A(P^A, P^B)}{\partial P^B} < 0, \qquad \forall P^B,$$

where P is the level of protection. Similarly,

$$\frac{\partial U_B(P^A, P^B)}{\partial P^A} < 0, \qquad \forall P^A.$$

ASSUMPTION 3. *For any fixed value of P^B, $U_A(P^A, P^B)$ is strictly increasing on $[0, R_A(P^B)]$ and strictly decreasing on $[R_A(P^B), \infty)$ as a function of P^A, where the position of the maximum may depend on P^B. Declining marginal returns to protectionist measures together with linear costs are sufficient to ensure this. This implies that there is a unique best response $R_A(P^B)$ by A to any choice by B. Similarly, for any fixed value of P^A, $U_B(P^A, P^B)$ is strictly increasing on $[0, R_B(P^A)]$ and strictly decreasing on $[R_B(P^A), \infty)$ as a function of P^B.*

ASSUMPTION 4. *A stability condition $\exists 0 < k < 1$ such that $R'_A(P^B) \leq k$, $\forall P^B$ guarantees that there will be no trade wars with unbounded increases in tariffs. Similarly, $R'_B(P^A) \leq k$ $\forall P^A$.*

ASSUMPTION 5. *$R''_A(P^A) \leq 0$, $\forall P^A$ and $R''_B(P^A) \leq 0$, $\forall P^A$. These represent nonincreasing marginal returns to increases in trade protection.*

ASSUMPTION 6. *$R_A(0) > 0$ and $R_B(0) > 0$. If the opponent has no tariffs or nontariff barriers, then some nonzero amount of protection is the best choice.*

PROPOSITION A1. *In a neighborhood of the noncooperative tariff structure, any utility function satisfying assumptions 1–6 is approximately*

$$U_A(P^A, P^B) = a_A(P^B - P_0^B) + b_A(P^A - P_0^A)^2 \tag{A1}$$

$$+ c_A(P^A - P_0^A)(P^B - P_0^B) + d_A(P^B - P_0^B)^2,$$

in which $a < 0$, $b < 0$, $c > 0$, and $|c/2b| < 1$. In this case, the reaction function for A is derived from equating the derivative to zero and is

$$R_A(P^B) = P_0^A - \frac{c_A}{2b_A}(P^B - P_0^B). \tag{A2}$$

Then this satisfies all the conditions if the following conditions hold. (Assumption 1 is satisfied automatically since U is a quadratic):

(1) For assumption 2 to be true at the equilibrium, we need $a < 0$.

(2) For assumption 3 to be true, we need $b < 0$.

(3) If A is to react to an increase with an increase and to a decrease with a decrease, we need $c > 0$.

(4) For assumption 4 to be true, we need $|c/2b| < 1$. This is a stability requirement. When this is the case, unbridled competition returns to an equilibrium level after a series of turns; if not, then any out-of-equilibrium situation would result in unbounded increases in protectionist measures.

(5) Assumption 5 is true always since the second partials of the reaction function are zero.

(6) For assumption 6 to be true, we need

$$P_0^A + \frac{c}{2b} P_0^B > 0 \tag{A3}$$

which is satisfied if $P_0^A > kP_0^B$ and $P_0^B > kP_0^A$, so that the equilibrium is not too far from even. Very uneven equilibria can occur with the general model, but the global quadratic model is then no longer suitable.

Appendix B

The table below gives a chronology of arms control and related treaties and agreements, including confidence- and security-building measures and measures related to transparency, nonproliferation, and defense conversion.

TABLE B1. *U.S. agreements since 1945*[a]

Agreement	Signed	Entered into force
Antarctic Treaty	1 December 1959	23 June 1961
"Hot Line" Agreement	20 June 1963	20 June 1963
Limited Test Ban Treaty	5 August 1963	10 October 1963
Outer Space Treaty	27 January 1967	10 October 1967
Treaty of Tlatelolco	14 February 1967	22 April 1968
Protocol II to the Treaty of Tlatelolco	1 April 1968	Ratified by U.S. 8 May 1971
Nonproliferation Treaty	1 July 1968	5 March 1970
Seabed Arms Control Treaty	11 February 1971	18 May 1972
"Accident Measures" Agreement	30 September 1971	30 September 1971
"Hot Line" Modernization Agreement	30 September 1971	30 September 1971
Biological Weapons Convention	10 April 1972	26 March 1975
"Incidents at Sea" Agreement	25 May 1972	25 May 1972
SALT I Interim Agreement	26 May 1972	3 October 1972
ABM Treaty	26 May 1972	3 October 1972

TABLE B1. *continued*

Agreement	Signed	Entered into force
Declaration of Basic Principles of Relations Between the U.S. and the U.S.S.R.	29 May 1972	29 May 1972
Prevention of Nuclear War Agreement Between the U.S. and U.S.S.R.	23 June 1973	23 June 1973
ABM Treaty Protocol	3 July 1974	24 May 1976
Threshold Test Ban treaty	3 July 1974	11 December 1990
Helsinki Final Act	1 August 1975	1 August 1975
PNE Treaty	28 May 1976	11 December 1990
ENMOD Convention	18 May 1977	5 October 1978
Protocol I to the Treaty of Tlatelolco	26 May 1977	Ratified by U.S. 19 November 1981
SALT II Treaty	18 June 1979	—[b]
Convention on the Physical Protection of Nuclear Material	3 March 1980	—
"Hot Line" Expansion Agreement	17 July 1984	17 July 1984
Stockholm Accord	Adopted 19 September 1986	Adopted 19 September 1986
Nuclear Risk Reduction Centers Agreement	15 September 1987	15 September 1987
INF Treaty	8 December 1987	1 June 1988
INF Diplomatic Note on "Weapons Delivery Vehicle"	12 May 1988	—
INF Agreed Minute	12 May 1988	1 June 1988
U.S.–U.S.S.R. Ballistic Missile Launch Notification Agreement	31 May 1988	31 May 1988
"Hot Line" MOU Modification Agreement	24 June 1988	24 June 1988
INF Inspection Procedures Agreement	24 June 1988	24 June 1988
INF Special Verification Commission MOU	20 December 1988	20 December 1988
Treaty of Tlatelolco IAEA Safeguards Agreement	17 February 1989	6 April 1989
INF continuous Monitoring Inspection Procedures Agreement	9 June 1989	9 June 1989
U.S.–U.S.S.R. Major Strategic Exercises Notification Agreement	23 September 1989	23 September 1989

TABLE B1. *continued*

Agreement	Signed	Entered into force
START Trial Verification and Stability Measures Agreement	23 September 1989	23 September 1989
START ICBM Verification Agreement	23 September 1989	23 September 1989
CW Verification and DATA Exchange MOU	23 September 1989	23 September 1989
INF Verification Implementation MOU	21 December 1980	21 December 1989
U.S.–U.S.S.R. CW Destruction Agreement	1 June 1990	Not yet entered into force
2 Plus 4 Treaty	12 September 1990	3 October 1990
The Vienna Document 1990	Adopted 17 November 1990	1 January 1991
CFE Treaty	19 November 1990	9 November 1992
Amendment I to the MOA on INF Verification	4 April 1991	4 April 1991
Amendment II to the MOA on the INF Verification	4 April 1991	4 April 1991
Amendment III to the MOA on INF Verification	11 December 1991	11 December 1991
Amendment IV to the MOA on INF Verification	11 December 1991	11 December 1991
START Treaty	31 July 1991	Not yet entered into force
The Vienna Document 1992	Adopted 4 March 1992	—
Treaty on Open Skies	24 March 1992	Not yet entered into force
Lisbon START Protocol	23 May 1992	—
Oslo Final Document on FE Implementation	5 June 1992	5 June 1992
U.S.–U.S.S.R. Joint Understanding on Strategic Offensive Arms	17 June 1992	—
Open Lands MOU	17 June 1992	17 June 1992
Korean Nuclear Nonproliferation Statement	Dated 17 June 1992	—
U.S. and Russian Agreement on Transportation and Destruction of Weapons Proliferation	17 June 1992	17 June 1992
Fissile Material Containers Agreement	17 June 1992	Not yet entered into force

TABLE B1. *continued*

Agreement	Signed	Entered into force
Armored Blankets Agreement	17 June 1992	17 June 1992
Emergency Response Equipment and Training Agreement	17 June 1992	17 June 1992
Joint Understanding Side Letter on Strategic Offensive Arms	18 June 1992	18 June 1992
FE 1A Concluding Act	10 July 1992	17 July 1992
U.S. DOD and Russian President's CAW Committee Agreement on CAW Destruction, Transport, or Storage	30 July 1992	30 July 1992
U.S. DOD and Russian MINATOM Agreement on Cargo and Guard Railcar Conversion Kits for Transportation of Nuclear Weapons and Material	28 August 1992	28 August 1992
U.S. and Russian Agreement on Disposition of HEU	Initialed 28 August 1992	Not yet entered into force
U.S. DOD and Russian MINATOM Agreement on Technical Assistance for Storage Facility Design for Fissile Material	6 October 1992	6 October 1992
U.S. and Belarussian Agreement on Emergency Response and Prevention of Proliferation of Weapons of Mass Destruction	22 October 1992	—
Emergency Response Equipment and Training Agreement	22 October 1992	22 October 1992
Export Control Systems Agreement	22 October 1992	22 October 1992
Continuous Communications Link Agreement	15 January 1993	15 January 1993
START II Treaty	3 January 1993	Not yet entered into force
Chemical Weapons Convention	13 January 1993	Not yet entered into force

[a]Abbreviations and acronyms are as follows: ABM = Antiballistic Missile, CFE = Conventional Forces in Europe; CW = Chemical Weapons; DOD = Department of Defense; ENMOD = Environmental Modification; HEU = Highly Enriched Uranium; IAEA = International Atomic Energy Agency; ICBM = Intercontinental Ballistic Missile; INF = Intermediate-range Nuclear Forces; MINATOM = Russian Nuclear Power Ministry; MOU = Memorandum of Understanding; PNE = Peaceful Nuclear Explosions; SALT = Strategic Arms Limitations Talks; START = Strategic Arms Reduction Talks.

[b]Dashes indicate missing information.

References

Abreu, Dilip. 1988. On the theory of infinitely repeated games with discounting. *Econometrica* 56:383–96.

Abreu, Dilip, David Pearce, and Ennio Stacchetti. 1986. Optimal cartel equilibria with imperfect monitoring. *Journal of Economic Theory* 39:251–69.

———. 1989. Renegotiation and symmetry in repeated games. Cowles Foundation discussion paper, Yale University, New Haven, Conn.

Arora, Seema, and Timothy N. Cason. 1995. An experiment in voluntary environmental regulation: Participation in EPA's 33/50 program. *Journal of Environmental Economics and Management* 28:271–86.

Barrett, Scott. 1994. Self-enforcing international environmental agreements. *Oxford Economic Papers* 46:878–94.

Bayard, Thomas O., and Kimberly Elliott. 1994. *Reciprocity and retaliation in U.S. trade policy.* Washington, D.C.: Institute of International Economics.

Bhagwati, Jagdish. 1990. *The world trading system at risk.* Princeton, N.J.: Princeton University Press.

Burley, Anne-Marie, and Walter Mattli. 1993. Europe before the court: A political theory of legal integration. *International Organization* 47:41–76.

———. 1991. Adjustment and compliance processes in international regulatory regimes. In *Preserving the Global Environment,* edited by Jessica Tuchman Mathews. New York: W.W. Norton.

Chayes, Abram, and Antonio Handler Chayes. 1990. From law enforcement to dispute settlement. *International Security* 14:147–64.

———. 1993a. The new sovereignty. Harvard University, Cambridge, Mass. Typescript.

———. 1993b. On compliance. *International Organization* 47:175–205.

Downs, George W., and David Rocke. 1990. *Tacit bargaining, arms races, and arms control.* Ann Arbor: University of Michigan Press.

———. 1995. *Optimal imperfection? Institutions and domestic politics in international relations.* Princeton, N.J.: Princeton University Press.

Duffy, Gloria. 1988. Conditions that affect arms control compliance. In *U.S.–Soviet Security Cooperation,* edited by Alexander George, Philip J. Farley, and Alexander Dallin. New York: Oxford University Press.

Goldblat, Jozef. 1993. *Arms control agreements: A handbook.* New York: Praeger.

Goldman, Emily. 1994. *Sunken treaties.* University Park: Pennsylvania State Press.

Goldstein, Judith, and Robert O. Keohane, eds. 1993. *Ideas and foreign policy.* Ithaca, N.Y.: Cornell University Press.

Grossman, Gene, and Elhanan Helpman. 1994. Protection for sale. *American Economic Review* 84:833–50.

Haas, Ernst. 1990. *When knowledge is power.* Berkeley: University of California Press.

Haas, Peter M., ed. 1992. *Knowledge, power, and international policy coordination.* Special issue, *International Organization* 46:1–390.

Haas, Peter M., Robert O. Keohane, and Marc A. Levy, eds. 1993. *Institutions for the earth: Sources of effective international environmental protection.* Cambridge, Mass.: MIT Press.

Hawkins, Keith. 1984. *Environment and enforcement: Regulation and the social definition of pollution.* Oxford Socio-legal Studies. Oxford: Clarendon Press.

Hudec, Robert E. 1990. Thinking about the new Section 301: Beyond good and evil. In *Aggressive unilateralism: America's 301 trade policy and the world trading system,* edited by Jagdish Bhagwati and Hugh T. Patrick. Ann Arbor: University of Michigan Press.

———. 1993. *Enforcing international trade law: The evolution of the modern GATT legal system.* Salem, N.H.: Butterworth.

Hungerford, Thomas L. 1991. GATT: A cooperative equilibrium in a noncooperative trading regime? *Journal of International Economics* 31:357–69.

Ikle, Fred Charles. 1961. After detection—what? *Foreign Affairs* 39:208–20.

Kandori, Michihiro. 1992. Social norms and community enforcement. *Review of Economic Studies* 59:63–80.

Kaufman, Robert. 1990. *Arms control during the pre-nuclear era.* New York: Columbia University Press.

Martin, Lisa L. 1992. *Coercive cooperation: Explaining multilateral economic sanctions.* Princeton, N.J.: Princeton University Press.

Mitchell, Ronald. 1993. Compliance theory: A synthesis. *Review of European Community and International Environmental Law (RECIEL)* 2:327–34.

———. 1994a. *Intentional oil pollution at sea: Environmental policy and treaty compliance.* Cambridge, Mass.: MIT Press.

———. 1994b. Regime design matters: Intentional oil pollution and treaty compliance. *International Organization* 48:425–58.

———. 1995. Altering consequences, opportunities, information, and values: Strategies of international social control. University of Oregon. Typescript.

Murdoch, James C., and Todd Sandler. 1994. The voluntary provision of a pure public good: The case of reduced CFC emissions and the Montreal Protocol. Iowa State University, Ames, Iowa. Typescript.

Ostrom, Elinor. 1990. *Governing the commons: The evolution of institutions for collective action.* Cambridge: Cambridge University Press.

Oye, Kenneth A. 1994. Comment on John Jackson. In *Managing the world economy,* edited by Peter B. Kenen. Washington, D.C.: Institute of International Economics.

Peterson, M.J. 1993. International fisheries management. In *Institutions for the earth: Sources of effective international environmental protection,* edited by Peter M. Haas, Robert O. Keohane, and Marc A. Levy. Cambridge, Mass.: MIT Press.

Scholz, John T. 1984. Voluntary compliance and regulatory enforcement. *Law and Policy* 6:385–404.

Sparrow, Malcolm, K. 1994. *Imposing duties: Government's changing approach to compliance.* Westport, Conn.: Praeger.

Staiger, Robert. 1995. International rules and institutions for trade policy. In *Handbook of International Economics,* vol. 2. Edited by Gene Grossman and Kenneth Rogoff. New York: North Holland.

Sykes, Alan O. 1990. Mandatory retaliation for breach of trade agreements: Some thoughts on the strategic design of Section 301. *Boston University International Law Journal* 8:301–31.

U.S. Arms Control and Disarmament Agency. 1990. *Arms control and disarmament agreements.* Washington, D.C.: U.S. Arms Control and Disarmament Agency.

———. 1991. The strategic arms reduction treaty, START data base.

———. 1992. Constructive unilateral threats in international commercial relations: The limited case for Section 301. *Law and Policy in International Business* 23:263–332.

Young, Oran. 1989. *International cooperation.* Ithaca, N.Y.: Cornell University Press.

———. 1994. *International governance: Protecting the environment in a stateless society.* Ithaca, N.Y.: Cornell University Press.

The Legalization of International Monetary Affairs

Beth A. Simmons

Sovereign control over money is one of the most closely guarded national prerogatives.[1] Creating, valuating, and controlling the distribution of national legal tender is viewed as an inherent right of a nation-state in the modern period. Yet over the course of the twentieth century, international rules of good monetary conduct have become "legalized" in the sense developed in this volume. This historic shift took place after World War II in an effort to bolster the confidence that had been shattered by the interwar monetary experience.[2] If the interwar years taught monetary policymakers anything, it was that economic prosperity required credible exchange-rate commitments, open markets, and nondiscriminatory economic arrangements. International legalization of monetary affairs was a way to inspire private actors to once again trade and invest across national borders.

Sensitivity to the sovereignty costs continues to preclude dense hard law in this area. This is especially obvious when compared to other areas of economic relations, such as trade in goods and services. The Bretton Woods institutions involved only three international legal obligations regarding the conduct of monetary policy. The best known of these was to establish and maintain a par value, an obligation that was formally eliminated by the Second Amendment to the International Monetary Fund's (IMF) Articles of Agreement in 1977. But two other obligations remain: to keep one's current account free from restrictions, and to maintain a unified exchange-rate

Thanks to William Clark and Brian Pollins, the editors of *International Organization* and this special volume, and two anonymous reviewers for very helpful comments. I would like to acknowledge the extremely helpful research assistance of Zachary Elkins and Conor O'Dwyer, who assisted with data management and analysis; Becky Curry, who assisted with the legal research; and Aaron Staines, Maria Vu, and Geoffrey Wong, who assisted with data collection and entry. I would also like to thank the Archives of the International Monetary Fund for access to documents. All errors remain my own.

1. Cohen 1998.
2. See Eichengreen 1992; and Simmons 1994.

International Organization 54, 3, Summer 2000, pp. 573–602

system. The first requires that if a bill comes due for imports or an external interest payment, national monetary authorities must make foreign exchange available to pay it. The second proscribes exchange-rate systems that favor certain transactions or trade partners over others. IMF members can voluntarily declare themselves bound by these rules (Article VIII status) or they can choose to maintain, though not augment, the restrictions that were in place when they joined the IMF (a form of grandfathering under Article XIV).

My premise is that legalization of international monetary relations helps governments make credible policy commitments to market actors. As I will argue, the central mechanism encouraging compliance is the desire to avoid reputational costs associated with reneging on a legal obligation. As Kenneth Abbott and Duncan Snidal suggest in this volume, legalization is a tool that enhances credibility by increasing the costs of reneging. The hard commitments encoded at Bretton Woods were thought to be necessary because the soft arrangements of the interwar years had proved useless. Governments have used commitment to the rules contained in the Articles of Agreement as a costly commitment to stable, liberal external monetary policies. This does not mean that compliance is perfect, but it is enhanced when other countries comply and when governments have a strong reputation for respecting the rule of law. When these conditions obtain, rule violation entails disproportionate reputational costs, as I shall argue.

In the first section of the article I examine the international monetary system prior to World War II and show that "hard" international legal obligations played virtually no role in monetary relations during that time. In the second section I demonstrate that the Bretton Woods system ushered in a new "public international law of money" that peaked just prior to the breakdown of the par value obligation in the 1970s. Although governments are no longer legally required to maintain fixed exchange rates, they can still (voluntarily) obligate themselves to maintain a unified exchange-rate system and to keep their current accounts free from restrictions. Thus the trajectory of legalization in this issue area is far from linear. In the third section I investigate why, given a choice, governments commit to and comply with the IMF's monetary rules. Since commitment to these rules is voluntary, why do governments obligate themselves to abide by them? I argue that governments are much more likely to choose to commit under conditions in which such a commitment would be credible, but that commitment is also conditioned on other countries' willingness to commit. In the fourth section I examine the conditions under which commitment affects behavior. Since the IMF is unlikely to enforce these rules in a direct way, what explains compliance? The findings suggest that the desire to avoid reputational costs is crucial. Costs are higher if comparable countries are complying, and if a state has heavily invested in maintaining a strong reputation for respecting the rule of law. In short, legalization strengthens commitment. It is this quality that makes formal treaty arrangements desirable in the first place.

The International Monetary System Before 1945: National Laws and International "Understandings"

The Nineteenth-Century Gold Standard

The stability of the international monetary system in the nineteenth century owed nothing to international legal agreements. Not a single international treaty addressed obligations of countries under the gold standard. Rather, the international system was anchored in national rules, often in the form of statutes, that specified the rights of private parties to import and export gold. In Britain, at the center of the system, the Peel Act of 1819[3] gave individuals the right to convert bank notes to gold by presenting them to the Bank of England. The Bank Charter Act (1844) extended to individuals the right to acquire notes for gold, and created a legal obligation on the part of the Bank of England to maintain gold backing pound for pound, for all outstanding Bank of England notes beyond the "fiduciary issue" of 14 million pounds.[4]

Although the gold standard certainly had a clear legal basis, there was nothing international about the legal structure on which it rested. It was, at most, a decentralized system of regulatory harmonization.[5] To access international capital and trade, other countries had an incentive to follow Britain onto gold. So in 1871 the German Empire made gold its standard (even though this required Germany to hold much more gold in reserve than did Britain). Switzerland and Belgium followed in 1878. France adopted the gold standard but restricted convertibility when the franc was weak. The Austro-Hungarian gulden floated until the passage of (what was purported to be) gold standard legislation in 1891. In 1900 the United States declared gold as the "standard unit of value," which put the country officially on the gold standard (though silver coins still circulated). None of these national decisions involved the international community in their making. Indeed, when international conferences did take place, they tended to favor bi-metalism.[6]

Nor was this system managed through international legal arrangements. Even if one does not accept the traditional description of balance-of-payments adjustment under the classical gold standard as fully "automatic," its cooperative aspects knew no international legal guidelines. W. M. Scammell described the adjustment mechanism as "quasi-organizational, being operated by a team of central bankers under the leadership of the Bank of England on behalf of the world community."[7] But at no point in the pre–World War I period could one point to an international legal framework within which such cooperation was to take place. It is not difficult to see why this should be so. This decentralized system of harmonized national rules seemed to provide a good degree of stability—at least for international traders and investors at

---

3. Amended in 1921.
4. Dam 1982, 23–25.
5. See, for example, the description by the MacMillan Committee on Finance and Industry, Cmd. 3897, HMSO 1931, as reprinted in Eichengreen 1985, 185–99.
6. Dam 1982, 23.
7. Scammell 1985, 105.

the industrialized core of the system.[8] As long as investors were confident that the system would be maintained,[9] there was little reason to design an elaborate international legal structure for its maintenance.

The Interwar Years

World War I disrupted not only the economic relationships but also the domestic political and social stability that underlay the confidence in the gold standard.[10] As a result, the interwar years were a "largely unsuccessful groping toward some form of organizational regulation of monetary affairs."[11] Increasingly, the major governments turned to negotiated agreements that had the feel of "soft law" as described by Abbott and Snidal. For example, the Brussels Conference of 1920 met to consider creating a new addition to the League of Nations, the Economic and Financial Commission, to which some responsibilities for economic stabilization might be delegated. In 1922 the governments of the major European countries met in Genoa to agree informally to the principles of a gold exchange standard, which would economize on gold by encouraging smaller financial centers to hold a portion of their reserves in foreign exchange rather than gold. Although this agreement did in fact have an important impact on the composition of reserves, it was at most a soft admonition to economize gold holding. When the Bank for International Settlements was created in 1930, governments were careful to limit their mutual obligations while solidifying the bank as their agent in the collection of reparations from Germany.[12] As the Permanent Court of International Arbitration noted, the international community had quite clearly "accepted [the] principle that a State is entitled to regulate its own currency."[13]

Virtually every important exchange-rate decision made in the interwar years was made unilaterally. On 21 September the British government implemented the Gold Standard (Amendment) Act of 1931, suspending payments of gold against legal tender and officially leaving the gold standard. Even as multilateral negotiations were in progress, the Roosevelt administration unilaterally imposed exchange controls and an export embargo.[14] Even when governments tried to coordinate their actions, diplomatic declarations were chosen over legal commitments. The Gold Bloc, formed in July 1933 among the governments of Belgium, France, Switzerland, and the Netherlands to cooperate to defend existing parities, was a "soft" legal arrangement created

---

8. Ford 1985.

9. Eichengreen writes extensively about the confidence that investors had in the prewar gold standard. Eichengreen 1992.

10. Simmons 1994.

11. Dam 1982, 50.

12. Simmons 1993.

13. *Case of Serbian Loans*, Permanent Court of International Justice, ser. A, nos. 20/21, 44, 1929, cited in Gold 1984b, 1533. Thus, researchers often speak of the "norms" of the gold standard (for example, Simmons 1994), but these were never codified in international agreements.

14. Presidential Proclamations 2039 (6 March 1933) and 2040 (9 March 1933); Executive orders 6111 (20 April 1933) and 6260 (28 August 1933). Cited in Dam 1982, 47, 55.

by declaration and communiqué, rather than a formal treaty. When France left the gold standard, for domestic reasons leaders needed multilateral cover and sought it in the form of the "Tripartite Agreement" of 1936. This agreement was the loosest of arrangements, in which Britain, the United States, and France issued separate declarations rather than sign a single document. Without mentioning devaluation, France announced the "readjustment" of its currency, while promising, as far as possible, to minimize the disturbance of such action on the international exchanges. France, Britain, and the United States agreed to arrange "for such consultations for this purpose as may prove necessary." The declarations also expressed the governments' intentions to take actions to relax the system of trade quotas and exchange controls that were in effect at that time and expressed the "trust that no country will attempt to obtain an unreasonable competitive exchange advantage and thereby hamper the effort to restore more stable economic relations which it is the aim of the three governments to promote."[15] Most historians of the period have concluded that the Tripartite Agreement did little to change international economic relations in the 1930s.[16] For our purposes, it was undoubtedly intended to create only the softest of obligations.

That governments tried at all to coordinate their monetary choices during this period had much to do with the growing incentives governments faced after World War I to externalize their problems of economic adjustment. The international monetary system was still dependent on national law, but the nature of the national rules had changed. Certainly governments could no longer passively accept internal adjustments in the face of mounting political demands to manage the economy. In contrast to the nineteenth century, during the 1930s a number of countries claimed to be on a "gold standard" even though gold had little to do with the money supply and hence held no implications for internal adjustment.[17] Once the national rules no longer commanded respect for internal adjustments, governments were increasingly faced with the need for international rules to put limits on external adjustments. Efforts to formalize international monetary relations arose from the need for credible limits on external adjustment.

The IMF and International Monetary Law: Toward the Formalization of "Rules of Good Conduct"

The legalization of international monetary relations burgeoned after World War II.[18] In rejecting the less formalized arrangements of the past century and establishing for

---

15. All quotations from the Tripartite Monetary Agreements of 25 September 1936 are from the version printed by the Bank for International Settlements, Monetary and Economic Department, Basle, January 1937. The sections quoted can be found nearly verbatim in all three declarations.

16. See Sauvy 1967, 224; Kindleberger 1986, 255, 257, 259; and Clarke 1977.

17. In the United States it was illegal after 1933 (Exec. order 6260) for a resident to hold gold coins or bullion. Sterilization funds in both the United States and Great Britain further severed the relationship between gold flows and international monetary policy.

18. The expression "rules of good conduct" is used by Gold 1965, passim.

the first time a public international law of money,[19] negotiators from the United States and the United Kingdom were consciously choosing an international legal framework to enhance the system's credibility. Moreover, the IMF was to be, among other things, a fund, the purpose of which was to extend loans to members in balance-of-payments trouble. This alone led to a huge increase in legal detail, since these rules are analogous to banking law or at least to banking practice, where terms of loans and their repayment are spelled out in contracts and often limited by statutes and regulations. The IMF was created by a multilateral treaty arrangement, by which signatories agree to pay in subscriptions in exchange for voting and drawing rights. Of course, the decision to create an intergovernmental organization and to codify basic rules required domestic ratification of all signatories. In the United States, this meant that the Articles of Agreement had to be ratified by two-thirds of the Senate and, because of the need for implementing legislation, a simple majority of both houses of Congress. With the entry into force of the IMF's Articles of Agreement, money—like activity on the seas and diplomatic relations among states—was drawn under the system of public international law and became newly subject to its broader norms and principles.[20]

Fixed Exchange Rates: The Rise and Fall of Legalization

The Articles of Agreement set forth two primary regulatory goals that reflected lessons drawn from the interwar years: governments should be obligated to peg exchange rates and to remove exchange controls and discriminatory practices that affected current transactions. Legalization was designed, of course, to fulfill the broader objectives of the IMF's founding members, especially those of the United Kingdom and United States. According to Article IV of the Articles of Agreement, "The essential purpose of the international monetary system is to provide a framework that facilitates the exchange of goods, services, and capital among countries, and . . . a principle objective is the continuing development of the underlying conditions that are necessary for financial and economic stability."[21] To this end, the original White Plan had advocated "the general policy of foreign exchange trading in open, free, and legal markets, and the abandonment as rapidly as conditions permit of restrictions on exchange controls." Controls that were once under the sovereign control of national governments now had to be justified to the international community and were collectively condoned only to the extent necessary "to carry out a purpose contributing to general prosperity."[22] In short, in the postwar monetary system, public international law was to be used as it had been for decades in trade relations: to

---

19. Gold 1984a, 801. A French plan was offered at the beginning of the postwar monetary negotiations. Although it played no direct role, it did indicate the French preference for agreement among the "principal nations" somewhat analogous to the Tripartite Agreement. The French plan saw an international institution as optional. Dam 1982, 76.

20. Gold 1980, 5. Nonetheless, legal treatments of these obligations are surprisingly few. See generally Denters 1996, 16–20.

21. Art. IV, sec. 1.

22. From the White Plan. Horsefield and De Vries 1969, 3:64.

help facilitate the international exchange of goods and services by providing for currency convertibility in open, free, and legal markets.

The international community thus explicitly recognized for the first time that exchange rates were properly a matter of international concern. To become a member of the IMF, a country had to communicate a "par value" for its currency by direct or indirect reference to gold. This might involve minor negotiations with the IMF staff, but it basically established par values very close to those prevailing just prior to membership. Members then had an obligation to maintain that par value within the margins prescribed in the articles.[23] Members were required, without exception, to consult with the IMF before making a change in their initial or subsequent par values; failing to do so constituted a breach of a legal obligation. And although the IMF could not propose a change in a member's par value, by using its resources it could influence a member's decisions to adopt a particular par value. In short, "the authority over exchange rates granted to the Fund by the original articles was unprecedented in international law."[24]

Not all members complied with the obligation to peg. Some were able to do so only by maintaining other undesirable (or illegal) practices, such as multiple currency arrangements or restrictions on current account, which will be analyzed later. Among the industrialized countries, Canada failed to comply and instituted generalized floating for many years,[25] and Germany and the Netherlands briefly were in breach as well.[26] The most spectacular instance of noncompliance—that of the United States in 1971—ultimately reversed the trend begun in the 1940s to harden exchange-rate obligations. Outside of the IMF's legal framework, the "Group of 10" (G-10) industrialized countries met in an attempt to stabilize exchange rates by loosening the margins. The ensuing "Smithsonian Agreement" was adopted as a temporary set of rules by the IMF's executive board on the same day that it was announced in the G-10 communiqué.[27] Rules for generalized floating were then negotiated by the "Group of 20"—again, outside of the legal framework of the IMF—and were adopted by the executive board as nonmandatory guidelines.[28] The heyday of multilateral

---

23. Art. IV, sec. 4. Furthermore, Art. IV, sec. 2 provided that "no member shall buy gold at a price above par value plus the prescribed margin, or sell gold at a price below par value minus the prescribed margin." A central bank could not enter into any gold transaction with another central bank other than at par without one or the other violating the articles.

24. Gold 1988, 48.

25. Canada's decision to float in 1950 was a violation of the Articles of Agreement, but the IMF did not want to force a showdown with Canada; instead it issued an explanation that amounted to pragmatic toleration of floating rates. No major currency followed Canada (at least for the next two decades), so the case was more of an aberration than a precedent.

26. Gold 1988, 31.

27. Executive board decision, Central Rates and Wider Margins: a Temporary Regime, 18 December 1971. See Dam 1982, 191. The board tried to reconcile the Smithsonian Agreement with the articles. The decision stated that the temporary arrangement "would enable members to observe the purposes of the IMF to the maximum extent possible during the temporary period preceding the resumption of effective par values with appropriate margins in accordance with the Articles." Gold 1979, 559.

28. The executive board decision called on members to "use their best endeavors to observe the guidelines." Decision of 13 June 1974 (IMF 1974, 112). The guidelines said that a member "should" intervene "to prevent or moderate sharp and disruptive fluctuations from day to day and from week to week, . . .

legalized exchange-rate relations were effectively over. It was only left for the IMF membership to officially acknowledge the reassertion of national sovereignty in exchange-rate relations by composing the Second Amendment to the Articles of Agreement, which took effect in 1977.

Remaining Monetary Obligations: Article VIII

Despite the softening of legal obligations with respect to the system of par values, governments who are members of the IMF do retain two important obligations in the conduct of their external monetary policy. Both of these are contained in Article VIII of the Articles of Agreement, which spells out the general obligations of members. These rules prohibit restrictions on the making of payments and transfers for current international transactions; they also prohibit multiple currency practices without the approval of the IMF itself.[29] Article VIII section 2(a) provides that governments must make foreign exchange available for goods, services, and invisibles.[30] By agreeing to this standard, governments obligate themselves to make available to their citizens foreign exchange to settle all legal international transactions (it remains up to the government to determine which are legal).[31] They also agree to refrain from delaying, limiting, or imposing charges on currency transfers if these have the effect of inhibiting or increasing the costs of making payments.[32] Interestingly, this provision appears to be the only part of the Bretton Woods Agreements that constitutes an obligation of member states toward their own residents.[33]

Multiple currency practices that establish different rates of exchange have always been prohibited by the Articles of Agreement. Article VIII section 3 creates a hard legal obligation to avoid such practices,[34] which were viewed as a threat to the original parity rule, potentially discriminatory, and always distortionary. As with the restrictions in section 2, the IMF could, however, approve temporarily such practices, which can serve to soften the proscription in the short run. Multiple currency practices were rampant after World War II: about a third of all the countries involved in the Bretton Woods negotiations had multiple currency systems in place. As late as

---

should not normally act aggressively with respect to the exchange value of its currency," should adopt a "target zone of rates," and should consult with the IMF.

29. Art. VIII, sec. 2, para. (a), and sec. 3. Member states are, however, permitted to maintain or impose exchange restrictions under certain conditions: (1) if they are necessary to regulate international capital movements (art. VI, sec. 3); (2) with the approval of the IMF (art. VIII, sec. 2 (a)); (3) if the IMF has declared a currency "scarce" (art. VII, sec. 3 (b)); and (4) if the exchange restrictions were effective at the time the state became a member of the IMF (art. XIV, sec. 2).

30. The restriction applies only to payments and transfers for current international transactions. The IMF articles explicitly permit the regulation of international capital movements (Art. VI, sec. 3).

31. See Executive Board Decision 1034 (60/27), 1 June 1960, para. 1, *Selected Decisions of the International Monetary Fund and Selected Documents*, 11:259 (Washington, D.C.: IMF). See also Horsefield and de Vries 1969, 3:260.

32. Edwards 1985, 391 (see fn. 39 for original documentary sources); and Horn 1985, 295.

33. Boehlhoff and Baumanns 1989, 108.

34. Art. VIII, sec. 3 says: "No member shall engage in, or permit any of its fiscal agencies referred to in Article V, Section 1 to engage in, discriminatory currency arrangements or multiple currency practices . . . except as authorized under this agreement or approved by the Fund."

1971, a major member, France, introduced a multiple exchange-rate system. The United Kingdom also maintained a separate investment rate as late as 1979.

Why were rules forbidding these practices considered necessary? For two general reasons: Governments may want to support developmental objectives that favor certain kinds of imports over others based on established state priorities.[35] More often, however, governments use exchange controls and multiple currency practices as one among a variety of methods to deal with balance-of-payments problems.[36] For either purpose, they may require exporters to surrender foreign currencies received in export sales to government authorities, at governmentally determined rates.[37] In turn, importers are required to obtain foreign currency from the governmental authority or authorized bank. Such systems allow for foreign currency rationing or import discrimination in which foreign currency is made available (or available at favorable rates) for some goods or some transactions but not others.[38]

The IMF has always viewed such systems of control as dangerous substitutes for economic adjustment and inhibitions to the development of free foreign exchange markets. However, because many of the IMF's founding members could not immediately achieve full convertibility at unified rates, Article VIII obligations are made voluntarily. Upon joining the IMF, new members can avail themselves of "transitional" arrangements, under Article XIV, which in effect "grandfather" practices that were in place on their accession to the Articles of Agreement.[39] Even so, Article XIV countries are expected to withdraw restrictions when they are no longer needed for balance-of-payments reasons[40] and are required to consult annually with the IMF about retaining restrictions inconsistent with Article VIII.[41] In the course of these consultations the IMF tries to persuade members gradually to move from "transitional" practices—foreign exchange rationing, multiple exchange rates, foreign exchange licensing systems—to the IMF's traditional approach: reduction of domestic inflation, comprehensive fiscal reform, devaluation if necessary, and simplification of exchange restrictions to remove their tax and subsidy effects. Once these fundamentals are in place the IMF usually urges the Article XIV country to commit itself to Article VIII status.[42]

---

35. See, for example, India and Article VIII, 11 July 1955, S424, Transitional Arrangements, Article VIII Country Studies (Washington, D.C.: IMF Archives).

36. See Edwards 1985, 381–82; and Gold 1988, 255.

37. Edwards 1985, 391. Surrender requirements are not prohibited, because surrender in itself is not considered to be an impediment to the making of payments. Gold 1984a, 813.

38. Edwards 1985, 382. A very comprehensive system of exchange controls might prohibit residents to transfer the state's currency to nonresidents except with the state's permission on a case-by-case basis, or prohibit residents to hold foreign currencies except with the state's permission.

39. Art. XIV, sec. 2. An Art. XIV country can also adapt its restrictions without the need for IMF approval. But an Art. XIV country cannot introduce new restrictions without approval, adapt multiple currency practices without IMF approval, nor maintain restrictions that the member cannot justify as necessary for balance-of-payments reasons. See Horsefield and De Vries 1969, 1:248–59.

40. Art. XIV, sec. 2.

41. Art. XIV, sec. 3.

42. Ideally, the IMF wants the removal of restrictions to coincide with the assumption of Art. VIII obligations, though it has recognized that this might not always be possible and that waiting for the complete removal of every last restriction would only serve to delay the making of such a commitment.

Legal Commitment: Expectations and Evidence

But why should a government voluntarily assume Article VIII obligations? And why should it continue to comply with them? After all, the articles specify neither a time period nor a set of criteria for ending the transitional period.[43] And although the IMF encourages countries they believe are in a position to do so to make an Article VIII commitment, the IMF does not provide direct positive or negative incentives for doing so.[44] Nor does it directly "enforce" these obligations.[45] It does publish data on states' policies from which one can infer compliance (see the data appendix). The executive board can also "approve" restrictions (or not) and has done so as an accompaniment to adjustment programs it is supporting. But the consequences of nonapproval are questionable, since the board does not generally make its decisions public.[46] The executive board can declare a member ineligible to use the IMF's resources if the member "fails to fulfill any of its obligations" under the articles,[47] and noncompliance sometimes does interrupt drawings under standby and extended arrangements.[48] But, in fact, the IMF has used these formal remedies very sparingly. Noncompliers rarely have to worry about retaliation directly from the IMF, since members that vote for some kind of punishment may be concerned about drawing a retaliatory

See Article VIII and Article XIV, memo prepared by Irving S. Friedman, Exchange Restrictions Department, 24 May 1955, S424, Transitional Arrangements, Art. VIII and XIV, September 1954–55, (IMF Archives). In a few cases, developing countries that were not in an especially strong position to accept Art. VIII had no restrictions in place, and the IMF urged them to go ahead and commit, since they had nothing to "grandfather" under Art. XIV. See Haiti, memo from H. Merle Cochran to Irving S. Friedman, 30 October 1953, C/Haiti/424.1, Trans. Arrange., Members' Intent to Use (IMF Archives); and Letter, Ivar Rooth, M.D., to Jose Garcia Ayber, Governor of the Central Bank of the Dominican Republic, 1 August 1953, C/Dominican Republic/424.1, Trans. Arrange., Members' Intent to Use (IMF Archives). These countries often turn out to be long-term noncompliers.

43. Horsefield and De Vries 1969, 2:225. The IMF staff discussed on various occasions the imposition of time limits for the removal of restrictions and the unification of exchange rates, but rejected them as impractical. Article VIII and Article XIV, memo prepared by Irving S. Friedman, 24 May 1955, S 424, Trans. Arrange. (IMF Archives). There were also debates over the IMF's legal authority to declare an end to the transitional period. Furthermore, there were debates in the early period about exactly what "transitional" referred to. Extract, Executive Board Informal Session 54/2, 19 November 1954, S424, Trans. Arrange. (IMF Archives).

44. However, sometimes countries in fairly tenuous balance-of-payments positions who were willing to accept Art. VIII obligations were provided standby arrangements. For example, see Costa Rica (1965), Executive Board Minutes, EBM/65/7, 29 January 1965, C/Costa Rica/424.1, Trans. Arrange., Members' Intent to Use (IMF Archives).

45. In 1948, the executive board explicitly disapproved France's multiple exchange-rate practice and declared France ineligible to use IMF resources, invoking Art. IV, sec. 6 sanctions. The sanction failed to induce France to adopt a unitary rate. The use of sanctions was perceived as a failure and never invoked again. Dam 1982, 132.

46. Although the board is not barred from publishing reports that communicate the board's views, doing so requires a two-thirds majority of the total voting power to make this decision. Gold 1979, 153.

47. Art. XV, sec. 2 (a).

48. According to Gold, "All standby arrangements include a uniform term on measures that directly or indirectly affect exchange rates. Under this term a member is precluded from making purchases under an arrangement if at any time during the period of the arrangement the member: 'i. imposes [or intensifies] restrictions on payments and transfers for current international transactions, or ii. introduces [or modifies] multiple currency practices, or iii. concludes bilateral payments agreements which are inconsistent with Art. VIII, or iv. imposes [or intensifies] import restrictions for balance of payments reasons.' " Gold 1988, 466.

vote in the future. The IMF is much more likely to use persuasion than to apply a remedy for continued noncompliance.[49]

Hypotheses about why countries commit and whether they comply relate to the function that international legal commitments play in international monetary relations. I have argued that the shift to legalization in the postwar regime was an effort to lend credibility to various monetary policy commitments that were shattered after World War I. Governments commit themselves in order to send a costly signal to market actors as well as other governments that they plan to maintain a stable, open, and nondiscriminatory stance. A legal commitment helps make this signal more credible. It does this through many of the mechanisms Abbott and Snidal outline in their paper. An Article VIII commitment is more costly to breach than are other kinds of policies. For one, breaching a commitment has consequences in domestic courts in cases in which contract performance is contested. Exchange contracts that reflect illegal or unapproved restrictions are required by the articles to be unenforceable in the courts of any member state.[50] This should, in theory at any rate, create disincentives to make exchange contracts with private or public entities that operate under national rules that do not comply with international obligations.[51]

More important, however, is the signal that an Article VIII commitment sends to markets. It indicates a serious intention not to interfere in free exchange and thus to protect property rights of those engaged in international transactions.[52] It is a potentially costly signal to send, since noncompliance could be expected to involve domestic political costs. Recall that the proscription of current account restrictions amounts to a right of access to foreign exchange to nationals. Abrogation, then, amounts to the denial of an expected right of a domestic constituency, which is likely to raise criticisms by affected groups. Of course for a signal to be credible, there must be a good possibility that it will be complied with. That is why almost every country considering a move to Article VIII status has tried to assure markets and the IMF staff that they are in a tenable balance-of-payments position.[53]

---

49. Gold 1979, 185

50. Art. VIII, sec. 2, para. (b). This provision was originally designed to support the par value system; in particular to assuage the United Kingdom that New York would not become a significant black market for discounted sterling the value of which the United Kingdom was unable to defend through gold sales. Gold 1989, 73. It was originally placed alongside the exchange-rate provisions (Art. IV). According to Gold, "If a contract is unenforceable as a result of the provision, a court may not decree performance of the contract or give damages for nonperformance. . . . The provision establishes a defense rather than a condition for the institution of proceedings." Gold 1989, 90.

51. In practice, many domestic courts have been reluctant to refuse to enforce such contracts, especially when the interests of national firms or major financial institutions are involved. Gold 1989, 6–7.

52. Archival materials thoroughly support such an interpretation. To cite two examples among many, executive board members, in discussing Argentina's acceptance, "thought that Article VIII status would add substantially to the domestic and external confidence in the intentions of the authorities." Argentina— Acceptance of Article VIII, sections 2, 3, and 4, EMB/68/122, 14 August 1968 (IMF Archives). Executive board members, in discussing Costa Rica's acceptance, noted, "The move to Article VIII status was further proof of its determination to maintain a liberal payments system." Costa Rica (1965), EBM/65/7, 29 January 1965, Trans. Arrange., Members' Intent to Use (IMF Archives).

53. Thus, "it may be assumed that it is countries with relatively strong balance of payments positions that would most likely feel able to assume Article VIII status." Article VIII and Article XIV, memo prepared by Irving S. Friedman, 24 May 1955, p. 5, S424, Trans. Arrange. (IMF Archives).

Thus our first hypothesis is that the decision to commit is tied to expectations regarding the ability to comply in the future.[54] The ability to comply is necessary to making a credible commitment. Accordingly, the commitment is likely to be useful only to those countries with a good chance of complying. Countries with economies that are vulnerable to highly volatile swings in their external position are likely to face future conditions in which current account restrictions provide a handy policy instrument in the short run. Since balance-of-payments problems are the main reason governments interfere with the current account in the first place, it is reasonable to expect that external economic pressure or excessive demands for external payments could discourage governments from making an Article VIII commitment. And why should they? Markets are not likely to respond positively when the commitment is incredible. Hence our first hypothesis: susceptibility to balance-of-payments pressures will make a government less likely to accept Article VIII obligations.

Furthermore, it is likely that one influence on the decision to accept Article VIII status is that others are doing so. If making a legal commitment is a way to credibly commitment in a competitive economic environment, then following the lead of one's major competitors may be necessary. A country's firms may find themselves at a competitive disadvantage in international transactions if competitors make commitments to refrain from foreign exchange restrictions while the home government does not. The risk of government interference could result in a premium charged by foreign firms on transactions with residents. For competitive reasons, a government might want to avoid such a premium and follow the suit of its major economic competitors. In addition, international socialization toward accepted standards of behavior, accelerated by the growing dominance of neoliberal economic ideas touted by the IMF itself, may reinforce expectations of openness.[55]

Governments therefore face something of a dilemma: there are costs to being the first to liberalize (including the possibility of direct balance-of-payments pressures), but there are also costs to lagging too far behind international or regional norms. Governments have keenly felt this dilemma in formulating their policies regarding Article VIII. The major Western European countries, for example, assumed Article VIII obligations in unison, since "None of the six countries wanted to move in advance of the other, and all of them preferred to come under Article VIII at the same time as the United Kingdom."[56] A similar decision was made by the African franc

---

54. Downs and Rocke have used this insight to develop an endogenous explanation of treaty commitments based on uncertainty over future compliance. Downs and Rocke 1995.

55. External normative influences are important in the work of Keck and Sikkink 1998; Legro 1997; Fisher 1981; Kratochwil 1989; and Finnemore 1996. Margaret Levi, in her study of compliance with conscription efforts, combines both rational and normative elements in describing a form of "contingent consent" in which some compliance is "the result of . . . incentives, but at least some compliance expresses a confirmation in the rightness of policies." Levi 1997, 18.

56. Implementation of Article XIV and Article VIII Decision, minutes of staff visit to the United Kingdom, 22 July 1960, S424, Trans. Arrange., Move to Article VIII Mission, minutes of meetings (IMF Archives). The IMF archives contain ample evidence that no European power wanted to pay the potential costs of being the first mover, yet none wanted to lag a decision by other countries in the region. Thus, "The French policy with regards to restrictions depends on the policy followed by other European countries, especially Great Britain. It might even be said in large measure it is conditioned by that policy."

zone countries three and a half decades later. When Argentina committed to Article VIII, executive board members indicated that they were "not surprised to see one more Latin American country assuming the obligation," since most of the other Article VIII countries were from Latin America. Board members predicted that "now that Argentina had assumed the obligations of Article VIII perhaps Brazil would also do the same soon and Chile would follow."[57] In discussions of the timing of Article VIII acceptance with the IMF, Peru's prime minister "agreed Peru should not jump out ahead of the others, but . . . definitely does not want to 'miss the boat.' "[58] These concerns are understandable if legal commitment is viewed as a way to reassure markets in a competitive economic environment. Although there may be few incentives to liberalize first, governments need to be cognizant of the signal they may be sending by refusing to commit, especially when other countries with whom they might compete for capital or trade have done so.

If a legal commitment to Article VIII is a way to improve access to capital and trade by in effect raising the costs of interfering in foreign exchange markets, then we should expect commitment to be influenced by two factors: (1) a basic ability to comply (which is necessary for a credible commitment), and (2) the commitment decisions of other countries (which avoids the costs of being the first to move and reduces the costs of lagging).

We should also consider a set of plausible control variables that could reveal a spurious correlation with these hypothesized relationships. I am not suggesting that a credible commitment is the only reason a government would commit to Article VIII but investigating whether it stands up to a range of plausible alternatives. The first is a straightforward argument based on domestic demands: commitment is likely to be a function of domestic policy demands, just like any other aspect of foreign economic policymaking.[59] Such arguments must consider the source and nature of domestic preferences and the extent to which the political system reflects these preferences. Article VIII provides a right of access to foreign exchange for residents and

---

F. A. G. Keesing, 1 July 1955. S424, Trans. Arrange., Art. VIII Country Studies (IMF Archives). For a similar position by the Netherlands, see Netherlands and Article VIII. 23 June 1955, S424, Trans. Arrange., Art. VIII Country Studies (IMF Archives). On the United Kingdom's unwillingness to move alone, see memo from Rooth to E. M. Bernstein, 20 May 1955, S424, Trans. Arrange., Art. VIII and XIV, Sept. 1954–55 (IMF Archives). On the incentives for a general snowball effect within Europe, see memo from F. A. G. Keesing, 13 May 1955, S424, Trans. Arrange., Art. VIII and XIV, 1954–55 (IMF Archives).

57. Argentina—Acceptance of Article VIII, sections 2, 3, and 4, p. 4, 14 August 1968, EMB/68/122 (IMF Archives).

58. Memo from Jorge del Canto to Per Jacobsson, IMF Managing Director, 23 September 1960, C/Peru/424.1, Trans. Arrange., Members' Intent to Use (IMF Archives). Peru was basically free from all restrictions in 1960, and IMF staff members wondered whether they should be encouraged to assume Art. VIII obligations as soon as possible or wait and go with the Europeans. In a handwritten note in the margins, Per Jacobsson wrote, "No. It would not profit Peru to move first—more advantageous to be 'drawn by movement' with others." Memo from Jorge del Canto to Per Jacobsson, 17 May 1960, C/Peru/424.1 (IMF Archives).

59. The literature linking foreign economic policymaking to domestic political demands is vast. Most of this work concentrates on demands for trade protection. See, for example, Aggarwal, Keohane, and Yoffie 1987; Alt et al. 1996; Destler and Odell 1987; Goodman, Spar, and Yoffie 1996; McKeown 1984; Milner 1988; and Rogowski 1989. For works on financial and monetary policy, see Simmons 1994; and Frieden 1991.

nonresidents, and demands for such a right are likely to be greater in countries where trade is an important part of the national economy. A right of free access to foreign exchange is valuable to importers: it provides a guarantee to foreign firms that the government is not likely to use interference in the foreign exchange market to intervene in international business transactions.[60] It is also likely to be favored by export groups, whom recent research has shown to be concerned with issues of reciprocity and retaliation.[61] For these reasons, economies that depend on trade are likely to be among the most willing to make legal commitments to free and open foreign exchange markets.[62]

The IMF staff, in their discussions of who was ready to commit, clearly recognized the incentives that trade dependence created. Indonesia was deemed unlikely to commit, for example, because "The restrictive system is somewhat peripheral to the broad economic issues in which the public are interested: foreign trade is only 6% of GDP. And non-nationals control the major industries" (jute and tea).[63] On the other hand, when Guyana made the Article VIII commitment, the executive board noted explicitly that "Guyana was one of those very few developing countries in the world whose imports and exports, taken separately, were larger than 50 per cent of GNP, and this necessarily meant that the country was highly vulnerable to swings both in capital and in trading magnitudes." Trade dependence made Guyana a good candidate for Article VIII but also implied a possible need for IMF assistance should liberalization prove destabilizing. A standby arrangement was considered simultaneously.[64]

Furthermore, we might expect that the demand for guaranteed foreign exchange access is most likely to be addressed by a democratic regime. The political organization around this issue area is likely to be that of civil society versus the state: on the one hand, it is difficult to conceive of a private interest that would organize to actively oppose free access to foreign exchange. On the other hand, the concentrated rents go to the government, as the dispenser of limited access to hard currency. If one of the primary characteristics of democracy is the extent to which it empowers civil demands vis-à-vis the state, and if it is also true that these demands are likely to favor those who want free access to foreign exchange, then we should expect democratic governance to be positively associated with the acceptance of Article VIII.

---

60. According to Horsefield and De Vries, for example, "Article VIII status had come to signify over the years either that a country had a sound international balance of payments position, or that if its payments position was threatened, it would avoid the use of exchange restrictions." Horsefield and De Vries 1969, 2:285–86.

61. Gilligan 1997.

62. Relatedly, the IMF staff thought that Art. VIII obligation created the most advantages for countries whose currencies tended to be traded internationally. See the staff discussion contained in Peru—Aspects of Article VIII, C/Peru/424.1, Trans. Arrange., Members' Intent to Use (IMF Archives).

63. Indonesia and Article VIII, 14 July 1955, S424, Trans. Arrange., Art. VIII Country Studies (IMF Archives).

64. Guyana—Acceptance of Obligations of Article VIII, Sections 2, 3, and 4, Initial Par Value, and Stand-by Arrangement, 13 February 1967, EMB/67/10, C/Guyana/424.1, Trans. Arrange., Members' Intent to Use (IMF Archives).

It is also important to control for the institutional incentives provided by the IMF for those who commit. An early inducement for countries to choose Article VIII status was the fact that multilateral surveillance applied only to Article XIV countries until the Second Amendment (revisions to Article IV) extended mandatory surveillance to the entire IMF membership.[65] Prior to 1977, governments willing to announce acceptance of Article VIII obligations could actually avoid multilateral surveillance.[66] Article XIV countries, on the other hand, were subject to wide-ranging, even invasive "consultations," during which the staff broadly reviewed the member's balance-of-payments position. The executive board would then follow up with an official "view" of the member's situation. Thus until 1977, members faced a perverse incentive to accept Article VIII obligations: the commitment gave them the ability to avoid discriminatory and potentially humiliating surveillance and formal board review. We can hypothesize that the acceptance rate was therefore higher, all else being equal, before 1977 than after.

Finally, controlling for time is appropriate in this analysis. One important reason is that countries may have been reluctant to commit to Article VIII in the early years of the IMF because it was unclear just how the executive board would interpret the obligation. Countries clearly did not want to commit and then be surprised that the executive board considered them in breach of their obligation.[67] As time went on, this kind of uncertainty could be expected to wane through approval decisions and executive board clarification.

Our control variables suggest that four other factors might influence commitment: (1) the degree of trade dependence of the economy, (2) whether the country is democratic, (3) whether those who commit are exempt from surveillance, and (4) the passage of time.

Before proceeding to more complicated analyses, it is useful to make a visual inspection of the data. The data set used is a panel of 138 countries. The only criterion for their inclusion was membership in the IMF by 1980. Of these countries, we have time varying and case varying data for 110 countries that have chosen Article VIII status since 1966. Using yearly observations for these countries, it is useful to construct a Kaplan-Meier "survival function" that describes the period of transition prior to making an Article VIII commitment (see Figure 1).[68]

---

65. James 1995, 773, 775.

66. Gold 1983, 474–75. Consultations with Art. VIII countries were established in 1960 but were completely voluntary. Horsefield and De Vries 1969, 2:246–47.

67. For example, the United Kingdom did not want the stigma of a board decision that they maintained an illegal multiple currency practice as a result of what the United Kingdom considered a legitimate way to control capital movements. Implementation of Article XIV and Article VIII Decision, minutes of staff visit to the United Kingdom, 27 July 1960, S424, Trans. Arrange., Move to Art. VIII Mission (IMF Archives). Uncertainty over board interpretation inhibited early commitment. Generally, see Policy Aspects of the Article VIII and Article XIV Problem, 21 October 1954, S424, Trans. Arrange., Art. VIII and XIV, 1954–55 (IMF Archives).

68. The literature usually terms the event of interest a "failure" and the time elapsed until its occurrence as "survival" regardless of the substantive problem modeled. Proponents of international openness and free markets would in this case view "survival" analysis as "transition" analysis, and an Art. VIII commitment as a "success"; those who favor closer government management of markets might agree that the customary appellations are in fact more apt.

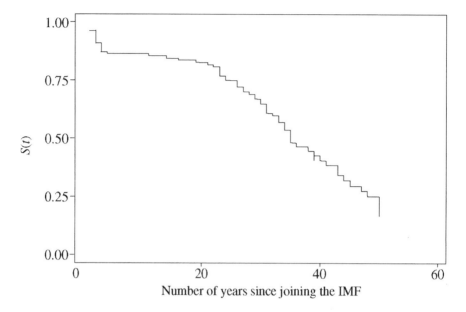

Note: The Kaplan-Meier estimator for maintaining Article XIV status beyond time *t* is the product of the probability of maintaining this status in time *t* and the preceding periods:

$$S(t) = \prod_{j=t0}^{t} \{(nj - dj)/nj\}$$

where *n* represents those cases that neither accepted Article VIII status nor were censored, and *d* represents the number of acceptances during the time period.

	Country-years at risk	Incidence rate	Number of countries	Survival time		
				25%	50%	75%
Total	3,125	.01999	110	24	35	50

FIGURE 1. *The Kaplan-Meier survival function: Duration of Article XIV status over time*

One fact becomes obvious from this visual representation of the data: the "transitional" regime could in fact last a long period of time for a number of countries. The Kaplan-Meier function estimates about a 25 percent chance of accepting Article VIII status in the first twenty-four years of IMF membership, a 50 percent chance within thirty-five years, and about a 75 percent chance after fifty years. Clearly, many countries have been in no rush to commit legally to keeping their current account free from restrictions.

What affects the rate at which governments make the commitment? Table 1 presents the findings of the Cox proportional hazard estimation for a combination of variables discussed earlier. (Note that ratios of more than 1 indicate an increase in the rate of Article VIII acceptance, and ratios of less than 1 indicate a reduction in the rate of acceptance. Thus the null hypothesis is that the hazard ratio is not significantly different from 1.) Consider first the ability to comply, which I argue is essential for a credible commitment. My expectation is that countries are more unlikely to make Article VIII obligations when their payments are volatile and they tend toward deficit. In the models developed here, balance-of-payments levels (the average balance of payments for the period as a whole) are interacted with balance-of-payments volatility.[69] This specification is meant to distinguish volatility effects conditional on whether the balance-of-payments position is relatively strong or weak. The results displayed in Table 1 show that, as anticipated, balance-of-payments volatility reduces the proportional hazard rate substantially. In model 3, it reduces the rate by (1 −.390), or .610, when mean deficits are equal to zero. Substantively, volatility is very likely to reduce the rate at which countries accept Article VIII obligations. Also as expected, countries that have better balance-of-payments positions are more likely to accept Article VIII obligations (36.4 percent more likely for every percentage point of balance of payments as a proportion of gross domestic product, GDP, according to model 3). Interestingly, the negative effects of volatility may be slightly greater in countries with better payments positions on average, as indicated by the statistically significant but substantively small impact of the interaction term. These findings about the balance of payments support the hypothesis that countries that are more capable of compliance are more likely to commit. The commitment is, in turn, more likely to be credible.

The next two variables, "universality" and "regional norm," are meant to test the proposition that taking on an obligation is likely to be contingent on similar actions by others. "Universality" is the proportion of all IMF members who have accepted Article VIII status, and "regional norm" is the proportion of countries within each subregion (as defined by the World Bank) that have done so. (All variable measures and sources are discussed in the data appendix.) Both of these variables have a large and positive influence on the acceptance rate. According to model 3, for example, every 1 percent increase in the proportion of IMF members accepting Article VIII increases the likelihood of acceptance by 38.5 percent. Similarly, a 1 percent increase in the regional proportion of Article VIII adherents increases a country's likelihood of acceptance by 4.1 percent. This translates into a 49 percent increase for every 10 percent increase in regional accession.[70] Clearly, as the number of countries who accept Article VIII increases, there is a greatly increased chance that an uncommitted government will do so. Note that this impact is significant even if we control for time ("year" in model 4). We can be fairly confident, then, that the universality and regional norms variables evaluated here do not simply reflect the fact that adherents

---

69. Reserve levels and volatility, as well as terms of trade volatility, were also analyzed, but because the results were insignificant they are not reported here.
70. Which is calculated by raising the estimated hazard ratio to the tenth power.

TABLE 1. *Influences on the rate of Article VIII acceptance*

	Rate of Article VIII acceptance (hazard ratios)			
	Model 1	*Model 2*	*Model 3*	*Model 4*
Average balance of payments	—	—	1.364**	1.352**
			(.145)	(.180)
Balance-of-payments volatility	—	—	.390**	.400*
			(.170)	(.205)
Balance-of-payments (volatility*mean)	—	—	.887**	.891**
			(.035)	(.046)
Universality	1.073***	1.330***	1.385***	1.553***
	(.015)	(.092)	(.111)	(.386)
Regional norm	1.030***	1.043***	1.045***	1.040***
	(.005)	(.009)	(.010)	(.010)
Surveillance	.608	.047***	.041***	.061**
	(.289)	(.042)	(.047)	(.087)
Openness	1.009***	1.015***	1.018***	1.018***
	(.003)	(.003)	(.004)	(.005)
Democracy	—	1.078*	1.081*	1.079*
		(.050)	(.044)	(.044)
Year	—	—	—	.904
				(.199)
N	1,988	1,757	1,754	1,754
Time "at risk"	2,517.97	2,296.98	2,294.98	2,294.98
Log likelihood	−182.45	−93.39	−90.15	−89.96
χ^2	132.12	75.63	66.09	74.76
Prob. $> \chi^2$	0.00	0.00	0.00	0.00

Note: Table shows estimated hazard rates using a Cox proportionate hazard model with time varying covariates. Robust standard errors are in parentheses.
   ***$p > |Z| = .01$.
   **$p > |Z| = .05$.
   *$p > |Z| = .10$.

increase over time. What most influences the acceptance rate is not time, but the proportion of adherents. This finding is consistent with the incentives of the competitive economic environment in which governments declare their legal adherence to Article VIII.

Domestic political demands that flow from trade openness also have an important impact on the acceptance rate. Openness to the international trade system raises the proportional hazard rate significantly. According to model 3, every one point increase in imports plus exports as a proportion of GDP increases the likelihood of Article VIII acceptance by 1.8 percent. This could account for a 67 percent difference in acceptance probability for countries with trade profiles as different as, say, Malaysia (imports plus exports totaling approximately 80 percent of GDP for the period under consideration) and the Philippines (where the corresponding figure is about 50 percent).[71] Certainly, the demands of importers and exporters have much to do with the government's willingness to commit. Interestingly, whether or not a country was democratic only marginally affected the decision, if at all. In the improbable event that a country transformed itself from a complete nondemocracy to a highly democratic society, the possible impact on the probability of accepting Article VIII would only be about 19 percent. Our confidence in this effect barely reaches standard levels of significance, however.[72]

There is also evidence that institutional incentives have made a big difference in Article VIII acceptance. "Surveillance" here is a dummy variable that takes on a value of zero prior to 1977 and 1 thereafter. Once surveillance has been extended to all countries—not just those availing themselves of the Article XIV transitional regime—the impact has been to reduce drastically the probability of accepting Article VIII, as we expected, though our confidence in this result is reduced somewhat by the exclusion of democracy as an independent explanation. The hazard ratio indicates that once the surveillance advantage of Article VIII states was removed, countries were anywhere from 40 percent to as much as 96 percent less likely to accept Article VIII status, other conditions held constant. The end of discriminatory surveillance seems to have mattered greatly to governments' willingness to commit. On the other hand, the simple passage of time had little effect. This could be because the uncertainty regarding obligations that motivated the inclusion of this variable was highly concentrated in the very earliest years of the IMF. There is little reason to believe that time itself accounts for changes in the rate of commitment.

The evidence suggests that governments are more likely to commit to Article VIII status when the commitment is credible and when other countries, especially countries in their own region, have done so as well. Although other factors influence the decision to commit, these results are consistent with the use of legal commitments as a signal to markets of a serious intent to maintain open and nondiscriminatory foreign exchange markets.

Who Complies? Explaining the Compliance Decision

Members of the IMF are legally required to comply with their commitments to keep the current account free from restrictions and to maintain unified exchange rates, and twenty-six members in our sample have perfect compliance records on both counts.[73] However, a number of Article VIII countries have far from a perfect record (see Tables 2 and 3). Most of the long-term noncompliers are concentrated in Latin

---

71. Calculated in this case by raising the estimated hazard ratio to the twenty-ninth power.
72. Subtracting the polity scores on autocracy from those on democracy, yielding a scale from –10 to 10, does not significantly alter this general conclusion.
73. Among the countries who were members of the IMF in 1980, as of 1997, Bahrain, Canada, Denmark, Djibouti, Finland, Gambia, Germany, Indonesia, Lebanon, Malaysia, Mauritius, New Zealand, Norway, Panama, Portugal, Qatar, Saudi Arabia, Seychelles, Spain, Sweden, Switzerland, Thailand, Trinidad and Tobago, United Arab Emirates, United States, and Yemen Arab Republic all had perfect records of compliance with their Art. VIII status.

TABLE 2. *Article VIII noncompliers, restrictions on current account (rates and years of noncompliance, 1967–95)*

Country	Rate of noncompliance (1967–95)	Years committed (1967–95)[a]	Dates of restrictions
Dominican Republic	1.000	29	1967–95
El Salvador	.931	29	1967–93
Jamaica	.862	29	1968–69, 1973–95
Guyana	.828	29	1967, 1971–93
Iceland	.750	12	1984–92
Chile	.722	18	1983–95
South Africa	.682	22	1979–93
Argentina	.630	27	1972–77, 1983–93
Fiji	.600	5	1989–92
Costa Rica	.586	29	1972–73, 1975, 1982–95
Guatemala	.552	29	1967–73, 1981–89
Peru	.552	29	1971–78, 1985–92
Nicaragua	.517	29	1979–93
Ecuador	.440	25	1983–93
Honduras	.414	29	1982–93
St. Lucia	.400	15	1981–86
St. Vincent	.357	14	1982–86
Morocco	.333	3	1993
Italy	.276	29	1975–82
Austria	.241	29	1967–73
Bolivia	.179	28	1982–86
Mexico	.172	29	1983–87
France	.138	29	1969–71, 1983
Haiti	.138	29	1968–71
Japan	.107	28	1968–70

Source: IMF, various years, *Exchange Arrangements and Restrictions.*

Note: Noncompliers are defined as countries that have declared themselves obligated by Article VIII but have implemented restrictions on current account. These are in apparent contravention of Article VIII, section 2(a), but no effort is made here to distinguish between "approved" and "unapproved" restrictions.

[a]Countries with fewer than two years of observations have been omitted.

America, though liberalization increased markedly in this region in the mid-to-late 1990s. Although data limitations prevent the inclusion of very recent years, almost all of the noncompliance associated with the global financial crisis of 1996–97 elicited foreign exchange restrictions rather than the implementation of multiple exchange rates. A few Article VIII countries have implemented one measure inconsistent with their obligations but not the other. Belgium, Hong Kong, and the Netherlands, for example, have in the past implemented multiple exchange rate systems but not restrictions on current account, whereas Austria, Korea, Singapore, and Japan have made the opposite choice.

What explains this variance among countries that chose to obligate themselves to openness? The strategy in this section is to examine only cases in which governments

TABLE 3. *Article VIII noncompliers, multiple exchange-rate systems (rates and years of noncompliance, 1967–95)*

Country	Rate of noncompliance (1967–95)	Years committed (1967–95)[a]	Dates of multiple exchange rates
Bahamas	1.000	24	1974–97
Costa Rica	.81	31	1967–91
Belgium/Luxembourg	.77	31	1967–90
Peru	.77	31	1968–91
Chile	.75	20	1983–97
Dominican Republic	.68	31	1973–91, 1996–97
Nicaragua	.68	31	1967–74, 1979–90
Venezuela	.67	21	1977–90
Argentina	.59	29	1972–77, 1982–92
South Africa	.54	24	1977–82, 1986–92
Bolivia	.43	30	1967, 1983, 1985–95
United Kingdom	.42	31	1967–79
Guyana	.39	31	1967–68, 1984–85, 1987–91, 1993–95
Ireland	.39	31	1967–78
El Salvador	.32	31	1982–91
Guatemala	.32	31	1985–94
Honduras	.32	31	1986–93, 1996–97
Jamaica	.29	31	1967–68, 1978–79, 1987–91
Mexico	.29	31	1983–91
Italy	.26	31	1973–74, 1976–78, 1980–82
France	.10	31	1972–74
Netherlands	.10	31	1972–74
Ecuador	.07	27	1972–73
Haiti	.06	31	1991–92
Hong Kong	.06	31	1970–71
Kuwait	.06	31	1970–71
Australia	.03	31	1968
Suriname	.03	31	1994

Source: IMF, various years, *Exchange Arrangements and Restrictions.*

Note: Noncompliers are defined as countries that have declared themselves obligated by Article VIII but have some form of multiple exchange-rate system. These are in apparent contravention of Article VIII, section 2(a), but no effort is made here to distinguish between "approved" and "unapproved" systems.

[a]Countries with fewer than two years of observations have been omitted.

have committed to Article VIII and then to explain the decision nevertheless to implement restrictions on current account or multiple exchange rate regimes.[74] The first and most obvious explanation for noncompliance is unexpected economic pressures that make the maintenance of an open current account and unified exchange rates

74. This is presented as a priori evidence of noncompliance, even though at this point I do not examine the technical question as to whether or not the executive board of the IMF has approved of the restrictions in place, thus rendering them "legal" temporarily.

very difficult. Certainly economic conditions are likely to have influenced Latin American noncompliance in the 1980s. Thus in the tests that follow I control for the changes in economic growth, current account balance, and current account volatility, all standardized over GDP.

If legalization is an attempt to make a commitment more credible, then governments should resist violating international law because they want to preserve their reputations as law abiding. The incentive for such a reputation in the monetary area is clear: governments want to convince markets that they provide a desirable venue for international trade and investment. Investors and suppliers seeking opportunities for international commerce should prefer to do business with firms in countries that provide a more certain legal framework with respect to the nondiscriminatory fulfillment of international contracts. Although there is no central enforcement of this obligation, the desire to avoid reputational costs should motivate compliance.

The question is, when will reputational costs have their greatest impact? My first hypothesis is that costs are greatest when a violator is an outlier among comparable countries. That is, rule violation is most costly when comparable countries manage to continue to comply. On the one hand, the more competitors are willing to comply, the greater the pressure for any one country to comply, even in the face of economic pressure to protect the national economy through restrictions or multiple exchange rates. On the other hand, if it is common for Article VIII countries in the region to disregard their commitment, this should increase the probability that any given country in that region will decide against compliance. Rampant violation makes it difficult for markets to single out any one violator for "punishment." Thus, we should expect compliance to be positively influenced by what other countries choose to do.

Consider next characteristics of the domestic polity itself. Several analysts have implied that compliance with international legal commitments is much more prevalent among liberal democracies, pointing to the constraining influence exercised by domestic groups who may have interests in or a preference for compliant behavior.[75] In this view participatory politics might put pressure on the government to comply, especially in the case where noncompliance involves curtailing the rights of residents to foreign exchange (it is less clear how this argument relates to the choice to implement or maintain a unified exchange-rate system). Others have argued that the most important characteristic of liberal democracy when it comes to international compliance is its strong domestic commitment to the rule of law. There are many variants of the argument—from Anne-Marie Slaughter's view that independent judiciaries in liberal democracies seem to share some of the same substantive approaches to law to a more general argument that domestic systems that value rule-based decision making and dispute resolution are also likely to respect rules internationally.[76] In essence, these are affinity arguments: they seem to suggest that domestic norms regarding limited government, respect for judicial processes, and regard for constitutional con-

---

75. See Young 1979; and Schachter 1991. See also Moravcsik 1997.
76. Slaughter 1995a. This captures the flavor of some of the democratic peace literature, for example, Doyle 1986; Dixon 1993; and Raymond 1994.

straints[77] "carry over" into the realm of international politics. They rest on an intuitively appealing assumption that policymakers and lawmakers are not able to park their normative perspectives at the water's edge.[78]

There are other reasons, however, to expect the rule of law to be associated with Article VIII compliance. Countries respecting the rule of law have a strong positive reputation for maintaining a stable framework for property rights. Markets expect them to maintain their commitments, and to undermine this expectation would prove costly. Countries that score low with respect to the rule of law do not have much to lose by noncompliance; erratic behavior is hardly surprising to investors and traders. I use an indicator for the rule of law that is especially appropriate to test the market's assessment of the reputation for rule of law: a six-point scale published by a political risk analysis firm expressly to assess the security of investments.[79] The scale represents the willingness of citizens peacefully to implement law and adjudicate disputes using established institutions. Higher scores on this six-point measure indicate the presence of such institutional characteristics as a strong court system, sound political institutions, and provisions for orderly succession. Low scores reflect an increased use of extra-legal activities in response to conflict and to settle disputes.

Since I have argued that the purpose of legalization is to make more credible monetary commits, that compliance is market enforced, and that markets prefer certainty in the legal framework, the comparison between the participatory characteristics of democracy and rule of law regimes should be especially telling. We have little reason to expect that democracy alone provides the stability that economic agents desire; on the contrary, popular participation along with weak guarantees for fair enforcement of property rights can endanger these rights. Clearly, these two variables are positively correlated (Pearson correlation $=.265$), but they are certainly conceptually distinct and may have very different effects on the decision to comply with Article VIII obligations. Thus we are able directly to compare two regime characteristics that are often conflated: democracy with its participatory dimensions on the one hand and the rule of law with its emphasis on procedural certainty on the other. Monetary compliance should therefore be conditioned by (1) compliance by other countries in the region, and (2) a country's reputation for respecting the rule of law. Participatory democracy is expected to have no effect.

The central explanation for compliance should revolve around these reputational factors. Still, it is important to control for other factors that could influence the compliance decision. Consistent with the reputational argument, it may be more costly for a country that is highly dependent on world trade to violate Article VIII. Certainly, retaliation would be more costly to nationals of such a country. Second, it is plausible that countries defending a fixed exchange rate might find it more difficult to maintain Article VIII obligations; countries that had shifted to more flexible regimes

77. "International law is not unlike constitutional law in that it imposes legal obligations on a government that in theory the government is not free to ignore or change." Fisher 1981, 30. Constitutional constraints most often rest on their shared normative acceptance, rather than on the certainty of their physical enforcement, providing another possible parallel to the international setting.
78. See Risse-Kappen 1995b; and Lumsdaine 1993.
79. See Knack and Keefer 1995, 225.

would not be under the same pressure to conserve foreign exchange for purposes of defending the currency's peg.[80] Third, use of the IMF's resources could provide an incentive to comply. Pressure from the IMF should be especially strong when countries are in need of a loan. Fourth, it may be the case that compliance is enhanced by the nesting of the Article VIII regime within a broader regime of free trade. Membership in the General Agreement on Tariffs and Trade (GATT) might encourage a country to maintain free and nondiscriminatory foreign exchange markets.[81] Finally, compliance may simply become easier with the passage of time. Thus the following control variables provide a small sample of other factors that could encourage compliance: (1) positive economic conditions, (2) a high degree of trade dependence, (3) flexible exchange rates, (4) use of IMF resources, (5) membership in the GATT, and (6) the passage of time.

In this case the compliance decision is modeled using logistical regression (logit), with the dependent variable taking on a value of 1 for the presence of restrictions or multiple exchange rates and zero for the absence of both. (Since we are analyzing only Article VIII countries, each instance of restrictions or multiple-rate systems is also a case of apparent noncompliance.) Because the data consist of observations across countries and over time, with a strong probability of temporal dependence among observations, a logit specification is used that takes explicit account of the nonindependence of observations.[82] The results are reported in Table 4.

One of the most important findings of this analysis is, again, the clustering of compliance behavior within regions. Article VIII countries are much more likely to put illegal restrictions on current account or use illegal multiple exchange-rate regimes if other countries in the region are doing so. The impact of regional behavior is substantial: the difference between a region with no violators compared to one with nearly all violators increased the probability of noncompliance by 79 percent. Could this be the result of common economic pressures sweeping the region? This explanation cannot be completely ruled out, but it is rendered less likely by the range of economic variables included in the specification. The inclusion of various measures of current account difficulty and GDP growth failed to wash out apparent regional convergence. Compliance decisions are apparently not being made on the basis of

---

80. The board clearly recognized this was the case: "It was quite evident that flexible rates made it easier for a country to eliminate payment and trade restrictions. This made the fact that several European countries were now accepting the obligations of Art. VIII on the basis of a fixed parity all the more significant." Peru's currency was still fluctuating. Executive board minutes, 8 February 1961, EBM/61/4., p. 15, C/Peru/424.1, Trans. Arrange., Members' Intent to Use (IMF Archives).

81. Indeed, the date of GATT's entry into force was conditioned on the acceptance of Art. VIII, sec. 2, 3, and 4 obligations by the contracting parties to the GATT. According to a memo circulated among the staff of the IMF, "The date of entry into force of the revised [GATT] rules concerning discrimination and quantitative restrictions is linked specifically to the date at which the obligations of Article VIII, Sections 2, 3, and 4 of the Fund Agreement become applicable to such contracting parties as are members of the Fund, the combined foreign trade of which constitutes at least 50 per cent of the aggregate foreign trade of all contracting parties." Article VIII and Article XIV, memo prepared by Irving S. Friedman, 24 May 1955 (IMF Archives).

82. Beck, Katz, and Tucker 1998. A counter vector was employed using the STATA routine made available on Richard Tucker's Web site at <http://www.fas.harvard.edu/~rtucker/papers/grouped/grouped3.html>. Three cubic splines were included in the analysis but are not reported here.

TABLE 4. *Influences on the decision to violate Article VIII obligations*

Explanatory variables	Model 1	Model 2	Model 3	Model 4
Constant	−17.8***	−17.13***	−17.3***	−17.9***
	(4.75)	(4.88)	(4.89)	(4.77)
Rule of law	−.340***	−.346***	−.272**	−.333***
	(.020)	(.119)	(.133)	(.120)
Democracy	.017*	.016	.018*	.018*
	(.010)	(.010)	(.010)	(.010)
Regional noncompliance	5.57***	5.47***	5.21***	5.45***
	(.554)	(.540)	(.567)	(.553)
Balance of payments/GDP $(t - 1)$	−.030**	−.031**	−.029**	−.030**
	(.013)	(.013)	(.013)	(.012)
Balance-of-payments volatility	.753***	.794***	.793***	.716***
	(.257)	(.262)	(.276)	(.266)
Change in GDP	−.055*	−.057*	−.056*	−.055*
	(.032)	(.032)	(.033)	(.031)
Openness	−.014***	−.014***	−.014***	−.014***
	(.003)	(.003)	(.003)	(.003)
Year	.198***	.188***	.186***	.203***
	(.051)	(.053)	(.052)	(.052)
Flexible exchange rates	—	.270	—	—
		(.404)		
Use of fund resources	—		.601	—
			(.404)	
GATT member		—	—	−.377
				(.334)
N	593	593	593	593
Wald χ^2	(11)	(12)	(12)	(12)
	207.63	207.04	215.52	220.2
Prob. $> \chi^2$	0.000	0.000	0.000	0.000
Log likelihood	−137.7	−137.4	−136.6	−137.3

Note: The dependent variable is an apparent Article VIII violation, either a restriction on current account or multiple exchange-rate system. This analysis covers Article VIII countries only. Logit coefficients are reported with correction for nonindependence of observations. Robust standard errors are in parentheses. Estimation includes three cubic splines, which are not reported here.

***$p > |Z| = .01$.
**$p > |Z| = .05$.
*$p > |Z| = .10$.

economic conditions alone, but with an eye to standards of regional behavior. The most obvious reason for this concern would be reputational consequences in a competitive international economic environment.

The domestic political variables tell an interesting story about regime characteristics. In contrast to theories of international behavior that concentrate on the law consciousness of democracies, the evidence presented here suggests that, in this set of countries, democracy may be associated with a greater tendency to violate the country's international monetary obligations.[83] Substantive interpretation of the coef-

---

83. This conclusion is not significantly altered by the use of the combined democracy-autocracy variable.

ficients reveals a highly asymmetrical impact; however, a move from zero to 5 on the democracy scale increases the chances of violating a commitment by only 2.89 percent, whereas a move from 5 to 10 on that scale increases the probability of violating by 10.8 percent. Why this might be so is not difficult to understand. A rich literature in political economy suggests that a potential cost of democracy is that the public does not always fully anticipate the consequences of its aggregate demands. For example, if democracies allow for macroeconomic policies that exhibit an inflationary bias,[84] participatory politics may complicate the international compliance problem. However, a strong domestic commitment to the rule of law contributed positively to Article VIII compliance. Again, the impact is somewhat asymmetrical for values on the explanatory variable. A move from 1 to 3 on the six-point rule-of-law scale reduced the probability of violating Article VIII by 17.7 percent, whereas a move from 4 to 6 reduced the probability of violating by about 4 percent. The effect of the rule of law is understandable in light of the argument about uncertainty and reputation: governments that have invested heavily in a reputation for respecting the rule of law—one aspect of which is protecting property rights—have a lot to lose by reneging on their international obligations.

None of the control variables affects these findings. As anticipated, a weakening balance of payments, as well as higher volatility, contributes to violation, as does a worsening business cycle. Governments of more open economies work hard to abide by their obligation of policy openness, consistent with our expectation. Surprisingly, compliance with these obligations does not improve over time; if anything, violations worsen over the years when other variables in the model are held constant. Flexible exchange rates, GATT membership, and the use of IMF resources may be important institutional contexts for international economic relations, but they do not systematically affect the compliance decision.

Conclusions

The legalization of some central aspects of the international monetary regime after World War II allows us to examine the conditions under which law can influence the behavior of governments in the choice of their international monetary policies. Historically, this policy area has been devoid of international legal rules. The classical gold standard did not depend on international legal commitments for its reputed stability. "Soft" international legal commitments began to develop only in the interwar years, largely in response to markets' shattered confidence in the ability of governments to maintain the commitments they had made unilaterally in the previous period. Driven by the need to limit the externalization of macroeconomic adjustment costs, some governments sought international commitments as a way to enhance certainty and reassure markets. However, these commitments were in the softest

---

84. See the review of this literature in Keech 1995.

possible form and did little to constrain behavior or encourage the confidence of economic agents.

The Bretton Woods agreement brought to an end the unbridled national legal sovereignty over monetary affairs. They hardly represent the triumph of legalization over market forces, however, as attested to by the breakdown of the original legal obligation to defend a par value system. Legal obligations cannot stifle market forces: capital mobility has made fixed rates very nearly unmanageable, treaty arrangements to the contrary notwithstanding. The end of the legal obligation to defend pegged rates is a clear reminder that legalization cannot be viewed in teleological terms. Obligations that increasingly frustrate major players as market conditions change are not likely to remain obligations for long.

Members of the IMF still have legal obligations regarding the conduct of their monetary policy. In fact, a growing number of members voluntarily assume these obligations every year. Article VIII Section 2(a) obligates members to keep their current accounts free from restrictions and proscribes the use of multiple exchange-rate systems. Conveniently, the IMF then publishes information on whether countries have imposed what the staff believes constitute restrictions or multiple rate systems. Thus it has been possible in this case to establish a precise account of, first, the rate of commitment and, second, the rate of compliance with international monetary law by looking at states' decisions to accept the obligations of nondiscriminatory current account convertibility and their subsequent behavior. My strategy in this article has been to model the factors contributing to the rate of Article VIII acceptance and to test a set of hypotheses regarding compliance with this commitment.

Legalization is one way governments attempt to make credible their international monetary commitments. The evidence shows that governments are hesitant to make international legal commitments if there is a significant risk that they will not be able to honor them in the future. The hazard models of the rate of acceptance of Article VIII indicate that commitment is associated with conditions that one can reasonably anticipate will make compliance possible. Balance-of-payments weakness and volatility could and did delay the acceptance of obligations for openness significantly. Furthermore, economic downturns and unanticipated balance-of-payments difficulties were associated with noncompliance among Article VIII countries. However, both the archival evidence and the quantitative analysis presented here suggest that governments wanted to be relatively sure they could comply before they committed legally to the open foreign exchange regime. Legal commitment was part of a strategy to make a credible commitment to maintain a liberal foreign exchange regime.

Among Article VIII countries, two regime effects had clear consequences for compliance. Surprisingly for those who view the international behavior of democracies as somehow distinctive with respect to law and obligation, the more democratic the Article VIII country, the more likely it may have been ($p = .10$) to place restrictions on current account. On the other hand, regimes that were based on clear principles of the rule of law were far more likely to comply with their commitments. This finding indicates that rules and popular pressures can and apparently sometimes do pull in opposite directions when it comes to international law compliance. There is no reason to think, based on these findings, that democracy itself is a positive influence on the rule of law in international relations. On the contrary, there is more reason to associate compliance with the extent to which the polity in question respects institutional channels for mediating domestic conflict and protecting property rights than with a participatory or competitive political system. Some analysts have argued that this finding can be understood as a normative constraint on foreign policy choice. But it is also consistent with rational market incentives, since rule-of-law regimes have more to lose reputationally than do capricious regimes in the event of a legal violation.

One of the most interesting findings of this research has been the evidence that commitment and compliance are related to the commitment and compliance patterns beyond one's own borders. The hazard model clearly indicates that the breadth of acceptance influenced acceptance by uncommitted governments. Both worldwide and regional acceptance of Article VIII status had this effect, even when controlling for time. Furthermore, the pervasiveness of restrictions within a region has a negative effect on the compliance decision among Article VIII countries. It is impossible to know from these associational effects, of course, exactly what kinds of mechanisms might be at play in such a relationship. I have argued that these kinds of regional and universal effects likely reflect the strategic nature of implementing restrictions: punishment by economic agents and retaliation or other pressures by trading partners, for example, may be minimal where restrictions are common (since it is prohibitively costly to punish everyone). Those who offer more normative explanations of state behavior might interpret this pattern as an example of the importance of regional norms of appropriate behavior. Or perhaps it is simply the case that although governments feel some moral obligation to obey the law, their willingness to comply breaks down as others abandon the rules at will. Although these tests cannot distinguish these distinct explanations, the ability to document a degree of contingent compliance provides a basis for disentangling the possible mechanisms in future research. What we can say is that compliance and commitment are likely influenced, for whatever reason, by the actions taken by other members of the international system.

This research has broader implications for the study of legalization and compliance with international legal obligations. It shows that legalization as a tool for commitment is limited by economic conditions and market forces. International monetary legalization can be characterized by an inverted "J" pattern: legalization was nonexistent under the classical gold standard and soft during the interwar years. It peaked between 1946 and 1971, when treaty obligations regulated the central relationship among currencies, and now involves definite obligations over a more limited range of policies. Much of the behavior that constitutes international monetary relations remains completely outside of legalized relationships, especially rules and practices with respect to the provision of liquidity.[85]

---

85. Art. VII, sec. 2 empowered the IMF to borrow from a member but also provided that no member should be obliged to lend to the IMF. Thus the General Agreement to Borrow was negotiated by the

Rather than debating whether compliance is pervasive or minimal,[86] my purpose here has been to examine the conditions under which compliance is likely. The study of international law compliance is rife with problems of conceptualization and measurement,[87] but in this case it has been possible to match a treaty obligation with authoritative assessments of behavior over time for a large number of countries and to match the suggested mechanisms with contextual archival materials. The evidence taken together points to law as a hook for making a credible commitment, with compliance largely "enforced" by the anticipation of reputational consequences.

Data Appendix

Dependent Variables

Article VIII Acceptance: Coded 1 if the country has accepted Article VIII status and zero if it remains subject to Article XIV transitional arrangements. Acceptance indicates the end of a "spell" for purposes of the Cox proportional hazard model.[88]

Violate: Coded 1 if restrictions exist and/or if a multiple exchange rate system is in place, zero otherwise. Since this dependent variable is used only to analyze policies of Article VIII countries, it is interpreted as noncompliance.[89]

Explanatory Variables

Universality: Proportion of current IMF members who have accepted Article VIII status.[90]

Regional norms: Proportion of current IMF members within each region who have accepted Article VIII status. Classification of economies by region (East and Southern Africa, West Africa, East Asia and Pacific, Eastern Europe and Central Asia, Rest of Europe, Middle East, North Africa, Americas) is based on World Bank categories.[91]

---

managing director and representatives of the signatory countries outside normal IMF channels. Reminiscent of the Tripartite Agreement, it was enshrined as a series of identical letters among participating countries. Swaps are also soft arrangements created by central banks and operating through the Bank of International Settlements. These were developed completely outside of the IMF framework. Dam 1982, 150. Nor are IMF standby arrangements a contract in the legal sense. Failure to carry out the performance criteria in the letter of intent is not a breach of any agreement and certainly not a breach of international law. All the "seal of approval" effects come despite the nonlegal nature of this commitment. The Executive board's decision of 20 September 1968 explicitly concerns the nonlegal status of standby arrangements. Gold 1979, 464–66.

86. On this point, compare Chayes and Chayes 1993 and 1995 and Henkin 1979 with Downs, Rocke, and Barsoom 1996.

87. These issues are discussed in Simmons 1998.

88. IMF various years, analytical appendix.

89. Ibid.

90. Ibid.

91. Ibid.

Surveillance: A dummy variable indicating whether the time period is before (coded zero) or after (coded 1) 1978, indicating a comprehensive regime of IMF surveillance for all members, whether Article XVI or Article VIII status.

Openness: Imports (total value of goods and services: sum of merchandise f.o.b., imports of nonfactor services, and factor payments at market prices in current U.S. dollars) plus exports (total value of goods and services; sum of merchandise f.o.b, exports of nonfactor services, and factor receipts at market prices in current U.S. dollars), as a proportion of GDP, multiplied by 100.[92]

Democracy: Democracy score (ranging from a low of zero to a high of 10) denoting the degree to which democratic institutions exist within each country.[93]

Mean balance of payments: The mean current account balance (the sum of net exports of goods and nonfactor services, net factor income, and net private transfers as a percentage of GDP, before official transfers) as a proportion of GDP for each country for the period under observation.[94]

Balance-of-payments volatility: The log of the standard deviation of current account balance as a proportion of GDP (defined earlier).[95]

Change in GDP: GDP average annual growth rate, for sum of GDP at factor cost and indirect taxes, less subsidies.[96]

Regional noncompliance: Proportion of current IMF members within each region who place restrictions on their current account and/or used multiple exchange-rate systems. Classification of economies by region (East and Southern Africa, West Africa, East Asia and Pacific, Eastern Europe and Central Asia, Rest of Europe, Middle East, North Africa, Americas) is based on World Bank categories. Since this explanatory variable is used only to analyze policies of Article VIII countries, it is interpreted as noncompliance.[97]

Rule of law: A six-point scale measuring the extent to which a country's domestic polity is based on practices and institutions that respect the rule of law.[98]

Use of IMF credit: Coded 1 if a country has made use of IMF credits during a given year and zero if it has not.[99]

Exchange-rate flexibility: Coded 1 if exchange rates are relatively flexible and zero if they are relatively inflexible; coded individually for each country-year.

GATT member: Coded 1 if a country had acceded to GATT and zero if had not.

92. World Bank 1995 and 1998, indicators (210 + 119)/38.

93. POLITY III data set. For a complete discussion of the conceptualization and coverage of this data set and comparisons with other measures of democracy, see Jaggers and Gurr 1995.

94. World Bank 1995 and 1998, indicator 181.

95. World Bank 1995 and 1998.

96. World Bank 1995 and 1998, indicator 181.

97. IMF, various years, analytical appendix.

98. International Country Risk Guide. For a full discussion of the conceptualization of this variable, see Knack and Keefer 1995.

99. World Bank 1995.

IV.
Critiques

M odern studies of international institutions began by identifying them as solutions to collective-action problems among states. States are often prevented from achieving mutually beneficial outcomes by high transaction costs and insufficient information. Institutions can improve these environmental conditions and thus enhance the prospects of cooperation. This "standard" account of institutions, with its roots in rationalist approaches, has been subject to criticism from a number of perspectives. Constructivists offer one of the most persistent critiques, arguing that the effects of institutions go well beyond changing a few aspects of the international environment and insisting that problems of mutual understanding and interpretation are central to institutional dynamics. Others challenge the ability of institutions and organizations to have the beneficial effects identified in the standard account, seeing instead repeated and predictable dysfunction. Still others, while remaining within the rationalist tradition, challenge the quality of empirical work in this tradition.

In one of the earliest theoretical critiques of modern rationalist scholarship on international regimes, Friedrich Kratochwil and John Gerard Ruggie (Chapter 11) argue that much ongoing research is misplaced because it neglects the central role of intersubjective meanings in regimes. The authors acknowledge that the renewed focus on regimes has strong theoretical roots and is progressive. However, they identify a central inconsistency in the work of most authors. International regimes, by definition, are based on states' "mutual expectations" about others' behavior.[1] Thus one cannot understand the logic and effects of regimes without considering the intersubjective meanings of regime norms and standards of behavior. Yet little empirical work concentrates on these intersubjective meanings, which would require careful interpretation of governments' justifications for their actions. Building on this foundational insight, Kratochwil and Ruggie offer some specific recommendations for future research that, in retrospect, are prescient of more recent trends in the literature. They call for a return to studying formal IOs as well as more

---

1. This emphasis on mutual expectations is consistent with the perspective of legal scholars such as Chayes and Chayes (Chapter 8).

informal systems of norms, called regimes. Studying formal organizations would allow scholars to take intersubjective meanings seriously by concentrating on some specific functions that organizations perform. For example, organizations provide transparency about behavior and expectations, serve as focal points for arguments about legitimacy, and act as forums for the development of consensual knowledge.

Beginning from a more policy-oriented perspective, Giulio Gallarotti (Chapter 12) launches a fundamental criticism of those who are optimistic about the ability of international organization and management to solve serious international problems. He notes that "international organization" does not just occasionally fail but fails systematically. Attempts to manage international conflict on an issue-by-issue basis, as is assumed in most work on regimes and institutions, are in most cases doomed to failure. Furthermore, international organization often has adverse, even perverse effects, such as intensifying conflict. Gallarotti then draws from existing theories to provide an analysis of when and why such systematic failure takes place. He argues that schemes to manage tightly coupled issues and relationships are particularly prone to collapse. One important and common reason for failure is that international management can unintentionally serve as a substitute for finding long-term solutions to underlying problems or for responsible policymaking actions by individual states. International organization can also have unintended negative effects by creating moral hazard problems, similar to those experienced in any type of insurance scheme. These systematic failures and the theoretically grounded reasons for them provide a challenge to those who see institutions as solutions to collective-action problems and provide the groundwork for developing alternative accounts of international institutions.

Michael Barnett and Martha Finnemore (Chapter 13), like Gallarotti, note that many IOs are dysfunctional. They draw on a Weberian analysis of bureaucracy both to explain this fact and to argue that IOs are far more powerful than recognized by standard rationalist, state-centered analyses. IOs are bureaucracies, with all the power and problems suggested by that word. Because they are bureaucracies, they make rules, which are a form of social knowledge. This knowledge, in turn, leads to redefinition of international problems, creates new types of actors in the international system, and leads actors to redefine their interests. However, the fact of bureaucracy also leads to systematic limitations of IO activities. They are driven by impersonal internal rules, and standards of appropriate behavior are defined relative to these rules. IOs can therefore become rigid, unable to respond to changing environments and new challenges. The result is inefficiency and frequent behavior that appears to be self-defeating.

Lisa Martin and Beth Simmons (Chapter 14) take the opportunity of surveying work on international institutions and organizations published in the first fifty years of International Organization *to advance a critique of theoretical and empirical work in the rationalist tradition and to suggest potentially productive new lines of research. They find that prior to the 1980s* International Organization *published a very substantial body of literature on IOs. Many of these articles contained important insights. However, this work failed to cumulate because of the lack of an overarching theoretical framework. That framework was provided by the emphasis on collective-action problems and transaction costs and led to a renaissance in the study of international institutions. Newer work has taken seriously questions both of institutional change and design (institutional endogeneity) and of institutional effects. However, empirical work on institutions suffers from a number of flaws, including selection bias and failure to take endogeneity seriously. Martin and Simmons suggest a number of theoretical moves that could address these issues and reinvigorate research on international institutions. One is to recognize institutions as simultaneously consequential and the object of state choices. Methods for doing so could be found, for example, in the study of domestic legislative institutions. Another move is to develop a more refined typology of institutional effects. Both of these steps would allow theoretical and empirical analyses to move beyond simple dichotomous arguments about whether "institutions matter" to more sophisticated, conditional statements about their effects.*

Overall, the literature on international institutions is exciting and progressive in its own right and provides a window on general debates in international relations. The theoretical and empirical articles collected here illustrate the range of approaches and debates in the literature and allow us to see why this field has attracted such great interest from scholars in the last two decades.

International Organization: A State of the Art on an Art of the State

Friedrich Kratochwil and John Gerard Ruggie

International organization as a field of study has had its ups and downs throughout the post-World War II era and throughout this century for that matter. In the interwar period, the fate of the field reflected the fate of the world it studied: a creative burst of work on "international government" after 1919, followed by a period of more cautious reassessment approaching the 1930s, and a gradual decline into irrelevance if not obscurity thereafter. Although they sometimes intersected, the fate of theory and the fate of practice were never all that closely linked after World War II. Indeed, it is possible to argue, with only slight exaggeration, that in recent years they have become inversely related: the academic study of international organization is more interesting, vibrant, and even compelling than ever before, whereas the world of actual international organizations has deteriorated in efficacy and performance. Today, international organization as a field of study is an area where the action is; few would so characterize international organizations as a field of practice.

Our purpose in this article is to try to figure out how and why the doctors can be thriving when the patient is moribund. To anticipate the answer without, we hope, unduly straining the metaphor, the reason is that the leading doctors have become biochemists and have stopped treating and in most cases even seeing patients. In the process, however, new discoveries have been made, new diagnostic techniques have been developed, and our understanding has deepened, raising the possibility of more effective treatment in the long run.

What we are suggesting, to pose the issue more directly, is that students of

The authors are grateful to Betty J. Starkey for bibliographical assistance, and to David Baldwin, Douglas Chalmers, Robert Jervis, Robert Keohane, Charles Lipson, Jack Snyder, and Mark Zacher for thoughtful comments on an earlier draft.

International Organization 40, 4, Autumn 1986, pp. 753–775

international organization have shifted their focus systematically away from international institutions, toward broader forms of international institutionalized behavior. We further contend that this shift does not represent a haphazard sequence of theoretical or topical "fads" but is rooted in a "core concern" or a set of puzzles which gives coherence and identity to this field of study.[1] The substantive core around which the various theoretical approaches have clustered is the problem of international governance. And the observable shifts in analytical foci can be understood as "progressive problem shifts," in the sense of Imre Lakatos's criterion for the heuristic fruitfulness of a research program.[2] This evolution has brought the field to its current focus on the concept of international regimes. To fully realize its potential, the research program must now seek to resolve some serious anomalies in the regime approach and to link up the informal ordering devices of international regimes with the formal institutional mechanisms of international organizations.

In the first section of this article, we present a review of the literature in order to trace its evolution. This review draws heavily on articles published in *International Organization,* the leading journal in the field since its first appearance in 1947, and a source that not only reflects but in considerable measure is also responsible for the evolution of the field. The second section critiques the currently prevalent epistemological practices in regime analysis and points toward lines of inquiry which might enhance the productive potential of the concept as an analytical tool. Finally, we briefly suggest a means of systematically linking up regimes and formal organizations in a manner that is already implicit in the literature.

Progressive analytical shifts

As a field of study, international organization has always concerned itself with the same phenomenon: in the words of a 1931 text, it is an attempt to describe and explain "how the modern Society of Nations governs itself."[3] In that text, the essence of government was assumed to comprise the coordination of group activities so as to conduct the public business, and the particular feature distinguishing international government was taken to lie in the necessity that it be consistent with national sovereignty. Few contempo-

---

1. Thomas Kuhn uses the notion "sets of puzzles" in his discussion of preludes to paradigms; see Kuhn, *The Structure of Scientific Revolutions* (Chicago: University of Chicago Press, 1962), and *The Essential Tension* (Chicago: University of Chicago Press, 1977).
2. The criterion of the fruitfulness of a research program, and issues connected with progressive versus degenerative problem shifts, were introduced by Imre Lakatos, "Falsification and the Methodology of Scientific Research Programmes," in Lakatos and Alan Musgrave, eds., *Criticisms and the Growth of Knowledge* (Cambridge: Cambridge University Press, 1970).
3. Edmund C. Mower, *International Government* (Boston: Heath, 1931).

rary students of international organization would want to alter this definition substantially.[4]

However, there have been identifiable shifts in how the phenomenon of international governance has been conceived, especially since World War II—so much so that the field is often described as being in permanent search of its own "dependent variable." Our reading of the literature reveals four major analytical foci, which we would place in roughly the following logical—and more or less chronological—order.

Formal institutions

The first is a formal institutional focus. Within it, the assumption was made or the premise was implicit that (1) international governance is whatever international organizations do; and (2) the formal attributes of international organizations, such as their charters, voting procedures, committee structures, and the like, account for what they do. To the extent that the actual operation of institutions was explored, the frame of reference was their constitutional mandate, and the purpose of the exercise was to discover how closely it was approximated.[5]

Institutional processes

The second analytical focus concerns the actual decision-making processes within international organizations. The assumption was gradually abandoned that the formal arrangements of international organizations explain what they do. This perspective originally emerged in the attempt to come to grips with the increasingly obvious discrepancies between constitutional designs and organizational practices. Some writers argued that the formal arrangements and objectives remained relevant and appropriate but were undermined or obstructed by such political considerations as cold war rivalry and such institutional factors as the veto in the UN Security Council, bloc voting in the UN General Assembly, and the like.[6] Others contended

4. The basic terms of the definition are entirely compatible with the most recent theoretical work in the field, Robert O. Keohane, *After Hegemony* (Princeton: Princeton University Press, 1984). The precise meaning of the terms of course has changed significantly, as we shall see presently.

5. A distinguished contribution to this literature is Leland M. Goodrich and Anne P. Simons, *The United Nations and the Maintenance of International Peace and Security* (Washington, D.C.: Brookings, 1955). See also Klaus Knorr, "The Bretton Woods Institutions in Transition," *International Organization* [hereafter cited as *IO*] 2 (February 1948); Walter R. Sharp. "The Institutional Framework for Technical Assistance," *IO* 7 (August 1953); and Henri Rolin, "The International Court of Justice and Domestic Jurisdiction," *IO* 8 (February 1954).

6. Norman J. Padelford, "The Use of the Veto," *IO* 2 (June 1948); Raymond Dennett, "Politics in the Security Council," *IO* 3 (August 1949); M. Margaret Ball, "Bloc Voting in the General Assembly," *IO* 5 (February 1951); Allan Hovey, Jr., "Obstructionism and the Rules of the General Assembly," *IO* 5 (August 1951); and Arlette Moldaver, "Repertoire of the Veto in the Security Council, 1946–1956," *IO* 11 (Spring 1957).

that the original designs themselves were unrealistic and needed to be changed.[7]

Over time, this perspective became more generalized, to explore overall patterns of influence shaping organizational outcomes.[8] The sources of influence which have been investigated include the power and prestige of individual states, the formation and functioning of the group system, organizational leadership positions, and bureaucratic politics. The outcomes that analysts have sought to explain have ranged from specific resolutions, programs, and budgets, to broader voting alignment and the general orientation of one or more international institutions.

Organizational role

In this third perspective, another assumption of the formal institutionalist approach was abandoned, namely, that international governance *is* whatever international organizations *do*. Instead, the focus shifted to the actual and potential roles of international organizations in a more broadly conceived process of international governance.[9] This perspective in turn subsumes three distinct clusters.

In the first cluster, the emphasis was on the roles of international organizations in the resolution of substantive international problems. Preventive diplomacy and peace-keeping were two such roles in the area of peace and security,[10] nuclear safeguarding by the International Atomic Energy Agency (IAEA) was another.[11] Facilitating decolonization received a good deal of

7. See, among others, Sir Gladwyn Jebb, "The Role of the United Nations," *IO* 6 (November 1952); A. Loveday, "Suggestions for the Reform of UN Economic and Social Machinery," *IO* 7 (August 1953); Wytze Corter, "GATT after Six Years: An Appraisal," *IO* 8 (February 1954); Lawrence S. Finkelstein, "Reviewing the UN Charter," *IO* 9 (May 1955); Robert E. Riggs, "Overselling the UN Charter—Fact or Myth," *IO* 14 (Spring 1960); and Inis L. Claude, Jr., "The Management of Power in the Changing United Nations," *IO* 15 (Spring 1961).

8. The most comprehensive work in this genre remains Robert W. Cox and Harold K. Jacobson, eds., *The Anatomy of Influence: Decision Making in International Organization* (New Haven: Yale University Press, 1973).

9. Inis L. Claude's landmark text, *Swords into Plowshares* (New York: Random House, 1959), both signaled and contributed to this shift.

10. Lincoln P. Bloomfield, ed., *International Force—A Symposium, IO* 17 (Spring 1973); James M. Boyd, "Cyprus: Episode in Peacekeeping," *IO* 20 (Winter 1966); Robert O. Matthews, "The Suez Canal Dispute: A Case Study in Peaceful Settlement," *IO* 21 (Winter 1967); Yashpal Tandon, "Consensus and Authority behind UN Peacekeeping Operations," *IO* 21 (Spring 1967); David P. Forsythe, "United Nations Intervention in Conflict Situations Revisited: A Framework for Analysis," *IO* 23 (Winter 1969); John Gerard Ruggie, "Contingencies, Constraints, and Collective Security: Perspectives on UN Involvement in International Disputes," *IO* 28 (Summer 1974); and Ernst B. Haas, "Regime Decay: Conflict Management and International Organization, 1945–1981," *IO* 37 (Spring 1983).

11. Robert E. Pendley and Lawrence Scheinman, "International Safeguarding as Institutionalized Collective Behavior," in John Gerard Ruggie and Ernst B. Haas, eds., special issue on international responses to technology, *IO* 29 (Summer 1975); and Joseph S. Nye, "Maintaining a Non-Proliferation Regime," in George H. Quester, ed., special issue on nuclear nonproliferation, *IO* 35 (Winter 1981).

attention in the political realm,[12] providing multilateral development assistance in the economic realm.[13] The potential role of international organizations in restructuring North-South relations preoccupied a substantial number of scholars throughout the 1970s,[14] as did the possible contributions of international organizations to managing the so-called global commons.[15] Most recently, analysts have challenged the presumption that the roles of international organizations in this regard are invariably positive; indeed, they have accused international organizations of occasionally exacerbating the problems they are designed to help resolve.[16]

The second cluster of the organizational-role perspective shifted the focus away from the solution of substantive problems per se, toward certain long-term institutional consequences of the failure to solve substantive problems through the available institutional means. This, of course, was the integrationist focus, particularly the neofunctionalist variety.[17] It was fueled by the fact that the jurisdictional scope of both the state and existing international organizations was increasingly outstripped by the functional scope of international problems. And it sought to explore the extent to which institutional adaptations to this fact might be conducive to the emergence of political forms "beyond the nation state."[18] Neofunctionalists assigned a major role in this process to international organizations, not simply as passive recipients of new tasks and authority but as active agents of "task expansion" and

12. Ernst B. Haas, "The Attempt to Terminate Colonization: Acceptance of the UN Trusteeship System," *IO* 7 (February 1953); John Fletcher-Cooke, "Some Reflections on the International Trusteeship System," *IO* 13 (Summer 1959); Harold K. Jacobson, "The United Nations and Colonialism: A Tentative Appraisal," *IO* 16 (Winter 1962); and David A. Kay, "The Politics of Decolonization: The New Nations and the United Nations Political Process," *IO* 21 (Autumn 1967).

13. Richard N. Gardner and Max F. Millikan, eds., special issue on international agencies and economic development, *IO* 22 (Winter 1968).

14. Among many other sources, see Branislav Gosovic and John Gerard Ruggie, "On the Creation of a New International Economic Order: Issue Linkage and the Seventh Special Session of the UN General Assembly," *IO* 30 (Spring 1976).

15. David A. Kay and Eugene B. Skolnikoff, eds., special issue on international institutions and the environmental crisis, *IO* 26 (Spring 1972); Ruggie and Haas, eds., special issue, *IO* 29 (Summer 1975); and Per Magnus Wijkman, "Managing the Global Commons," *IO* 36 (Summer 1982).

16. The most extreme form of this criticism recently has come from the political right in the United States; cf. Burton Yale Pines, ed., *A World without the U.N.: What Would Happen If the United Nations Shut Down* (Washington, D.C.: Heritage Foundation, 1984). But the same position has long been an article of faith on the political left as well; cf. Cheryl Payer, "The Perpetuation of Dependence: The IMF and the Third World," *Monthly Review* 23 (September 1971), and Payer, "The World Bank and the Small Farmers," *Journal of Peace Research* 16, no. 2 (1979); and the special issue of *Development Dialogue,* no. 2 (1980).

17. Various approaches to the study of integration were summarized and assessed in Leon N. Lindberg and Stuart A. Scheingold, eds., special issue on regional integration, *IO* 24 (Autumn 1970).

18. Ernst B. Haas, *Beyond the Nation State: Functionalism and International Organization* (Stanford: Stanford University Press, 1964).

"spillover."[19] Other approaches concerned themselves less with institutional changes than with attitudinal changes, whether among national elites, international delegates, or mass publics.[20]

The third cluster within the organizational-role perspective began with a critique of the transformational expectations of integration theory and then shifted the focus onto a more general concern with how international institutions "reflect and to some extent magnify or modify" the characteristic features of the international system.[21] Here, international organizations have been viewed as potential dispensers of collective legitimacy,[22] vehicles in the international politics of agenda formation,[23] forums for the creation of transgovernmental coalitions as well as instruments of transgovernmental policy coordination,[24] and as means through which the global dominance structure is enhanced or can possibly come to be undermined.[25]

The theme that unifies all works of this genre is that the process of global governance is not coterminous with the activities of international organiza-

19. In addition to Haas, ibid., see Philippe C. Schmitter, "Three Neo-Functionalist Hypotheses about International Integration," *IO* 23 (Winter 1969); Leon N. Lindberg and Stuart A. Scheingold, *Europe's Would-Be Polity: Patterns of Change in the European Community* (Englewood Cliffs, N.J.: Prentice-Hall, 1970); Joseph S. Nye, *Peace in Parts: Integration and Conflict in Regional Organization* (Boston: Little, Brown, 1971). For a critique of the neofunctionalist model, see Roger D. Hansen "Regional Integration: Reflection on a Decade of Theoretical Efforts," *World Politics* 21 (January 1969).

20. Henry H. Kerr, Jr., "Changing Attitudes through International Participation: European Parliamentarians and Integration," *IO* 27 (Winter 1973); Peter Wolf, "International Organizations and Attitude Change: A Re-examination of the Functionalist Approach," *IO* 27 (Summer 1973); David A. Karns, "The Effect of Interparliamentary Meetings on the Foreign Policy Attitudes of the United States Congressmen," *IO* 31 (Summer 1977); and Ronald Inglehart, "Public Opinion and Regional Integration," *IO* 24 (Autumn 1970).

21. The phrase is Stanley Hoffmann's in "International Organization and the International System," *IO* 24 (Summer 1970). A similar position was advanced earlier by Oran R. Young, "The United Nations and the International System," *IO* 22 (Autumn 1968).

22. Inis L. Claude, Jr., "Collective Legitimization as a Political Function of the United Nations," *IO* 20 (Summer 1966); cf. Jerome Slater, "The Limits of Legitimization in International Organizations: The Organization of American States and the Dominican Crisis," *IO* 23 (Winter 1969).

23. A representative sampling would include Kay and Skolnikoff, eds., special issue, *IO* 26 (Spring 1972); Robert Russell, "Transgovernmental Interaction in the International Monetary System, 1960–1972," *IO* 27 (Autumn 1973); Thomas Weiss and Robert Jordan, "Bureaucratic Politics and the World Food Conference," *World Politics* 28 (April 1976); Raymond F. Hopkins, "The International Role of 'Domestic' Bureaucracy," *IO* 30 (Summer 1976); and John Gerard Ruggie, "On the Problem of 'The Global Problematique': What Roles for International Organizations?" *Alternatives* 5 (January 1980).

24. The major analytical piece initiating this genre was Robert O. Keohane and Joseph S. Nye, "Transgovernmental Relations and International Organizations," *World Politics* 27 (October 1974); cf. their earlier edited work on transnational relations and world politics, *IO* 25 (Summer 1971).

25. Robert Cox's recent work has been at the forefront of exploring this aspect of international organization: "Labor and Hegemony," *IO* 31 (Summer 1977); "The Crisis of World Order and the Problem of International Organization in the 1980's," *International Journal* 35 (Spring 1980); and "Gramsci, Hegemony and International Relations: An Essay in Method," *Millenium: Journal of International Studies* 12 (Summer 1983).

tions but that these organizations do play some role in that broader process. The objective was to identify their role.

International regimes

The current preoccupation in the field is with the phenomenon of international regimes. Regimes are broadly defined as governing arrangements constructed by states to coordinate their expectations and organize aspects of international behavior in various issue-areas. They thus comprise a normative element, state practice, and organizational roles.[26] Examples include the trade regime, the monetary regime, the oceans regime, and others. The focus on regimes was a direct response both to the intellectual odyssey that we have just traced as well as to certain developments in the world of international relations from the 1970s on.

When the presumed identity between international organizations and international governance was explicitly rejected, the precise roles of organizations *in* international governance became a central concern. But, apart from the focus on integration, no overarching conception was developed *of* international governance itself. And the integrationists themselves soon abandoned their early notions, ending up with a formulation of integration that did little more than recapitulate the condition of interdependence which was assumed to trigger integration in the first place.[27] Thus, for a time the field of international organization lacked any systematic conception of its traditional analytical core: international governance. The introduction of the concept of regimes reflected an attempt to fill this void. International regimes were thought to express both the parameters and the perimeters of international governance.[28]

The impact of international affairs during the 1970s and beyond came in the form of an anomaly for which no ready-made explanation was at hand. Important changes occurred in the international system, associated with the relative decline of U.S. hegemony: the achievement of nuclear parity by the Soviet Union; the economic resurgence of Europe and Japan; the success of OPEC together with the severe international economic dislocations that followed it. Specific agreements that had been negotiated after World War II were violated, and institutional arrangements, in money and trade above all,

26. The most extensive analytical exploration of the concept may be found in Stephen D. Krasner, ed., *International Regimes* (Ithaca, N.Y.: Cornell University Press, 1983), most of which was first published as a special issue of *IO* in Spring 1982. Page references will be to the book.

27. Robert O. Keohane and Joseph S. Nye, "International Interdependence and Integration," in Fred I. Greenstein and Nelson W. Polsby, eds., *Handbook of Political Science,* vol. 8 (Reading, Mass.: Addison-Wesley, 1975). The point is also implicit in Ernst Haas's self-criticism, "Turbulent Fields and the Theory of Regional Integration," *IO* 30 (Spring 1976).

28. John Gerard Ruggie, "International Responses to Technology: Concepts and Trends," *IO* 29 (Summer 1975).

came under enormous strain. Yet—and here is the anomaly—governments on the whole did not respond to the difficulties confronting them in beggar-thy-neighbor terms. Neither systemic factors nor formal institutions alone apparently could account for this outcome. One way to resolve the anomaly was to question the extent to which U.S. hegemony in point of fact had eroded.[29] Another, and by ro means entirely incompatible route, was via the concept of international regimes. The argument was advanced that regimes continued in some measure to constrain and condition the behavior of states toward one another, despite systemic change and institutional erosion. In this light, international regimes were seen to enjoy a degree of relative autonomy, though of an unknown duration.[30]

In sum, in order to resolve both disciplinary and real-world puzzles, the process of international governance has come to be associated with the concept of international regimes, occupying an ontological space some-where between the level of formal institutions on the one hand and systemic factors on the other. Hence, the notion that the concern with international regimes is but another academic fad from which the field has suffered throughout the postwar period itself betrays a misunderstanding of the con-siderable intellectual continuity that has brought the field to the present point.[31]

These shifts in analytical foci of course have never been complete; not everyone in the field at any one time works within the same perspective, and once introduced into the field no perspective ever disappears altogether. To provide some sense of relative orders of magnitude and of changes in them over time, a brief review of all articles ever published in *IO* may be of help. Figure 1 summarizes their analytical foci, defined as they are in the text, except that "international integration" as a focus has been separated out from the more general category of "organizational roles" in order to high-light a particular evolutionary pattern.

Two trends are striking. First, the formal institutional focus has declined steadily from the very beginning and now accounts for fewer than 5 percent of the total. Second, the category of "general international relations" has dominated every other from the mid-1960s on and now accounts for over 60 percent of the total. A comprehensive sociology of knowledge, not only of the field but also of the journal, would be required to explain fully this latter

---

29. This is the tack taken by Susan Strange, "Still an Extraordinary Power: America's Role in a Global Monetary System," in Raymond E. Lombra and William E. Witte, eds., *Political Economy of International and Domestic Monetary Relations* (Ames: Iowa State University Press, 1982); and Bruce Russett, "The Mysterious Case of Vanishing Hegemony: Or, Is Mark Twain Really Dead?" *IO* 39 (Spring 1985).

30. See Krasner, "Introduction," *International Regimes,* and Keohane, *After Hegemony,* for discussions of this thesis.

31. The fad-fettish is argued by Susan Strange, "Cave! Hic Dragones: A Critique of Regime Analysis," in Krasner, ed., *International Regimes*.

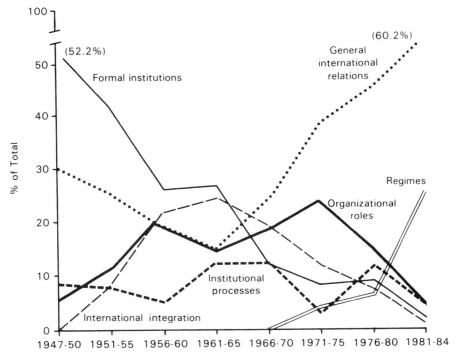

FIGURE 1. *Analytical foci of contributions to International Organization.*
Source. International Organization, 1947–84.

trend. But in part at least it reflects the loss of an analytical core of which we spoke above, which the concept of regimes was designed to provide. As Figure 1 also shows, the focus on regimes emerged suddenly in the 1970s and now ranks in second place.

In addition, there exists an interesting relationship between studies of organizational roles, international integration, and regimes. The first phase of organizational-role studies, it will be recalled, had a substantive focus, namely the contributions of international organizations to resolving the various problems confronting the international community. It was overtaken by integration studies by 1960, the concern of which was the impact of international organizations not on solving the substance but on changing the process of international governance. When integration studies declined about ten years later, they were overtaken in turn by studies that rejected the specific focus on integration as an outcome but continued to concern themselves with the role of organizations in the general process of international governance. And the decline of this latter phase of organizational-role studies clearly coincides with the emergence of regime studies, suggesting a fairly direct lineage.

Conflict and cooperation

These shifts in analytical foci have been accompanied by an analytical shift of a very different sort, perhaps most clearly expressed in the premises of recent methodological approaches. Take the rational-choice approach as one instance.[32] It raises the promise and offers the possibility that two strands of thinking about international relations which have been distinct if not oppositional in the past may become unified. Typically, the opposition has been expressed in the conflict/cooperation dichotomy. It has been widely assumed throughout the history of modern international relations theory that there exists one realm of international life which is intrinsically conflictual and another which is intrinsically more cooperative. Moreover, it has been inferred from this premise that these two realms of international life require (from the vantage point of conflict studies) or make possible (from the vantage point of cooperation studies) two very different modes of analysis. Realism and to a lesser extent Marxism have tended to dominate the former strand, and liberalism in its many guises—Ricardian trade theory, Wilsonian idealism, functionalism, and interdependence imperatives—the latter.

What we find in the recent literature inspired by the rational-choice perspective, on the contrary, is the claim that *both* conflict *and* cooperation can be explained by a *single* logical apparatus.[33] Moreover, the differences between the two branches now are understood to reflect situational determinants not structural determinants. In game-theoretic terms, such situational factors include how many rounds are played in a game resembling an iterated Prisoner's Dilemma, how much the value of future payoffs is discounted in comparison with immediate payoffs, whether or not swift and decisive defection from cooperation is possible, and so on.[34] Interestingly, developments in some neo-Marxist approaches have proceeded on precisely

32. The public-choice approach to the study of international organization began with the use of public goods theory in the early 1970s, went on to explore the theory of property rights later in the decade, and has come to focus on game theory and microeconomic theories of market failure to explain patterns of international governance. See, respectively, Bruce M. Russett and John D. Sullivan, "Collective Goods and International Organizations," *IO* 25 (Autumn 1971); and John Gerard Ruggie, "Collective Goods and Future International Collaboration," *American Political Science Review* 66 (September 1972); John A. C. Conybeare, "International Organization and the Theory of Property Rights," *IO* 34 (Summer 1980); and Keohane, *After Hegemony*. A useful review of the relevant literature may be found in Bruno S. Frey, "The Public Choice View of International Political Economy," *IO* 38 (Winter 1984).

33. In the context of rational-choice theory generally, the argument was first articulated by John Harsanyi, "Rational Choice Models of Political Behavior vs. Functionalist and Conformist Theories," *World Politics* 21 (July 1969). In the international relations literature, it is implicit in Robert Jervis, "Cooperation under the Security Dilemma," *World Politics* 30 (January 1978), and explicit in Robert Axelrod, "The Emergence of Cooperation among Egoists," *American Political Science Review* 75 (June 1981), as well as in Keohane, *After Hegemony*.

34. Robert Jervis first made these points in his paper "Security Regimes," in Krasner, ed., *International Regimes*. For a more extended discussion see Charles Lipson, "International Cooperation in Economic and Security Affairs," *World Politics* 37 (October 1984).

analogous lines, insofar as the traditional opposites, unity and rivalry, have been collapsed within a single "world system" framework, or insofar as the question of unity versus rivalry has been derived from the presence or absence of "hegemony" in the Gramscian sense of the term.[35] Approaches informed by hermeneutics and language philosophy are reaching much the same conclusions as well.[36] And in each case, the concept of regimes is found to be a useful focal point for analysis.

In summary, that branch of the study of international relations which calls itself international organization is lively and productive. It is once again focusing squarely on the phenomenon of international governance, and it is pursuing its object of study in innovative ways that are bringing it closer to the theoretical core of more general international relations work. These are no mean accomplishments. And they are not diminished by the fact that serious problems remain to be resolved.

Problems in the practice of regime analysis

One of the major criticisms made of the regimes concept is its "wooliness" and "imprecision."[37] The point is well taken. There is no agreement in the literature even on such basic issues as boundary conditions: Where does one regime end and another begin? What is the threshold between nonregime and regime? Embedding regimes in "meta-regimes," or "nesting" one within another, typifies the problem; it does not resolve it.[38] The same is true of the proposal that any set of patterned or conventionalized behavior be considered as prima facie evidence for the existence of a regime.[39]

The only cure for wooliness and imprecision is, of course, to make the concept of regimes less so. Definitions can still be refined, but only up to a point. Two fundamental impediments stand in the way. One is absolute: ultimately, there exists no external Archimedian point from which regimes can be viewed as they "truly" are. This is so because regimes are conceptual creations not concrete entities. As with any analytical construction in the human sciences, the concept of regimes will reflect commonsense understandings, actor preferences, and the particular purposes for which analyses

---

35. Immanuel Wallerstein, "The Rise and Future Demise of the World Capitalist System: Concepts for Comparative Analysis," *Comparative Studies in Society and History* 16 (September 1974); and Cox, "Labor and Hegemony," "The Crisis of World Order," and "Gramsci, Hegemony, and International Relations."

36. Richard K. Ashley, "The Poverty of Neorealism," *IO* 38 (Spring 1984), and Friedrich Kratochwil, "Errors Have Their Advantage," *IO* 38 (Spring 1984).

37. See Susan Strange, in Krasner, ed., *International Regimes.*

38. This route is taken by Vinod K. Aggarwal, *Liberal Protectionism: The International Politics of Organized Textile Trade* (Berkeley: University of California Press, 1985).

39. Oran R. Young, "Regime Dynamics: The Rise and Fall of International Regimes," in Krasner, ed., *International Regimes.*

are undertaken. Ultimately, therefore, the concept of regimes, like the concept of "power," or "state," or "revolution," will remain a "contestable concept."[40]

Well short of this absolute impediment stands another. It is not insuperable, but a great deal of work will have to be done in order to overcome it. The problem is this: the practice of regime analysis is wracked by epistemological anomalies—anomalies that more often than not go unnoticed in the literature. These anomalies debilitate any endeavor to achieve clarity and precision in the concept of regimes and to enhance its productive capacity as an analytical tool. In the paragraphs that follow, we flag three related epistemological problem areas. Without pretending that we can resolve them here, we hope merely to obtain their entry into the disciplinary discourse.

Ontology versus epistemology

International regimes are commonly defined as social institutions around which expectations converge in international issue-areas. The emphasis on convergent expectations as the constitutive basis of regimes gives regimes an inescapable intersubjective quality. It follows that we *know* regimes by their principled and shared understandings of desirable and acceptable forms of social behavior. Hence, the ontology of regimes rests upon a strong element of intersubjectivity.

Now, consider the fact that the prevailing epistemological position in regime analysis is almost entirely positivistic in orientation. Before it does anything else, positivism posits a radical separation of subject and object. It then focuses on the "objective" forces that move actors in their social interactions. Finally, intersubjective meaning, where it is considered at all, is inferred from behavior.

Here, then, we have the most debilitating problem of all: epistemology fundamentally contradicts ontology! Small wonder that so much disagreement exists on what should be fairly straightforward empirical questions: Did Bretton Woods "collapse" in 1971–73, or was the change "norm governed"? Are recent trade restraints indicative of dangerous protectionism or not? How is it that the Non-Proliferation Treaty in 1985 successfully passed yet another review, when so many states that voluntarily adhere to it protest its inequitable terms? And on and on.

In many such puzzling instances, actor *behavior* has failed adequately to convey intersubjective *meaning*. And intersubjective meaning, in turn, seems to have had considerable influence on actor behavior. It is precisely this factor that limits the practical utility of the otherwise fascinating insights into the collaborative potential of rational egoists which are derived from

---

40. On "contestable concepts," see William Connally, *The Terms of Political Discourse*, 2d ed. (Princeton: Princeton University Press, 1983).

laboratory or game-theoretic situations.[41] To put the problem in its simplest terms: in the simulated world, actors cannot communicate *and* engage in behavior; they are condemned to communicate *through* behavior. In the real world, the situation of course differs fundamentally. Here, the very essence of international regimes is expressed in cases such as that of France in 1968, asking for "sympathy and understanding" from its trading partners, as France invoked emergency measures against imports after the May disturbances of that year—and getting both from GATT (General Agreement on Tariffs and Trade) even though *no* objective basis existed in fact or in GATT law for doing so. But a positivist epistemology simply cannot accommodate itself to so intersubjective an ontology. Hence, the case is treated in the literature as illustrating cynicism, complicity, and the erosion of respect for the GATT regime.[42]

The contradiction between ontology and epistemology has elicited surprisingly little concern in the regimes literature.[43] Once it is realized just how problematical the contradiction is, however, what options exist to deal with it? One possibility would be to try to deny it somehow. Theodore Abel's classic neopositivist response to the challenge posed by Weber's concept of *Verstehen* might serve as a model: the concept aids in "the context discovery," Abel contended, but ultimately it is not a method relevant to "the context of validation." Hence it poses no challenge.[44] This response may have been viable a generation ago, but it no longer is. Interpretive epistemologies that stress the intimate relationship between validation and the uncovering of intersubjective meanings are simply too well developed today to be easily dismissed by charges of subjectivism[45]—or, more likely in the arena of international relations theory, of idealism.

---

41. Most notable among such works is Robert Axelrod's *Evolution of Cooperation* (New York: Basic, 1984), and Axelrod, "Modeling the Evolution of Norms" (Paper delivered at the annual meeting of the American Political Science Association, New Orleans, 29 August–1 September 1985). For an attempt to incorporate progressively more "reflective" logical procedures into sequential Prisoner's Dilemma situations and to expose them to more realistic data sets, see Hayward R. Alker, James Bennett, and Dwain Mefford, "Generalized Precedent Logics for Resolving Insecurity Dilemmas," *International Interactions* 7, no. 2 (1980), and Hayward Alker and Akihiro Tanaka, "Resolution Possibilities in 'Historical' Prisoners' Dilemmas" (Paper delivered at the annual meeting of the International Studies Association, Philadelphia, 18 March 1981).

42. This case, and the more general problem of interpretation which it reflects, are discussed by John Gerard Ruggie, "International Regimes, Transactions, and Change: Embedded Liberalism in the Postwar Economic Order," in Krasner, ed., *International Regimes*.

43. In the basic regime text, *International Regimes*, edited by Krasner, intersubjectivity is stressed by Ruggie, "Embedded Liberalism," and by Donald J. Puchala and Raymond F. Hopkins, "International Regimes: Lessons from Inductive Analysis," but no systematic epistemological discussion is undertaken in the volume.

44. Theodore F. Abel, "The Operation Called *Verstehen*," *American Journal of Sociology* 54 (November 1948).

45. For a good selection of readings that begins with Weber, includes the neopositivist response, the Wittgensteinian school, phenomenology, and ethnomethodology, and ends with hermeneutics and critical theory, see Fred R. Dallmayr and Thomas A. McCarthy, *Understanding and Social Inquiry* (Notre Dame: University of Notre Dame Press, 1977).

A second possibility would be to try to formulate a rendition of the inter-subjective ontology which is compatible with positivist epistemology. In view of the influence currently enjoyed in international relations theory by analogies and metaphors drawn from microeconomics, one plausible means of executing this maneuver would be to follow the economists down the road of "revealed preferences"—that consumption behavior, for example, reveals true consumer preferences. If our epistemology does not enable us to uncover meaning, the analogous reasoning would hold, then let us look for "revealed meaning," that is, for "objective" surrogates. It should suffice to point out that this is a solution by displacement: it displaces the problem into the realm of assumption—namely that "objective" surrogates can capture "intersubjective" reality—which of course is not uncharacteristic of the manner in which economists handle difficult problems.

That leaves us with the third and only viable option, of opening up the positivist epistemology to more interpretive strains, more closely attuned to the reality of regimes. Experimentation along these lines has begun. Ernst Haas has been moving steadily toward his own brand of an "evolutionary epistemology," wherein consensual knowledge about various aspects of the human condition becomes one of the forces behind the rise and decline of international regimes.[46] Robert Cox has advanced an unconventional historical materialist epistemology, which gives pride of place to shifting intersubjective frameworks of human discourse and practice.[47] Epistemological positions derived from the "universal pragmatics" of Jürgen Habermas, or informed by the "interpretive analytics" of Michel Foucault, have been found fruitful.[48] Other possibilities have been probed as well.[49] The burden of our discussion is not to advocate any one such alternative but to urge that their consideration be delayed no longer.

Norms in explanation

There is a closely related problem having to do with models of explanation. The standard positivist model works with an initial condition plus a

46. The position is signaled in Ernst B. Haas, "Words Can Hurt You; Or, Who Said What to Whom about Regimes," in Krasner, ed., *International Regimes;* and elaborated in Haas, "What Is Progress in the Study of International Organization?" which has been published only in Japanese translation.

47. Robert W. Cox, "Social Forces, States, and World Orders: Beyond International Relations Theory," and, especially, "Postscript 1985," both in Robert O. Keohane, ed., *Neorealism and Its Critics* (New York: Columbia University Press, 1986).

48. See, respectively, Friedrich Kratochwil, "Rules, Norms, and Decisions: On the Conditions of Practical and Legal Reasoning in International Relations" (Manuscript, Columbia University, 1986); and John Gerard Ruggie, *Planetary Politics: Ecology and the Organization of Global Political Space* (New York: Columbia University Press, forthcoming).

49. For example, a nondeterministic dialectical formulation of states' conceptions of world order is sketched out by Hayward R. Alker, "Dialectical Foundations of Global Disparities," *International Studies Quarterly* 25 (March 1981); and of the mutual recognition among states of competencies to act in collectively prescribed ways, by Richard Ashley, "Poverty of Neorealism."

covering law, on the basis of which it hypothesizes or predicts an occurrence. Even a single counterfactual occurrence may be taken to refute the covering law.[50] (A probabilistic formulation would, of course, appropriately modify the criteria for refutation, but it would not alter the basic structure of the explanation.)

Now consider the fact that what distinguishes international regimes from other international phenomena—from strategic interaction, let us say—is a specifically normative element.[51] Indeed, one of the four analytical components of the concept of regimes is specified to be norms—"standards of behavior defined in terms of rights and obligations." And it has become customary to maintain that change in the normative structure of regimes produces change *of,* as opposed merely to *within,* regimes.[52]

The positivist model of explanation is not easily applied to cases in which norms, so defined, are a significant element in the phenomena to be explained. Alas, the positivist model reigns in regime analysis. Two problems in particular need to be raised.[53]

First, unlike the initial conditions in positivist explanations, norms can be thought of only with great difficulty as "causing" occurrences. Norms may "guide" behavior, they may "inspire" behavior, they may "rationalize" or "justify" behavior, they may express "mutual expectations" about behavior, or they may be ignored. But they do not effect cause in the sense that a bullet through the heart causes death or an uncontrolled surge in the money supply causes price inflation. Hence, where norms are involved, the first component of the positivist model of explanation is problematical.

The second is even more so. For norms are counterfactually valid. No single counterfactual occurrence refutes a norm. Not even many such occurrences necessarily do. Does driving while under the influence of alcohol refute the law (norm) against drunk driving? Does it when half the population is implicated? To be sure, the law (norm) is *violated* thereby. But whether or not violations also invalidate or refute a law (norm) will depend upon a host of other factors, not the least of which is how the community assesses the violation and responds to it. What is true of drunk driving is

50. On the importance of the logical form of *modus tollens* in the hypothetical deductive explanation scheme, see Karl Popper, *The Logic of Scientific Discovery* (New York: Harper & Row, 1968), chaps. 3 and 4.

51. One of the distinctive characteristics of strategic interaction is that ultimately it rests upon a *unilateral* calculation of verbal and nonverbal cues: "A's expectation of B will include an estimation of B's expectations of A. This process of replication, it must be noted, is not an interaction between two states, but rather a process in which decision-makers in one state work out the consequences of their beliefs about the world; a world they believe to include decision-makers in other states, also working out the consequences of their beliefs. The expectations which are so formed are the expectations of one state, but they refer to other states." Paul Keal, *Unspoken Rules and Superpower Dominance* (London: Macmillan, 1984), p. 31.

52. See Krasner, "Introduction," *International Regimes.*

53. Some of these and related issues are discussed more extensively in Kratochwil, "The Force of Prescriptions," *IO* 38 (Autumn 1984).

equally true of the norms of nondiscrimination in international trade, free and stable currency exchanges, and adequate compensation for expropriated foreign property.

Indeed, it is possible to go further and argue that norms need not "exist" at all in a formal sense in order to be valid. It is often said, for example, that the Bretton Woods monetary regime did not exist prior to 1958, because only then did the Europeans assume the obligation of full currency convertibility for transactions on current account. But surely the norms of the regime guided the behavior of European states *toward* that event for some years before it actually took place. Thus, neither the violation of norms, nor, in some special circumstances, even their "nonexistence," necessarily refutes their validity.

Let it be understood that we are not advocating a coup whereby the reign of positivist explanation is replaced by explanatory anarchy. But we would insist that, just as epistemology has to match ontology, so too does the explanatory model have to be compatible with the basic nature of the particular scientific enterprise at hand. The impact of norms within international regimes is not a passive process, which can be ascertained analogously to that of Newtonian laws governing the collision of two bodies. Hence, the common practice of treating norms as "variables"—be they independent, dependent, intervening, or otherwise—should be severely curtailed. So too should be the preoccupation with the "violation" of norms as the beginning, middle, and end of the compliance story. Precisely because state behavior within regimes *is* interpreted by other states, the rationales and justifications for behavior which are proffered, together with pleas for understanding or admissions of guilt, as well as the responsiveness to such reasoning on the part of other states, all are absolutely critical component parts of any explanation involving the efficacy of norms. Indeed, such communicative dynamics may tell us far more about how robust a regime is than overt behavior alone. And only where noncompliance is widespread, persistent, and unexcused—that is, presumably, in limiting cases—will an explanatory model that rests on overt behavior alone suffice.[54]

To be sure, communicative dynamics may be influenced by such extracontextual factors as state power, but that is no warrant for ignoring them. On the contrary, it suggests a potentially important relationship to be explored.[55] Similarly, the fact that verbal behavior may lend itself to manipula-

54. Account should also be taken of that fact that different types of norms—implicit versus explicit, constraining versus enabling, and so on—function differently in social relations. Consult Edna Ullman-Margalit, *The Emergence of Norms* (Oxford: Clarendon, 1977), and H. L. A. Hart, *The Concept of Law* (Oxford: Oxford University Press, 1961). Moreover, compliance too is a variegated and complex phenomenon, as discussed by Oran R. Young, *Compliance and Public Authority* (Baltimore: Johns Hopkins University Press, 1979).

55. It is well established that the so-called hegemonic stability thesis, for example, leaves a good deal about regimes still to be accounted for. See the original formulation and test by

tion suggests only that it be treated as judiciously as any other piece of scientific evidence.

The hierarchy of analytical components

The concept of international regimes is said to be a composite of four analytical component parts: principles ("beliefs of fact, causation, and rectitude"), norms ("standards of behavior defined in terms of rights and obligations"), rules ("specific prescriptions and proscriptions for action"), and decision-making procedures ("prevailing practices for making and implementing collective choice").[56] At first blush, the four fit together neatly in the specific case that was uppermost in everyone's mind when this conception was initially hammered out: the GATT-based trade regime.[57] The principle that liberalized trade is good for global welfare and international peace was readily translated by states into such norms as nondiscrimination, which in turn suggested the most-favored-nation rule, all of which led to negotiated tariff reductions based on reciprocal concessions. But matters were complicated right from the start by the fact that GATT contained not one but at least *two* such "scripts," and that the second stood in stark contrast to the first. The second ran from the responsibility of governments to stabilize their domestic economies on through the norm of safeguarding the balance of payments and, under certain circumstances, domestic producers, to rules defining specific GATT safeguarding provisions, and finally to establishing mechanisms of multilateral surveillance over their operations.[58] Different governments of course weighted these two scripts differently, but over time they seem not to have been unduly perturbed by the need to live with the ambiguity of their juxtaposition. Ambiguity, however, *is* more troublesome

---

Robert O. Keohane, "Theory of Hegemonic Stability and Changes in International Economic Regimes," in Ole Holsti et al., eds., *Change in the International System* (Boulder: Westview, 1980); and, most recently, Duncan Snidal, "The Limits of Hegemonic Stability Theory," *IO* 39 (Autumn 1985). One of the few contemporary realists who take the relationship between power and norms to be at all problematical and worthy of serious examination is Stephen D. Krasner, as in his thoughtful study of these issues in *Structural Conflict: The Third World against Global Liberalism* (Berkeley: University of California Press, 1985). We can agree with much of what Krasner has to say about the efficacy of norms, principles of legitimacy, and "movements of thought"—indeed, Krasner even invokes hermeneutics. And yet, in the end, we remain perplexed at how he reconciles this position with his fervent commitment to positivist realism.

56. Krasner, "Introduction," *International Regimes*, p. 2.

57. These issues were discussed at length at the October 1980 UCLA conference in preparation for the regimes book edited by Krasner.

58. The interplay between these two scripts forms the basis of Ruggie's interpretation of the postwar trade and monetary regimes presented in "Embedded Liberalism."

for analysts, *even when* it is a deliberate creation of policy makers.[59] And therein lies another epistemological tale.

The notion still prevails in the regimes literature that the four analytical components are related instrumentally and that the greater the coherence among them is, the stronger the regime will be.[60] There is an a priori attractiveness to this notion, in the 'sense that our collective research program would be eased considerably were it to obtain. But reality is not so obliging. Let us take up first the instrumentalist idea.

A basic epistemological problem with instrumentalism is its presumption that it is always possible to separate goals (presumably expressed in principles and norms) from means (presumably expressed in rules and procedures), and to order them in a superordinate-subordinate relationship. But this relationship need not hold. As R. S. Summers has aptly remarked: "However true this might be of constructing houses or other artifacts, it is not always so in law. In law when available means limit and in part define the goal, the means and the goal thus defined are to that extent inseparable."[61] What is true of law may also be true of regimes, for, as Kenneth Waltz has argued persuasively, international collaboration is shaped primarily by the availability and acceptability of means not by the desirability of ends.[62] Thus, notions such as reciprocity in the trade regime are *neither* its ends *nor* its means: in a quintessential way, they *are* the regime—they *are* the principled and shared understandings that the regime comprises.

The idea that the four regime components should also be coherent, and that coherence indicates regime strength, is even more profoundly problematical. The basic epistemological problem with this notion is its presumption that, once the machinery is in place, actors merely remain programmed by it. But this is clearly not so. Actors not only reproduce normative structures, they also change them by their very practice, as underlying conditions change, as new constraints or possibilities emerge, or as new claimants make their presence felt. Lawyers call this "interstitial lawmaking,"[63] and sociologists, the process of "structuration."[64] Only under

59. The proclivity of international relations theorists to resolve ambiguity and contradiction in images of international order, and the schema on the basis of which they do so, are explored by John Gerard Ruggie, "Changing Frameworks of International Collective Behavior: On the Complementarity of Contradictory Tendencies," in Nazli Choucri and Thomas Robinson, eds., *Forecasting in International Relations* (San Francisco: Freeman, 1978).

60. Cf. Haas, "Regime Decay."

61. R. S. Summers, "Naive Instrumentalism and the Law," in P. S. Hacker and J. Raz, eds., *Law, Morality, and Society* (Oxford: Clarendon, 1977).

62. Kenneth N. Waltz, *Theory of International Politics* (Reading, Mass.: Addison-Wesley, 1979), p. 109.

63. This is simply another name for the role of precedent in legal interpretation and development.

64. Anthony Giddens, *A Contemporary Critique of Historical Materialism* (Berkeley: University of California Press, 1981), p. 19: "According to the theory of structuration, all social action consists of social practices, situated in time-space, and organized in a skilled and knowl-

extremely unusual circumstances could we imagine parallel and simultaneous changes having taken place in each of the four component parts of regimes such that they remained coherent—assuming that they were so at the outset. In any case the robustness of international regimes has little to do with how coherent they remain—how coherent is the very robust U.S. Constitution?—but depends on the extent to which evolving and even diverging practices of actors express principled reasoning and shared understandings.

We have now reached the same conclusion through three different routes: the conventional epistemological approaches in regime studies do not and cannot suffice. Allow us, before ending this section, to resist the claim that *we* have opened up a proverbial Pandora's box. The box was opened when the discipline gravitated toward an intersubjective ontology in the study of international regimes. We have merely pointed out that this first, critical choice has consequences and implications that have not yet been adequately addressed. No discipline can resolve anomalies or reduce the wooliness of concepts when its ontological posture is contradicted by its epistemological orientation, models of explanation, and the presumed relationships among its constitutive analytical constructs. The problems we have pointed to are not insuperable, but their resolution will require the incorporation into prevailing approaches of insights and methods derived from the interpretive sciences.[65]

Regimes and organizations

The progressive shift in the literature toward the study of international regimes has been guided by an abiding concern with the structures and processes of international governance. Despite remaining problems with this framework of analysis, the most serious of which were flagged in the previous section, a great deal has been accomplished in a relatively short span of time. Along the way, however, as Figure 1 indicated, international institutions of a formal kind have been left behind. This fact is of academic interest because of the ever-present danger of theory getting out of touch with prac-

---

edgeable fashion by human agents. But such knowledgeability is always 'bounded' by unacknowledged conditions of action on the one side, and unintended consequences of action on the other. . . . By the duality of structure I mean that the structured properties of social systems are simultaneously the *medium and outcome of social acts*."

65. Representative approaches may be found in Richard Bernstein, *Praxis and Action* (Philadelphia: University of Pennsylvania Press, 1971); Stephen Toulmin, *Human Understanding* (Princeton: Princeton University Press, 1972); Clifford Geertz, *The Interpretation of Cultures* (New York: Basic, 1973); Paul Connerton, *Critical Sociology* (New York: Penguin, 1976); Dallmayr and McCarthy, *Social Inquiry;* T. K. Seung, *Structuralism and Hermeneutics* (New York: Columbia University Press, 1982); Donald Polkinghorne, *Methodology of the Human Sciences* (Albany: State University of New York Press, 1983); and Hubert L. Dreyfus and Paul Rabinow, *Michel Foucault: Beyond Structuralism and Hermeneutics* (Chicago: University of Chicago Press, 1983).

tice. But it is also of more than academic interest. The secretary general of the United Nations, to cite but one serious practical instance, has lamented that the malfunctioning of that institution seriously inhibits interstate collaboration in the peace and security field.[66] This is not the place to take up detailed institutional shortcomings in the world of international organizations. Nor would we be the ones to propose a return to the institutionalist approaches of yesteryear. Nevertheless, in order for the research program of international regimes *both* to contribute to ongoing policy concerns *and* better reflect the complex and sometimes ambiguous policy realm, it is necessary to link up regimes in some fashion with the formal mechanisms through which real-world actors operate. In point of fact, the outlines of such linkages are already implicit in the regime approach. Our purpose in this final section is no more than to underscore the specific dimensions that are highlighted by an interpretive epistemology.

There has been a great deal of interest in the regimes literature recently in what can be described as the "organizational-design" approach. The key issue underlying this approach is to discern what range of international policy problems can best be handled by different kinds of institutional arrangements, such as simple norms of coordination, the reallocation of international property rights, or authoritative control through formal organizations. For example, an international fishing authority would probably be less appropriate and less able to avoid the early exhaustion of fisheries' stock than would the ascription of exclusive property rights to states. Where problems of liability enter the picture, however, as in ship-based pollution, authoritative procedures for settling disputes would become necessary. The work of Oliver Williamson and William Ouchi is very suggestive here, demonstrating the relative efficacy of the institutionalization of behavior through "hierarchies" versus through transaction-based informal means.[67] Robert Keohane has pioneered this territory in his "functional" theory of international regimes, from which organizational designs can be similarly derived.[68]

For its part, an interpretive epistemology would emphasize three additional dimensions of the organizational-design issue. The intersubjective

66. United Nations, *Report of the Secretary-General on the Work of the Organization, 1982* (A/37/1).

67. Oliver Williamson, *Markets and Hierarchies* (New York: Free, 1975), and William Ouchi and Oliver Williamson, "The Markets and Hierarchies Program of Research: Origins, Implications, Prospects," in William Joyce and Andrew van de Ven, eds., *Organization Design* (New York: Wiley, 1981). From the legal literature, see Guido Calabresi and Douglas Melamed, "Property Rules, Liability Rules, and Inalienability: One View of the Cathedral," *Harvard Law Review* 85 (April 1972); Philip Heyemann, "The Problem of Coordination: Bargaining with Rules," *Harvard Law Review* 86 (March 1973); and Susan Rose-Ackerman, "Inalienability and the Theory of Property Rights," *Columbia Law Review* 85 (June 1985).

68. Keohane, *After Hegemony*. Some policy recommendations that flow from the approach are spelled out by Robert O. Keohane and Joseph S. Nye, "Two Cheers for Multilateralism," *Foreign Policy* 60 (Fall 1985).

basis of international regimes suggests that *transparency* of actor behavior and expectations within regimes is one of their core requirements. And, as has been shown in such diverse issue-areas as international trade, investment, nuclear nonproliferation, and human rights, international organizations can be particularly effective instruments by which to create such transparency.[69] The appropriate design of the mechanisms by which international organizations do so, therefore, should be given every bit as much consideration as the design of the mechanisms of substantive problem solving.

The second is *legitimation*. A regime can be perfectly rationally designed but erode because its legitimacy is undermined.[70] Or a regime that is a logical nonstarter can be the object of endless negotiations because a significant constituency views its aims to be legitimate.[71] If a regime enjoys both it is described as being "stable" or "hegemonic." The important point to note is that international organizations, because of their trappings of universality, are the major venue within which the global legitimation struggle over international regimes is carried out today. Work in this genre goes back at least to Inis Claude and includes important recent contributions by Robert Cox and Stephen Krasner.[72]

The third dimension we would describe as *epistemic*. Stephen Toulmin has posed the issue well: "The problem of human understanding is a twofold one. Man knows, and he is also conscious that he knows. We acquire, possess, and make use of our knowledge; but at the same time, we are aware of our own activities as knowers."[73] In the international arena, neither the processes whereby knowledge becomes more extensive nor the means whereby reflection on knowledge deepens are passive or automatic. They are intensely political. And for better or for worse, international organizations have maneuvered themselves into the position of being the vehicle through which both types of knowledge enter onto the international agenda.[74] As Ernst Haas has sought to show in his seminal work, in these

69. The GATT multilateral surveillance mechanisms are, of course, its chief institutional means of establishing intersubjectively acceptable interpretations of what actors are up to. For a treatment of investment which highlights this dimension, see Charles Lipson, *Standing Guard: Protecting Foreign Capital in the Nineteenth and Twentieth Centuries* (Berkeley: University of California Press, 1985); for nonproliferation, see Nye, "Maintaining a Nonproliferation Regime," and for human rights, John Gerard Ruggie, "Human Rights and the Future International Community *Daedalus* 112 (Fall 1983). The impact of intergovernmental information systems is analyzed by Ernst B. Haas and John Gerard Ruggie, "What Message in the Medium of Information Systems?" *International Studies Quarterly* 26 (June 1982).

70. Puchala and Hopkins, "International Regimes," in Krasner, ed., *International Regimes*, discuss the decline of colonialism in terms that include this dimension.

71. The New International Economic Order is a prime example.

72. See Claude, "Collective Legitimization"; Cox, "Labor and Hegemony," "The Crisis of World Order," and "Gramsci, Hegemony, and International Relations"; and Krasner, *Structural Conflict*.

73. Toulmin, *Human Understanding*, p. 1.

74. Ruggie analyzes this process in "On the Problem of 'The Global Problematique.' "

processes of global epistemic politics lie the seeds of the future demand for international regimes.[75]

In short, the institutional-design approach, complemented by a concern with transparency creation, the legitimation struggle, and epistemic politics, can push the heuristic fruitfulness of the regime research program "forward" yet another step, linking it "back" to the study of international organizations.

Conclusion

In this article, we set out to present a "state of the art" of the field of international organization circa 1985. Our conclusions can be restated very quickly. In the first section, we tried to dispel the notion that the field has been floundering from one "dependent variable" to another, as academic fashions have dictated. On the contrary, the analytical shifts have been progressive and cumulative and have been guided by an overriding concern with what has always preoccupied students of international organization: how the modern society of nations governs itself.

In the second section we pointed out, however, that the currently ascendant regimes approach is internally inconsistent in a manner that has deleterious effects. The reason for its inconsistency is the tension between its ontological posture and its prevailing epistemological practices. In contrast to the epistemological ideal of positivism, which insists on a separation of "object" and "subject," we proposed a more interpretive approach that would open up regime analysis to the communicative rather than merely the referential functions of norms in social interactions. Thus, what constitutes a breach of an obligation undertaken within a regime is not simply an "objective description" of a fact but an intersubjective appraisal. Likewise, what constitutes reciprocity or reasonableness of behavior within regime contexts is not an issue that can be resolved simply by a monological treatment of "objective information," as is characteristic of a propositional language. For regimes are inherently dialogical in character. To be sure, in circumstances that require little interpretation on the part of the relevant actors— because the environment is placid, because shared knowledge prevails, or because coercion determines outcomes—interpretive epistemologies will not be required. But we do not take such occurrences to be broadly representative of contemporary international regimes. For the more general universe of cases, once it was decided that the ontology of regimes consists of an intersubjective basis—and the consensus definition of regimes suggests

75. Haas, "Words Can Hurt You," and Haas, "Why Collaborate? Issue-Linkage and International Regimes," *World Politics* 32 (April 1980).

as much—then what Frank Lentricchia has called "spectator epistemology" ipso facto became insufficient.[76]

Finally, in our third section, we identified some linkages between the analytical construct of international regimes and the concrete entities of international organizations. Students of international organization have already assimilated from the organizational design school the lesson that the provision of routine and predictable policy frameworks is not synonymous with the construction of formal hierarchies. An interpretive epistemology would suggest further that international organizations can contribute to the effectiveness of informal ordering mechanisms, such as regimes, by their ability to enhance (or diminish) intersubjective expectations and normatively stabilized meanings, which are the very bases of regimes. International organizations do so, we pointed out, through the modalities of transparency creation, focusing the legitimation struggle, and devising future regime agendas via epistemic politics. Thus reinvigorated, the study of formal organizations may yet come to reinvigorate the practice of formal organizations.

76. Frank Lentricchia, *Criticism and Social Change* (Chicago: University of Chicago Press, 1983), p. 3.

The Limits of International Organization: Systematic Failure in the Management of International Relations

Giulio M. Gallarotti

"Nothing in excess" is the warning inscribed on the Temple of Apollo at Delphi and echoed in the literature and mythology of ancient Greece. According to the logic of excesses, too much of anything—even a "good" thing—can be detrimental. This lesson appears to be as relevant for international organization (IO) as it is for other social contexts.[1] Just as poorly managed or "bad" IO can be harmful, "good" IO in excess can have adverse effects.

On the one hand, IO can be counterproductive when management is of the wrong kind or is executed poorly. Critics of the Food and Agriculture Organization, for example, argue that the institution's administration supports a model of agricultural development that is antithetical to private sector growth and therefore inhibits general economic development in Third World countries.[2] On the other hand, excessive IO can be bad even when the management is apparently good. Some have argued, for example, that the provision of abundant liquidity to debt-ridden nations creates a moral hazard in that it gives debtors fewer incentives to promote the economic changes

An earlier version of this article was presented at a seminar sponsored by the Program on International Politics, Economics, and Security (PIPES) at the University of Chicago in May 1989. I gratefully acknowledge the comments of the seminar participants as well as the suggestions of Riccardo Fiorito, Jeff Frieden, Robert Jervis, Stephen Krasner, Duncan Snidal, and the anonymous referees of *International Organization*.

1. Throughout this article, I refer to international organization (IO) and international organizations (IOs) in keeping with the following distinction made in the mainstream IO literature: the term "IO" refers to both the formal (institutionalized) and informal (noninstitutionalized) processes of management, while the term "IOs" refers to the institutions engaged in the formal processes of management. IOs are thus a subset of IO. See J. Martin Rochester, "The Rise and Fall of International Organization as a Field of Study," *International Organization* 40 (Autumn 1986), pp. 753–75; Friedrich Kratochwil and John Gerard Ruggie, "International Organization: A State of the Art on an Art of the State," *International Organization* 40 (Autumn 1986), pp. 777–813; and Inis Claude, *Swords into Plowshares*, 4th ed. (Random House: New York, 1984).

2. See Roger Brooks, "Africa Is Starving and the United Nations Shares the Blame," *Backgrounder* 480, Heritage Foundation, January 1986.

International Organization 45, 2, Spring 1991, pp. 183–220

that would make them less dependent on foreign lending.[3] In this case, as with the recent case of savings and loans bailouts in the United States, it appears that safety has it price. Similarly, food aid, as traditionally practiced with respect to less developed countries (LDCs), has often served to compound problems of hunger and food dependence because of its "disincentive effects" on domestic food production.[4] And, finally, too much IO may be undesirable if it is costly and has no appreciable effect on international relations.

While IO can be said to "fail" in any of these ways, it is most antithetical to orderly international relations when its failures make international problems worse or generate new problems—that is, when IO itself is a destabilizing force in world politics. In his first annual report on the work of the United Nations (UN), Secretary-General Javier Pérez de Cuéllar sensitized the international community to such destabilizing failings in the multilateral management of interdependence by citing the adverse effects that UN resolutions can have on international security and by admitting that the misuse of the UN has contributed to the global problems facing the organization.[5] In light of the failures of IO, bureaucrats and scholars alike need to reassess the role of multilateral management and its effects on international relations within and across issue-areas. Or, more formally, they need to take into account the limitations of IO when considering the optimal scope and level of multilateral management.[6]

As Friedrich Kratochwil, John Ruggie, and J. Martin Rochester have argued, recent scholarship has increasingly strayed from the study of IO as distinct from world politics and has relinquished much in terms of the normative foundations of the traditional literature on IO. A result is that the processes of IO and international relations have been conflated in a way that makes the specific assessment of managerial processes and institutions more difficult. Furthermore, the analytic modes and conclusions generated by recent work have insufficiently addressed issues that contribute to social engineering at the level of multilateral management; that is, they have provided little food for consumption on the part of international bureaucrats

3. General arguments on moral hazard in the international monetary system have most recently been made by Charles Kindleberger in *The International Economic Order* (Cambridge, Mass.: MIT Press, 1988).

4. See Raymond Hopkins, "Reform in the International Food Aid Regime: The Role of Consensual Knowledge," *International Organization* (forthcoming).

5. Javier Pérez de Cuéllar, *Report of the Secretary-General on the Work of the Organization,* no. A/37/1 (New York: United Nations, 1982).

6. The scope of IO is defined by neofunctionalists as the range of issue-specific tasks involved in a managerial scheme, while the level is defined as the "central institutional capacity to handle a particular [issue-specific] task." See Joseph Nye, "Comparing Common Markets: A Revised Neo-Functionalist Model," in Leon Lindberg and Stuart Scheingold, eds., *Regional Integration* (Cambridge, Mass.: Harvard University Press, 1971), p. 201; and Philippe Schmitter, "Three Neo-Functional Hypotheses About Integration," *International Organization* 13 (Winter 1969), p. 162.

and national policymakers.[7] Historically, the study of IO has to a large extent been coterminous with the study of the structures, roles, and goals of international institutions. The traditional literature has placed much emphasis on institutional origins and developments in the frameworks and objectives of specific organizations and has paid considerably less attention to the effects of these organizations on international relations. Moreover, when scholars have assessed the effects, they have tended to offer a rather benign vision in which the process of multilateral management is characterized as invariably contributing to the stabilization of relations among nations and in which the limitations of management are ignored or downplayed. Thus, traditional contributions to the IO literature have been heavy on the positive side (the stabilizing outcomes of management) and light on the negative side (the failures of management), whereas the recent contributions have been instrumental in addressing the negative side but have taken a somewhat restricted approach to organizational failure. To use Kratochwil and Ruggie's analogy, while the doctor has more recently stopped visiting the patient altogether, the doctor has traditionally visited the patient without systematically diagnosing illness.[8]

In addressing these limitations in the IO literature, this article presents a typology of the systematic (inherent rather than mistake-related) failures of IO. In doing so, it brings the processes and institutions of multilateral management back into focus as phenomena that are sui generis and therefore distinct from the underlying relations they oversee. While its conclusions about the nature of overmanaged relations and the partial solutions that it offers are intended to serve as potential normative guidelines, its focus on the effects of IO is intended to complement the traditional focus on the roles, goals, and structures of international institutions. Thus, by emphasizing the destabilizing effects of IO and presenting a less benign view of the management of international relations, the article makes a contribution toward filling in the negative side of the managerial ledger. In Kratochwil and Ruggie's terms, the present enterprise once more attends to the patient, but with an emphasis on diagnosing illness.

The article begins with a discussion of the managerial approach to IO and the recent revisionist scholarship. It then confronts the managerial vision of IO by offering a more general theoretical approach to understanding the destabilizing effects of multilateral management than has commonly been taken in the critical IO literature. In presenting a typology of systematic failures, it seeks to bridge the gaps in our understanding of why many different institutions and managerial schemes fail. That IO has virtues and can

---

7. See Kratochwil and Ruggie, "International Organization"; and Rochester, "The Rise and Fall of International Organization as a Field of Study." Regarding the normative rationale for the study of IO, see also John Gerard Ruggie, "The United States and the United Nations: Toward a New Realism," *International Organization* 39 (Spring 1985), p. 345.

8. Kratochwil and Ruggie, "International Organization."

have a positive impact on international relations is not denied. Nevertheless, the article concludes that it is often in the best interest of stable international relations in and across issue-areas to be regulated by IOs that are limited in their scope or level of management. In addressing the general issue of IO failure, rather than addressing why a particular institution or managerial scheme fails, the analysis is thus intended to serve both as a focal point for understanding critical approaches to the study of IO and as an alternative rationale for eliminating the excesses of multilateral management.[9]

The managerial approach to international organization

Traditional IO scholars have tended to take a rather benign view of the process of multilateral management.[10] For these scholars, IO at best provides the necessary management dictated by the growing complexity of interdependence within and between issue-areas. At worst, this management appears as a benign redundancy in functions insofar as it is targeted to bring about order that is already existent in some set of relations. The tone of the literature has for the most part been uncritical both on a systematic and a general level,[11] and any explicit or implicit critiques that have been offered have tended to be issue- or case-specific.[12]

9. Regime analysts and neoliberal institutionalists have argued that big government can be redundant and is unnecessary when limited forms of management are sufficient. But the viability of smaller government is all the more compelling when big government is subject to organizational failure.

10. As Conybeare notes, "Federalists, functionalists, neofunctionalists, and pluralists all agree as to the inherent desirability of world government. . . . It would not be a caricature to infer from the modern IO literature that the world needs more supranational authority to manage interdependence, public goods, and externalities in general." See John Conybeare, "International Organization and the Theory of Property Rights," *International Organization* 34 (Summer 1980), pp. 307–8. The critical focus of my article, however, is not the modern IO literature per se but, rather, those strands in the IO and international relations literature that uncritically profess the need for the extensive multilateral management of international relations and support the benign view of IO from which this prescription stems. Some strands are not overtly managerial in orientation. And in many cases, as pointed out in my article, the logics of their arguments are not antithetical to the usefulness and importance of limited forms of IO.

11. Critiques of domestic government have been far more prevalent and systematic than have general critiques of IO. For a typical example of the former, see Richard Rose, "What If Anything Is Wrong with Big Government?" *Journal of Public Policy* 1 (February 1981), pp. 5–36. An inquiry into the reasons for this neglect would be speculative. Perhaps it is simply a matter of specialization, with IO failing to attract the attention of erstwhile critics of big domestic government who are specialized in domestic political issues. Or perhaps the unpleasant effects of IO are not felt on an individual level to the same extent as the unpleasant effects of domestic government are. IOs do not conscript or tax individuals, for example. Their dues come from nations rather than individuals; their laws do not affect individuals directly; and there is no authoritarian appropriation of human capital and resources. Quite simply, there are fewer reasons for individuals to be angry with IO.

12. There are, of course, exceptions to this trend, notably in the classic literature on integration and interdependence. But even these show limitations. Early neofunctionalists argued that IO can have adverse effects on specific interest groups and elites within nations but have said

According to the functionalists, the growth of technology, the awareness of its possible adverse and positive effects, and the spread and intensification of demands for higher material welfare place increasing pressure on nations to seek what Ernst Haas calls "managerial leadership" at the multilateral level.[13] The growth of "common activities and interests across nations," argues David Mitrany, requires a concomitant growth in the "common administrative agencies" that manage interdependence. International government must grow so that it remains "co-extensive with international activities." Hence, like the activities it must oversee, international management must itself become "all-embracing and all-pervasive."[14] In this sense, the growth of IO is consistent with the ongoing evolution and greater centralization of functions in human society. For a working peace system, notes Mitrany, nations must collectively "take over and coordinate activities hitherto controlled by the nation state, just as the state increasingly has to take over activities which until now have been carried on by local bodies."[15] Thus, the goal of global security is reached through a process involving "a sufficient addition" of managerial functions, which together "would create increasingly deep and wide strata of peace."[16]

For neofunctionalists, the causal link between technological and welfare problems on the one hand and international management on the other is mediated by interest groups and elites, but the vision of IO is quite similar. For them, the process of spillover is the forcing variable.[17] As the pressures for integration spread laterally and vertically, the level and scope of international management must be expanded. According to Haas, the problems of international security, economic development, and technological and scientific interdependence require an "upgrading of common interests" among nations, which is only realizable within "the framework of supranational institutions." The intensification of this "upgrading" in turn requires "continuing supranational activity."[18] For Ruggie, the impact of scientific and technological interdependence on international relations necessitates a "col-

---

much less about the adverse impact on international order and relations between nations. Haas noted that organizations can sometimes fail to achieve their goals, but he did not go on to explore the possible negative consequences of this failure. Morse noted that IO can adversely affect nations by limiting their autonomy, but he did not pursue the manifold consequences of this constraint. See Ernst Haas, *The Uniting of Europe* (Stanford, Calif.: Stanford University Press, 1958), pp. 288–89; Ernst Haas, *Beyond the Nation-State* (Stanford, Calif.: Stanford University Press, 1964), p. 126; and Edward Morse, *Modernization and the Transformation of International Relations* (New York: Free Press, 1966), p. 100.

13. Haas, *Beyond the Nation-State*, p. 31.

14. David Mitrany, *A Working Peace System* (Chicago: Quadrangle, 1966), pp. 52, 63, and 97.

15. Ibid., p. 37.

16. Ibid., p. 98.

17. Of course, even for neofunctionalists, spillover is not a given. Integration has been conceptualized as positive, stagnant, and negative.

18. See Haas, *Beyond the Nation-State*, p. 459; and Haas, *The Uniting of Europe*, p. 287.

lective response" based on "mutual accountability."[19] The collective response will be manifest in "greater amounts of joint services and joint production, and a greater degree of joint regulation of national activities."[20] For Eugene Skolnikoff, this interdependence requires that nation-states "accept a degree of international regulation and control over their nominally domestic activities that goes well beyond the situation today."[21]

Traditional scholarship in the field of modernization and interdependence has similarly argued that the greater interpenetration of the social and economic spheres that occurs with industrialization necessitates a collective approach to the specific needs of nations. Edward Morse, for example, indicates that "modernization is accompanied by increased levels and types of interdependences among societies, which require . . . a high level of cooperation."[22] This interdependence, adds Morse, makes "international coordination of policies highly desirable" because the "attainment of basic domestic policy goals" can no longer be realized through independent actions.[23]

These managerialist strands in the traditional literature on IO and interdependence have numerous counterparts in the general literature on international relations. For example, Seyom Brown and Larry Fabian would address the problem of the global commons with a comprehensive oceans authority, an international scientific commission on global resources and ecologies, a global weather and climate organization, and an outer space project agency.[24] Stanley Hoffmann, in mainstream fashion, argues that the future of the world order will depend on the growth of IO as a means of integrating inherently conflictual interests and realizing joint gains both in a political and an economic context.[25] In explicating the assumptions underlying Hoffmann's vision, Richard Cooper states that "where trust is not complete, some form of international organization may be helpful to police the rules and supervise the imposition of penalties for violations of the rules."[26] Regarding the international political economy, the exhortations of Fred Block and Robert Solomon are characteristic. According to Block, "If

19. John Gerard Ruggie, "International Responses to Technology: Concepts and Trends," *International Organization* 29 (Summer 1975), pp. 557–83.

20. John Gerard Ruggie, "Collective Goods and Future International Collaboration," *American Political Science Review* 66 (September 1972), p. 875.

21. Eugene Skolnikoff, *The International Imperatives of Technology* (Berkeley, Calif.: Institute of International Studies, 1972), p. 153.

22. Morse, *Modernization and the Transformation of International Relations,* p. 80.

23. Ibid., pp. 85 and 93.

24. Seyom Brown and Larry L. Fabian, "Toward Mutual Accountability in Nonterrestrial Realms," *International Organization* 29 (Summer 1975), pp. 887–92.

25. Stanley Hoffmann, "International Organization and the International System," in Leland Goodrich and David Kay, eds., *International Organization: Politics and Process* (Madison: University of Wisconsin Press, 1973).

26. Richard Cooper, "Prolegomena to the Choice of an International Monetary System," in C. Fred Bergsten and Lawrence Krause, eds., *World Politics and International Economics* (Washington, D.C.: Brookings Institution, 1975), p. 83.

our goal is the improvement of human welfare, this requires subordinating market forces to conscious human will."[27] Similarly, Solomon argues, "Cooperation and joint management are still necessary. . . . The international system has tended to follow the evolution that has occurred within individual countries. One of the major lessons learned in the thirties . . . is that the pursuit of self-interest by individual entities in an economy does not necessarily bring about optimal results for the economy as a whole."[28] The high point of this managerialism in international economic relations is embodied in Irving Friedman's call for a "new Bretton Woods."[29]

More recently, scholars have taken a much more systematically critical approach to IO and have qualified the traditional arguments about the need for extensive supranational government. IO has been attacked both from the right and the left and both in theoretical and nontheoretical treatises. On the right, the ongoing studies of the Heritage Foundation have expounded a vision of IO, especially as manifest in the UN, as a destabilizing force in international politics because of the inflammatory way it mediates disputes (for example, supporting the positions of guerrilla groups) and the way it generates other managerial failures.[30] A frequent critique of the UN is that it perpetuates underdevelopment because its approach is biased against market solutions. In exploring the ways in which UN management in and across issue-areas makes the world a more "dangerous place," Abraham Yeselson and Anthony Gaglione have adopted the same destabilizing view of the UN.[31] Others have underscored that deficiencies in the managerial structures of the UN are the sources of its failure and inefficiencies.[32]

27. Fred Block, *The Origins of International Economic Disorder* (Berkeley: University of California Press, 1977), p. 225.

28. Robert Solomon, *The International Monetary System, 1945–1981* (New York: Harper & Row, 1982), p. 379.

29. See Irving Friedman, *Toward World Prosperity: Reshaping the World Money System* (Lexington, Mass.: Lexington Books, 1987), p. 273. More specifically, Friedman calls for a resuscitation of the managerial instruments of the Bretton Woods system, which he and many others believed were strong. Actually, the system reflected rather weak management in configuring monetary relations. Relations carried on in a rather haphazard way with occasional multilateral (G-10) and unilateral (U.S.) management.

30. In its journal, *Backgrounder,* the Heritage Foundation has published numerous studies that take a critical view of UN operations. See especially Juliana Geran Pilon, "The Center on Transnational Corporations: How the UN Injures Poor Nations," *Backgrounder* 608, October 1987; Thomas Gulick, "How the U.N. Aids Marxist Guerrilla Groups," *Backgrounder* 177, April 1982; and Brooks, "Africa Is Starving and the United Nations Shares the Blame." See also Charles Lichenstein et al., *The United Nations: Its Problems and What to Do About Them* (Washington, D.C.: Heritage Foundation, 1986); and Burton Yale Pines, ed., *A World Without a U.N.* (Washington, D.C.: Heritage Foundation, 1984).

31. See the following works by Abraham Yeselson and Anthony Gaglione: "The Use of the United Nations in World Politics," in Steven Spiegel, ed., *At Issue: Politics in the World Arena* (New York: St. Martin's Press, 1981), pp. 392–99; and *A Dangerous Place* (New York: Viking Press, 1974).

32. Robert Jackson argued, for example, that the UN could be likened to "some prehistoric monster, incapable of intelligently controlling itself. This is not because it lacks intelligent and capable officials, but because it is so organized that managerial direction is impossible." Jackson is quoted in "The United Nations Agencies: A Case for Emergency Treatment," *Economist,*

The leftist literature on IO has tended to take the same pejorative view of supranational structures of governance that leftists normally take of domestic structures of governance: both types institutionalize class hegemony. In the case of supranational government, leftists speak of economic (capitalist) classes of nations as well as social classes. Most of their studies are targeted at specific organizations, while some contributions exhibit a general orientation.[33]

On a more theoretical level, proponents of rational choice and public choice approaches to IO have argued that supranational management is either redundant or the source of inefficiencies in the relations between nations. John Conybeare argues that the market can sufficiently allocate goods and address international problems in relations that do not exhibit high levels of publicness and that supranational management in these relations is unnecessary and would only replicate the outcomes generated by less centralized schemes.[34] John Ruggie and Per Magnus Wijkman marshal similar, albeit more restrictive, arguments.[35] Roland Vaubel sees the collusive and redistributive nature of international collaboration as inherently imposing welfare losses on the international system in general as well as on specific subnational groups.[36]

At the same time that scholars have taken a more critical approach to IO, they have also taken a more decentralized approach to the possibilities for order and cooperation in international politics. This trend is particularly evident in the regime and neoliberal institutionalist contributions to the international relations literature. According to proponents of the decentralized approach, institutions serve as facilitators of cooperation. This suggests positive, rather than critical, sentiments about the role of IO. Where they

---

2 December 1989, p. 23. See also David Pitt, "Power in the UN Superbureaucracy: A Modern Byzantium," and Johan Galtung, "A Typology of United Nations Organizations," in David Pitt and Thomas Weiss, eds., *The Nature of United Nations Bureaucracies* (Boulder, Colo.: Westview Press, 1986), pp. 23–38 and 59–83, respectively.

33. See, for example, Ismail Abdalla, "The Inadequacy and Loss of Legitimacy of the International Monetary Fund," *Development*, vol. 22, Society for International Development, Rome, 1980, pp. 46–65; Cheryl Payer, *The Debt Trap: The International Monetary Fund and the Third World* (New York: Monthly Review Press, 1974); Cheryl Payer, *The World Bank: A Critical Analysis* (New York: Monthly Review Press, 1982); Teresa Hayter, *Aid as Imperialism* (New York: Penguin, 1974); Robert Cox, "The Crisis in World Order and the Problem of International Organization in the 1980s," *International Journal* 35 (Spring 1980), pp. 370–95; Robert Cox, "Labor and Hegemony," *International Organization* 31 (Summer 1977), pp. 385–424; and Peter Cocks, "Toward a Marxist Theory of European Integration," *International Organization* 34 (Winter 1980), pp. 1–40.

34. Conybeare, "International Organization and the Theory of Property Rights."

35. Ruggie and Wijkman, however, are generally positive about the functions of IO with respect to confronting issues of publicness. See Ruggie, "Collective Goods and Future International Collaboration"; and Per Magnus Wijkman, "Managing the Global Commons," *International Organization* 36 (Summer 1982), pp. 511–36.

36. Roland Vaubel, "A Public Choice Approach to International Organization," *Public Choice*, vol. 51, 1986, pp. 39–57.

depart from traditional managerial approaches, however, is in their sensitivity to the conditionality of management. Since relations in and across issue-areas are seen as heterogeneous, rather than homogeneous, the requirements for regulation will vary in scope and level. Some constellations of relations (particularly those with preexisting norms about appropriate policies) will require institutions only to reduce the organization or transaction costs of cooperation, while others will require more careful and extensive regulation.[37]

Although the revisionist literature on IO offers a valuable counterbalance to the traditional managerial view, it nevertheless exhibits limitations in its identification and analysis of organizational failure. The existing critical literature, for example, tends to be disproportionately specific in its targets and orientation. While the work of Yeselson and Gaglione, the studies from the Heritage Foundation, and the literature on bureaucratic failure are specifically targeted toward the UN, the leftist literature has commonly focused on the World Bank, International Monetary Fund, and the UN. Even the work that appears to be of a more general orientation is still quite restricted and sometimes insufficiently systematic in its identification of IO failure. General leftist critiques, such as those of Robert Cox and Teresa Hayter,[38] are fundamentally restricted to the adverse distributional effects of the institutionalization of First World hegemony and are much less concerned with instabilities within classes of nations. Conybeare, Wijkman, and Ruggie are more concerned with why IO might be unnecessary than with how and why IO fails. Although Vaubel is both general and systematic in the identification of IO failure, he is more concerned with the inefficiencies than with the destabilizing effects of IO, and his analysis of inefficiencies is restricted to those generated by the collusive and redistributional nature of IO.

In contrast to the revisionist literature, which offers a restricted critique

37. See the contributions to *International Organization,* vol. 36, Spring 1982, a special issue on regimes. See also Robert Keohane, *After Hegemony* (Princeton, N.J.: Princeton University Press, 1984); and Robert Keohane and Joseph Nye, *Power and Interdependence,* 2d ed. (Glenview, Ill.: Scott, Foresman, 1985). For surveys of the literature on regimes and neoliberal institutionalism, see Stephan Haggard and Beth Simmons, "Theories of International Regimes," *International Organization* 41 (Summer 1987), pp. 491–517; and Joseph Grieco, "Anarchy and the Limits of Cooperation: A Realist Critique of the Newest Liberal Institutionalism," *International Organization* 42 (Summer 1988), pp. 485–507. For other works that are concerned with less managed relations, see Conybeare, "International Organization and the Theory of Property Rights"; Wijkman, "Managing the Global Commons"; W. Max Corden, "The Logic of the International Monetary Non-System," in Fritz Machlup, Gerhard Fels, and Hubertus Muller-Groeling, eds., *Reflections on a Troubled World Economy: Essays in Honor of Herbert Giersch* (New York: St. Martin's Press, 1983), pp. 59–74; W. Max Corden, "Fiscal Policies, Current Accounts and Real Exchange Rates: In Search of a Logic of International Policy Coordination," *Weltwirtschaftliches,* vol. 122, 1986, pp. 423–38; Roland Vaubel, "Coordination or Competition Among National Macro-Economic Policies?" in Machlup, Fels, and Muller-Groeling, *Reflections on a Troubled World Economy,* pp. 3–28; and Martin Feldstein, "Let the Market Decide," *Economist,* 3 December 1988, pp. 21–24.

38. See Cox, "The Crisis in World Order and the Problem of International Organization in the 1980s"; Cox, "Labor and Hegemony"; and Hayter, *Aid as Imperialism.*

of how IO can fail *within* specific issues and institutions, the following general critique of managerialism offers a typology of systematic organizational failure and suggests how IO can fail *across* issues and institutions.

Critique of managerialism: the systematic failure of international organization

The failures of IO, defined here as the negative or destabilizing effects of IO on international relations, can generally be classified as either unsystematic or systematic. While unsystematic failures are related to mistakes or malfunctions in the management of international problems, systematic failures are considered inherent in or endemic to IO.[39] There is no systematic reason, for example, why one supranational organization would make the mistake of overmanaging relations while another would not; why one would be too extreme in demanding adherence to its rules while another would not; or, more generally, why one institution or managerial scheme would be characterized by or result in poor management. While unsystematic failures are stochastic and have a chaotic distribution, systematic failures are determined by bias (by the roles, functions, and goals of IO, which naturally encourage failure) and have an identifiable pattern in their distribution. IO can fail systematically in four general ways that will be summarized briefly here and discussed in detail below.

First, IO can be destabilizing when it attempts to manage complex, tightly coupled systems. Because management of complex relations and issues is one of the goals of IO and because these complex systems are difficult to understand and therefore manage successfully, there are inherent possibilities for destabilizing management.[40]

Second, IO can be destabilizing when its solutions discourage nations from pursuing more substantive or long-term resolutions to international problems, including disputes, or when it serves as a substitute for responsible

---

39. This dual categorization of managerial failure is somewhat problematic because what some consider to be random mistakes of bureaucrats may be seen by others as problems endemic to the bureaucratic structure of IO. Similarly, depending on the manner in which malfunction is defined, IO can be said to malfunction systematically or unsystematically. Further research may improve upon the present typology by suggesting a better differentiation both between and within categories. Nevertheless, the dual categorization is useful as a first-cut approach to the general failures in the process of international management. The alternative presentation of undifferentiated failure does little service to the normative and theoretical importance of distinguishing endemic failures from failures that are more stochastic.

A point that deserves emphasis here is that while IO is by nature prone to several types of failure, it does not follow that IO will invariably fail. A simple analogy is that the inherent or genetic predisposition to diabetes does not always manifest itself as disease.

40. The mainstream IO literature has tended to offer a "complexity" rationale for supranational government: as interdependence becomes more complex and issue-spaces increase in density, the need for IO to orchestrate relations also increases.

domestic or foreign policy. It is in the nature of supranational management to generate solutions and resolutions (output) that address international problems, and to the extent that it does so, it reduces the incentives of nations to come up with better alternatives.

Third, IO can actually intensify international disputes under several circumstances: when it is used as a weapon of confrontational statecraft, when it encourages confrontational solutions to problems, when it creates roadblocks to the resolution of disputes, when it is a source of destabilizing linkages, when it is a source of predatory or confrontational collusion, and when it takes sides in international disputes. In the case of international disputes, IO is by nature prone to confer greater legitimacy to one of the competing factions and thereby shift the moral balance of power. Like other instruments of international competition, then, IO support can be an important instrument of statecraft. This was evident, for example, in President Kennedy's desire to have the approval of the Organization of American States before confronting the Soviets on the issue of Cuban missiles.

Fourth, IO can have destabilizing effects when it is a source of moral hazard. Supranational management is fundamentally based on the desire to prevent crises or provide insurance against the untoward effects of potential crises that emanate from a state's irresponsible behavior. In mitigating the adverse consequences of this behavior, IO reduces the incentives for the state to eliminate the underlying problem, which is the behavior itself.

The principal element of failure in the first category—the management of complex, tightly coupled systems—is essentially a technical one: cooperation yields inferior outcomes because of the technical difficulty of managing systems of relations and issues. The principal element of failure in the other three categories—which we can label adverse substitution, dispute intensification, and moral hazard—is not technical: a technical basis for cooperation does exist, but the political systems act in ways that can make cooperation destabilizing.

Managing complex, tightly coupled systems

Organizations often attempt to manage systems whose problems emanate from what Charles Perrow would refer to as the "complex, tightly coupled" nature of international relations.[41] As with any cybernetic system, the feedback effects of the systems of relations and issues are complicated and frequently unpredictable. And as with any complex chaotic system, these systems commonly exhibit what the chaos literature refers to as a sensitivity

---

41. The subject of complex, tightly coupled systems is formally explored by Perrow in the context of accidents which involve nuclear power, chemicals, and other high-risk technology and which have adverse effects on the various ecosystems. See Charles Perrow, *Normal Accidents: Living with High-Risk Technologies* (New York: Basic Books, 1984).

to initial conditions, or a macrosensitivity to developments in microconditions. Their complexity and unpredictability are thus a function of the numerous and highly conditional connections between the many variables that contribute to systemic outcomes. As Perrow argues, the complexity of tightly coupled systems makes it impossible to manage them in a way that avoids periodic crises; in other words, catastrophes and accidents are "normal" and are the rule rather than the exception.[42] Not only is IO incapable of avoiding crises, but IO often causes or exacerbates problems by offering solutions that have unpredictable and destabilizing effects.[43]

Contributors to the literature on interdependence, most notably Robert Keohane, Joseph Nye, Richard Cooper, and James Rosenau, have essentially viewed the international political economy as a system with the characteristics noted above and have emphasized the complexity of interdependence emanating from process and issue density (the tight linkage of different economic processes and international issues).[44] The literature has also highlighted the similarities between international political economic relations and the processes of systems theory and chaotic systems: feedback processes are numerous and not fully understood; knowledge about principal relationships is often indirect and inferred; there are strong systemic sensitivities to small changes in underlying conditions; policies and actions are connected in complicated constellations of relations; and simple policy initiatives often generate unintended systemic outcomes.[45]

The period from the mid-1940s to the present, for example, has been one in which international monetary schemes have been aimed at instituting and managing equilibrium exchange rates while economists have continually argued that we do not know what equilibrium rates are *ex ante* and can only know what they are *ex post*. Gottfried Haberler's statement on the equilibrium value of the dollar is representative: "With all due respect, it must be said that we, economists as well as ministers and other officials, simply do

---

42. Ibid.

43. Economists of the Austrian school have underscored this point with respect to attempts at managing complex systems such as markets and prices. Centrally planned economies, contrived price systems, and other forms of control, they argue, produce outcomes that are Pareto-inferior and significantly worse than those effected by a market approach. See, for example, the following works of Friedrich Hayek: *Individualism and Economic Order* (Chicago: University of Chicago Press, 1948), p. 187; *Law, Legislation and Liberty,* vol. 1 (Chicago: University of Chicago Press, 1973), pp. 48–50; and *The Fatal Conceit: The Errors of Socialism* (Chicago: University of Chicago Press, 1988), pp. 85–88.

44. See Keohane and Nye, *Power and Interdependence;* Richard Cooper, *The Economics of Interdependence* (New York: Council on Foreign Relations, 1968); and James Rosenau, *Turbulence in World Politics* (Princeton, N.J.: Princeton University Press, 1990).

45. For a discussion of systems in international politics, see Robert Jervis, "Systems Theories and International Politics," in Paul Gordon Lauren, ed., *Diplomacy* (New York: Free Press, 1979), pp. 212–43. On the subject of chaos, see James Gleick, *Chaos: Making a New Science* (New York: Penguin, 1988).

not know enough to say what the equilibrium exchange rate is.''[46] More generally, William Branson argues that the management of exchange rates is well beyond our state-of-the-art methods of rational organization: "With this range of disagreement on [the] economic analysis [of exchange rate equilibration], how are negotiators to reach agreement? The topic is one for the National Science Foundation, not a new Bretton Woods.''[47]

There is significant disagreement on a plethora of issues, not the least of which is what economic indicators are a valid reflection of equilibrium. It has been commonly thought that equilibrium is determined on the real side: the exchange rate at which trade balance is encouraged. But even this long-honored wisdom has been called to task both on the empirical and the theoretical side. The U.S. deficit with Japan budged only hesitantly from 1985 to 1987, while the dollar lost 50 percent of its value vis-à-vis the yen during this period. Japanese retail pricing trends showed that the yen-denominated prices of American goods in Japan had remained almost unchanged. Evidently, Japanese importers enjoyed the greater purchasing power of the yen but did not pass the savings on to the Japanese consumer. Hence, the decline of the dollar vis-à-vis the yen effected a redistribution from American exporters and Japanese consumers to Japanese middlemen, rather than eradicating the bilateral trade imbalance. Outcomes such as this have led some economists, Jagdish Bhagwati and Robert Mundell included, to question whether any continued change in the dollar will significantly dent the trade deficit. They argue that because competition in industrial markets is imperfect and because nations can counteract an appreciating currency with more protectionism so as to maintain a trade balance, exchange rates are rendered less effective in adjusting trade flows.[48]

Attempts at managing the complex, tightly coupled system of political economic relations have created a trail of international events that leads to the graveyard of misguided social engineering. The Louvre Accord of February 1987, for example, was negotiated and adopted by the G-7 for the purpose of strengthening the dollar following its sharp two-year decline. It ended up having just the opposite effect in the short run because it was perceived by the market as a signal of the dollar's weakness rather than its strength, and the resulting run against the dollar brought it well below the Louvre target. The G-7 did not anticipate this negative feedback. As it turned out, the intervention scheme initiated a destabilizing self-fulfilling prophecy: investors, thinking that the fall of the dollar was not yet over, took actions that brought such an outcome about. If the accord had not been concluded,

46. Gottfried Haberler, "The International Monetary System: Recent Developments in Perspective," *Aussenwirtschaft,* vol. 42, 1987, p. 379.
47. William Branson, "The Coordination of Exchange Rate Policy," *Brookings Papers on Economic Activity,* no. 1, 1986, p. 176.
48. See "Passing the Buck," *Economist,* 11 February 1989.

the market might have been prepared to accept the Louvre target. In other words, less management might have brought about a better outcome.[49]

Unfortunately, the Louvre story does not end there. U.S. authorities tried to counteract the destabilizing speculation by raising interest rates and demanding specific macroeconomic policies from other G-7 nations. These actions destabilized financial markets during the period in which the Dow speculative balloon was most inflated. The October crash followed. Haberler bluntly called the Louvre Accord "a striking example of how *not* to fix exchange rates."[50] Pointing out the dangers involved when less than well conceived and organized schemes are used in an attempt to manage complex systems, he argued that "the foreign exchange market, like the stock market, is a very delicate and sensitive mechanism that does not lend itself to continued manipulation by a loosely organized group of nations."[51] In this case, the solution made the problem worse because the approach in counteracting the adverse effects of the initial managerial miscalculation was essentially a linear solution to a tightly coupled problem. Decision makers proceeded as if moods in domestic financial markets were isolated from international policy initiatives. They erroneously assumed that policies geared toward the defense of the dollar in international forums would not feed back adversely onto perceptions of prevailing trends in domestic financial markets.[52]

The Louvre Accord was presented to the public in a way that reduced rather than increased confidence. "The accord," noted one journalist, "focused attention on the weakest elements of cooperation. Every time [James] Baker spoke he offered a new version of what the accord was expected to

---

49. For discussions of the Louvre Accord and its results, see "The Show Can't Go On," *Economist*, 21 November 1987, pp. 13–14; Haberler, "The International Monetary System"; and Yoichi Funabashi, *Managing the Dollar: From the Plaza to the Louvre* (Washington, D.C.: Institute for International Economics, 1988), pp. 187–92. It is not clear that defenders of the Louvre Accord are correct in attributing positive externalities to it. The argument that even misaligned rates stabilize trade flows assumes that volatility following the imposition of the exchange rate was less than it would have been if the rate had been allowed to converge by market forces. There is more evidence to suggest that, on the contrary, the imposition and market reaction to it created more volatility than would have otherwise occurred.

50. Haberler, "The International Monetary System," p. 383.

51. Ibid., p. 381.

52. The direction of swings in response to changes or developments in financial markets, currency markets, and other complex systems is difficult to predict, as are the perceptions of investors and other actors. This brings up the question of whether these systems would be more manageable if actors knew more about the manifold effects of different policies. In some situations, even supposedly prudent policies may have adverse effects if actors in systems are adapting to rather than passively accepting policy. (Such adaptive microbehavior typifies complex, tightly coupled systems.) But this could also be the case when actors are cognitively rigid. For example, given a particular nervous state in currency markets, investors may interpret any kind of interest rate policy (even the most prudent one based on knowledge of how currency markets work) as signaling trouble for a currency. An interest rate hike to prop up the dollar, for instance, may be perceived as a signal that the dollar is weak. A rate decrease may be perceived as a signal that U.S. policymakers will let the dollar slip. And finally, no change in the interest rate may be taken as indecision on the part of U.S. policymakers and perceived as a sign of trouble.

achieve, and of the roles of the various partner countries' policies. . . . Each new disagreement with West Germany . . . made the Louvre agreement seem hollower than it really was."[53] The April 1987 communiqué of the G-7 on the state of monetary relations was an especially glaring failure. Baker called the April meeting of the G-7 "quite successful," but the communiqué failed to make mention of any specific intentions to support the dollar. A strong-dollar statement was necessary to get the dollar out of its bearish state, given that trade figures for February were announced in mid-April and were dismal, causing dismay among dollar holders. James Vick of Manufactures Hanover Trust reflected how the market in general perceived this omission and what it indicated about G-7 intentions when he commented that the G-7 "seemed to be accepting the current level of the dollar and the downward direction."[54] This perception was reinforced by the G-7's approval of the new rate around "the most current levels."[55] These outcomes were further manifestations of the strong sensitivity of macroproperties to apparently small developments in international markets.

The managerial pattern continued under James Brady. In November 1988, following the election of Bush, the dollar declined sharply. This was met with intervention both by the Federal Reserve Bank and by several European central banks to keep the dollar from declining to a new low against the yen. On the second day of this intervention, Brady made the following statement: "Markets go up and down. I really don't worry about it very much."[56] The statement was perceived as signaling that the commitment of the G-7 was not strong and that the dollar might fall even more. This led to foreign exchange trading that ran counter to the intervention of the central banks (and, of course, imposed losses on the banks that had purchased depreciating dollars). One New York banker said, "We've had Brady make several statements early on that have not given the indication that he recognizes or has the judgment to understand that he has a profound impact on the market-place."[57]

In the cases of both the Louvre Accord and the Plaza Accord that preceded it, policymakers failed to accept a fundamental lesson: exchange rates are not imposed upon markets; they are determined by markets.[58] In 1987, after Louvre ranges were established and defended, Baker and the G-7 kept talking (telling the market what equilibrium rates were), but the market failed to

53. See "Almighty Fallen," *Economist,* 14 November 1987, p. 11.
54. James Vick, quoted by Funabashi in *Managing the Dollar,* pp. 189–90.
55. Funabashi, *Managing the Dollar.*
56. See "Brady Avoiding Critics as Group of 7 Gathers," *The New York Times,* 2 February 1989, p. D-1.
57. Ibid.
58. Rates were imposed much more frequently under the Bretton Woods regime in the 1950s and 1960s than they have been recently. But the size and the sensitivity of exchange markets were considerably smaller than they are now. And, in fact, the destabilizing money flows of the 1960s attest to the difficulty of sustaining rates misaligned with respect to the market rate.

listen.[59] In both cases, agreements were ill-conceived because they were attempting to coordinate unstable policy preferences.[60] The outcome was that the nations violated both the letter and the spirit of the agreements, thereby producing bad relations among the participants.[61] These events served to further destabilize financial markets. Investors perceived that the G-7 was unable to impose order on the international monetary system, and this in turn fed back domestically and internationally to create pessimistic investment moods.[62] Decision makers continued to remain out of touch with the complete range of reactions to the nature and effectiveness of their multilateral policy initiatives. And these reactions continued to be principal sources of instability in financial and exchange markets.[63] In sum, for reasons relating to the limitations of regulating complex economic systems, the Louvre and Plaza schemes produced some cures that ended up being worse than the diseases.

The outcomes of policy coordination in recent years are quite consistent with recent theoretical findings regarding the pursuit of collective macroeconomic management in the face of disagreements on the fundamental workings of national and international economies and in the face of limited information. Jeffrey Frankel and Katherine Rockett, for example, have shown that in cases in which nations disagree on the macroeconomic models (an expected situation, since macroeconomies themselves constitute complex, tightly coupled systems) and in which the effects of economic policy are not perfectly predictable because of the complexity and tightly coupled nature of causal relations in economic markets, macroeconomic policy coordination

59. See Funabashi, *Managing the Dollar,* p. 190.

60. See ibid., pp. 28, 29, 34, 205–7, 214, and 228.

' 61. Especially distasteful were the U.S. threats; the U.S. insistence on a high yen rate; the constant changes in negotiating forums, including at various times the G-2, G-3, G-5, and G-7; and the attempts at unilateral management of the dollar rate, characterized by "talking the dollar down" when others refused to accommodate the downward trend of the dollar. See ibid., pp. 53, 182, 217, and 235–37.

62. An alternative interpretation of the Louvre and Plaza episodes might be that large and responsive capital markets, in combination with high mobility in the flow of goods and capital, have made it necessary for advanced industrial nations to coordinate their economic policies and that failures are a small price to pay for the necessary long-term management. No one would argue that coordination is not valuable or that the market can resolve all economic problems. But the Louvre and Plaza agreements generated significant instabilities that most likely would not have occurred in the absence of intervention. Even the necessity of long-term coordination is no excuse for generating market instability that has short-run effects and might in turn generate lasting effects. Given the adverse outcomes of linear managerial approaches taken in the past, it seems all the more inexcusable to turn to them again and again in the present.

63. For reasons relating to the unpredictability of international reactions to the construction of international managerial schemes in the area of the debt problem, Kindleberger appears cautious about the desirability of even attempting to develop collaborative multilateral solutions. If such attempts were made and fail, he argues, and if this generated pessimistic forecasts about developments in the issue-area, the problem is likely to be exacerbated. See Kindleberger, *The International Economic Order,* p. 12.

can almost as likely be bad for nations in terms of welfare as it can be good. In some instances, constellations of uncoordinated unilateral actions would be preferable to cooperation, especially the type of cooperation founded on linear approaches to market interventions.[64]

These findings point to a common failure for any organization solving problems in complex, tightly coupled systems. There are side effects, many of which are unforseeable. With respect to the problem of economic development, Paul Streeten notes that "scientists may have a solution to every problem, but development has a problem for every solution."[65] Such conditions put a premium on nonlinear solutions to the problem of poverty. "Single actions which look technically correct," he emphasizes, "can be worse than useless if they are not accompanied by supplementary actions."[66] This is especially true about managing nations toward higher levels of economic development. According to Streeten, "Development is . . . like a jigsaw puzzle. To be effective, several actions must be taken together, in the right order; rural education has to be combined with the improvement of rural amenities or the educated will leave the countryside. The new seeds have to be applied with fertilizers and water at the right time; there must be extension services and roads to get the food to the markets."[67]

Adverse substitution

Nations are continually faced with difficult domestic and international problems whose resolution entails political, economic, or social costs. Although IO can alleviate short-run pressures and provide nations with an "out" from more costly solutions, doing so can be counterproductive in that it discourages nations from seeking more substantive and longer-term resolutions to their problems. To the extent that time horizons are short (which is certainly the case in domestic political systems where political survival is predicated on short-run imperatives) and national leaders are sensitive to differing domestic costs of competing solutions to domestic and international problems (which also appears to be the case), nations will be encouraged to substitute less costly and less viable multilateral schemes for more costly and substantive solutions.[68] The problem of substitution is systematic be-

64. See Jeffrey Frankel and Katherine Rockett, "International Macroeconomic Policy Coordination when Policymakers Do Not Agree on the Model," *American Economic Review* 78 (June 1988), pp. 318–40.

65. Paul Streeten, "The United Nations: Unhappy Family," in Pitt and Weiss, *The Nature of United Nations Bureaucracies*, p. 187.

66. Ibid.

67. Ibid.

68. It has, in fact, been a long-standing characteristic of international economic summitry for leaders to use international agreements to reduce some of their domestic economic and political costs. See Robert Putnam and Nicholas Bayne, *Hanging Together: Cooperation and Conflict in the Seven-Power Summits* (Cambridge, Mass.: Harvard University Press, 1987); and Vaubel, "A Public Choice Approach to International Organization."

cause it is in the nature of IO to solve international and domestic problems. But because of jurisdictional limitations and the bargaining process, the solutions offered by IO are often not substantive.

Secretary-General Pérez de Cuéllar pointed to one of the largest and most prevalent drawbacks of IO substitution in his first annual report on the work of the UN: "There is a tendency in the United Nations for governments to act as though the passage of a resolution absolved them from further responsibility for the subject in question."[69] Particularly in the case of dispute resolution, the tendency has been to offer flimsy "patch job" solutions that reduce the incentives for disputants to find a better way of resolving their differences. This point was emphasized by James Stegenga in his 1968 assessment of the effects of UN efforts in Cyprus: "UNFICYP [the UN Peace-keeping Force in Cyprus] is vulnerable to the charge that it may very well be inhibiting settlement. By helping to protect and thus consolidate the abnormal status quo and by reducing the sense of urgency felt by both sides, the Force may actually be making a negative contribution to what in the long run is the most important requirement, a viable political order."[70] Yeselson and Gaglione have questioned whether the UN Emergency Force (UNEF) efforts in the Middle East have had the same negative effect by providing an inferior substitute for a viable resolution in the region.[71]

Patrick Garrity has recently argued that UN peacekeeping efforts have allowed U.S. policymakers to postpone crucial security decisions that eventually must be made.[72] In this regard, we must question the effects of the UN in general and its solutions in particular on the relations between the superpowers. In the UN General Assembly, majorities have always favored one superpower over the other, offering more support to the United States in the early decades and more to the Soviet Union in later decades. Historically, the UN has provided a rational incentive for one of the superpowers to try to marshall collective support for a UN resolution against the other and thereby extract some desired action or policy through collective confrontation rather than through direct negotiations that would involve some form of concessions or quid pro quos. In short, given the tendency of UN members to automatically side with the appropriate superpower, collective confrontation via the UN has provided the superpowers with a relatively costless substitute for more costly direct bargaining. As Yeselson and Gaglione have observed, "Victories at the [UN] were cheap. They involved no

---

69. Pérez de Cuéllar, *Report of the Secretary-General on the Work of the Organization,* p. 3.

70. James Stegenga, *The United Nations Force in Cyprus* (Columbus: Ohio State University Press, 1968), p. 186.

71. See Yeselson and Gaglione, *A Dangerous Place.*

72. See Patrick Garrity, "The United Nations and Peacekeeping," in Pines, *A World Without a U.N.,* p. 155. See also Ruggie's response to Garrity, "The United States and the United Nations," p. 348.

cost in blood and very little in treasure, and they lent an aura of righteousness to . . . foreign policy.''[73]

For the same or similar reasons, the diversion of important issues or controversies into IOs that are mainly ceremonial forums (which many are) is often counterproductive. Nations may perceive negotiations in international forums either as viable substitutes for more fruitful negotiations at the bilateral or multilateral level or as viable substitutes for real cooperation.[74] The result, as Robert Rothstein pointed out in his study of the UN Conference on Trade and Development (UNCTAD) is that "the situation may get worse simply because living with an increasingly ceremonial process is much easier than trying to reform it. . . . And, of course, the most obvious consequences ought to be reemphasized: problems get worse, time is lost, and resources are expended."[75]

Critics of IO-orchestrated development schemes argue that the public funds of IOs are inferior substitutes for private investments in the Third World and tend to generate negative externalities. IO funds are often tied to government planning that is antithetical to market processes. Because regulated economies are less attractive to international investors, this has the effect of driving out private investment, which is especially bad given the link between economic development and the growth of the private sector in underdeveloped nations.[76] Roger Brooks makes a related point with respect to agricultural development in Africa.[77]

Food aid, as commonly practiced before the 1970s, has encouraged LDCs to substitute food transfers for domestic agricultural production. This has served to reduce agricultural self-sufficiency in the long run through disincentive effects on local food production, thus compounding the problems of hunger and food dependence in underdeveloped nations. Moreover, food

73. Yeselson and Gaglione, *A Dangerous Place,* p. 178.

74. The literature on collective action suggests that sometimes it is to the benefit of a community as a whole for people not to have private substitutes for poor public services. The fact that they have such substitutes encourages them to exit (vote with their feet) rather than use their voice to contribute to the improvement of those services. For example, communities will be less likely to have poor public schools if private schools do not exist. This will encourage the wealthiest and most educated to contribute to collective action schemes designed to improve the school system. Collective action is enhanced to the extent that private substitutes for public goods are unavailable. One could make an interesting argument about the destabilizing nature of the "star wars" program on these grounds. The program's technology would increase the risk of war among the superpowers because if developed (even by both) it would represent a substitute for further cooperation. For a discussion about the adverse effects of private substitutes, see Russell Hardin, *Collective Action* (Baltimore, Md.: Johns Hopkins University Press, 1982), p. 73.

75. Robert Rothstein, *Global Bargaining: UNCTAD and the Quest for a New International Economic Order* (Princeton, N.J.: Princeton University Press, 1979), p. 20.

76. Data show that development is positively correlated with the growth of the private sector. See Edward Erickson and Daniel Sumner, "The U.N. and Economic Development," in Pines, *A World Without a U.N.,* pp. 1–22. See also Pilon, "The Center on Transnational Corporations."

77. See Brooks, "Africa Is Starving and the United Nations Shares the Blame."

transfers have disrupted local systems of food production and distribution, generated extremely expensive subsidy programs, created administrative nightmares, and encouraged corruption.[78]

It is interesting, Inis Claude notes, that some of the fiercest enemies of IO have been strong proponents of world government (federalists).[79] This animosity is not surprising, however, according to the federalist logic. As an unsatisfactory substitute for more comprehensive managerial arrangements, IO serves as a "palliative" that reduces the fervor for real world government. In this sense, IO is more antithetical to international government than anarchy is. Agreeing with this assessment, Claude has argued that world government requires an existing community. IO can delay or prevent that community from arising because it reduces the sense of urgency for real and substantive community building.[80] Consistent with this same line of argument, Adam Roberts and Benedict Kingsbury have argued that the UN has actually worked against international security in its function as a perceived potential substitute for arms control. "By presenting a mythological alternative to armaments," they argue, "it may distract attention from other possibly more fruitful approaches to the urgent problem of controlling and limiting military force."[81]

IO sometimes functions as another kind of substitute: a substitute for responsible domestic policies. In this function, IO can be destabilizing in the long run not only at the national level but also at the international level if domestic disorder spills over into international relations. In the case of the Plaza Accord, for example, the United States was given a way of escaping necessary and costly adjustments in government spending: bringing down the dollar through intervention was preferred to bringing down the dollar by cutting the budget, which would have brought interest rates down.[82] Defenders of the conditionality policies of multilateral lending institutions have used the substitution logic to justify their argument that unconditional lending would only make loans a substitute for responsible macroeconomic and foreign economic policy management.[83] In the case of the Bretton Woods

---

78. Hopkins identifies these problems as central targets for multilateral food aid reform in the 1970s and 1980s. See Hopkins, "Reform in the International Food Aid Regime."

79. See Claude, *Swords into Plowshares*, pp. 417–19.

80. Ibid.

81. Adam Roberts and Benedict Kingsbury, "The UN's Roles in a Divided World," in Adam Roberts and Benedict Kingsbury, eds., *United Nations, Divided World* (Oxford: Oxford University Press, 1988), p. 11. The problem is not a matter of nations believing that the UN is a real and significant instrument of world peace and that they therefore avoid other means of addressing global security issues. Rather, the problem is that any positive perceptions of the security-enhancing potential of the UN may alter their incentives to apply their full resources to other strategies. This suggests an element of moral hazard, a subject discussed in a later section of my article.

82. See Funabashi, *Managing the Dollar*, p. 41.

83. It is impossible to definitively state that in the absence of IO, nations would act more responsibly or make the necessary hard choices required for long-run stability in their econ-

system, liquidity became a substitute for adjustment. External adjustment was constrained by means of fixed exchange rates and rules governing trade policy, while internal adjustment was no longer accepted as a viable means of eradicating external payment imbalances.[84] In another context of adverse substitution, Vaubel argues that as a forum for collusion, IO can make it easier for governments to pursue unstable economic policies. Monetary collaboration, for example, can shield policymakers from criticism over high inflation by bringing inflation rates into conformity.[85]

Jan Tumlir and others have argued that it should be a principal goal of IO to limit this substitution and enhance responsible policies at home. According to Tumlir, IO should "help national governments . . . discharge those basic domestic functions on which the economic stability of their societies depends in the long run."[86] If nations would all follow responsible policies at home, then IO would be less necessary. Certainly this argument is common in the context of international economic relations. As a recent article in the *Economist* noted, economic ministers could "think of cooperation as a boring means to an end, not as a glorious goal in its own right. Because if they all stayed home and adopted sensible domestic policies there would be precious little need for cooperation on trade or exchange rates."[87] A similar view was offered by Max Corden: "It can be argued that if countries make adequate use of the policy instruments available to them, there is no need for coordination of policies. . . . One can thus imagine countries reacting quickly and atomistically to the events from outside them, including the consequences of other countries' stabilization policies. And if their policies are

---

omies. Certainly, nations might seek other ways to avoid making hard choices. However, to the extent that IO provides additional "outs" or, alternatively, fails to close off less responsible avenues, it augments or maintains the possibilities for destabilizing policy choices in the long run.

84. Some might argue that this tendency toward substitution was not as apparent to the founders of the Bretton Woods system, since their principal goal was to provide nations with liquidity as a way to avoid market intervention (prompted by balance-of-payments disequilibria) in the short run and thus give them the opportunity to develop more incremental adjustment policies in the long run. Furthermore, the fixed exchange rates and the circumscription of internal adjustment were a reaction to the problems that prevailed during the interwar period. The point to be made here is that the opportunities for adverse substitution which IO provides can as likely be unintended as intended. For a discussion of the early objectives of the Bretton Woods system, see Richard Gardner, *Sterling-Dollar Diplomacy: Anglo–American Collaboration in the Reconstruction of Multilateral Trade* (Oxford: Clarendon Press, 1956), chap. 5.

85. In "A Public Choice Approach to International Organization," pp. 47–49, Vaubel cites evidence that inflation tends to be higher among nations that exhibit more convergent inflation rates.

86. See Jan Tumlir, *Protectionism: Trade Policy in Democratic Societies* (Washington, D.C.: American Enterprise Institute, 1985), p. 12. On a related note, critics of super-301 and strategic American trade policy argue that these initiatives represent a destabilizing substitute for a long-term resolution to the trade deficit, which would require the elimination of the underlying microeconomic and macroeconomic causes. See "The Snit List," *Economist*, 3 June 1989, pp. 30–31.

87. *Economist*, 26 September 1987, p. 56.

intelligent and speedy, they will achieve whatever stabilization they wish to achieve."[88]

The argument for responsible domestic policies reflects the belief that domestic problems have a tendency to spill over and become international problems. In the economic realm, excessive internal deficits and inflation alter exchange rates, and this in turn influences external positions. Differential rates of inflation in a fixed exchange rate system redistribute trade surpluses to nations with low inflation. While these effects are unintentional (externalities), there are also intentional actions (policies) that are instituted to redistribute external surpluses—for example, tariff barriers and exchange controls keep imports down and capital in. Both externalities and policies can therefore be quite destabilizing internationally.[89] Similarly, in the political realm, domestic problems can become international problems. For example, oppressive authoritarian regimes may find foreign adventurism a necessary remedy to quell domestic unrest.

Dispute intensification

IO can be a destabilizing force when it intensifies disputes. Because IO can lend moral force to the foreign policy positions of nations, it has the tendency to be used by them as a means of statecraft to further their global interests. To the extent that these interests create confrontational behavior, IO generates utility not only as a forum in which accusations are made and brinkmanship is practiced in front of the community of states but also as a vehicle through which collusion and alliance building are effected.

In general, scholars have tended to underplay these and other negative uses of IO that interfere with negotiations and make agreements difficult to achieve. Rather than serving as vehicles to resolve conflict, IOs are often used to promote or magnify conflict. As Claude has noted, they frequently function as arenas "for the conduct of international political warfare."[90] The UN, for example, has historically served as a forum to embarrass nations. In 1956, Western nations brought up the Hungarian issue for the purpose of embarrassing the Soviet Union. The Soviets vindicated themselves in 1965 when they brought up the Dominican Republic issue to embarrass the United States. As Yeselson and Gaglione have pointed out, "Real negotiations

---

88. See W. Max Corden, "The Coordination of Stabilization Policies Among Countries," in Albert Ando, Richard Herring, and Richard Marston, eds., *International Aspects of Stabilization Policies* (Boston: Federal Reserve Bank of Boston, 1977), pp. 139–40.

89. See Giulio M. Gallarotti, "Toward a Business-Cycle Model of Tariffs," *International Organization* 39 (Winter 1985), pp. 155–87. The success of GATT in lowering tariffs may be counterproductive, given the fact that nations often substitute nontariff barriers. These barriers are more protectionist and more distorting of trade flows, since producers cannot compensate for them by managing prices and costs. This illustrates the fact that IO can channel policy into less stabilizing instruments.

90. Claude, *Swords into Plowshares*, p. 446.

require that the parties define differences as narrowly as possible, avoid recrimination, and exclude extremists from discussions. At the UN, issues are widened, insults are common, and the most violent spokesmen frequently dominate the debate. The effects of such deliberately provocative discussions is to contaminate efforts to achieve peaceful settlements."[91]

The "safety valve" rationale for IO, which reflects the famous Churchill quote "better to jaw, jaw than war, war,"[92] is based on the erroneous assumption that battle among diplomats is a perfect substitute for battle in the fields. In fact, however, "war jaw" in the UN merely compounds conflicts, as Maurice Tugwell has pointed out.[93] For example, the verbal aggression traditionally marshaled toward the United States by the Soviet Union and involving the use of terminology such as "racist," "imperialist," "anti-peace," and "neocolonial" served to compound confrontations outside of the UN both directly and indirectly, since it prompted as well as justified the arms buildups and supported the extremist views of Cold Warriors in domestic debates over foreign policy. In this respect, Jeane Kirkpatrick, former U.S. Ambassador to the UN, was probably justified in saying that she has "never believed that the release of aggression is healthy or therapeutic" and that "it is a sorry state of affairs when the United Nations, which was conceived as an instrument for the building of peace, is now justified as an instrument for the release of aggression."[94] She was also at least partially correct in calling the UN a "dangerous place."[95]

The UN was historically used as an instrument of Cold War competition, with each superpower marshaling voting alliances against the other. Claude underscored the point that the superpowers competed for control of the organization and viewed it as the ultimate ally in the Cold War, while Ruggie added that the Soviets considered it "a vehicle to delegitimize the postwar international order constructed by the capitalist nations."[96] Yeselson and Gaglione have noted that what many have seen as UN failures in cooperation are in fact successful instances of the organization's use as a weapon to embarrass nations.[97] According to them, much can be understood about the UN if it is seen as a tool of statecraft in the Cold War. To say that this use has substituted for more direct confrontation assumes that the marshaling of alliances which occurred earlier outside the UN was subsequently re-

91. Yeselson and Gaglione, "The Use of the United Nations in World Politics," p. 396.

92. See Maurice Tugwell, "The UN as the World's Safety Valve," in Pines, *A World Without a U.N.*, pp. 157–74. The Churchill quote is from his speech on 26 June 1954 in Washington, D.C.

93. Tugwell, "The UN as the World's Safety Valve," p. 157.

94. Jeane Kirkpatrick, speech before the Anti-Defamation League on 11 February 1982 in Palm Beach, Fla., pp. 11–12.

95. Kirkpatrick, quoted by the Associated Press, 29 October 1982.

96. See Claude, *Swords into Plowshares,* pp. 89–94; and Ruggie, "The United States and the United Nations," p. 354.

97. Yeselson and Gaglione, *A Dangerous Place,* pp. 31–43.

placed by the formation of voting blocs within the UN forum. This is not the case, however, since confrontations within the UN were merely added to confrontations outside it. In this sense, according to Tugwell, instead of acting as a "safety valve," the UN became "a threat to peace."[98] This is also evident in the fact that the organization has actively taken part in conflicts and either escalated them, as in the Korean War, or intervened to suppress them, as in the siding with Kasavubu in the Katangan revolt led by Tsombe. In the latter case, Belgian Prime Minister Paul Henry Spaak cited the intervention in the Congo affairs as a "UN war operation."[99]

In addition to these direct effects, IO has had indirect international and domestic effects that run counter to the ideals of multilateral cooperation. The constant attacks of the UN on Israel, South Africa, and Rhodesia, for example, have had the unfortunate effects of strengthening the political position of "hawks" in Israel and of providing racial extremists in the African nations with a weapon to use against moderates.[100] For this reason, nations have become reluctant to bring disputes or problems to IOs that have historically been mobilized against them. Israel, a victim of Egyptian and Syrian attack in 1973, chose not to bring the problem to the UN Security Council because of the anti-Israeli sentiment there. The Soviets bypassed the UN often during the earlier period in which the Western coalition dominated the organization, and the United States has done so following the organization's shift to Soviet and Third World domination. Claude underscored this point with respect to the earlier period: "To the degree that the United States succeeded in using the [UN] as a pro-Western device, it reduced the utility of the organization as an agency of conciliation and stabilization in the Cold War."[101]

98. Tugwell, "The U.N. as the World's Safety Valve," p. 158.

99. The ultimate outcome in this intervention was markedly different from the original intention "not to take any action which would make [the UN] a party to internal conflicts in the country." See UN Security Council, *Official Records,* meeting no. 872, 7 July 1960, p. 5.

100. See Yeselson and Gaglione, *A Dangerous Place,* p. 203. With respect to the indirect effects of IOs on African politics, Jackson and Roseberg see a quite different deleterious effect. By accepting African nations as members regardless of their political regimes, IOs serve to legitimate oppressive political systems. See Robert Jackson and Carl Roseberg, "Why Africa's Weak States Persist: The Empirical and Juridical in Statehood," *World Politics* 35 (October 1982), pp. 1–24.

101. See Claude, *Swords into Plowshares,* p. 130. Some analysts might interpret the 1990 involvement of the UN in the Iraq–Kuwait crisis as a breakdown in the deleterious Cold War use of the organization and argue that with superpower agreement the UN can be a positive force in abating and preventing crises in global security. There are several problems with this interpretation. The first and most obvious is that it is premature to draw conclusions, given that the crisis is still in progress at the time of the writing of this article. The second is that we have to question whether the UN initiated or followed the U.S. lead in attempting to resolve the crisis. The United States, defending its geopolitical and resource-security interests in the Middle East, played the major role with regard to constructing a unified response to the invasion of Kuwait. Insofar as the 1990 UN resolutions called for actions that the United States and its allies had already committed themselves to, the organization merely served as a stamp of approval or vehicle for legitimating the actions. The European Community has, in fact, at the

In resolving smaller controversies or contentious issues, IO has often created roadblocks to the resolution of more important issues. For example, the 1948 Security Council resolution endorsing self-determination in Kashmir drove a major wedge into Indian–Pakistani relations, while resolutions favoring South Korea fueled bad North–South Korean sentiment. The result was that substantive relation improvements were impeded. In the greater scheme of international relations, it may have been better for the resolutions not to have been made, regardless of their short-run successes in addressing injustices.[102]

Furthermore, as a facilitator of issue linkage, IO has often had negative rather than positive effects. Scholars have argued that linkage leads to greater possibilities for exchange and bargaining and thus enhances the potential for substantive agreements. "Clustering of issues," according to Keohane, "facilitates side-payments among these issues: more potential *quids* are available for the *quo*."[103] Although linkage can be stabilizing if it encourages cooperation, it can have destabilizing effects if it instead fuels conflict. In 1974, the Arab states traded votes with the Black African nations in the UN: the former pledged their vote to silence the South African delegation in exchange for the latter's vote in support of the Palestine Liberation Organization (PLO). This not only intensified old disputes but also brought new participants into the disputes. In IOs, voting alliances whose purposes revolve principally around confrontation are quite the rule rather than the exception.[104]

Along this line of logic, it is not the case that IO always enhances the conditions favorable to cooperation or dispute resolution. In the case of dispute mediation, IO may restrict, rather than expand, the number of mediators. The restriction occurs as a result of nations being identified as biased either because they took a particular position on an issue in IO debates or because they failed to take sides. For example, India's abstinence on a UN

---

time of the writing of this article made a collective request to the Security Council to pursue air blockade in addition to naval and ground coverage. Critics of the confrontational style within the UN forum might argue that since nations are committed to a confrontational response to the invasion outside this forum, it would behoove the UN to expend its energies toward engineering a diplomatic resolution. This would reduce the possibilities of pan-Arab antagonism (especially from Iraq, Iran, Yemen, and Jordan) toward the UN and would place the organization in a better position to fulfill its role with respect to resolving other disputes in the Middle East. Given the fact that Hussein has threatened war in response to the UN resolutions, we have to question whether confrontational resolutions are counterproductive and whether the UN has served as a positive force.

102. See Yeselson and Gaglione, "The Use of the United Nations in World Politics," p. 396.

103. Keohane, *After Hegemony,* p. 91. See also Robert Keohane, "The Demand for International Regimes," *International Organization* 36 (Spring 1982), pp. 325–56; and Robert Tollison and Thomas Willett, "An Economic Theory of Mutually Advantageous Linkages in International Negotiations," *International Organization* 33 (Autumn 1979), pp. 425–50.

104. See Yeselson and Gaglione, "The Use of the United Nations in World Politics," p. 397.

vote regarding Soviet intervention in Hungary discredited India as a Cold War mediator in the eyes of the United States. The potential for such outcomes is high, given that IO normally puts nations in a position of appearing to choose sides on divisive issues whether they elect to vote or not. This destabilizing transitivity can manifest itself also in terms of the effects of inner-IO confrontations on outer-IO negotiations. In 1973, for example, Americans were quite apprehensive about Chinese–South Korean interaction in the UN, given its potential effects on Chinese–U.S. rapprochement.

This tendency of "leaning" international support to one side or another is not peculiar to IO but is a characteristic of such social functions in general. When IO takes sides, however, it can have adverse effects on both the longevity and the intensity of a dispute. As Yeselson and Gaglione have observed, "Victorious states are emboldened by the vindication of their policies, and losers are embittered by injustice."[105] Taking sides without regard to consequences—even in the form of condemning what is considered an illegitimate use of force, as in the cases of the Israeli occupation of Arab territories in 1967, the Falklands invasion of 1982, and Soviet intervention in Afghanistan in 1979—encourages the use of counterforce.[106] Critics have often lamented the overt UN support of groups such as the PLO, the Southwest African People's Organization (SWAPO), the African National Congress (ANC), and the Pan-African Congress (PAC) and have argued that these groups use UN support as a legitimization of violent methods.[107] The following statement by PLO spokesman Massur on the murder of two Israelis by a PLO terrorist group in 1975 is revealing: "We sponsored the operation because it is our right to fight for our rights, and the whole world sponsored it . . . because the [UN] General Assembly has approved the right of the Palestinians to pursue their struggle *with all means* to gain usurped rights."[108] In the Falklands case, it is difficult to separate the aggressive Argentine foreign policy of the late 1960s and the 1970s from the fact that the Falklands problem had been linked to decolonization by the UN after 1965. Great Britain asserted its sovereignty over the islands throughout the century, but

105. Ibid., p. 395.

106. See Roberts and Kingsbury, "The UN's Roles in a Divided World," p. 19.

107. See Gulick, "How the U.N. Aids Marxist Guerrilla Groups." It appears that this support has been uneven in a most destabilizing way, given the recent UN decision to allow South Africa to break Resolution 435 and confront SWAPO rebels in Namibia.

108. Massur, quoted in ibid., p. 4. The argument that IO is supposed to promote change and that the PLO and ANC are therefore justified in their use of the UN to promote conflict in the Middle East and Africa presents some problems. First, it assumes that people think it worth the costs of conflict intensification, including death and destruction, to promote change. Many would not think so. Second, it assumes that any parties advocating changes to some status quo are justified in using IOs to promote conflict. In fact, nations have historically been encouraged to bring their disputes to IOs as a way of avoiding conflict. Finally, there are both peaceful and conflictual avenues to change. Some think it a bad precedent for IOs to expend resources in anything but peaceful solutions. Certainly the traditional spirit of IO suggests diplomatic approaches to resolving conflicts of interests.

it was not until after 1965 that Argentine terrorism and militarism became pronounced.[109] The problem was probably compounded when the General Assembly passed a resolution in December 1976 praising the Argentine government for "facilitat[ing] the process of decolonization" and thus legitimized its confrontational methods of using verbal and military aggression in resolving the problem.[110]

Finally, and most obviously, IO can be destabilizing by stimulating cooperation in the negative form of predatory collusion. When nations collude for the purpose of exploitation, redistribution, or aggression, collective action is bad, just as it is bad for economic efficiency when firms with market power collude to restrict output. Nations perceive confrontational alliances as bad, just as consumer nations perceive international commodity cartels as bad. Depending on the goals of cooperation, it is sometimes in the interest of peaceful international relations for collective action and prisoners' dilemma problems to exist.

Moral hazard

Situations involving moral hazard are those in which a nation is relieved of the obligation of incurring the full costs of its social, economic, or political actions because some protective scheme allows it to impose those costs onto other nations through risk sharing. The problem of generating moral hazard has been most extensively discussed in the context of the social inefficiencies of insurance. An inherent problem of insurance is that it encourages individuals to be more reckless in the management of their possessions and consequently raises the risk of losses, which in turn imposes greater costs on society. Similarly, an inherent problem of IO is that by helping to ward off catastrophes or by insuring nations against them, it discourages individually responsible behavior on their part.

There are numerous examples in which IOs have functioned as providers of insurance. The International Energy Agency (IEA) has traditionally insured against energy shortages through resource-sharing schemes. The es-

109. Operation Condor in 1966 and the immediate reception of this terrorist operation on the part of the Argentine masses suggest a sharp turning point in Argentine policy toward the Falklands in the mid-1960s. See W. Michael Reisman and Andrew Willard, eds., *International Incidents* (Princeton, N.J.: Princeton University Press, 1988), pp. 121–22.

110. In 1974, the newspaper *Cronica* began a campaign for the invasion of the Falklands. In January 1976, the Argentine foreign minister predicted a head-on collision with Great Britain. Just one month later, an Argentine destroyer fired on the British research ship *Shakleton*. See ibid., pp. 122–27. UN involvement may have contributed to the Falklands episode by exacerbating the domestic antagonism toward Great Britain and driving policy toward a more militant response. While this is somewhat speculative, one thing is certain: in its resolutions and other involvement in this matter, the UN provided sources of legitimacy that could be used by Argentina as justification for confrontational approaches to the problem. This in itself violated the traditional spirit of the UN objective to encourage peaceful diplomatic resolution of international disputes.

cape clauses of the General Agreement on Tariffs and Trade (GATT) have provided partial insurance to domestic industries in distress and alleviated balance-of-payments difficulties. The Financial Support Fund, agreed to by members of the Organization for Economic Cooperation and Development (OECD) but never instituted, was meant to serve as a lender of last resort that would spread the risk of loans given to nations in economic difficulty. The compensatory and contingency finance facilities of the International Monetary Fund (IMF) were instituted specifically as insurance against sudden economic disruptions that negatively affect the balance of payments. And the Lomé Convention's Compensatory Finance Scheme for Exports (STABEX) was instituted as insurance against a sudden decline in the key exports of the African, Caribbean, and Pacific nations.

In their various protective or safeguard functions, these and other IOs have frequently generated adverse effects in encouraging nations to be reckless in the management of their domestic economies. As Charles Kindleberger has argued with respect to the debt problem, last-resort and crisis lenders reduce the incentives of nations to make the internal economic adjustments necessary for long-term domestic stability. The fact that trade deficits can be financed through external funds allows nations to overinflate without worrying about the adverse effects of high prices on their trade balances. The guarantee of external sources of liquidity also allows nations to increase government spending, to prolong or expand their budget deficits, to smooth over exchange rate mismanagement, and, worst of all, to compound their foreign debt.[111] These domestic problems, spread over many nations, have the capacity to spill over and become international problems. For optimal stability in the international economic system, Kindleberger thus prescribes a lender whose commitment is uncertain: "Because of moral hazard, there should be some ambiguity about whether there will or will not be a lender of last resort."[112] Shrinking the safety net would encourage nations to manage their external accounts and macroeconomies in a manner that makes them more self-sufficient in the long run and is conducive to both domestic and international stability.

The logic of moral hazard suggests that managerial schemes can create conditions that cut against the spirit of their original purposes. In the case of the Plaza Accord, for example, cooperation provided a multilateral substitute for addressing U.S. economic problems. Instead of encouraging U.S. policymakers to bring interest rates down by instituting domestic measures to reduce their budget deficit, the G-7 stepped in to manage the dollar. In the short run, this redistributed some of the costs of the large U.S. deficit

---

111. Historical limitations in the demands and enforcement of conditionality have given nations more leeway than is good for their own long-run economic stability.

112. See Kindleberger, *The International Economic Order*, p. 39. See also Charles Kindleberger, "The International Monetary System," in *International Money: A Collection of Essays* (London: Allen & Unwin, 1981), pp. 297–300.

to the community of industrialized nations. But because it also reduced the incentives for the U.S. government to manage its deficit more cautiously, the deficit worsened and has become a significant potential source of international economic instability.

A better approach: limited international organization

Managerial prescriptions for IO and proscriptions against deregulating relations have led to a predilection for big supranational government. However, as Keohane and Nye have pointed out, supranational institutions "are not desirable for their own sake."[113] Nor does a high level or large scope of international management ensure optimal results. More limited forms of IO are in fact preferable in many cases, particularly those in which IO is prone to managerial failures of the types noted above and those in which the interactive patterns among nations are less conflictual and thus more representative of coordination games than of stag hunt or prisoners' dilemma. Contributors to the revisionist literature on IO and the literature on cooperation have recognized the negative effects and conditionality of management and have provided a partial solution to these problems by recommending more limited managerial functions for IOs.

In determining the proper level and scope of IO, we should begin by questioning to what extent stable international relations in the past have been the result of extensive management. Contrary to common assumptions, history shows that extensive management of international relations in both orderly and disorderly periods has been more the exception than the rule. IOs have rarely been constructed to manage any issue-area extensively or even effectively. The constitutions of IOs, like most other constitutions, have commonly been so vague as to tolerate a wide range of behavior on the part of actors both close to and far from implicit principles. Rule breaking has been tolerated, escape mechanisms have always been pervasive, and the problems of compliance have been compounded by the lack or general underdevelopment of enforcement instruments.[114]

The calls for an escape from the present "nonsystem" (nonmanagement) of monetary relations and an adoption of a new Bretton Woods system on the part of managerialists such as Irving Friedman are rather curious considering that some have questioned whether management under the old Bret-

---

113. Keohane and Nye, *Power and Interdependence*, p. 274.

114. Interestingly, Puchala has argued that during the first half of the European Community's existence, much of its success was actually attributable to weaknesses in getting nations to follow rules. The Community has, however, shown itself to be much stronger in the second half of its existence in both generating legislation and encouraging adherence. See Donald Puchala, "Domestic Politics and Regional Harmonization in the European Communities," *World Politics* 27 (July 1975), pp. 496–520.

ton Woods plan was extensive or strong.[115] Robert Solomon has observed that under the old Bretton Woods system

> there were no accepted rules to govern changes in par values, yet such changes were necessary as economic policies and conditions diverged among nations. Furthermore, there was no systematic means for increasing countries' reserves in a growing world economy. The growth of reserves was the haphazard result of the outcome of the U.S. balance of payments, which then, as now, depended on developments in other countries as well as in the United States. For these two reasons alone, it may be concluded that the nostalgic desire to get away from the present "nonsystem" is a product of emotion rather than careful analysis.[116]

Furthermore, those who unequivocally profess the evils of decentralization and the superiority of extensive regulation ("bigger government is better") are sometimes guilty of overestimating the destabilizing elements in international relations and their effects on international politics, underestimating those forces which naturally inhibit nations from behaving predatorially in anarchic environments, and overestimating the capacity of IO to solve problems. Common rationales for extensive supranational management have centered around the conviction that international relations are permeated by prisoners' dilemmas, stag hunts, security dilemmas, and public goods problems. Under such conditions, even the least expansionist and aggressive nations would be rationally driven to participate in destabilizing behavior such as arms races, trade wars, and competitive depreciation. The result of the "pursuit of self-interest by each," Keohane and Nye have argued, would thus be a "disaster for all."[117] But as the growing literature on cooperation suggests, the incidence and the adverse effects of predatory games have been overstated. The games that nations play are much more varied than the traditional literature on international relations has suggested, and the effects of conflictual games can vary in their level of adversity. Moreover, even under conditions that are potentially destabilizing, such as relative gains maximization, cooperative outcomes are still possible. Interactional patterns, according to this literature, are not so inherently unstable that they cannot often converge toward orderly equilibria under more limited international management. As Keohane and Nye note, "Issues lacking conflicts of interests may need very little institutional structure."[118]

115. In "Fiscal Policies, Current Accounts and Real Exchange Rates," p. 426, Corden sees the post–Bretton Woods period as a period of decentralized monetary relations, "an international laissez faire system."

116. Robert Solomon, "Issues at the IMF Meeting," *Journal of Commerce*, October 1979, p. 4.

117. Keohane and Nye, *Power and Interdependence*, p. 274.

118. Ibid., p. 273. For other contributions to this literature, see John Conybeare, "Public Goods, Prisoners' Dilemmas and the International Political Economy," *International Studies*

The fears of less centralized management, which are frequently founded on the misconception that prisoners' dilemmas and stag hunts are ubiquitous in international relations, systematically discount the costs of predation. Imposing suckers' payoffs onto other nations incurs significant costs that are independent of those costs incurred as a result of retaliation. This is not to say that exploitation does not pay; rather, the point is that it does not pay as much as many believe and that, moreover, managerialists tend to mistake other games for prisoners' dilemma and stag hunt. With tariffs, for instance, there are obvious deadweight losses with respect to social welfare. Tariffs are conducive to inflation, which bears high economic and political costs. They raise the cost of domestic production as well as reduce the efficiency of a nation's capital stock in the long run by shielding domestic industries from competition and making it difficult to import foreign capital and inputs. Declining capital efficiency will also have adverse effects on wages in the long run. Finally, tariffs can adversely affect a nation's capital balance if investors perceive them as a sign of external difficulties or mercantilistic policy styles.[119] Competitive depreciation causes not only inflation but capital flight. Depreciation can also adversely affect current balances if a nation's demand for imports and others' demand for its exports are inelastic.[120] Brinkmanship and wars can incur preponderant political as well as economic costs, as the Cuban crisis, the Vietnam War, and the Falklands War have demonstrated. The more prolonged and unsuccessful the adventurism, the greater are the costs.

The fears of decentralization are also fueled by a propensity to see disorder where it may not exist. For example, external imbalances are not in themselves a sign of economic disorder, any more than traders exchanging resources are a sign of market disorder. Much depends on the structure of the imbalances. In the present external imbalance between the United States and Japan, the former is running a current deficit against the latter, and the latter is running a capital deficit against the former. There are some important

Quarterly 28 (March 1984), pp. 5–22; Conybeare, "International Organization and the Theory of Property Rights"; Arthur Stein, "Coordination and Collaboration: Regimes in an Anarchic World," *International Organization* 36 (Spring 1982), pp. 299–324; Duncan Snidal, "Coordination Versus Prisoners' Dilemma: Implications for International Cooperation and Regimes," *American Political Science Review* 79 (December 1985), pp. 923–42; Duncan Snidal, "Relative Gains Don't Prevent International Cooperation," paper presented at the annual meeting of the American Political Science Association, Atlanta, Ga., 31 August 1989; Timothy McKeown, "Hegemonic Stability Theory and 19th Century Tariff Levels in Europe," *International Organization* 37 (Winter 1983), pp. 73–92; R. Harrison Wagner, "The Theory of Games and the Problem of International Cooperation," *American Political Science Review* 77 (June 1983), pp. 330–46; and Robert Axelrod, *The Evolution of Cooperation* (New York: Basic Books, 1984).

119. The conventional argument about the advantages of optimal tariffs assumes that other nations will not retaliate.

120. In "The Logic of the International Monetary Non-System," p. 65, Corden implies that these predatory costs increase on the margin, thus suggesting that the restraints against predation will rise as predation increases.

gains from trade in this reciprocal imbalance: Japan is helping finance the U.S. budget deficit in exchange for the exportation of goods.[121]

Various forms of limited IO have been suggested in the recent literature on cooperation and the critical literature on IO as a partial solution to the problems of managerial failure and the conditionality of international management.[122] The transaction costs approach to IO, for example, has modest aspirations for the functions of institutions. Keohane and Nye specifically cite them as facilitators "of bargaining among member states that leads to mutually beneficial cooperation."[123] In this sense, order is institutionally assisted rather than managed. Institutions, they argue, can "set the international agenda and act as catalysts for coalition formation and as arenas for political initiatives and linkage by weak states."[124] The principal function of IOs in this case would be the reduction of organization costs, such as those deriving from asymmetric information, deception, irresponsibility, uncertainty, risk, and unstable expectations, all of which are potential impediments to stable relations and exchange patterns. Cost reduction can be effected through limited functions relevant to the roles of gathering and disseminating data and information about the preferences of nations, facilitating side-payments and communication, and reducing the costs of decision making. In general, in cases in which the construction of extensive managerial schemes (what Keohane refers to as "control" schemes) is fraught with problems or is unnecessary, less ambitious schemes become desirable.[125]

The literature on regimes has also suggested substitutes for control schemes. According to this literature, preexisting norms and principles can reduce the need for extensive management in several ways.[126] First, they can render strategic interactional patterns less conflictual by altering payoffs. For example, they can make defection more costly. Second, they can facilitate intertemporal cooperation by generating expectations of reciprocity or, in more static games, by enhancing expectations of "nice" moves. And, third, in specific issue-areas where coordination games predominate, as described by Arthur Stein, or where spontaneous regimes exist, as described by Oran Young, the preexisting norms and principles either obviate the need for

121. See Corden, "Fiscal Policies, Current Accounts and Real Exchange Rates," p. 436. This is not to say that the imbalance cannot be politically destabilizing.

122. Even those contributors to the literature on cooperation who are quite sympathetic to the role of IO in world politics note that limited forms of multilateral management can be desirable and effective given the proper underlying conditions in relations among nations. See especially Keohane and Nye, *Power and Interdependence*, pp. 274–76; and Ruggie, "Collective Goods and Future International Collaboration," p. 888.

123. Keohane and Nye, *Power and Interdependence*, p. 274.

124. Ibid., p. 35.

125. Ibid., pp. 35 and 274. See also Keohane, *After Hegemony;* and Keohane, "The Demand for International Regimes."

126. See the special issue of *International Organization,* vol. 36, Spring 1982.

extensive regulation or eliminate the need for formal institution building.[127] The stable patterns of interaction in specific issue-areas, Duncan Snidal has argued, can be maintained through more modest functions concerned with "codification and elaboration of an existing or latent convention" and with "providing information and communication to facilitate the smooth operation of the convention."[128] In other words, by performing limited functions with regard to preexisting focal points, management can facilitate the convergence of expectations about international behavior.[129]

Ruggie has noted that epistemic communities can be viable substitutes for extensive control schemes.[130] They are capable, for instance, of generating stable structures of expectations that are conducive to nonconflictual relations. Some of the limited management functions in the case of communities concerned with technology, for example, relate to facilitating efficient exchange through consensus about how and under which conditions transactions can be effected.

As Keohane and Nye have pointed out and as the public choice literature on IO has demonstrated, in cases in which nations can agree upon reasonable entitlement rules, an institutionally assisted market solution is superior to an extensive managerial scheme.[131] The conventional minimum-support functions in these cases are the definition, adjudication, and enforcement of property rights; the dissemination of information about preferences; and other functions related to the elimination of market distortions such as externalities. Conybeare has noted that in international environmental law, for example, there has been an impressive evolution that "illustrates the ability of states operating in a market exchange environment to develop a system of property rights and liability rules consistent with global welfare, in the absence of any overarching supranational IO directly intervening to force

127. See Stein, "Coordination and Collaboration"; and Oran Young, "Regime Dynamics: The Rise and Fall of International Regimes," *International Organization* 36 (Spring 1982), pp. 277–98. See also Wagner, "The Theory of Games and the Problem of International Cooperation"; and Snidal, "Coordination Versus Prisoners' Dilemma."
128. Snidal, "Coordination Versus Prisoners' Dilemma," p. 932. Even with more conflictual payoff structures, such as that of prisoners' dilemma, notes Wagner, functions relating to the dissemination of information about preferences and potential choices can play an essential role in bringing about cooperative outcomes. Furthermore, in cases in which conflictual games generate horizontal proliferation (interissue linkage in games), modest managerial assistance is required to arrive at mutually beneficial equilibria. Snidal argues that to the extent that horizontal properties emerge, the game "becomes embedded in a broader social context, and cooperation is increasingly possible with less centralized enforcement." See Snidal, ibid., p. 939; and Wagner, "The Theory of Games and the Problem of International Cooperation."
129. For a discussion of the role of focal points in generating mutually beneficial outcomes in games, see Thomas Schelling, *The Strategy of Conflict* (Cambridge, Mass.: Harvard University Press, 1980).
130. Ruggie, "International Responses to Technology."
131. See Keohane and Nye, *Power and Interdependence*, p. 274; Conybeare, "International Organization and the Theory of Property Rights"; Vaubel, "A Public Choice Approach to International Organization"; and Wijkman, "Managing the Global Commons."

states to internalize the effects of externalities."[132] Wijkman, who notes that environmental problems have historically been dealt with through the market approach of subdividing internationally shared resources into "national inheritances," has argued that this approach would be viable with regard to the deep seabed and the continental margin (which are less costly to subdivide than other environments) and possibly with regard to the orbital spectrum as well.[133]

Even the traditional literature on IO, which has a strong managerial orientation, exhibits strands of logic that attest to the utility of limited IO. The functionalist concept of "technical self-determination" suggests that the nature of technological problems will dictate the scope and level of supranational regulation. Although the mainstream vision of functional interdependence foresees a growing need for the integration and management of technical issues, there is nothing in the logic to suggest that decentralized solutions in which each nation addresses a problem independently of other nations cannot sometimes be viable. If autarkic solutions to technical and welfare problems do not suffice, IO can serve minor functions in facilitating stable relations. Moreover, limited technical integration need not spill over into greater political integration.[134] Neofunctionalists acknowledge that IO is sometimes ineffective in achieving specified goals.[135] If this is because the goals are set too high, as in the case of grand collaborative schemes, it may be preferable to moderate the targeted level of cooperation, since failure may serve to delegitimize cooperation not only in the short run but also in the long run.[136] Edward Morse has argued that in some ways modernization breeds conditions that abate conflict and tension in international politics, thereby reducing the need for international management. In bringing low politics to the fore (for example, making issues relating to welfare and technology as important as those relating to power and status), the content of foreign policies becomes less threatening because conflicts are diverted into the positive-sum contexts of economics and technology.[137]

The literature on collective action suggests another reason that limited IO can be viable. Russell Hardin, for example, has argued that it is easier to eradicate public "bads" than to procure or create public goods, since the goal of collective action in the former is more focused and since nations are likely to experience more "disutility" from bads than utility from goods.[138] In cases in which the elimination of bads is the primary goal, limited IO can

132. Conybeare, "International Organization and the Theory of Property Rights," p. 314.

133. Wijkman, "Managing the Global Commons," p. 527.

134. See Mitrany, *A Working Peace System,* pp. 28 and 73.

135. See, for example, Haas, *Beyond the Nation-State,* p. 126.

136. In *Power and Interdependence,* p. 276, Keohane and Nye make a similar point with respect to viable moderated management of crisis versus nonviable control management.

137. See Morse, *Modernization and the Transformation of International Relations,* p. 85.

138. See Hardin, *Collective Action,* pp. 62–65.

be effective. Moreover, the classic Olsonian treatment of collective action suggests that IOs with limited membership are more effective than large IOs in both eliminating bads and procuring goods.[139] Historically, however, the target of IO has tended to be the management of goods with little publicness. As Ruggie has pointed out, it has been "the production of [private] goods and services which accounts for most of the activities of international organization."[140] This essentially means that IO has historically been redundant in its managerial functions and has expended more managerial capital than is necessary, since relations involving private goods require the least supranational regulation.[141]

That limited IO can be effective, however, does not mean that it will be. For IO to be a viable means of contributing to order in international relations, the environment in which it functions must be conducive to the effectiveness of supranational management in general. It appears from the logic in this article that IO will be more effective in the management of relatively simple constellations of intra- or inter-issue relations than in the management of complex chaotic systems in which relations between relevant variables are difficult to understand and forecast. With respect to the complexity of the two major issue-areas of international economic and security relations, it is interesting to note that management will most likely be effective where it is least likely to emerge. The processes involved in economic cooperation are much more complex according to Perrow's definition than those involved in security cooperation, but cooperation in security relations has historically been much less visible than that in economic relations.[142]

Moreover, IO will be more effective when it facilitates or encourages substantive and long-term solutions to problems than when it offers short-run and ad hoc approaches to them. UN peacekeeping functions, for example, have historically specialized in the latter approaches to abating conflict.[143] As valuable as these may be in insulating and desensitizing conflict, they need to be bolstered by viable schemes that raise and maintain the incentives for nations to continue pursuing substantive and lasting settle-

---

139. See Mancur Olson, *The Logic of Collective Action* (Cambridge, Mass.: Harvard University Press, 1965).

140. Ruggie, "Collective Goods and Future International Collaboration," p. 888.

141. See ibid.; Conybeare, "International Organization and the Theory of Property Rights"; and Wijkman, "Managing the Global Commons."

142. Jervis argues that cooperation is more likely to occur in economic relations than in security relations because the underlying strategic structure of the former is positive-sum, while that of the latter is closer to zero-sum. See Robert Jervis, "Security Regimes," *International Organization* 36 (Spring 1982), pp. 357–78. Of course, a disaggregation of economic relations would show a significant variation in the complexity of the various forms, ranging from commodity agreements, which are relatively simple, to macroeconomic coordination, which is highly complex.

143. See Brian Urquhart, "International Peace and Security," *Foreign Affairs* 60 (Fall 1981), pp. 1–16.

ments to their foreign relations problems.[144] Economic cooperation among the G-7 has also had a history of ineffectiveness because it has remained open to and often encouraged domestic and foreign policies that are inconsistent with the intentions and spirit of substantive economic policy coordination. Economic summitry has exhibited a tendency to be a legitimator of national economic policies as well as an instrument of domestic politics, rather than serving exclusively as a forum for substantive negotiations.[145] While the United States was able to use macroeconomic coordination in the 1980s as a means of escaping tough but necessary adjustments in spending,[146] future effectiveness in coordination will depend on the resolve of nations to limit such domestic policy responses. Similarly, with regard to the debt problem, strengthening conditionality will make international monetary management more effective in the long run. Greater conditionality can be even more effective if accompanied by some uncertainties regarding the provision of crisis liquidity in the international system, as suggested by Kindleberger. Absolute guarantees not only generate excessive moral hazard in the management of debt but also make conditionality more difficult to maintain.

Finally, IO is more likely to be effective when it does not put itself in a position to be a vehicle of international competition. In managing international conflicts and disputes, the UN has had mixed results. Notwithstanding its value as a forum for positive interactions, it has (even when siding with a position that seems morally correct) added fuel to international fires by intentionally or unintentionally producing instruments of confrontation and competition. By discouraging confrontational rhetoric and debate and making other adjustments in style or function, the UN might be more effective in reducing international tensions. The argument that a world with an imperfect UN is preferred to a world without a UN does not sufficiently justify the continuation of a style of dispute settlement that exhibits destabilizing characteristics.

Conclusions

Contributors to the IO literature have traditionally been overly optimistic about the ability of multilateral management to stabilize international relations and have generally ignored the fact that IO can be a source of, rather

144. These schemes require neither extensive scope nor extensive level. Their effect depends on their ability to address the right issues in the right ways. Depending on underlying strategic structures in specific relational contexts, institutions that assist cooperation may be more substantive means of generating positive outcomes than institutions that manage cooperation. Often, as has been suggested in this article, big and broad functions make it more difficult to substantively address issues.

145. See Putnam and Bayne, *Hanging Together*.

146. Critics of super-301 would identify a similar motive behind the U.S. trade policy toward Asia.

than a remedy for, disorder in and across issue-areas. Although recent revisionist scholars have recognized the destabilizing effects of IO, they have taken a somewhat restrictive view of organizational failure. In addressing the general issue of the ways in which IO can fail and outlining the conditions under which more limited and less centralized modes of regulation are preferable, this article has sought to develop a set of guidelines that are pertinent to decision making and serve as a rationale for eliminating the excesses of IO. The findings of the article have implications not only for policymaking but also for theory and research in the field of international relations.

According to conventional theories of cooperation and conflict, the sources of international disorder are the underlying strategic structures of relations between nations. However, the findings presented here suggest that disorder springs from more heterogeneous sources. Important sources of disorder—sources that are seemingly unlikely and have thus tended to be overlooked—are the solutions proffered by IOs. While these solutions are intended to moderate or eliminate the disorder created by strategic structures, they often have the opposite effect of exacerbating existing problems or creating new ones. Theories thus need to endogenize these origins of disorder. They also need to expand their menu of dependent variables, which has traditionally been limited to the roles, goals, and functions of IOs. Far more attention needs to be paid to the effects (impact) of management in shaping international outcomes. The finding emphasized here with regard to impact is that IO has the potential for negative as well as positive results, a finding that supports the view that conflict and cooperation coexist in close proximity and even overlap in international relations.[147]

Recent research has tended to blur the distinction between international relations on the one hand and the schemes and institutions that are created to manage these relations on the other hand. In other words, it has failed to distinguish the forest from the trees. By focusing on the processes of IO, this article has attempted to avoid this pitfall. More work in this direction is needed, however, particularly with regard to better differentiating the impact as well as the roles, goals, and functions of IO.[148] Which specific IOs are more likely to generate moral hazard?[149] Which are more likely to generate inferior substitutes? Questions such as these only partially reflect the theoretical and empirical issues that need to be addressed.

Finally, international bureaucrats and national policymakers, like schol-

147. Nowhere is this more evident than in alliance relations. See Paul Diesing and Glenn Snyder, *Conflict Among Nations* (Princeton, N.J.: Princeton University Press, 1977), chap. 6.

148. Jervis, for one, has differentiated between security and international economic regimes in terms of viability and stability. See Jervis, "Security Regimes."

149. Discussions of moral hazard in international politics have generally focused on monetary relations, but the possibilities for moral hazard appear to be more far-reaching. Jervis and Nye, for example, make interesting albeit brief allusions to possibilities for moral hazard in security relations. See Jervis, "Security Regimes," p. 368; and Joseph Nye, "Nuclear Learning," *International Organization* 41 (Summer 1987), p. 390.

ars, need to be more sensitized to the complexity of the effects of IO when considering optimal responses to international problems. The problems themselves should not comprise the sole criteria according to which managerial schemes are constructed but must instead be carefully considered in conjunction with the likely effects generated by these schemes. In other words, the specific roles, functions, and goals of IO should be dictated both by the nature or underlying strategic structures of the international problems and by the potential positive and negative effects of possible managed solutions. Such a "conditional orientation" toward organizational design seems best adapted to the realities of IO failure and the underlying relations among nations.

The Politics, Power, and Pathologies of International Organizations

Michael N. Barnett and Martha Finnemore

Do international organizations really do what their creators intend them to do? In the past century the number of international organizations (IOs) has increased exponentially, and we have a variety of vigorous theories to explain why they have been created. Most of these theories explain IO creation as a response to problems of incomplete information, transaction costs, and other barriers to Pareto efficiency and welfare improvement for their members. Research flowing from these theories, however, has paid little attention to how IOs actually behave after they are created. Closer scrutiny would reveal that many IOs stray from the efficiency goals these theories impute and that many IOs exercise power autonomously in ways unintended and unanticipated by states at their creation. Understanding how this is so requires a reconsideration of IOs and what they do.

In this article we develop a constructivist approach rooted in sociological institutionalism to explain both the power of IOs and their propensity for dysfunctional, even pathological, behavior. Drawing on long-standing Weberian arguments about bureaucracy and sociological institutionalist approaches to organizational behavior, we argue that the rational-legal authority that IOs embody gives them power independent of the states that created them and channels that power in particular directions. Bureaucracies, by definition, make rules, but in so doing they also create social knowledge. They define shared international tasks (like "development"), create and define new categories of actors (like "refugee"), create new interests for actors (like "promoting human rights"), and transfer models of political organization around the world (like markets and democracy.) However, the same normative valuation on impersonal, generalized rules that defines bureaucracies and makes them powerful in

We are grateful to John Boli, Raymond Duvall, Ernst Haas, Peter Haas, Robert Keohane, Keith Krause, Jeffrey Legro, John Malley, Craig Murphy, M. J. Peterson, Mark Pollack, Andrew Moravcsik, Thomas Risse, Duncan Snidal, Steve Weber, Thomas Weiss, and two anonymous referees for their comments. We are especially grateful for the careful attention of the editors of *International Organization*. Earlier versions of this article were presented at the 1997 APSA meeting, the 1997 ISA meeting, and at various fora. We also acknowledge financial assistance from the Smith Richardson Foundation and the United States Institute of Peace.

International Organization 53, 4, Autumn 1999, pp. 699–732

modern life can also make them unresponsive to their environments, obsessed with their own rules at the expense of primary missions, and ultimately lead to inefficient, self-defeating behavior. We are not the first to suggest that IOs are more than the reflection of state preferences and that they can be autonomous and powerful actors in global politics.[1] Nor are we the first to note that IOs, like all organizations, can be dysfunctional and inefficient.[2] However, our emphasis on the way that characteristics of bureaucracy as a generic cultural form shape IO behavior provides a different and very broad basis for thinking about how IOs influence world politics.[3]

Developing an alternative approach to thinking about IOs is only worthwhile if it produces significant insights and new opportunities for research on major debates in the field. Our approach allows us to weigh in with new perspectives on at least three such debates. First, it offers a different view of the power of IOs and whether or how they matter in world politics. This issue has been at the core of the neoliberal-institutionalists' debate with neorealists for years.[4] We show in this article how neo-liberal-institutionalists actually disadvantage themselves in their argument with real-ists by looking at only one facet of IO power. Global organizations do more than just facilitate cooperation by helping states to overcome market failures, collective action dilemmas, and problems associated with interdependent social choice. They also create actors, specify responsibilities and authority among them, and define the work these actors should do, giving it meaning and normative value. Even when they lack material resources, IOs exercise power as they constitute and construct the social world.[5]

Second and related, our perspective provides a theoretical basis for treating IOs as autonomous actors in world politics and thus presents a challenge to the statist ontol-ogy prevailing in international relations theories. Despite all their attention to inter-national institutions, one result of the theoretical orientation of neoliberal institution-alists and regimes theorists is that they treat IOs the way pluralists treat the state. IOs are mechanisms through which others (usually states) act; they are not purposive actors. The regimes literature is particularly clear on this point. Regimes are "prin-ciples, norms, rules, and decision-making procedures;" they are not actors.[6] Weber's insights about the normative power of the rational-legal authority that bureaucracies embody and its implications for the ways bureaucracies produce and control social knowledge provide a basis for challenging this view and treating IOs as agents, not just as structure.

---

1. For Gramscian approaches, see Cox 1980, 1992, and 1996; and Murphy 1995. For Society of States approaches, see Hurrell and Woods 1995. For the epistemic communities literature, see Haas 1992. For IO decision-making literature, see Cox et al. 1974; Cox and Jacobson 1977; Cox 1996; and Ness and Brechin 1988. For a rational choice perspective, see Snidal 1996.

2. Haas 1990.

3. Because the neorealist and neoliberal arguments we engage have focused on intergovernmental organizations rather than nongovernmental ones, and because Weberian arguments from which we draw deal primarily with public bureaucracy, we too focus on intergovernmental organizations in this article and use the term *international organizations* in that way.

4. Baldwin 1993.

5. See Finnemore 1993 and 1996b; and McNeely 1995.

6. Krasner 1983b.

Third, our perspective offers a different vantage point from which to assess the desirability of IOs. While realists and some policymakers have taken up this issue, surprisingly few other students of IOs have been critical of their performance or desirability.[7] Part of this optimism stems from central tenets of classical liberalism, which has long viewed IOs as a peaceful way to manage rapid technological change and globalization, far preferable to the obvious alternative—war.[8] Also contributing to this uncritical stance is the normative judgment about IOs that is built into the theoretical assumptions of most neoliberal and regimes scholars and the economic organization theories on which they draw. IOs exist, in this view, only because they are Pareto improving and solve problems for states. Consequently, if an IO exists, it must be because it is more useful than other alternatives since, by theoretical axiom, states will pull the plug on any IO that does not perform. We find this assumption unsatisfying. IOs often produce undesirable and even self-defeating outcomes repeatedly, without punishment much less dismantlement, and we, as theorists, want to understand why. International relations scholars are familiar with principal-agent problems and the ways in which bureaucratic politics can compromise organizational effectiveness, but these approaches have rarely been applied to IOs. Further, these approaches by no means exhaust sources of dysfunction. We examine one such source that flows from the same rational-legal characteristics that make IOs authoritative and powerful. Drawing from research in sociology and anthropology, we show how the very features that make bureaucracies powerful can also be their weakness.

The claims we make in this article flow from an analysis of the "social stuff" of which bureaucracy is made. We are asking a standard constructivist question about what makes the world hang together or, as Alexander Wendt puts it, "how are things in the world put together so that they have the properties they do."[9] In this sense, our explanation of IO behavior is constitutive and differs from most other international relations approaches. This approach does not make our explanation "mere description," since understanding the constitution of things does essential work in explaining how those things behave and what causes outcomes. Just as understanding how the double-helix DNA molecule is constituted materially makes possible causal arguments about genetics, disease, and other biological processes, so understanding how bureaucracies are constituted socially allows us to hypothesize about the behavior of IOs and the effects this social form might have in world politics. This type of constitutive explanation does not allow us to offer law-like statements such as "if X happens, then Y must follow." Rather, by providing a more complete understanding of what bureaucracy is, we can provide explanations of how certain kinds of bureaucratic behavior are possible, or even probable, and why.[10]

We begin by examining the assumptions underlying different branches of organization theory and exploring their implications for the study of IOs. We argue that assumptions drawn from economics that undergird neoliberal and neorealist treat-

---

7. See Mearsheimer 1994; and Helms 1996.
8. See Commission on Global Governance 1995; Jacobson 1979, 1; and Doyle 1997.
9. See Ruggie 1998; and Wendt 1998.
10. Wendt 1998.

ments of IOs do not always reflect the empirical situation of most IOs commonly studied by political scientists. Further, they provide research hypotheses about only some aspects of IOs (like why they are created) and not others (like what they do). We then introduce sociological arguments that help remedy these problems.

In the second section we develop a constructivist approach from these sociological arguments to examine the power wielded by IOs and the sources of their influence. Liberal and realist theories only make predictions about, and consequently only look for, a very limited range of welfare-improving effects caused by IOs. Sociological theories, however, expect and explain a much broader range of impacts organizations can have and specifically highlight their role in constructing actors, interests, and social purpose. We provide illustrations from the UN system to show how IOs do, in fact, have such powerful effects in contemporary world politics. In the third section we explore the dysfunctional behavior of IOs, which we define as behavior that undermines the stated goals of the organization. International relations theorists are familiar with several types of theories that might explain such behavior. Some locate the source of dysfunction in material factors, others focus on cultural factors. Some theories locate the source of dysfunction outside the organization, others locate it inside. We construct a typology, mapping these theories according to the source of dysfunction they emphasize, and show that the same internally generated cultural forces that give IOs their power and autonomy can also be a source of dysfunctional behavior. We use the term *pathologies* to describe such instances when IO dysfunction can be traced to bureaucratic culture. We conclude by discussing how our perspective helps to widen the research agenda for IOs.

Theoretical Approaches to Organizations

Within social science there are two broad strands of theorizing about organizations. One is economistic and rooted in assumptions of instrumental rationality and efficiency concerns; the other is sociological and focused on issues of legitimacy and power.[11] The different assumptions embedded within each type of theory focus attention on different kinds of questions about organizations and provide insights on different kinds of problems.

The economistic approach comes, not surprisingly, out of economics departments and business schools for whom the fundamental theoretical problem, laid out first by Ronald Coase and more recently by Oliver Williamson, is why we have business firms. Within standard microeconomic logic, it should be much more efficient to conduct all transactions through markets rather than "hierarchies" or organizations. Consequently, the fact that economic life is dominated by huge organizations (business firms) is an anomaly. The body of theory developed to explain the existence and power of firms focuses on organizations as efficient solutions to contracting problems, incomplete information, and other market imperfections.[12]

---

11. See Powell and DiMaggio 1991, chap. 1; and Grandori 1993.
12. See Williamson 1975 and 1985; and Coase 1937.

This body of organization theory informs neoliberal and neorealist debates over international institutions. Following Kenneth Waltz, neoliberals and neorealists understand world politics to be analogous to a market filled with utility-maximizing competitors.[13] Thus, like the economists, they see organizations as welfare-improving solutions to problems of incomplete information and high transaction costs.[14] Neoliberals and realists disagree about the degree to which constraints of anarchy, an interest in relative versus absolute gains, and fears of cheating will scuttle international institutional arrangements or hobble their effectiveness, but both agree, implicitly or explicitly, that IOs help states further their interests where they are allowed to work.[15] State power may be exercised in political battles inside IOs over where, on the Pareto frontier, political bargains fall, but the notion that IOs are instruments created to serve state interests is not much questioned by neorealist or neoliberal scholars.[16] After all, why else would states set up these organizations and continue to support them if they did not serve state interests?

Approaches from sociology provide one set of answers to this question. They provide reasons why, in fact, organizations that are not efficient or effective servants of member interests might exist. In so doing, they lead us to look for kinds of power and sources of autonomy in organizations that economists overlook. Different approaches within sociology treat organizations in different ways, but as a group they stand in sharp contrast to the economists' approaches in at least two important respects: they offer a different conception of the relationship between organizations and their environments, and they provide a basis for understanding organizational autonomy.

IOs and their environment.   The environment assumed by economic approaches to organizations is socially very thin and devoid of social rules, cultural content, or even other actors beyond those constructing the organization. Competition, exchange, and consequent pressures for efficiency are the dominant environmental characteristics driving the formation and behavior of organizations. Sociologists, by contrast, study organizations in a wider world of nonmarket situations, and, consequently, they begin with no such assumptions. Organizations are treated as "social facts" to be investigated; whether they do what they claim or do it efficiently is an empirical question, not a theoretical assumption of these approaches. Organizations respond not only to other actors pursuing material interests in the environment but also to normative and cultural forces that shape how organizations see the world and conceptualize their own missions. Environments can "select" or favor organizations for reasons other than efficient or responsive behavior. For example, organizations may be created and supported for reasons of legitimacy and normative fit rather than efficient output; they may be created not for what they do but for what they are—for what they represent symbolically and the values they embody.[17]

13. Waltz 1979.
14. See Vaubel 1991, 27; and Dillon, Ilgen, and Willett 1991.
15. Baldwin 1993.
16. Krasner 1991.
17. See DiMaggio and Powell 1983; Scott 1992; Meyer and Scott 1992, 1–5; Powell and DiMaggio 1991; Weber 1994; and Finnemore 1996a.

Empirically, organizational environments can take many forms. Some organizations exist in competitive environments that create strong pressures for efficient or responsive behavior, but many do not. Some organizations operate with clear criteria for "success" (like firms that have balance sheets), whereas others (like political science departments) operate with much vaguer missions, with few clear criteria for success or failure and no serious threat of elimination. Our point is simply that when we choose a theoretical framework, we should choose one whose assumptions approximate the empirical conditions of the IO we are analyzing, and that we should be aware of the biases created by those assumptions. Economistic approaches make certain assumptions about the environment in which IOs are embedded that drive researchers who use them to look for certain kinds of effects and not others. Specifying different or more varied environments for IOs would lead us to look for different and more varied effects in world politics.[18]

IO autonomy.   Following economistic logic, regime theory and the broad range of scholars working within it generally treat IOs as creations of states designed to further state interests.[19] Analysis of subsequent IO behavior focuses on processes of aggregating member state preferences through strategic interaction within the structure of the IO. IOs, then, are simply epiphenomena of state interaction; they are, to quote Waltz's definition of reductionism, "understood by knowing the attributes and the interactions of [their] parts."[20]

These theories thus treat IOs as empty shells or impersonal policy machinery to be manipulated by other actors. Political bargains shape the machinery at its creation, states may politick hard within the machinery in pursuit of their policy goals, and the machinery's norms and rules may constrain what states can do, but the machinery itself is passive. IOs are not purposive political actors in their own right and have no ontological independence. To the extent that IOs do, in fact, take on a life of their own, they breach the "limits of realism" as well as of neoliberalism by violating the ontological structures of these theories.[21]

The regimes concept spawned a huge literature on interstate cooperation that is remarkably consistent in its treatment of IOs as structure rather than agents. Much of the neoliberal institutionalist literature has been devoted to exploring the ways in which regimes (and IOs) can act as intervening variables, mediating between states' pursuit of self-interest and political outcomes by changing the structure of opportunities and constraints facing states through their control over information, in particular.[22] Although this line of scholarship accords IOs some causal status (since they demonstrably change outcomes), it does not grant them autonomy and purpose inde-

---

18. Researchers applying these economistic approaches have become increasingly aware of the mismatch between the assumptions of their models and the empirics of IOs. See Snidal 1996.

19. Note that empirically this is not the case; most IOs now are created by other IOs. See Shanks, Jacobson, and Kaplan 1996.

20. Waltz 1979, 18.

21. Krasner 1983a, 355–68; but see Finnemore 1996b; and Rittberger 1993.

22. See Keohane 1984; and Baldwin 1993.

pendent of the states that comprise them. Another branch of liberalism has recently divorced itself from the statist ontology and focuses instead on the preferences of social groups as the causal engine of world politics, but, again, this view simply argues for attention to a different group of agents involved in the construction of IOs and competing for access to IO mechanisms. It does not offer a fundamentally different conception of IOs.[23]

The relevant question to ask about this conceptualization is whether it is a reasonable approximation of the empirical condition of most IOs. Our reading of detailed empirical case studies of IO activity suggests not. Yes, IOs are constrained by states, but the notion that they are passive mechanisms with no independent agendas of their own is not borne out by any detailed empirical study of an IO that we have found. Field studies of the European Union provide evidence of independent roles for "eurocrats."[24] Studies of the World Bank consistently identify an independent culture and agendas for action.[25] Studies of recent UN peacekeeping and reconstruction efforts similarly document a UN agenda that frequently leads to conflict with member states.[26] Accounts of the UN High Commission on Refugees (UNHCR) routinely note how its autonomy and authority has grown over the years. Not only are IOs independent actors with their own agendas, but they may embody multiple agendas and contain multiple sources of agency—a problem we take up later.

Principal-agent analysis, which has been increasingly employed by students of international relations to examine organizational dynamics, could potentially provide a sophisticated approach to understanding IO autonomy.[27] Building on theories of rational choice and of representation, these analysts understand IOs as "agents" of states ("principals"). The analysis is concerned with whether agents are responsible delegates of their principals, whether agents smuggle in and pursue their own preferences, and how principals can construct various mechanisms to keep their agents honest.[28] This framework provides a means of treating IOs as actors in their own right with independent interests and capabilities. Autonomous action by IOs is to be expected in this perspective. It would also explain a number of the nonresponsive and pathological behaviors that concern us because we know that monitoring and shirking problems are pervasive in these principal-agent relationships and that these relationships can often get stuck at suboptimal equilibria.

The problem with applying principal-agent analysis to the study of IOs is that it requires a priori theoretical specification of what IOs want. Principal-agent dynamics are fueled by the disjuncture between what agents want and what principals want. To produce any insights, those two sets of interests cannot be identical. In economics this type of analysis is usually applied to preexisting agents and principals (clients

23. Moravcsik 1997.
24. See Pollack 1997; Ross 1995; and Zabusky 1995; but see Moravcsik 1999.
25. See Ascher 1983; Ayres 1983; Ferguson 1990; Escobar 1995; Wade 1996; Nelson 1995; and Finnemore 1996a.
26. Joint Evaluation of Emergency Assistance to Rwanda 1996.
27. See Pollack 1997; Lake 1996; Vaubel 1991; and Dillon, Ilgen, and Willett 1991.
28. See Pratt and Zeckhauser 1985; and Kiewit and McCubbins 1991.

hiring lawyers, patients visiting doctors) whose ongoing independent existence makes specification of independent interests relatively straightforward. The lawyer or the doctor would probably be in business even if you and I did not take our problems to them. IOs, on the other hand, are often created by the principals (states) and given mission statements written by the principals. How, then, can we impute independent preferences a priori?

Scholars of American politics have made some progress in producing substantive theoretical propositions about what U.S. bureaucratic agencies want. Beginning with the pioneering work of William Niskanen, scholars theorized that bureaucracies had interests defined by the absolute or relative size of their budget and the expansion or protection of their turf. At first these interests were imputed, and later they became more closely investigated, substantiated, and in some cases modified or rejected altogether.[29]

Realism and liberalism, however, provide no basis for asserting independent utility functions for IOs. Ontologically, these are theories about states. They provide no basis for imputing interests to IOs beyond the goals states (that is, principals) give them. Simply adopting the rather battered Niskanen hypothesis seems less than promising given the glaring anomalies—for example, the opposition of many NATO and OSCE (Organization for Security and Cooperation in Europe) bureaucrats to those organizations' recent expansion and institutionalization. There are good reasons to assume that organizations care about their resource base and turf, but there is no reason to presume that such matters exhaust or even dominate their interests. Indeed, ethnographic studies of IOs describe a world in which organizational goals are strongly shaped by norms of the profession that dominate the bureaucracy and in which interests themselves are varied, often in flux, debated, and worked out through interactions between the staff of the bureaucracy and the world in which they are embedded.[30]

Various strands of sociological theory can help us investigate the goals and behavior of IOs by offering a very different analytical orientation than the one used by economists. Beginning with Weber, sociologists have explored the notion that bureaucracy is a peculiarly modern cultural form that embodies certain values and can have its own distinct agenda and behavioral dispositions. Rather than treating organizations as mere arenas or mechanisms through which other actors pursue interests, many sociological approaches explore the social content of the organization—its culture, its legitimacy concerns, dominant norms that govern behavior and shape interests, and the relationship of these to a larger normative and cultural environment. Rather than assuming behavior that corresponds to efficiency criteria alone, these approaches recognize that organizations also are bound up with power and social control in ways that can eclipse efficiency concerns.

29. See Niskanen 1971; Miller and Moe 1983; Weingast and Moran 1983; Moe 1984; and Sigelman 1986.
30. See Ascher 1983; Zabusky 1995; Barnett 1997b; and Wade 1996.

The Power of IOs

IOs can become autonomous sites of authority, independent from the state "principals" who may have created them, because of power flowing from at least two sources: (1) the legitimacy of the rational-legal authority they embody, and (2) control over technical expertise and information. The first of these is almost entirely neglected by the political science literature, and the second, we argue, has been conceived of very narrowly, leading scholars to overlook some of the most basic and consequential forms of IO influence. Taken together, these two features provide a theoretical basis for treating IOs as autonomous actors in contemporary world politics by identifying sources of support for them, independent of states, in the larger social environment. Since rational-legal authority and control over expertise are part of what defines and constitutes any bureaucracy (a bureaucracy would not be a bureaucracy without them), the autonomy that flows from them is best understood as a constitutive effect, an effect of the way bureaucracy is constituted, which, in turn, makes possible (and in that sense causes) other processes and effects in global politics.

Sources of IO Autonomy and Authority

To understand how IOs can become autonomous sites of authority we turn to Weber and his classic study of bureaucratization. Weber was deeply ambivalent about the increasingly bureaucratic world in which he lived and was well-attuned to the vices as well as the virtues of this new social form of authority.[31] Bureaucracies are rightly considered a grand achievement, he thought. They provide a framework for social interaction that can respond to the increasingly technical demands of modern life in a stable, predictable, and nonviolent way; they exemplify rationality and are technically superior to previous forms of rule because they bring precision, knowledge, and continuity to increasingly complex social tasks.[32] But such technical and rational achievements, according to Weber, come at a steep price. Bureaucracies are political creatures that can be autonomous from their creators and can come to dominate the societies they were created to serve, because of both the normative appeal of rational-legal authority in modern life and the bureaucracy's control over technical expertise and information. We consider each in turn.

Bureaucracies embody a form of authority, rational-legal authority, that modernity views as particularly legitimate and good. In contrast to earlier forms of authority that were invested in a leader, legitimate modern authority is invested in legalities, procedures, and rules and thus rendered impersonal. This authority is "rational" in that it deploys socially recognized relevant knowledge to create rules that determine how goals will be pursued. The very fact that they embody rationality is what makes bureaucracies powerful and makes people willing to submit to this kind of authority.

---

31. See Weber 1978, 196–97; Weber 1947; Mouzelis 1967; and Beetham 1985 and 1996.
32. See Schaar 1984, 120; Weber 1978, 973; and Beetham 1985, 69.

According to Weber,

> in legal authority, submission does not rest upon the belief and devotion to charismatically gifted persons. . . or upon piety toward a personal lord and master who is defined by an ordered tradition. . . . Rather submission under legal authority is based upon an *impersonal* bond to the generally defined and functional "duty of office." The official duty—like the corresponding right to exercise authority: the "jurisdictional competency"—is fixed by *rationally established* norms, by enactments, decrees, and regulations in such a manner that the legitimacy of the authority becomes the legality of the general rule, which is purposely thought out, enacted, and announced with formal correctness.[33]

When bureaucrats do something contrary to your interests or that you do not like, they defend themselves by saying "Sorry, those are the rules" or "just doing my job." "The rules" and "the job" are the source of great power in modern society. It is because bureaucrats in IOs are performing "duties of office" and implementing "rationally established norms" that they are powerful.

A second basis of autonomy and authority, intimately connected to the first, is bureaucratic control over information and expertise. A bureaucracy's autonomy derives from specialized technical knowledge, training, and experience that is not immediately available to other actors. While such knowledge might help the bureaucracy carry out the directives of politicians more efficiently, Weber stressed that it also gives bureaucracies power over politicians (and other actors). It invites and at times requires bureaucracies to shape policy, not just implement it.[34]

The irony in both of these features of authority is that they make bureaucracies powerful precisely by creating the appearance of depoliticization. The power of IOs, and bureaucracies generally, is that they present themselves as impersonal, technocratic, and neutral—as not exercising power but instead as serving others; the presentation and acceptance of these claims is critical to their legitimacy and authority.[35] Weber, however, saw through these claims. According to him, the depoliticized character of bureaucracy that legitimates it could be a myth: "Behind the functional purposes [of bureaucracy], of course, 'ideas of culture-values' usually stand."[36] Bureaucracies always serve some social purpose or set of cultural values. That purpose may be normatively "good," as Weber believed the Prussian nationalism around him was, but there was no a priori reason to assume this.

In addition to embodying cultural values from the larger environment that might be desirable or not, bureaucracies also carry with them behavioral dispositions and values flowing from the rationality that legitimates them as a cultural form. Some of these, like the celebration of knowledge and expertise, Weber admired. Others concerned him greatly, and his descriptions of bureaucracy as an "iron cage" and bureaucrats as "specialists without spirit" are hardly an endorsement of the bureaucratic

---

33. Gerth and Mills 1978, 299 (italics in original).
34. See Gerth and Mills 1978, 233; Beetham 1985, 74–75; and Schaar 1984, 120.
35. We thank John Boli for this insight. Also see Fisher 1997; Ferguson 1990; Shore and Wright 1997; and Burley and Mattli 1993.
36. Gerth and Mills 1978, 199.

form.[37] Bureaucracy can undermine personal freedom in important ways. The very impersonal, rule-bound character that empowers bureaucracy also dehumanizes it. Bureaucracies often exercise their power in repressive ways, in the name of general rules because rules are their raison d'être. This tendency is exacerbated by the way bureaucracies select and reward narrowed professionals seeking secure careers internally—people who are "lacking in heroism, human spontaneity, and inventiveness."[38] Following Weber, we investigate rather than assume the "goodness" of bureaucracy.

Weber's insights provide a powerful critique of the ways in which international relations scholars have treated IOs. The legitimacy of rational-legal authority suggests that IOs may have an authority independent of the policies and interests of states that create them, a possibility obscured by the technical and apolitical treatment of IOs by both realists and neoliberals. Nor have realists and neoliberals considered how control over information hands IOs a basis of autonomy. Susan Strange, at the forefront among realists in claiming that information is power, has emphatically stated that IOs are simply the agents of states. Neoliberals have tended to treat information in a highly technocratic and depoliticized way, failing to see how information is power.[39] As IOs create transparencies and level information asymmetries among states (a common policy prescription of neoliberals) they create new information asymmetries between IOs and states. Given the neoliberal assumption that IOs have no goals independent of states, such asymmetries are unimportant; but if IOs have autonomous values and behavioral predispositions, then such asymmetries may be highly consequential.

Examples of the ways in which IOs have become autonomous because of their embodiment of technical rationality and control over information are not hard to find. The UN's peacekeepers derive part of their authority from the claim that they are independent, objective, neutral actors who simply implement Security Council resolutions. UN officials routinely use this language to describe their role and are explicit that they understand this to be the basis of their influence. As a consequence, UN officials spend considerable time and energy attempting to maintain the image that they are not the instrument of any great power and must be seen as representatives of "the international community" as embodied in the rules and resolutions of the UN.[40] The World Bank is widely recognized to have exercised power over development policies far greater than its budget, as a percentage of North/South aid flows, would suggest because of the expertise it houses. While competing sites of expertise in development have proliferated in recent years, for decades after its founding the World Bank was a magnet for the "best and brightest" among "development experts." Its staff had and continues to have impressive credentials from the most pres-

---

37. See Weber [1930] 1978, 181–83; and Clegg 1994a, 152–55.
38. Gerth and Mills 1978, 216, 50, 299. For the extreme manifestation of this bureaucratic characteristic, see Arendt 1977.
39. See Strange 1997; and Keohane 1984.
40. See David Rieff, "The Institution that Saw No Evil," *The New Republic*, 12 February 1996, 19–24; and Barnett 1997b.

tigious universities and the elaborate models, reports, and research groups it has sponsored over the years were widely influential among the "development experts" in the field. This expertise, coupled with its claim to "neutrality" and its "apolitical" technocratic decision-making style, have given the World Bank an authoritative voice with which it has successfully dictated the content, direction, and scope of global development over the past fifty years.[41] Similarly, official standing and long experience with relief efforts have endowed the UNHCR with "expert" status and consequent authority in refugee matters. This expertise, coupled with its role in implementing international refugee conventions and law ("the rules" regarding refugees), has allowed the UNHCR to make life and death decisions about refugees without consulting the refugees, themselves, and to compromise the authority of states in various ways in setting up refugee camps.[42] Note that, as these examples show, technical knowledge and expertise need not be "scientific" in nature to create autonomy and power for IOs.

The Power of IOs

If IOs have autonomy and authority in the world, what do they do with it? A growing body of research in sociology and anthropology has examined ways in which IOs exercise power by virtue of their culturally constructed status as sites of authority; we distill from this research three broad types of IO power. We examine how IOs (1) classify the world, creating categories of actors and action; (2) fix meanings in the social world; and (3) articulate and diffuse new norms, principles, and actors around the globe. All of these sources of power flow from the ability of IOs to structure knowledge.[43]

Classification.   An elementary feature of bureaucracies is that they classify and organize information and knowledge. This classification process is bound up with power. "Bureaucracies," writes Don Handelman, "are ways of making, ordering, and knowing social worlds." They do this by "moving persons among social categories or by inventing and applying such categories."[44] The ability to classify objects, to shift their very definition and identity, is one of bureaucracy's greatest sources of power. This power is frequently treated by the objects of that power as accomplished through caprice and without regard to their circumstances but is legitimated and justified by bureaucrats with reference to the rules and regulations of the bureaucracy. Consequences of this bureaucratic exercise of power may be identity defining, or even life threatening.

Consider the evolving definition of "refugee." The category "refugee" is not at all straightforward and must be distinguished from other categories of individuals who

41. See Wade 1996; Ayres 1983; Ascher 1983; Finnemore 1996b; and Nelson 1995.
42. See Malkki 1996; Hartigan 1992; and Harrell-Bond 1989.
43. See Foucault 1977, 27; and Clegg 1994b, 156–59. International relations theory typically disregards the negative side of the knowledge and power equation. For an example, see Haas 1992.
44. Handelman 1995, 280. See also Starr 1992; and Wright 1994, 22.

are "temporarily" and "involuntarily" living outside their country of origin—displaced persons, exiles, economic migrants, guest workers, diaspora communities, and those seeking political asylum. The debate over the meaning of "refugee" has been waged in and around the UNHCR. The UNHCR's legal and operational definition of the category strongly influences decisions about who is a refugee and shapes UNHCR staff decisions in the field—decisions that have a tremendous effect on the life circumstance of thousands of people.[45] These categories are not only political and legal but also discursive, shaping a view among UNHCR officials that refugees must, by definition, be powerless, and that as powerless actors they do not have to be consulted in decisions such as asylum and repatriation that will directly and dramatically affect them.[46] Guy Gran similarly describes how the World Bank sets up criteria to define someone as a peasant in order to distinguish them from a farmer, day laborer, and other categories. The classification matters because only certain classes of people are recognized by the World Bank's development machinery as having knowledge that is relevant in solving development problems.[47] Categorization and classification are a ubiquitous feature of bureaucratization that has potentially important implications for those being classified. To classify is to engage in an act of power.

The fixing of meanings.   IOs exercise power by virtue of their ability to fix meanings, which is related to classification.[48] Naming or labeling the social context establishes the parameters, the very boundaries, of acceptable action. Because actors are oriented toward objects and objectives on the basis of the meaning that they have for them, being able to invest situations with a particular meaning constitutes an important source of power.[49] IOs do not act alone in this regard, but their organizational resources contribute mightily to this end.

There is strong evidence of this power from development studies. Arturo Escobar explores how the institutionalization of the concept of "development" after World War II spawned a huge international apparatus and how this apparatus has now spread its tentacles in domestic and international politics through the discourse of development. The discourse of development, created and arbitrated in large part by IOs, determines not only what constitutes the activity (what development is) but also who (or what) is considered powerful and privileged, that is, who gets to do the developing (usually the state or IOs) and who is the object of development (local groups).[50]

Similarly, the end of the Cold War encouraged a reexamination of the definition of security.[51] IOs have been at the forefront of this debate, arguing that security pertains not only to states but also to individuals and that the threats to security may be

45. See Weiss and Pasic 1997; Goodwin-Gill 1996; and Anonymous 1997.
46. See Harrell-Bond 1989; Walkup 1997; and Malkki 1996.
47. Gran 1986.
48. See Williams 1996; Clegg 1994b; Bourdieu 1994; Carr [1939] 1964; and Keeley 1990.
49. Blumer 1969.
50. See Gupta 1998; Escobar 1995; Cooper and Packard 1998; Gran 1986; Ferguson 1990; and Wade 1996.
51. See Matthews 1989; and Krause and Williams 1996.

economic, environmental, and political as well as military.[52] In forwarding these alternative definitions of security, officials from various IOs are empowering a different set of actors and legitimating an alternative set of practices. Specifically, when security meant safety from invading national armies, it privileged state officials and invested power in military establishments. These alternative definitions of security shift attention away from states and toward the individuals who are frequently threatened by their own government, away from military practices and toward other features of social life that might represent a more immediate and daily danger to the lives of individuals.

One consequence of these redefined meanings of development and security is that they legitimate, and even require, increased levels of IO intervention in the domestic affairs of states—particularly Third World states. This is fairly obvious in the realm of development. The World Bank, the International Monetary Fund (IMF), and other development institutions have established a web of interventions that affect nearly every phase of the economy and polity in many Third World states. As "rural development," "basic human needs," and "structural adjustment" became incorporated into the meaning of development, IOs were permitted, even required, to become intimately involved in the domestic workings of developing polities by posting inhouse "advisors" to run monetary policy, reorganizing the political economy of entire rural regions, regulating family and reproductive practices, and mediating between governments and their citizens in a variety of ways.[53]

The consequences of redefining security may be similar. Democratization, human rights, and the environment have all now become tied to international peace and security, and IOs justify their interventions in member states on these grounds, particularly in developing states. For example, during the anti-apartheid struggle in South Africa, human rights abuses came to be classified as security threats by the UN Security Council and provided grounds for UN involvement there. Now, that linkage between human rights and security has become a staple of the post–Cold War environment. Widespread human rights abuses anywhere are now cause for UN intervention, and, conversely, the UN cannot carry out peacekeeping missions without promoting human rights.[54] Similarly, environmental disasters in Eastern Europe and the newly independent states of the former Soviet Union and water rights allocations in the Middle East have also come to be discussed under the rubric of "environmental security" and are thus grounds for IO intervention. The United Nations Development Program argues that there is an important link between human security and sustainable development and implicitly argues for greater intervention in the management of environment as a means to promote human security.[55]

Diffusion of norms.   Having established rules and norms, IOs are eager to spread the benefits of their expertise and often act as conveyor belts for the transmission of

---

52. See UN Development Program 1994; and Boutros-Ghali 1995.
53. See Escobar 1995; Ferguson 1990; and Feldstein 1998.
54. World Conference on Human Rights 1993.
55. UN Development Program 1994.

norms and models of "good" political behavior.[56] There is nothing accidental or unintended about this role. Officials in IOs often insist that part of their mission is to spread, inculcate, and enforce global values and norms. They are the "missionaries" of our time. Armed with a notion of progress, an idea of how to create the better life, and some understanding of the conversion process, many IO elites have as their stated purpose a desire to shape state practices by establishing, articulating, and transmitting norms that define what constitutes acceptable and legitimate state behavior. To be sure, their success depends on more than their persuasive capacities, for their rhetoric must be supported by power, sometimes (but not always) state power. But to overlook how state power and organizational missionaries work in tandem and the ways in which IO officials channel and shape states' exercise of power is to disregard a fundamental feature of value diffusion.[57]

Consider decolonization as an example. The UN Charter announced an intent to universalize sovereignty as a constitutive principle of the society of states at a time when over half the globe was under some kind of colonial rule; it also established an institutional apparatus to achieve that end (most prominently the Trusteeship Council and the Special Committee on Colonialism). These actions had several consequences. One was to eliminate certain categories of acceptable action for powerful states. Those states that attempted to retain their colonial privileges were increasingly viewed as illegitimate by other states. Another consequence was to empower international bureaucrats (at the Trusteeship Council) to set norms and standards for "stateness." Finally, the UN helped to ensure that throughout decolonization the sovereignty of these new states was coupled with territorial inviolability. Colonial boundaries often divided ethnic and tribal groups, and the UN was quite concerned that in the process of "self-determination," these governments containing "multiple" or "partial" selves might attempt to create a whole personality through territorial adjustment—a fear shared by many of these newly decolonized states. The UN encouraged the acceptance of the norm of sovereignty-as-territorial-integrity through resolutions, monitoring devices, commissions, and one famous peacekeeping episode in Congo in the 1960s.[58]

Note that, as with other IO powers, norm diffusion, too, has an expansionary dynamic. Developing states continue to be popular targets for norm diffusion by IOs, even after they are independent. The UN and the European Union are now actively involved in police training in non-Western states because they believe Western policing practices will be more conducive to democratization processes and the establishment of civil society. But having a professional police establishment assumes that there is a professional judiciary and penal system where criminals can be tried and jailed; and a professional judiciary, in turn, presupposes that there are lawyers that can come before the court. Trained lawyers presuppose a code of law. The result is a package of reforms sponsored by IOs aimed at transforming non-Western societies

56. See Katzenstein 1996; Finnemore 1996b; and Legro 1997.
57. See Alger 1963, 425; and Claude 1966, 373.
58. See McNeely 1995; and Jackson 1993.

into Western societies.[59] Again, while Western states are involved in these activities and therefore their values and interests are part of the reasons for this process, international bureaucrats involved in these activities may not see themselves as doing the bidding for these states but rather as expressing the interests and values of the bureaucracy.

Other examples of this kind of norm diffusion are not hard to find. The IMF and the World Bank are explicit about their role as transmitters of norms and principles from advanced market economies to less-developed economies.[60] The IMF's Articles of Agreement specifically assign it this task of incorporating less-developed economies into the world economy, which turns out to mean teaching them how to "be" market economies. The World Bank, similarly, has a major role in arbitrating the meaning of development and norms of behavior appropriate to the task of developing oneself, as was discussed earlier. The end of the Cold War has opened up a whole new set of states to this kind of norm diffusion task for IOs. According to former Secretary of Defense William Perry, one of the functions of NATO expansion is to inculcate "modern" values and norms into the Eastern European countries and their militaries.[61] The European Bank for Reconstruction and Development has, as part of its mandate, the job of spreading democracy and private enterprise. The OSCE is striving to create a community based on shared values, among these respect for democracy and human rights. This linkage is also strong at the UN as evident in *The Agenda for Democratization* and *The Agenda for Peace*.[62] Once democratization and human rights are tied to international peace and security, the distinctions between international and domestic governance become effectively erased and IOs have license to intervene almost anywhere in an authoritative and legitimate manner.[63]

Realists and neoliberals may well look at these effects and argue that the classificatory schemes, meanings, and norms associated with IOs are mostly favored by strong states. Consequently, they would argue, the power we attribute to IOs is simply epiphenomenal of state power. This argument is certainly one theoretical possibility, but it is not the only one and must be tested against others. Our concern is that because these theories provide no ontological independence for IOs, they have no way to test for autonomy nor have they any theoretical cause or inclination to test for it since, by theoretical axiom, autonomy cannot exist. The one empirical domain in which the statist view has been explicitly challenged is the European Union, and empirical studies there have hardly produced obvious victory for the "intergovernmentalist" approach.[64] Recent empirical studies in the areas of human rights, weapons taboos, and environmental practices also cast doubt on the statist approach by providing evidence about the ways in which nongovernmental and intergovernmen-

59. Call and Barnett forthcoming.
60. Wade 1996.
61. See Perry 1996; and Ruggie 1996.
62. Boutros-Ghali 1995 and 1996a,b.
63. Keen and Hendrie, however, suggest that nongovernmental organizations and IOs can be the long-term beneficiaries of intervention. See Keen 1994; and Hendrie 1997.
64. See Burley and Mattli 1993; Pollack 1997; and Sandholtz 1993.

tal organizations successfully promote policies that are not (or not initially) supported by strong states.[65] Certainly there are occasions when strong states do drive IO behavior, but there are also times when other forces are at work that eclipse or significantly dampen the effects of states on IOs. Which causal mechanisms produce which effects under which conditions is a set of relationships that can be understood only by intensive empirical study of how these organizations actually do their business—research that would trace the origins and evolution of IO policies, the processes by which they are implemented, discrepancies between implementation and policy, and overall effects of these policies.

The Pathologies of IOs

Bureaucracies are created, propagated, and valued in modern society because of their supposed rationality and effectiveness in carrying out social tasks. These same considerations presumably also apply to IOs. Ironically, though, the folk wisdom about bureaucracies is that they are inefficient and unresponsive. Bureaucracies are infamous for creating and implementing policies that defy rational logic, for acting in ways that are at odds with their stated mission, and for refusing requests of and turning their backs on those to whom they are officially responsible.[66] Scholars of U.S. bureaucracy have recognized this problem and have devoted considerable energy to understanding a wide range of undesirable and inefficient bureaucratic behaviors caused by bureaucratic capture and slack and to exploring the conditions under which "suboptimal equilibria" may arise in organizational structures. Similarly, scholars researching foreign policy decision making and, more recently, those interested in learning in foreign policy have investigated organizational dynamics that produce self-defeating and inefficient behavior in those contexts.[67]

IOs, too, are prone to dysfunctional behaviors, but international relations scholars have rarely investigated this, in part, we suspect, because the theoretical apparatus they use provides few grounds for expecting undesirable IO behavior.[68] The state-centric utility-maximizing frameworks most international relations scholars have borrowed from economics simply assume that IOs are reasonably responsive to state interests (or, at least, more responsive than alternatives), otherwise states would withdraw from them. This assumption, however, is a necessary theoretical axiom of these frameworks; it is rarely treated as a hypothesis subject to empirical investigation.[69] With little theoretical reason to expect suboptimal or self-defeating behavior in IOs, these scholars do not look for it and have had little to say about it. Policymakers, however, have been quicker to perceive and address these problems and are putting

---

65. See Keck and Sikkink 1998; Wapner 1996; Price 1997; and Thomas forthcoming.
66. March and Olsen 1989, chap. 5.
67. See Nye 1987; Haas 1990; Haas and Haas 1995; and Sagan 1993.
68. Two exceptions are Gallaroti 1991; and Snidal 1996.
69. Snidal 1996.

	Internal	External
Material	Bureaucratic politics	Realism/ neoliberal institutionalism
Cultural	Bureaucratic culture	World polity model

FIGURE 1. *Theories of international organization dysfunction*

them on the political agenda. It is time for scholars, too, to begin to explore these issues more fully.

In this section we present several bodies of theorizing that might explain dysfunctional IO behavior, which we define as behavior that undermines the IO's stated objectives. Thus our vantage point for judging dysfunction (and later pathology) is the publicly proclaimed mission of the organization. There may be occasions when overall organizational dysfunction is, in fact, functional for certain members or others involved in the IO's work, but given our analysis of the way claims of efficiency and effectiveness act to legitimate rational-legal authority in our culture, whether organizations actually do what they claim and accomplish their missions is a particularly important issue to examine. Several bodies of theory provide some basis for understanding dysfunctional behavior by IOs, each of which emphasizes a different locus of causality for such behavior. Analyzing these causes, we construct a typology of these explanations that locates them in relation to one another. Then, drawing on the work of James March and Johan Olsen, Paul DiMaggio and Walter Powell, and other sociological institutionalists, we elaborate how the same sources of bureaucratic power, sketched earlier, can cause dysfunctional behavior. We term this particular type of dysfunction *pathology*.[70] We identify five features of bureaucracy that might produce pathology, and using examples from the UN system we illustrate the way these might work in IOs.

Extant theories about dysfunction can be categorized in two dimensions: (1) whether they locate the cause of IO dysfunction inside or outside the organization, and (2) whether they trace the causes to material or cultural forces. Mapping theories on these dimensions creates the typology shown in Figure 1.

Within each cell we have identified a representative body of theory familiar to most international relations scholars. Explanations of IO dysfunction that emphasize the pursuit of material interests within an organization typically examine how competition among subunits over material resources leads the organization to make deci-

---

70. Karl Deutsch used the concept of pathology in a way similar to our usage. We thank Hayward Alker for this point. Deutsch 1963, 170.

sions and engage in behaviors that are inefficient or undesirable as judged against some ideal policy that would better allow the IO to achieve its stated goals. Bureaucratic politics is the best-known theory here, and though current scholars of international politics have not widely adopted this perspective to explain IO behavior, it is relatively well developed in the older IO literature.[71] Graham Allison's central argument is that the "name of the game is politics: bargaining along regularized circuits among players positioned hierarchically within the government. Government behavior can thus be understood as . . . results of these bargaining games."[72] In this view, decisions are not made after a rational decision process but rather through a competitive bargaining process over turf, budgets, and staff that may benefit parts of the organization at the expense of overall goals.

Another body of literature traces IO dysfunctional behavior to the material forces located outside the organization. Realist and neoliberal theories might posit that state preferences and constraints are responsible for understanding IO dysfunctional behavior. In this view IOs are not to blame for bad outcomes, states are. IOs do not have the luxury of choosing the optimal policy but rather are frequently forced to chose between the bad and the awful because more desirable policies are denied to them by states who do not agree among themselves and/or do not wish to see the IO fulfill its mandate in some particular instance. As Robert Keohane observed, IOs often engage in policies not because they are strong and have autonomy but because they are weak and have none.[73] The important point of these theories is that they trace IO dysfunctional behavior back to the environmental conditions established by, or the explicit preferences of, states.

Cultural theories also have internal and external variants. We should note that many advocates of cultural theories would reject the claim that an organization can be understood apart from its environment or that culture is separable from the material world. Instead they would stress how the organization is permeated by that environment, defined in both material and cultural terms, in which it is embedded. Many are also quite sensitive to the ways in which resource constraints and the material power of important actors will shape organizational culture. That said, these arguments clearly differ from the previous two types in their emphasis on ideational and cultural factors and clearly differ among themselves in the motors of behavior emphasized. For analytical clarity we divide cultural theories according to whether they see the primary causes of the IO's dysfunctional behavior as deriving from the culture of the organization (internal) or of the environment (external).

The world polity model exemplifies theories that look to external culture to understand an IO's dysfunctional behavior. There are two reasons to expect dysfunctional behavior here. First, because IO practices reflect a search for symbolic legitimacy rather than efficiency, IO behavior might be only remotely connected to the efficient implementation of its goals and more closely coupled to legitimacy criteria that come

---

71. See Allison 1971; Haas 1990; Cox et al. 1974; and Cox and Jacobson 1977.
72. See Allison 1971, 144; and Bendor and Hammond 1992.
73. Personal communication to the authors.

from the cultural environment.[74] For instance, many arms-export control regimes now have a multilateral character not because of any evidence that this architecture is the most efficient way to monitor and prevent arms exports but rather because multilateralism has attained a degree of legitimacy that is not empirically connected to any efficiency criteria.[75] Second, the world polity is full of contradictions; for instance, a liberal world polity has several defining principles, including market economics and human equality, that might conflict at any one moment. Thus, environments are often ambiguous about missions and contain varied, often conflicting, functional, normative, and legitimacy imperatives.[76] Because they are embedded in that cultural environment, IOs can mirror and reproduce those contradictions, which, in turn, can lead to contradictory and ultimately dysfunctional behavior.

Finally, organizations frequently develop distinctive internal cultures that can promote dysfunctional behavior, behavior that we call "pathological." The basic logic of this argument flows directly from our previous observations about the nature of bureaucracy as a social form. Bureaucracies are established as rationalized means to accomplish collective goals and to spread particular values. To do this, bureaucracies create social knowledge and develop expertise as they act upon the world (and thus exercise power). But the way bureaucracies are constituted to accomplish these ends can, ironically, create a cultural disposition toward undesirable and ultimately self-defeating behavior.[77] Two features of the modern bureaucratic form are particularly important in this regard. The first is the simple fact that bureaucracies are organized around rules, routines, and standard operating procedures designed to trigger a standard and predictable response to environmental stimuli. These rules can be formal or informal, but in either case they tell actors which action is appropriate in response to a specific stimuli, request, or demand. This kind of routinization is, after all, precisely what bureaucracies are supposed to exhibit—it is what makes them effective and competent in performing complex social tasks. However, the presence of such rules also compromises the extent to which means-ends rationality drives organizational behavior. Rules and routines may come to obscure overall missions and larger social goals. They may create "ritualized behavior" in bureaucrats and construct a very parochial normative environment within the organization whose connection to the larger social environment is tenuous at best.[78]

Second, bureaucracies specialize and compartmentalize. They create a division of labor on the logic that because individuals have only so much time, knowledge, and expertise, specialization will allow the organization to emulate a rational decision-making process.[79] Again, this is one of the virtues of bureaucracy in that it provides a way of overcoming the limitations of individual rationality and knowledge by embedding those individuals in a structure that takes advantage of their competencies with-

74. See Meyer and Rowan 1977; Meyer and Zucker 1989; Weber 1994; and Finnemore 1996a.
75. Lipson 1999.
76. McNeely 1995.
77. See Vaughan 1996; and Lipartito 1995.
78. See March and Olsen 1989, 21–27; and Meyer and Rowan 1977.
79. See March and Olsen 1989, 26–27; and March 1997.

out having to rely on their weaknesses. However, it, too, has some negative consequences. Just as rules can eclipse goals, concentrated expertise and specialization can
(and perhaps must) limit bureaucrats' field of vision and create subcultures within
bureaucracy that are distinct from those of the larger environment. Professional training plays a particularly strong role here since this is one widespread way we disseminate specialized knowledge and credential "experts." Such training often gives experts, indeed is designed to give them, a distinctive worldview and normative
commitments, which, when concentrated in a subunit of an organization, can have
pronounced effects on behavior.[80]

Once in place, an organization's culture, understood as the rules, rituals, and beliefs that are embedded in the organization (and its subunits), has important consequences for the way individuals who inhabit that organization make sense of the
world. It provides interpretive frames that individuals use to generate meaning.[81]
This is more than just bounded rationality; in this view, actors' rationality itself, the
very means and ends that they value, are shaped by the organizational culture.[82]
Divisions and subunits within the organization may develop their own cognitive
frameworks that are consistent with but still distinct from the larger organization,
further complicating this process.

All organizations have their own culture (or cultures) that shape their behavior.
The effects of bureaucratic culture, however, need not be dysfunctional. Indeed, specific organizational cultures may be valued and actively promoted as a source of
"good" behavior, as students of business culture know very well. Organizational
culture is tied to "good" and "bad" behavior, alike, and the effects of organizational
culture on behavior are an empirical question to be researched.

To further such research, we draw from studies in sociology and anthropology to
explore five mechanisms by which bureaucratic culture can breed pathologies in IOs:
the irrationality of rationalization, universalism, normalization of deviance, organizational insulation, and cultural contestation. The first three of these mechanisms all
flow from defining features of bureaucracy itself. Consequently, we expect them to
be present in any bureaucracy to a limited degree. Their severity may be increased,
however, by specific empirical conditions of the organization. Vague mission, weak
feedback from the environment, and strong professionalism all have the potential to
exacerbate these mechanisms and to create two others, organizational insulation and
cultural contestation, through processes we describe later. Our claim, therefore, is
that the very nature of bureaucracy—the "social stuff" of which it is made—creates
behavioral predispositions that make bureaucracy prone to these kinds of behaviors.[83] But the connection between these mechanisms and pathological behavior is
probabilistic, not deterministic, and is consistent with our constitutive analysis.
Whether, in fact, mission-defeating behavior occurs depends on empirical condi-

---

80. See DiMaggio and Powell 1983; and Schien 1996.
81. See Starr 1992, 160; Douglas 1986; and Berger and Luckman 1966, chap. 1.
82. See Campbell 1998, 378; Alvesson 1996; Burrell and Morgan 1979; Dobbin 1994; and Immergut
1998, 14–19.
83. Wendt 1998.

tions. We identify three such conditions that are particularly important (mission, feedback, and professionals) and discuss how they intensify these inherent predispositions and activate or create additional ones.

Irrationality of rationalization.   Weber recognized that the "rationalization" processes at which bureaucracies excelled could be taken to extremes and ultimately become irrational if the rules and procedures that enabled bureaucracies to do their jobs became ends in themselves. Rather than designing the most appropriate and efficient rules and procedures to accomplish their missions, bureaucracies often tailor their missions to fit the existing, well-known, and comfortable rulebook.[84] Thus, means (rules and procedures) may become so embedded and powerful that they determine ends and the way the organization defines its goals. One observer of the World Bank noted how, at an operational level, the bank did not decide on development goals and collect data necessary to pursue them. Rather, it continued to use existing data-collection procedures and formulated goals and development plans from those data alone.[85] UN-mandated elections may be another instance where means become ends in themselves. The "end" pursued in the many troubled states where the UN has been involved in reconstruction is presumably some kind of peaceful, stable, just government. Toward that end, the UN has developed a repertoire of instruments and responses that are largely intended to promote something akin to a democratic government. Among those various repertoires, elections have become privileged as a measure of "success" and a signal of an operation's successful conclusion. Consequently, UN (and other IO) officials have conducted elections even when evidence suggests that such elections are either premature or perhaps even counterproductive (frequently acknowledged as much by state and UN officials).[86] In places like Bosnia elections have ratified precisely the outcome the UN and outside powers had intervened to prevent—ethnic cleansing—and in places like Africa elections are criticized as exacerbating the very ethnic tensions they were ostensibly designed to quell.

UN peacekeeping might also provide examples. As the UN began to involve itself in various "second-generation operations" that entailed the management and reconciliation of domestic conflicts it turned to the only instrument that was readily available in sufficient numbers—peacekeeping units. Peacekeepers, however, are military troops, trained to handle interstate conflict and to be interposed between two contending national armies, operating with their consent. Some UN staff, state officials, and peacekeeping scholars worried that peacekeepers might be inappropriate for the demands of handling domestic security. They feared that peacekeepers would transfer the skills and attitudes that had been honed for one environment to another without fully considering the adjustments required. According to some observers, peacekeepers did just that: they carried their interstate conflict equipment and mindset into new situations and so created a more aggressive and offensively minded posture than

---

84. Beetham 1985, 76.
85. See Ferguson 1990; and Nelson 1995.
86. Paris 1997.

would otherwise have been the case. The result was operations that undermined the objectives of the mandate.[87]

Bureaucratic universalism. A second source of pathology in IOs derives from the fact that bureaucracies "orchestrate numerous local contexts at once."[88] Bureaucrats necessarily flatten diversity because they are supposed to generate universal rules and categories that are, by design, inattentive to contextual and particularistic concerns. Part of the justification for this, of course, is the bureaucratic view that technical knowledge is transferable across circumstances. Sometimes this is a good assumption, but not always; when particular circumstances are not appropriate to the generalized knowledge being applied, the results can be disastrous.[89]

Many critics of the IMF's handling of the Asian financial crises have argued that the IMF inappropriately applied a standardized formula of budget cuts plus high interest rates to combat rapid currency depreciation without appreciating the unique and local causes of this depreciation. These governments were not profligate spenders, and austerity policies did little to reassure investors, yet the IMF prescribed roughly the same remedy that it had in Latin America. The result, by the IMF's later admission, was to make matters worse.[90]

Similarly, many of those who worked in peacekeeping operations in Cambodia were transferred to peacekeeping operations in Bosnia or Somalia on the assumption that the knowledge gained in one location would be applicable to others. Although some technical skills can be transferred across contexts, not all knowledge and organizational lessons derived from one context are appropriate elsewhere. The UN has a longstanding commitment to neutrality, which operationally translates into the view that the UN should avoid the use of force and the appearance of partiality. This knowledge was employed with some success by UN envoy Yasushi Akashi in Cambodia. After his stint in Cambodia, he became the UN Special Representative in Yugoslavia. As many critics of Akashi have argued, however, his commitment to these rules, combined with his failure to recognize that Bosnia was substantially different from Cambodia, led him to fail to use force to defend the safe havens when it was appropriate and likely to be effective.[91]

Normalization of deviance. We derive a third type of pathology from Diane Vaughan's study of the space shuttle *Challenger* disaster in which she chronicles the way exceptions to rules (deviance) over time become routinized and normal parts of procedures.[92] Bureaucracies establish rules to provide a predictable response to environmental stimuli in ways that safeguard against decisions that might lead to accidents and faulty decisions. At times, however, bureaucracies make small, calculated

---

87. See Featherston 1995; Chopra, Eknes, and Nordbo 1995; and Hirsch and Oakley 1995, chap. 6.
88. Heyman 1995, 262.
89. Haas 1990, chap. 3.
90. See Feldstein 1998; Radelet and Sachs 1999; and Kapur 1998.
91. Rieff 1996.
92. Vaughan 1996.

deviations from established rules because of new environmental or institutional developments, explicitly calculating that bending the rules in this instance does not create excessive risk of policy failure. Over time, these exceptions can become the rule—they become normal, not exceptions at all: they can become institutionalized to the point where deviance is "normalized." The result of this process is that what at time t_1 might be weighed seriously and debated as a potentially unacceptable risk or dangerous procedure comes to be treated as normal at time t_n. Indeed, because of staff turnover, those making decisions at a later point in time might be unaware that the now-routine behavior was ever viewed as risky or dangerous.

We are unaware of any studies that have examined this normalization of deviance in IO decision making, though one example of deviance normalization comes to mind. Before 1980 the UNHCR viewed repatriation as only one of three durable solutions to refugee crises (the others being third-country asylum and host-country integration). In its view, repatriation had to be both safe and voluntary because forced repatriation violates the international legal principle of nonrefoulement, which is the cornerstone of international refugee law and codified in the UNHCR's convention. Prior to 1980, UNHCR's discussions of repatriation emphasized that the principles of safety and voluntariness must be safeguarded at all costs. According to many commentators, however, the UNHCR has steadily lowered the barriers to repatriation over the years. Evidence for this can be found in international protection manuals, the UNHCR Executive Committee resolutions, and discourse that now weighs repatriation and the principle of nonrefoulement against other goals such a peace building. This was a steady and incremental development as initial deviations from organizational norms accumulated over time and led to a normalization of deviance. The result was a lowering of the barriers to repatriation and an increase in the frequency of involuntary repatriation.[93]

Insulation.   Organizations vary greatly in the degree to which they receive and process feedback from their environment about performance. Those insulated from such feedback often develop internal cultures and worldviews that do not promote the goals and expectations of those outside the organization who created it and whom it serves. These distinctive worldviews can create the conditions for pathological behavior when parochial classification and categorization schemes come to define reality—how bureaucrats understand the world—such that they routinely ignore information that is essential to the accomplishment of their goals.[94]

Two causes of insulation seem particularly applicable to IOs. The first is professionalism. Professional training does more than impart technical knowledge. It actively seeks to shape the normative orientation and worldviews of those who are trained. Doctors are trained to value life above all else, soldiers are trained to sacri-

---

93. See Chimni 1993, 447; Amnesty International 1997a,b; Human Rights Watch 1997; Zieck 1997, 433, 434, 438–39; and Barbara Crossette, "The Shield for Exiles Is Lowered," *The New York Times,* 22 December 1996, 4-1.

94. See Berger and Luckman 1967, chap. 1; Douglas 1986; Bruner 1990; March and Olsen 1989; and Starr 1992.

fice life for certain strategic objectives, and economists are trained to value efficiency. Bureaucracies, by their nature, concentrate professionals inside organizations, and concentrations of people with the same expertise or professional training can create an organizational worldview distinct from the larger environment. Second, organizations for whom "successful performance" is difficult to measure—that is, they are valued for what they represent rather than for what they do and do not "compete" with other organizations on the basis of output—are protected from selection and performance pressures that economistic models simply assume will operate. The absence of a competitive environment that selects out inefficient practices coupled with already existing tendencies toward institutionalization of rules and procedures insulates the organization from feedback and increases the likelihood of pathologies.

IOs vary greatly in the degree to which the professionals they recruit have distinctive worldviews and the degree to which they face competitive pressures, but it is clearly the case that these factors insulate some IOs to some degree and in so doing create a tendency toward pathology. The World Bank, for example, has been dominated for much of its history by economists, which, at least in part, has contributed to many critiques of the bank's policies. In one such critique James Ferguson opens his study of the World Bank's activity in Lesotho by comparing the bank's introductory description of Lesotho in its report on that country to facts on the ground; he shows how the bank "creates" a world that has little resemblance to what historians, geographers, or demographers see on the ground in Lesotho but is uniquely suited to the bank's organizational abilities and presents precisely the problems the bank knows how to solve. This is not simply "staggeringly bad scholarship," Ferguson argues, but a way of making the world intelligible and meaningful from a particular perspective—the World Bank's.[95] The problem, however, is that this different worldview translates into a record of development failures, which Ferguson explores in detail.

Insulation contributes to and is caused by another well-known feature of organizations—the absence of effective feedback loops that allow the organization to evaluate its efforts and use new information to correct established routines. This is surely a "rational" procedure in any social task but is one that many organizations, including IOs, fail to perform.[96] Many scholars and journalists, and even the current head of the World Bank, have noticed that the bank has accumulated a rather distinctive record of "failures" but continues to operate with the same criteria and has shown a marked lack of interest in evaluating the effectiveness of its own projects.[97] The same is true of other IOs. Jarat Chopra observes that the lessons-learned conferences that were established after Somalia were structurally arranged so that no information could come out that would blemish the UN's record. Such attempts at face saving, Chopra cautions, make it more likely that these maladies will go uncorrected.[98] Sometimes

---

95. Ferguson 1990, 25–73.
96. March and Olsen 1989, chap. 5; Haas 1990.
97. See Wade 1996, 14–17; Nelson 1995, chaps. 6, 7; and Richard Stevenson, "The Chief Banker for the Nations at the Bottom of the Heap," *New York Times*, 14 September 1997, sec. 3, 1, 12–14.
98. Chopra 1996.

new evaluative criteria are hoisted in order to demonstrate that the failures were not really failures but successes.

Cultural contestation.   Organizational coherence is an accomplishment rather than a given. Organizational control within a putative hierarchy is always incomplete, creating pockets of autonomy and political battles within the bureaucracy.[99] This is partly a product of the fact that bureaucracies are organized around the principle of division-of-labor, and different divisions tend to be staffed by individuals who are "experts" in their assigned tasks. These different divisions may battle over budgets or material resources and so follow the bureaucratic politics model, but they may also clash because of distinct internal cultures that grow up inside different parts of the organization. Different segments of the organization may develop different ways of making sense of the world, experience different local environments, and receive different stimuli from outside; they may also be populated by different mixes of professions or shaped by different historical experiences. All of these would contribute to the development of different local cultures within the organization and different ways of perceiving the environment and the organization's overall mission. Organizations may try to minimize complications from these divisions by arranging these demands hierarchically, but to the extent that hierarchy resolves conflict by squelching input from some subunits in favor of others, the organization loses the benefits of a division of labor that it was supposed to provide. More commonly, though, attempts to reconcile competing worldviews hierarchically are simply incomplete. Most organizations develop overlapping and contradictory sets of preferences among subgroups.[100] Consequently, different constituencies representing different normative views will suggest different tasks and goals for the organization, resulting in a clash of competing perspectives that generates pathological tendencies.

The existence of cultural contestation might be particularly true of high-profile and expansive IOs like the UN that have vague missions, broad and politicized constituencies, and lots of divisions that are developed over time and in response to new environmental demands. Arguably a number of the more spectacular debacles in recent UN peacekeeping operations might be interpreted as the product of these contradictions.

Consider the conflict between the UN's humanitarian missions and the value it places on impartiality and neutrality. Within the organization there are many who view impartiality as a core constitutive principle of UN action. On the one hand, the UN's moral standing, its authority, and its ability to persuade all rest on this principle. On the other hand, the principles of humanitarianism require the UN to give aid to those in need—values that are particularly strong in a number of UN relief and humanitarian agencies. These two norms of neutrality and humanitarian assistance, and the parts of the bureaucracy most devoted to them, come into direct conflict in those situations where providing humanitarian relief might jeopardize the UN's

99. See Clegg 1994a, 30; Vaughan 1996, 64; and Martin 1992.
100. Haas 1990, 188.

vaunted principle of neutrality. Bosnia is the classic case in point. On the one hand, the "all necessary means" provision of Security Council resolutions gave the UN authority to deliver humanitarian aid and protect civilians in the safe havens. On the other hand, the UN abstained from "taking sides" because of the fear that such actions would compromise its neutrality and future effectiveness. The result of these conflicts was a string of contradictory policies that failed to provide adequately for the UN's expanding humanitarian charges.[101] According to Shashi Tharoor, a UN official intimately involved in these decisions, "It is extremely difficult to make war and peace with the same people on the same territory at the same time."[102]

UNHCR provides another possible example of cultural contestation. Historically, the UNHCR's Protection Division has articulated a legalistic approach toward refugee matters and thus tends to view the UNHCR and itself as the refugee's lawyer and as the protector of refugee rights under international law. Those that inhabit the UNHCR's regional bureaus, however, have been characterized as taking a less "narrow" view of the organization's mission, stressing that the UNHCR must take into account the causes of refugee flows and state pressures. These cultural conflicts have been particularly evident, according to many observers, when the UNHCR contemplates a repatriation exercise in areas of political instability and conflict: protection officers demand that the refugees' rights, including the right of nonrefoulement, be safeguarded, whereas the regional bureaus are more willing to undertake a risky repatriation exercise if it might serve broader organizational goals, such as satisfying the interests of member states, and regional goals, such as facilitating a peace agreement.[103]

Although bureaucratic culture is not the only source of IO dysfunction, it is a potentially powerful one that creates broad patterns of behavior that should interest international relations scholars. None of the sources of pathologies sketched here is likely to appear in isolation in any empirical domain. These processes interact and feed on each other in ways that will require further theorizing and research. Moreover, while we have highlighted the organization's internal characteristics, we must always bear in mind that the external environment presses upon and shapes the internal characteristics of the organization in a host of ways. Cultural contestation within an organization frequently originates from and remains linked to normative contradictions in the larger environment. Demands from states can be extremely important determinants of IO behavior and may override internal cultural dynamics, but they can also set them in place if conflicting state demands result in the creation of organizational structures or missions that are prone to pathology. As we begin to explore dysfunctional and pathological behavior, we must bear in mind the complex relationship between different causal pathways, remaining closely attentive to both the internal organizational dynamics and the IO's environment.

101. See Barnett 1997a; David Rieff, "We Hate You," *New Yorker*, 4 September 1995, 41–48; David Rieff, "The Institution That Saw No Evil," *The New Republic*, 12 February 1996, 19–24; and Rieff 1996.
102. Quoted in Weiss 1996, 85; also see Rieff 1996, 166, 170, 193.
103. See Kennedy 1986; and Lawyers Committee for Human Rights 1991.

Conclusion

For all the attention international relations scholars have paid to international institutions over the past several decades, we know very little about the internal workings of IOs or about the effects they have in the world. Our ignorance, we suspect, is in large part a product of the theoretical lens we have applied. From an economistic perspective, the theoretically interesting question to ask about IOs is why they are created in the first place. Economists want to know why we have firms; political scientists want to know why we have IOs. In both cases, the question flows naturally from first theoretical principles. If you think that the world looks like a microeconomic market—anarchy, firms (or states) competing to maximize their utilities—what is anomalous and therefore theoretically interesting is cooperation. Consequently, our research tends to focus on the bargains states strike to make or reshape IOs. Scholars pay very little attention to what goes on subsequently in their day-to-day operations or even the larger effects that they might have on the world.

Viewing IOs through a constructivist or sociological lens, as we suggest here, reveals features of IO behavior that should concern international relations scholars because they bear on debates central to our field—debates about whether and how international institutions matter and debates about the adequacy of a statist ontology in an era of globalization and political change. Three implications of this alternative approach are particularly important. First, this approach provides a basis for treating IOs as purposive actors. Mainstream approaches in political science that are informed by economic theories have tended to locate agency in the states that comprise IO membership and treat IOs as mere arenas in which states pursue their policies. By exploring the normative support for bureaucratic authority in the broader international culture and the way IOs use that authority to construct the social world, we provide reasons why IOs may have autonomy from state members and why it may make sense analytically to treat them as ontologically independent. Second, by providing a basis for that autonomy we also open up the possibility that IOs are powerful actors who can have independent effects on the world. We have suggested various ways to think about how IOs are powerful actors in global politics, all of which encourage greater consideration of how IOs affect not only discrete outcomes but also the constitutive basis of global politics.

Third, this approach also draws attention to normative evaluations of IOs and questions what appears to us to be rather uncritical optimism about IO behavior. Contemporary international relations scholars have been quick to recognize the positive contributions that IOs can make, and we, too, are similarly impressed. But for all their desirable qualities, bureaucracies can also be inefficient, ineffective, repressive, and unaccountable. International relations scholars, however, have shown little interest in investigating these less savory and more distressing effects. The liberal Wilsonian tradition tends to see IOs as promoters of peace, engines of progress, and agents for emancipation. Neoliberals have focused on the impressive way in which IOs help states to overcome collective action problems and achieve durable cooperation. Realists have focused on their role as stabilizing forces in world politics. Constructivists, too, have tended to focus on the more humane and other-regarding features of IOs, but there is nothing about social construction that necessitates "good" outcomes. We do not mean to imply that IOs are "bad"; we mean only to point out theoretical reasons why undesirable behavior may occur and suggest that normative evaluation of IO behavior should be an empirical and ethical matter, not an analytic assumption.

References

Alger, Chadwick. 1963. United Nations Participation as a Learning Process. *Public Opinion Quarterly* 27 (3):411–26.

Allison, Graham. 1971. *Essence of Decision*. Boston: Little, Brown.

Alvesson, Mats. 1996. *Cultural Perspectives on Organizations*. New York: Cambridge University Press.

Amnesty International. 1997a. In Search of Safety: The Forcibly Displaced and Human Rights in Africa. AI Index, 20 June, AFR 01/05/97. Available from <www.amnesty.org/ailib/aipub/1997/10100597.htm>.

———. 1997b. Rwanda: Human Rights Overlooked in Mass Repatriation. Available from <www.amnesty.org/ailib/aipub/1997/AFR/147002797.htm>.

Anonymous. 1997. The UNHCR Note on International Protection You Won't See. *International Journal of Refugee Law* 9 (2):267–73.

Arendt, Hannah. 1977. *Eichmann in Jerusalem: A Report on the Banality of Evil*. New York: Penguin.

Ascher, William. 1983. New Development Approaches and the Adaptability of International Agencies: The Case of the World Bank. *International Organization* 37 (3):415–39.

Ayres, Robert L. 1983. *Banking on the Poor: The World Bank and World Poverty*. Cambridge, Mass.: MIT Press.

Baldwin, David, ed. 1993. *Neorealism and Neoliberalism*. New York: Columbia University Press.

Barnett, Michael. 1997a. The Politics of Indifference at the United Nations and Genocide in Rwanda and Bosnia. In *This Time We Knew: Western Responses to Genocide in Bosnia*, edited by Thomas Cushman and Stjepan Mestrovic, 128–62. New York: New York University Press.

———. 1997b. The UN Security Council, Indifference, and Genocide in Rwanda. *Cultural Anthropology* 12 (4):551–78.

Beetham, David. 1985. *Max Weber and the Theory of Modern Politics*. New York: Polity.

———. 1996. *Bureaucracy*. 2d ed. Minneapolis: University of Minnesota Press.

Bendor, Jonathan, and Thomas Hammond. 1992. Rethinking Allison's Models. *American Political Science Review* 82 (2):301–22.

Berger, Peter, and Thomas Luckmann. 1966. *The Social Construction of Reality*. New York: Doubleday.

Blumer, Herbert. 1969. *Symbolic Interactionism: Perspective and Method*. Englewood Cliffs, N.J.: Prentice-Hall.

Bourdieu, Pierre. 1994. On Symbolic Power. In *Language and Symbolic Power*, edited by Pierre Bourdieu, 163–70. Chicago: University of Chicago Press.

Boutros-Ghali, Boutros. 1995. *Agenda for Peace*. 2d ed. New York: UN Press.

———. 1996a. Global Leadership After the Cold War. *Foreign Affairs* 75:86–98.

———. 1996b. *Agenda for Democratization*. New York: UN Press.

Bruner, Jerome. 1990. *Acts of Meaning*. Cambridge, Mass.: Harvard University Press.

Burley, Anne-Marie, and Walter Mattli. 1993. Europe Before the Court: A Political Theory of Integration. *International Organization* 47 (1):41–76.

Burrell, Gibson, and Gareth Morgan. 1979. *Sociological Paradigms and Organizational Analysis*. London: Heinemann.

Call, Chuck, and Michael Barnett. Forthcoming. Looking for a Few Good Cops: Peacekeeping, Peacebuilding, and U.N. Civilian Police. *International Peacekeeping*.

Campbell, John. 1998. Institutional Analysis and the Role of Ideas in Political Economy. *Theory and Society* 27:377–409.

Carr, Edward H. [1939] 1964. *The Twenty Year's Crisis*. New York: Harper Torchbooks.

Chimni, B. 1993. The Meaning of Words and the Role of UNHCR in Voluntary Repatriation. *International Journal of Refugee Law* 5 (3):442–60.

Chopra, Jarat. 1996. Fighting for Truth at the UN. *Crosslines Global Report*, 26 November, 7–9.

Chopra, Jarat, Age Eknes, and Toralv Nordbo. 1995. *Fighting for Hope in Somalia*. Oslo: NUPI.

Claude, Inis L., Jr. 1966. Collective Legitimization as a Political Function of the United Nations. *International Organization* 20 (3):337–67.

Clegg, Stewart. 1994a. Power and Institutions in the Theory of Organizations. In *Toward a New Theory of Organizations*, edited by John Hassard and Martin Parker, 24–49. New York: Routledge.

———. 1994b. Weber and Foucault: Social Theory for the Study of Organizations. *Organization* 1 (1): 149–78.

Coase, Ronald. 1937. The Nature of the Firm. *Economica* 4 (November):386–405.

Commission on Global Governance. 1995. *Our Global Neighborhood*. New York: Oxford University Press.

Cooper, Frederick, and Randy Packard, eds. 1998. *International Development and the Social Sciences*. Berkeley: University of California Press.

Cox, Robert. 1980. The Crisis of World Order and the Problem of International Organization in the 1980s. *International Journal* 35 (2):370–95.

———. 1992. Multilateralism and World Order. *Review of International Studies* 18 (2):161–80.

———. 1996. The Executive Head: An Essay on Leadership in International Organization. In *Approaches to World Order*, edited by Robert Cox, 317–48. New York: Cambridge University Press.

Cox, Robert, and Harold Jacobson. 1977. Decision Making. *International Social Science Journal* 29 (1):115–33.

Cox, Robert, Harold Jacobson, Gerard Curzon, Victoria Curzon, Joseph Nye, Lawrence Scheinman, James Sewell, and Susan Strange. 1974. *The Anatomy of Influence: Decision Making in International Organization*. New Haven, Conn.: Yale University Press.

Deutsch, Karl. 1963. *The Nerves of Government: Models of Political Communication and Control*. Glencoe, Ill.: Free Press.

Dillon, Patricia, Thomas Ilgen, and Thomas Willett. 1991. Approaches to the Study of International Organizations: Major Paradigms in Economics and Political Science. In *The Political Economy of International Organizations: A Public Choice Approach*, edited by Ronald Vaubel and Thomas Willett, 79–99. Boulder, Colo.: Westview Press.

DiMaggio, Paul J., and Walter W. Powell. 1983. The Iron Cage Revisited: Institutional Isomorphism and Collective Rationality in Organizational Fields. *American Sociological Review* 48:147–60.

Dobbin, Frank. 1994. Cultural Models of Organization: The Social Construction of Rational Organizing Principles. In *The Sociology of Culture*, edited by Diana Crane, 117–42. Boston: Basil Blackwell.

Douglas, Mary. 1986. *How Institutions Think*. Syracuse, N.Y.: Syracuse University Press.

Doyle, Michael. 1997. *Ways of War and Peace*. New York: Norton.

Escobar, Arturo. 1995. *Encountering Development: The Making and Unmaking of the Third World*. Princeton, N.J.: Princeton University Press.

Featherston, A. B. 1995. Habitus in Cooperating for Peace: A Critique of Peacekeeping. In *The New Agenda for Global Security: Cooperating for Peace and Beyond*, edited by Stephanie Lawson, 101–18. St. Leonards, Australia: Unwin and Hyman.

Feld, Werner J., and Robert S. Jordan, with Leon Hurwitz. 1988. *International Organizations: A Comparative Approach*. 2d ed. New York: Praeger.

Feldstein, Martin. 1998. Refocusing the IMF. *Foreign Affairs* 77 (2):20–33.

Ferguson, James. 1990. *The Anti-Politics Machine: "Development," Depoliticization, and Bureaucratic Domination in Lesotho*. New York: Cambridge University Press.

Finnemore, Martha. 1993. International Organizations as Teachers of Norms: The United Nations Educational, Scientific, and Cultural Organization and Science Policy. *International Organization* 47: 565–97.

————. 1996a. Norms, Culture, and World Politics: Insights from Sociology's Institutionalism. *International Organization* 50 (2):325–47.

————. 1996b. *National Interests in International Society*. Ithaca, N.Y.: Cornell University Press.

Fisher, William. 1997. Doing Good? The Politics and Antipolitics of NGO Practices. *Annual Review of Anthropology* 26:439–64.

Foucault, Michel. 1977. *Discipline and Punish*. New York: Vintage Press.

Gallaroti, Guilio. 1991. The Limits of International Organization. *International Organization* 45 (2):183–220.

Gerth, H. H., and C. Wright Mills. 1978. *From Max Weber: Essays in Sociology*. New York: Oxford University Press.

Goodwin-Gill, Guy. 1996. *Refugee in International Law*. New York: Oxford Clarendon.

Gran, Guy. 1986. Beyond African Famines: Whose Knowledge Matters? *Alternatives* 11:275–96.

Grandori, Anna. 1993. Notes on the Use of Power and Efficiency Constructs in the Economics and Sociology of Organizations. In *Interdisciplinary Perspectives on Organizational Studies*, edited by S. Lindenberg and H. Schreuder, 61–78. New York: Pergamon

Gupta, Akhil. 1998. *Postcolonial Developments: Agriculture in the Making of Modern India*. Durham, N.C.: Duke University Press.

Haas, Ernst. 1990. *When Knowledge Is Power*. Berkeley: University of California Press.

Haas, Ernst, and Peter Haas. 1995. Learning to Learn: Improving International Governance. *Global Governance* 1 (3):255–85.

Haas, Peter, ed. 1992. Epistemic Communities. *International Organization* 46 (1). Special issue.

Handelman, Don. 1995. Comment. *Current Anthropology* 36 (2):280–81.

Harrell-Bond, Barbara. 1989. Repatriation: Under What Conditions Is It the Most Desirable Solution for Refugees? *African Studies Review* 32 (1):41–69.

Hartigan, Kevin. 1992. Matching Humanitarian Norms with Cold, Hard Interests: The Making of Refugee Policies in Mexico and Honduras, 1980–89. *International Organization* 46:709–30.

Helms, Jesse. 1996. Saving the UN. *Foreign Affairs* 75 (5):2–7.

Hendrie, Barbara. 1997. Knowledge and Power: A Critique of an International Relief Operation. *Disasters* 21 (1):57–76.

Heyman, Josiah McC. 1995. Putting Power in the Anthropology of Bureaucracy. *Current Anthropology* 36 (2):261–77.

Hirsch, John, and Robert Oakley. 1995. *Somalia and Operation Restore Hope: Reflections on Peacemaking and Peacekeeping*. Washington, D.C.: USIP Press.

Human Rights Watch. 1997. Uncertain Refuge: International Failures to Protect Refugees. Vol. 1, no. 9 (April).

Hurrell, Andrew, and Ngaire Woods. 1995. Globalisation and Inequality. *Millennium* 24 (3):447–70.

Immergut, Ellen. 1998. The Theoretical Core of the New Institutionalism. *Politics and Society* 26 (1):5–34.

Jackson, Robert. 1993. The Weight of Ideas in Decolonization: Normative Change in International Relations. In *Ideas and Foreign Policy*, edited by Judith Goldstein and Robert O. Keohane, 111–38. Ithaca, N.Y.: Cornell University Press.

Jacobson, Harold. 1979. *Networks of Interdependence*. New York: Alfred A. Knopf.

Joint Evaluation of Emergency Assistance to Rwanda. 1996. *The International Response to Conflict and Genocide: Lessons from the Rwanda Experience*. 5 vols. Copenhagen: Steering Committee of the Joint Evaluation of Emergency Assistance to Rwanda.

Kapur, Devesh. 1998. The IMF: A Cure or a Curse? *Foreign Policy* 111:114–29.

Katzenstein, Peter J., ed. 1996. *The Culture of National Security: Identity and Norms in World Politics*. New York: Columbia University Press.

Keck, Margaret, and Kathryn Sikkink. 1998. *Activists Beyond Borders*. Ithaca, N.Y.: Cornell University Press.

Keeley, James. 1990. Toward a Foucauldian Analysis of International Regimes. *International Organization* 44 (1):83–105.

Keen, David. 1994. *The Benefits of Famine: A Political Economy of Famine and Relief in Southwestern Sudan, 1983–89*. Princeton, N.J.: Princeton University Press

Kennedy, David. 1986. International Refugee Protection. *Human Rights Quarterly* 8:1–9.

Keohane, Robert O. 1984. *After Hegemony*. Princeton, N.J.: Princeton University Press.

Kiewiet, D. Roderick, and Matthew McCubbins. 1991. *The Logic of Delegation*. Chicago: University of Chicago Press.

Krasner, Stephen D. 1991. Global Communications and National Power: Life on the Pareto Frontier. *World Politics* 43 (3):336–66.

———. 1983a. Regimes and the Limits of Realism: Regimes as Autonomous Variables. In *International Regimes*, edited by Stephen Krasner, 355–68. Ithaca, N.Y.: Cornell University Press.

Krasner, Stephen D., ed. 1983b. *International Regimes*. Ithaca, N.Y.: Cornell University Press.

Krause, Keith, and Michael Williams. 1996. Broadening the Agenda of Security Studies: Politics and Methods. *Mershon International Studies Review* 40 (2):229–54.

Lake, David. 1996. Anarchy, Hierarchy, and the Variety of International Relations. *International Organization* 50 (1):1–34.

Lawyers Committee for Human Rights. 1991. *General Principles Relating to the Promotion of Refugee Repatriation*. New York: Lawyers Committee for Human Rights.

Legro, Jeffrey. 1997. Which Norms Matter? Revisiting the "Failure" of Internationalism. *International Organization* 51 (1):31–64.

Lipartito, Kenneth. 1995. Culture and the Practice of Business History. *Business and Economic History* 24 (2):1–41.

Lipson, Michael. 1999. International Cooperation on Export Controls: Nonproliferation, Globalization, and Multilateralism. Ph.D. diss., University of Wisconsin, Madison.

Malkki, Liisa. 1996. Speechless Emissaries: Refugees, Humanitarianism, and Dehistoricization. *Cultural Anthropology* 11 (3):377–404.

March, James. 1988. *Decisions and Organizations*. Boston: Basil Blackwell.

———. 1997. Understanding How Decisions Happen in Organizations. In *Organizational Decision Making*, edited by Z. Shapira, 9–33. New York: Cambridge University Press.

March, James, and Johan P. Olsen. 1989. *Rediscovering Institutions: The Organizational Basis of Politics*. New York: Free Press.

Martin, Joan. 1992. *Cultures in Organizations: Three Perspectives*. New York: Oxford University Press.

Matthews, Jessica Tuchman. 1989. Redefining Security. *Foreign Affairs* 68 (2):162–77.

McNeely, Connie. 1995. *Constructing the Nation-State: International Organization and Prescriptive Action*. Westport, Conn.: Greenwood Press.

Mearsheimer, John. 1994. The False Promise of International Institutions. *International Security* 19 (3):5–49.

Meyer, John W., and Brian Rowan. 1977. Institutionalized Organizations: Formal Structure as Myth and Ceremony. *American Journal of Sociology* 83:340–63.

Meyer, John W., and W. Richard Scott. 1992. *Organizational Environments: Ritual and Rationality*. Newbury Park, Calif.: Sage.

Meyer, Marshall, and Lynne Zucker. 1989. *Permanently Failing Organizations*. Newbury Park: Sage Press.

Miller, Gary, and Terry M. Moe. 1983. Bureaucrats, Legislators, and the Size of Government. *American Political Science Review* 77 (June):297–322.

Moe, Terry M. 1984. The New Economics of Organization. *American Journal of Political Science* 28:739–77.

Moravcsik, Andrew. 1997. Taking Preferences Seriously: Liberal Theory and International Politics. *International Organization* 51 (4):513–54.

———. 1999. A New Statecraft? Supranational Entrepreneurs and International Cooperation. *International Organization* 53 (2):267–306.

Mouzelis, Nicos. 1967. *Organization and Bureaucracy*. Chicago: Aldine.

Murphy, Craig. 1994. *International Organizations and Industrial Change*. New York: Oxford University Press.

Nelson, Paul. 1995. *The World Bank and Non-Governmental Organizations*. New York: St. Martin's Press.

Ness, Gayl, and Steven Brechin. 1988. Bridging the Gap: International Organizations as Organizations. *International Organization* 42 (2):245–73.

Niskanen, William A. 1971. *Bureaucracy and Representative Government*. Chicago: Aldine.

Paris, Roland. 1997. Peacebuilding and the Limits of Liberal Internationalism. *International Security* 22 (2):54–89.

Perry, William. 1996. Defense in an Age of Hope. *Foreign Affairs* 75 (6):64–79.

Pollack, Mark. 1997. Delegation, Agency, and Agenda-Setting in the European Community. *International Organization* 51 (1):99–134.

Powell, Walter W., and Paul J. DiMaggio, eds. 1991. *The New Institutionalism in Organizational Analysis*. Chicago: University of Chicago Press.

Pratt, John, and Richard J. Zeckhauser. 1985. *Principals and Agents: The Structure of Business*. Boston: Harvard Business School Press.

Price, Richard. 1997. *The Chemical Weapons Taboo*. Ithaca, N.Y.: Cornell University Press.

Radelet, Steven, and Jeffrey Sach. 1999. What Have We Learned, So Far, From the Asian Financial Crisis? Harvard Institute for International Development, 4 January. Available from <www.hiid.harvard.edu/pub/other/aea122.pdf>.

Rieff, David. 1996. *Slaughterhouse*. New York: Simon and Schuster.

Rittberger, Volker, ed. 1993. *Regime Theory and International Relations*. Oxford: Clarendon Press.

Ross, George. 1995. *Jacques Delors and European Integration*. New York: Oxford University Press.

Ruggie, John. 1996. *Winning the Peace*. New York: Columbia University Press.

———. 1998. What Makes the World Hang Together. *International Organization* 52 (3):855–86.

Sandholtz, Wayne. 1993. Choosing Union: Monetary Politics and Maastricht. *International Organization* 47:1–40.

Sagan, Scott. 1993. *The Limits of Safety: Organizations, Accidents, and Nuclear Weapons*. Princeton, N.J.: Princeton University Press.

Schaar, John. 1984. Legitimacy in the Modern State. In *Legitimacy and the State*, edited by William Connolly, 104–33. Oxford: Basil Blackwell.

Schien, Edgar. 1996. Culture: The Missing Concept in Organization Studies. *Administrative Studies Quarterly* 41:229–40.

Scott, W. Richard. 1992. *Organizations: Rational, Natural, and Open Systems*. 3d ed. Englewood Cliffs, N.J.: Prentice-Hall.

Shanks, Cheryl, Harold K. Jacobson, and Jeffrey H. Kaplan. 1996. Inertia and Change in the Constellation of Intergovernmental Organizations, 1981–1992. *International Organization* 50 (4):593–627.

Shapira, Zur, ed. 1997. *Organizational Decision*. New York: Cambridge University Press.

Shore, Cris, and Susan Wright. 1997. Policy: A New Field of Anthropology. In *Anthropology of Policy: Critical Perspectives on Governance and Power*, edited by Cris Shore and Susan Wright, 3–41. New York: Routledge Press.

Sigelman, Lee. 1986. The Bureaucratic Budget Maximizer: An Assumption Examined. *Public Budgeting and Finance* (spring):50–59.

Snidal, Duncan. 1996. Political Economy and International Institutions. *International Review of Law and Economics* 16:121–37.

Starr, Paul. 1992. Social Categories and Claims in the Liberal State. In *How Classification Works: Nelson Goodman Among the Social Sciences*, edited by Mary Douglas and David Hull, 154–79. Edinburgh: Edinburgh University Press.

Strange, Susan. 1997. *The Retreat of the State*. New York: Cambridge University Press.

Thomas, Daniel C. Forthcoming. *The Helsinki Effect: International Norms, Human Rights, and Demise of Communism*. Princeton, N.J.: Princeton University Press.

UN Development Program. 1994. *Human Development Report 1994*. New York: Oxford University Press.

UN Peacekeeping Missions. 1994. The Lessons from Cambodia. Asia Pacific Issues, Analysis from the East-West Center, No. 11, March.

Vaubel, Roland. 1991. A Public Choice View of International Organization. In *The Political Economy of International Organizations*, edited by Roland Vaubel and Thomas Willett, 27–45. Boulder, Colo.: Westview Press.

Vaughan, Diane. 1996. *The Challenger Launch Decision*. Chicago: University of Chicago Press.

Wade, Robert. 1996. Japan, the World Bank, and the Art of Paradigm Maintenance: The East Asian Miracle in Political Perspective. *New Left Review* 217:3–36.

Walkup, Mark. 1997. Policy Dysfunction in Humanitarian Organizations: The Role of Coping Strategies, Institutions, and Organizational Culture. *Journal of Refugee Studies* 10 (1):37–60.

Waltz, Kenneth. 1979. *Theory of International Politics*. Reading, Mass.: Addison-Wesley.

Wapner, Paul. 1996. *Environmental Activism and World Civic Politics*. Albany: State University of New York Press.

Weber, Max. 1947. *Theory of Social and Economic Organization*. New York: Oxford University Press.

———. [1930] 1968. *The Protestant Ethic and the Spirit of Capitalism*. New York: Routledge.

———. 1978. Bureaucracy. In *From Max Weber: Essays in Sociology*, edited by H. H. Gerth and C. Wright Mills, 196–44. New York: Oxford

Weber, Steven. Origins of the European Bank for Reconstruction and Development. *International Organization* 48(1):1–38.

Weingast, Barry R., and Mark Moran. 1983. Bureaucratic Discretion or Congressional Control: Regulatory Policymaking by the Federal Trade Commission. *Journal of Political Economy* 91 (October):765–800.

Weiss, Thomas. 1996. Collective Spinelessness: U.N. Actions in the Former Yugoslavia. In *The World and Yugoslavia's Wars*, edited by Richard Ullman, 59–96. New York: Council on Foreign Relations Press.

Weiss, Tom, and Amir Pasic. 1997. Reinventing UNHCR: Enterprising Humanitarians in the Former Yugoslavia, 1991–95. *Global Governance* 3 (1):41–58.

Wendt, Alexander. 1995. Constructing International Politics. *International Security* 20 (1):71–81.

———. 1998. Constitution and Causation in International Relations. *Review of International Studies* 24 (4):101–17. Special issue.

Williams, Michael. 1996. Hobbes and International Relations: A Reconsideration. *International Organization* 50 (2):213–37.

Williamson, Oliver. 1975. *Markets and Hierarchies, Analysis and Antitrust Implications: A Study in the Economics of Internal Organization*. New York: Free Press.

———. 1985. *The Economic Institutions of Capitalism: Firms, Markets, Relational Contracting*. New York: Free Press.

World Conference on Human Rights. 1993. Vienna Declaration on Human Rights, adopted 14–25 June. UN Document A/CONF.157/24 (Part I), 20; A/CONF.157/23 DPI/1394/Rev.1 DPI/1676 (95.I.21), 448; DPI/1707 ST/HR/2/Rev.4, 383.

Wright, Susan. 1994. "Culture" in Anthropology and Organizational Studies. In *Anthropology of Organizations*, edited by Susan Wright, 1–31. New York: Routledge.

Zabusky, Stacia. 1995. *Launching Europe*. Princeton, N.J.: Princeton University Press.

Zieck, Marjoleine. 1997. *UNHCR and Voluntary Repatriation of Refugees: A Legal Analysis*. The Hague: Martinus Nijhoff.

Theories and Empirical Studies
of International Institutions
Lisa L. Martin and Beth A. Simmons

The role of international institutions has been central to the study of world politics at least since the conclusion of World War II. Much of this research was, and continues to be, pioneered in the pages of *International Organization*. In this article we take stock of past work on international institutions, trace the evolution of major themes in scholarship over time, and highlight areas for productive new research. Our central argument is that research should increasingly turn to the question of how institutions matter in shaping the behavior of important actors in world politics. New research efforts should emphasize observable implications of alternative theories of institutions. We advocate approaching international institutions as both the object of strategic choice and a constraint on actors' behavior, an idea that is familiar to scholars of domestic institutions but has been neglected in much of the debate between realist and institutionalist scholars of international relations.

The article is organized into three major sections. The first section provides an analytical review of the development of studies of international institutions. From the beginning, the pages of *IO* have been filled with insightful studies of institutions, in some cases asking questions consistent with the research agenda we propose in this essay. But the lack of a disciplinary foundation in the early years meant that many good insights were simply lost, not integrated into other scholars' research. With the professionalization of the discipline since the late 1950s, scholarship on international institutions has become more theoretically informed, and empirical research has begun more often to conform to social-scientific standards of evidence, with results that provide both caution and inspiration for future research. One of the most consequential developments for our understanding of international institutions came in the early 1970s, when a new generation of scholars developed insights that opened up inquiry beyond that of formal organizations, providing intellectual bridgeheads to the study of institutions more generally.

Our thanks for comments on previous versions go to Marc Busch, Peter Katzenstein, Bob Keohane, Steve Krasner, and participants in the *IO* fiftieth anniversary issue conference.

International Organization 52, 4, Autumn 1998, pp. 729–757

The second section explicitly addresses a theme that arises from the review of scholarship on institutions: whether international politics needs to be treated as *sui generis*, with its own theories and approaches that are distinct from other fields of political science, or whether it fruitfully can draw on theories of domestic politics. As our review shows, developments in studies of American politics, such as studies of voting and coalitional behavior, have often influenced the way that scholars approached international institutions. Most of these efforts did not pay off with major insights. The functionalist approach to institutions adopted in the 1980s owed little to theories of domestic politics, drawing more on economic models. Today, we see the pendulum swinging back, as more scholars turn to modern theories initially developed to study domestic political phenomena (see Helen Milner's article in this issue). Here, we assess whether these new attempts are likely to be any more successful than previous efforts.

The third section turns to the problem of research agendas. Where does scholarship on international institutions go next? Our primary argument in this section is that attention needs to focus on *how*, not just *whether*, international institutions matter for world politics. Too often over the last decade and a half the focal point of debate has been crudely dichotomous: institutions matter, or they do not. This shaping of the agenda has obscured more productive and interesting questions about variation in the types and degree of institutional effects, variations that were in fact well documented in the less theoretical but well-researched case studies of the journal's earliest years. Of course, we do not suggest a return to idiographic institutional analysis. Rather, we suggest a number of lines of theoretically informed analysis that may lead to research that both asks better questions and is more subject to empirical testing. These paths include more serious analysis of the distributional effects of institutions, the relation between international institutions and domestic politics, the problem of unanticipated consequences, and a typology of institutional effects.

The Evolution of an Idea: Institutions in International Politics

Early Studies of the Institutionalization of the Postwar World

The "poles" of realism and idealism—of which much is made in graduate seminars— had little to do with the highly practical organizational analysis that dominated the pages of *IO* in the first decades after the war. The focus of attention was on how well these newly established institutions met the problems that they were designed to solve. On this score, few scholarly accounts were overly optimistic. Overwhelmed by the magnitude of the political and economic reconstruction effort, few judged postwar organizations as up to the task. Central to this debate was a highly realistic understanding that international politics would shape and limit the effectiveness of postwar institutions; virtually no one predicted that these would triumph over politics. The UN,[1] the General Agreement on Tariffs and Trade (GATT),[2] the International Monetary Fund[3] —all were the subject of highly critical review.

A number of important studies grappled explicitly with the impact of these institutions on the policies of the major powers and the outcomes for the central political and military competition between them. The answers, predictably, were derived from little more than informed counterfactual reasoning, but they displayed a sensitivity to the broad range of possible impacts that institutions such as the League and the UN could have on the major powers. In their examination of the ideal of collective security, Howard C. Johnson and Gerhart Niemeyer squarely inquired into the role that norms, backed by organizations such as the UN, play in affecting states' behavior. They asked whether states were "prepared to use force or the threat of force for the sake of public law and order rather than for the sake of their national advantage in relation to that of other states. . . . How has the behavior of states been affected by these standards?"[4] Though ultimately more confident in the balance of power than in norms embodied in the rule of law, these scholars were correct to push for a mechanism that might explain the effects of institutions on behavior: "We cannot claim to have learned much about the League experiment until we know *how* it has affected the problem of harnessing and controlling the factors of force and their role in the relations of power."[5]

A flurry of studies in the early 1950s suggested possible answers. Pointing to the U.S. role in decolonization and military aid for Korea, collective institutions were said to raise U.S. "consciousness of broader issues" that might affect American interests and thereby make the U.S. more responsive to world opinion.[6] By subjecting policies to global scrutiny—a mechanism not unlike those of transparency and reputation central to the literature in the 1980s—the UN was viewed as having had an (admittedly marginal) effect on some of the most central issues of world politics.

Though lacking the elaborate theoretical apparatus of current research, early studies of postwar organizations had many of the same insights that have informed "modern" institutionalism. Paralleling much contemporary argument on the form of cooperation,[7] one study as early as 1949 argued that multilateralism was precluded in cases where there were significant bargaining advantages and discrimination advantages of proceeding bilaterally.[8] Foreshadowing more theoretically sophisticated treatments of informal versus formal agreements,[9] studies of GATT as early as 1954 recognized that some agreements gain strength through their informal nature, and

---

1. See Goodrich 1947, 18; Fox 1951; Hoffmann 1956; Claude 1963; and Malin 1947. But for the optimistic view, see Bloomfield 1960.
2. Gorter 1954.
3. See Knorr 1948; and Kindleberger 1951a.
4. Johnson and Niemeyer 1954, 27.
5. Niemeyer 1952, 558 (italics added).
6. Cohen 1951. For a parallel analysis of institutional effects on Soviet behavior, see Rudzinski 1951.
7. See Oye 1992; and Martin 1992b.
8. Little 1949.
9. Lipson 1991.

prescient of the regimes literature viewed the value of GATT as "a focal point on which many divergent views on appropriate commercial policy converge."[10] Lacking a theoretical hook on which to hang these observations, and without a professionalized critical mass of scholars to develop these insights, many important findings were only rediscovered and advanced more than two decades later.

Nowhere is this more true than in the rediscovery of the relationship between international institutions and domestic politics. The idea that international institutions can influence state behavior by acting through domestic political channels was recognized by scholars writing in the mid-1950s. Referring to the example of the International Finance Corporation, B. E. Matecki wrote that international organizations could be "idea generating centers" with the ability to set in motion national forces that directly influence the making of national policy.[11] Reflecting on the efforts of the Council of Europe to gain acceptance of its vision for Europe in national capitals, an early study by A. Glenn Mowers pointed out the conscious strategy of direct lobbying of national governments through national parliaments.[12] And in a fascinating study of the role of the Security Council in influencing Dutch colonial policy, Whitney Perkins pointed to the crucial interaction between authoritative international decisions and democratic politics: "By defiance of the Security Council the Dutch alerted powerful monitors who allied their strength with domestic forces in requiring them to live up to principles [of decolonization]."[13] "In this type of interaction between democratic governments and the UN emerge some of the essential elements of a world political process."[14] Anticipating a mechanism for institutional effects that have recently resurfaced in contemporary studies, he concluded that "The role of the UN is to exert pressures designed to enable the loser in public sentiment to accept the consequences of its loss."[15] This research approach reflected an effort to flesh out the mechanisms by which the policies and perspectives of international institutions could work through national politics.

In short, the early postwar literature on international institutions, while highly focused on formal organizations, was far less naive and legalistic, more politically sensitive and insightful than it is often given credit for being. Early insights included the recognition that the nature of the international political system provided a context for the effectiveness of international institutions, that institutional effectiveness should be subject to empirical investigation, and that elaborate organizational structure is not always the best approach to achieving international cooperation. Moreover, the best of this early literature was concerned not merely with *whether* international institutions had an impact, but *how* one might think about a mechanism for their effects. Transparency, reputation, and legitimacy as well as domestic political pressures were suggested in various strands of thought. But there was no conceptual

---

10. Gorter 1954, 1, 8.
11. Matecki 1956.
12. Mowers 1964.
13. Perkins 1958, 40.
14. Ibid., 26.
15. Ibid., 42

framework that could tie these insights together; nor was there a systematic comparative enterprise to check for their regularity. Rather, another research agenda, replete with fancy methodological tools imported from American politics, was to demote these questions in favor of an only partially fruitful examination of the internal politics of international organizations.

The Influence of Behavioralism:
Politics Within International Institutions

If few thought international organization would liberate the world from politics, it arguably became important to understand who has power in these organizations and how that power was being exercised. Especially since the use of the veto had apparently rendered the Security Council toothless, concern began to focus on the development of rules and norms in the General Assembly. The supposed "specter" of bloc voting in that forum—increasingly of concern to American scholars and policymakers as the Cold War extended its gelid reach—became a central concern.[16]

This debate took what appears today to be an odd early direction. Perhaps due to new and exciting work in U.S. legislative behavior, the research program quickly became focused on how to describe patterns of voting in the General Assembly, without a systematic attempt to sort out the usefulness of the voting behavior approach. Despite warnings that the international system was fundamentally different from domestic political systems,[17] this research program easily accepted that voting in the UN was a proxy for power in that institution. Certainly there were skeptics: Rupert Emerson and Inis L. Claude, for example, cautioned that voting in an international body does not have the same function as in a democratically elected parliament; an international conference is a negotiating rather than a legislative body. Voting in such a situation, they noted, was unlikely to play a deliberative role, since such votes were no more than propaganda efforts.[18] Few of these studies explicitly defended their assumption that General Assembly resolutions somehow mattered to the conduct of world politics. But the fascination with the method for analyzing voting behavior overcame fairly readily the caution that the domestic–international logic should be subject to close scrutiny. Moreover, the hope of providing an explicitly political (legislative) model inspired by American politics may have been a reaction against the overly "anarchic" systems analysis of the late 1950s.[19]

Much of this work can be traced directly to developments in the study of American politics. Hayward Alker and Bruce Russett's study *International Politics in the Gen-*

---

16. For one of the earliest studies of bloc voting, see Ball 1951. For a study focusing primarily on the behavior of the Commonwealth countries, see Carter 1950. Concern with the influence of the Commonwealth grew as former British colonies gained independence and membership in the early 1960s. See Millar 1962.

17. Hoffmann 1960, 1–4.

18. Emerson and Claude 1952. See also Jebb 1952.

19. Alker and Russett 1965, 145, explicitly refer to Liska 1957 and Kaplan 1957. They argue that "[i]t is simply erroneous to think of international politics as anarchic, chaotic, and utterly unlike national politics." Alker and Russett 1965, 147.

eral Assembly, for example, acknowledged "that studies of the American political process by Robert Dahl, Duncan Macrae,[20] and David Truman were theoretically and methodologically suggestive of ways in which roll-call data could be used to test for the existence of a pluralistic political process in a quasi-legislative international organization."[21] Influenced by James March[22] and Robert Dahl, this study sought to understand various influences on UN voting behavior across issue areas in which the dimensions of power and influence were likely to differ. Certainly, one factor influencing this research agenda was the priority given to reproducible and "objective" forms of social science; the focus on General Assembly voting was acknowledged to be an artifact of the availability of fairly complete voting records.[23]

Largely related to the ferment in American voting studies, politics within the UN dominated the research agenda for most of the decade from the mid-1960s. Central was the concern to explain why certain countries had a tendency to vote together, to vote in blocs, or to form "legislative coalitions."[24] Also obviously inspired by American politics, another branch of inquiry focused on the determinants of successfully running for elective UN office.[25] Much of this literature was methodologically rather than conceptually driven and highly inductive with respect to its major empirical findings.[26] Little effort was made to explore the extent to which the concept of representation or the winning of elections in the domestic setting could travel meaningfully to an international institution. The research program lost steam under heavy fire from scholars who demanded a stronger justification for focusing on the General Assembly as a microcosm for world politics.[27]

Partially in response to the critique that the General Assembly was hardly the center of world politics, and partially influenced by another trend in American politics growing out of the study of bureaucratic politics and political systems, another research path was taken by Robert Cox and Harold Jacobson's study of eight specialized agencies within the UN.[28] In their edited volume, the focus was on the structure and process of influence associated with these institutions and their outputs, rather than on their formal character. Reflecting once again a major thread in American politics, the underlying assumption was that international organizations could be fruitfully analyzed as distinct political systems in which one could trace out patterns of influence: "The legal and formal character and the content of the decision is less important than the balance of forces that it expresses and the inclination that it gives to the further direction of events."[29]

20. MacRae 1958.
21. Alker and Russett 1965, vii.
22. March 1955.
23. On objectivity, see Alker and Russett 1965, 2–3; on availability of data see p. 19.
24. See Riggs 1958; Hovet 1958; Keohane 1967, 1969; Weigert and Riggs 1969; Gareau 1970; Alker 1970; Volgy 1973; and Harbert 1976.
25. See Volgy and Quistgard 1974; and Singer and Sensenig 1963.
26. See, for example, Rieselbach 1960.
27. For two systematic reviews of the quantitative research on the UN and international organizations, see Riggs et al. 1970; and Alger 1970.
28. Cox and Jacobson 1973.
29. Ibid.

The work of Cox and Jacobson also encouraged the study of international organizations to consider a more transgovernmental model of their influences. Whereas other research inspired by behavioralism typically assumed a unified model of state interests and actors, this work focused on transgovernmental coalitions involving parts of governments and parts of international organizations. One of the most important insights generated was highly consonant with developments in transgovernmental relations that had come on the intellectual scene in the 1970s:[30] the observation that one channel through which international organizations could affect state policies was through the potential alliances that could form between international bureaucracies and domestic pressure groups at the national level.[31] Although this was an interesting insight, and case studies tended to confirm the importance of such "transnational coalitions" for policy implementation, their effect on policy formulation remains unclear.[32] Meanwhile, the issues facing the international community changed drastically in the early 1970s, giving rise to a new approach to the study of international institutions, discussed in the following section.

Finally, a strand of research stimulated by Ernst Haas's "neofunctional approach" to integration also left a telling mark on the study of empirical effects of international institutions in the 1970s. Neofunctionalism ascribed a dynamic role to individuals and interest groups in the process of integrating pluralist communities.[33] By virtue of their participation in the policymaking process of an integrating community, interest groups and other participants were hypothesized to "learn" about the rewards of such involvement and undergo attitudinal changes inclining them favorably toward the integrative system. According to Haas, "political integration is the process whereby actors shift their loyalties, expectations, and political activities toward a new center, whose institutions possess or demand jurisdiction over preexisting national states."[34] The implications for empirical research on such institutions were readily drawn: those who participate in international organizations should exhibit altered attitudes toward their usefulness and effectiveness.

American politics provided yet another methodological instrument that dovetailed nicely with what was thought to be an empirically testable proposition of Haas's theory: survey research! From the late 1950s into the early 1980s, a plethora of studies tried to establish whether international organizations could contribute to "learning," whether cognitive or affective.[35] The attitudes of civil servants,[36] political appointees, and even national legislators[37] were scrutinized for evidence that the length or nature of their association with various kinds of international organizations had induced attitudinal change. The impact of methods from American politics was obvi-

---

30. Keohane and Nye 1974.

31. See Cox 1969, 225; and Cox and Jacobson 1973, 214.

32. See, for example, Russell 1973; and Keohane 1978.

33. See Haas 1958; and Pentland 1973.

34. Haas 1958, 10.

35. See Kelman 1962; Alger 1965; and Jacobson 1967. See also Wolf 1974, 352–53; and Volgy and Quistgard 1975.

36. See Ernst 1978; and Peck 1979.

37. See Bonham 1970; Kerr 1973; Riggs 1977; and Karns 1977.

ous: in some cases, indicators were used that precisely paralleled the "thermometers" used by the National Opinion Survey Research project.

Three problems bedeviled this research approach for years. First, it failed to produce consensus on the effect of international institutions on attitudes.[38] Second, attitudes were never reconnected with outcomes, policies, or actions.[39] Third, researchers were never able to overcome the problem of recruitment bias, which itself accounted for most of the positive attitudes held by personnel associated with international institutions. As neofunctionalism as a theoretical orientation lost favor over the course of the 1970s and integrative international organizations such as the European Community and the UN seemed to stagnate in the face of growing world problems beyond their purview, this research program declined, though today a version is pursued primarily in studies that attempt to document mass attitudes toward the European Union.

Politics Beyond Formal Organizations:
The Rise of International Regimes

As the study of international institutions progressed over the post–World War II years, the gulf between international politics and formal organization arrangements began to open in ways that were not easy to reconcile. The major international conflict for a rising generation of scholars—the Vietnam War—raged beyond the formal declarations of the UN. Two decades of predictable monetary relations under the Bretton Woods institutions were shattered by a unilateral decision by the United States in 1971 to close the gold window and later to float the dollar. The rise of the Organization of Petroleum Exporting Countries and their apparent power to upset previously understood arrangements with respect to oil pricing and availability took place outside the structure of traditional international organizations, as did consumers' response later in the decade. For some, the proper normative response seemed to be to strengthen international organizations to deal with rising problems of interdependence.[40] Others more familiar with the public choice literature argued that a proper extension of property rights, largely underway in areas such as environmental protection, rather than a formal extension of supranational authority per sc, was the answer to solving problems of collective action.[41] Overall, few doubted that international life was "organized," but, increasingly, it became apparent that much of the earlier focus

38. Studies that failed to confirm expectations of attitudinal change include Siverson 1973; and Bonham 1970. A few studies even found negative impacts on attitudes due to association with international organizations: Smith 1973; and Pendergast 1976.

39. To the extent that such associations affected outcomes, the results were generally innocuous. See, for example, Mathiason 1972.

40. Brown and Fabian, for example, modestly call for "a comprehensive ocean authority, an outer space projects agency, a global weather and climate organization, and an international scientific commission on global resources and technologies." See Brown and Fabian 1975. See also Ruggie 1972, 890, 891; and Gosovic and Ruggie 1976.

41. Conybeare 1980.

on formal structures and multilateral treaty-based agreements, especially the UN, had been overdrawn.[42]

The events of the early 1970s gave rise to the study of "international regimes," defined as rules, norms, principles, and procedures that focus expectations regarding international behavior. Clearly, the regimes movement represented an effort to substitute an understanding of international organization with an understanding of international governance more broadly.[43] It also demoted the study of international organizations as actors: prior to the study of international regimes an inquiry into the effects of international institutions meant inquiring into how effectively a particular agency performed its job, for example, the efficiency with which the World Health Organization vaccinated the world's needy children.[44] When regimes analysts looked for effects, these were understood to be outcomes influenced by a constellation of rules rather than tasks performed by a collective international agency.

But just what effects regimes analysis sought to uncover has changed as the research program has unfolded.[45] A first collective effort by the scholarly community to address regime effects was primarily interested in the distributive consequences of the norms of the international food regime, arguing that it is important to consider the "ways in which the global food regime affects . . . wealth, power, autonomy, community, nutritional well-being, . . . and sometimes physical survival."[46] In this view, regime "effects" were to be reckoned in terms of the distributive consequences of the behavior of a myriad of producers, distributors, and consumers, and, in a minor way, by international organizations and state bureaucracies. Certainly, there was in this early volume little thought that regimes were somehow efficient or efficiency-improving outcomes, as later theorizing would imply; rather, the food regime was characterized by "broad and endemic inadequacies," which are the result of national policies that are "internationally bargained and coordinated . . . by multilateral agreement or unilateral dictate."[47]

Further research on international regimes moved thinking in three important directions. First, distributive consequences soon fell from the center of consideration as research began to focus on how international regimes are created and transformed in the first place as well as the behavioral consequences of norms or rules,[48] rather than the distributive consequences of behavior itself. (We argue later that attention to distributive issues ought to be restored.) Second, in one (though not dominant) strand

---

42. On skepticism regarding the centrality of the GATT regime, see Strange 1988. On the declining importance of "public international agencies" in general and the FAO in particular, see McLin 1979.

43. See, for example, Hopkins and Puchala 1978, especially 598.

44. Hoole 1977. The focus on international organizations as actors providing collective or redistributive goods has a long history. See Kindleberger 1951a; Ascher 1952; Wood 1952; Loveday 1953; Sharp 1953; and Gregg 1966.

45. We focus here on effects of international regimes because, as argued later, we think this is the question on which future research should concentrate. For a review of theories that purport to explain international regimes, see Haggard and Simmons 1987.

46. Hopkins and Puchala 1978, 598.

47. Ibid., 615–16.

48. Krasner 1983b, introduction and conclusion.

of research, attention to the normative aspects of international regimes led naturally to consideration of the subjective meaning of such norms and to a research paradigm that was in sympathy with developments in constructivist schools of thought.[49] (See the essay by Martha Finnemore and Kathryn Sikkink in this issue of *IO*.)

Third, by the mid-1980s explanations of international regimes became intertwined with explanations of international cooperation more generally. The work of Robert Keohane especially drew from functionalist approaches that emphasized the efficiency reasons for rules and agreements among regime participants.[50] Based on rationality assumptions shared by a growing literature in political economy, this research sought to show that international institutions provided a way for states to overcome problems of collective action, high transaction costs, and information deficits or asymmetries. This approach has produced a number of insights, which we will discuss and extend later. But its analytical bite—derived from its focus on states as unified rational actors—was purchased at the expense of earlier insights relating to transnational coalitions and, especially, domestic politics. Furthermore, the strength of this approach has largely been its ability to explain the creation and maintenance of international institutions. It has been weaker in delineating their effects on state behavior and other significant outcomes, an issue to which we will return.

This weakness opened the way for an important realist counterthrust in the late 1980s: the challenge to show that international institutions affect state behavior in any significant way. Some realists, particularly neorealists, raised logical and empirical objections to the institutionalist research agenda. On the logical side, Joseph Grieco[51] and John Mearsheimer argued that relative-gains concerns prevent states from intensive cooperation. The essence of their argument was that since the benefits of cooperation could be translated into military advantages, states would be fearful that such benefits would disproportionately flow to potential adversaries and therefore would be reluctant to cooperate in substantial, sustained ways. Responses by Duncan Snidal and Robert Powell showed that, even if states did put substantial weight on such relative-gains concerns, the circumstances under which they would greatly inhibit cooperation were quite limited. Mearsheimer, in his extensive challenge to institutionalism, also argued that the empirical evidence showing that institutions changed patterns of state behavior was weak, especially in the area of security affairs. While we might dispute the extreme conclusions drawn by Mearsheimer, we take seriously his challenge to provide stronger empirical evidence. In the third section of this article we suggest lines of institutionalist analysis that should lend themselves to rigorous empirical testing, avoiding some of the inferential traps and fallacies that Mearsheimer and other realists have identified.[52]

---

49. See Haas 1983; and Ruggie 1972.
50. Keohane 1984.
51. See Grieco 1988; and Mearsheimer 1994.
52. See Snidal 1991; and Powell 1991. See also Baldwin 1993.

Institutions Across the Level-of-Analysis Divide:
Insights from Domestic Politics

Early studies of international institutions were often motivated by the attempt to apply new methods used in the study of domestic politics. As just reviewed, studies of voting behavior in the General Assembly, electoral success in the UN governing structure, and surveys regarding attitudinal change as a result of international organization experience are all prime examples. Similar studies continue today, for example, in calculations of power indexes for member states of the European Union.[53] These approaches have not, however, been widely influential recently and have been subject to trenchant criticisms.[54] In spite of this less-than-promising experience, scholars today are turning once again to models of domestic politics to suggest new questions and approaches to the study of international institutions. In this section, we briefly consider whether these new approaches are more likely to bear fruit.

We find reasons to be relatively optimistic about today's attempts to transport models across levels of analysis, as long as such attempts are undertaken with some caution. In particular, we see substantial potential in looking at theories of domestic institutions that are rooted in noncooperative game theory. Rationalist theories of institutions that fall into the category of the "new institutionalism" have applicability at both the domestic and international levels. Virtually all the early attempts to apply techniques and research strategies from domestic politics to the international level were implicitly based on the assumption that agreements among actors are enforceable. Indeed, this was the *only* assumption under which it made sense to look at the politics that underlay voting and decision making in international institutions at all. Models that assume that agreements will be enforced by a neutral third party are especially inappropriate for the international setting; calculating voting power in the General Assembly in a world of unenforceable agreements may have more than a passing resemblance to arranging deck chairs on the Titanic. Thus, it is not surprising that these models have not had great influence when transported to the international level.

However, recent models of domestic institutions as a rule draw, often explicitly, on noncooperative game theory. The basic assumptions of noncooperative game theory are that actors are rational, strategic, and opportunistic, and that no outside actor will step in to enforce agreements. Therefore, agreements that will make a difference must be self-enforcing. These conditions are remarkably similar to the usual characterization of international politics as a situation of anarchy and self-help.[55] As long as models use the same basic assumptions about the nature of actors and their environment, the potential for learning across the level-of-analysis divide could be enormous.

53. Hosli 1993.
54. Garrett and Tsebelis 1996.
55. Waltz 1979.

As one example, consider what international relations scholars might learn from looking at current debates on the nature of legislative institutions.[56] Analogously to how realist theory portrays states with a mixture of common and conflicting interests but without supranational enforcement, these models treat legislators as self-interested, individualistic actors in a situation where they must cooperate with one another to achieve mutual benefits.[57] They ask how legislators under these conditions might construct institutions—such as committees or parties—that will allow them to reach goals such as reelection.[58] Similarly, international relations scholars are interested in how states or other entities design institutional forms (organizations, procedures, informal cooperative arrangements, treaty arrangements) that assist in the realization of their objectives. The point is *not*, as much of the earlier literature assumed, that "legislative activity" at the international level is interesting per se. The power of the analogy rests solely on how actors choose strategies to cope with similar strategic environments. In general, we suggest that more progress can be made by drawing out the aspects of domestic politics that are characterized by attempts to cooperate by actors with mixed motives, who cannot turn easily to external enforcement, and applying them selectively to the study of international relations.

The debate about legislative organization, which we argue may provide insights into international institutions more generally, has been roughly organized into a contrast between informational and distributional models. Informational models concentrate on the ways in which legislative structures allow legislators to learn about the policies they are adopting, thus avoiding inefficient outcomes.[59] Researchers have argued that properly structured legislative committees can efficiently signal information about the effects of proposed policies to the floor, and that informational concerns can explain both the pattern of appointment of legislators to committees and the decision making rules under which committees operate. All of these claims have stimulated intense empirical investigation, which has been challenged by the distributional perspective discussed later. Informational models can be used to extend and clarify arguments in the international literature that stress the role of institutions in the provision of information, as Keohane has argued, and in the learning process, as Ernst and Peter Haas have emphasized. They can lead to predictions about the conditions under which international institutions can effectively provide policy-relevant information to states, about the kinds of institutions that can provide credible information, and about the effects of such information provision on patterns of state behavior. An example of an issue area where these effects might be prominent is environ-

---

56. The work on legislative institutions is just one example of the application of noncooperative game theory to domestic institutions. But since it is a particularly well-developed literature, we concentrate on it here, without wishing to imply that this is the only branch of research on domestic institutions that may have interesting analogies to international institutions.

57. Shepsle and Weingast 1995.

58. Although much of the work on legislative organization concentrates on the American context, in recent years creative efforts have been made to develop such models in non-U.S. settings. See Huber 1996b; Tsebelis and Money 1995; Ramseyer and Rosenbluth 1993; G. Cox 1987; and Shugart and Carey 1992.

59. See Gilligan and Krehbiel 1990; and Krehbiel 1991.

mental institutions, where it is highly likely that the ability of organizations to provide reliable, credible information about the effects of human activities on the environment is a key factor in explaining the success or failure of negotiations on environmental treaties. Another possible application might be the creation of international financial institutions, such as the Bank for International Settlements, an original function of which was to provide credible information to markets on German creditworthiness.[60] Within the European Union, the Commission's role as a relatively independent collector of policy-relevant information is a plausible explanation for its ability to exercise considerable influence over policy outcomes.[61]

Distributional models, on the other hand, assume that information is not all that problematic. Instead, they concentrate on the fact that legislators are heterogeneous in their tastes, caring differentially about various issues.[62] Achieving mutual gains, in this framework, means cutting deals that will stick across different issues. Since exchanges of votes cannot always be simultaneous, legislators have developed structures such as committees and agenda-setting rules that allow them to put together majorities on the issues of most intense particularistic interest to them. This structure provides predictions about the distribution of benefits to individual legislators. Distributional benefits flow through appointment to powerful legislative committees. Like researchers in the informational tradition, those in the distributional tradition have used such models to explain and predict various aspects of legislative organization. For example, they argue that committees will be composed of preference outliers— those legislators who care most intensely about particular issues—and that such committees will be granted agenda-setting power, which is necessary to keep cross-issue deals from unraveling on the floor. Distributional models may be especially useful in exploring in a rigorous fashion the role of international institutions in facilitating or hampering mutually beneficial issue linkages that have been an important research agenda in international relations.[63]

The debate between informational and distributional models of legislative organization has been highly productive, in both theoretical and empirical terms. It has provided new insights into the types of problems confronted by legislators, the types of solutions available to them, and the role of institutions in democracies. On the empirical side, it has generated a plethora of alternative observable implications, for example, about the composition of congressional committees or the conditions under which actors gain gatekeeping or amendment power. Empirical research on both sides has led to deep insights about how the structure of institutions, such as legislative committees, influences their ability to help individuals overcome collective-action problems, and the conditions under which individuals will be willing to delegate substantial decision-making authority to such institutions. Both types of questions are highly relevant and essential to an understanding of the role of institutions in international politics as well. For example, the informational model suggests

---

60. Simmons 1993.
61. See Haas 1989; and Bernauer 1995.
62. Weingast and Marshall 1988.
63. On issue linkage, see Stein 1980; and Martin 1992c.

that institutions should be most influential in promoting cooperation when they are relatively independent, "expert" sources of information and when such information is scarce and valuable to states. We should expect this model to be most useful in international issue areas characterized by information asymmetries or in the development of expert knowledge (such as financial and banking regulation). The distributional model predicts that institutions will be most successful in allowing for credible cross-issue deals between states when those with the most intense interest in any particular issue dominate policymaking on that dimension and when institutional mechanisms inhibit states from reneging on cross-issue deals, even if performance on different dimensions is not simultaneous. Institutions that try to cope with environmental protection and development needs in the same package (such as UNCED and the Agenda 21 program) provide a plausible example. For our interests, another striking analogy between the international arena and the legislative literature is the degree to which the terms of the debate—information versus distribution—reflect the emerging debate about the significance of international institutions.

In many essential respects the problems faced by individual legislators mirror those faced by individual states in the international system. Individual actors face situations in which they must cooperate in order to achieve benefits but also face temptations to defect from cooperative arrangements. No external authority exists to enforce cooperative agreements; they must be self-enforcing. Self-enforcement takes the form of exclusion from the benefits of cooperation, a coercive measure. Given these analogies, there is every reason to expect that some of the methods, insights, and results of these new studies of legislators could usefully inform new studies of international institutions, *in spite of the fact that legislators (usually) operate in a more densely institutionalized environment.*[64] More generally, rationalist models of institutions that have been developed in domestic settings have the potential to be translated to the international level. As long as we are considering mixed-motive situations in which actors must cooperate in order to pursue their objectives, the incentives to construct institutions to structure and encourage cooperation are similar.

How Institutions Matter

Since the 1980s, work on international institutions has been defined for the most part by the demand that scholars respond to a realist agenda: to prove that institutions have a significant effect on state behavior. While structuring the debate in this manner may have stimulated direct theoretical confrontation, it has also obscured some important and tractable research paths. Allowing realism to set the research agenda has meant that models of international institutions have rarely taken domestic poli-

---

64. One could make a similar argument about domestic theories of delegation. See Epstein and O'Halloran 1997; Lohmann and O'Halloran 1994; and Lupia and McCubbins 1994. The analogy between politicians deciding to delegate authority to bureaucrats or committees and states delegating authority to international institutions is strong.

tics seriously, treating the state as a unit. The debate has also been reduced to a dichotomy: either institutions matter or they do not. Insufficient attention has been given to the mechanisms through which we might expect institutional effects to work. Institutionalists, in response to realism, have treated institutions largely as independent variables, while playing down earlier insights that international institutions are themselves the objects of strategic state choice. Treating institutions as dependent variables has mistakenly been understood as an implicit admission that they are epiphenomenal, with no independent effect on patterns of behavior.[65]

Although it has been important to go beyond merely explaining the existence of international institutions, productive new lines of research emerge if we accept that institutions are *simultaneously causes and effects*; that is, institutions are both the objects of state choice and consequential. In a rationalist, equilibrium framework, this statement is obvious and unexceptionable: states choose and design institutions. States do so because they face certain problems that can be resolved through institutional mechanisms. They choose institutions because of their intended effects. Once constructed, institutions will constrain and shape behavior, even as they are constantly challenged and reformed by their member states. In this section, we outline a number of lines of research that show promise to take us beyond the "do they matter or don't they" structure of research on international institutions.

The following research agenda is firmly in the rationalist tradition. Although this approach allows for substantial variation in patterns of preferences over outcomes, and indeed provides predictions about outcomes based on exogenous change in such preferences, it provides relatively little explanatory leverage with respect to the sources of change in such preferences. A few words on how this agenda is related to the constructivist research program may be in order. To the degree that constructivist approaches prove powerful at making changes in actors' fundamental goals endogenous, providing refutable hypotheses about the conditions for such change, the constructivist and rationalist approaches will be complementary. Although rationalist approaches are generally powerful for explaining how policy preferences change when external constraints or information conditions change, alternative approaches, such as constructivism, are necessary for explaining more fundamental, internal changes in actors' goals. However, the rationalist research program has much to contribute even without strong theories about the reasons for change in actors' goals. One of the core insights of theories of strategic interaction is that, regardless of actors' specific preferences, they will tend to face generic types of cooperation problems over and over again. Many situations give rise to incentives to renege on deals or to behave in time-inconsistent ways that make actors happy in the short run but regretful in the long run. Likewise, many situations of strategic interaction give rise to benefits from cooperation, and conflicts over how to divide up this surplus will plague cooperative efforts. Thus, considerations of how to prevent cheating and how to resolve distributional conflict, to give two prominent examples, are central to theories of cooperation regardless of the specific goals of actors. Rationalist ap-

65. Mearsheimer 1994.

proaches are powerful because they suggest observable implications about patterns of cooperation in the face of such dilemmas, even absent the kind of precise information about preferences that scholars desire. It is to such dilemmas that we now turn our attention.

Collaboration Versus Coordination Problems

The most productive institutionalist research agenda thus far in international relations has been the rationalist–functionalist agenda, originating with Keohane's *After Hegemony* and Steve Krasner's edited volume on international regimes.[66] This work was informed by a fundamentally important insight, inspired by the metaphor of the Prisoners'Dilemma (PD). Individually rational action by states could impede mutually beneficial cooperation. Institutions would be effective to the degree that they allowed states to avoid short-term temptations to renege, thus realizing available mutual benefits.

Some authors, recognizing that PD was only one type of collective-action problem, drew a distinction between collaboration and coordination problems.[67] Collaboration problems, like PD, are characterized by individual incentives to defect and the existence of equilibria that are not Pareto optimal. Thus, the problem states face in this situation is finding ways to bind themselves and others in order to reach the Pareto frontier. In contrast, coordination games are characterized by the existence of multiple Pareto-optimal equilibria. The problem states face in this situation is not to avoid temptations to defect, but to choose among these equilibria. Such choice may be relatively simple and resolved by identification of a focal point, if the equilibria are not sharply differentiated from one another in terms of the distribution of benefits.[68] But some coordination games, like the paradigmatic Battle of the Sexes, involve multiple equilibria over which the actors have strongly divergent preferences. Initially, most authors argued that institutions would have little effect on patterns of state behavior in coordination games, predicting substantial institutional effects only in collaboration situations. Interestingly, these arguments led both to expectations about institutional effects on state behavior and to state incentives to delegate authority to institutions, consistent with the kind of equilibrium analysis we find most promising for future research.

As the logic of modern game theory has become more deeply integrated into international relations theory, and as authors have recognized the limitations of the collaboration–coordination distinction, we have begun to see work that integrates the efficiency concerns associated with collaboration and the distributional concerns associated with coordination. Krasner made a seminal contribution to this line of analysis.[69] He argued that when states are attempting to cooperate with one another, achieving efficiency gains—reaching the Pareto frontier—is only one of the challenges they

66. See Keohane 1984; and Krasner 1983b.
67. See Snidal 1985a; Stein 1983; and Martin 1992b.
68. Garrett and Weingast 1993.
69. Krasner 1991.

face and often not the most difficult one. Many equilibria may exist along the Pareto frontier, and specifying one of these as the locus of cooperation, through bargaining and the exercise of state power, dominates empirical examples of international cooperation. Krasner's insight is perfectly compatible with the folk theorems of noncooperative game theory that show that repeated play of a PD-type game gives rise to many—in fact, infinite—equilibria. Thus, repetition transforms collaboration problems into coordination problems. In most circumstances, states have simultaneously to worry about reaching efficient outcomes and resolving distributional conflict.

Once we recognize this fact, our approach to international institutions becomes both more complex and more closely related to traditional international relations concerns about power and bargaining. To be effective, institutions cannot merely resolve collaboration problems through monitoring and other informational functions. They must also provide a mechanism for resolving distributional conflict. For example, institutions may construct focal points, identifying one possible equilibrium as the default or "obvious" one, thus reducing state-to-state bargaining about the choice of a particular pattern of outcomes. The role of the European Court of Justice (ECJ), discussed elsewhere in this article, is captured in part by this type of constructed focal-point analysis. The Basle Banking Committee's role in devising international standards for prudential banking practices similarly helped to coordinate national regulations where a number of plausible solutions were available.[70] Where states fear that the benefits of cooperation are disproportionately flowing to others, institutions can provide reliable information about state behavior and the realized benefits of cooperation to allay such fears. Trade institutions perform many functions; one function that could stand more analytical scrutiny is the provision of such information about the distribution of benefits among members. Another way institutions could mitigate distributional conflict is to "keep account" of deals struck, compromises made, and gains achieved, particularly in complex multi-issue institutions. The networks created within the supranational institutions of the European Union, for example, provide the necessary scope for issue-linkage and institutional memory to perform the function of assuring that all members, over time, achieve a reasonably fair share of the benefits of cooperation.[71] Unless the problem of equilibrium selection is resolved, all the third-party monitoring in the world will not allow for stable international cooperation.

Thus, a promising line of research will involve bringing distributional issues back into the study of international institutions, issues that were in fact the focus of some of the early regimes literature discussed earlier. Institutions may interact with distributional conflict in a number of ways. Most simply, they reflect and solidify settlements of distributional conflict that have been established through more traditional means. These means include the exercise of state power, which Krasner emphasizes, market dominance, and alternative methods of bargaining such as making trades across issues.[72] In this perspective, institutions can make a difference if they lock in a

70. Simmons 1998.
71. Pollack 1997.
72. Fearon 1994a.

particular equilibrium, providing stability. But rather than merely reflecting power in an epiphenomenal fashion, as realists would have it, institutions in this formulation prevent potential challengers from undermining existing patterns of cooperation, explaining why powerful states may choose to institutionalize these patterns rather than relying solely on ad hoc cooperation.

Institutions may also serve a less controversial signaling function, therefore minimizing bargaining costs. This would be the case if institutions construct focal points or if they primarily keep account of the pattern of benefits over time, as discussed earlier. In either case, they effectively increase path dependence. Once a particular equilibrium is chosen, institutions lock it in. Researching the ways in which institutions do this—how do they enhance path dependence, and under what conditions?—would be intriguing. Normative questions also rise to the top of the agenda once we recognize the lock-in role of institutions. If they do in fact solidify a pattern of cooperation preferred by the most powerful, we should question the ethical status of institutions, turning our attention to equity, as well as efficiency, questions.

In the most traditional, state-centric terms, institutions reflect and enhance state power; in Tony Evans and Peter Wilson's words, they are "arenas for acting out power relations."[73] On the other end of the spectrum, we may want to ask about situations in which institutions play a more active role in resolving distributional conflict. Perhaps institutions sometimes do more than lock in equilibria chosen through the exercise of state power, having an independent part in the selection of equilibria. Such an argument has been made most clearly in the case of the ECJ. Here, Geoffrey Garrett and Barry R. Weingast find that there are a number of ways in which the European Community could have realized its goal of completing the internal market.[74] The ECJ made a big difference in the course of European integration because it was able to construct a focal point by choosing one of these mechanisms, that of mutual recognition. This choice had clear distributional implications but was accepted by member states because it was a Pareto improvement over the reversion point of failing to complete the internal market. A distinct research tradition emphasizes the legitimizing role that international institutions can play in focal-point selection. Some scholars point out that institutionally and legally enshrined focal points can gain a high degree of legitimacy both internationally and domestically.[75] This legitimacy, in turn, has important political consequences.[76]

To develop a research agenda on how institutions resolve problems of multiple equilibria and distribution, we would have to build on these insights to ask conditional questions. When are states, particularly the powerful, willing to turn the problem of equilibrium selection over to an institution? What kinds of institutions are most likely to perform this function effectively—those that are strategic or those that

73. Evans and Wilson 1992.

74. Garrett and Weingast 1993. They also argue that the multiple equilibria were not sharply distinguished from one another in terms of efficiency and do not concentrate on distributional conflict among equilibria. They have been criticized on these points. See Burley and Mattli 1993.

75. See Franck 1990; and Peck 1996, 237.

76. Claude 1966, 367.

are naive; those that rely on political decision making or those that rely heavily on relatively independent experts and/or judicial processes; those that broadly reflect the membership of the institution or those that are dominated by the powerful? Under what conditions are constructed focal points likely to gain international recognition and acceptance? Overall, bringing the traditional international relations focus on distributional conflict back into the study of international institutions holds the potential for generating researchable questions that are both positive and normative in nature.

International Institutions and Domestic Politics

In allowing their agenda to be defined by responding to the realist challenge, institutionalists have generally neglected the role of domestic politics. States have been treated as rational unitary actors and assigned preferences and beliefs. This framework has been productive in allowing us to outline the broad ways in which institutions can change patterns of behavior. But in privileging the state as an actor, we have neglected the ways in which other actors in international politics might use institutions (a central insight of earlier studies of transgovernmental organization) and the ways in which the nature or interests of the state itself are potentially changed by the actions of institutions (an implication of the early neofunctionalist literature). Here we outline a few lines of analysis that should be fruitful for integrating domestic politics and international institutions in a systematic manner, rather than treating domestic politics as a residual category of explanation. Because the lines of analysis here have foundations in specific analytical frameworks with explicit assumptions, applying them to the problem of international institutions should result in productive research paths, rather than merely the proliferation of possible "explanatory variables" that has characterized many attempts to integrate domestic politics and international relations. We should note that bringing domestic politics back into the study of international institutions is an agenda that should be understood as analytically distinct from that of applying institutionalist models developed in the domestic setting to the international level, an agenda addressed elsewhere in this article.

As we will argue, one of the more fundamental ways in which international institutions can change state behavior is by substituting for domestic practices. If policies formerly made by domestic institutions are now made on the international level, it is reasonable to expect substantial changes in the patterns of world politics. Three related questions are central to understanding the relations between domestic and international institutions. First, under what conditions might domestic actors be willing to substitute international for domestic institutions? Second, are particular domestic actors regularly advantaged by the ability to transfer policymaking authority to the international level? Third, to what extent can international institutional decisions and rules be enforced by domestic institutions, and what are the implications for compliance? These questions are tied together by the assumption that domestic actors intentionally delegate policymaking authority to the international level when this action furthers pursuit of their interests.

Domestic institutions can at times be a barrier to the realization of benefits for society as a whole. Failures of domestic institutions can arise through a number of mechanisms. Perhaps most obviously, domestic institutions can be captured by preference outliers who hold policy hostage to their demands. Recent research suggests that this may be the case with respect to the settlement of territorial disputes between bordering states in some regions: repeated failure to ratify border agreements in the legislature is one of the most important domestic political conditions associated with the willingness of states to submit their disputes to international arbitration.[77] More generally, this situation is likely to arise when some actors, such as those looking for particularistic benefits, find it easier to organize than do actors more concerned with the welfare of the average citizen. Such is the story often told about trade policy. Import-competing producers and others with an interest in protectionist policies may find it easier to organize than those who favor free trade, a coalition of exporters and consumers. This differential ability to organize will bias policy in favor of protection, decreasing overall welfare. Transferring the policymaking process to the international level, where exporters can see that they have a stake in organization in order to gain the opening of foreign markets, can facilitate a more evenhanded representation of interests. Those actors who have the most to gain from pursuit of general welfare—such as executives elected by a national constituency—will show the most interest in turning to international institutions under such circumstances. Judith Goldstein provides an analysis along these lines when she explains the paradox of the U.S. president agreeing to bilateral dispute-resolution panels in the U.S.–Canada Free Trade Act (FTA), in spite of the fact that these panels predictably decide cases in a way that tends to deny protection to U.S. producers.[78]

We can identify other incentives for domestic actors to transfer policymaking to the international level. One common problem with institutions that are under the control of political actors is that of time-inconsistent preferences. Although running an unexpectedly high level of inflation today may bring immediate benefits to politicians up for reelection, for example, allowing monetary policy to be made by politicians will introduce a welfare-decreasing inflationary bias to the economy. Putting additional constraints on policy, for example, by joining a system of fixed exchange rates or a common currency area, can provide a mechanism to overcome this time-inconsistency problem, as argued by proponents of a single European currency. In general, if pursuit of gains over time involves short-term sacrifices, turning to international institutions can be an attractive option for domestic policymakers.

A second and related question about domestic politics is whether particular kinds of actors will regularly see an advantage in turning to the international level. At the simplest level, it seems likely that "internationalist" actors—those heavily engaged in international transactions,[79] those who share the norms of international society,[80]

77. Simmons 1998.
78. See Goldstein 1996; and Gilligan 1997.
79. Frieden 1991.
80. Sikkink 1993a.

or those who have a stake in a transnational or global resource[81] —will have an interest in turning to the international level. This may especially be the case when such groups or parties are consistently in a minority position in domestic politics. Drawing on these ideas, we could begin to develop hypotheses about the kinds of domestic interest groups that will most favor transferring some authority to the international level.

Certain domestic institutional actors may also have a tendency to benefit from international-level policymaking. One such actor, which is just beginning to enter political scientists' analysis of international institutions, is the judiciary. Increasingly, international agreements are legal in form. This means that they often are interpreted by domestic courts, and that judges can use international law as a basis on which to make judgments.[82] Because international law provides this particular actor with an additional resource by which to pursue agendas, whether bureaucratic or ideological, we might expect that the judiciary in general tends to be sympathetic to international institutions.

Overall, as we work toward more sophisticated specification of the causal mechanisms through which institutions can influence behavior, we will have to pay much more attention to domestic politics than studies of international institutions have thus far. The development of general theories of domestic politics provides an opening for systematic development of propositions about domestic actors. We no longer need to treat the domestic level as merely the source of state preferences, nor as a residual category to explain anomalies or patterns of variation that cannot be explained by international factors. Instead, we can move toward genuinely interactive theories of domestic politics and international institutions, specifying the conditions under which certain actors are likely to prefer that policy be made on the international level. This focus allows us to specify conditions likely to lead to the delegation of policymaking authority to the international level, some of which we have outlined here.

Unanticipated Consequences

In a rationalist framework, institutions are both the object of state choice and consequential. The link that ties these two aspects of institutions together, and allows the analyst to develop refutable propositions about institutions within an equilibrium framework, is the ability of actors to anticipate the consequences of particular types of institutions. For example, in the preceding discussion of domestic politics, we assumed consistently that domestic actors were able to gauge with some degree of accuracy the ways in which working within international institutions would affect their ability to pursue their material or ideational goals.

The rationalist approach stands in distinction to a historical or sociological approach to institutions.[83] These approaches see institutions as more deeply rooted and

---

81. Young 1979.
82. See Alter 1996; and Conforti 1993.
83. See Steinmo, Thelen, and Longstreth 1992; and Pierson 1996b. Historical institutionalism stresses the path-dependent nature of institutions, explaining why apparently inefficient institutions persist. Socio-

draw attention to their unanticipated consequences. Although we may question whether many international institutions reach the same degree of "taken-for-grantedness" that we see in domestic politics or smaller-scale social relations, it seems undeniable that they sometimes have effects that surprise their member states. It is important to differentiate between unintended and unanticipated effects. Effects may be anticipated but unintended. For example, it is generally expected that arrangements to lower the rate of inflation will lead to somewhat higher levels of unemployment. Thus, higher unemployment is an anticipated, although unintended, consequence of stringent monetary policies. It is best understood as a price actors are sometimes willing to bear to gain the benefits of low inflation. Such unintended but anticipated consequences of institutions present little challenge to a rationalist approach, since they fit neatly into a typical cost-benefit analysis. Genuinely unanticipated effects, however, present a larger challenge.

Specific examples of apparently unanticipated consequences of international institutions are not difficult to find. States that believed that human-rights accords were nothing but meaningless scraps of paper found themselves surprised by the ability of transnational actors to use these commitments to force governments to change their policies.[84] In the European Community, few anticipated that the ECJ would have the widespread influence on policy that it has.[85] Prime Minister Margaret Thatcher was apparently quite surprised at the results of agreeing to change voting rules within the European Community, such as the adoption of qualified-majority voting, which she accepted in the Single European Act.[86]

How might a rationalist approach deal with these events? One productive approach might be to attempt to specify the conditions under which unanticipated consequences are most likely. This specification would at least allow us to suggest when a simple rationalist model will provide substantial explanatory leverage and when it might become necessary to integrate the insights of other schools of thought. If unanticipated consequences dominate political outcomes, we would have to draw on alternatives to rationalist models in a way that goes far beyond using them as a way to specify preferences and goals. Here, we begin specifying when unanticipated consequences are most likely to confound patterns of international cooperation.

Inductively, it appears that changes in secondary rules—that is, rules about rules—are the changes most likely to work in unexpected ways. Changes in voting rules within an institution, for example, can give rise to new coalitions and previously suppressed expressions of interest, leading to unpredicted policy outcomes. Changes in decision-making procedures can have even more widespread and unexpected effects if they open the policy process to input from new actors. Many examples of unanticipated consequences arise from decision-making procedures that provide access to nongovernmental and transnational actors, as, for example, Kathryn Sik-

---

logical institutionalism emphasizes the social nature of institutions, stressing their role in defining individuals' identities and the fact that many important institutions come to be taken for granted and therefore not seen as susceptible to reform.

84. Sikkink 1993a.
85. Burley and Mattli 1993.
86. Moravcsik 1991.

kink's work has shown.[87] Both as sources of new information and as strategic actors in their own right, such groups are often able to use new points of access to gain unexpected leverage over policy. Changes in decision-making rules will have widespread effects on a variety of substantive rules and are thus more likely to have unanticipated effects on outcomes than changes in substantive rules themselves. If this observation is correct, we should see more unanticipated consequences in situations that have relatively complex and permutable secondary rules, such as legalized institutions. Traditional state-to-state bargaining with a unit veto, which has little secondary rule structure, should provide less opportunity for nonstate actors or coalitions of the weak to influence outcomes unexpectedly.

One question that often arises, especially in the international arena, is why governments are willing to live with unanticipated outcomes. After all, participation in international institutions is voluntary. If unpleasant and unexpected outcomes frequently occur, states as sovereign actors retain the right to pull out of institutions. Why might they choose to remain in? The trivial answer is that the benefits of remaining in are greater than the costs. But we can turn this answer into something nontrivial by thinking about the conditions when institutional membership is likely to provide the greatest benefits. Some of these have been spelled out in functionalist theory. Keohane argues that the demand for international institutions will be greatest under conditions of interdependence, when states face a dense network of relations with one another and where information is somewhat scarce.[88] We could generalize that states are least likely to be willing to withdraw from an institution in the face of unanticipated consequences when they are dealing with issues that exhibit increasing returns to scale, which, in turn, create conditions of path dependence. Consider the creation of regional trading arrangements in the 1990s. These arrangements provide their members with economic benefits, and those on the outside of the arrangements find themselves losing investment and trading opportunities. We therefore see eastern European, Caribbean, and other states clamoring to become members of the relevant regional trading arrangements. This is a good example of how increasing returns to scale create a high demand for institutional membership. Under these conditions, it seems likely that these states will be willing to put up with a high level of unexpected outcomes before they would seriously consider withdrawing from an institution. However, this example begs the question of whether trade agreements are likely to have substantial unanticipated effects. They are only likely to do so in the case of rapid technological change or large international economic shocks, such as the oil shocks of the 1970s.

Typology of Institutional Effects

As we turn our attention to the problem of how, not just whether, international institutions matter, it becomes essential to understand alternative mechanisms through which institutions might exert their effects. To prod our thinking in this direction, we

87. Sikkink 1993a.
88. Keohane 1983a.

introduce a preliminary typology of institutional effects. The reasoning behind this typology is that different institutions, or perhaps similar institutions in different settings, will have different types of effects. Specifying these effects will not only allow us to develop better insights into the causal mechanisms underlying the interaction between institutions and states or societies. It will also provide for more testable propositions about how and when we should expect institutions to exert substantial effects on behavior.

The typology we suggest is analytically informed but aims first to provide a language for describing patterns of change in state behavior after creation of an international institution. Here we spell out the typology and present some illustrative examples. The next step will be to link the typology to causal processes, and we suggest some preliminary ideas along these lines. We begin by suggesting two types of institutional effects: *convergence* and *divergence* effects. Of course, the null hypothesis is that institutions have no effect. Development of a clearer analytical framework may force us to consider situations in which we combine effects: for example, perhaps some types of states are subject to convergence effects and others to divergence effects.

We begin with convergence effects, since the logic of most rationalist, economistic, and functionalist theories of international institutions leads us to expect such effects. These models posit goals that states find it difficult to achieve on their own, whether for reasons of time-inconsistent preferences, collective-action problems, old-fashioned domestic political stalemate, or other failures of unilateral state action. In this functionalist logic, states turn to international institutions to resolve such problems; institutions allow them to achieve benefits unavailable through unilateral action of existing state structures. Functionalist analysis sees international institutions as important because they help states to solve problems. Many of these problems have their roots in the failures of domestic institutions, and their resolution involves turning some types of authority over to the international level. Once policy is delegated to an international institution, state behavior will converge: members will tend to adopt similar monetary, trade, or defense policies.

What has been missing from functionalist accounts of institutionalization is the systematic connection between domestic political conditions and incentives to construct and comply with international institutions. But once we recognize that international institutions may make a difference because they effectively substitute for domestic practices (making policy decisions, setting policy goals, or undertaking monitoring activities), our attention turns to the domestic political conditions that make such substitution a reasonable policy alternative. If domestic institutions are the source of persistent policy failure, if they somehow prevent the realization of societal preferences, or if they interfere with the pursuit of mutual benefits with other states, turning functions over to the international level can enhance national welfare.[89] Monetary policy is a prime example of this logic. Other examples might

---

89. Some would argue that this process is antidemocratic. See Vaubel 1986. However, such an argument rests on weak foundations. First, it assumes that domestic institutions are necessarily responsive to

include trade policy, if domestic trade policy institutions are captured by protectionists; or environmental policy, if domestic institutions encourage a short-term rather than a long-term perspective on the problem. Thinking about the logic of substitution requires much more attention to inefficient domestic politics than most functional theories have provided to date.

A classic example of international institutions acting as substitutes for domestic institutions and therefore having convergence effects lies in arguments about why high-inflation states such as Italy might choose to enter the European Monetary Union (EMU).[90] High inflation is a public bad, leading to lower overall welfare than low inflation. However, the short-term benefits to politicians from allowing spurts of unanticipated inflation make it difficult to achieve low rates of inflation unless institutions that set monetary policy are independent of political influence.[91] Thus, transferring authority to an institution that is relatively insulated from political influence, and that itself has a preference for low inflation, can provide overall welfare benefits for the country. This is the logic that leads a state like Italy to take the unusual step (for a relatively rich, developed country) of transferring a core aspect of sovereignty—control over the currency—to a European Central Bank.

Given this logic of delegation, states that become members of the EMU should see a convergence in their rates of inflation.[92] Although the debate rages among economists about whether the European Monetary System has in fact worked in this manner,[93] there is little doubt that one of the major motivations for monetary union is for high-inflation states to "import" low German rates of inflation, leading to similar inflation rates in all member states. If we looked at the variation in inflation rates prior to entry into monetary union (or into a monetary system more generally), and compared it to inflation rates after entry, we should see a decline in the level of variation.

Although monetary union is a prominent and intriguing example of convergence effects, we can imagine a similar dynamic in other issue areas as well. Environmental institutions should lead to convergence of environmental indicators, such as carbon dioxide emissions.[94] Human-rights institutions acting as substitutes should lead members to adopt increasingly similar human-rights practices. Even if full convergence does not occur, the major effect of an institution that is acting as a substitute will be to bring state practices more closely in line with one another.

A convergence effect could be measured and identified by decreased variation in relevant indicators of state practices, whether inflation rates, pollution, or human-

national preferences. For the kinds of reasons just discussed, such as time-inconsistent preferences, or institutional capture, this assumption is often false. Second, the argument assumes that international institutions are necessarily more difficult to monitor, constrain, and influence than domestic institutions. Although this may be a reasonable assumption for some kinds of societal actors and some states, it is not universally true.

90. For a contrasting argument on the logic of EMU, see Gruber 1996.
91. Rogoff 1985.
92. Fratianni and von Hagen 1992.
93. See Giavazzi and Giovannini 1989; and Weber 1991.
94. Levy 1993.

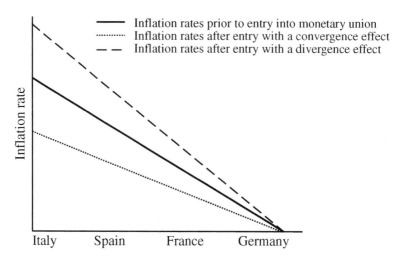

FIGURE 1. *International institutions with convergence or divergence effects*

rights abuses. The existence of a convergence effect could also be identified through graphical means. Figure 1 gives an example. On the *x*-axis, states are arrayed in order of their performance on the outcome dimension, say inflation rates. These rates are indicated on the *y*-axis. The solid line indicates inflation rates prior to entry into monetary union. Its steep slope indicates that the states exhibit substantial variation in inflation rates. The dotted line represents the outcome of monetary union acting as substitute, causing convergence in inflation rates. The more shallow slope indicates less variation than observed before entry into monetary union.

The notion that international institutions might substitute for domestic ones underlies functionalist theories of institutions. However, some empirical work on the effects of institutions has found a pattern quite different from the convergence of outcomes predicted by such a mechanism. Instead, some authors have found that the primary effect of institutions is to exaggerate preexisting patterns of behavior. For example, Andrew Moravcsik has found, in a regional comparison of human-rights institutions, that these institutions only led to an improvement in practices in those states that already exhibited a high level of respect for human rights.[95] Thus, West European states, through participation in institutions, have improved their already very good human-rights records, whereas Latin American states, according to his evidence, show little impact of institutional participation.

This pattern suggests that international institutions sometimes lead to divergence of state practices, in effect complementing and magnifying preexisting tendencies rather than overriding them. In this case, institutions will have a divergence effect. This effect results when states whose initial practice falls far from institutional guidelines will show little change from behavior, whereas those near the guidelines move

---

95. Moravcsik 1995.

even closer to them. In contrast, a convergence effect appears when institutions exert their greatest influence on precisely those states whose behavior deviates substantially from institutional norms. Divergence is likely to emerge when institutions exaggerate domestically generated tendencies of state behavior or when they primarily mimic domestic institutions. Anne-Marie Slaughter has argued something along these lines in pointing out that liberal states are the ones most likely to create and abide by relatively liberal international institutions.[96] According to this logic, liberal institutions will change the behavior of liberal states but not illiberal ones, leading to divergence of state behavior.

A divergence effect means that those states that already come close to institutional norms will move further toward them, whereas the behavior of those that deviate from such norms will remain unchanged. If we were to develop a measure of state behavior, we would see a divergence effect in increased variation of state behavior after institutional creation. We can also illustrate divergence effects graphically, as in Figure 1. Here, institutional effects result in a steeper line, indicating greater divergence in the relevant outcome variable. For ease of comparison, we continue to use the EMU-inflation example. Although such an outcome seems unlikely in practice, for the sake of argument we could imagine that monetary union that allowed for decentralized, unconstrained fiscal policymaking while providing additional resources to cover national debts could lead to such a perverse outcome. Another, perhaps more plausible, example of a divergence effect is in the area of overseas development aid. In the 1970s, OECD countries agreed to devote a set percentage of their GDP, 0.7 percent, to development assistance. Although some countries have come close to providing this level of aid and use the target figure as a tool in domestic debates, others have wholly neglected this target and instead decreased the percentage of their national income that they devote to foreign aid.

If this typology provides a useful way to describe alternative institutional effects, the next challenge is to begin to link up these patterns of behavior to alternative causal mechanisms. This project appears promising, and we outline preliminary ideas here. As suggested earlier, institutions that lead to convergence of state behavior link up nicely to the functionalist approach that has dominated studies of international institutions, regimes, and organizations over the last fifteen years. In this situation, the failure of domestic institutions or of unilateral state action creates incentives to rely on international mechanisms. The kinds of problems that would prompt states to use international institutions that lead to convergence of behavior are relatively well understood. They include time-inconsistency problems that create incentives for states to bind themselves and collective-action problems among states or within polities. When states turn to international institutions as the result of such problems, and when these institutions are operating as intended, we would expect to see convergence of state behavior.

The conditions that would prompt states to use institutions that lead to divergence of behavior are not as well understood. We can begin by noting that states facing

96. Slaughter 1995.

collective-action problems, such as a PD or a coordination game, would be unlikely to rely on an institution that exaggerated differences in state behavior. The fundamental problem in such cases is to create incentives for states to adopt similar policies: free trade, stringent fiscal policies, arms control, and so on.[97] In such a situation, an institution that led to increased divergence of state practice would quickly become irrelevant as states ignored its constraints. Thus, one initial expectation is that institutions should not lead to divergence in situations where incentives exist to adopt similar policies, as when strong externalities to divergent or unilateral state behavior exist. Perhaps this helps us understand why we appear to see some divergence effects in the human-rights issue area. Although human rights are a matter of concern around the globe, human-rights practices usually do not involve the kinds of externalities and incentives for strategic interaction that exist in issue areas such as the environment or monetary policy.[98]

However, lack of externalities does not provide a direct answer to why divergence would occur. To understand this effect, it is likely that we need to consider domestic politics, returning us to an argument made earlier in this article. International agreements, even those without enforcement mechanisms such as the OECD aid target, can provide "hooks" by which interest groups that favor the international agreement can increase their influence on the domestic agenda. For example, in Scandinavian countries the OECD target has become a potent arguing point in parliamentary debates. In states without a well-organized group to grab onto this hook, or in those with a more closed political process, agreements without enforcement mechanisms or substantial pressure from other states to comply are unlikely to have any effect. These contrasting domestic political dynamics are likely to give rise to divergence of state behavior among members of the institution.

A rationalist research agenda for the study of international institutions is rich and promising. This agenda begins by recognizing that, in equilibrium, institutions are both causes and effects, and that empirical researchers must begin to consider the question of how institutions matter, not just whether they do. Thinking in these terms turns our attention to the problem of how institutions might resolve bargaining and distributional conflict as well as the more recognized problems of cheating. It forces us to differentiate anticipated from unanticipated effects of institutions and to ask about the conditions under which unanticipated effects are most likely. Rationalist theories provide a mechanism for bringing domestic politics more systematically into the study of international institutions, an area of research that has been slighted by the development of the field thus far. Finally, a rationalist approach allows us to

---

97. There may be some coordination situations, for example, some discussed by Simmons, in which the solution to the coordination problem does not involve adoption of similar policies by all states but clear division of responsibilities among states. See Simmons 1994. The Bretton Woods systems, for example, coordinated state behavior by creating expectations that the United States would behave differently from other members of the system.

98. Donnelly surveys the landscape of human rights regimes. See Donnelly 1986. There may be exceptions to the generalization that international strategic interaction on human rights is minimal, for example, when severe human-rights abuses lead to massive refugee flows. This kind of logic could lead to testable propositions within the issue area, for example, that institutions should function differently when such externalities exist than under "normal" circumstances.

begin differentiating between different types of institutional effects and developing refutable propositions about the conditions under which we are most likely to observe such effects.

Conclusions

Studies of international institutions have varied in their theoretical sophistication and frequency over time but have remained a staple of international relations research and the pages of *IO* over the last fifty years. In this article we have examined the development of these studies and outlined some promising directions for future research on international institutions. Early studies of institutions were very much problem-driven, focusing on the problems of the postwar world that some hoped international organizations could solve. Although on balance realistic and insightful, the results of these studies failed to cumulate, likely due to the lack of a disciplinary or theoretical framework in which to situate the studies. A more scientific approach showed itself in a newer wave of work on institutions, drawing on methods and models of American politics. But because these models were in general poorly suited to the realities of international politics, they failed to generate substantial new insights. It was not until the 1980s, with the development of work on international regimes and functionalist theories, that a more progressive research program on institutions arose.

One failing of the current research program, however, has been its intense focus on proving that institutions matter, without sufficient attention to constructing well-delineated causal mechanisms or explaining variation in institutional effects. We consider two approaches that might move research beyond this impasse. First, we ask whether applying recent models of domestic politics might be more successful than have past attempts. We find scope for optimism here, since modern theories of domestic institutions typically draw on similar assumptions of unenforceable agreements and opportunistic behavior by individuals that characterize most work in international relations. Finally, we turn to some more specific research directions that are likely to give rise to important and testable propositions. These include more careful consideration of distributional issues, the role of domestic politics, unanticipated consequences, and a typology of institutional effects.

As we consider international institutions as both objects of strategic choice and consequential, allowing them to serve as both dependent and independent variables in our models, the potential for increasing our understanding of institutions and of international politics in general is substantial, as preliminary empirical work has begun to show. The earliest work on international institutions produced insights that failed to add up to much because of the lack of an analytical framework in which to situate these insights; the next generation of work had the benefit of such a framework, but one that was poorly suited to the task at hand. In this article, we hope to have identified lines of research that will combine the best of both worlds: theoretically grounded research on institutions that draws on assumptions that are appropriate for the persistent problems of international relations.